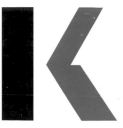

Kaplan Publishing are constantly finding new ways to make a difference to your studies and our exciting online resources really do offer something different to students looking for exam success.

This book comes with free MyKaplan online resources so that you can study anytime, anywhere

Having purchased this book, you have access to the following online study materials:

CONTENT	ACCA (including FFA,FAB,FMA)		FIA (excluding FFA,FAB,FMA)	
	Text	Kit	Text	Kit
iPaper version of the book	✓	✓	✓	✓
Interactive electronic version of the book	✓			
Progress tests with instant answers	✓			
Material updates	✓	✓	✓	✓
Latest official ACCA exam questions*		✓		
Extra question assistance using the signpost icon*		✓		
Timed questions with an online tutor debrief using the clock icon*		✓		
Interim assessment including questions and answers	✓		✓	
Technical articles	✓	✓	✓	✓

* Excludes F1, F2, F3, FFA, FAB, FMA

Kaplan 4 Success
muwra2

How to access your online resources

Kaplan Financial students will already have a MyKaplan account and these extra resources will be available to you online. You do not need to register again, as this process was completed when you enrolled. If you are having problems accessing online materials, please ask your course administrator.

If you are already a registered MyKaplan user go to www.MyKaplan.co.uk and log in. Select the 'add a book' feature and enter the ISBN number of this book and the unique pass key at the bottom of this card. Then click 'finished' or 'add another book'. You may add as many books as you have purchased from this screen.

If you purchased through Kaplan Flexible Learning or via the Kaplan Publishing website you will automatically receive an e-mail invitation to MyKaplan. Please register your details using this email to gain access to your content. If you do not receive the e-mail or book content, please contact Kaplan Flexible Learning.

If you are a new MyKaplan user register at www.MyKaplan.co.uk and click on the link contained in the email we sent you to activate your account. Then select the 'add a book' feature, enter the ISBN number of this book and the unique pass key at the bottom of this card. Then click 'finished' or 'add another book'.

Your Code and Information

This code can only be used once for the registration of one book online. This registration and your online content will expire when the final sittings for the examinations covered by this book have taken place. Please allow one hour from the time you submit your book details for us to process your request.

Please scratch the film to access your MyKaplan code.

Please be aware that this code is case-sensitive and you will need to include the dashes within the passcode, but not when entering the ISBN. For further technical support, please visit www.MyKaplan.co.uk

KAPLAN

PUBLISHING

Professional Examinations

Paper P7 (INT & UK)

ADVANCED AUDIT AND ASSURANCE

EXAM KIT

British Library Cataloguing-in-Publication Data

A catalogue record for this book is available from the British Library.

Published by:

Kaplan Publishing UK

Unit 2 The Business Centre

Molly Millar's Lane

Wokingham

Berkshire

RG41 2QZ

ISBN: 978-1-78415-056-3

© Kaplan Financial Limited, 2014

Printed and bound in Great Britain

Acknowledgements

The past ACCA examination questions are the copyright of the Association of Chartered Certified Accountants. The original answers to the questions from June 1994 onwards were produced by the examiners themselves and have been adapted by Kaplan Publishing.

We are grateful to the Association of Chartered Certified Accountants for permission to reproduce past examination questions. The answers have been prepared by Kaplan Publishing.

CONTENTS

Section

Key features in this edition

In addition to providing a wide ranging bank of real past exam questions, we have also included in this edition:

- An analysis of all of the recent new syllabus examination papers.

- Paper specific information and advice on exam technique.

- Our recommended approach to make your revision for this particular subject as effective as possible.

  This includes step by step guidance on how best to use our Kaplan material (Complete text, pocket notes and exam kit) at this stage in your studies.

- Enhanced tutorial answers packed with specific key answer tips, technical tutorial notes and exam technique tips from our experienced tutors.

- Complementary online resources including full tutor debriefs and question assistance to point you in the right direction when you get stuck.

You will find a wealth of other resources to help you with your studies on the following sites:

www.MyKaplan.co.uk

www.accaglobal.com/students/

Quality and accuracy are of the utmost importance to us so if you spot an error in any of our products, please send an email to mykaplanreporting@kaplan.com with full details.

Our Quality Co-ordinator will work with our technical team to verify the error and take action to ensure it is corrected in future editions.

INDEX TO QUESTIONS AND ANSWERS

INTRODUCTION

The style of current Paper P7 exam questions is different to older versions of the syllabus and changes have been made to questions in order to reflect changes in question style and syllabus updates.

Accordingly any older ACCA questions within this kit have been adapted to reflect the new style of paper and the new guidance. If changed in any way from the original version, this is indicated in the end column of the index below with the mark *(A)*.

Note that all of the questions within the kit are past ACCA exam questions.

The pilot paper is included at the end of the kit.

KEY TO THE INDEX

PAPER ENHANCEMENTS

We have added the following enhancements to the answers in this exam kit:

Key answer tips

All answers include key answer tips to help your understanding of each question.

Tutorial note

All answers include more tutorial notes to explain some of the technical points in more detail.

Top tutor tips

For selected questions, we "walk through the answer" giving guidance on how to approach the questions with helpful 'tips from a top tutor', together with technical tutor notes.

These answers are indicated with the "footsteps" icon in the index.

ONLINE ENHANCEMENTS

 Timed question with Online tutor debrief

For selected questions, we recommend that they are to be completed in full exam conditions (i.e. properly timed in a closed book environment).

In addition to the examiner's technical answer, enhanced with key answer tips and tutorial notes in this exam kit, you can find an answer debrief online by a top tutor that:

- works through the question in full

- points out how to approach the question

- discusses how to ensure that the easy marks are obtained as quickly as possible, and

- emphasises how to tackle exam questions and exam technique.

These questions are indicated with the "clock" icon in the index.

 Online question assistance

Have you ever looked at a question and not know where to start, or got stuck part way through?

For selected questions, we have produced "Online question assistance" offering different levels of guidance, such as:

- ensuring that you understand the question requirements fully, highlighting key terms and the meaning of the verbs used

- how to read the question proactively, with knowledge of the requirements, to identify the topic areas covered

- assessing the detailed content of the question body, pointing out key information and explaining why it is important

- help in devising a plan of attack

With this assistance, you should then be able to attempt your answer confident that you know what is expected of you.

These questions are indicated with the "signpost" icon in the index.

Section A-Type Questions

Section B-Type Questions

Professional/ethical considerations and practice management

Assignments

Completion and Reporting

UK Syllabus only

ANALYSIS OF PAST PAPERS

The table below summarises the key topics that have been tested in the new syllabus examinations to date.

	Jun 09	Dec 09	Jun 10	Dec 10	Jun 11	Dec 11	Jun 12	Dec 12	Jun 13	Dec 13	Jun 14
Regulatory Environment											
Regulatory framework		✓	✓								
Money laundering		✓					✓				✓
Professional & Ethical											
Laws and regulations							✓			✓	
Code of ethics	✓	✓	✓	✓	✓	✓	✓	✓	✓	✓	✓
Fraud and error	✓		✓						✓		
Professional liability			✓						✓		
Practice Management											
Quality control		✓	✓		✓	✓		✓	✓		✓
Obtaining professional work				✓							
Tendering	✓							✓			
Professional appointments	✓				✓						
Assignments											
Audit planning:											
Professional scepticism							✓				
Audit risk			✓			✓			✓		✓
Business risk	✓				✓			✓			
Material misstatement		✓			✓	✓	✓	✓		✓	
Understanding client	✓										
Audit evidence:											
Sufficient/appropriate											
Specific procedures	✓	✓	✓	✓	✓	✓	✓	✓	✓	✓	
Analytical procedures	✓	✓			✓	✓		✓	✓		
Related parties					✓						
Written representations											
Work of experts							✓				
Work of internal audit											
Group audit			✓		✓		✓	✓	✓		✓
Audit evaluation/review											
Review procedures											
Matters and evidence	✓	✓		✓	✓		✓	✓	✓	✓	✓
Initial engagements					✓						

	Jun 09	Dec 09	Jun 10	Dec 10	Jun 11	Dec 11	Jun 12	Dec 12	Jun 13	Dec 13	Jun 14
Comparatives					✓						
Other info.				✓							
Subsequent events		✓		✓							
Going concern			✓		✓					✓	✓
Written reps						✓					
Audit related services											
Interim review	✓							✓			
Due diligence					✓					✓	
Assurance services											
Levels of assurance											
Prospective financial information		✓					✓				✓
Social/environmental audit				✓			✓				
Forensic audit			✓			✓		✓	✓		
Internal audit			✓								
Outsourcing			✓					✓			✓
Insolvency (UK only)					✓		✓				✓
Reporting											
Audit reports											
Form and content	✓	✓	✓	✓	✓	✓	✓	✓	✓	✓	✓
Special purpose audit											
Reports to management				✓							
Current Issues											
Ethics and corporate governance					✓	✓		✓			
Going concern											✓
Transnational audit	✓										
Joint audits								✓			

13

KAPLAN PUBLISHING

EXAM TECHNIQUE

- Use the allocated **15 minutes reading and planning time** at the beginning of the exam:
    - read the questions and examination requirements carefully, and
    - begin planning your answers.

    See the Paper Specific Information for advice on how to use this time for this paper.

- **Divide the time** you spend on questions in proportion to the marks on offer:
    - there are 1.8 minutes available per mark in the examination
    - within that, try to allow time at the end of each question to review your answer and address any obvious issues

    Whatever happens, always keep your eye on the clock and **do not over run on any part of any question!**

- Spend the last **five minutes** of the examination:
    - reading through your answers, and
    - **making any additions or corrections.**

- If you **get completely stuck** with a question:
    - leave space in your answer book, and
    - **return to it later.**

- Stick to the question and **tailor your answer** to what you are asked.
    - pay particular attention to the verbs in the question.

- If you do not understand what a question is asking, **state your assumptions.**

    Even if you do not answer in precisely the way the examiner hoped, you should be given some credit, if your assumptions are reasonable.

- You should do everything you can to make things easy for the marker.

    The marker will find it easier to identify the points you have made if your **answers are legible.**

- **Written questions:**

    Your answer should:
    - Have a clear structure
    - Be concise: get to the point!
    - Address a broad range of points: it is usually better to write a little about a lot of different points than a great deal about one or two points.

- **Reports, memos and other documents:**

    Some questions ask you to present your answer in the form of a report, a memo, a letter or other document.

    Make sure that you use the correct format – there could be easy marks to gain here.

PAPER SPECIFIC INFORMATION

THE EXAM

FORMAT OF THE P7 EXAM

		Number of marks
Section A:	2 compulsory questions	
	Question 1:	35
	Question 2:	25
Section B:	2 questions from 3 (20 marks each)	40
		_____
		100
		_____

Total time allowed: 3 hours plus 15 minutes reading and planning time.

Note that:

- Questions 1 and 2 normally focus on reasonably large scenarios. The first question usually requires some form of risk assessment. The second question normally considers another form of engagement or a specialised area of audit, such as group auditing.

- Most of the marks available for question 1 are for applying your knowledge of audit procedures to the scenario, rather than simple 'knowledge dumping.'

- The question requirements normally include:

  - a requirement to perform a review of evidence gathered on an assurance assignment. You are normally asked to discuss what 'matters you would now consider' and what 'further procedures you would recommend.'

  - a discussion of the ethical and professional issues relevant to a few short scenarios.

  - reporting, typically audit reports, although reports to those charged with governance are also possible. You normally have to discuss the impact of certain issues on the wording of the report and the assurance opinion offered.

- Questions are no longer restricted to particular topics. Any topic could appear on any question, including within the compulsory questions (1 and 2).

- All requirements will be broken into numerous sub-requirements that test a range of topics.

- The majority of marks available on P7 are for applying your knowledge to specific case studies. There is little scope for 'knowledge dumping,' so only do this if the question specifically asks for it, e.g. when a definition is requested.

- Current issues and developments within the profession are examinable. For these types of questions it is likely that a technical article on the relevant topic will be issued in the months preceding the exam. Students are advised to check for any recent technical articles published by the ACCA Examining Team. Examiner's reports emphasise the need for students to read up on current issues and recommend that students do not solely depend on the text books for this exam.

- Discussion questions are generally disliked by students, possibly because there is no right or wrong answer. The way to approach these questions is to provide a balanced argument. Where a statement is given that you are required to discuss, give reasons why you agree with the statement and reasons why you disagree with the statement.

UK VARIANT SPECIFIC INFORMATION

The following are the key differences between the UK and INT variant exams:

- Q1 requirement in the UK exam will not be broken down in the same way as the INT variant. This may appear to make the question more difficult however this means that the marking scheme will be more flexible. It is recommended that you use the INT variant papers as a guide for how many marks are typically awarded for the different requirements and apply this in your exam. The questions included in this exam kit are from the INT papers so take notice of the breakdown of the marks to help you.

- Questions on ethics and audit reports will require knowledge of UK guidance e.g. FRC Ethical Standards and ISA 700 (UK and Ireland). The basic knowledge is the same for UK and INT but there are some variations in ethical safeguards and the format of a UK audit report.

- Insolvency is a syllabus area which is only relevant for UK variant exams. This will not necessarily be examined every sitting. If it is examined it is likely to be one requirement that is changed from the INT variant paper.

- Practise the UK specific questions in the Complete Text and this exam kit to help prepare you for any UK specific questions.

PASS MARK

The pass mark for all ACCA Qualification examination papers is 50%.

READING AND PLANNING TIME

Remember that all three hour paper based examinations have an additional 15 minutes reading and planning time.

ACCA GUIDANCE

ACCA guidance on the use of this time is as follows:

This additional time is allowed at the beginning of the examination to allow candidates to read the questions and to begin planning their answers before they start to write in their answer books.

This time should be used to ensure that all the information and, in particular, the exam requirements are properly read and understood.

During this time, candidates may only annotate their question paper. They may not write anything in their answer booklets until told to do so by the invigilator.

KAPLAN GUIDANCE

In relation to P7, we recommend that you take the following approach with your reading and planning time:

- **Skim through the whole paper**, assessing the level of difficulty of each question and identifying which **two** of the section B questions you wish to attempt.

- **Write down** on the question paper next to the mark allocation **the amount of time you should spend on each part.** Do this for each part of every question.

- **Decide the order** in which you think you will attempt each question:

  This is a personal choice and you have time on the revision phase to try out different approaches, for example, if you sit mock exams.

  A common approach is to tackle the question you think is the easiest and you are most comfortable with first.

  Others may prefer to tackle the longest questions first as this has the most marks attributable and you cannot afford to leave this question to last and find that you have run out of time to complete it fully. The examiner has commented that students who do not attempt Q1 first tend to do badly in the exam.

  It is usual, however, that students tackle their least favourite topic and/or the most difficult question last.

  Whatever your approach, you must make sure that you leave enough time to attempt all questions fully and be very strict with yourself in timing each question.

- **Read the requirements** and then the detail of the questions **1 and 2** carefully.

  Always read the requirement first as this enables you to **focus on the detail of the question with the specific task in mind.**

  For written questions:

  Take notice of the format required (e.g. briefing notes, memo, report) and identify the recipient of the answer. You need to do this to judge the level of sophistication required in your answer and whether the use of a formal reply is appropriate.

  P7 marks are normally awarded for depth of explanation and discussion. For this reason lists and bullet points should be avoided unless specifically requested. Always plan the structure of your answer and use sub-headings, as this always improves the quality and clarity of your response. You may also be asked to write a report or a memo. Professional marks are awarded for these questions so do not ignore their format.

  For all questions:

  Spot the easy marks to be gained in a question.

  Make sure that you do these parts first when you tackle the question.

  By covering all questions you can often help yourself as you may find that facts in one question may remind you of things you should put into your answer relating to a different question.

  With your plan of attack in mind, **start answering your chosen question** with your plan to hand, as soon as you are allowed to start.

Always keep your eye on the clock and do not over run on any part of any question!

DETAILED SYLLABUS

The detailed syllabus and study guide written by the ACCA can be found at:

www.accaglobal.com/students/

KAPLAN'S RECOMMENDED REVISION APPROACH

QUESTION PRACTICE IS THE KEY TO SUCCESS

Success in professional examinations relies upon you acquiring a firm grasp of the required knowledge at the tuition phase. In order to be able to do the questions, knowledge is essential.

However, the difference between success and failure often hinges on your exam technique on the day and making the most of the revision phase of your studies.

The **Kaplan complete text** is the starting point, designed to provide the underpinning knowledge to tackle all questions. However, in the revision phase, pouring over text books is not the answer.

Kaplan online progress tests help you consolidate your knowledge and understanding and are a useful tool to check whether you can remember key topic areas.

Kaplan pocket notes are designed to help you quickly revise a topic area, however you then need to practice questions. There is a need to progress to full exam standard questions as soon as possible, and to tie your exam technique and technical knowledge together.

The importance of question practice cannot be over-emphasised.

The recommended approach below is designed by expert tutors in the field, in conjunction with their knowledge of the examiner and their recent real exams.

The approach taken for the fundamental papers is to revise by topic area. However, with the professional stage papers, a multi topic approach is required to answer the scenario based questions.

You need to practice as many questions as possible in the time you have left.

OUR AIM

Our aim is to get you to the stage where you can attempt exam standard questions confidently, to time, in a closed book environment, with no supplementary help (i.e. to simulate the real examination experience).

Practising your exam technique on real past examination questions, in timed conditions, is also vitally important for you to assess your progress and identify areas of weakness that may need more attention in the final run up to the examination.

In order to achieve this we recognise that initially you may feel the need to practice some questions with open book help and exceed the required time.

The approach below shows you which questions you should use to build up to coping with exam standard question practice, and references to the sources of information available should you need to revisit a topic area in more detail.

Remember that in the real examination, all you have to do is:

- attempt all questions required by the exam

- only spend the allotted time on each question, and

- get at least 50% of the marks allocated!

Try and practice this approach on every question you attempt from now to the real exam.

EXAMINER COMMENTS

We have included the examiners comments to the specific new syllabus examination questions in this kit for you to see the main pitfalls that students fall into with regard to technical content.

However, too many times in the general section of the report, the examiner comments that students had failed due to:

- "misallocation of time"

- "running out of time" and

- showing signs of "spending too much time on an earlier questions and clearly rushing the answer to a subsequent question".

Good exam technique is vital.

THE KAPLAN PAPER P7 REVISION PLAN

Stage 1: Assess areas of strengths and weaknesses

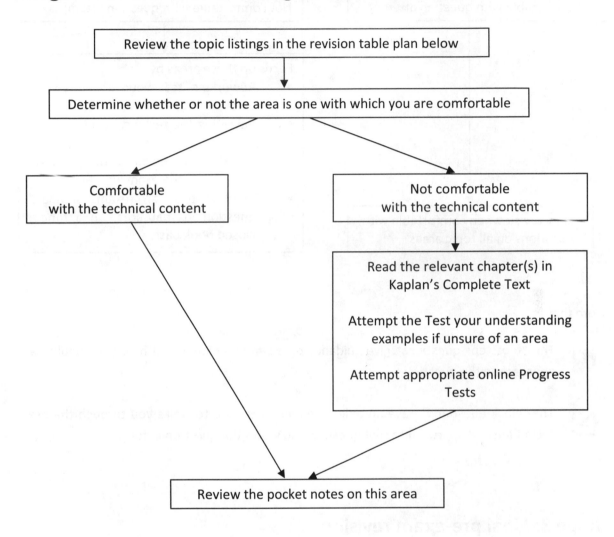

Stage 2: Practice questions

Follow the order of revision of topics as recommended in the revision table plan below and attempt the questions in the order suggested.

Try to avoid referring to text books and notes and the model answer until you have completed your attempt.

Try to answer the question in the allotted time.

Review your attempt with the model answer and assess how much of the answer you achieved in the allocated exam time.

Fill in the self-assessment box below and decide on your best course of action.

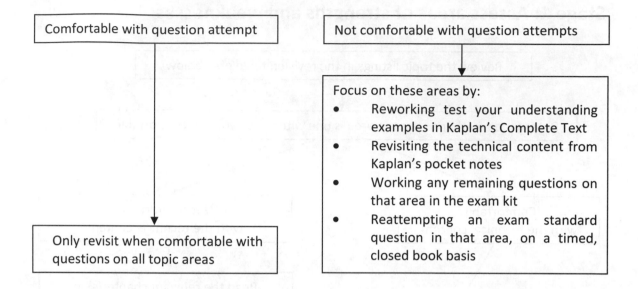

Comfortable with question attempt

Not comfortable with question attempts

Focus on these areas by:

* Reworking test your understanding examples in Kaplan's Complete Text
* Revisiting the technical content from Kaplan's pocket notes
* Working any remaining questions on that area in the exam kit
* Reattempting an exam standard question in that area, on a timed, closed book basis

Only revisit when comfortable with questions on all topic areas

Note that :

 The "footsteps questions" give guidance on exam techniques and how you should have approached the question.

 The "clock questions" have an online debrief where a tutor talks you through the exam technique and approach to that question and works the question in full.

Stage 3: Final pre-exam revision

We recommend that you **attempt at least one three hour mock examination** containing a set of previously unseen exam standard questions.

It is important that you get a feel for the breadth of coverage of a real exam without advanced knowledge of the topic areas covered – just as you will expect to see on the real exam day.

Ideally this mock should be sat in timed, closed book, real exam conditions and could be:

* a mock examination offered by your tuition provider, and/or

* the pilot paper in the back of this exam kit, and/or

* the last real examination paper (available shortly afterwards on MyKaplan with "enhanced walk through answers" and a full "tutor debrief").

KAPLAN'S DETAILED REVISION PLAN

	Topics	Complete Text (and Pocket Note) Chapter	Questions to attempt	Tutor guidance	Date attempted	Self assessment
1	Audit planning, risk assessment and materiality including group audits	9 & 10	1, 3, 5, 7, 11	Audit risk, business and risk of material misstatement is fundamental to P7. However, rather than discussing definitions you need to be able to perform a risk assessment for specific information given in a scenario. It is imperative to understand the difference between the three types of risk in order to answer the question correctly.		
2	Audit procedures	11	1, 3, 5, 7, 11	Throughout the P7 exam you will be required to provide examples of principle audit procedures. The assertions you are testing will usually be very narrowly defined and this represents a significant step up from F8. You therefore need to know the sorts of procedures available to an auditor and then rehearse applying them to specific scenarios.		
3	Non-audit engagements	15 – 21	2, 4, 8, 14, 40, 42	There are many non-audit engagements that you could be asked to discuss. Therefore ensure that you know: the typical sorts of engagement; how they are planned; how they are performed; and how they are reviewed. You also need to consider the ethical/professional impact of an auditor accepting these engagements.		

4	Evaluation and review procedures	12	26, 27, 29, 31, 37	At the review stage of an audit you need to consider a number of issues: whether there is sufficient appropriate evidence on file; if the audit plan has been followed; whether there are any material errors in the information under review; and the impact of these issues on the reports you will have to issue.		
5	Ethics and professional issues	2 – 8	19, 20, 21, 35, 23	You need to be able to discuss and apply the code of ethics to given scenarios. In addition you also need to consider a wide range of practice management issues, such as: internal quality control; legal requirements; commercial strategy; and professional liability.		
6	Engagement reporting	13 & 14	44, 45, 46, 47, 48	One of the fundamental weaknesses identified by the examiner is a lack of understanding regarding the nature of audit report modifications. It is therefore important that you are able to assess a scenario and identify how it might impact upon your audit opinion. You also need to be able to discuss the content and purpose of reports to those charged with governance.		

Note that not all of the questions are referred to in the programme above. We have recommended an approach to build up from the basic to exam standard questions.

The remaining questions are available in the kit for extra practice for those who require more question on some areas.

Section 1

PRACTICE QUESTIONS – SECTION A

1 STOW GROUP *Walk in the footsteps of a top tutor*

You are an audit manager in Compton & Co, responsible for the audit of the Stow Group (the Group). You are planning the audit of the Group financial statements for the year ending 31 December 2013. The Group's projected profit before tax for the year is $200 million and projected total assets at 31 December are $2,500 million.

The Group is a car manufacturer. Its operations are divided between a number of subsidiaries, some of which focus on manufacturing and distributing the cars, while others deal mainly with marketing and retail. All components of the Group have the same year end. The Group audit engagement partner, Chad Woodstock, has just sent you the following email.

To: Audit manager

From: Chad Woodstock, audit partner

Subject: The Stow Group – audit planning

Hello

We need to start planning the audit of The Stow Group. Yesterday I met with the Group finance director, Marta Bidford, and we discussed some restructuring of the Group which has taken place this year. A new wholly-owned subsidiary has been acquired – Zennor Co, which is located overseas in Farland. Another subsidiary, Broadway Co, was disposed of.

I have provided you with a summary of issues which I discussed with Marta, and using this information I would like you to prepare briefing notes for my use in which you:

(a) (i) **Explain the risks of material misstatement to be considered in planning the Group audit, commenting on their materiality to the Group financial statements; and** **(12 marks)**

   (ii) **Identify any further information that may be needed.** **(4 marks)**

(b) **Recommend the principal audit procedures to be performed in respect of the disposal of Broadway Co.** **(8 marks)**

Marta has told me that Zennor Co has a well established internal audit team. She has suggested that we use the internal audit team as much as possible when performing our audit of Zennor Co as this will reduce the audit fee. The Group audit committee appreciates that with the audit of the new subsidiary there will be some increase in our costs, but has requested that the audit fee for the Group as a whole is not increased from last year's fee. I have provided you with some information about the internal audit team and in your briefing notes I would like you to:

(c) **Discuss how Marta's suggestion impacts on the planning of the audit of Zennor Co's and of the Group's financial statements, and comment on any ethical issue raised.** **(7 marks)**

Thank you.

Acquisition of Zennor Co

In order to expand overseas, the Group acquired 100% of the share capital of Zennor Co on 1 February 2013. Zennor Co is located in Farland, where it owns a chain of car dealerships. Zennor Co's financial statements are prepared using International Financial Reporting Standards and are measured and presented using the local currency of Farland, the Dingu. At the present time, the exchange rate is 4 Dingu = $1. Zennor Co has the same year end as the Group, and its projected profit for the year ending 31 December 2013 is 90 million Dingu, with projected assets at the same date of 800 million Dingu.

Zennor Co is supplied with cars from the Group's manufacturing plant. The cars are sent on cargo ships and take approximately six weeks to reach the main port in Farland, where they are stored until delivered to the dealerships. At today's date there are cars in transit to Zennor Co with a selling price of $58 million.

A local firm of auditors was engaged by the Group to perform a due diligence review on Zennor Co prior to its acquisition. The Group's statement of financial position recognises goodwill at acquisition of $60 million.

Compton & Co was appointed as auditor of Zennor Co on 1 March 2013.

Disposal of Broadway Co

On 1 September 2013, the Group disposed of its wholly-owned subsidiary, Broadway Co, for proceeds of $180 million. Broadway Co operated a distribution centre in this country. The Group's statement of profit or loss includes a profit of $25 million in respect of the disposal.

Broadway Co was acquired by a retail organisation, the Cornwall Group, which wished to bring its distribution operations in house in order to save costs. Compton & Co resigned as auditor to Broadway Co on 15 September 2013 to be replaced by the principal auditor of the Cornwall Group.

Zennor Co – Internal audit team

The internal audit team was established several years ago and is headed up by a qualified accountant, Jo Evesham, who has a lot of experience in designing systems and controls. Jo and her team monitor the effectiveness of operating and financial reporting controls, and report to the board of directors. Zennor Co does not have an audit committee as corporate governance rules in Farland do not require an internal audit function or an audit committee to be established.

During the year, the internal audit team performed several value for money exercises such as reviewing the terms negotiated with suppliers.

Required:

Respond to the instructions in the partner's email. (31 marks)

Note: The mark allocation is shown against each of the instructions in the partner's email above.

Professional marks will be awarded for the structure and presentation of the briefing notes and for the clarity of explanations. (4 marks)

(Total: 35 marks)

2   BALTIMORE   *Walk in the footsteps of a top tutor*

You are a manager in the business advisory department of Goleen & Co. Your firm has been approached to provide assurance to Baltimore Co, a company which is not an audit client of your firm, on a potential acquisition. You have just had a conversation with Mark Clear, Baltimore Co's managing director, who made the following comments:

'Baltimore Co is a book publisher specialising in publishing textbooks and academic journals. In the last few years the market has changed significantly, with the majority of customers purchasing books from online sellers. This has led to a reduction in profits, and we recognise that we need to diversify our product range in order to survive. As a result of this, we decided to offer a subscription-based website to customers, which would provide the customer with access to our full range of textbooks and journals online.

'On investigating how to set up this website, we found that we lack sufficient knowledge and resources to develop it ourselves and began to look for another company which has the necessary skills, with a view to acquiring the company. We have identified Mizzen Co as a potential acquisition, and we have approached the bank for a loan which will be used to finance the acquisition if it goes ahead.

'Baltimore Co has not previously acquired another company. We would like to engage your firm to provide guidance regarding the acquisition. I understand that a due diligence review would be advisable prior to deciding on whether to go ahead with the acquisition, but the other directors are not sure that this is required, and they don't understand what the review would involve. They are also unsure about the type of conclusion that would be issued and whether it would be similar to the opinion in an audit report.

'To help me brief the other directors and using the information I have provided, I would like you to:

(a)   Discuss THREE benefits to Baltimore Co of a due diligence review being performed on Mizzen Co. (6 marks)

(b)   Identify and explain the matters which you would focus on in your due diligence review and recommend the additional information which you will need to perform your work. (16 marks)

(c)   Describe the type of conclusion which would be issued for a due diligence report and compare this to an audit report.' (3 marks)

Mark Clear has sent you the following information about Mizzen Co:

Company background

Mizzen Co was established four years ago by two university graduates, Vic Sandhu and Lou Lien, who secured funds from a venture capitalist company, BizGrow, to set up the company. Vic and Lou created a new type of website interface which has proven extremely popular, and which led to the company growing rapidly and building a good reputation. They continue to innovate and have won awards for website design. Vic and Lou have a minority shareholding in Mizzen Co.

Mizzen Co employs 50 people and operates from premises owned by BizGrow, for which a nominal rent of $1,000 is paid annually. The company uses few assets other than computer equipment and fixtures and fittings. The biggest expense is wages and salaries and due to increased demand for website development, freelance specialists have been used in the last six months. According to the most recent audited financial statements, Mizzen Co has a bank balance of $500,000.

The company has three revenue streams:

(1)   Developing and maintaining websites for corporate customers. Mizzen Co charges a one-off fee to its customers for the initial development of a website and for maintaining the website for two years. The amount of this fee depends on the size and complexity of the website and averages at $10,000 per website. The customer can then choose to pay another one-off fee, averaging $2,000, for Mizzen Co to provide maintenance for a further five years.

(2)   Mizzen Co has also developed a subscription-based website on which it provides access to technical material for computer specialists. Customers pay an annual fee of $250 which gives them unlimited access to the website. This accounts for approximately 30% of Mizzen Co's total revenue.

(3)   The company has built up several customer databases which are made available, for a fee, to other companies for marketing purposes. This is the smallest revenue stream, accounting for approximately 20% of Mizzen Co's total revenue.

Extracts from audited financial statements

Statement of profit or loss and other comprehensive income

	Year ended 30 September 2013 $000	Year ended 30 September 2012 $000	Year ended 30 September 2011 $000	Year ended 30 September 2010 $000
Revenue	4,268	3,450	2,150	500
Operating expenses	(2,118)	(2,010)	(1,290)	(1,000)
Operating profit/(loss)	2,150	1,440	860	(500)
Finance costs	(250)	(250)	(250)	–
Profit/(loss) before tax	1,900	1,190	610	(500)
Tax expense	(475)	(300)	(140)	–
Profit/(loss) for the year	1,425	890	470	(500)

There were no items of other comprehensive income recognised in any year.

Required:

Respond to the request from Mark Clear.

Note: The mark allocation is shown against each of the instructions from Mark Clear above.

(Total: 25 marks)

3   PARKER   *Walk in the footsteps of a top tutor*

You are an audit manager in Hound & Co, responsible for the audit of Parker Co, a new audit client of your firm. You are planning the audit of Parker Co's financial statements for the year ending 30 June 2013, and you have just attended a meeting with Ruth Collie, the finance director of Parker Co, where she gave you the projected results for the year. Parker Co designs and manufactures health and beauty products including cosmetics.

You have just received an email from Harry Shepherd, the audit engagement partner:

To: Audit manager

From: Harry Shepherd, Partner

Hello

I understand you met with Ruth Collie at Parker Co recently and that you are planning the forthcoming audit. To bring me up to date on this new client, I would like you to use the information obtained in your meeting to prepare briefing notes for my use in which you:

(a)   Perform preliminary analytical procedures and evaluate the audit risks to be considered in planning the audit of the financial statements, and identify and explain any additional information that would be relevant to your evaluation; and
(24 marks)

(b)   Discuss any ethical issues raised and recommend the relevant actions to be taken by our firm.   **(7 marks)**

Thank you

Parker Co – Statement of profit or loss and other comprehensive income

	Notes	30 June 2013 Projected $000	30 June 2012 Actual $000
Revenue		7,800	8,500
Cost of sales	1	(5,680)	(5,800)
		———	———
Gross profit		2,120	2,700
Operating expenses		(1,230)	(1,378)
		———	———
Operating profit		890	1,322
Finance costs		(155)	(125)
		———	———
Profit before tax		735	1,197
Taxation		(70)	(300)
		———	———
Profit for the year		665	897
		———	———

Note 1: Cost of sales includes $250,000 relating to a provision for a potential fine payable. The advertising regulatory authority has issued a notice of a $450,000 fine payable by Parker Co due to alleged inappropriate claims made in an advertising campaign. The fine is being disputed and the matter should be resolved in August 2013.

Parker Co – Statement of financial position

	Notes	30 June 2013 Projected $000	30 June 2012 Actual $000
Non-current assets			
Property, plant and equipment		21,500	19,400
Intangible asset – development costs	2	2,250	–
		———	———
		23,750	19,400
Current assets			
Inventory		2,600	2,165
Trade receivables		900	800
Cash		–	1,000
		———	———
		3,500	3,965
		———	———
Total assets		27,250	23,365
		———	———

Equity

Share capital		8,000	8,000
Revaluation reserve	3	2,500	2,000
Retained earnings		1,275	1,455
		———	———
		11,775	11,455

Non-current liabilities

2% preference shares	3,125	3,125
Bank loan	3,800	2,600
Obligations under finance leases	4,900	4,000
	11,825	9,725

Current liabilities

Trade payables	1,340	1,000
Taxation	50	300
Obligations under finance leases	860	685
Provisions	500	200
Overdraft	900	–
	———	———
	3,650	2,185
	———	———
Total equity and liabilities	27,250	23,365
	———	———

Human resources

In December 2012 Parker Co's internal audit team performed a review of the operation of controls over the processing of overtime payments in the human resources department. The review found that the company's specified internal controls procedures in relation to the processing of overtime payments and associated tax payments were not always being followed. Until December 2012 this processing was split between the human resources and finance departments. Since then, the processing has been entirely carried out by the finance department.

Expansion plans

Management is planning to expand Parker Co's operations into a new market relating to beauty salons. This is a growing market, and there is synergy because Parker Co's products can be sold and used in the salons. Expansion would be through the acquisition of an existing company which operates beauty salons. A potential target, Beauty Boost Co, has been identified and preliminary discussions have taken place between the management of the two companies. Parker Co's managing director has asked for our firm's advice about the potential acquisition, and specifically regarding the financing of the transaction. Beauty Boost Co is an audit client of our firm, so we have considerable knowledge of its business.

Required:

Respond to the email from the audit partner. (31 marks)

Note: The split of the mark allocation is shown within the partner's email.

Professional marks will be awarded for the presentation, logical flow and clarity of explanation of the briefing notes. (4 marks)

(Total: 35 marks)

4   RETRIEVER *Walk in the footsteps of a top tutor*

(a)   Kennel & Co, a firm of Chartered Certified Accountants, is the external audit provider for the Retriever Group (the Group), a manufacturer of mobile phones and laptop computers. The Group obtained a stock exchange listing in July 2012. The audit of the consolidated financial statements for the year ended 28 February 2013 is nearing completion.

You are a manager in the audit department of Kennel & Co, responsible for conducting engagement quality control reviews on listed audit clients. You have discussed the Group audit with some of the junior members of the audit team, one of whom made the following comments about how it was planned and carried out:

'The audit has been quite time-pressured. The audit manager told the juniors not to perform some of the planned audit procedures on items such as directors' emoluments and share capital as they are considered to be low risk. He also instructed us not to use the firm's statistical sampling methods in selecting trade receivables balances for testing, as it would be quicker to pick the sample based on our own judgement.

'Two of the juniors were given the tasks of auditing trade payables and going concern. The audit manager asked us to review each other's work as it would be good training for us, and he didn't have time to review everything.

'I was discussing the Group's tax position with the financial controller, when she said that she was struggling to calculate the deferred tax asset that should be recognised. The deferred tax asset has arisen because several of the Group's subsidiaries have been loss making this year, creating unutilised tax losses. As I had just studied deferred tax at college I did the calculation of the Group's deferred tax position for her. The audit manager said this saved time as we now would not have to audit the deferred tax figure.

'The financial controller also asked for my advice as to how the tax losses could be utilised by the Group in the future. I provided her with some tax planning recommendations, for which she was very grateful.'

Required:

In relation to the audit of the Retriever Group, evaluate the quality control, ethical and other professional matters arising in respect of the planning and performance of the Group audit.   (13 marks)

(b)   The audit committee of the Group has contacted Kennel & Co to discuss an incident that took place on 1 June 2013. On that date, there was a burglary at the Group's warehouse where inventory is stored prior to despatch to customers. CCTV filmed the thieves loading a lorry belonging to the Group with boxes containing finished goods. The last inventory count took place on 30 April 2013.

The Group has insurance cover in place and Kennel & Co's forensic accounting department has been asked to provide a forensic accounting service to determine the amount to be claimed in respect of the burglary. The insurance covers the cost of assets lost as a result of thefts.

It is thought that the amount of the claim will be immaterial to the Group's financial statements, and there is no ethical threat in Kennel & Co's forensic accounting department providing the forensic accounting service.

Required:

In respect of the theft and the associated insurance claim:

(i)   **Identify and explain the matters to be considered, and the steps to be taken in planning the forensic accounting service; and**

(ii) **Recommend the procedures to be performed in determining the amount of the claim.**

Note: The total marks will be split equally between each part.   **(12 marks)**

(Total: 25 marks)

5   GROHL *Walk in the footsteps of a top tutor*

(a)   You are a manager in Foo & Co, responsible for the audit of Grohl Co, a company which produces circuit boards which are sold to manufacturers of electrical equipment such as computers and mobile phones. It is the first time that you have managed this audit client, taking over from the previous audit manager, Bob Halen, last month. The audit planning for the year ended 30 November 2012 is about to commence, and you have just received an email from Mia Vai, the audit engagement partner.

To: Audit manager

From: Mia Vai, Audit partner, Foo & Co

Subject: Grohl Co – audit planning

Hello

I am meeting with the other audit partners tomorrow to discuss forthcoming audits and related issues. I understand that you recently had a meeting with Mo Satriani, the finance director of Grohl Co. Using the information from your meeting, I would like you to prepare briefing notes for my use in which you:

(i)   **Evaluate the business risks faced by Grohl Co;**   **(12 marks)**

(ii) **Identify and explain FOUR risks of material misstatement to be considered in planning the audit; and**   **(8 marks)**

(iii) **Discuss any ethical issues raised, and recommend the relevant actions to be taken by our firm.**   **(8 marks)**

Thank you.

Comments made by Mo Satriani in your meeting

Business overview

Grohl Co's principal business activity remains the production of circuit boards. One of the key materials used in production is copper wiring, all of which is imported. As a cost cutting measure, in April 2012 a contract with a new overseas supplier was signed, and all of the company's copper wiring is now supplied under this contract. Purchases are denominated in a foreign currency, but the company does not use forward exchange contracts in relation to its imports of copper wiring.

Grohl Co has two production facilities, one of which produces goods for the export market, and the other produces goods for the domestic market. About half of its goods are exported, but the export market is suffering due to competition from cheaper producers overseas. Most domestic sales are made under contract with approximately 20 customers.

Recent developments

In early November 2012, production was halted for a week at the production facility which supplies the domestic market. A number of customers had returned goods, claiming faults in the circuit boards supplied. On inspection, it was found that the copper used in the circuit boards was corroded and therefore unsuitable for use. The corrosion is difficult to spot as it cannot be identified by eye, and relies on electrical testing. All customers were contacted immediately and, where necessary, products recalled and replaced. The corroded copper remaining in inventory has been identified and separated from the rest of the copper.

Work has recently started on a new production line which will ensure that Grohl Co meets new regulatory requirements prohibiting the use of certain chemicals, which come into force in March 2013. In July 2012, a loan of $30 million with an interest rate of 4% was negotiated with Grohl Co's bank, the main purpose of the loan being to fund the capital expenditure necessary for the new production line. $2.5 million of the loan represents an overdraft which was converted into long-term finance.

Other matters

Several of Grohl Co's executive directors and the financial controller left in October 2012, to set up a company specialising in the recycling of old electronic equipment. This new company is not considered to be in competition with Grohl Co's operations. The directors left on good terms, and replacements for the directors have been recruited. One of Foo & Co's audit managers, Bob Halen, is being interviewed for the role of financial controller at Grohl Co. Bob is a good candidate for the position, as he developed good knowledge of Grohl Co's business when he was managing the audit.

At Grohl Co's most recent board meeting, the audit fee was discussed. The board members expressed concern over the size of the audit fee, given the company's loss for the year. The board members would like to know whether the audit can be performed on a contingent fee basis.

Financial Information provided by Mo Satriani

Extract from draft statement of profit or loss for the year ended 30 November 2012

	2012 Draft	2011 Actual
	$000	$000
Revenue	12,500	13,800
Operating costs	(12,000)	(12,800)
Operating profit	500	1,000
Finance costs	(800)	(800)
Profit/(loss) before tax	(300)	200

The draft statement of financial position has not yet been prepared, but Mo states that the total assets of Grohl Co at 30 November 2012 are $180 million, and cash at bank is $130,000. Based on draft figures, the company's current ratio is 1.1, and the quick ratio is 0.8.

Required:

Respond to the email from the audit partner. **(28 marks)**

Note: The split of the mark allocation is shown within the partner's email.

Professional marks will be awarded for the presentation, structure, logical flow and clarity of your answer. **(4 marks)**

(b) You have just received a phone call from Mo Satriani, Grohl Co's finance director, in which he made the following comments:

'There is something I forgot to mention in our meeting. Our business insurance covers us for specific occasions when business is interrupted. I put in a claim on 28 November 2012 for $5 million which I have estimated to cover the period when our production was halted due to the problem with the corroded copper. This is not yet recognised in the financial statements, but I want to make an adjustment to recognise the $5 million as a receivable as at 30 November.'

Required:

Comment on the matters that should be considered, and recommend the audit procedures to be performed, in respect of the insurance claim. **(8 marks)**

(Total: 40 marks)

6 JOVI GROUP *Walk in the footsteps of a top tutor*

(a) You are a manager in Sambora & Co, responsible for the audit of the Jovi Group (the Group), which is listed. The Group's main activity is steel manufacturing and it comprises a parent company and five subsidiaries. Sambora & Co currently audits all components of the Group.

You are working on the audit of the Group's financial statements for the year ended 30 June 2012. This morning the audit engagement partner left a note for you:

'**Hello**

The audit senior has provided you with the draft consolidated financial statements and accompanying notes which summarise the key audit findings and some background information.

At the planning stage, materiality was initially determined to be $900,000, and was calculated based on the assumption that the Jovi Group is a high risk client due to its listed status. During the audit, a number of issues arose which meant that we needed to revise the materiality level for the financial statements as a whole. The revised level of materiality is now determined to be $700,000. One of the audit juniors was unsure as to why the materiality level had been revised. There are two matters you need to deal with:

(i) Explain why auditors may need to reassess materiality as the audit progresses. **(4 marks)**

(ii)   Assess the implications of the key audit findings for the completion of the audit. Your assessment must consider whether the key audit findings indicate a risk of material misstatement. Where the key audit findings refer to audit evidence, you must also consider the adequacy of the audit evidence obtained, but you do not need to recommend further specific procedures.   **(18 marks)**

Thank you'

The Group's draft consolidated financial statements, with notes referenced to key audit findings, are shown below:

Draft consolidated statement of profit or loss

	Note	30 June 2012 Draft $000	30 June 2011 Actual $000
Revenue	1	98,795	103,100
Cost of sales		(75,250)	(74,560)
Gross profit		23,545	28,540
Operating expenses	2	(14,900)	(17,500)
Operating profit		8,645	11,040
Share of profit of associate		1,010	900
Finance costs		(380)	(340)
Profit before tax		9,275	11,600
Taxation		(3,200)	(3,500)
Profit for the year		6,075	8,100
Other comprehensive income/expense for the year, net of tax:			
Gains on property revaluation	3	800	–
Actuarial losses on defined benefit plan	4	(1,100)	(200)
Other comprehensive income/expense		(300)	(200)
Total comprehensive income for the year		5,775	7,900

Notes: Key audit findings – statement of profit or loss

(1)   Revenue has been stable for all components of the Group with the exception of one subsidiary, Copeland Co, which has recognised a 25% decrease in revenue.

(2)   Operating expenses for the year to June 2012 is shown net of a profit on a property disposal of $2 million. Our evidence includes agreeing the cash receipts to bank statement and sale documentation, and we have confirmed that the property has been removed from the non-current asset register. The audit junior noted when reviewing the sale document, that there is an option to repurchase the property in five years time, but did not discuss the matter with management.

(3)   The property revaluation relates to the Group's head office. The audit team have not obtained evidence on the revaluation, as the gain was immaterial based on the initial calculation of materiality.

(4)   The actuarial loss is attributed to an unexpected stock market crash. The Group's pension plan is managed by Axle Co – a firm of independent fund managers who maintain the necessary accounting records relating to the plan. Axle Co has supplied written representation as to the value of the defined benefit plan's assets and liabilities at 30 June 2012. No other audit work has been performed other than to agree the figure from the financial statements to supporting documentation supplied by Axle Co.

Draft consolidated statement of financial position

	Note	30 June 2012 Draft $000	30 June 2011 Actual $000
ASSETS			
Non-current assets			
Property, plant and equipment		81,800	76,300
Goodwill	5	5,350	5,350
Investment in associate	6	4,230	4,230
Assets classified as held for sale	7	7,800	–
		99,180	85,880
Current assets			
Inventory		8,600	8,000
Receivables		8,540	7,800
Cash and cash equivalents		2,100	2,420
		19,240	18,220
Total assets		118,420	104,100
EQUITY AND LIABILITIES			
Equity			
Share capital		12,500	12,500
Revaluation reserve		3,300	2,500
Retained earnings		33,600	29,400
Non-controlling interest	8	4,350	4,000
Total equity		53,750	48,400

Non-current liabilities

Defined benefit pension plan		10,820	9,250
Long-term borrowings	9	43,000	35,000
Deferred tax		1,950	1,350
Total non-current liabilities		55,770	45,600

Current liabilities

Trade and other payables	6,200	7,300
Provisions	2,700	2,800
Total current liabilities	8,900	10,100
Total liabilities	64,670	55,700
Total equity and liabilities	118,420	104,100

Notes: Key audit findings – statement of financial position

(5)   The goodwill relates to each of the subsidiaries in the Group. Management has confirmed in writing that goodwill is stated correctly, and our other audit procedure was to arithmetically check the impairment review conducted by management.

(6)   The associate is a 30% holding in James Co, purchased to provide investment income. The audit team have not obtained evidence regarding the associate as there is no movement in the amount recognised in the statement of financial position.

(7)   The assets held for sale relate to a trading division of one of the subsidiaries, which represents one third of that subsidiary's net assets. The sale of the division was announced in May 2012, and is expected to be complete by 31 December 2012. Audit evidence obtained includes a review of the sales agreement and confirmation from the buyer, obtained in July 2012, that the sale will take place.

(8)   Two of the Group's subsidiaries are partly owned by shareholders external to the Group.

(9)   A loan of $8 million was taken out in October 2011, carrying an interest rate of 2%, payable annually in arrears. The terms of the loan have been confirmed to documentation provided by the bank.

Required:

Respond to the note from the audit engagement partner.   **(22 marks)**

Note: The split of the mark allocation is shown within the partner's note.

(b) The audit engagement partner now sends a further note regarding the Jovi Group:

'The Group finance director has just informed me that last week the Group purchased 100% of the share capital of May Co, a company located overseas in Farland. The Group audit committee has suggested that due to the distant location of May Co, a joint audit could be performed, starting with the next financial statements for the year ending 30 June 2013. May Co's current auditors are a small local firm called Moore & Co who operate only in Farland.'

Required:

Discuss the advantages and disadvantages of a joint audit being performed on the financial statements of May Co. **(6 marks)**

(Total: 28 marks)

7 CROW *Walk in the footsteps of a top tutor*

You are a manager in Magpie & Co, responsible for the audit of the CS Group. An extract from the permanent audit file describing the CS Group's history and operations is shown below:

Permanent file (extract)

Crow Co was incorporated 100 years ago. It was founded by Joseph Crow, who established a small pottery making tableware such as dishes, plates and cups. The products quickly grew popular, with one range of products becoming highly sought after when it was used at a royal wedding. The company's products have retained their popularity over the decades, and the Crow brand enjoys a strong identity and good market share.

Ten years ago, Crow Co made its first acquisition by purchasing 100% of the share capital of Starling Co. Both companies benefited from the newly formed CS Group, as Starling Co itself had a strong brand name in the pottery market. The CS Group has a history of steady profitability and stable management.

Crow Co and Starling Co have a financial year ending 31 July 2012, and your firm has audited both companies for several years.

(a) You have received an email from Jo Daw, the audit engagement partner:

> **To: Audit manager**
>
> **From: Jo Daw**
>
> **Regarding: CS Group audit planning**
>
> Hello
>
> I have just been to a meeting with Steve Eagle, the finance director of the CS Group. We were discussing recent events which will have a bearing on our forthcoming audit, and my notes from the meeting are attached to this email. One of the issues discussed is the change in group structure due to the acquisition of Canary Co earlier this year. Our firm has been appointed as auditor of Canary Co, which has a year ending 30 June 2012, and the terms of the engagement have been agreed with the client. We need to start planning the audits of the three components of the Group, and of the consolidated financial statements.

Using the attached information, you are required to:

(i) Identify and explain the implications of the acquisition of Canary Co for the audit planning of the individual and consolidated financial statements of the CS Group **(8 marks)**

(ii) Evaluate the risks of material misstatement to be considered in the audit planning of the individual and consolidated financial statements of the CS Group; and **(18 marks)**

(iii) Recommend the principal audit procedures to be performed in respect of the goodwill initially recognised on the acquisition of Canary Co. **(5 marks)**

Thank you.

Attachment: Notes from meeting with Steve Eagle, finance director of the CS Group

Acquisition of Canary Co

The most significant event for the CS Group this year was the acquisition of Canary Co, which took place on 1 February 2012. Crow Co purchased all of Canary Co's equity shares for cash consideration of $125 million, and further contingent consideration of $30 million will be paid on the third anniversary of the acquisition, if the Group's revenue grows by at least 8% per annum. Crow Co engaged an external provider to perform due diligence on Canary Co, whose report indicated that the fair value of Canary Co's net assets was estimated to be $110 million at the date of acquisition. Goodwill arising on the acquisition has been calculated as follows:

	$ million
Fair value of consideration:	
Cash consideration	125
Contingent consideration	30
	———
	155
Less: fair value of identifiable net assets acquired	(110)
	———
Goodwill	45
	———

To help finance the acquisition, Crow Co issued loan stock at par on 31 January 2012, raising cash of $100 million. The loan has a five-year term, and will be repaid at a premium of $20 million. 5% interest is payable annually in arrears. It is Group accounting policy to recognise financial liabilities at amortised cost.

Canary Co manufactures pottery figurines and ornaments. The company is considered a good strategic fit to the Group, as its products are luxury items like those of Crow Co and Starling Co, and its acquisition will enable the Group to diversify into a different market. Approximately 30% of its sales are made online, and it is hoped that online sales can soon be introduced for the rest of the Group's products. Canary Co has only ever operated as a single company, so this is the first year that it is part of a group of companies.

Financial performance and position

The Group has performed well this year, with forecast consolidated revenue for the year to 31 July 2012 of $135 million (2011 – $125 million), and profit before tax of $8.5 million (2011 – $8.4 million). A breakdown of the Group's forecast revenue and profit is shown below:

	Crow Co $ million	Starling Co $ million	Canary Co $ million	CS Group $ million
Revenue	69	50	16	135
Profit before tax	3.5	3	2	8.5

Note: Canary Co's results have been included from 1 February 2012 (date of acquisition), and forecast up to 31 July 2012, the CS Group's financial year end.

The forecast consolidated statement of financial position at 31 July 2012 recognises total assets of $550 million.

Other matters

Starling Co received a grant of $35 million on 1 March 2012 in relation to redevelopment of its main manufacturing site. The government is providing grants to companies for capital expenditure on environmentally friendly assets. Starling Co has spent $25 million of the amount received on solar panels which generate electricity, and intends to spend the remaining $10 million on upgrading its production and packaging lines.

On 1 January 2012, a new IT system was introduced to Crow Co and Starling Co, with the aim of improving financial reporting controls and to standardise processes across the two companies. Unfortunately, Starling Co's finance director left the company last week.

Required:

Respond to the email from the partner.   **(31 marks)**

Note: the split of the mark allocation is shown within the email.

(b)   Magpie & Co's ethics partner, Robin Finch, leaves a note on your desk:

'I have just had a conversation with Steve Eagle concerning the CS Group. He would like the audit engagement partner to attend the CS Group's board meetings on a monthly basis so that our firm can be made aware of any issues relating to the audit as soon as possible. Also, Steve asked if one of our audit managers could be seconded to Starling Co in temporary replacement of its finance director who recently left, and asked for our help in recruiting a permanent replacement. Please provide me with a response to Steve which evaluates the ethical implications of his requests.'

Required:

Respond to the note from the partner.   **(6 marks)**

(Total: 37 marks)

8   HAWK *Walk in the footsteps of a top tutor*

(a)   You are a manager in Lapwing & Co. One of your audit clients is Hawk Co which operates commercial real estate properties typically comprising several floors of retail units and leisure facilities such as cinemas and health clubs, which are rented out to provide rental income.

Your firm has just been approached to provide an additional engagement for Hawk Co, to review and provide a report on the company's business plan, including forecast financial statements for the 12-month period to 31 May 2013. Hawk Co is in the process of negotiating a new bank loan of $30 million and the report on the business plan is at the request of the bank. It is anticipated that the loan would be advanced in August 2012 and would carry an interest rate of 4%. The report would be provided by your firm's business advisory department and a second partner review will be conducted which will reduce any threat to objectivity to an acceptable level.

Extracts from the forecast financial statements included in the business plan are given below:

Statement of Profit or Loss (extract)

	Note	FORECAST 12 months to 31 May 2013	UNAUDITED 12 months to 31 May 2012
		$000	$000
Revenue		25,000	20,600
Operating expenses		(16,550)	(14,420)
Operating profit		8,450	6,180
Profit on disposal of Beak Retail	1	4,720	–
Finance costs		(2,650)	(1,690)
Profit before tax		10,520	4,490

Statement of financial position

	Note	FORECAST 12 months to 31 May 2013	UNAUDITED 12 months to 31 May 2012
Assets		$000	$000
Non-current assets			
Property, plant and equipment	2	330,150	293,000
Current assets			
Inventory		500	450
Receivables		3,600	3,300
Cash and cash equivalents		2,250	3,750
		6,350	7,500
Total assets		336,500	300,500

Equity and liabilities
Equity

Share capital		105,000	100,000
Retained earnings		93,400	92,600
Total equity		**198,400**	**192,600**
Non-current liabilities			
Long-term borrowings	2	82,500	52,500
Deferred tax		50,000	50,000
Current liabilities			
Trade payables		5,600	5,400
Total liabilities		**138,100**	**107,900**
Total equity and liabilities		**336,500**	**300,500**

Notes:

(1)   Beak Retail is a retail park which is underperforming. Its sale is currently being negotiated, and is expected to take place in September 2012.

(2)   Hawk Co is planning to invest the cash raised from the bank loan in a new retail and leisure park which is being developed jointly with another company, Kestrel Co.

Required:

In respect of the engagement to provide a report on Hawk Co's business plan:

(i)   **Identify and explain the matters that should be considered in agreeing the terms of the engagement, and**

Note: You are NOT required to consider ethical threats to objectivity.

(6 marks)

(ii)   **Recommend the procedures that should be performed in order to examine and report on the forecast financial statements of Hawk Co for the year to 31 May 2013.**
(13 marks)

(b) You are also responsible for the audit of Osprey Co, which has a financial year ended 31 May 2012. The audit engagement partner, Bill Kingfisher, sent you the following email this morning:

To: Audit manager

From: Bill Kingfisher, audit engagement partner, Osprey Co

Regarding: Environmental incident

Hello

Osprey Co's finance director called me yesterday to explain that unfortunately over the last few weeks, one of its four factories leaked a small amount of toxic chemicals into the atmosphere. The factory's operations were halted immediately and a decision has been taken to permanently close the site. Though this is a significant event for the company and will result in relocation and some restructuring of operations, it is not considered to be a threat to its going concern status. Costs of closure of the factory have been estimated to be $1.25 million, which is expected to be material to the financial statements, and a provision has been set up in respect of these costs.

Osprey Co is keen to highlight its previous excellent record on socio-environmental matters. Management is preparing a report to be published with the financial statements which will describe the commitment of the company to socio-environmental matters, and state its target of reducing environmental damage caused by its operations. The report will contain a selection of targets and key performance indicators to show performance in areas such as energy use, water consumption and employee satisfaction. Our firm may be asked to provide an assurance report on the key performance indicators.

I am asking you to prepare briefing notes for my use in which you:

(i) Recommend the principal audit procedures to be performed in respect of the costs of closure of the factory   **(6 marks)**

(ii) Discuss the difficulties in measuring and reporting on environmental and social performance.   **(4 marks)**

Thank you.

Required:

Respond to the partner's email.   **(10 marks)**

Note: the split of the mark allocation is shown within the partner's email.

Professional marks will be awarded in part (b) for the presentation and clarity of your answer.   **(4 marks)**

(Total: 33 marks)

9 **OAK** *Walk in the footsteps of a top tutor*

(a) You are a manager in Maple & Co, responsible for the audit of Oak Co, a listed company. Oak Co manufactures electrical appliances such as televisions and radios, which are then sold to retail outlets. You are aware that during the last year, Oak Co lost several customer contracts to overseas competitors. However, a new division has been created to sell its products directly to individual customers via a new website, which was launched on 1 November 2011.

You are about to commence planning the audit for the year ending 31 December 2011, and you have received an email from Holly Elm, the audit engagement partner.

To: Audit manager

From: Holly Elm, Audit partner

Subject: Oak Co – audit planning

Hello

(i) I would like you to start planning the audit of Oak Co. You need to perform a preliminary analytical review on the financial information and accompanying notes provided by Rowan Birch, the finance director of Oak Co. Using this information and the results of your analytical review, please prepare notes for inclusion in the planning section of the working papers, which identify and explain the principal audit risks to be considered in planning the final audit. Your notes should include any calculations performed. **(23 marks)**

(ii) Please also recommend the principal audit procedures which should be performed in respect of:

(1) the recognition and measurement of the share-based payment plan, and

(2) the classification of the new lease. **(8 marks)**

Thank you.

Financial information provided by Rowan Birch:

Statement of profit or loss (extract from management accounts)

	Note	11 months to 30 November 2011 $000	11 months to 30 November 2010 $000
Revenue		25,700	29,300
Cost of sales		(15,420)	(15,900)
Gross profit		10,280	13,400
Operating expenses	(1)	(6,200)	(7,750)
Operating profit		4,080	5,650
Finance costs		(1,500)	(1,500)
Profit before tax		2,580	4,150

Statement of financial position

	Note	30 November 2011	30 November 2010
ASSETS		$000	$000
Non-current assets			
Property plant and equipment	(2), (3)	90,000	75,750
Intangible assets	(4)	1,250	–
		91,250	75,750
Current assets			
Inventory		1,800	1,715
Trade receivables		4,928	4,815
Cash and cash equivalents		100	2,350
		6,828	8,880
Total assets		98,078	84,630
EQUITY AND LIABILITIES			
Equity			
Share capital		20,000	20,000
Revaluation reserve	(3)	10,000	–
Retained earnings		32,278	34,895
Total equity		62,278	54,895
Non-current liabilities			
Long-term borrowings	(5)	25,000	25,000
Provisions	(6)	1,000	1,250
Finance lease payable	(2)	5,000	–
		31,000	26,250
Current liabilities			
Bank overdraft	(7)	1,300	–
Trade and other payables		3,500	3,485
		4,800	3,485
Total liabilities		35,800	29,735
Total equity and liabilities		98,078	84,630

Notes:

(1) Oak Co established an equity-settled share-based payment plan for its executives on 1 January 2011. 250 executives and senior managers have received 100 share options each, which vest on 31 December 2013 if the executive remains in employment at that date, and if Oak Co's share price increases by 10% per annum. No expense has been recognised this year as Oak Co's share price has fallen by 5% in the last six months, and so it is felt that the condition relating to the share price will not be met this year end.

(2) On 1 July 2011, Oak Co entered into a lease which has been accounted for as a finance lease and capitalised at $5 million. The leased property is used as the head office for Oak Co's new website development and sales division. The lease term is for five years and the fair value of the property at the inception of the lease was $20 million.

(3) On 30 June 2011 Oak Co's properties were revalued by an independent expert.

(4) A significant amount has been invested in the new website, which is seen as a major strategic development for the company. The website has generated minimal sales since its launch last month, and advertising campaigns are currently being conducted to promote the site.

(5) The long-term borrowings are due to be repaid in two equal instalments on 30 September 2012 and 2013. Oak Co is in the process of renegotiating the loan, to extend the repayment dates, and to increase the amount of the loan.

(6) The provision relates to product warranties offered by the company.

(7) The overdraft limit agreed with Oak Co's bank is $1.5 million.

Required:

Respond to the email from the audit partner. (31 marks)

Note: the split of the mark allocation is shown within the partner's email.

Professional marks will be awarded for the presentation and clarity of your answer.
(2 marks)

(b) Maple & Co is suffering from declining revenue, and as a result of this, another audit manager has been asked to consider how to improve the firm's profitability. In a conversation with you this morning he mentioned the following:

'We really need to make our audits more efficient. I think we should fix materiality at the planning stage at the maximum possible materiality level for all audits, as this would reduce the work we need to do.

I also think we can cut the firm's overheads by reducing our spending on training. We spend a lot on expensive training courses for junior members of the audit team, and on Continuing Professional Development for our qualified members of staff.

We could also guarantee our clients that all audits will be completed quicker than last year. Reducing the time spent on each assignment will improve the firm's efficiency and enable us to take on more audit clients.'

Required:

Comment on the practice management and quality control issues raised by the audit manager's suggestions to improve the audit firm's profitability. (6 marks)

(Total: 39 marks)

10 WILLOW CO *Walk in the footsteps of a top tutor*

Willow Co is a print supplier to businesses, printing catalogues, leaflets, training manuals and stationery to order. It specialises in using 100% recycled paper in its printing, a fact which is promoted heavily in its advertising.

You are a senior audit manager in Bark & Co, and you have just been placed in charge of the audit of Willow Co. The audit for the year ended 31 August 2011 is nearing completion, and the audit engagement partner, Jasmine Berry, has sent you an email:

To: Audit manager

From: Jasmine Berry, Audit partner

Subject: Audit completion and other issues – Willow Co

Hello

The manager previously assigned to the audit of Willow Co has been moved to another urgent assignment, so thank you for stepping in to take on the manager's role this late in the audit. The audit report is due to be issued in two weeks' time, and the audit senior has prepared a summary of matters for your consideration.

I have been asked to attend a meeting with the audit committee of Willow Co tomorrow, so I need you to update me on how the audit has progressed. I am asking you to prepare briefing notes for my use in which you:

Assess the audit implications of the THREE issues related to audit work raised by the audit senior. Your assessment should consider the sufficiency of evidence obtained, explain any adjustments that may be necessary to the financial statements, and describe the impact on the audit report if these adjustments are not made. You should also recommend any further audit procedures necessary. **(15 marks)**

Explain the matters, other than the three issues related to audit work raised by the audit senior, which should be brought to the attention of the audit committee of Willow Co.

(8 marks)

Thanks

Summary of issues for manager's attention, prepared by audit senior

Materiality has been determined as follows:

$800,000 for assets and liabilities

$250,000 for income and expenses

Issues related to audit work performed:

(i)   Audit work on inventory

Audit procedures performed at the inventory count indicated that printed inventory items with a value of $130,000 were potentially obsolete. These items were mainly out of date training manuals. The finance director, Cherry Laurel, has not written off this inventory as she argues that the paper on which the items are printed can be recycled and used again in future printing orders. However, the items appear not to be recyclable as they are coated in plastic. The junior who performed the audit work on inventory has requested a written representation from management to confirm that the items can be recycled and no further procedures relevant to these items have been performed.

(ii)   **Audit work on provisions**

Willow Co is involved in a court case with a competitor, Aspen Co, which alleges that a design used in Willow Co's printed material copies one of Aspen Co's designs which are protected under copyright. Our evidence obtained is a verbal confirmation from Willow Co's lawyers that a claim of $125,000 has been made against Willow Co, which is probable to be paid. Cherry Laurel has not made a provision, arguing that it is immaterial. Cherry refused our request to ask the lawyers to confirm their opinion on the matter in writing, saying it is not worth bothering the lawyers again on such a trivial matter.

(iii)   **Audit work on current assets**

Willow Co made a loan of $6,000 to Cherry Laurel, the finance director, on 30 June 2011. The amount is recognised as a current asset. The loan carries an interest rate of 4% which we have confirmed to be the market rate for short-term loans and we have concluded that the loan is an arm's length transaction. Cherry has provided written confirmation that she intends to repay the loan by 31 March 2012. The only other audit work performed was to agree the cash payment to the cash book. Details of the loan made to Cherry have not been separately disclosed in the financial statements.

Other issues for your attention:

Property revaluations

Willow Co currently adopts an accounting policy of recognising properties at cost. During the audit of non-current assets Willow Co's property manager said that the company is considering a change of accounting policy so that properties would be recognised at fair value from 1 January 2012.

Non-current asset register

The audit of non-current assets was delayed by a week. We had asked for the non-current asset register reconciliation to be completed by the client prior to commencement of our audit procedures on non-current assets, but it seems that the person responsible for the reconciliation went on holiday having forgotten to prepare the reconciliation. This happened on last year's audit as well, and the issue was discussed with the audit committee at that time.

Procurement procedures

We found during our testing of trade payables that an approved supplier list is not maintained, and invoices received are not always matched back to goods received notes. This was mentioned to the procurement manager, who said that suppliers are switched fairly often, depending on which supplier is the cheapest, so it would be difficult to maintain an up-to-date approved supplier list.

Financial controller

Mia Fern, Willow Co's financial controller, owns a holiday home overseas. It appears that she offered the audit team free use of the holiday home for three weeks after the audit, as a reward for the team's hard work. She also bought lunch for the audit team on most days.

Required:

Respond to the partner's email.   (23 marks)

Note: the split of the mark allocation is shown within the email.

Professional marks will be awarded for the format and clarity of your answer.   (2 marks)

(Total: 25 marks)

11 BILL *Walk in the footsteps of a top tutor*

(a) You are a senior audit manager in Suki & Co, a firm of Chartered Certified Accountants. This morning you have been re-assigned to the audit of Bill Co, a long-standing audit client of your firm, as the manager previously assigned to the client has been taken ill. Bill Co has a year ending 30 June 2011, and the audit planning has been largely completed by the previously assigned audit manager, Tara Lafayette, who had been recruited by your firm four months ago.

Bill Co is a property development company, specialising in the regeneration and refurbishment of old industrial buildings, which are sold for commercial or residential use. All property developments are performed under specifically negotiated fixed-price contracts. The company was founded 35 years ago by two brothers, Alex and Ben Bradley, who own the majority of the company's share capital. Alex and Ben are nearing retirement age, and are planning to sell the company within the next two years. The forecast revenue for the year ending 30 June 2011 is $10.8 million, and the forecast profit before tax is $2.5 million. The forecast statement of financial position recognises total assets of $95 million.

You have just received the following email from the audit engagement partner:

To:	Audit manager
From:	Audit partner
Regarding: Bill Co – audit planning	

Hello

Thanks for taking on the role of audit manager for the forthcoming audit of Bill Co.

(i) I have just received some information on two significant issues that have arisen over the last week, from Sam Compton, the company's finance director. This information is provided in attachment 1.

I am asking you to prepare briefing notes, for my use, in which you explain the matters that should be considered in relation to the treatment of these two issues in the financial statements, and also explain the risks of material misstatement relating to them. I also want you to recommend the planned audit procedures that should be performed in order to address those risks.

(16 marks)

(ii) In addition, please critically evaluate the planning that has been completed by the previously assigned audit manager. Relevant details are provided in attachment 2, which contains notes made by her, and placed on the current year audit file. Make sure you include discussion of any ethical matters arising from the notes, and recommend any actions you think necessary.

(11 marks)

Thanks.

Attachment 1: Information from Sam Compton, finance director of Bill Co

In the last week, two significant issues have arisen at Bill Co. The first issue concerns a major contract involving the development of an old riverside warehouse into a conference centre in Bridgetown. An architect working on the development has discovered that the property will need significant additional structural improvements, the extra cost of which is estimated to be $350,000. The contract was originally forecast to make a profit of $200,000. The development is currently about one third complete, and will take a further 15 months to finish, including this additional construction work. The customer has been told that the completion of the contract will be delayed by around two months. However, the contract price is fixed, and so the additional costs must be covered by Bill Co.

The second issue concerns one of Bill Co's specialist divisions, which trades under the name 'Treasured Homes' and which deals exclusively in the redevelopment of non-industrial historic buildings such as castles and forts. These buildings are usually acquired as uninhabitable ruins, and are then developed into luxury residences for wealthy individuals. The management of Bill Co decided last week to sell this division, as although it is profitable, it generates a lower margin than other business divisions. 'Treasured Homes' operates separately from the rest of the business, and generates approximately 15% of the total revenue of the company. In a board minute dated 1 June 2011, it was noted that 'interest has already been expressed in this division from a potential buyer, and it is hoped that sale negotiations will soon commence, leading to sale in August 2011. There is a specific office building and some other tangible assets that will be sold as part of the deal. These assets are recorded at $7.6 million in the financial statements. No redundancies will be necessary as employees' contracts will transfer to the new owners.'

Attachment 2:

Planning Summary: Bill Co, year ending 30 June 2011, prepared by Tara Lafayette, manager previously assigned to the audit

The planning for the forthcoming audit is almost complete. Time has been saved by not carrying out procedures considered unnecessary for this long-standing audit client. Forecast accounts have been obtained and placed on file, and discussions held with management concerning business developments during the year. Analytical procedures have been performed on the statement of profits and losses, but not on the statement of financial position, as there did not appear to be any significant movements in assets or liabilities since last year.

Management confirmed that there have been no changes to accounting systems and controls in the financial year. For this reason we do not need to carry out walk-through tests or review our documentation of the systems and controls.

Management also confirmed that there have been no changes to business operations, other than the potential sale of 'Treasured Homes'. All divisions are operating normally, generating sufficient profit and cash. For this reason, the business risk of Bill Co is assessed as low, and no further comments or discussions about business operations have been placed on file.

The matter that will demand the most audit work is the valuation of properties currently under development, especially the determination of the percentage completion of each development at the reporting date. Historically, we have engaged a property valuation expert to provide a report on this area. However, Bill Co has recently employed a newly qualified architect, who will be happy to provide us with evidence concerning the stage of completion of each property development contract at the year end. Using this person to produce a report on all properties being developed will save time and costs.

Bill Co has recently completed the development of a luxury new office building in Newtown. Several of the office units are empty, and the management of Bill Co has offered the office space to our firm for a nominal rent of $100 per year.

Required:

Respond to the partner's email. **(27 marks)**

Note: The split of the mark allocation is shown within the partner's email.

Professional marks will be awarded for the format and clarity of your response.

(2 marks)

(b) Ben and Alex Bradley have a sister, Jo, who runs an interior design company, Lantern Co. During a review of board minutes, performed as part of the planning of Bill Co's audit, it was discovered that Bill Co has paid $225,000 to Lantern Co during the year, in respect of refurbishment of development properties. On further enquiry, it was also found that Lantern Co leases an office space from Bill Co, under an informal arrangement between the two companies.

Required:

(i)   **Explain the inherent limitations which mean that auditors may not identify related parties and related party transactions; and** **(4 marks)**

(ii) **Recommend the audit procedures to be performed in relation to Bill Co's transactions with Lantern Co.** **(4 marks)**

(Total: 37 marks)

12 BUTLER & CO *Walk in the footsteps of a top tutor*

(a) Butler Co is a new audit client of your firm. You are the manager responsible for the audit of the financial statements for the year ended 31 May 2011. Butler Co designs and manufactures aircraft engines and spare parts, and is a subsidiary of a multi-national group. Extracts from the draft financial statements are shown below:

Statement of financial position	31 May 2011 Draft $ million	31 May 2010 Actual $ million
Assets		
Non-current assets		
Intangible assets (note 1)	200	180
Property, plant and equipment (note 2)	1,300	1,200
Deferred tax asset (note 3)	235	20
Financial assets	25	35
	1,760	1,435
Current assets		
Inventory	1,300	800
Trade receivables	2,100	1,860
	3,400	2,660
Total assets	5,160	4,095
Equity and liabilities		
Equity		
Share capital	300	300
Retained earnings	(525)	95
	(225)	395
Non-current liabilities		
Long-term borrowings (note 4)	1,900	1,350
Provisions (note 5)	185	150
	2,085	1,500
Current liabilities		
Short-term borrowings (note 6)	800	400
Trade payables	2,500	1,800
	3,300	2,200
Total equity and liabilities	5,160	4,095

Notes to the statement of financial position:

Note 1   Intangible assets comprise goodwill on the acquisition of subsidiaries ($80 million), and development costs capitalised on engine development projects ($120 million).

Note 2   Property, plant and equipment includes land and buildings valued at $25 million, over which a fixed charge exists.

Note 3   The deferred tax asset has arisen following several loss-making years suffered by the company. The asset represents the tax benefit of unutilised tax losses carried forward.

Note 4   Long-term borrowings include a debenture due for repayment in July 2012, and a loan from Butler Co's parent company due for repayment in December 2012.

Note 5   Provisions relate to warranties provided to customers.

Note 6   Short-term borrowings comprise an overdraft ($25 million), a short term loan ($60 million) due for repayment in August 2011, and a bank loan ($715 million) repayable in September 2011.

You have received an email from the audit partner responsible for the audit of Butler Co:

To:	Audit manager
From:	Audit partner
Regarding: Butler Co – going concern issues	

Hello

I understand that the audit work on Butler Co commences this week. I am concerned about the future of the company, as against a background of economic recession, sales have been declining, several significant customer contracts have been cancelled unexpectedly, and competition from overseas has damaged the market share previously enjoyed by Butler Co.

(i)   Please prepare briefing notes, for my use, in which you identify and explain any matters arising from your review of the draft statement of financial position, and the cash flow forecast, which may cast significant doubt on the company's ability to continue as a going concern. The cash flow forecast has just been sent to me from the client, and is attached. It covers only the first three months of the next financial year, the client is currently preparing the forecasts for the whole 12 month period. Please be sceptical when reviewing the forecast, as the assumptions may be optimistic.   **(10 marks)**

(ii)   In addition, please recommend the principal audit procedures to be carried out on the cash flow forecast. Your recommendations can be included in a separate section of the briefing notes.   **(8 marks)**

Thanks.

Attachment: Cash flow forecast for the three months to 31 August 2011

	June 2011 $ million	July 2011 $ million	August 2011 $ million
Cash inflows			
Cash receipts from customers (note 1)	175	195	220
Loan receipt (note 2)		150	
Government subsidy (note 3)			50
Sales of financial assets	50		
Total cash inflows	225	345	270
Cash outflows			
Operating cash outflows	200	200	290
Interest payments	40	40	40
Loan repayment			60
Total cash outflows	240	240	390
Net cash flow for the month	(15)	105	(120)
Opening cash	(25)	(40)	65
Closing cash	(40)	65	(55)

Notes to the cash flow forecast:

This cash flow forecast has been prepared by the management of Butler Co, and is based on the following assumptions:

(1)   Cash receipts from customers should accelerate given the anticipated improvement in economic conditions. In addition, the company has committed extra resources to the credit control function, in order to speed up collection of overdue debts.

(2)   The loan expected to be received in July 2011 is currently being negotiated with our parent company, Rubery Co.

(3)   The government subsidy will be received once our application has been approved. The subsidy is awarded to companies which operate in areas of high unemployment and it subsidises the wages and salaries paid to staff.

Required:

Respond to the email from the audit partner.   **(18 marks)**

Note: The split of the mark allocation is shown within the partner's email. Professional marks will be awarded for presentation, and for the clarity of explanations provided.   **(2 marks)**

(b)   Given the information provided relating to Butler Co, it is likely that the auditor may conclude on completion of all necessary audit procedures, that the use of the going concern assumption in the financial statements is appropriate, but that a material uncertainty, or several uncertainties, exist regarding the company's ability to continue as a going concern.

Required:

If audit procedures indicate that one or more material uncertainties exist regarding Butler Co's ability to continue as a going concern:

Explain the matters that should be considered in forming the audit opinion and the potential impacts on the auditor's report.   **(7 marks)**

(Total: 27 marks)

13   JOLIE CO *Walk in the footsteps of a top tutor*

Jolie Co is a large company, operating in the retail industry, with a year ended 30 November 2010. You are a manager in Jen & Co, responsible for the audit of Jolie Co, and you have recently attended a planning meeting with Mo Pitt, the finance director of the company. As this is the first year that your firm will be acting as auditor for Jolie Co, you need to gain an understanding of the business risks facing the new client. Notes from your meeting are as follows:

Jolie Co sells clothing, with a strategy of selling high fashion items under the JLC brand name. New ranges of clothes are introduced to stores every eight weeks. The company relies on a team of highly skilled designers to develop new fashion ranges. The designers must be able to anticipate and quickly respond to changes in consumer preferences.

There is a high staff turnover in the design team.

Most sales are made in-store, but there is also a very popular catalogue, from which customers can place an order on-line, or over the phone. The company has recently upgraded the computer system and improved the website, at significant cost, in order to integrate the website sales directly into the general ledger, and to provide an easier interface for customers to use when ordering and entering their credit card details. The new on-line sales system has allowed overseas sales for the first time.

The system for phone ordering has recently been outsourced. The contract for outsourcing went out to tender and Jolie Co awarded the contract to the company offering the least cost. The company providing the service uses an overseas phone call centre where staff costs are very low.

Jolie Co has recently joined the Ethical Trading Initiative. This is a 'fair-trade' initiative, which means that any products bearing the JLC brand name must have been produced in a manner which is clean and safe for employees, and minimises the environmental impact of the manufacturing process. A significant advertising campaign promoting Jolie Co's involvement with this initiative has recently taken place. The JLC brand name was purchased a number of years ago and is recognised at cost as an intangible asset, which is not amortised. The brand represents 12% of the total assets recognised on the statement of financial position.

The company owns numerous distribution centres, some of which operate close to residential areas. A licence to operate the distribution centres is issued by each local government authority in which a centre is located. One of the conditions of the licence is that deliveries must only take place between 8 am and 6 pm. The authority also monitors the noise level of each centre, and can revoke the operating licence if a certain noise limit is breached. Two licences were revoked for a period of three months during the year.

You have just received the following e-mail from the audit engagement partner, Toni Pacino:

To: Audit manager

From: Toni Pacino

Regarding: Audit planning for Jolie Co

I would like you to begin the audit planning for our new audit client, Jolie Co. Mo Pitt has just sent to me extracts from Jolie Co's draft accounts and comparative figures, which should help you to prepare some briefing notes which will be used at the audit planning meeting. I understand you met recently with Mo, and I am sure you discussed a variety of issues relevant to the audit planning. In your briefing notes, you should evaluate the business risks facing Jolie Co. The notes will be used to brief the audit team members about the issues facing the client, and to help them gain some business understanding of Jolie Co.

Thanks, Toni

Extract from draft statement of profit or loss:

Year ending 30 November	2010 Draft	2009 Actual
	$ million	$ million
Revenue:		
Retail outlets	1,030	1,140
Phone and on-line sales	425	395
Total revenue	**1,455**	**1,535**
Operating profit	245	275
Finance costs	(25)	(22)
Profit before tax	**220**	**253**

Additional information:

Number of stores	210	208
Average revenue per store	$4.905 million	$5.77 million
Number of phone orders	680,000	790,000
Number of on-line orders	1,020,000	526,667
Average spend per order	$250	$300

Required:

(a)   Respond to the e-mail from the partner.   **(15 marks)**

        Professional marks will be awarded in part (a) for the format of the answer and the clarity of the evaluation.   **(2 marks)**

(b)   Using the information provided, identify and explain FIVE risks of material misstatement in the financial statements of Jolie Co.

                                                                                            (10 marks)

(c)   Recommend the principal audit procedures to be performed in respect of the valuation of the JLC brand name.   **(5 marks)**

                                                                                    (Total: 32 marks)

14   NEWMAN & CO   *Walk in the footsteps of a top tutor*

You are a manager in Newman & Co, a global firm of Chartered Certified Accountants. You are responsible for evaluating proposed engagements and for recommending to a team of partners whether or not an engagement should be accepted by your firm.

Eastwood Co, a listed company, is an existing audit client and is an international mail services operator, with a global network including 220 countries and 300,000 employees. The company offers mail and freight services to individual and corporate customers, as well as storage and logistical services.

Eastwood Co takes its corporate social responsibility seriously, and publishes social and environmental key performance indicators (KPIs) in a Sustainability Report, which is published with the financial statements in the annual report. Partly in response to requests from shareholders and pressure groups, Eastwood Co's management has decided that in the forthcoming annual report, the KPIs should be accompanied by an independent assurance report. An approach has been made to your firm to provide this report in addition to the audit.

To help in your evaluation of this potential engagement, you have been given an extract from the draft Sustainability Report, containing some of the KPIs published by Eastwood Co. In total, 25 environmental KPIs, and 50 social KPIs are disclosed.

Extract from Sustainability Report:

Year ended 31 October	2010 Draft	2009 Actual
CO_2 emissions (million tonnes)	26.8	28.3
Energy use (million kilowatt hours)	4,895	5,250
Charitable donations ($ million)	10.5	8.2
Number of serious accidents in the workplace	60	68
Average annual spend on training per employee	$180	$175

You have also had a meeting with Ali Monroe, the manager responsible for the audit of Eastwood Co, and notes of the meeting are given below:

> **Notes from meeting with audit manager, Ali Monroe**
>
> Newman & Co has audited Eastwood Co for three years, and it is a major audit client of our firm, due to its global presence and recent listing on two major stock exchanges. The audit is managed from our office in Oldtown, which is also the location of the global headquarters of Eastwood Co.
>
> We have not done any work on the KPIs, other than review them for consistency, as we would with any 'other information' issued with the financial statements. The KPIs are produced by Eastwood Co's Sustainability Department, located in Fartown.
>
> We have performed audit procedures on the charitable donations, as this is disclosed in a note to the financial statements, and our evidence indicates that there have been donations of $9 million this year, which is the amount disclosed in the note. However, the draft KPI is a different figure – $10.5 million, and this is the figure highlighted in the draft Chairman's Statement as well as the draft Sustainability Report. $9 million is material to the financial statements.
>
> The audit work is nearly complete, and the annual report is to be published in about four weeks, in time for the company meeting, scheduled for 31 January 2011.

Your firm has recently established a sustainability reporting assurance team based in Oldtown, and if the engagement to report on the Sustainability Report is accepted, it would be performed by members of that team, who would not be involved with the audit.

Required:

(a)   Identify and explain the matters that should be considered in evaluating the invitation to perform an assurance engagement on the Sustainability Report of Eastwood Co.   **(12 marks)**

(b)   Recommend procedures that could be used to verify the following draft KPIs:

   (i)   The number of serious accidents in the workplace; and

   (ii)   The average annual spend on training per employee.   **(6 marks)**

You have a trainee accountant assigned to you, who has read the notes taken at your meeting with Ali Monroe.

She is unsure of the implications of the charitable donations being disclosed as a different figure in the financial statements compared with the other information published in the annual report.

Required:

(c)   Prepare briefing notes to be used in a discussion with the trainee accountant, in which you:

   (i)   Explain the responsibility of the auditor in relation to other information published with the financial statements; and

   (ii)   Recommend the action to be taken by Newman & Co if the figure relating to charitable donations in the other information is not amended.   **(8 marks)**

   Professional marks will be awarded in part (c) for the format and clarity of your answer.   **(2 marks)**

                                                                                                      (Total: 28 marks)

15 GRISSOM GROUP (A) *Walk in the footsteps of a top tutor*

You are a senior audit manager in Vegas & Co, responsible for the audit of the Grissom Group, which has been an audit client for several years. The group companies all have a financial year ending 30 June 2010, and you are currently planning the final audit of the consolidated financial statements. The group's operations focus on the manufacture and marketing of confectionery and savoury snacks. Information about several matters relevant to the group audit is given below. These matters are all potentially material to the consolidated financial statements. None of the companies in the group are listed.

Grissom Co

This is a non-trading parent company, which wholly owns three subsidiaries – Willows Co, Hodges Co and Brass Co, all of which are involved with the core manufacturing and marketing operations of the group. This year, the directors decided to diversify the group's activities in order to reduce risk exposure. Non-controlling interests representing long-term investments have been made in two companies – an internet-based travel agent, and a chain of pet shops. In the consolidated statement of financial position, these investments are accounted for as associates, as Grissom Co is able to exert significant influence over the companies.

As part of their remuneration, the directors of Grissom Co receive a bonus based on the profit before tax of the group. In April 2010, the group finance director resigned from office after a disagreement with the chief executive officer over changes to accounting estimates. A new group finance director is yet to be appointed.

Willows Co

This company manufactures and distributes chocolate bars and cakes. In July 2009, production was relocated to a new, very large factory. One of the conditions of the planning permission for the new factory is that Willows Co must, at the end of the useful life of the factory, dismantle the premises and repair any environmental damage caused to the land on which it is situated.

Hodges Co

This company's operations involve the manufacture and distribution of packaged nuts and dried fruit. The government paid a grant in November 2009 to Hodges Co, to assist with costs associated with installing new, environmentally friendly, packing lines in its factories. The packing lines must reduce energy use by 25% as part of the conditions of the grant, and they began operating in February 2010.

Brass Co

This company is a new and significant acquisition, purchased in January 2010. It is located overseas, in Chocland, a developing country, and has been purchased to supply cocoa beans, a major ingredient for the goods produced by Willows Co. It is now supplying approximately half of the ingredients used in Willow Co's manufacturing. Chocland has not adopted International Financial Reporting Standards, meaning that Brass Co's financial statements are prepared using local accounting rules. The company uses local currency to measure and present its financial statements.

Further information

Your firm audits all components of the group with the exception of Brass Co, which is audited by a small local firm, Sidle & Co, based in Chocland. Audit regulations in Chocland are not based on International Standards on Auditing.

To:	Audit Manager
From:	Warwick Stokes
Re:	Grissom Group Audit Planning

Hello

I need you to get started on the planning for the audit of the consolidated financial statements of the Grissom Group. We will be holding an audit planning meeting next week, so can you put together some briefing notes to be used at that meeting? I want you to evaluate the principal audit risks, but do not consider issues to do with reliance on another auditor, as that will be dealt with separately. The briefing notes will be the basis of a discussion with the audit team.

Thanks,

Warwick.

Required:

(a) **Respond to the email from the engagement partner.** **(18 marks)**

   Professional marks will be awarded in part (a), for the format of the answer, and for the clarity of the evaluation. **(2 marks)**

(b) **Explain the factors that should be considered, and the procedures that should be performed, in deciding the extent of reliance to be placed on the work of Sidle & Co.** **(8 marks)**

(c) **Recommend the principal audit procedures that should be performed on:**

   (i) **The classification of non-controlling investments made by Grissom Co**
   (4 marks)

   (ii) **The condition attached to the grant received by Hodges Co.** **(4 marks)**

   (Total: 36 marks)

16 PAPAYA CO (A) *Walk in the footsteps of a top tutor*

(a) ISA 520 *Analytical Procedures* requires that the auditor performs analytical procedures during the initial risk assessment stage of the audit. These procedures, also known as preliminary analytical review, are usually performed before the year end, as part of the planning of the final audit.

   Required:

   (i) **Explain, using examples, the reasons for performing analytical procedures as part of risk assessment; and**

   (ii) **Discuss the limitations of performing analytical procedures at the planning stage of the final audit.** **(6 marks)**

(b) **Explain and differentiate between the terms 'overall audit strategy' and 'audit plan'.** **(4 marks)**

You are the manager responsible for the audit of Papaya Co, a listed company, which operates a chain of supermarkets, with a year ending 31 December 2009. There are three business segments operated by the company – two segments are supermarket chains which operate under internally generated brand names, and the third segment is a new financial services division.

The first business segment comprises stores branded as 'Papaya Mart'. This segment makes up three-quarters of the supermarkets of the company, and are large 'out of town' stores, located on retail parks on the edge of towns and cities. These stores sell a wide variety of items, including food and drink, clothing, household goods, and electrical appliances. In September 2009, the first overseas Papaya Mart opened in Farland. This expansion was a huge drain on cash resources, as it involved significant capital expenditure, as well as an expensive advertising campaign to introduce the Papaya Mart brand in Farland.

The second business segment comprises the rest of the supermarkets, which are much smaller stores, located in city centres, and branded as 'Papaya Express'. The Express stores offer a reduced range of products, focussing on food and drink, especially ready meals and other convenience items.

The company also established a financial services division on 1 January 2009, which offers loans, insurance services and credit cards to customers.

The audit engagement partner has today sent to you the following email.

To:	Audit Manager
From:	Audit Partner
Re:	Notes from meeting held 29 November 2009

Hello

We are due to hold the audit planning meeting for Papaya Co next week. In preparation for this, I am asking you to produce some briefing notes which assess the risks of material misstatement relevant to our new audit client. The notes that were taken at a recent meeting with the client are attached to the email.

Thanks,

A. Partner

Notes from meeting held 29 November 2009

On 31 August 2009, Papaya Co received notice from a government body that it is under investigation, along with three other companies operating supermarket chains, for alleged collusion and price fixing activities. If it is found guilty, significant financial penalties will be imposed on Papaya Co. The company is vigorously defending its case.

To help cash flows in a year of expansion, the company raised finance by issuing debentures which are potentially convertible into equity on maturity in 2015.

To manage the risk associated with overseas expansion, in October 2009, the company entered for the first time into several forward exchange contracts which end in February 2010. The contracts were acquired at no cost to Papaya Co and are categorised as 'fair value through profit or loss' financial instruments.

The property market has slumped this year, and significant losses were made on the sale of some plots of land which were originally acquired for development potential. The decision to sell the land was made as it is becoming increasingly difficult for the company to receive planning permission to build supermarkets on the land. Land is recognised at cost in the statement of financial position.

Papaya Co has 35 warehouses which store non-perishable items of inventory. Due to new regulation, each warehouse is required to undergo a major health and safety inspection every three years. All warehouses were inspected in January 2009, at a cost of $25,000 for each inspection.

(c)   **Using the specific information provided in respect of Papaya Co explain the information that you would require in order to perform analytical procedures during the planning of the audit.** (6 marks)

(d)   **Respond to the email from the partner.** (16 marks)

   Professional marks will be awarded in part (d) for the format of the answer, and for the clarity of assessment provided. (2 marks)

(Total: 34 marks)

17   BLUEBELL CO *Walk in the footsteps of a top tutor*

Bluebell Co operates a chain of 95 luxury hotels. This year's results show a return to profitability for the company, following several years of losses. Hotel trade journals show that on average, revenue in the industry has increased by around 20% this year. Despite improved profitability, Bluebell Co has poor liquidity, and is currently trying to secure further long-term finance.

You have been the manager responsible for the audit of Bluebell Co for the last four years. Extracts from the draft financial statements for the year ended 30 November 2008 are shown below:

Extracts from the Statement of profit or loss		
	2008	*2007*
	$m	*$m*
Revenue (note 1)	890	713
Operating expenses (note 2)	(835)	(690)
Other operating income (note 3)	135	10
Operating profit	190	33
Finance charges	(45)	(43)
Profit/(loss) before tax	145	(10)

Note 1: Revenue recognition

Revenue comprises sales of hotel rooms, conference and meeting rooms. Revenue is recognised when a room is occupied. A 20% deposit is taken when the room is booked.

Note 2: Significant items included in operating expenses:		
	2008	*2007*
	$m	*$m*
Share-based payment expense (i)	138	–
Damaged property repair expenses (ii)	100	–

(i) In June 2008 Bluebell Co granted 50 million share options to executives and employees of the company. The cost of the share option scheme is being recognised over the three year vesting period of the scheme. It is currently assumed that all of the options will vest and the expense is calculated on that basis. Bluebell Co operates in a tax jurisdiction in which no deferred tax consequences arise from share-based payment schemes.

(ii) In September 2008, three hotels situated near a major river were severely damaged by a flood. All of the hotels, which were constructed by Bluebell Co only two years ago, need extensive repairs and refurbishment at an estimated cost of $100 million, which has been provided in full. All of the buildings are insured for damage caused by flooding.

Note 3: Other operating income includes:		
	2008	*2007*
	$m	*$m*
Profit on property disposal (iii)	125	10

(iii) Eight properties were sold in March 2008 to Daffodil Fund Enterprises (DFE). Bluebell Co entered into a management contract with DFE and is continuing to operate the eight hotels under a 15 year agreement. Under the terms of the management contract, Bluebell Co receives an annual financial return based on the profit made by the eight hotels. At the end of the contract, Bluebell Co has the option to repurchase the hotels, and it is likely that the option will be exercised.

Extracts from the Statement of Financial Position	*2008*	*2007*
	$m	*$m*
Property, plant and equipment (note 4)	1,265	1,135
Deferred tax asset (note 5)	285	335
Deferred tax liability (note 6)	(735)	(638)
Total assets	2,870	2,230

Note 4: Property, Plant and Equipment (extract)

On 31 October 2008 all of Bluebell Co's owned hotels were revalued. A revaluation gain of $250 million has been recognised in the statement of changes in equity and in the statement of financial position.

Note 5: Deferred Tax Asset (extract)

The deferred tax asset represents unutilised tax losses which accumulated in the loss making periods 2004–2007 inclusive. Bluebell Co is confident that future taxable trading profits will be generated in order for the tax losses to be utilised.

Note 6: Deferred Tax Liability (extract)	*Temporary differences relating to Property, plant and equipment*
	$m
1 December 2007	638
Charged to equity	88
Charged to tax expense	9
	———
30 November 2008	735
	———

Required:

(a) Using the specific information provided, identify and explain the risks of material misstatement to be addressed when planning the final audit of Bluebell Co for the year ended 30 November 2008. **(14 marks)**

(b) Describe the principal audit procedures to be carried out in respect of the following:

    (i) The measurement of the share-based payment expense **(6 marks)**

    (ii) The recoverability of the deferred tax asset. **(4 marks)**

A new internal auditor, Daisy Rosepetal, has recently joined Bluebell Co. She has been asked by management to establish and to monitor a variety of social and environmental Key Performance Indicators (KPIs). Daisy has no experience in this area, and has asked you for some advice. It has been agreed with Bluebell Co's audit committee that you are to provide guidance to Daisy to help her in this part of her role, and that this does not impair the objectivity of the audit.

(c) Recommend EIGHT KPIs which could be used to monitor Bluebell Co's social and environmental performance, and outline the nature of evidence that should be available to provide assurance on the accuracy of the KPIs recommended. Your answer should be in the form of briefing notes to be used at a meeting with Daisy Rosepetal. **(10 marks)**

Note: Requirement (c) includes 2 professional marks.

(Total: 34 marks)

18 ROSIE CO *Walk in the footsteps of a top tutor*

Rosie Co is the parent company of an expanding group of companies. The group's main business activity is the manufacture of engine parts. In January 2008 the acquisition of Dylan Co was completed, and the group is currently considering the acquisition of Maxwell Co, a large company which would increase the group's operating facilities by around 40%. All subsidiaries are wholly owned. The group structure is summarised below:

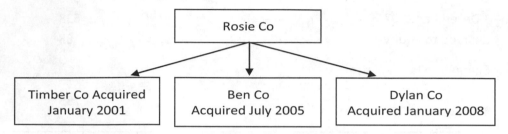

You are an audit manager in Chien & Co, a firm of Chartered Certified Accountants, and you are reviewing the working papers completed on the final audit of Rosie Co and the Rosie Group for the year ended 31 January 2008. Your firm has audited all current components of the group for several years, but the target company Maxwell Co is audited by a different firm.

The management of Rosie Co has provided the audit team with some information about Maxwell Co to aid business understanding, but little audit work is considered necessary as the acquisition, if it goes ahead, will be after the audit report has been issued. Information provided includes audited financial statements for the year ended 31 January 2008, an organisational structure, several customer contracts, and prospective financial information for the next two years. This seems to be all of the information that the directors of Rosie Co have available. The finance director, Leo Sabat is hoping that the other directors will agree that an externally provided due diligence investigation should be carried out urgently, before any investment decision is made, however the other directors feel this is not needed, as the financial statements of Maxwell Co have already been audited. Leo has asked you to prepare a report to explain to the other directors the purpose of due diligence, and the difference between due diligence and an audit of financial statements, which will be presented at the next board meeting. Goodwill on the acquisition of Dylan Co is recognised in the consolidated statement of financial position at $750,000. The calculation provided by the client is shown below:

	$000
Cost of Investment:	
Cash consideration	2,500
Deferred consideration payable 31 January 2009	1,500
Contingent consideration payable 31 January 2012 if Dylan Co's revenue grows 5% per annum	1,000
	–––––
	5,000
Net assets acquired	(4,250)
	–––––
Goodwill on acquisition	750
	–––––

All of the figures in the schedule above are material to the financial statements of Rosie Co and the Rosie Group.

Required:

(a) **Prepare a report to Leo Sabat (the finance director), in which you should:**

    (i) **Describe the purpose, and evaluate the benefits of a due diligence investigation to the potential purchaser of a company; and** **(10 marks)**

    (ii) **Compare the scope of a due diligence investigation with that of an audit of financial statements.** **(4 marks)**

    Note: **Requirement (a) includes 2 professional marks.**

(b) (i) **Explain the matters you should consider, and the evidence you would expect to find in respect of the carrying value of the cost of investment of Dylan Co in the financial statements of Rosie Co; and** **(7 marks)**

    (ii) **State the principal audit procedures to be performed on the consolidation schedule of the Rosie Group.** **(4 marks)**

(c) Maxwell Co is audited by Lead & Co, a firm of Chartered Certified Accountants. Leo Sabat has enquired as to whether your firm would be prepared to conduct a joint audit in cooperation with Lead & Co, on the future financial statements of Maxwell Co if the acquisition goes ahead. Leo Sabat thinks that this would enable your firm to improve group audit efficiency, without losing the cumulative experience that Lead & Co has built up while acting as auditor to Maxwell Co.

Required:

Define 'joint audit', and assess the advantages and disadvantages of the audit of Maxwell Co being conducted on a 'joint basis'. **(7 marks)**

(Total: 32 marks)

 Online question assistance

Section 2

PRACTICE QUESTIONS – SECTION B

PROFESSIONAL/ETHICAL CONSIDERATIONS AND PRACTICE MANAGEMENT

19   CHESTER & CO *Walk in the footsteps of a top tutor*

You are an audit manager in Chester & Co, and you are reviewing three situations which have recently arisen with respect to potential and existing audit clients of your firm.

Tetbury Co's managing director, Juan Stanton, has approached Chester & Co to invite the firm to tender for its audit. Tetbury Co is a small, owner-managed company providing financial services such as arranging mortgages and advising on pension plans. The company's previous auditors recently resigned. Juan Stanton states that this was due to 'a disagreement on the accounting treatment of commission earned, and because they thought our controls were not very good.' You are aware that Tetbury Co has been investigated by the financial services authority for alleged noncompliance with its regulations. As well as performing the audit, Juan would like Chester & Co to give business development advice.

The audit of Stratford Co's financial statements for the year ended 30 November 2013 will commence shortly. You are aware that the company is in financial difficulties. Stratford Co's managing director, Colin Charlecote, has requested that the audit engagement partner accompanies him to a meeting with the bank where a new loan will be discussed, and the draft financial statements reviewed. Colin has hinted that if the partner does not accompany him to the meeting, he will put the audit out to tender. In addition, an invoice relating to interim audit work performed in August 2013 has not yet been paid.

Banbury Co is a listed entity, and its audit committee has asked Chester & Co to perform an actuarial valuation on the company's defined benefit pension plan. One of the audit partners is a qualified actuary and has the necessary skills and expertise to perform the service. Banbury Co has a year ending 28 February 2014, and the audit planning is due to commence next week. Its financial statements for the year ended 28 February 2013, in respect of which the audit report was unmodified, included total assets of $35 million and a pension liability of $105,000.

Required:

Identify and discuss the ethical and other professional issues raised, and recommend any actions that should be taken in respect of:

(a)	Tetbury Co	(8 marks)
(b)	Stratford Co; and	(6 marks)
(c)	Banbury Co.	(6 marks)

(Total: 20 marks)

20 WELLER & CO *Walk in the footsteps of a top tutor*

(a) You are an audit manager in Weller & Co, an audit firm which operates as part of an international network of firms. This morning you received a note from a partner regarding a potential new audit client:

'I have been approached by the audit committee of the Plant Group, which operates in the mobile telecommunications sector. Our firm has been invited to tender for the audit of the individual and group financial statements for the year ending 31 March 2013, and I would like your help in preparing the tender document. This would be a major new client for our firm's telecoms audit department.

The Plant Group comprises a parent company and six subsidiaries, one of which is located overseas. The audit committee is looking for a cost effective audit, and hopes that the strength of the Plant Group's governance and internal control mean that the audit can be conducted quickly, with a proposed deadline of 31 May 2013. The Plant Group has expanded rapidly in the last few years and significant finance was raised in July 2012 through a stock exchange listing.'

Required:

Identify and explain the specific matters to be included in the tender document for the audit of the Plant Group. **(8 marks)**

(b) Weller & Co is facing competition from other audit firms, and the partners have been considering how the firm's revenue could be increased. Two suggestions have been made:

(1) Audit partners and managers can be encouraged to sell non-audit services to audit clients by including in their remuneration package a bonus for successful sales.

(2) All audit managers should suggest to their audit clients that as well as providing the external audit service, Weller & Co can provide the internal audit service as part of an 'extended audit' service.

Required:

Comment on the ethical and professional issues raised by the suggestions to increase the firm's revenue. **(8 marks)**

(Total: 16 marks)

21 RAVEN *Walk in the footsteps of a top tutor*

You are a senior manager in the audit department of Raven & Co. You are reviewing two situations which have arisen in respect of audit clients, which were recently discussed at the monthly audit managers' meeting:

Grouse Co is a significant audit client which develops software packages. Its managing director, Max Partridge, has contacted one of your firm's partners regarding a potential business opportunity. The proposal is that Grouse Co and Raven & Co could jointly develop accounting and tax calculation software, and that revenue from sales of the software would be equally split between the two firms. Max thinks that Raven & Co's audit clients would be a good customer base for the product.

Plover Co is a private hospital which provides elective medical services, such as laser eye surgery to improve eyesight. The audit of its financial statements for the year ended 31 March 2012 is currently taking place. The audit senior overheard one of the surgeons who performs laser surgery saying to his colleague that he is hoping to finish his medical qualification soon, and that he was glad that Plover Co did not check his references before employing him. While completing the subsequent events audit procedures, the audit senior found a letter from a patient's solicitor claiming compensation from Plover Co in relation to alleged medical negligence resulting in injury to the patient.

Required:

Identify and discuss the ethical, commercial and other professional issues raised, and recommend any actions that should be taken in respect of:

(a)   **Grouse Co; and**   (8 marks)

(b)   **Plover Co.**   (7 marks)

(Total: 15 marks)

22 WEXFORD *Walk in the footsteps of a top tutor*

(a)   Your firm has been approached by Wexford Co to provide the annual audit. Wexford Co operates a chain of bookshops across the country. The shops sell stationery such as diaries and calendars, as well as new books. The financial year will end on 31 July 2011, and this will be the first year that an audit is required, as previously the company was exempt from audit due to its small size.

The potential audit engagement partner, Wendy Kwan, recently attended a meeting with Ravi Shah, managing director of Wexford Co regarding the audit appointment. In this meeting, Ravi made the following comments:

'Wexford Co is a small, owner-managed business. I run the company, along with my sister, Rita, and we employ a part-qualified accountant to do the bookkeeping and prepare the annual accounts. The accountant prepares management accounts at the end of every quarter, but Rita and I rarely do more than quickly review the sales figures. We understand that due to the company's size, we now need to have the accounts audited. It would make sense if your firm could prepare the accounts and do the audit at the same time. We don't want a cash flow statement prepared, as it is not required for tax purposes, and would not be used by us.

Next year we are planning to acquire another company, one of our competitors, which I believe is an existing audit client of your firm. For this reason, we require that your audit procedures do not include reading the minutes of board meetings, as we have been discussing some confidential matters regarding this potential acquisition.'

Required:

Identify and explain the professional and ethical matters that should be considered in deciding whether to accept the appointment as auditor of Wexford Co.

(10 marks)

(b)   Wexford Co's financial statements for the year ended 31 July 2010 included the following balances:

Profit before tax $50,000

Inventory $25,000

Total assets $350,000

The inventory comprised stocks of books, diaries, calendars and greetings cards.

Required:

In relation to opening balances where the financial statements for the prior period were not audited:

Explain the audit procedures required by ISA 510 *Initial Audit Engagements – Opening Balances*, and recommend the specific audit procedures to be applied to Wexford Co's opening balance of inventory.   **(8 marks)**

(Total: 18 marks)

23   NEESON & CO   *Walk in the footsteps of a top tutor*

(a)   You are a manager in Neeson & Co, a firm of Chartered Certified Accountants, with three offices and 12 partners. About one third of the firm's clients are audit clients, the remainder are clients for whom Neeson & Co performs tax, accounting and business advisory services. The firm is considering how to generate more revenue, and you have been asked to evaluate two suggestions made by the firm's business development manager.

(i)   An advertisement could be placed in national newspapers to attract new clients. The draft advertisement has been given to you for review:

> Neeson & Co is the largest and most professional accountancy and audit provider in the country. We offer a range of services in addition to audit, which are guaranteed to improve your business efficiency and save you tax.
>
> If you are unhappy with your auditors, we can offer a second opinion on the report that has been given.
>
> Introductory offer: for all new clients we offer a 25% discount when both audit and tax services are provided. Our rates are approved by ACCA.

(8 marks)

(ii)   A new partner with experience in the banking sector has joined Neeson & Co. It has been suggested that the partner could specialise in offering a corporate finance service to clients. In particular, the partner could advise clients on raising debt finance, and would negotiate with the client's bank or other provider of finance on behalf of the client. The fee charged for this service would be contingent on the client obtaining the finance with a borrowing cost below market rate.   **(5 marks)**

Required:

Evaluate each of the suggestions made above, commenting on the ethical and professional issues raised.

Note: the mark allocation is shown against each of the issues.(b) You have set up an internal discussion board, on which current issues are debated by employees and partners of Neeson & Co. One posting to the board concerned the compulsory rotation of audit firms, whereby it has been suggested in the press that after a pre-determined period, an audit firm must resign from office, to be replaced by a new audit provider.

Required:

(i)   **Explain the ethical threats created by a long association with an audit client.**
                                                                              (3 marks)

(ii)   **Evaluate the advantages and disadvantages of compulsory audit firm rotation.**
                                                                              (4 marks)

                                                                       (Total: 20 marks)

24   CARTER & CO   *Walk in the footsteps of a top tutor*

You are a manager in the audit department of Carter & Co, and you are dealing with several ethical and professional matters raised at recent management meetings, all of which relate to audit clients of your firm.

(1)   Fernwood Co has a year ending 30 June 2010. During this year, the company established a pension plan for its employees, and this year end the company will be recognising for the first time a pension deficit on the statement of financial position, in accordance with IAS 19 Employee Benefits. The finance director of Fernwood Co has contacted the audit engagement partner, asking if your firm can provide a valuation service in respect of the amount recognised.

(2)   The finance director of Hall Co has requested that a certain audit senior, Kia Nelson, be assigned to the audit team. This senior has not previously been assigned to the audit of Hall Co. On further investigation it transpired that Kia Nelson is the sister of Hall Co's financial controller.

(3)   Collier Co has until recently kept important documents such as title deeds and insurance certificates in a safe at its head office. However, following a number of thefts from the head office the directors have asked if the documents could be held securely at Carter & Co's premises. The partners of Carter & Co are considering offering a custodial service to all clients, some of whom may want to deposit tangible assets such as paintings purchased as investments for safekeeping. The fee charged for this service would depend on the value of item deposited as well as the length of the safekeeping arrangement.

(4)   Several audit clients have requested that Carter & Co provide technical training on financial reporting and tax issues. This is not a service that the firm wishes to provide, and it has referred the audit clients to a training firm, Gates Co, which is paying a referral fee to Carter & Co for each audit client which is referred.

Required:

Identify and evaluate the ethical and other professional issues raised, in respect of:

(a)   Fernwood Co   **(6 marks)**

(b)   Hall Co   **(6 marks)**

(c)   Collier Co   **(5 marks)**

(d)   Gates Co.   **(3 marks)**

                                                                                                  (Total: 20 marks)

25   **CLIFDEN & CO**   *Walk in the footsteps of a top tutor*

 Timed question with Online tutor debrief

(a)   IFAC's Code of Ethics for Professional Accountants states that a professional accountant is required to comply with five fundamental principles, one of which is the principle of 'professional competence and due care'.

Required:

Explain what is meant by the term 'professional competence and due care', and outline how firms of Chartered Certified Accountants can ensure that the principle is complied with. **(4 marks)**

(b)   You are a senior manager in Clifden & Co, and you are responsible for the audit of Headford Co, a manufacturer of plastic toys which are exported all over the world. The following matter has been brought to your attention by the audit senior, who has just completed the planning of the forthcoming audit for the year ending 30 June 2009:

During a discussion with the production manager, it was revealed that there have been some quality control problems with the toys manufactured between March and May 2009. It was discovered that some of the plastic used in the manufacture of the company's products had been contaminated with a dangerous chemical which has the potential to explode if it is exposed to high temperatures. Headford Co did not recall any of the products which had been manufactured during that time from customers, as management felt that the risk of any injury being caused was remote.

Your firm has been invited to tender for the provision of the external audit service to Cong Co. You are aware that Cong Co operates in the same industry as Headford Co, and that the two companies often enter into highly publicised, aggressive advertising campaigns featuring very similar products. Cong Co is a much larger company than Headford Co, and there would be the opportunity to offer some non-audit services as well as the external audit.

Required:

Assess the ethical and professional issues raised, and recommend any actions necessary in respect of:

(i)   **the contaminated plastic used by Headford Co; and** (8 marks)

(ii)   **the invitation to audit Cong Co.** (5 marks)

(Total: 17 marks)

ASSIGNMENTS

26   DASSET *Walk in the footsteps of a top tutor*

Dasset Co operates in the coal mining industry. The company owns ten mines across the country from which coal is extracted before being sold onto customers who are energy providers. Coal mining companies operate under licence from the National Coal Mining Authority, an organisation which monitors the environmental impact of coal mining operations, and requires coal mines to be operated in compliance with strict health and safety regulations.

You are an audit manager in Burton & Co, responsible for the audit of Dasset Co and you are reviewing the audit working papers for the year ended 31 August 2013. The draft financial statements recognise profit before tax of $18 million and total assets of $175 million. The audit senior has left a note for your attention:

Accident at the Ledge Hill Mine

On 15 August 2013, there was an accident at the Ledge Hill Mine, where several of the tunnels in the mine collapsed, causing other tunnels to become flooded. This has resulted in one-third of the mine becoming inaccessible and for safety reasons, the tunnels will be permanently closed. However, Dasset Co's management thinks that the rest of the mine can remain operational, as long as improvements are made to ensure that the mine meets health and safety regulations.

Luckily no one was injured in the accident. However, the collapse caused subsidence which has damaged several residential properties in a village located above the mine. A surveyor has been commissioned to report on whether the properties need to be demolished or whether they can be safely repaired. A group of 20 residents has been relocated to rental properties in the local area and Dasset Co is meeting all expenses in relation to this.

The Ledge Hill Mine was acquired several years ago and is recognised in the draft statement of financial position at $10 million. As no employees were injured in the accident, Dasset Co's management has decided not to report the accident to the National Coal Mining Authority.

Required:

In respect of the accident at the Ledge Hill Mine:

(a)   (i)   Comment on the matters which you should consider; and

       (ii)   Describe the audit evidence which you should expect to find,

      in undertaking your review of the audit working papers and financial statements of Dasset Co.

      Note: The total marks will be split equally between each part.   **(14 marks)**

(b   In relation to management's decision not to report the accident to the National Coal Mining Authority, discuss Burton & Co's responsibilities and recommend the actions which should be taken by the firm.   **(6 marks)**

                                             (Total: 20 marks)

27   SETTER STORES   *Walk in the footsteps of a top tutor*

You are the manager responsible for the audit of Setter Stores Co, a company which operates supermarkets across the country. The final audit for the year ended 31 January 2013 is nearing completion and you are reviewing the audit working papers. The draft financial statements recognise total assets of $300 million, revenue of $620 million and profit before tax of $47.5 million.

Three issues from the audit working papers are summarised below:

(a)   **Assets held for sale**

      Setter Stores Co owns a number of properties which have been classified as assets held for sale in the statement of financial position. The notes to the financial statements state that the properties are all due to be sold within one year. On classification as held for sale, in October 2012, the properties were re-measured from carrying value of $26 million to fair value less cost to sell of $24 million, which is the amount recognised in the statement of financial position at the year end.   **(8 marks)**

(b)   **Sale and leaseback arrangement**

      A sale and leaseback arrangement involving a large property complex was entered into on 31 January 2013. The property complex is a large warehousing facility, which was sold for $37 million, its fair value at the date of the disposal. The facility had a carrying value at that date of $27 million. The only accounting entry recognised in respect of the proceeds raised was to record the cash received and recognise a non-current liability classified as 'Obligations under finance lease'. The lease term is for 20 years, the same as the remaining useful life of the property complex, and Setter Stores Co retains the risks and rewards associated with the asset.   **(7 marks)**

(c)   **Distribution licence**

      The statement of financial position includes an intangible asset of $15 million, which is the cost of a distribution licence acquired on 1 September 2012. The licence gives Setter Stores Co the exclusive right to distribute a popular branded soft drink in its stores for a period of five years.   **(5 marks)**

Required:

Comment on the matters to be considered, and explain the audit evidence you should expect to find during your file review in respect of each of the issues described above.

Note: The split of the mark allocation is shown against each of the issues above.

(Total: 20 marks)

28   SPANIEL *Walk in the footsteps of a top tutor*

You are a manager in Groom & Co, a firm of Chartered Certified Accountants. You have just attended a monthly meeting of audit partners and managers at which client-related matters were discussed. Information in relation to two clients, which were discussed at the meeting, is given below:

(a)   **Spaniel Co**

The audit report on the financial statements of Spaniel Co, a long-standing audit client, for the year ended 31 December 2012 was issued in April 2013, and was unmodified. In May 2013, Spaniel Co's audit committee contacted the audit engagement partner to discuss a fraud that had been discovered. The company's internal auditors estimate that $4.5 million has been stolen in a payroll fraud, which has been operating since May 2012.

The audit engagement partner commented that neither tests of controls nor substantive audit procedures were conducted on payroll in the audit of the latest financial statements as in previous years' audits there were no deficiencies found in controls over payroll. The total assets recognised in Spaniel Co's financial statements at 31 December 2012 were $80 million. Spaniel Co is considering suing Groom & Co for the total amount of cash stolen from the company, claiming that the audit firm was negligent in conducting the audit.

Required:

Explain the matters that should be considered in determining whether Groom & Co is liable to Spaniel Co in respect of the fraud. **(12 marks)**

(b)   **Bulldog Co**

Bulldog Co is a clothing manufacturer, which has recently expanded its operations overseas. To manage exposure to cash flows denominated in foreign currencies, the company has set up a treasury management function, which is responsible for entering into hedge transactions such as forward exchange contracts. These transactions are likely to be material to the financial statements. The audit partner is about to commence planning the audit for the year ending 31 July 2013.

Required:

Discuss why the audit of financial instruments is particularly challenging, and explain the matters to be considered in planning the audit of Bulldog Co's forward exchange contracts. **(8 marks)**

(Total: 20 marks)

29   KOBAIN *Walk in the footsteps of a top tutor*

(a)   'Revenue recognition should always be approached as a high risk area of the audit.'

Required:

Discuss this statement.   **(6 marks)**

(b)   You are a manager in Beck & Co, responsible for the audit of Kobain Co, a new audit client of your firm, with a financial year ended 31 July 2012. Kobain Co's draft financial statements recognise total assets of $55 million, and profit before tax of $15 million. The audit is nearing completion and you are reviewing the audit files.

Kobain Co designs and creates high-value items of jewellery. Approximately half of the jewellery is sold in Kobain Co's own retail outlets. The other half is sold by external vendors under a consignment stock arrangement, the terms of which specify that Kobain Co retains the ability to change the selling price of the jewellery, and that the vendor is required to return any unsold jewellery after a period of nine months. When the vendor sells an item of jewellery to a customer, legal title passes from Kobain Co to the customer.

On delivery of the jewellery to the external vendors, Kobain Co recognises revenue and derecognises inventory. At 31 July 2012, jewellery at cost price of $3 million is held at external vendors. Revenue of $4 million has been recognised in respect of this jewellery.

Required:

Comment on the matters that should be considered, and explain the audit evidence you should expect to find in your file review in respect of the consignment stock arrangement.   **(6 marks)**

(c)   Your firm also performs the audit of Jarvis Co, a company which installs windows. Jarvis Co uses sales representatives to make direct sales to customers. The sales representatives earn a small salary, and also earn a sales commission of 20% of the sales they generate.

Jarvis Co's sales manager has discovered that one of the sales representatives has been operating a fraud, in which he was submitting false claims for sales commission based on non-existent sales. The sales representative started to work at Jarvis Co in January 2012. The forensic investigation department of your firm has been engaged to quantify the amount of the fraud.

Required:

Recommend the procedures that should be used in the forensic investigation to quantify the amount of the fraud.   **(4 marks)**

                                                                    (Total: 16 marks)

30 HERON *Walk in the footsteps of a top tutor*

(a) You are a manager in Lark & Co, responsible for the audit of Heron Co, an owner-managed business which operates a chain of bars and restaurants. This is your firm's first year auditing the client and the audit for the year ended 31 March 2012 is underway. The audit senior sends a note for your attention:

'When I was auditing revenue I noticed something strange. Heron Co's revenue, which is almost entirely cash-based, is recognised at $5.5 million in the draft financial statements. However, the accounting system shows that till receipts for cash paid by customers amount to only $3.5 million. This seemed odd, so I questioned Ava Gull, the financial controller about this. She said that Jack Heron, the company's owner, deals with cash receipts and posts through journals dealing with cash and revenue. Ava asked Jack the reason for these journals but he refused to give an explanation.

'While auditing cash, I noticed a payment of $2 million made by electronic transfer from the company's bank account to an overseas financial institution. The bank statement showed that the transfer was authorised by Jack Heron, but no other documentation regarding the transfer was available.

'Alarmed by the size of this transaction, and the lack of evidence to support it, I questioned Jack Heron, asking him about the source of cash receipts and the reason for electronic transfer. He would not give any answers and became quite aggressive.'

Required:

(i) **Discuss the implications of the circumstances described in the audit senior's note; and** **(6 marks)**

(ii) **Explain the nature of any reporting that should take place by the audit senior.** **(3 marks)**

(b) You are also responsible for the audit of Coot Co, and you are currently reviewing the working papers of the audit for the year ended 28 February 2012. In the working papers dealing with payroll, the audit junior has commented as follows:

'Several new employees have been added to the company's payroll during the year, with combined payments of $125,000 being made to them. There does not appear to be any authorisation for these additions. When I questioned the payroll supervisor who made the amendments, she said that no authorisation was needed because the new employees are only working for the company on a temporary basis. However, when discussing staffing levels with management, it was stated that no new employees have been taken on this year. Other than the tests of controls planned, no other audit work has been performed.'

Required:

In relation to the audit of Coot Co's payroll:

Explain the meaning of the term 'professional scepticism', and recommend any further actions that should be taken by the auditor. **(6 marks)**

(Total: 15 marks)

31   FIR   *Walk in the footsteps of a top tutor*

You are a manager in the audit department of Beech & Co, responsible for the audits of Fir Co, Spruce Co and Pine Co. Each company has a financial year ended 31 July 2011, and the audits of all companies are nearing completion. The following issues have arisen in relation to the audit of accounting estimates and fair values:

(a)   **Fir Co**

Fir Co is a company involved in energy production. It owns several nuclear power stations, which have a remaining estimated useful life of 20 years. Fir Co intends to decommission the power stations at the end of their useful life and the statement of financial position at 31 July 2011 recognises a material provision in respect of decommissioning costs of $97 million (2010 – $110 million). A brief note to the financial statements discloses the opening and closing value of the provision but no other information is provided.

Required:

Comment on the matters that should be considered, and explain the audit evidence you should expect to find in your file review in respect of the decommissioning provision.   **(8 marks)**

(b)   **Spruce Co**

Spruce Co is also involved in energy production. It has a trading division which manages a portfolio of complex financial instruments such as derivatives. The portfolio is material to the financial statements. Due to the specialist nature of these financial instruments, an auditor's expert was engaged to assist in obtaining sufficient appropriate audit evidence relating to the fair value of the financial instruments. The objectivity, capabilities and competence of the expert were confirmed prior to their engagement.

Required:

Explain the procedures that should be performed in evaluating the adequacy of the auditor's expert's work.   **(5 marks)**

(c)   **Pine Co**

Pine Co operates a warehousing and distribution service, and owns 120 properties. During the year ended 31 July 2011, management changed its estimate of the useful life of all properties, extending the life on average by 10 years. The financial statements contain a retrospective adjustment, which increases opening non-current assets and equity by a material amount. Information in respect of the change in estimate has not been disclosed in the notes to the financial statements.

Required:

Identify and explain the potential implications for the auditor's report of the accounting treatment of the change in accounting estimates.   **(5 marks)**

(Total: 18 marks)

32   CHESTNUT *Walk in the footsteps of a top tutor*

You are an audit manager in Cedar & Co, responsible for the audit of Chestnut Co, a large company which provides information technology services to business customers. The finance director of Chestnut Co, Jack Privet, contacted you this morning, saying:

'I was alerted yesterday to a fraud being conducted by members of our sales team. It appears that several sales representatives have been claiming reimbursement for fictitious travel and client entertaining expenses and inflating actual expenses incurred. Specifically, it has been alleged that the sales representatives have claimed on expenses for items such as gifts for clients and office supplies which were never actually purchased, claimed for business-class airline tickets but in reality had purchased economy tickets, claimed for non-existent business mileage and used the company credit card to purchase items for personal use.

I am very worried about the scale of this fraud, as travel and client entertainment is one of our biggest expenses. All of the alleged fraudsters have been suspended pending an investigation, which I would like your firm to conduct. We will prosecute these employees to attempt to recoup our losses if evidence shows that a fraud has indeed occurred, so your firm would need to provide an expert witness in the event of a court case. Can we meet tomorrow to discuss this potential assignment?'

Chestnut Co has a small internal audit department and in previous years the evidence obtained by Cedar & Co as part of the external audit has indicated that the control environment of the company is generally good. The audit opinion on the financial statements for the year ended 31 March 2011 was unmodified.

Required:

(a)   Assess the ethical and professional issues raised by the request for your firm to investigate the alleged fraudulent activity. **(6 marks)**

(b)   Explain the matters that should be discussed in the meeting with Jack Privet in respect of planning the investigation into the alleged fraudulent activity. **(6 marks)**

(c)   Evaluate the arguments for and against the prohibition of auditors providing non-audit services to audit clients. **(6 marks)**

(Total: 18 marks)

33   JACOB *Walk in the footsteps of a top tutor*

Jacob Co, an audit client of your firm, is a large privately owned company whose operations involve a repair and maintenance service for domestic customers. The company offers a range of services, such as plumbing and electrical repairs and maintenance, and the repair of domestic appliances such as washing machines and cookers, as well as dealing with emergencies such as damage caused by flooding. All work is covered by a two-year warranty.

The directors of Jacob Co have been seeking to acquire expertise in the repair and maintenance of swimming pools and hot-tubs as this is a service increasingly requested, but not offered by the company. They have recently identified Locke Co as a potential acquisition. Preliminary discussions have been held between the directors of the two companies with a view to the acquisition of Locke Co by Jacob Co. This will be the first acquisition performed by the current management team of Jacob Co. Your firm has been asked to perform a due diligence review on Locke Co prior to further discussions taking place. You have been provided with the following information regarding Locke Co:

Locke Co is owner-managed, with three of the five board members being the original founders of the company, which was incorporated thirty years ago. The head office is located in a prestigious building, which is owned by the founders' family estate. The company recently acquired a separate piece of land on which a new head office is to be built.

The company has grown rapidly in the last three years as more affluent customers can afford the cost of installing and maintaining swimming pools and hot-tubs. The expansion was funded by a significant bank loan. The company relies on an overdraft facility in the winter months when less operating cash inflows arise from maintenance work.

Locke Co enjoys a good reputation, though this was tarnished last year by a complaint by a famous actor who claimed that, following maintenance of his swimming pool by Locke Co's employees, the water contained a chemical which damaged his skin. A court case is on-going and is attracting media attention.

The company's financial year end is 31 August. Its accounting function is outsourced to Austin Co, a local provider of accounting and tax services.

Required:

(a)   Explain THREE potential benefits of an externally provided due diligence review to Jacob Co. **(6 marks)**

(b)   Recommend additional information which should be made available for your firm's due diligence review, and explain the need for the information. **(12 marks)**

(Total: 18 marks)

34   **CLOONEY CO** *Walk in the footsteps of a top tutor*

Clooney Co is one of the world's leading leisure travel providers, operating under several brand names to sell package holidays. The company catered for more than 10 million customers in the last 12 months. Draft figures for the year ended 30 September 2010 show revenue of $3,200 million, profit before tax of $150 million, and total assets of $4,100 million. Clooney Co's executives earn a bonus based on the profit before tax of the company.

You are the manager responsible for the audit of Clooney Co. The final audit is nearing completion, and the following points have been noted by the audit senior for your attention:

In July 2010, thousands of holiday-makers were left stranded abroad after the company operating the main airline chartered by Clooney Co went into liquidation. The holiday-makers were forced to wait an average of two weeks before they could be returned home using an alternative airline. They have formed a group which is claiming compensation for the time they were forced to spend abroad, with the total claim amounting to $20 million. The items which the group is claiming compensation for include accommodation and subsistence costs, lost income and distress caused by the situation. The claim has not been recognised or disclosed in the draft financial statements, as management argues that the full amount payable will be covered by Clooney Co's insurance.

One part of the company's activities, operating under the Shelly's Cruises brand, provides cruise holidays. Due to economic recession, the revenue of the Shelly's Cruises business segment has fallen by 25% this year, and profit before tax has fallen by 35%. Shelly's Cruises contributed $640 million to total revenue in the year to 30 September 2010, and has identifiable assets of $235 million, including several large cruise liners. The Shelly's Cruises brand is not recognised as an intangible asset, as it has been internally generated.

On 15 November 2010, Clooney Co acquired Craig Co, a company offering adventure holidays for independent travellers. Craig Co represents a significant acquisition, but this has not been referred to in the financial statements.

Required:

Comment on the matters that you should consider, and state the audit evidence you should expect to find in your review of the audit working papers for the year ended September 2010 in respect of:

(a)	The compensation claim,	**(8 marks)**
(b)	Shelly's Cruises, and	**(7 marks)**
(c)	The acquisition of Craig Co.	**(5 marks)**

(Total: 20 marks)

35 BANANA CO *Walk in the footsteps of a top tutor*

You are a manager in Grape & Co, a firm of Chartered Certified Accountants. You have been temporarily assigned as audit manager to the audit of Banana Co, because the engagement manager has been taken ill. The final audit of Banana Co for the year ended 30 September 2009 is nearing completion, and you are now reviewing the audit files and discussing the audit with the junior members of the audit team. Banana Co designs and manufactures equipment such as cranes and scaffolding, which are used in the construction industry. The equipment usually follows a standard design, but sometimes Banana Co designs specific items for customers according to contractually agreed specifications. The draft financial statements show revenue of $12.5 million, net profit of $400,000, and total assets of $78 million.

The following information has come to your attention during your review of the audit files:

During the year, a new range of manufacturing plant was introduced to the factories operated by Banana Co. All factory employees received training from an external training firm on how to safely operate the machinery, at a total cost of $500,000. The training costs have been capitalised into the cost of the new machinery, as the finance director argues that the training is necessary in order for the machinery to generate an economic benefit.

After the year end, Cherry Co, a major customer with whom Banana Co has several significant contracts, announced its insolvency, and that procedures to shut down the company had commenced. The administrators of Cherry Co have suggested that the company may be able to pay approximately 25% of the amounts owed to its trade payables. A trade receivable of $300,000 is recognised on Banana Co's statement of financial position in respect of this customer.

In addition, one of the junior members of the audit team voiced concerns over how the audit had been managed. The junior said the following: 'I have only worked on two audits prior to being assigned to the audit team of Banana Co. I was expecting to attend a meeting at the start of the audit, where the partner and other senior members of the audit team discussed the audit, but no meeting was held. In addition, the audit manager has been away on holiday for three weeks, and left a senior in charge. However, the senior was busy with other assignments, so was not always available.

I was given the task of auditing the goodwill which arose on an acquisition made during the year. I also worked on the audit of inventory, and attended the inventory count, which was quite complicated, as Banana Co has a lot of work-in-progress. I tried to be as useful as possible during the count, and helped the client's staff count some of the raw materials. As I had been to the inventory count, I was asked by the audit senior to challenge the finance director regarding the adequacy of the provision against inventory, which the senior felt was significantly understated.

Lastly, we found that we were running out of time to complete our audit procedures. The audit senior advised that we should reduce the sample sizes used in our tests as a way of saving time. He also suggested that if we picked an item as part of our sample for which it would be time consuming to find the relevant evidence, then we should pick a different item which would be quicker to audit.'

Required:

In respect of the specific information provided:

(a) **Comment on the matters to be considered, and explain the audit evidence you should expect to find during your file review in respect of:**

   (i) **The training costs that have been capitalised into the cost of the new machinery; and**

   (ii) **The trade receivable recognised in relation to Cherry Co.** **(12 marks)**

(b) **Evaluate the audit junior's concerns regarding the management of the audit of Banana Co.** **(10 marks)**

(c) There are specific regulatory obligations imposed on accountants and auditors in relation to detecting and reporting money laundering activities. You have been asked to provide a training session to the new audit juniors on auditors' responsibilities in relation to money laundering.

   Required:

   Prepare briefing notes to be used at your training session in which you:

   (i) **Explain the term 'money laundering'. Illustrate your explanation with examples of money laundering offences, including those which could be committed by the accountant; and**

   (ii) **Explain the policies and procedures that a firm of Chartered Certified Accountants should establish in order to meet its responsibilities in relation to money laundering.** **(10 marks)**

   Professional marks will be awarded in part (c) for the format of the answer, and the quality of the explanations provided. **(2 marks)**

   (Total: 34 marks)

36   APRICOT CO *Walk in the footsteps of a top tutor*

Your audit client, Apricot Co, is intending to purchase a new warehouse at a cost of $500,000. One of the directors of the company, Pik Choi, has agreed to make the necessary finance available through a director's loan to the company. This arrangement has been approved by the other directors, and the cash will be provided on 30 March 2010, one day before the purchase is due to be completed. Pik's financial advisor has asked to see a cash flow projection of Apricot Co for the next three months. Your firm has been asked to provide an assurance report to Pik's financial advisor on this prospective financial information.

The cash flow forecast is shown below:

	January 2010 $000	February 2010 $000	March 2010 $000
Operating cash receipts:			
Cash sales	125	135	140
Receipts from credit sales	580	600	625
Operating cash payments:			
Purchases of inventory	(410)	(425)	(425)
Salaries	(100)	(100)	(100)
Overheads	(175)	(175)	(175)
Other cash flows:			
Dividend payment		(80)	
Purchase of new licence	(35)		
Fixtures for new warehouse			(60)
Loan receipt			500
Payment for warehouse			(500)
Cash flow for the month	(15)	(45)	5
Opening cash	100	85	40
Closing cash	85	40	45

The following information is relevant:

(1)   Apricot Co is a wholesaler of catering equipment and frozen food. Its customers are mostly restaurant chains and fast food outlets.

(2)   Customers who pay in cash receive a 10% discount. Analysis has been provided showing that for sales made on credit, 20% of customers pay in the month of the sale, 60% pay after 45 days, 10% after 65 days, 5% after 90 days, and the remainder are bad debts.

(3)   Apricot Co pays for all purchases within 30 days in order to take advantage of a 12% discount from suppliers.

(4)   Overheads are mainly property rentals, utility bills, insurance premiums and general office expenses.

(5)   Apricot Co needs to have a health and safety licence as it sells food. Each licence is valid for one year and is issued once an inspection has taken place.

(6)   A profit forecast has also been prepared for the year ending 31 December 2010 to help with internal planning and budgeting.

This is the first time that Apricot Co has requested an assurance report, and the directors are unsure about the contents of the report that your firm will issue. They understand that it is similar in format to an audit report, but that the specific contents are not the same.

Required:

(a)   Recommend the procedures that should be performed on the cash flow forecast for the three months ending 31 March 2010 in order to provide an assurance report as requested by Apricot Co.   **(11 marks)**

(b)   Explain the main contents of the report that will be issued on the prospective financial information.   **(5 marks)**

(Total: 16 marks)

37   ROBSTER CO *Walk in the footsteps of a top tutor*

 Timed question with Online tutor debrief

Robster Co is a company which manufactures tractors and other machinery to be used in the agricultural industry. You are the manager responsible for the audit of Robster Co, and you are reviewing the audit working papers for the year ended 28 February 2009. The draft financial statements show revenue of $10.5 million, profit before tax of $3.2 million, and total assets of $45 million.

Two matters have been brought to your attention by the audit senior, both of which relate to assets recognised in the statement of financial position for the first time this year:

Leases

In July 2008, Robster Co entered into five new finance leases of land and buildings. The leases have been capitalised and the statement of financial position includes leased assets presented as non-current assets at a value of $3.6 million, and a total finance lease payable of $3.2 million presented as a non-current liability.

Financial assets

Non-current assets include financial assets recognised at $1.26 million. A note to the financial statements describes these financial assets as investments classified as 'fair value through profit or loss', and the investments are described in the note as 'held for trading'. The investments are all shares in listed companies. A gain of $350,000 has been recognised in net profit in respect of the revaluation of these investments.

Required:

(a) In your review of the audit working papers, comment on the matters you should consider, and state the audit evidence you should expect to find in respect of:

   (i)   the leases; and   (8 marks)

   (ii) the financial assets.   (5 marks)

You are aware that Robster Co is seeking a listing in September 2009. The listing rules in this jurisdiction require that interim financial information is published half-way through the accounting period, and that the information should be accompanied by a review report issued by the company's independent auditor.

Required:

(b) Explain the principal analytical procedures that should be used to gather evidence in a review of interim financial information.   (4 marks)

                                                                    (Total: 17 marks)

38   DRAGON GROUP *Walk in the footsteps of a top tutor*

 Timed question with Online tutor debrief

(a) Explain FOUR reasons why a firm of auditors may decide NOT to seek re-election as auditor.   (6 marks)

The Dragon Group is a large group of companies operating in the furniture retail trade. The group has expanded rapidly in the last three years, by acquiring several subsidiaries each year. The management of the parent company, Dragon Co, a listed company, has decided to put the audit of the group and all subsidiaries out to tender, as the current audit firm is not seeking re-election. The financial year end of the Dragon Group is 30 September 2009.

You are a senior manager in Unicorn & Co, a global firm of Chartered Certified Accountants, with offices in over 150 countries across the world. Unicorn & Co has been invited to tender for the Dragon Group audit (including the audit of all subsidiaries). You manage a department within the firm which specialises in the audit of retail companies, and you have been assigned the task of drafting the tender document. You recently held a meeting with Edmund Jalousie, the group finance director, in which you discussed the current group structure, recent acquisitions, and the group's plans for future expansion.

Meeting notes – Dragon Group

Group structure

The parent company owns 20 subsidiaries, all of which are wholly owned. Half of the subsidiaries are located in the same country as the parent, and half overseas. Most of the foreign subsidiaries report under the same financial reporting framework as Dragon Co, but several prepare financial statements using local accounting rules.

Acquisitions during the year

Two companies were purchased in March 2009, both located in this country:

(i) Mermaid Co, a company which operates 20 furniture retail outlets. The audit opinion expressed by the incumbent auditors on the financial statements for the year ended 30 September 2008 was qualified by a disagreement over the non-disclosure of a contingent liability. The contingent liability relates to a court case which is still on-going.

(ii) Minotaur Co, a large company, whose operations are distribution and warehousing. This represents a diversification away from retail, and it is hoped that the Dragon Group will benefit from significant economies of scale as a result of the acquisition.

Other matters

The acquisitive strategy of the group over the last few years has led to significant growth. Group revenue has increased by 25% in the last three years, and is predicted to increase by a further 35% in the next four years as the acquisition of more subsidiaries is planned. The Dragon Group has raised finance for the acquisitions in the past by becoming listed on the stock exchanges of three different countries. A new listing on a foreign stock exchange is planned for January 2010. For this reason, management would like the group audit completed by 31 December 2009.

Required:

(b) Recommend and describe the principal matters to be included in your firm's tender document to provide the audit service to the Dragon Group. **(10 marks)**

(c) Using the specific information provided, evaluate the matters that should be considered before accepting the audit engagement, in the event of your firm being successful in the tender. **(7 marks)**

   Professional marks will be awarded in part (c) for the clarity and presentation of the evaluation. **(2 marks)**

(d) (i) Define 'transnational audit', and explain the relevance of the term to the audit of the Dragon Group **(3 marks)**

   (ii) Discuss TWO features of a transnational audit that may contribute to a high level of audit risk in such an engagement **(4 marks)**

(Total: 32 marks)

 Calculate your allowed time, allocate the time to the separate parts..............

39   POPPY CO (A) *Walk in the footsteps of a top tutor*

(a)   Financial statements often contain material balances recognised at fair value. For auditors, this leads to additional audit risk.

Required:

Discuss this statement.   **(7 marks)**

(b)   You are the manager responsible for the audit of Poppy Co, a manufacturing company with a year ended 31 October 2008. In the last year, several investment properties have been purchased to utilise surplus funds and to provide rental income. The properties have been revalued at the yearend in accordance with IAS 40 *Investment Property*, they are recognised on the statement of financial position at a fair value of $8 million, and the total assets of Poppy Co are $160 million at 31 October 2008. An external valuer has been used to provide the fair value for each property.

Required:

(i)   **Recommend the enquiries to be made in respect of the external valuer, before placing any reliance on their work, and explain the reason for the enquiries**   **(7 marks)**

(ii)   **Identify and explain the principal audit procedures to be performed on the valuation of the investment properties.**   **(6 marks)**

                                                                                            (Total: 20 marks)

40   CROCUS CO *Walk in the footsteps of a top tutor*

(a)   **Define the following terms:**

(i)   **Forensic Accounting**

(ii)   **Forensic Investigation**

(iii)   **Forensic Auditing.**   **(6 marks)**

You are a manager in the forensic investigation department of your audit firm. The directors of a local manufacturing company, Crocus Co, have contacted your department regarding a suspected fraud, which has recently been discovered operating in the company, and you have been asked to look into the matter further. You have held a preliminary discussion with Gita Thrales, the finance director of Crocus Co, the notes of this conversation are shown below:

Notes of discussion with Gita Thrales

Four months ago Crocus Co shut down one of its five factories, in response to deteriorating market conditions, with all staff employed at the factory made redundant on the date of closure.

While monitoring the monthly management accounts, Gita performs analytical procedures on salary expenses. She found that the monthly total payroll expense had reduced by 3% in the months following the factory closure – not as much as expected, given that 20% of the total staff of the company had been made redundant. Initial investigations performed last week by Gita revealed that many of the employees who had been made redundant had actually remained on the payroll records, and salary payments in respect of these individuals were still being made every month, with all payments going into the same bank account. As soon as she realised that there may be a fraud being conducted within the company, Gita stopped any further payments in respect of the redundant employees. She contacted our firm as she is unsure how to proceed, and would like our firm's specialist department to conduct an investigation.

Gita says that the senior accountant, Miles Rutland, has been absent from work since she conducted her initial investigation last week, and it has been impossible to contact him. Gita believes that he may have been involved with the suspected fraud.

Gita has asked whether your department would be able to provide a forensic investigation, but is unsure what this would involve. Crocus Co is not an audit client of your firm.

Required:

(b) **Prepare a report to be sent to Gita Thrales (the finance director), in which you:**

    (i) **Describe the objectives of a forensic investigation; and**

    (ii) **Explain the steps involved in a forensic investigation into the payroll fraud, including examples of procedures that could be used to gather evidence.**

    Note: Requirement (b) includes 3 professional marks.　　　　　　　　**(14 marks)**

(c) **Assess how the fundamental ethical principles of IFAC's Code of Ethics for Professional Accountants should be applied to the provision of a forensic investigation service.**　　　　　　　　**(6 marks)**

　　　　　　　　　　　　　　　　　　　　　　　　　　(Total: 26 marks)

41　SEYMOUR

You are the manager responsible for the audit of Seymour Co. The company offers information, proprietary foods and medical innovations designed to improve the quality of life. (Proprietary foods are marketed under and protected by registered names.) The draft consolidated financial statements for the year ended 30 September 2006 show revenue of $74.4 million (2005 – $69.2 million), profit before taxation of $13.2 million (2005 – $15.8 million) and total assets of $53.3 million (2005 – $40.5 million).

The following issues arising during the final audit have been noted on a schedule of points for your attention:

(a) In 2001, Seymour had been awarded a 20-year patent on a new drug, Tournose, that was also approved for food use. The drug had been developed at a cost of $4 million which is being amortized over the life of the patent. The patent cost $11,600. In September 2006 a competitor announced the successful completion of preliminary trials on an alternative drug with the same beneficial properties as Tournose. The alternative drug is expected to be readily available in two years time.　　**(7 marks)**

(b)   Seymour offers health-related information services through a wholly-owned subsidiary, Aragon Co. Goodwill of $1.8 million recognized on the purchase of Aragon in October 2004 is included at cost in the consolidated statement of financial position. At 30 September 2006 Seymour's investment in Aragon is shown at cost, $4.5 million, in its separate financial statements. Aragon's draft financial statements for the year ended 30 September 2006 show a loss before taxation of $0.6 million (2005 – $0.5 million loss) and total assets of $4.9 million (2005 – $5.7 million). The notes to Aragon's financial statements disclose that they have been prepared on a going concern basis that assumes that Seymour will continue to provide financial support.   **(7 marks)**

(c)   In November 2006 Seymour announced the recall and discontinuation of a range of petcare products. The product recall was prompted by the high level of customer returns due to claims of poor quality. For the year to 30 September 2006, the product range represented $8.9 million of consolidated revenue (2005 – $9.6 million) and $1.3 million loss before tax (2005 – $0.4 million profit before tax). The results of the 'petcare' operations are disclosed separately on the face of the statement of profit or loss.   **(6 marks)**

Required:

For each of the above issues:

(i)   comment on the matters that you should consider; and

(ii)   state the audit evidence that you should expect to find,

in undertaking your review of the audit working papers and financial statements of Seymour Co for the year ended 30 September 2006.

Note: The mark allocation is shown against each of the three issues.

(Total: 20 marks)

42   RBG

The activities of the Retail and Business Group (RBG) comprise retailing of general merchandize and luxury goods. RBG has developed an internal audit function over many years. Employee turnover in the internal audit department has risen, with high performing employees moving to other departments and less successful ones moving out. The external auditors, Grey & Co have suggested that RBG outsources its internal audit function to experienced auditors.

Your firm, York & Co, has been invited to tender for the provision of internal audit services to RBG for the three years to 31 December 2009. The appointment will include an evaluation of organisational risk, financial compliance, information technology control and systems audits, and fraud investigation. As the prospective assignment manager, you have been asked to identify the principal matters to be presented in your firm's written submission. The invitation to tender indicates that written submissions will be used as a means of shortlisting candidates to make a detailed presentation to RBG's Audit and Risk Management Committee.

You have obtained the following information from RBG:

(1) The Audit and Risk Management Committee receives annual reports from the head of internal audit on the controls over operational, financial and compliance risks.

(2) RBG has a comprehensive system of budgetary control including monthly performance reviews of both financial and non-financial indicators.

(3) Financial extracts ($m):

	Six months to 30 June 2006 Draft	Year to 31 December 2005 Actual
Revenue	387	751
Profit before tax	46	83

(4) A substantial proportion of RBG's revenue is generated through retail outlets in department stores and shopping centres. Many of the rents payable for these premises are contingent on revenues earned.

Required:

(a) **Briefly describe potential advantages and disadvantages to RBG of outsourcing its internal audit services.** **(6 marks)**

(b) **Describe the principal matters that should be included in your firm's submission to provide internal audit services to RBG.** **(10 marks)**

(c) **Explain the possible impact of RBG outsourcing its internal audit services on the audit of the financial statements by Grey & Co.** **(4 marks)**

(Total: 20 marks)

Note: The mark allocation is shown against each of the three issues. **(20 marks)**

COMPLETION AND REPORTING

43 BURFORD *Walk in the footsteps of a top tutor*

(a) You are the manager responsible for the audit of Burford Co, a company which designs and manufactures engine parts. The audit of the financial statements for the year ended 31 July 2013 is nearing completion and you are reviewing the working papers of the going concern section of the audit file. The draft financial statements recognise a loss of $500,000 (2012 – profit of $760,000), and total assets of $13.8 million (2012 – $14.4 million).

The audit senior has left the following note for your attention:

'I have performed analytical review on Burford Co's year-end financial statements. The current ratio is 0.8 (2012 – 1.2), the quick ratio is 0.5 (2012 – 1.6). The latest management accounts show that ratios have deteriorated further since the year end, and the company now has a cash balance of only $25,000. Burford Co has a long-term loan outstanding of $80,000 with a covenant attached, which states that if the current ratio falls below 0.75, the loan can be immediately recalled by the lender.'

You are also aware that one of Burford Co's best-selling products, the QuickFire, has become technically obsolete during 2013 as customers now prefer more environmentally friendly engine parts. Historically, the QuickFire has generated 45% of the company's revenue. In response to customers' preference, $1.3 million has been spent on designing a new product, the GreenFire, due for launch in February 2014, which will be marketed as an environmentally friendly product.

A cash flow forecast has been prepared for the year to 31 July 2014, indicating that based on certain assumptions, the company's cash balance is predicted to increase to $220,000 by the end of the forecast period. Assumptions include:

(1)   The successful launch of the GreenFire product,

(2)   The sale of plant and machinery which was used to manufacture the QuickFire, generating cash proceeds of $50,000, forecast to take place in January 2014,

(3)   A reduction in payroll costs of 15%, caused by redundancies in the QuickFire manufacturing plant, and

(4)   The receipt of a grant of $30,000 from a government department which encourages innovation in environmentally friendly products, scheduled to be received in February 2014.

Required:

(i)   **Identify and explain the matters which cast doubt on the going concern status of Burford Co.**   **(6 marks)**

(ii)   **Explain the audit evidence you should expect to find in your file review in respect of the cash flow forecast.**   **(8 marks)**

(b)   Having completed the file review, you have concluded that the use of the going concern assumption is appropriate, but that there is significant doubt over Burford Co's ability to continue as a going concern. You have advised the company's audit committee that a note is required in the financial statements to describe the significant doubt over going concern. The audit committee is reluctant to include a detailed note to the financial statements due to fears that the note will highlight the company's problems and cause further financial difficulties, but have agreed that a brief note will be included.

Required:

In respect of the note on going concern to be included in Burford Co's financial statements, discuss the implications for the audit report and outline any further actions to be taken by the auditor.   **(6 marks)**

(Total: 20 marks)

44   POODLE *Walk in the footsteps of a top tutor*

You are the manager responsible for the audit of the Poodle Group (the Group) and you are completing the audit of the consolidated financial statements for the year ended 31 March 2013. The draft consolidated financial statements recognise revenue of $18 million (2012 – $17 million), profit before tax of $2 million (2012 – $3 million) and total assets of $58 million (2012 – $59 million). Your firm audits all of the components of the Group, apart from an overseas subsidiary, Toy Co, which is audited by a small local firm of accountants and auditors.

The audit senior has left a file note for your attention. You are aware that the Group's annual report and financial statements are due to be released next week, and the Group is very reluctant to make any adjustments in respect of the matters described.

(a)   **Toy Co**

The component auditors of Toy Co, the overseas subsidiary, have been instructed to provide the Group audit team with details of a court case which is ongoing. An ex-employee is suing Toy Co for unfair dismissal and has claimed $500,000 damages against the company. To comply with local legislation, Toy Co's individual financial statements are prepared using a local financial reporting framework. Under that local financial reporting framework, a provision is only recognised if a cash outflow is virtually certain to arise. The component auditors obtained verbal confirmation from Toy Co's legal advisors that the damages are probable, but not virtually certain to be paid, and no provision has been recognised in either the individual or consolidated financial statements. No other audit evidence has been obtained by the component auditors. **(7 marks)**

(b)   **Trade receivable**

On 1 June 2013, a notice was received from administrators dealing with the winding up of Terrier Co, following its insolvency. The notice stated that the company should be in a position to pay approximately 10% of the amounts owed to its trade payables. Poodle Co, the parent company of the Group, includes a balance of $1.6 million owed by Terrier Co in its trade receivables. **(7 marks)**

(c)   **Chairman's statement**

The draft chairman's statement, to be included in the Group's annual report, was received yesterday. The chairman comments on the performance of the Group, stating that he is pleased that revenue has increased by 20% in the year.   **(6 marks)**

Required:

In respect of each of the matters described:

(i)   **Assess the implications for the completion of the Group audit, explaining any adjustments that may be necessary to the consolidated financial statements, and recommending any further procedures necessary; and**

(ii)   **Describe the impact on the Group audit report if these adjustments are not made.**

Note: The split of the mark allocation is shown above against each of the parts.

(Total: 20 marks)

45 HENDRIX *Walk in the footsteps of a top tutor*

(a) You are the manager responsible for the audit of Dylan Co, a listed company, and you are reviewing the working papers of the audit file for the year ended 30 September 2012. The audit senior has left a note for your attention:

'Dylan Co outsources its entire payroll, invoicing and credit control functions to Hendrix Co. In August 2012, Hendrix Co suffered a computer virus attack on its operating system, resulting in the destruction of its accounting records, including those relating to Dylan Co. We have therefore been unable to perform the planned audit procedures on payroll, revenue and receivables, all of which are material to the financial statements. Hendrix Co has manually reconstructed the relevant figures as far as possible, and has supplied a written statement to confirm that they are as accurate as possible, given the loss of accounting records.'

Required:

(i)   **Comment on the actions that should be taken by the auditor, and the implications for the auditor's report; and**   **(7 marks)**

(ii) **Discuss the quality control procedures that should be carried out by the audit firm prior to the audit report being issued.**   **(3 marks)**

(b) You are also responsible for the audit of Squire Co, a listed company, and you are completing the review of its interim financial statements for the six months ended 31 October 2012. Squire Co is a car manufacturer, and historically has offered a three-year warranty on cars sold. The financial statements for the year ended 30 April 2012 included a warranty provision of $1.5 million and recognised total assets of $27.5 million. You are aware that on 1 July 2012, due to cost cutting measures, Squire Co stopped offering warranties on cars sold. The interim financial statements for the six months ended 31 October 2012 do not recognise any warranty provision. Total assets are $30 million at 31 October 2012.

Required:

Assess the matters that should be considered in forming a conclusion on Squire Co's interim financial statements, and the implications for the review report.

(6 marks)

(Total: 16 marks)

46 SNIPE *Walk in the footsteps of a top tutor*

You are the partner responsible for performing an engagement quality control review on the audit of Snipe Co. You are currently reviewing the audit working papers and draft audit report on the financial statements of Snipe Co for the year ended 31 January 2012. The draft financial statements recognise revenue of $8.5 million, profit before tax of $1 million, and total assets of $175 million.

(a) During the year Snipe Co's factory was extended by the self-construction of a new processing area, at a total cost of $5 million. Included in the costs capitalised are borrowing costs of $100,000, incurred during the six-month period of construction. A loan of $4 million carrying an interest rate of 5% was taken out in respect of the construction on 1 March 2011, when construction started. The new processing area was ready for use on 1 September 2011, and began to be used on 1 December 2011. Its estimated useful life is 15 years.

Required:

In respect of your file review of non-current assets:

Comment on the matters that should be considered, and the evidence you would expect to find regarding the new processing area. **(8 marks)**

(b)   Snipe Co has in place a defined benefit pension plan for its employees. An actuarial valuation on 31 January 2012 indicated that the plan is in deficit by $10.5 million. The deficit is not recognised in the statement of financial position. An extract from the draft audit report is given below:

Auditor's opinion

In our opinion, because of the significance of the matter discussed below, the financial statements do not give a true and fair view of the financial position of Snipe Co as at 31 January 2012, and of its financial performance and cash flows for the year then ended in accordance with International Financial Reporting Standards.

Explanation of adverse opinion in relation to pension

The financial statements do not include the company's pension plan. This deliberate omission contravenes accepted accounting practice and means that the accounts are not properly prepared.

Required:

Critically appraise the extract from the proposed audit report of Snipe Co for the year ended 31 January 2012.

Note: you are NOT required to re-draft the extract of the audit report. **(7 marks)**

(Total: 15 marks)

47   YEW *Walk in the footsteps of a top tutor*

(a)   You are the manager responsible for the audit of Yew Co, a company which designs and develops aircraft engines. The audit for the year ended 31 July 2011 is nearing completion and the audit senior has left the following file note for your attention:

'I have just returned from a meeting with the management of Yew Co, and there is a matter I want to bring to your attention. Yew Co's statement of financial position recognises an intangible asset of $12.5 million in respect of capitalised research and development costs relating to new aircraft engine designs. However, market research conducted by Yew Co in relation to these new designs indicated that there would be little demand in the near future for such designs. Management has provided written representation that they agree with the results of the market research.

Currently, Yew Co has a cash balance of only $125,000 and members of the management team have expressed concerns that the company is finding it difficult to raise additional finance.

The new aircraft designs have been discussed in the chairman's statement which is to be published with the financial statements. The discussion states that 'developments of new engine designs are underway, and we believe that these new designs will become a significant source of income for Yew Co in the next 12 months.'

Yew Co's draft financial statements include profit before tax of $23 million, and total assets of $210 million. Yew Co is due to publish its annual report next week, so we need to consider the impact of this matter urgently.'

Required:

Discuss the implications of the audit senior's file note on the completion of the audit and on the auditor's report, recommending any further actions that should be taken by the auditor. **(12 marks)**

(b) You are responsible for answering technical queries from other managers and partners of your firm. An audit partner left the following note on your desk this morning:

(i) 'I am about to draft the audit report for my client, Sycamore Co. I am going on holiday tomorrow and want to have the audit report signed and dated before I leave. The only thing outstanding is the written representation from management – I have verbally confirmed the contents with the finance director who agreed to send the representations to the audit manager within the next few days. I presume this is acceptable?' **(3 marks)**

(ii) 'We are auditing Sycamore Co for the first time. The prior period financial statements were audited by another firm. We are aware that the auditor's report on the prior period was qualified due to a material misstatement of trade receivables. We have obtained sufficient appropriate evidence that the matter giving rise to the misstatement has been resolved and I am happy to issue an unmodified opinion. But should I refer to the prior year modification in this year's auditor's report?' **(3 marks)**

Required:

Respond to the audit partner's comments.

Note: the split of the mark allocation is shown within the question.

(Total: 18 marks)

48 **NASSAU GROUP** *Walk in the footsteps of a top tutor*

(a) You are the manager responsible for the audit of the Nassau Group, which comprises a parent company and six subsidiaries. The audit of all individual companies' financial statements is almost complete, and you are currently carrying out the audit of the consolidated financial statements. One of the subsidiaries, Exuma Co, is audited by another firm, Jalousie & Co. Your firm has fulfilled the necessary requirements of ISA 600 Special Considerations – Audits of Group Financial Statements (Including the Work of Component Auditors) and is satisfied as to the competence and independence of Jalousie & Co.

You have received from Jalousie & Co the draft audit report on Exuma Co's financial statements, an extract from which is shown below:

'Basis for Qualified Opinion (extract)

The company is facing financial damages of $2 million in respect of an on-going court case, more fully explained in note 12 to the financial statements. Management has not recognised a provision but has disclosed the situation as a contingent liability. Under International Financial Reporting Standards, a provision should be made if there is an obligation as a result of a past event, a probable outflow of economic benefit, and a reliable estimate can be made. Audit evidence concludes that these criteria have been met, and it is our opinion that a provision of $2 million should be recognised. Accordingly, net profit and shareholders' equity would have been reduced by $2 million if the provision had been recognised.

Qualified Opinion (extract)

In our opinion, except for effects of the matter described in the Basis for Qualified Opinion paragraph, the financial statements give a true and fair view of the financial position of Exuma Co as at 31 March 2011...'

An extract of Note 12 to Exuma Co's financial statements is shown below:

Note 12 (extract)

The company is the subject of a court case concerning an alleged breach of planning regulations. The plaintiff is claiming compensation of $2 million. The management of Exuma Co, after seeking legal advice, believe that there is only a 20% chance of a successful claim being made against the company.

Figures extracted from the draft financial statements for the year ending 31 March 2011 are as follows:

	Nassau Group	Exuma Co
	$ million	$ million
Profit before tax	20	4
Total assets	85	20

Required:

Identify and explain the matters that should be considered, and actions that should be taken by the group audit engagement team, in forming an opinion on the consolidated financial statements of the Nassau Group. **(10 marks)**

(b) A trainee accountant, Jo Castries, is assigned to your audit team. This is the first group audit that Jo has worked on. Jo made the following comment regarding the group audit:

'I understand that in a group audit engagement, one of the requirements is to design and perform audit procedures on the consolidation process. Please explain to me the principal audit procedures that are performed on the consolidation process.'

Required:

Respond to the trainee accountant's question. **(8 marks)**

(Total: 18 marks)

49   WILLIS CO *Walk in the footsteps of a top tutor*

(a)   You are the manager responsible for the audit of Willis Co, a large client of your audit firm, operating in the pharmaceutical industry. The audit work for the year ended 30 August 2010 is nearly complete, and you are reviewing the draft audit report which has been prepared by the audit senior. You are aware that Willis Co is developing a new drug and has incurred significant research and development costs during the year, most of which have been capitalised as an intangible asset. The asset is recognised at a value of $4.4 million, the total assets recognised on the draft statement of financial position are $55 million, and Willis Co has a draft profit before tax of $3.1 million. Having reviewed the audit working papers, you are also aware that management has not allowed the audit team access to the results of scientific tests and trials performed on the new drug being developed. An extract from the draft audit report is shown below:

Basis of opinion (extract)

Evidence available to us in respect of the intangible asset capitalised was limited, because of restrictions imposed on our work by management. As a result of this we have been unable to verify the appropriateness of the amount capitalised, and we are worried that the asset may be overvalued. Because of the significance of the item, and the lack of integrity shown by management, we have been unable to form a view on the financial statements as a whole.

Opinion (extract): Disclaimer on view given by financial statements

Because of the lack of evidence that we could gain over the intangible asset, we are unable to form an opinion as to whether the financial statements are properly prepared in accordance with the relevant financial reporting framework.

Required:

(i)   **Critically appraise the draft audit report of Willis Co for the year ended 30 August 2010, prepared by the audit senior**

Note: You are NOT required to re-draft the extracts from the audit report.

(10 marks)

(ii)   **Identify and explain any other matters to be considered, and the actions to be taken by the auditor, in respect of the management-imposed limitation on scope.** **(5 marks)**

(b)   You are also responsible for the audit of Moore Co, with a year ended 30 September 2010. The following notes have been left for your attention by the audit senior:

'Our audit testing performed so far on trade payables revealed some internal control deficiencies. Supplier statement reconciliations have not always been performed by the client, and invoices were often not approved before payment. We have found a few errors in the payables ledger and the individual accounts of suppliers making up the trade payables balance, the total of which is material to the statement of financial position.'

Required:

Recommend the further actions that should be taken by the auditor, and outline any reporting requirements in respect of the internal control deficiencies identified.

(5 marks)

(Total: 20 marks)

50 GRIMES CO (A) *Walk in the footsteps of a top tutor*

(a) You are the partner responsible for the audit of Grimes Co, for the year ended 30 April 2010. The final audit has been completed and you have asked the audit manager to draft the audit report. The manager is aware that there is guidance for auditors relating to audit reports in ISA 706 *Emphasis of Matter Paragraphs and Other Matter Paragraphs in the Independent Auditor's Report*. The manager has asked for your assistance in this matter.

Required:

(i) **Define an 'Emphasis of Matter paragraph' and explain, providing examples, the use of such a paragraph** **(6 marks)**

(ii) **Define an 'Other Matter paragraph' and explain, providing examples, the use of such a paragraph.**

Note: You are not required to produce draft paragraphs. **(4 marks)**

(b) You are also responsible for providing direction to more junior members of the audit department of your firm on technical matters. Several recent recruits have asked for guidance in the area of auditor's liability. They are keen to understand how an audit firm can reduce its exposure to claims of negligence. They have also heard that in some countries, it is possible to restrict liability by making a liability limitation agreement with an audit client.

Required:

(i) **Explain FOUR methods that may be used by an audit firm to reduce exposure to litigation claims** **(4 marks)**

(ii) **Assess the potential implications for the profession, of audit firms signing a liability limitation agreement with their audit clients.** **(6 marks)**

(Total: 20 marks)

51 LYCHEE CO (A) *Walk in the footsteps of a top tutor*

(a) Guidance on subsequent events is given in ISA 560 (Redrafted) Subsequent Events.

Required:

Explain the auditor's responsibility in relation to subsequent events. **(6 marks)**

(b) You are the manager responsible for the audit of Lychee Co, a manufacturing company with a year ended 30 September 2009. The audit work has been completed and reviewed and you are due to issue the audit report in three days. The draft audit opinion is unmodified. The financial statements show revenue for the year ended 30 September 2009 of $15 million, net profit of $3 million, and total assets at the yearend are $80 million.

The finance director of Lychee Co telephoned you this morning to tell you about the announcement yesterday, of a significant restructuring of Lychee Co, which will take place over the next six months. The restructuring will involve the closure of a factory, and its relocation to another part of the country. There will be some redundancies and the estimated cost of closure is $250,000. The financial statements have not been amended in respect of this matter.

Required:

In respect of the announcement of the restructuring:

(i) Comment on the financial reporting implications, and advise the further audit procedures to be performed; and **(6 marks)**

(ii) Recommend the actions to be taken by the auditor if the financial statements are not amended. **(4 marks)**

(Total: 16 marks)

52 PLUTO CO (A) *Walk in the footsteps of a top tutor*

 Timed question with Online tutor debrief

(a) **Explain the term 'fraudulent financial reporting', illustrating your explanation with examples.** **(4 marks)**

You are the partner responsible for performing an engagement quality control review on the audit of Pluto Co, a listed company. You are currently reviewing the engagement partner's proposed audit report on the financial statements of Pluto Co for the year ended 31 March 2009. During the year the company has undergone significant reorganisation, involving the discontinuance of two major business segments. Extracts of the proposed audit report are shown below:

Adverse opinion arising from disagreement about application of IAS 37

The directors have not recognised a provision in relation to redundancy costs associated with the reorganisation during the year. The reason is that they do not feel that a reliable estimate of the amount can be made, and so the recognition criteria of IAS 37 have not been met. We disagree with the directors as we feel that an estimate can be made. This matter is more fully explained in a note to the financial statements. We feel that this is a material misstatement as the profit for the year is overstated.

In our opinion, the financial statements do not show a true and fair view of the financial position of the company as of 31 March 2009, and of its financial performance and its cash flows for the year then ended in accordance with International Financial Reporting Standards.

Emphasis of matter paragraph

The directors have decided not to disclose the Earnings per Share for 2009, as they feel that the figure is materially distorted by significant discontinued operations in the year. Our opinion is not qualified in respect of this matter.

Required:

(b) Critically appraise the proposed audit report of Pluto Co for the year ended 31 March 2009.

Note: you are NOT required to re-draft the extracts from the audit report. (9 marks)

(c) Explain the matters to be considered in deciding who is eligible to perform an engagement quality control review for a listed client. (4 marks)

(Total: 17 marks)

 Calculate your allowed time, allocate the time to the separate parts..............

53 DEXTER CO (A)   *Walk in the footsteps of a top tutor*

(a) Compare and contrast the responsibilities of management, and of auditors, in relation to the assessment of going concern. You should include a description of the procedures used in this assessment where relevant. (7 marks)

You are the manager responsible for performing hot reviews on audit files where there is a potential disagreement between your firm and the client regarding a material issue. You are reviewing the going concern section of the audit file of Dexter Co, a client with considerable cash flow difficulties, and other, less significant operational indicators of going concern problems. The working papers indicate that Dexter Co is currently trying to raise finance to fund operating cash flows, and state that if the finance is not received, there is significant doubt over the going concern status of the company. The working papers conclude that the going concern assumption is appropriate, but it is recommended that the financial statements should contain a note explaining the cash flow problems faced by the company, along with a description of the finance being sought, and an evaluation of the going concern status of the company. The directors do not wish to include the note in the financial statements.

Required:

(b) Consider and comment on the possible reasons why the directors of Dexter Co are reluctant to provide the note to the financial statements. (5 marks)

(c) Identify and discuss the implications for the audit report if:

(i)   the directors refuse to disclose the note (4 marks)

(ii) the directors agree to disclose the note. (4 marks)

(Total: 20 marks)

 Online question assistance

54 BLOD CO (A) *Walk in the footsteps of a top tutor*

You are the manager responsible for the audit of Blod Co, a listed company, for the year ended 31 March 2008. Your firm was appointed as auditors of Blod Co in September 2007. The audit work has been completed, and you are reviewing the working papers in order to draft a report to those charged with governance. The statement of financial position shows total assets of $78 million (2007 – $66 million). The main business activity of Blod Co is the manufacture of farm machinery.

During the audit of property, plant and equipment it was discovered that controls over capital expenditure transactions had deteriorated during the year. Authorisation had not been gained for the purchase of office equipment with a cost of $225,000. No material errors in the financial statements were revealed by audit procedures performed on property, plant and equipment.

An internally generated brand name has been included in the statement of financial position at a fair value of $10 million. Audit working papers show that the matter was discussed with the financial controller, who stated that the $10 million represents the present value of future cash flows estimated to be generated by the brand name. The member of the audit team who completed the work programme on intangible assets has noted that this treatment appears to be in breach of IAS 38 *Intangible Assets*, and that the management refuses to derecognise the asset.

Problems were experienced in the audit of inventories. Due to an oversight by the internal auditors of Blod Co, the external audit team did not receive a copy of inventory counting procedures prior to attending the count. This caused a delay at the beginning of the inventory count, when the audit team had to quickly familiarise themselves with the procedures. In addition, on the final audit, when the audit senior requested documentation to support the final inventory valuation, it took two weeks for the information to be received because the accountant who had prepared the schedules had mislaid them.

Required:

(a) (i) Identify the main purpose of including 'findings from the audit' (management letter points) in a report to those charged with governance. **(2 marks)**

   (ii) From the information provided above, recommend the matters which should be included as 'findings from the audit' in your report to those charged with governance, and explain the reason for their inclusion. **(7 marks)**

The finance director of Blod Co, Uma Thorton, has requested that your firm type the financial statements in the form to be presented to shareholders at the forthcoming company general meeting. Uma has also commented that the previous auditors did not use a liability disclaimer in their audit report, and would like more information about the use of liability disclaimer paragraphs.

Required:

(b) Discuss the ethical issues raised by the request for your firm to type the financial statements of Blod Co. **(3 marks)**

(c) In the context of a standard unmodified audit report, describe the content of a liability disclaimer paragraph, and discuss the main arguments for and against the use of a liability disclaimer paragraph. **(5 marks)**

(Total: 17 marks)

UK SYLLABUS ONLY

55 **COXON** *Walk in the footsteps of a top tutor*

Hunt & Co has provided non-audit services such as corporate finance and tax planning for Coxon Ltd in the past. Coxon Ltd ran a chain of high street stores selling books, CDs and computer games. Unfortunately, it could not compete with internet sites selling the same goods at a much cheaper price, and since 2012 the company had been loss making. The company was placed into compulsory liquidation last week due to being unable to pay its debts as they fall due.

The finance director, James Corgan, has contacted your firm, seeking advice on several issues to do with the liquidation; his comments are shown in the note below:

'We had thought for some time that the company was in financial difficulties, having lost market share to competitors, but we hoped to turn the company around. Things came to a head in January 2014 when the accounts showed a net liabilities position for the first time, and several loan covenants had been breached. However, we decided to continue to trade in order to maximise cash inflows, keep staff employed for a few months longer, and try to negotiate finance from new providers. During this period we continued to order goods from several suppliers.

However, the cash position deteriorated and in May 2014 creditors applied to the court for the compulsory winding up of the company. The court has appointed liquidators who are about to commence the winding up.

As you can imagine, myself and the other directors are very worried about the situation. Please provide me with explanations on the following matters. We have heard that we may be personally liable for some of the company's debts. Is this correct, and what are the potential consequences for us? Also, can you explain the impact of the compulsory liquidation process for our employees and for creditors?'

Required:

Respond to the instructions in the note from the finance director. **(13 marks)**

56 **HAWK (A)** *Walk in the footsteps of a top tutor*

(a) You are a manager in Lapwing & Co. One of your audit clients is Hawk Ltd which operates commercial real estate properties typically comprising several floors of retail units and leisure facilities such as cinemas and health clubs, which are rented out to provide rental income.

Your firm has just been approached to provide an additional engagement for Hawk Ltd, to review and provide a report on the company's business plan, including forecast financial statements for the 12-month period to 31 May 2013. Hawk Ltd is in the process of negotiating a new bank loan of £30 million and the report on the business plan is at the request of the bank. It is anticipated that the loan would be advanced in August 2012 and would carry an interest rate of 4%. The report would be provided by your firm's business advisory department and a second partner review will be conducted which will reduce any threat to objectivity to an acceptable level.

Extracts from the forecast financial statements included in the business plan are given below:

Statement of comprehensive income (extract)

	Note	FORECAST 12 months to 31 May 2013	UNAUDITED 12 months to 31 May 2012
		$000	$000
Revenue		25,000	20,600
Operating expenses		(16,550)	(14,420)
Operating profit		8,450	6,180
Profit on disposal of Beak Retail	1	4,720	–
Finance costs		(2,650)	(1,690)
Profit before tax		10,520	4,490

Statement of financial position

	Note	FORECAST 12 months to 31 May 2013	UNAUDITED 12 months to 31 May 2012
Assets		$000	$000
Non-current assets			
Property, plant and equipment	2	330,150	293,000
Current assets			
Inventory		500	450
Receivables		3,600	3,300
Cash and cash equivalents		2,250	3,750
		6,350	7,500
Total assets		336,500	300,500
Equity and liabilities			
Equity			
Share capital		105,000	100,000
Retained earnings		93,400	92,600
Total equity		198,400	192,600

Non-current liabilities			
Long-term borrowings	2	82,500	52,500
Deferred tax		50,000	50,000
Current liabilities			
Trade payables		5,600	5,400
		———	———
Total liabilities		138,100	107,900
		———	———
Total equity and liabilities		336,500	300,500
		———	———

Notes:

(1) Beak Retail is a retail park which is underperforming. Its sale is currently being negotiated, and is expected to take place in September 2012.

(2) Hawk Ltd is planning to invest the cash raised from the bank loan in a new retail and leisure park which is being developed jointly with another company, Kestrel Ltd.

Required:

In respect of the engagement to provide a report on Hawk Ltd's business plan:

(i) **Identify and explain the matters that should be considered in agreeing the terms of the engagement; and Note: You are NOT required to consider ethical threats to objectivity.** **(6 marks)**

(ii) **Recommend the procedures that should be performed in order to examine and report on the forecast financial statements of Hawk Ltd for the year to 31 May 2013.** **(10 marks)**

(b) You are also responsible for the audit of Jay Ltd, a company with a year ended 30 September 2011, in relation to which an unmodified audit report was issued in December 2011. Jay Ltd operates two separate divisions both of which manufacture food supplements – 'Jay Sport' manufactures food supplements targeted at athletes, and 'Jay Plus' is targeted at the general public. The audit engagement partner, Bill Kingfisher, sent you the following email this morning:

To: Audit manager

From: Bill Kingfisher, audit engagement partner, Jay Ltd

Regarding: Jay Ltd – financial results

Hello

I have just received some worrying news from the finance director of Jay Ltd. The company's latest results are not looking good – I have attached an extract from the latest management accounts for your information.

It seems that one of the key ingredients used in the 'Jay Sport' range has been found to have harmful side effects, so very few sales from that range have been made in the current financial year. The company is struggling to manage its working capital and meet interest payments on loans.

In light of all this, the directors are anxious about the future of the company, and I have been asked to attend a meeting with them tomorrow to discuss their concerns over the financial performance and position of Jay Ltd.

I am asking you to prepare briefing notes for my use in the meeting with the directors, in which you:

(i)   Examine the financial position of Jay Ltd and determine whether the company is insolvent; and **(4 marks)**

(ii)   Evaluate, reaching a recommendation, the options available to the directors in terms of the future of the company. **(9 marks)**

Thank you.

Attachment: Extract from Jay Ltd's management accounts at 31 May 2012 (unaudited)

Statement of financial position

	£000
Property, plant and equipment	12,800
Inventory	500
Trade receivables	400
Cash	0
Total assets	13,700
Share capital	100
Retained earnings	(1,050)
Long-term borrowings (secured with a fixed charge over property, plant and equipment)	12,000
Trade payables (including employees' wages of £300,000)	1,250
Bank overdraft	1,400
Total equity and liabilities	13,700

Statement of Comprehensive Income (extract)

	£000	£000	£000
Revenue	50	1,450	1,500
Operating costs	(800)	(1,200)	(2,000)
Operating loss/profit	(750)	250	(500)
Finance costs			(800)
Loss before tax			(1,300)

Required:

Respond to the partner's email. (13 marks)

Note: the split of the mark allocation is shown within the partner's email.

Professional marks will be awarded in part (b) for the presentation and clarity of your answer. (4 marks)

(Total: 33 marks)

57   BUTLER (A)   *Walk in the footsteps of a top tutor*

(a)   Butler Ltd is a new audit client of your firm. You are the manager responsible for the audit of the financial statements for the year ended 31 May 2011. Butler Ltd designs and manufactures aircraft engines and spare parts, and is a subsidiary of a multi-national group. Extracts from the draft financial statements are shown below:

Statement of financial position	31 May 2011 Draft	31 May 2010 Actual
Assets	£ million	£ million
Non-current assets		
Intangible assets (note 1)	200	180
Property, plant and equipment (note 2)	1,300	1,200
Deferred tax asset (note 3)	235	20
Financial assets	25	35
	1,760	1,435
Current assets		
Inventory	1,300	800
Trade receivables	2,100	1,860
	3,400	2,660
Total assets	5,160	4,095
Equity and liabilities		
Equity		
Share capital	300	300
Retained earnings	(525)	95
	(225)	395
Non-current liabilities		
Long-term borrowings (note 4)	1,900	1,350
Provisions (note 5)	185	150
	2,085	1,500

Current liabilities		
Short-term borrowings (note 6)	800	400
Trade payables	2,500	1,800
	3,300	2,200
Total equity and liabilities	5,160	4,095

Notes to the statement of financial position:

Note 1   Intangible assets comprise goodwill on the acquisition of subsidiaries (£80 million), and development costs capitalised on engine development projects (£120 million).

Note 2   Property, plant and equipment includes land and buildings valued at £25 million, over which a fixed charge exists.

Note 3   The deferred tax asset has arisen following several loss-making years suffered by the company. The asset represents the tax benefit of unutilised tax losses carried forward.

Note 4   Long-term borrowings include a debenture due for repayment in July 2012, and a loan from Butler Ltd's parent company due for repayment in December 2012.

Note 5   Provisions relate to warranties provided to customers.

Note 6   Short-term borrowings comprise an overdraft (£25 million), a short-term loan (£60 million) due for repayment in August 2011, and a bank loan (£715 million) repayable in September 2011.

You have received an email from the audit partner responsible for the audit of Butler Ltd:

To: Audit manager

From: Audit partner

Regarding: Butler Ltd – going concern issues

Hello

I understand that the audit work on Butler Ltd commences this week. I am concerned about the future of the company, as against a background of economic recession, sales have been declining, several significant customer contracts have been cancelled unexpectedly, and competition from overseas has damaged the market share previously enjoyed by Butler Ltd.

(i)   Please prepare briefing notes, for my use, in which you identify and explain any matters arising from your review of the draft statement of financial position, and the cash flow forecast, which may cast significant doubt on the company's ability to continue as a going concern. The cash flow forecast has just been sent to me from the client, and is attached. It covers only the first three months of the next financial year, the client is currently preparing the forecasts for the whole 12 month period. Please be sceptical when reviewing the forecast, as the assumptions may be optimistic.   **(10 marks)**

(ii)   In addition, please recommend the principal audit procedures to be carried out on the cash flow forecast. Your recommendations can be included in a separate section of the briefing notes.   **(8 marks)**

Thanks.

Attachment: Cash flow forecast for the three months to 31 August 2011

	June 2011 £ million	July 2011 £ million	August 2011 £ million
Cash inflows			
Cash receipts from customers (note 1)	175	195	220
Loan receipt (note 2)		150	
Government subsidy (note 3)			50
Sales of financial assets	50		
Total cash inflows	225	345	270
Cash outflows			
Operating cash outflows	200	200	290
Interest payments	40	40	40
Loan repayment			60
Total cash outflows	240	240	390
Net cash flow for the month	(15)	105	(120)
Opening cash	(25)	(40)	65
Closing cash	(40)	65	(55)

Notes to the cash flow forecast:

This cash flow forecast has been prepared by the management of Butler Ltd, and is based on the following assumptions:

(1)   Cash receipts from customers should accelerate given the anticipated improvement in economic conditions. In addition, the company has committed extra resources to the credit control function, in order to speed up collection of overdue debts.

(2)   The loan expected to be received in July 2011 is currently being negotiated with our parent company, Rubery Ltd.

(3)   The government subsidy will be received once our application has been approved. The subsidy is awarded to companies which operate in areas of high unemployment and it subsidises the wages and salaries paid to staff.

Required:

Respond to the email from the audit partner.   **(18 marks)**

Note: The split of the mark allocation is shown within the partner's email. Professional marks will be awarded for presentation, and for the clarity of explanations provided. **(2 marks)**

(b) The management of Butler Ltd is concerned that given the company's poor liquidity position, the company could be placed into compulsory liquidation.

Required:

(i) Explain the procedures involved in placing a company into compulsory liquidation; and **(4 marks)**

(ii) Explain the consequences of a compulsory liquidation for Butler Ltd's payables (creditors), employees and shareholders. **(3 marks)**

(Total: 27 marks)

58 ASPECTS OF INSOLVENCY *Walk in the footsteps of a top tutor*

(a) Explain the differences between fraudulent and wrongful trading and the consequences for company directors. **(6 marks)**

(b) Explain how an auditor would determine whether a company is insolvent under the provisions of the UK Insolvency Act 1986. **(2 marks)**

(c) State the circumstances under which a company may be obliged to liquidate. **(2 marks)**

(d) Explain the consequences of compulsory liquidation and how it may affect company stakeholders. **(5 marks)**

(e) Explain the meaning of and describe procedures involved in a member's voluntary liquidation. **(5 marks)**

(Total: 20 marks)

INT SYLLABUS ONLY

59 **PUBLIC SECTOR ORGANISATIONS** *Walk in the footsteps of a top tutor*

(a) Define the terms 'performance audit' and 'performance information'. **(2 marks)**

(b) Suggest 4 performance targets which could be measured for each of the following public sector organisations:

   (i) Local police department **(2 marks)**

   (ii) Local hospital **(2 marks)**

   (iii) Local council **(2 marks)**

(c) State 2 stakeholder groups that would rely on the performance information produced by the public sector organisations in part (b) and explain what they might use that information for. **(6 marks)**

(d) Explain the difficulties encountered by auditors when auditing performance information. **(6 marks)**

(Total: 20 marks)

Section 3

ANSWERS TO PRACTICE QUESTIONS – SECTION A

Tutorial note

These model answers are considerably longer and more detailed than would be expected from any candidate in the examination. They should be used as a guide to the form, style and technical standard (but not length) of answer that candidates should aim to achieve. However, these answers may not include all valid points mentioned by a candidate – credit will be given to candidates mentioning such points.

1   STOW GROUP   *Walk in the footsteps of a top tutor*

Key answer tips

Part (a) requires you to explain the risks of material misstatement, commenting on their materiality. A risk of material misstatement needs to relate to the financial statements in some way – figures, disclosures, basis of preparation. Ultimately, the FS will be materially misstated if the client has not complied with the relevant accounting standard. Your answer should give reasons why the accounting treatment is wrong.

Materiality calculations are the easy marks to earn. If there is a figure mentioned in the scenario, calculate the percentage of profits or assets it represents and state whether this is material or not material. As a general rule of thumb use the lower materiality thresholds: 5% PBT, 1% Assets, 0.5% Revenue.

The question also asks for any further information that may be needed. This is a common requirement in more recent exams and you should try to identify other information that would help you with your risk assessment.

Part (b) asks for 'principal' audit procedures in respect of the disposal. Principal procedures are the procedures that should be performed to obtain the best quality evidence or the most important evidence.

Part (c) is a straightforward requirement considering whether reliance can be placed on the work of the internal audit department, including any ethical issues.

There are four professional marks available for the **structure, presentation of the briefing notes and the clarity of the explanations.** Your answer should be labelled 'Briefing Notes'. You should identify who the briefing notes are intended for. For the introduction, use the words from the requirement. The body of the answer should have a clear structure including underlined headings for each risk. Don't forget to include a conclusion summarising the key points identified.

Briefing notes

To: Audit Partner

From: Audit Manager

Subject: Planning issues for the Stow Group, year ending 31 December 2013

Introduction

These briefing notes contain an explanation of the risks of material misstatement to be considered in planning the audit of the Stow Group. The risks which have been explained focus on a restructuring of the Group which has taken place during the year. Materiality has been considered where information permits, and further information which would be useful in planning the audit has also been identified. The briefing notes also contain recommended audit procedures to be performed in respect of the disposal of Broadway Co. In addition, the Group finance director's suggestion that our firm makes use of the new subsidiary's internal audit team when performing our audit has been discussed, along with the ethical implication of the suggestion.

(a) (i)

and (ii) **Zennor Co**

Materiality of Zennor Co

To evaluate the materiality of Zennor Co to the Group, its profit and assets need to be retranslated into $. At the stated exchange rate of 4 Dingu = $1, its projected profit for the year is $22.5 million (90 million Dingu/4) and its projected total assets are $200 million (800 million Dingu/4).

Zennor Co's profit represents 11.3% of Group projected profit for the year (22.5/200), and its assets represent 8% of Group total assets (200/2,500). Zennor Co is therefore material to the Group and may be considered to be a significant component of it. A significant component is one which is identified by the auditor as being of individual financial significance to the group. Zennor Co is likely to be considered a significant component due to its risk profile and the change in group structure which has occurred in the year.

The goodwill arising on the acquisition of Zennor Co amounts to 2.4% (60/2,500) of Group assets and is material.

Because the balances above, including goodwill, are based on a foreign currency, they will need to be retranslated at the year end using the closing exchange rate to determine and conclude on materiality as at the year end.

Materiality needs to be assessed based on the new, enlarged group structure. Materiality for the group financial statements as a whole will be determined when establishing the overall group audit strategy. The addition of Zennor Co to the group during the year is likely to cause materiality to be different from previous years, possibly affecting audit strategy and the extent of testing in some areas.

Risks of material misstatement

Retranslation of Zennor Co's financial statements

According to IAS 21 *The Effects of Changes in Foreign Exchange Rates*, the assets and liabilities of Zennor Co should be retranslated using the closing exchange rate. Its income and expenses should be retranslated at the exchange rates at the dates of the transactions.

The risk is that incorrect exchange rates are used for the retranslations. This could result in over/understatement of the assets, liabilities, income and expenses that are consolidated, including goodwill. It would also mean that the exchange gains and losses arising on retranslation and to be included in Group other comprehensive income are incorrectly determined.

Measurement and recognition of exchange gains and losses

The calculation of exchange gains and losses can be complex, and there is a risk that it is not calculated correctly, or that some elements are omitted, for example, the exchange gain or loss on goodwill may be missed out of the calculation.

IAS 21 states that exchange gains and losses arising as a result of the retranslation of the subsidiary's balances are recognised in other comprehensive income. The risk is incorrect classification, for example, the gain or loss could be recognised incorrectly as part of profit for the year

Initial measurement of goodwill

In order for goodwill to be calculated, the assets and liabilities of Zennor Co must have been identified and measured at fair value at the date of acquisition. Risks of material misstatement arise because the various components of goodwill each have specific risks attached, for example:

- Not all assets and liabilities may have been identified, for example, contingent liabilities and contingent assets may be omitted

- Fair value is subjective and based on assumptions which may not be valid.

There is also a risk that the cost of investment is not stated correctly, for example, that any contingent consideration has not been included in the calculation.

Subsequent measurement of goodwill

According to IFRS 3 *Business Combinations*, goodwill should be subject to an impairment review on an annual basis. The risk is that a review has not taken place, and so goodwill is overstated and Group operating expenses understated if impairment losses have not been recognised.

Consolidation of income and expenses

Zennor Co was acquired on 1 February 2013 and its income and expenses should have been consolidated from that date. There is a risk that the full year's income and expenses have been consolidated, leading to a risk of overstated Group profit.

Disclosure

Extensive disclosures are required by IFRS 3 to be included in the notes to the Group financial statements, for example, to include the acquisition date, reason for the acquisition and a description of the factors which make up the goodwill acquired. The risk is that disclosures are incomplete or not understandable.

Intra-group transactions

There will be a significant volume of intra-group transactions as the Group is supplying Zennor Co with inventory. There is a risk that intra-group sales, purchases, payables and receivables are not eliminated, leading to overstated revenue, cost of sales, payables and receivables in the Group financial statements.

There is also a risk that intercompany transactions are not identified in either/both companies' accounting systems.

The intra-group transactions are by definition related party transactions according to IAS 24 *Related Party Disclosures*, because Zennor Co is under the control of the Group. No disclosure of the transactions is required in the Group financial statements in respect of intra-group transactions because they are eliminated on consolidation. However, both the individual financial statements of the Group company supplying Zennor Co and the financial statements of Zennor Co must contain notes disclosing details of the intra-group transactions. There is a risk that this disclosure is not provided.

In addition, the cars may be supplied including a profit margin or mark up, in which case a provision for unrealised profit should be recognised in the Group financial statements. If this is not accounted for, Group inventory will be overstated, and operating profit will be overstated.

Completeness of inventory

There is a risk that cars which are in transit to Zennor Co at the year end may be omitted from inventory. The cars spend a significant amount of time in transit and awaiting delivery to Zennor Co, and without a good system of controls in place, it is likely that items of inventory will be missing from the Group's current assets as they may have been recorded as despatched from the seller but not yet as received by Zennor Co.

The inventory in transit to Zennor Co represents 2.3% of Group total assets (58/2,500) and is therefore material to the consolidated financial statements.

Tutorial note

Credit will also be awarded where answers discuss the issue of whether the arrangement is a consignment inventory arrangement, and the relevant risks of material misstatement.

Further information in relation to Zennor Co:

- Prior years' financial statements and auditor's reports.
- Minutes of meetings where the acquisition was discussed.
- Business background, e.g. from the company's website or trade journals.
- Copies of systems documentation from the internal audit team.
- Confirmation from Zennor Co's previous auditors of any matters which they wish to bring to our attention.
- Projected financial statements for the year to 31 December 2013.
- A copy of the due diligence report.
- Copies of prior year tax computations.

Tutorial note

Credit will also be awarded for discussions of risks of material misstatement and relevant audit procedures relating to the initial audit of Zennor Co by Compton & Co, e.g. increased risk of misstatement of opening balances and comparatives.

Broadway Co

Materiality

The profit made on the disposal of Broadway Co represents 12.5% of Group profit for the year (25/200) and the transaction is therefore material to the Group financial statements.

Given that the subsidiary was sold for $180 million and that a profit on disposal of $25 million was recognised, the Group's financial statements must have derecognised net assets of $155 million on the disposal. This amounts to 6.2% of the Group's assets and is material. This is assuming that the profit on disposal has been correctly calculated, which is a risk factor discussed below.

Risk of material misstatement

Derecognition of assets and liabilities

On the disposal of Broadway Co, all of its assets and liabilities which had been recognised in the Group financial statements should have been derecognised at their carrying value, including any goodwill in respect of the company.

There is therefore a risk that not all assets, liabilities and goodwill have been derecognised leading to overstatement of those balances and an incorrect profit on disposal being calculated and included in Group profit for the year.

Profit consolidated prior to disposal

There is a risk that Broadway Co's income for the year has been incorrectly consolidated. It should have been included in Group profit up to the date that control passed and any profit included after that point would mean overstatement of Group profit for the year.

Calculation of profit on disposal

There is a risk that the profit on disposal has not been accurately calculated, e.g. that the proceeds received have not been measured at fair value as required by IFRS 10 *Consolidated Financial Statements*, or that elements of the calculation are missing.

Classification and disclosure of profit on disposal

IAS 1 *Presentation of Financial Statements* requires separate disclosure on the face of the financial statements of material items to enhance the understanding of performance during the year. The profit of $25 million is material, so separate disclosure is necessary. The risk is that the profit is not separately disclosed, e.g. is netted from operating expenses, leading to material misstatement.

Extensive disclosure requirements exist in relation to subsidiaries disposed of, e.g. IAS 7 *Statement of Cash Flows* requires a note which analyses the assets and liabilities of the subsidiary at the date of disposal. There is a risk that not all necessary notes to the financial statements are provided.

Tutorial note

It is possible that Broadway Co represents a disposal group and a discontinued operation, and credit will be awarded for discussion of relevant risks of material misstatement and audit procedures in respect of these issues.

Treatment of the disposal in parent company individual financial statements

The parent company's financial statements should derecognise the original cost of investment and recognise a profit on disposal based on the difference between the proceeds of $180 million and the cost of investment. Risk arises if the investment has not been derecognised or the profit has been incorrectly calculated.

Tax on disposal

There should be an accrual in both the parent company and the Group financial statements for the tax due on the disposal. This should be calculated based on the profit recognised in the parent company. There is a risk that the tax is not accrued for, leading to overstated profit and understated liabilities. There is also a risk that the tax calculation is not accurate.

Tutorial note

As Compton & Co is no longer the auditor of Broadway Co, there is no need for any further information in relation to audit planning, other than that needed to perform the audit procedures listed below.

(b)   **Procedures to be performed on the disposal of Broadway Co**

- Obtain the statement of financial position of Broadway Co as at 1 September 2013 to confirm the value of assets and liabilities which have been derecognised from the Group.

- Review prior year Group financial statements and audit working papers to confirm the amount of goodwill that exists in respect of Broadway Co and trace to confirm it is derecognised from the Group on disposal.

- Confirm that the Stow Group is no longer listed as a shareholder of the company.

- Obtain legal documentation in relation to the disposal to confirm the date of the disposal and confirm that Broadway Co's profit has been consolidated up to this date only.

- Agree or reconcile the profit recognised in the Group financial statements to Broadway Co's individual accounts as at 1 September 2013.

- Perform substantive analytical procedures to gain assurance that the amount of profit consolidated from 1 January to 1 September 2013 appears reasonable and in line with expectations based on prior year profit.

- Reperform management's calculation of profit on disposal in the Group financial statements.

- Agree the proceeds received of $180 million to legal documentation, and to cash book/bank statements.

- Confirm that $180 million is the fair value of proceeds on disposal and that no deferred or contingent consideration is receivable in the future.

- Review the Group statement of profit or loss and other comprehensive income to confirm that the profit on disposal is correctly disclosed as part of profit for the year (not in other comprehensive income) on a separate line.

- Using a disclosure checklist, confirm that all necessary information has been provided in the notes to the Group financial statements.

- Obtain the parent company's statement of financial position to confirm that the cost of investment is derecognised.

- Using prior year financial statements and audit working papers, agree the cost of investment derecognised to prior year's figure.

- Reperform the calculation of profit on disposal in the parent company's financial statements.

- Reconcile the profit on disposal recognised in the parent company's financial statements to the profit recognised in the Group financial statements.

- Obtain management's estimate of the tax due on disposal, reperform the calculation and confirm the amount is properly accrued at parent company and at Group level.

- Review any correspondence with tax authorities regarding the tax due.

- Possibly the tax will be paid in the subsequent events period, in which case the payment can be agreed to cash book and bank statement.

(c)   **Internal audit team and ethical issue**

It is not improper for Marta to suggest that Compton & Co use the work of Zennor Co's internal audit team. ISA 610 *Using the Work of Internal Auditors* contains requirements relating to the evaluation of the internal audit function to determine in what areas, and to what extent, the work of internal audit can be used by the external audit firm.

It would be beneficial for Compton & Co to use the internal audit team as it may result in a more efficient audit strategy, for example, the internal audit team's monitoring of controls should have resulted in a strong control environment, so a less substantive approach can be used on the audit.

In addition, the internal audit team should be able to provide Compton & Co with systems documentation and information on control activities which have been implemented. This will help the audit firm to build its knowledge and understanding of the new audit client. The internal audit team will also be able to assist Compton & Co in gaining more general business understanding with respect to the new subsidiary.

Compton & Co may also decide to rely on audit work performed by the internal audit team, for example, they may be asked to attend inventory counts of cars held at the port and awaiting delivery to Zennor Co.

All of the benefits described above are particularly significant given Zennor Co's overseas location, as reliance on the internal audit team would reduce travel time and costs which would be incurred if the external auditor had to perform the work themselves. However, there will be a limit to the amount of work that can be delegated to the internal audit team.

Before deciding to what extent the work of internal audit can be used, ISA 610 requires the external auditor to evaluate various matters, including the extent to which the internal audit function's organisation status and policies and procedures support the objectivity of the function; the level of competence of the internal audit team; and whether the internal audit function applies a systematic and disciplined approach, including quality control. To perform these evaluations the external auditor may wish, for example, to discuss the work of the team with Jo Evesham including a consideration of the level of supervision, review and documentation of work performed, and also review the qualifications held by members of the team.

The fact that the internal audit team does not report to an independent audit committee may reduce the reliance that can be placed on their work as it affects the objectivity of work performed.

If Compton & Co chooses to use the work of the internal audit team, this will be relevant to the audit of both Zennor Co's individual financial statements, and the Group financial statements and will affect the audit strategy of both.

Marta states that reliance on the internal audit team will reduce the external audit fee, and the Group audit committee has requested that the Group audit fee remains the same as last year. This implies an intimidation threat to objectivity. IESBA's (IFAC) *Code of Ethics for Professional Accountants* states that an audit firm being pressured to reduce inappropriately the extent of work performed in order to reduce fees is an example of an intimidation threat. It should be brought to Marta's attention that the audit fee will not necessarily be reduced by reliance on internal audit, especially as this is the first year that Compton & Co have audited Zennor Co, so there will be a lot of work to be performed in developing knowledge and understanding of the client whether or not the firm chooses to rely on the work of the internal audit team.

Conclusion

The Stow Group's financial statements contain a high risk of material misstatement this year end, due to the restructuring which has taken place. The audit plan will contain numerous audit procedures to reduce the identified risks to an acceptable level. Compton & Co may choose to place reliance on Zennor Co's internal audit team, but only after careful consideration of their competence and objectivity, and communication between the external and internal audit teams must be carefully planned for.

Examiner's comments

This 35 mark question involved the Stow Group, which had undergone some reorganisation during the year. A subsidiary had been disposed of, and a new foreign subsidiary had been acquired. Information was provided in the form of notes of a meeting that had been held with the Group's finance director. The notes described the acquisition of the foreign subsidiary Zennor Co and the goodwill arising on the acquisition, the disposal of Broadway Co, and gave information about some trading between group companies. In addition, some detail was provided on Zennor Co's internal audit team.

As is typical in Question One, the requirements were based on planning the audit. The first requirement, for 12 marks, asked candidates to explain the risks of material misstatement to be considered in planning the Group audit, and to comment on materiality. This type of requirement is standard for P7, many candidates made a reasonable attempt at this requirement. Almost all candidates could at least identify several risks of material misstatement and determine their materiality, however the quality of explanation varied dramatically between scripts.

The best dealt with issues included the acquisition of the new subsidiary, with the majority of candidates correctly retranslating its figures into the Group's currency and discussing the risks relating to the re-translation process. Other matters generally well dealt with was the measurement of goodwill on acquisition and the risks associated with the elimination of balances arising on transactions between Group companies.

The main weakness seen in candidate's answers to this requirement was that of inadequately explained risks of material misstatements. While most candidates could identify a risk, only a small minority could adequately explain the risk. For example, having identified a risk, say in the recognition of goodwill, some candidates would simple suggest that 'this should be accounted for properly' or that 'the auditor must ensure that this is calculated properly', or simply 'this needs to be accounted for in accordance with accounting standards'.

Unfortunately this type of comment does not adequately answer the question requirement and where candidates supplied this type of explanation in their answers they would be unlikely to generate sufficient marks to pass this question requirement. Candidates are reminded that practicing past questions and carefully reviewing the model answers are the best way to prepare for this type of requirement, in order to understand exactly what is being asked for in the question requirement and to develop skill in explaining the risks identified.

Very few candidates picked up on some of the less obvious risks of material misstatement such as the tax implication of the disposal of Broadway.

Other common errors and weaknesses in answering this requirement included:

Discussing business risks and failing to develop these into risks of material misstatement.

Discussing detection risks, which are not part of the risk of material misstatement.

Incorrectly calculating the amount of profit that should be consolidated for the subsidiaries during the year.

Stating that Zennor Co's assets and liabilities should be recognised on a time-apportioned basis due to the subsidiary being acquired part way through the year.

Stating that goodwill on acquisition should be cancelled out and not recognised in the group accounts because it is an inter-company transaction.

Discussing that Broadway Co's assets and liabilities should be classified as held for sale at the year end, when in fact the subsidiary had been sold some months prior to the year end.

Providing long discussions on the use of component auditors at the year end, which was not relevant to the scenario.

Simply saying that a balance is material without demonstrating that this is the case.

Requirement (a) (ii), for 4 marks, asked candidates, in the context of planning the Group audit, to identify further information that would be needed. Answers to this requirement were very mixed. Sound answers identified that information such as the due diligence report on the acquisition of Zennor Co and its previous years financial statements and audit reports would useful in planning the audit, as well as business background given that it is a first-year audit. Some answers gave audit procedures rather than information requirements, which was not asked for. Again candidates are encouraged to review similar past exam requirements and their model answers to gain an understanding of the type of information that would be useful in planning the audit.

The next requirement was for 8 marks, and required candidates to recommend the principal audit procedures to be performed in respect of the disposal of Broadway Co. While there does seem to have been an improvement in the way that some candidates describe audit procedures, with many candidates scoring enough marks to pass this requirement, many answers were too vague to score well on this requirement. It was common to see procedures suggested such as 'agree to supporting documentation', or simply 'discuss with management' without any suggestion of what documentation should be looked at, and for what purpose, or the relevant matters that may be discussed with management. Procedures need to be specific to score well.

Requirement (c), for 7 marks, focused on a suggestion by the Group's finance director that the external audit firm should use Zennor Co's internal audit team as much as possible in order to reduce the audit fee. Some information was provided about the internal audit team, the work they had performed, and the fact that it reports to the board of directors in the absence of an audit committee. The finance director had also requested that the audit fee should not be increased from the previous year. Candidates were asked to discuss how the finance director's suggestions impact on audit planning and to comment on relevant ethical issues.

This requirement was generally quite well answered. Most candidates knew the main requirements of the relevant ISA and could to some extent apply them to the scenario. Many candidates picked up on the fact that Zennor Co not having an audit committee would impact on the control environment of the company, and that the work of the internal audit team would need to be evaluated before any reliance could be placed on it. Most candidates could describe the impact that using the work of internal audit could have on the overall audit strategy, though this was often only very briefly mentioned, and few candidates suggested the type of work that the internal audit team could perform with relevance to the audit. On the whole though, this issue was quite well dealt with. The issue in relation to the audit fee was also generally well answered. Almost all candidates could identify the ethical threats raised, and attempted to evaluate them in the context of the scenario. However a significant minority of candidates thought that the finance director's suggestion was some kind of contingent fee arrangement, which was not correct, and there were the usual suggestions that the finance director should be 'disciplined' or 'sacked' due to her improper suggestions, which did not earn credit.

To summarise on this question, the answers on risk of material misstatement were unsatisfactory, especially given that this is a regularly examined area. Candidates need to improve on the quality of their explanations of the risks identified. Simply stating that a balance or transaction may be 'risky' without explaining why, and calculating its materiality is not enough to score well in this type of question. There were also relatively easy marks lost in many scripts where candidates had failed to provide any additional information requests, or due to audit procedures being inadequately described. For many candidates the requirement where they demonstrated the best level of understanding was in relation to internal audit and ethical matters.

ACCA marking scheme		
		Marks
(a) (i) **Risks of material misstatement, materiality and further information requests**		
Generally up to 1½ marks for each risk identified and explained (to a maximum of 4 marks for identification only):		
Zennor Co		
– Retranslation of Zennor Co's financial statements using incorrect exchange rate		
– Treatment of exchange gains and losses arising on retranslation		
– Goodwill not measured correctly at initial recognition		
– Goodwill not tested for impairment before the year end		
– Time apportionment of Zennor Co's income and expenses not correct		
– Incomplete or inadequate disclosure		
– Cancellation of intercompany balances		
– Disclosure of related party transactions		
– Completeness of inventory		
Broadway Co		
– Derecognition of assets, liabilities and goodwill		
– Time apportionment of profit up to date of disposal		
– Calculation of profit on disposal		
– Classification and presentation regarding the disposal		
– Treatment in parent company financial statements		
– Accrual for tax payable		
Generally 1 mark for each of the following calculations/comments on materiality:		
– Appropriate retranslation of Zennor Co figures into $		
– Calculate materiality of Zennor Co to the Group		
– Determine if Zennor Co is a significant component of the Group		
– Calculate materiality of goodwill arising on acquisition		
– Calculate materiality of inventory in transit to the Group		
Maximum		12
(ii) 1 mark for each piece of additional information identified:		
– Prior years' financial statements and auditor's reports		
– Minutes of meetings where the acquisition was discussed		
– Business background, e.g. from the company's website or trade journals		
– Copies of systems documentation from the internal audit team		
– Confirmation from Zennor Co's previous auditors of any matters that they wish to bring to our attention		
– Projected financial statements for the year to 31 December 2013		
– A copy of the due diligence report		
– Copies of prior year tax computations		
Maximum		4

(b)	**Audit procedures**		
	Generally 1 mark for each well described audit procedure:		
	– Confirm the value of assets and liabilities which have been derecognised from the Group		
	– Confirm goodwill that exists is derecognised from the Group		
	– Confirm that the Stow Group is no longer listed as a shareholder of the company		
	– Obtain legal documentation in relation to the disposal to confirm the date of the disposal and confirm that Broadway Co's profit has been consolidated up to this date only		
	– Agree or reconcile the profit recognised in the Group financial statements to Broadway Co's individual accounts as at 1 September 2013		
	– Analytical procedures to gain assurance that the amount of profit consolidated from 1 January to 1 September 2013 appears reasonable		
	– Reperform management's calculation of profit on disposal in the Group financial statements		
	– Agree proceeds received to legal documentation/cash book/bank statements		
	– Confirm that no deferred or contingent consideration is receivable in the future		
	– Confirm that the profit on disposal is correctly disclosed as part of profit for the year		
	– Confirm that all necessary notes are given in the Group financial statements		
	– Obtain the parent company's statement of financial position to confirm that the cost of investment is derecognised		
	– Reperform the calculation of profit on disposal in the individual financial statements		
	– Reconcile the profit on disposal recognised in the parent company's financial statements to the profit recognised in the Group financial statements		
	– Obtain management's estimate of the tax due on disposal, reperform the calculation and confirm the amount is properly accrued at parent company and at Group level		
	– Review any correspondence with tax authorities regarding the tax due		
	– If the tax is paid in the subsequent events period, agree to cash book and bank statement		
		Maximum	8
(c)	**Reliance on internal audit**		
	Generally 1 mark for each discussion point:		
	– Impact on audit strategy, e.g. reliance on controls		
	– Impact on audit planning, e.g. systems documentation/business understanding		
	– Specific work can be performed, e.g. inventory counts		
	– Could lead to significant reduction in audit costs, e.g. travel costs can be avoided		
	– Need to evaluate how much reliance can be placed (objectivity, competence, quality control, etc) – up to 3 marks		
	– Reliance will impact Group audit as well as individual audit		
	– Pressure on fee is an intimidation threat		
	– Fee unlikely to be maintained given the change in Group structure		
		Maximum	7
	Professional marks to be awarded for:		
	– Use of headings		
	– Introduction		
	– Logical flow/presentation		
	– Conclusion		
		Maximum	4
Total			35

2   BALTIMORE *Walk in the footsteps of a top tutor*

Key answer tips

Part (a) requires discussion of the benefits of a due diligence review being performed prior to the acquisition of a company. There were indications in the scenario that the client did not have the skill to do this and you are expected to identify these points and use them in your answer.

Part (b) asked for matters to focus on during the due diligence review. A due diligence review is performed to find information relevant to the client's decision regarding the acquisition. Therefore you should identify the matters that might deter them from going ahead with the acquisition or might encourage them to go ahead with the acquisition.

Part (c) is a straightforward requirement asking for the type of conclusion, i.e. level of assurance, to be issued on the due diligence review and to compare this to an audit.

(a)   **Three benefits of due diligence to Baltimore Co**

One of the objectives of a due diligence review is for the assets and liabilities of the target company to be identified and valued. Therefore a benefit of due diligence to Baltimore Co is to gain an understanding of the nature of assets and liabilities which are being acquired, as not all assets and liabilities of Mizzen Co are recognised in its financial statements. For example, Mizzen Co has built up several customer databases, which, being internally generated, will not be recognised as assets in its statement of financial position, but these could be valuable assets to Baltimore Co.

A second benefit is that the due diligence review should uncover more information about operational issues, which may then help Baltimore Co's management to decide whether to go ahead with the acquisition. For example, only one of Mizzen Co's revenue streams appears to be directly relevant to Baltimore Co's expansion plans, so more information is needed about the other operations of Mizzen Co to determine how they may be of benefit to Baltimore Co. The due diligence review should cover a wide range of issues, such as reviews of the company's legal and tax positions, which may uncover significant matters.

An externally provided due diligence review, as opposed to a review conducted by management of Baltimore Co, is likely to provide information in a time-efficient, impartial manner. Baltimore Co's management has not previously dealt with an acquisition, whereas the audit firm has the financial and business understanding and expertise to provide a quality due diligence review. A review report issued by Goleen & Co will add credibility to the planned acquisition, which may help secure the bank loan which is needed to fund the acquisition.

Tutorial note

Credit will be awarded for other relevant benefits which are discussed.

(b)   **Matters to focus on in the due diligence review**

Equity owners of Mizzen Co and involvement of BizGrow

The nature of the involvement of the venture capitalist company, BizGrow, is a crucial issue which must be the starting point of the due diligence review. Venture capitalists provide equity when a company is incorporated, and typically look for an exit route within three to seven years. Mizzen Co was incorporated four years ago, so it will be important to determine whether BizGrow retains its original equity holding in Mizzen Co, and if so, whether the acquisition of BizGrow's shares by Baltimore Co would be compatible with the planned exit route.

Key skills and expertise

It appears that the original founders of Mizzen Co, Vic Sandhu and Lou Lien, are crucial to the success of Mizzen Co and it would be in Baltimore Co's interests to keep them involved with the business. However, Vic and Lou may wish to focus on further work involving IT innovation rather than Baltimore Co's planned website and without Vic and Lou's expertise the acquisition may be much less worthwhile. However, there could be other employed personnel with the necessary skills and experience to meet Baltimore Co's needs, or much of the skill and expertise could be provided from freelancers, who will not be part of the acquisition.

Internally generated intangible assets

Mizzen Co is likely to have several important internally generated intangible assets, which will not be recognised in its individual accounts but must be identified and measured as part of the due diligence review. First, Vic and Lou have innovated and developed new website interfaces, and the review must determine the nature of this intellectual property (IP), and whether it belongs to Vic and Lou or to Mizzen Co. The measurement of this asset will be very difficult, and it is likely to form an important part of the acquisition deal if Baltimore Co want to acquire the IP to use in its new website.

There are also several customer databases which need to be measured and included in the list of assets acquired, which again may be difficult to measure in value. It is important for the due diligence review to confirm the relevance of the databases to Baltimore Co's operations, and that the databases contain up-to-date information.

Premises

Mizzen Co currently operates from premises owned by BizGrow and pays a nominal rent for this. Presumably if the acquisition were to go ahead, this arrangement would cease. The due diligence review should consider the need for new premises to be found for Mizzen Co and the associated costs. Possibly there is room for Mizzen Co to operate from Baltimore Co's premises as the operations do not appear to need a large space. The rental agreement may be fixed for a period of time and cancellation may incur a penalty.

Other tangible assets

Mizzen Co appears to own only items such as computer equipment and fixtures and fittings. It needs to be clarified whether these assets are owned or held under lease, and also whether any other tangible assets, such as vehicles, are used in the business. Any commitments for future purchases of tangible assets should be reviewed.

Accounting policy on revenue recognition

Mizzen Co has some fairly complex revenue streams, and the due diligence review should establish that the accounting policies in place are reasonable and in line with IAS 18 *Revenue*. The revenue generated from website development and maintenance should be split into two components, with the revenue for website development recognised once the website has been provided to the customer, but the revenue for maintenance spread over the contract period. There is a risk that revenue is recognised too early, inflating Mizzen Co's profit.

The revenue recognition policy for annual subscriptions should also be scrutinized, with revenue relating to future periods being deferred.

Sustainability and relevance of revenue streams

The financial statements indicate that revenue has increased each year, and that in the last year it has increased by 23.7%. This is an impressive growth rate and work must be done to analyse the likelihood of revenue streams being maintained and further growth being achieved. For example, the proportion of website development and two year maintenance contracts which are renewed should be investigated. Not all of Mizzen Co's revenue streams seem very relevant to Baltimore Co's operations, so how these may be managed post-acquisition should be considered.

Operating expenses

The financial extracts indicate a potentially unusual trend in relation to operating expenses. In 2011 and 2012, operating expenses represented 60% and 58.3% of revenue respectively. In 2013, this had reduced to 49.6%. This may be due to economies of scale being achieved as the company grows, or possibly expenses are understated or revenue overstated in 2013. As freelance web designers have been used in 2013, operating expenses may have been expected to have increased in proportion to revenue. The due diligence review should perform detailed analysis on the operating costs incurred by the company to gain assurance that expenses are complete and accurately recorded.

With the exception of 2010, the finance cost has remained static at $250,000 per annum. The due diligence review must uncover what this finance cost relates to, and whether it will continue post-acquisition. It may be a bank loan or it could be a payment made to BizGrow, as venture capitalist companies often impose a management charge on companies which they have invested in. Baltimore Co will need to understand the nature of any liability in relation to this finance charge.

Cash position and cash management

Mizzen Co's cash position should be confirmed. Given that the company appears to have limited need for capital expenditure and working capital, and given the level of profits which has been made in the last three years, it could be expected that the company would be cash-rich. The due diligence review should confirm how the cash generated by the company since incorporation has been used, for example, in dividend payments to BizGrow and to Vic and Lou.

Additional information required

- Contract or legal documentation describing the nature of the investment which BizGrow made when Mizzen Co was incorporated, and detailing the planned exit route.

- A register of shareholders showing all shareholders of Mizzen Co.

- An organisational structure, in order to identify the members of management and key personnel and their roles within Mizzen Co.

- A list of employees and their roles within the company, and their related obligations including salary, holiday entitlements, retirement plans, health insurance and other benefits provided by Mizzen Co, and details of compensation to be paid in the case of redundancy.

- A list of freelance web designers used by Mizzen Co, and a description of the work they perform.

- The key terms of contracts or agreements with freelance web designers.

- A list of all IT innovations which have been created and developed by Mizzen Co, and details of any patent or copyright agreements relating to them.

- Agreements with employees regarding assignment of intellectual property and confidentiality.

- Copies of the customer databases showing contact details of all people or companies included on the list.

- A list of companies which have contracts with Mizzen Co for website development and maintenance.

- A copy of all contracts with customers for review of the period for which maintenance is to be provided.

- A breakdown of the revenue which has been generated from making each database available to other companies, and the dates when they were made available.

- A summary of the controls which are in place to ensure that the database details are regularly updated.

- A copy of the rental agreement with BizGrow, to determine whether any penalty is payable on cancellation.

- Non-current asset register showing descriptions and values of all assets used in the business.

- Copies of any lease agreements, for example, leases of computer equipment, photocopiers, etc.

- Details of any capital expenditure budgets for previous accounting periods, and any planned capital expenditure in the future.

- Mizzen Co's stated accounting policy on revenue recognition.

- Systems and controls documentation over the processing of revenue receipts.

- An analysis of expenses included in operating expenses for each year and copies of documentation relating to ongoing expenses, such as salaries and other overheads.

- Copies of management accounts to agree expenses in the audited accounts are in line and to perform more detailed analytical review.

- The full set of financial statements and auditor's reports for each year since the company's incorporation, to:
    - Confirm the assets and liabilities recognised
    - Agree the level of dividends paid each year
    - Review all of the accounting policies used in preparing the financial statements
    - Find the details of any related party transactions that have occurred
    - Review the statement of cash flows for each year.
- Any agreements with banks or other external providers of finance, including finance advanced and relevant finance charges, or confirmation that no such finance has been provided to Mizzen Co.

Tutorial note

Credit will be awarded for other relevant information which would be required as part of the due diligence review.

(c) **Due diligence conclusion**

Due diligence is a specific example of a direct reporting assurance engagement. The form of the report issued in this type of engagement is covered by ISAE 3000 *Assurance Engagements other than Audits or Reviews of Historical Financial Information*, and ISRE 2400 *Engagements to Review Historical Financial Statements* also contains relevant guidance.

The main difference between a review report and an audit report is the level of assurance that is given. In a review report a conclusion is expressed in a negative form. The conclusion would start with the wording 'based on our review, nothing has come to our attention...'

This type of conclusion is used because the nature of a due diligence review is that only limited assurance has been obtained over the subject matter. The procedures used in a review engagement are mainly enquiry and analytical review which can only provide limited assurance.

Tutorial note

Credit is equally awarded where answers discuss the due diligence assignment as being based on agreed upon procedures, in which case no assurance is provided.

In comparison, in an audit of historical information, the auditor will use a wide variety of procedures to obtain evidence to give reasonable assurance that the financial statements are free from material misstatement. This means that an opinion expressed in a positive form can be given.

Examiner's comments

This question focused on due diligence, a topic that has appeared in P7 examinations several times previous to this sitting. The scenario described a due diligence assignment to be performed on the target company Mizzen Co, at the request of Baltimore Co. The history and activities of the target company was described in some detail, and some financial information provided for the last four years. For Baltimore Co this would be their first acquisition, and was being considered as a means to diversify the company's operations.

Requirement (a) was for 6 marks, and asked candidates to discuss three benefits to Baltimore Co of a due diligence review being performed on Mizzen Co. While some reasonable answers were given, possibly by candidates who had practiced the past exam question containing a similar requirement, on the whole answers were unsatisfactory. The following factors contributed to inadequate performance in relation to this requirement:

- Writing answers that were much too brief for the marks available – it was common to see three sentences given as an answer to this requirement, which cannot be enough for a 6 mark requirement.

- At the other extreme, some very lengthy answers were given that usually failed to answer the question requirement and instead either simply wrote in detail on how a due diligence assignment should be performed, or suggested in some detail the operational benefits to Baltimore Co of acquiring Mizzen Co.

- Many answers failed to limit to three benefits and instead provided a bullet point list of benefits that were not discussed at all.

Requirement (b) was the main part of the question, and asked candidates, for 16 marks, to identify and explain the matters that the due diligence review would focus on, and to recommend the additional information needed.

The answers provided to this requirement were extremely mixed in quality. There were some exceptionally sound answers, explaining relevant matters in sufficient depth, and using the financial information provided to come up with reasonable points. These answers also provided relevant requests for additional information.

However, the majority of answers were unsatisfactory. Most candidates picked up at least a few marks by identifying some of the matters that the review would focus on, but many candidates let themselves down by failing to explain the matters that they had identified in any real depth. It was common for answers to simply contain a list of bullet points with very little explanation at all, and only a limited amount of marks can be awarded to answers of this type.

Some points were better dealt with, including the following:

- Most answers picked up on the fact that Mizzen Co used premises owned by the venture capitalist company, and the fact that this arrangement would probably cease on the acquisition.

- Many candidates realised that the two founders of Mizzen Co were crucial to the company's success and that without them the acquisition would probably be pointless.

- Many candidates used the financial information to some extent, though sometimes only in a very limited way, but most picked up on the fact that Mizzen Co was paying finance charges, and so information would be needed to understand what those charges relate to.

- Many answers considered that revenue recognition would be a matter to focus on due to the relatively complex nature of the company's revenue streams.

- Some answers performed a little analytical review on the financial information to reveal that expenses were not increasing in line with revenue, and that this would need to be investigated.

The answers that were unsatisfactory, as well as containing inadequately explained points as mentioned above, also tended to focus too much on financial reporting matters, for example giving very lengthy discussions on the calculation of goodwill. While the accounting treatment of some items certainly was relevant to the answer, just focussing on these matters meant that candidates did not provide a broad enough range of comments to score well.

Another factor leading to poor marks for this requirement was that many candidates simply failed to recommend any additional information at all that would be needed in the review. Many candidates missed out on marks here, for example for recommending that a statement of financial position, management accounts and cash flow forecasts would be needed.

Some candidates supplied a lengthy discussion of matters relating to the acceptance of the due diligence assignment, such as agreeing fees and clarifying deadlines, which was not asked for.

Requirement (c) was for 3 marks, and required candidates to describe the type of conclusion that would be issued for a due diligence report and to compare this to an audit report. This was well answered by most candidates, who compared the type of assurance that could be offered for a due diligence assignment with that given in an audit report, and linked this to the type of work that is carried out. Credit was awarded for different types of answers, as some discussed due diligence as being performed as agreed upon procedures rather than a review engagement, either of which is appropriate.

	ACCA marking scheme	Marks
(a)	**Benefit of due diligence** Up to 2 marks for each benefit discussed for a maximum of three benefits: – Identification of assets and liabilities – Valuation of assets and liabilities – Review of operational issues – Examination of financial position and performance – Added credibility and expertise – Added value for negotiation of purchase price – Other advice can be given, e.g. on obtaining finance Maximum	6
(b)	**Areas to focus on and additional information** Generally up to 1½ marks for each explanation of area to focus on: – Equity owners of Mizzen Co and involvement of BizGrow – Key skills and expertise – Internally generated intangible assets – Premises – Other intangible assets – Accounting policy on revenue recognition – Sustainability and relevance of revenue streams – Operating expenses – Finance charges – Cash management	

1 mark for each specific additional information recommended:
– Contract or legal documentation dealing with BizGrow's investment in Mizzen Co
– A register of shareholders showing all shareholders of Mizzen Co
– An organisational structure
– A list of employees and their role within the company, obligations and compensation
– A list of freelance web designers used by Mizzen Co, and a description of the work they perform
– The key terms of contracts or agreements with freelance web designers
– A list of all IT innovations which have been created and developed by Mizzen Co, and details of any patent or copyright agreements relating to them
– Agreements with employees regarding assignment of intellectual property and confidentiality
– Copies of the customer databases
– A list of companies which have contracts with Mizzen Co for website development and maintenance
– A copy of all contracts with customers for review of the period for maintenance
– A breakdown of the revenue that has been generated from making each database available to other companies, and the dates when they were made available
– A summary of the controls which are in place to ensure that the database details are regularly updated
– A copy of the premises rental agreement with BizGrow
– Non-current asset register showing descriptions and values of all assets used in the business
– Copies of any lease agreements
– Details of any capital expenditure budgets for previous accounting periods, and any planned capital expenditure in the future
– Mizzen Co's stated accounting policy on revenue recognition
– Systems and controls documentation over the processing of revenue receipts
– Analysis of expenses included in operating expenses for each year and copies of documentation relating to ongoing expenses such as salaries and other overheads
– Copies of management accounts to agree expenses in the audited accounts are in line and to perform more detailed analytical review
– The full set of financial statements and auditor's reports
– Any agreements with banks or other external providers of finance

	Maximum	16

(c) **Conclusion on due diligence**
Generally 1 mark for each discussion point:
– Due diligence report to express conclusion of negative assurance
– Limited assurance due to nature of work performed
– Audit opinion is a positive opinion of reasonable assurance

	Maximum	3

Total		25

3   PARKER *Walk in the footsteps of a top tutor*

Key answer tips

Part (a) requires analytical procedures to be performed to help identify audit risks as well as any additional information relevant to the evaluation of audit risk. The mark allocation did not specify the split between analytical procedures, audit risks and additional information. Students who had practised lots of past papers would have been able to use their experience to judge the approximate split of marks. This demonstrates the importance of past paper practise as a key element of preparation for this exam.

Be careful not to spend too much time on the calculations to the detriment of talking about the numbers and explaining the audit risks. A good approach to take is to choose 5 or 6 key ratios or trends, calculate them and then move on to writing about the risks. Try to link the results of the calculations with the information in the scenario for a more rounded answer.

Remember that audit risks are the risks of material misstatement and any detection risks such as the client being new, as was the case with Parker Co.

Part (b) asks for discussion of the ethical issues raised. As ethical issues are always examined, this should be straightforward. To discuss the ethical issues they should be identified, explained, considered in terms of their significance and relevant safeguards should be suggested.

There are four professional marks available for the **structure, presentation of the briefing notes and the clarity of the explanations.** Your answer should be labelled 'Briefing Notes'. You should identify who the briefing notes are intended for. For the introduction, use the words from the requirement. The body of the answer should have a clear structure including headings for each risk. Don't forget to include a conclusion summarising the key points identified.

Briefing notes

To: Audit Partner

From: Audit Manager

Regarding: Audit planning issues in relation to Parker Co

Introduction

These briefing notes include the results of a preliminary analytical review and evaluate the audit risks to be considered in planning the audit of Parker Co for the year ending 30 June 2013, and identify additional information required. In addition, ethical issues will be discussed and appropriate actions recommended.

(a)   **Results of preliminary analytical review and audit risk evaluation**

The appendix to the briefing notes contains the detailed results of the analytical review performed, which are evaluated in the following section.

Profitability

Parker Co's profitability has declined, with gross profit falling by 21.5% and operating profit by 32.7%. The company's revenue has fallen by 8.2%.

Ratio analysis shows that both gross and operating margins have fallen, the projected gross profit margin at the year end is 27.2% (2012 – 31.8%) and the projected operating margin is 11.4% (2012 – 15.6%). The return on capital employed also shows significant decline, falling from 6.2% to 3.8%. The declines can be explained by a price cutting strategy, difficult economic conditions, and the costs of the legal claim of the company amplify the fall in profitability.

The trends in profitability cause going concern issues. If the company's results do not improve next year, for example, if the new organic range of goods is not successful, the company may become loss-making, especially if margins are squeezed by further price cuts.

Some further information would be helpful to make a more detailed assessment of profitability, for example, an analysis of revenue and profit by product range, which would allow margins to be calculated for individual product ranges to identify those that are particularly underperforming. In addition, the results of any market research that has been performed on the new organic product range to evaluate the potential of the development to generate future profit.

Further adjustments may be necessary to the financial statements, which may reduce the current year's profit further. These adjustments relate to possible incorrect accounting treatments applied to the provision, development costs, finance costs and tax expense, which are discussed later in the briefing notes.

Liquidity

The company's cash position has deteriorated dramatically during the year, moving from a positive cash balance of $1 million, to a projected overdraft of $900,000 at the year end. Analytical review shows that the current and quick ratios have both deteriorated, and it is projected that current assets will not cover current liabilities, as the current ratio projected at the year end is 0.96 (2012 – 1.8). Parker Co will therefore find it difficult to pay liabilities as they fall due, increasing the going concern risk.

Payables days have increased from 63 days to 86 days; this indicates that the company is experiencing difficulties making payments to suppliers as they fall due. This could result in supplier relationships deteriorating and they may stop supplying Parker Co if they see them as a 'risky' customer. Suppliers may also restrict the credit terms offered to Parker Co, causing further working capital problems.

Receivables days have increased from 34 to 42; this could be as a result of poor credit control. A significant control deficiency could affect our overall risk assessment of the client. Alternatively, the increased receivables balance could be the result of irrecoverable debts that require a provision to be made against them; this could further affect profit levels if such a provision is required.

The current and quick ratios will deteriorate further if an adjustment is necessary in respect of the provision, which has been recognised for a potential penalty payment (discussed further below).

Working capital also seems to be a problem, with inventory holding period, receivables collection period and trade payables period all increasing. The inventory holding period is perhaps the most significant, increasing from 136 days to 167 days. This shows that a large amount of working capital is tied up in inventory, and it is likely that some of these goods are obsolete (for example, ranges of cosmetics that are out of fashion) and will never generate a cash flow.

This creates a further audit risk, that the inventory is overstated and needs to be written off to net realisable value. Any write off necessary will put further pressure on the gross profit margin.

To help the risk assessment in relation to cash management, a statement of cash flows projected to the year end would be useful. This is important in order to analyse the main cash generating activities and, more importantly, where cash has been used during the year. A cash flow forecast for at least the next 12 months would also help with going concern assessment.

Solvency

Parker Co's gearing ratio is projected to increase from 0.8 to 1. This indicates a high level of gearing, and the company may, as a result, find it difficult to raise further finance if required, again increasing the going concern risk. The company extended its bank loan during the year and now also has a significant overdraft. It seems very reliant on finance from its bank, and it may be that the bank will be reluctant to offer any further finance, especially in the current economic climate.

It will be important to obtain the details of the bank loan and overdraft, as this will impact on the going concern assessment. In particular, additional information is needed on the overdraft limit to determine how close the current and projected overdraft is to the limit.

The interest cover has fallen from 10.6 to 5.7. Based on these figures, there still appears to be plenty of profit to cover the finance charges, but of course there is a lack of cash in the company, meaning that payments of interest and capital may be difficult.

Finance charge

The finance charge expensed in the statement of profit or loss and other comprehensive income appears very low when compared to the company's level of interest bearing debt and its overdraft. To illustrate, the year-end interest bearing debt and overdraft is $12.725 million ($11.825 million non-current liabilities + $900,000 overdraft), which when compared to the finance charge for the year of $155,000 implies an overall interest rate on all interest bearing debt of only 1.2%. This seems very low, especially when the preference shares have an interest rate of 2%.

This rough calculation indicates that finance charges may be understated. This may also be the case for the comparative figures and creates significant audit risk. If the finance cost needs to be increased, this will further reduce profit before tax and could cause either or both years to become loss-making.

There is a risk that the dividend paid to preference shareholders has been incorrectly accounted for as a distribution from retained earnings, but the correct treatment would be to include the dividend within finance charges, in accordance with IFRS 7 *Financial Instruments: Disclosures*.

Further information is needed, such as the dates that new finance leases were taken out, the interest rates applicable to each interest-bearing balance and the annual payment due to preference shareholders. This will help to assess whether the finance charge is at risk of understatement.

Tax expense

The effective tax rate based on the projected figures for 2013 is 9.5% (70/735), compared to 25% (300/1,197) in 2012. The tax expense for 2013 seems low and it is possible that a proper estimate has not yet been made of tax payable. The statement of financial position shows a tax payable figure of $50,000 whereas the tax expense is $70,000. This also indicates that the tax figures are not correct and will need to be adjusted.

Provision

A provision in relation to a fine against the company has been recognised in cost of sales. There are two audit risks in relation to this item. First, the provision may not be measured correctly. $450,000 is the amount of the potential amount payable, but only $250,000 has been provided. According to IAS 37 *Provisions, Contingent Liabilities and Contingent Assets*, a provision should be recognised where there is a present obligation as a result of a past event, a probable outflow of economic benefit and a reliable estimate can be made. Assuming that these criteria have been met, it would be reasonable to expect the full amount of the fine against the company to be provided. Therefore there is a risk that profit is overstated and current liabilities are understated by $200,000. Additional information is needed from management to understand the rationale behind the amount that has been provided.

Furthermore, the provision has been charged to cost of sales. This is not the normal classification of items of this type, which would usually be classified as an operating expense. A presentation risk therefore arises, which affects the gross and operating profit figures. If the full amount of the provision were recognised in operating expenses, the operating margin for 2013 would only be 8.9%.

Development cost

A significant amount, $2.25 million, has been capitalised during the year in relation to costs arising on development of the new organic product range. This represents 8.3% of total assets. There is a risk that this has been inappropriately capitalised, as IAS 38 *Intangible Assets* only permits the capitalisation of development costs as an internally generated intangible asset when certain criteria have been met. There is therefore a risk that non-current assets and operating profit are overstated by $2.25 million if the criteria have not been met, for example, if market research does not demonstrate that the new product will generate a future economic benefit. There is also a risk that inappropriate expenses, such as revenue expenses or costs of developing a brand name for the organic range of products, have been capitalised incorrectly.

This is a significant risk, as if an adjustment were necessary to write off the intangible asset, the profit for the year of $665,000 would become a loss for the year of $1.585 million, and retained earnings would become retained losses of $975,000. This adds to the going concern risk facing Parker Co.

Revaluation of properties

A revaluation during the year has led to an increase in the revaluation reserve of $500,000, representing 1.8% of total assets. Despite the valuations being performed by an independent expert, we should be alert to the risk that non-current assets could be overstated in value. This is especially the case given that Parker Co faces solvency problems resulting in potential management bias to improve the financial position of the company. Information is needed on the expert to ensure the valuation is objective, thereby reducing the audit risk.

There is also a risk that depreciation was not re-measured at the point of the revaluation, leading to understated expenses.

The revaluation should also have a deferred tax consequence according to IAS 12 *Income Taxes*, as the revaluation gives rise to a taxable temporary difference. If a deferred tax liability is not recognised, the statement of financial position is at risk of misstatement through understated liabilities. Currently there is no deferred tax liability recognised, indicating that liabilities are understated. The same is true for the comparative figures, so an adjustment may be needed in the opening balances.

Finally, a further audit risk is incorrect or inadequate disclosure in the notes to the financial statements. IAS 16 *Property, Plant and Equipment* requires extensive disclosure of matters such as the methods and significant assumptions used to estimate fair values, the effective date of the revaluation and whether an independent valuer was used, as well as numerical disclosures. The revaluation gain should also be disclosed as Other Comprehensive Income and there is a risk that this disclosure is not made. The financial statements provided by Ruth Collie do not contain any items of Other Comprehensive Income and the risk is that the financial statements have not been prepared in accordance with IAS 1 *Presentation of Financial Statements*.

Payroll

Parker Co's internal audit team found control deficiencies when auditing the processing of overtime payments. Additional information is needed on the nature of the deficiencies in order to determine the significance of them, and to plan our approach to the audit of overtime payments. The fact that the processing is no longer carried out by human resources could indicate that the problems were significant. We also need to know the monetary value of the overtime payments to determine its materiality to the financial statements.

The fact that the finance function is now performing the processing will affect our assessment of control risk. On one hand, finance department members should be familiar with the operation of internal controls and understand their importance, which would reduce control risk. However, as all of the processing is now done by one department there is less segregation of duty, which could lead to higher control risk.

New client

Parker Co is a new client, and therefore our firm lacks cumulative knowledge and experience of the business. This increases our detection risk somewhat, but this will be mitigated by thorough planning, including developing an understanding of the business including the internal control environment.

There may also be risks attached to the comparative information and opening balances, especially as the audit risk evaluation has highlighted some potential areas of concern.

Appendix: Results of preliminary analytical review

Profitability:	2013	2012
Gross profit margin:		
Gross profit/revenue	2,120/7,800 = 27.2%	2,700/8,500 = 31.8%
Operating profit margin:		
Operating profit/revenue	890/7,800 = 11.4%	1,322/8,500 = 15.6%
Operating profit margin for 2013 adjusted to include full amount of provision	890 – 200/7,800 = 8.9%	
Return on capital employed:		
Operating profit/capital employed	890/11,775 + 11,825 = 3.8%	1,322/11,455 + 9,725 = 6.2%
Return on capital employed adjusted to include full amount of provision	890 – 200/11,775 + 11,825 = 2.9%	
Liquidity:		
Current ratio:		
Current assets/current liabilities	3,500/3,650 = 0.96	3,965/2,185 = 1.8
Quick ratio:		
Current assets – inventory/current liabilities	3,500 – 2,600/3,650 = 0.25	3,965 – 2,165/2,185 = 0.82
Inventory holding period:		
Inventory/cost of sales × 365	2,600/5,680 × 365 = 167 days	2,165/5,800 × 365 = 136 days
Receivables collection period: Receivables/revenue × 365	900/7,800 × 365 = 42 days	800/8,500 × 365 = 34 days
Trade payables payment period:		
Trade payables/cost of sales × 365	1,340/5,680 × 365 = 86 days	1,000/5,800 × 365 = 63 days
Gearing:		
Gearing ratio:		
Long-term liabilities/equity	11,825/11,775 = 1	9,725/11,455 = 0.8
Interest cover:		
Operating profit/finance costs	890/155 = 5.7	1,322/125 = 10.6

Tutorial note

Credit will be awarded for calculation of ratios on alternative bases and using different assumptions, as long as stated. Credit will also be awarded for relevant trend analysis.

(b) **Ethical matters**

Parker Co is intending to acquire Beauty Boost Co, which is an audit client of our firm. This raises an ethical issue, as the auditor could be involved with advising both the acquirer and the intended target company in relation to the acquisition, which could create a conflict of interest. IESBA's (IFAC) *Code of Ethics for Professional Accountants* states that in relation to the fundamental principle of objectivity, an auditor should not allow bias, conflict of interest or undue influence of others to override professional or business judgements.

IESBA's Code requires that, when faced with a potential conflict of interest, an auditor shall evaluate the significance of any threats and apply safeguards when necessary to eliminate the threats or reduce them to an acceptable level.

An important safeguard is that both parties should be notified of the potential conflict of interest in relation to the planned acquisition. The notification should outline that a conflict of interest may exist and consent should be obtained from both Parker Co and Beauty Boost Co for our firm, Hound & Co, to act for both in relation to the acquisition. If the requested consent is not obtained, the auditor should not continue to act for one of the parties in relation to this matter.

- The auditor shall also determine whether to apply one or more of the following additional safeguards:
- The use of separate engagement teams
- Procedures to prevent access to information (for example, strict physical separation of such teams, confidential and secure data filing)
- Clear guidelines for members of the engagement team on issues of security and confidentiality
- The use of confidentiality agreements signed by employees and partners of the firm; and
- Regular review of the application of safeguards by a senior individual not involved with relevant client engagements.

If the conflict of interest creates a threat to objectivity or confidentiality that cannot be eliminated or reduced to an acceptable level through the application of safeguards, Hound & Co should not advise Parker Co regarding the acquisition.

Parker Co has specifically requested advice on financing the acquisition. IESBA's Code has specific guidance on such activities, which are corporate finance activities.

The provision of such services can create advocacy and self-review threats to objectivity. The advocacy threat arises as the audit firm could be put in a position of promoting the audit client's interests, for example, when negotiating financial arrangements. The self-review threat arises because the financing arrangements will directly affect amounts that will be reported in the financial statements on which the firm will provide an opinion.

The significance of any threat must be evaluated and safeguards applied when necessary to eliminate the threat or reduce it to an acceptable level. Examples of such safeguards include:

- Using professionals who are not members of the audit team to perform the corporate finance service; or
- Having a professional who was not involved in providing the corporate finance service to the client advise the audit team on the service and review the accounting treatment and any financial statement treatment.

The extent of the self-review threat should be evaluated, for example, by considering the materiality of the potential financing transactions to the financial statements, and the degree of subjectivity involved in determining the amounts to be recognised.

Where no safeguards could reduce the threat to an acceptable level, the corporate finance advice should not be provided.

Conclusion

These briefing notes have evaluated the audit risks to be considered in planning the audit of Parker Co, and going concern has been highlighted as a particular area of concern. Preliminary analytical review determined that Parker Co is facing problems with profitability, cash flow and long-term solvency. Our audit approach should focus on this issue. In addition, some specific areas of risk in relation to provisions, finance charges, tax and non-current assets have been identified. Further information as specified in the briefing notes should be requested from the client in order to complete our audit planning.

Our firm should also consider the ethical issues raised by acting for Parker Co and for its potential target acquisition. Furthermore, the provision of a specific corporate finance service to Parker Co must be evaluated as safeguards will be needed to reduce threats to an acceptable level.

Examiner's comments

This 35 mark question had two question requirements, and typically for Question 1, involved the planning stages of an audit engagement. The scenario was based on Parker Co, a new audit client, and information was provided in the form of extracts from financial statements, and notes from a meeting with the company's finance director.

The notes covered matters including a brief business review, financing arrangements, internal control issues, and future plans for expansion.

As this style of question appears regularly it was no surprise that most candidates seemed well prepared for a question on audit planning, and there were some detailed and well-focused answers. However there were some common problems seen in candidates' answers, which will be discussed below.

Requirement (a) was for 24 marks and asked candidates to perform analytical procedures and evaluate audit risks to be considered in planning the audit of Parker Co, and also to identify and explain additional information relevant to the evaluation. Looking first at the audit risk evaluation, this was generally reasonably well attempted, with most answers working through the information given in the scenario to identify and then discuss the audit risks. Almost all answers spotted the going concern risk facing Parker Co, and could evaluate it appropriately.

The majority of answers also included commentary on the internal control weakness in payroll, and a discussion of several risks of material misstatement including classification and measurement of a provision, a revaluation of properties, and the classification of leases. Each of these had been clearly signposted in the scenario as issues related to audit planning.

Fewer candidates picked up on the less obvious audit risks. This was often because analytical review had not been conducted, or it had been done but then not used to help identify audit risks. One of the purposes of performing analytical review is to help the auditor to identify potential risks of material misstatement, and there were many audit risks that could have been identified in this scenario from properly prepared analytical review.

For example the increase in inventory days indicates potentially obsolete inventory which may be overvalued and the deterioration in margins and interest cover add weight to the company's going concern problems. It is therefore important that when asked to perform analytical review that candidates do not just calculate trends and ratios but go on to assess them as part of the evaluation of audit risk. Calculating trends and ratios and then leaving them unused in the written part of the answer is poor exam technique and to some extent a waste of time.

Some candidates did no analytical review at all, which meant that as well as not picking up marks for relevant calculations, they also failed to achieve marks on identifying some audit risks. There were also many scripts that focused exclusively on calculating trends rather than ratios, which often resulted in less detailed answers. A significant number of answers included incorrect calculations, with gearing ratios and return on capital employed being the most commonly mis-calculated.

The areas of audit risk that were generally well dealt with in this scenario included the following:

- Going concern – this was mentioned in almost every answer, and usually was quite well evaluated in some detail, with the majority of answers linking their analytical review to a discussion of the company's going concern problems. It was also pleasing to see that many candidates developed the risk into financial statement implications, particularly that going concern issues may need disclosure in a note to the financial statements.

- Provision for fine payable – most answers included a discussion relating to the measurement of the provision, which usually referred to the relevant financial reporting requirements. Whether the expense should be classified in cost of sales was also discussed in most answers.

- Development costs – this was usually very well evaluated, with almost all candidates appreciating that the development costs could include in error items of research expenditure that should not be capitalised, and that development costs may not meet the criteria for capitalisation due to Parker Co's lack of cash and the competitive nature of the market. Sound answers considered the impact on profit if the development costs had to be expensed.

- Property revaluations – the majority of candidates appreciated that the revaluations could have been done to improve the appearance of the statement of financial position, and many answers included a comment relating the auditor having to be sceptical when auditing the valuation of the properties.

- Finance costs – the relatively small increase in the finance cost compared to the increase in borrowings was often identified and well evaluated.

- Internal control deficiency – most answers included a section evaluating the deficiencies uncovered by the company's internal audit team, and its implication for audit risk.

- First year audit – this was identified as an issue in most answers, with the most common audit planning issue discussed being the lack of familiarity of the audit team with Parker Co, and that extra care would need to be taken when auditing opening balances. Sound answers also considered the appropriateness of accounting policies.

Some issues were less well evaluated:

- Trends and their implications – while most candidates could correctly calculate trends, for example the percentage decreases in revenue, cost of sales and operating expenses, many then went on to discuss the trends incorrectly, for example saying that the trend indicated a potential understatement of expenses when it should have been overstatement, or vice versa.

- Provisions – this was where even quite competent answers were often let down by an obvious lack of understanding of bookkeeping, with many answers stating that the provision should not be an expense at all, but should only impact on liabilities.

- Brand – many answers asserted that the company's brand was overvalued and should be tested for impairment. In fact there was no brand recognised in the financial statements at all, indicating that the extract from the financial statements had not been reviewed carefully enough.

- Change in accounting policy – many answers suggested that the property revaluation was a change in accounting policy, despite there being a revaluation reserve in the comparative figures.

- Taxation – few scripts picked up on the very low tax expense and tax liability, and even fewer calculated an effective tax rate which would have identified a significant risk of understatement.

Some of the problems noted above arise from lack of knowledge, others from poor exam technique. It is vital with this type of question to spend enough time reading the information provided, including the extracts from the financial statements, and to think about how the information gives rise to risk factors. It is obvious that when faced with an audit risk scenario, many candidates see a heading or word, for example 'brand' and write an answer point that is totally irrelevant to the scenario.

As well as asking for analytical review and audit risk evaluation, this requirement also asked candidates for additional information that would help in the evaluation. Most answers contained at least a few requests for additional information, often those relating to the evaluation of going concern risk, such as cash flow forecasts and market research findings. It was pleasing to see in many scripts a wide range of information requests, and candidates are encouraged to read the model answer to this requirement in preparing for paper P7, to see examples of the kind of information requests included. Some answers however overlooked this part of the requirement, missing out on marks.

Other problems often seen in answers that scored less well on this requirement included the following:

- Long sections at the start of the answer describing the audit risk model in enormous depth.

- Discussions of client acceptance matters such as the need for know your client procedures.

- Detailed description of analytical procedure and its use in the audit (including at completion stage) with no application at all to the scenario.

- Concentration on going concern risk and very little discussion of any other risk.

- Repeating long sections of wording from the question requirement.

Requirement (b) asked candidates to discuss any ethical issues raised and recommend actions to be taken by the audit firm. This was for 8 marks. Clearly many candidates were comfortable, producing satisfactory answers covering a range of ethical matters relevant to the audit firm. The ethical issues most commonly dealt with were conflict of interest, confidentiality and the self-review and advocacy threats, all associated with the planned acquisition by Parker Co of one of the audit firm's existing audit clients.

It was satisfactory to see that in general terms answers on ethics have improved somewhat compared to previous sittings in that they tend to discuss ethical threats rather than just identify them, and many answers used an appropriate framework to identify and explain threats, evaluate their significance, and recommend appropriate safeguards.

The ethical issues in respect of confidentiality and conflicts of interest were particularly well discussed, as was the self-review threat associated with providing a non-audit service to Parker Co.

However, there were still many answers, which often failed to recommend actions to be taken by the audit firm.

Also, some answers tended to identify almost every possible threat without really explaining their relevance to the scenario. There also is an increasing trend for answers to consider ethical matters that have little, if anything, to do with the audit, and sometimes make little sense, for example whether it is 'ethical' for Parker Co's management to develop a new organic product range, or whether the company's management 'lacks integrity' for the company's going concern problems. Candidates are strongly advised to focus their answer on ethical threats directly related to the planning and performance of the audit.

Finally there were 4 professional marks available for Question 1, which were awarded for the structure of the answer, and for the clarity of explanations given and evaluation performed. Almost all candidates used a reasonable structure, with appropriate use of headings, and having an introduction. Fewer candidates provided a conclusion to their briefing notes. Though not essential, it is recommended that the calculations provided as part of analytical review are given in a separate section of the briefing notes, and then referred to in the main text, as this creates a well-structured answer. Again, not essential, but as part of exam technique candidates may want to consider having their requests for additional information as a separate part of the answer, presented in a clear list. Generally the presentation of answers was satisfactory, though as mentioned earlier in this report, a significant number of candidates have such illegible handwriting that it is very difficult to award many marks to the answer they have provided.

ACCA marking scheme		
		Marks
(a)	Audit risk evaluation, preliminary analytical review and additional information requests In relation to the matters listed below: Up to 2 marks for each audit risk/area from preliminary analytical review evaluated 1 mark for each ratio and comparative calculated (½ mark for a trend) to a maximum of 6 marks 1 mark for each additional information request to a maximum of 5 marks	
	• Profitability	
	• Liquidity	
	• Solvency	
	• Going concern	
	• Provisions	
	• Finance costs	
	• Tax expense	
	• Development costs	
	• Property revaluation	
	• Overtime payments control risk	
	• New client detection risk	
	• Opening balances	
	Maximum	24

(b)	**Ethical matters**		
	Generally 1 mark per comment:		
	• Conflict of interest threat to objectivity		
	• Evaluate significance of threat and potential safeguards		
	• Contact both parties to request consent to act		
	• Identify safeguards (1 mark each)		
	• If consent not obtained cannot act for both parties		
	• Explain why corporate finance service creates advocacy threat		
	• Explain why corporate finance service creates self-review threat		
	• Identify safeguards (1 mark each)		
		Maximum	7
	Professional marks for the overall presentation, structure and logical flow of the briefing notes, and for the clarity of the evaluation and explanations provided.		
		Maximum	4
Total			**35**

4 RETRIEVER *Walk in the footsteps of a top tutor*

Key answer tips

Part (a) requires evaluation of quality control, ethical and other professional matters arising. Whilst this requirement is often covered in Q4 of the exam, students should be prepared for any syllabus area being tested in any question of the exam.

Typical issues to look out for in such a question are: whether the work has been assigned to the appropriate level of staff, whether sufficient time has been allocated for the audit, whether sufficient appropriate evidence has been obtained (e.g. have the ISA's been followed), whether any ethical threats are apparent (e.g. threats to objectivity or competence).

Part (b) deals with a forensic accounting service for a client who has been burgled and requested assistance determining the amount of the insurance claim. The question is split into two sections: matters to be considered when planning and procedures to be performed. Forensic accounting was the subject of a technical article in 2008 and this provides guidance on how to plan and perform such engagements. For the procedures, a common sense approach can be taken to quantify the extent of the loss.

(a) There are many concerns raised regarding quality control. Audits should be conducted with adherence to ISA 220 *Quality Control for an Audit of Financial Statements* and it seems that this has not happened in relation to the audit of the Retriever Group, which is especially concerning, given the Group obtaining a listing during the year. It would seem that the level of staffing on this assignment is insufficient, and that tasks have been delegated inappropriately to junior members of staff.

Time pressure

The junior's first comment is that the audit was time pressured. All audits should be planned to ensure that adequate time can be spent to obtain sufficient appropriate audit evidence to support the audit opinion. It seems that the audit is being rushed and the juniors instructed not to perform work properly, and that review procedures are not being conducted appropriately. All of this increases the detection risk of the audit and, ultimately, could lead to an inappropriate opinion being given.

The juniors have been told not to carry out some planned procedures on allegedly low risk areas of the audit because of time pressure. It is not acceptable to cut corners by leaving out audit procedures. Even if the balances are considered to be low risk, they could still contain misstatements. Directors' emoluments are related party transactions and are material by their nature and so should not be ignored. Any modifications to the planned audit procedures should be discussed with, and approved by, senior members of the audit team and should only occur for genuine reasons.

Method of selecting sample

ISA 530 *Audit Sampling* requires that the auditor shall select items for the sample in such a way that each sampling unit in the population has a chance of selection. The audit manager favours non-statistical sampling as a quick way to select a sample, instead of the firm's usual statistical sampling method. There is a risk that changing the way that items are selected for testing will not provide sufficient, reliable audit evidence as the sample selected may no longer be representative of the population as a whole. Or that an insufficient number of items may be selected for testing. The juniors may not understand how to pick a sample without the use of the audit firm's statistical selection method, and there is a risk that the sample may be biased towards items that appear 'easy to audit'. Again, this instruction from the audit manager is a departure from planned audit procedures, made worse by deviating from the audit firm's standard auditing methods, and likely to increase detection risk.

Audit of going concern

Going concern can be a difficult area to audit, and given the Group's listed status and the fact that losses appear to have been made this year, it seems unwise to delegate such an important area of the audit to an audit junior. The audit of going concern involves many subjective areas, such as evaluating assumptions made by management, analysing profit and cash flow forecasts and forming an overall opinion on the viability of the business. Therefore the going concern audit programme should be performed by a more senior and more experienced member of the audit team. This issue shows that the audit has not been well planned as appropriate delegation of work is a key part of direction and supervision, essential elements of good quality control.

Review of work

The juniors have been asked to review each other's work which is unacceptable. ISA 220 requires that the engagement partner shall take responsibility for reviews being performed in accordance with the firm's review policies and procedures. Ideally, work should be reviewed by a person more senior and/or experienced than the person who conducted the work. Audit juniors reviewing each other's work are unlikely to spot mistakes, errors of judgement and inappropriate conclusions on work performed. The audit manager should be reviewing all of the work of the juniors, with the audit partner taking overall responsibility that all work has been appropriately reviewed.

Deferred tax

It is concerning that the client's financial controller is not able to calculate the deferred tax figure. This could indicate a lack of competence in the preparation of the financial statements, and the audit firm should consider if this impacts the overall assessment of audit risk.

The main issue is that the junior prepared the calculation for the client. IESBA's (IFAC) *Code of Ethics for Professional Accountants* states that providing an audit client with accounting and bookkeeping services, such as preparing accounting records or financial statements, creates a self-review threat when the firm subsequently audits the financial statements. The significance of the threat depends on the materiality of the balance and its level of subjectivity.

Clients often request technical assistance from the external auditor, and such services do not, generally, create threats to independence provided the firm does not assume a management responsibility for the client. However, the audit junior has gone beyond providing assistance and has calculated a figure to be included in the financial statements. The Group is listed and generally the provision of bookkeeping services is not allowed to listed clients.

IESBA's Code states that, except in emergency situations, in the case of an audit client that is a public interest entity, a firm shall not prepare tax calculations of current and deferred tax liabilities (or assets) for the purpose of preparing accounting entries that are material to the financial statements on which the firm will express an opinion.

The calculation of a deferred tax asset is not mechanical and involves judgements and assumptions in measuring the balance and evaluating its recoverability. The audit junior may be able to perform a calculation, but is unlikely to have sufficient detailed knowledge of the business and its projected future trading profits to be able to competently assess the deferred tax position. The calculation has not been reviewed and poses a high audit risk, as well as creating an ethical issue for the audit firm.

The deferred tax balance calculated by the junior should be assessed for materiality, carefully reviewed or re-performed, and discussed with management. It is unclear why the junior was discussing the Group's tax position with the financial controller, as this is not the type of task that should normally be given to an audit junior.

Tax planning

The audit junior should not be advising the client on tax planning matters. This is an example of a non-audit service, which can create self-review and advocacy threats to independence. As discussed above, the audit junior does not have the appropriate level of skill and knowledge to perform such work.

The junior's work on tax indicates that the audit has not been properly supervised, and that the junior does not seem to understand the ethical implications created. As part of a good quality control system, all members of the audit team should understand the objectives of the work they have been allocated and the limit to their responsibilities.

(b)   (i)   **Planning a forensic investigation**

Planning the investigation will involve consideration of similar matters to those involved in planning an audit.

The planning should commence with a meeting with the client at which the investigation is discussed. In particular, the investigation team should develop an understanding of the events surrounding the theft and the actions taken by the client since it occurred. Matters that should be clarified with the client include:

- The objective of the investigation – to quantify the amount to be claimed under the insurance cover
- Whether the client has informed the police and the actions taken by the police so far
- Whether the thieves have been captured and any stolen goods recovered
- Whether the thieves are suspected to be employees of the Group
- Any planned deadline by which time the insurance claim needs to be submitted
- Whether the client has contacted the insurance company and discussed the events leading to the potential claim.

The insurance policy should be scrutinised to clarify the exact terms of the insurance, to ensure that both the finished goods and stolen lorry will be included in the claim. The period of the insurance cover should be checked, to ensure that the date of the theft is covered, and the client should confirm that payments to the insurance company are up to date, to ensure the cover has not lapsed.

The audit firm should also consider the resources that will be needed to conduct the work. Kennel & Co has a forensic accounting department, so will have staff with relevant skills, but the firm should consider if staff with specific experience of insurance claims work are available.

The client should confirm that the investigation team will have full access to information required, and are able to discuss the matter with the police and the insurance company without fear of breaching confidentiality.

The output of the investigation should be confirmed, which is likely to be a report addressed to the insurance company. It should be clarified that the report is not to be distributed to any other parties. Kennel & Co should also confirm whether they would be required to act as expert witness in the event of the thieves being caught and prosecuted.

Tutorial note

Credit will also be awarded for explanations of acceptance issues such as the need for a separate engagement letter drawn up to cover the forensic investigation, outlining the responsibilities of the investigation team and of the client. Fees should also be discussed and agreed.

(ii) **Procedures**

- Watch the CCTV to form an impression of the quantity of goods stolen, for example, how many boxes were loaded onto the lorry.

- If possible, from the CCTV, determine if the boxes contain either mobile phones or laptop computers.

- Inspect the boxes of goods remaining in the warehouse to determine how many items of finished goods are in each box.

- Agree the cost of an individual mobile phone and laptop computer to accounting records, such as cost cards.

- Perform an inventory count on the boxes of goods remaining in the warehouse and reconcile to the latest inventory movement records.

- Discuss the case with the police to establish if any of the goods have been recovered and if, in the opinion of the police, this is likely to happen.

- Obtain details of the stolen lorry, for example the licence plate, and agree the lorry back to the non-current asset register where its carrying value should be shown.

Examiner's comments

This question was for 25 marks, and contained two separate requirements in relation to the same client, the Retriever Group. The first requirement was largely based around quality control and ethics, the second to do with a forensic investigation. The scenario provided was not long, and candidates did not appear to be time pressured when attempting this question.

Requirement (a) was for 13 marks. The scenario described various matters that had arisen during the performance of the audit as described one of the audit juniors, including time pressure, deviations from the audit plan, and the type of work that had been performed by the audit juniors, some of which was inappropriate. The requirement asked candidates to evaluate the quality control, ethical and other professional issues arising in the planning and performance of the audit. Answers on the whole were satisfactory, and candidates seemed comfortable with applying their knowledge of quality control requirements and ethical threats to the scenario.

Most answers were well structured, working through each piece of information and discussing the matters in a relevant way. There were a number of scripts where the maximum marks were awarded for this requirement.

The common strengths seen in many answers included:

- Identifying that the audit had not been planned well, as it was time pressured and the allocation of tasks to audit juniors was not commensurate with their knowledge and experience.

- Discussing the problems in the direction and supervision of the audit, including the significant issue of the audit manager instructing the juniors not to follow planned audit procedures.

- Appreciating that review procedures were not being performed in accordance with ISA requirements, and that audit juniors did not know the limit of their responsibilities.

- Explaining the ethical threats caused by the audit junior's inappropriate work on deferred tax and tax planning.

- Describing the lack of competence and integrity of the audit manager in allowing the audit to be performed to such poor quality.
- Recommending that the audit team members receive training on quality control and ethical issues, and that the audit files should be subject to a detailed quality control review with a view to some areas of the audit possibly being re-performed.

It was especially encouraging to see that most candidates were not just able to identify the problems but could also explain and evaluate them to some extent.

There were satisfactory answers to this requirement, but some answers tended to simply describe the relevant ISA and ISQC requirements in relation to quality control with little application to the scenario. Some answers also tended to suggest that the audit team members should all be disciplined and / or reported to ACCA for 'misconduct'.

Requirement (b) was for 12 marks and contained a short scenario describing a burglary that had occurred at the Retriever Group. The Group's audit committee had asked the audit firm's forensic accounting department to provide a forensic accounting service to determine the amount to be claimed on the Group's insurance policy.

The requirement asked candidates to identify and explain the matters to be considered and steps to be taken in planning the forensic investigation, and for the procedures to be performed. Unfortunately answers to this requirement were overall unsatisfactory indicating that this is not a well understood part of the syllabus.

Some answers tended to include one or more of the following in relation to the first part of the requirement:

- A lengthy discussion of what a forensic investigation is, including long definitions, with no application to the scenario – this was not asked for. This tended to be based on rote learning and earned few, if any marks.
- An assumption that management had already quantified the amount to be claimed, and that the forensic investigation would 'audit' that amount – leading to mostly irrelevant answer points.
- A discussion about fraud and the lack of integrity of management for 'allowing' the fraud to take place - this was often accompanied by lengthy speculation about the control deficiencies that failed to prevent the burglary from happening.
- A focus on whether adequate safeguards could be put in place to allow the audit firm's forensic accounting department to perform the investigation – this is a valid consideration to an extent, but the question did clearly state that there was no ethical threat.
- A discussion on the accounting treatment necessary for the stolen goods – again, not asked for.

In relation to the second part of the requirement, while some answers gave well described and relevant procedures to quantify the loss, many focused exclusively on determining the volume of goods stolen and said nothing about the value of them. Many suggested discussing the amount to be claimed with the insurance provider and comparing our figure with theirs, clearly not understanding the point of the forensic investigation being to provide the amount to be claimed in the first place. On the plus side, most answers included suggestions that a reconciliation should be performed between the latest inventory count records and the amount of goods currently in the warehouse, though these were not often presented as procedures.

On the whole it was clear that many candidates were unprepared for a question requirement of this type, and that again it is apparent that a significant number of candidates rely on rote learnt knowledge and have difficulty to develop relevant answer points for a given scenario. Some candidates barely attempted this requirement, which for scripts achieving a mark that is a marginal fail is obviously a significant issue.

ACCA marking scheme		
		Marks
(a)	**Quality control, ethical and other professional matters** Up to 2 marks for each matter evaluated (up to a maximum 3 marks for identification only) • Time pressure • Planned procedures ignored on potentially material item • Sampling method changed – increases sampling risk • Inappropriate review by juniors • Inappropriate delegation of tasks • Deferred tax – management not competent • Deferred tax – self-review/management responsibility threat • Tax planning – non-audit service with advocacy threat • Junior lacks experience for this work regardless of ethical issues • Junior not supervised/directed appropriately • Overall conclusion	
	Maximum	13
(b) (i)	**Planning the forensic investigation** Up to 1½ marks for each planning matter identified and explained (up to a maximum 2 marks for identification only) • Develop understanding of the events surrounding the theft • Meeting with client to discuss the investigation • Confirm insurance policy details (period covered, what is covered) • Agree output of investigation • Confirm access to necessary information • Discuss confidentiality and ability to discuss with police/insurance company • Consider resources for the investigation team • Deadlines/fees	
(ii)	**Procedures to be performed** 1 mark for each specific procedure recommended: • Watch the CCTV to form an impression of the quantity of goods stolen • If possible, from the CCTV, determine the type of goods stolen • Determine how many items of finished goods are in each box • Agree the cost of an individual item to accounting records such as cost cards • Perform an inventory count on the boxes of goods remaining in the warehouse and reconcile to the latest inventory movement records • Discuss the case with the police to establish if any of the goods have been recovered and if, in the opinion of the police, this is likely to happen • Obtain details of the stolen lorry and agree to the non-current asset register	
	Maximum	12
Total		**25**

5 **GROHL** *Walk in the footsteps of a top tutor*

Key answer tips

Part (a) (i) and (ii) requires evaluation of both business risks and risks of material misstatement. This is a common requirement as it enables the examiner to ensure that students understand both types of risks. Business risks should be considered from the perspective of the client i.e. risks to profit, cash flow, reputation, survival of the company. Risks of material misstatement are the risks to the financial statements. For risks of material misstatement it is important to identify the balances or disclosures that could be wrong and to explain why this might be the case. Risks of material misstatement result from non-compliance with accounting standards so try to remember the relevant accounting standard and what the accounting treatment should be. Vague answers stating that there is a risk that the relevant accounting standard might not have been followed will not earn marks. State the requirements of the standards.

Part (a) (iii) asks for discussion of ethical issues. Whilst this requirement is often covered in Q4 of the exam, students should be prepared for any syllabus area being tested in any question of the exam.

There are four professional marks available for the **structure, presentation of the briefing notes and the clarity of the explanations.** Your answer should be labelled 'Briefing Notes'. You should identify who the briefing notes are intended for. For the introduction, use the words from the requirement. The body of the answer should have a clear structure including headings for each risk. Don't forget to include a conclusion summarising the key points identified.

Part (b) deals with matters and procedures in respect of an insurance claim. Matters questions require consideration of the materiality of the claim, discussion of the appropriate accounting treatment for the potential receivable and the risk to the financial statements if the matter is not accounted for correctly.

Procedures should be specific enough that another audit team member would know what to do if they were asked to perform the procedure. Be as specific as possible to ensure the marks are awarded.

(a) **Briefing notes**

  To: Audit Partner

  From: Audit Manager

  Regarding: Audit planning and ethical issues in respect of Grohl Co

  Introduction

  These briefing notes evaluate the business risks facing Grohl Co, and identify and explain four risks of material misstatement to be considered in planning the audit of the financial statements for the year ended 30 November 2012. In addition, two ethical issues are discussed and relevant actions recommended.

(i) **Business risks**

Imported goods – exchange rate fluctuations

Grohl Co relies on a key component of its production process being imported from overseas. This exposes the company to exchange rate volatility and consequentially cash flow fluctuations. The company chooses not to mitigate this risk by using forward exchange contracts, which may not be a wise strategy for a business so reliant on imports. Exchange gains and losses can also cause volatility in profits, and as the company already has a loss for the year, any adverse movements in exchange rates may quickly increase this loss.

Imported goods – transportation issues

Heavy reliance on imports means that transportation costs will be high, and with fuel costs continuing to increase this will put pressure on Grohl Co's margins. It is not just the cost that is an issue – reliance on imports is risky as supply could be disrupted due to aviation problems, such as the grounding of aircraft after volcanic eruptions or terrorist activities.

Reliance on imported goods increases the likelihood of a stock out. Unless Grohl Co keeps a reasonable level of copper wiring as inventory, production would have to be halted if supply were interrupted, creating idle time and inefficiencies, and causing loss of customer goodwill.

Reliance on single supplier

All of Grohl Co's copper wiring is supplied by one overseas supplier. This level of reliance is extremely risky, as any disruption to the supplier's operations, for example, due to financial difficulties or political interference, could result in the curtailment of supply, leading to similar problems of stock outs and halted production as discussed above.

Quality control issues

Since appointing the new supplier of copper wiring, Grohl Co has subsequently experienced quality control issues with circuit boards, which could result in losing customers (discussed further below). This may have been due to changing supplier as part of a cost-cutting exercise. Given that the new supplier is overseas, it may make resolving the quality control issues more difficult. Additional costs may have to be incurred to ensure the quality of goods received, for example, extra costs in relation to electrical testing of the copper wiring. The company's operating margins for 2012 are already low at only 4% (2011 – 7.2%), and additional costs will put further pressure on margins.

High-technology and competitive industry

Grohl Co sells into a high-technology industry, with computers and mobile phones being subject to rapid product development. It is likely that Grohl Co will need to adapt quickly to changing demands in the marketplace, but it may not have the resources to do this.

Grohl Co operates in a very competitive market. With many suppliers chasing the same customer base, there will be extreme pressure to cut prices in order to remain competitive. As discussed above, the company's operating margins are already low, so competition based on price would not seem to be an option.

Reliance on key customers

Grohl Co relies on only 20 key customers to generate its domestic revenue, which accounts for approximately half of its total revenue. In a competitive market, it may be difficult to retain customers without cutting prices, which will place further pressure on profit margins. In addition, the product quality issue in November could mean that some contracts are cancelled, despite Grohl Co's swift action to recall defective items, meaning a potentially significant loss of revenue.

Furthermore, Grohl Co will have to refund dissatisfied customers or supply alternative products to them, putting strain on cash flows and operating margins.

Regulatory issues

New regulations come into force within a few months of the year end. It would appear that the existing production facilities do not comply with these regulations, and work has only recently begun on the new and regulation-compliant production line, so it is very unlikely that the new regulations can be complied with in time. This creates a significant compliance risk for Grohl Co, which could lead to investigation by the regulatory authority, and non-compliance may result in forced cessation of production, fines, penalties and bad publicity. There may also be additional on-going costs involved in complying with the new regulations, for example, monitoring costs, as well as the costs of the necessary capital expenditure.

Additional finance taken out – liquidity/solvency issues

A loan representing 16.7% of total assets was taken out during the year. This is a significant amount, increasing the company's gearing, and creating an obligation to fund interest payments of $1.2 million per annum, as well as repayments of capital in the future. Grohl Co does not appear to be cash-rich, with only $130,000 cash available at the year end, and having built up an overdraft of $2.5 million in July, working capital management may be a long-term problem for the company. The current and quick ratios also indicate that Grohl Co would struggle to pay debts as they fall due.

Profitability

The draft statement of profit or loss indicates that revenue has fallen by 9.4%, and operating profit fallen by 50%. Overall, the company has made a loss for the year. In 2012 finance charges are not covered by operating profit, and it would seem that finance charges may not yet include the additional interest on the new loan, which would amount to $500,000 ($30m × 4% × 5/12). The inclusion of this additional cost would increase the loss for the year to $800,000. This may indicate going concern problems for the company.

Change in key management

The loss of several directors during the year is a business risk as it means that the company may lose important experience and skills. It will take time for the new directors to build up business knowledge and to develop and begin to implement successful business strategies.

(ii)   **Risks of material misstatement**

Foreign currency transactions – initial recognition

The majority of Grohl Co's copper wiring is imported, leading to risk in the accounting treatment of foreign currency transactions. According to IAS 21 *The Effects of Changes in Foreign Exchange Rates,* foreign currency transactions should be initially recognised having been translated using the spot rate, or an average rate may be used if exchange rates do not fluctuate significantly. The risk on initial recognition is that an inappropriate exchange rate has been used in the translation of the amount, causing an inaccurate expense, current liability and inventory valuation to be recorded, which may be over or understated in value.

Foreign currency transactions – exchange gains and losses

Further risk arises in the accounting treatment of balances relating to foreign currency at the year end. Payables denominated in a foreign currency must be retranslated using the closing rate, with exchange gains or losses recognised in profit or loss for the year. The risk is that the year end retranslation does not take place, or that an inappropriate exchange rate is used for the retranslation, leading to over or understated current liabilities and operating expenses. Risk also exists relating to transactions that are settled within the year, if the correct exchange gain or loss has not been included in profit. Inventory should not be retranslated at the year end as it is a non-monetary item, so any retranslation of inventory would result in over or undervaluation of inventory and profit.

Product recall – obsolete inventory

There is a quantity of copper wiring which appears to have no realisable value as it has been corroded and cannot be used in the production of circuit boards. This inventory should be written off, as according to IAS 2 *Inventories,* measurement should be at the lower of cost and net realisable value. The risk is that inventory has not been reduced in value, leading to overstated current assets and overstated operating profit. The risk is heightened if Grohl Co has not adequately identified and separated the corroded copper wiring from the rest of its inventory. This is quite likely, given that the corrosion cannot be spotted visually and relies on the copper being tested.

Product recall – refunds to customers

Due to the faulty items being recalled, some customers may have demanded a refund instead of a replacement circuit board. If the customer had already paid for the goods, a provision should be recognised for the refund, as the original sale and subsequent product recall would create an obligation. If the customer had not already paid for the goods and did not want a replacement, then the balance on the customer's receivables account should be written off. Depending on whether the customer had paid before the year end, there is a risk of overstated profits and either understated provisions or overstated current assets if the necessary adjustment for any refunds is not made.

Additional finance – capitalisation of new production line

The new production process would appear to be a significant piece of capital expenditure, and it is crucial that directly attributable costs are appropriately capitalised according to IAS 16 Property, *Plant and Equipment* and IAS *23 Borrowing Costs.* Directly attributable finance costs must be capitalised during the period of construction of the processing line, and if they have not been capitalised, non-current assets will be understated and profit understated. There is also a risk that due to the company's low level of profit, there is pressure on management to understate expenses. This could be achieved by treating items of revenue expenditure as capital expenditure, which would overstate non-current assets and overstate profit.

New regulations – valuation of existing production facilities

There is a risk that the existing production facilities are impaired. This is due to the new regulations which come into force next year, and may make at least part of the existing facilities redundant when the new production line is ready for use. IAS 36 *Impairment of Assets* identifies adverse changes in the legal environment as an external indicator of potential impairment. If management does not perform an impairment review to identify the recoverable amount of the production facilities, then the carrying value may be overstated. Profit would also be overstated if the necessary impairment loss were not recognised.

Additional finance – measurement and disclosure of loan

The loan taken out is a financial liability and must be accounted for in accordance with IFRS *9 Financial Instruments,* which states that financial liabilities must be classified and measured at amortised cost using the effective interest method (unless an option is taken to measure at fair value). The risk is that amortised cost has not been applied, meaning that finance costs have not accrued on the loan. The fact that the finance cost in the draft statement of profit or loss has remained static indicates that this may have happened, resulting in understated finance costs and understated liabilities.

There is also a risk that necessary disclosures under IFRS *7 Financial Instruments: Disclosures* have not been made. The notes to the financial statements should contain narrative and numerical disclosures regarding risk exposures, and given the materiality of the loan, it is likely that disclosure would be necessary.

Tutorial note

More than the required number of four risks of material misstatement have been identified and explained in the answer above. Credit will be awarded for any four relevant risks, such as cut-off problems in relation to overseas transactions.

(iii) **Ethical issues**

An audit manager of Foo & Co is being interviewed for the position of financial controller at Grohl Co. This creates a potential ethical threat. According to IFAC's *Code of Ethics for Professional Accountants,* familiarity or intimidation threats may be created by employment with an audit client.

The familiarity threat is caused by the relationship that Bob Halen will have with the audit team, having worked at the firm. This may cause the audit team to lose objectivity, fail to challenge him sufficiently and lose professional skepticism. The more junior members of the audit team may also feel intimidated by him as his previous position was as audit manager. He will also be aware of the firm's audit methodology and procedures, making it easier for him to circumvent procedures.

IFAC's Code states that if a former member of the audit team or partner of the firm has joined the audit client in a position that can influence the preparation of the financial statements, and a significant connection remains between the firm and the individual, the threat would be so significant that no safeguards could reduce the threat to an acceptable level. Therefore it is crucial that Foo & Co ensures that no significant connection between the audit firm and Bob Halen remains, for example, by ensuring that he does not continue to participate or appear to participate in the firm's business or professional activities, and by making sure that he is not owed any material sum of money from the audit firm. If a significant connection were to remain, then the threat to objectivity would be unacceptably high, and Foo & Co would have to consider resigning as auditors of Grohl Co.

In the event of Bob Halen accepting the position and no significant connection between him and the firm remaining, the existence and significance of familiarity and intimidation threats would need to be considered and appropriate safeguards, such as modifying the audit plan and changing the composition of the audit team, put in place.

Any work that Bob Halen may have recently performed on Grohl Co should be subject to review, as there may have been a self-interest threat if Bob knew he was going to apply for the role at the same time as performing work for the client. However, as audit planning has yet to commence, this may not be an important issue.

Foo & Co should have in place policies and procedures which require members of an audit team to notify the audit firm when entering employment negotiations with the client, as required by IFAC's Code. The firm's policies and procedures should be reviewed to ensure they are adequate and they may need to be communicated again to members of staff.

Tutorial note

It is not certain or even implied that Bob has deliberately tried to hide his intention to join Grohl Co – but credit will be awarded where candidates assume this to be the case. Equally, credit will be awarded for comments recognising that it is appropriate that Bob has been removed from the audit team.

As to the comment regarding whether the audit can be conducted on a contingent fee basis, this is not allowed according to IFAC's Code. Contingent fee arrangements in respect of audit engagements create self-interest threats to the auditor's objectivity and independence that are so significant that they cannot be eliminated or reduced to an acceptable level by the application of any safeguards.

The audit fee must not depend on contingencies such as whether the auditor's report on the financial statements is qualified or unqualified. The basis for the calculation of the audit fee is agreed with the audited entity each year before significant audit work is undertaken.

Conclusion

The audit of Grohl Co should be approached as high risk, due to the number of business risks and risks of material misstatement explained in these briefing notes. An audit strategy must be developed to minimise the overall level of audit risk, and strong quality control procedures must be adhered to throughout the audit. In addition, the ethical issue relating to Bob Halen must be brought to the attention of our firm's Ethics Partner as soon as possible.

(b) **Matters to consider**

The amount of $5 million that has been claimed is material to the draft financial statements, representing 2.7% of total assets. It represents 40% of revenue for the year, and if adjusted would turn the loss currently recognised of $300,000 to a profit of $4.7 million.

The claim represents a contingent asset, which, according to IAS *37 Provisions, Contingent Liabilities and Contingent Assets* should not be recognised until such time as the inflow of economic benefits is virtually certain. If the inflow of benefits is probable rather than virtually certain, then the matter should only be disclosed in a note to the financial statements.

The issue here is whether the amount claimed can be considered as virtually certain or even probable to be received. The business insurance taken out by Grohl Co might only cover business interruption caused by certain circumstances or events, such as terrorist acts or natural disasters. And it may only apply if the whole business operation is curtailed, rather than just activities in one location.

The amount claimed appears unrealistic. Production was halted for one week at one location only, so to claim an amount equivalent to 40% of the company's total annual revenue seems extreme, making it very unlikely that the claim would be approved by the insurance provider.

For these reasons, an adjustment to the financial statements would seem inappropriate, certainly until confirmation has been received from the insurance provider. If the financial statements are adjusted to include a receivable of $5 million, the audit firm should consider this as a very high risk issue, because of the potential impact on the auditor's report of the potentially material and possibly pervasive misstatement.

Recommended procedures

- Obtain a copy of the insurance claim made and confirm that $5 million is the amount claimed.

- Enquire as to the basis of the $5 million claimed, and review any supporting documentation such as extracts of management accounts showing lost income for the period of halted production.

- Scrutinise the terms of Grohl Co's insurance policy, to determine whether production halted in Grohl Co's circumstances would be covered.

- Seek permission to contact the insurance provider to enquire as to the status of the claim, and attempt to receive written confirmation of the likelihood of any payment being made.

- Review correspondence between Grohl Co and the insurance provider, looking for confirmation of any amounts to be paid.

- Contact Grohl Co's lawyers to enquire if there have been any legal repercussions arising from the insurance claim, for example, the insurance company may have disputed the claim and the matter may now be in the hands of legal experts.

Examiner's comments

This question was for 40 marks, and was split into four question requirements. As is typical for question one, the scenario and requirements involved the planning of the audit, and information was given on the business background and recent developments of the client company, as well as some financial information. There were also ethical issues embedded in the scenario.

It was clear that the majority of candidates were familiar with audit planning questions and seemed comfortable with the style of the question and with the amount of information that had been given in the scenario. There was little evidence of time pressure despite the length of the question.

Requirement (a) (i) was for 12 marks, and asked candidates to evaluate the business risks faced by the company.

This was by far the best answered requirement of the exam, with most candidates identifying and explaining a range of relevant business risks, which on the whole were developed in enough detail. Most candidates tended to be able to discuss at least six different business risks, with foreign exchange issues, the loss of several executives, reliance on a single supplier and too few customers, and the problems of operating in a high technology industry being the most commonly risks discussed.

For candidates who achieved lower marks on this requirement, the problem was that they did not develop their discussion enough to achieve the maximum marks per point. Some of the answers just repeated the business issue as stated in the question without discussing any of the impact on the business at all. Most candidates discussed going concern, which was relevant, but instead of relating going concern to specific matters such as liquidity problems and the large loan, it was simply mentioned as a conclusion in relation to every business risk discussed, and therefore was not specific enough to earn credit.

Many answers could have been improved in relation to business risk evaluation by including some simple analysis of the financial information made available, for example through the calculation of profit margins and trends. This would have been an easy way to develop the point that financial performance was suffering, as well as liquidity being poor.

Requirement (a) (ii) was for 8 marks, and was less well answered. Candidates were asked to identify and explain four risks of material misstatement to be considered in planning the audit. (Note the UK and IRL adapted papers had a slightly different requirement with no specific number of risks of material misstatement required and a mark allocation for (a) (i) and (a) (ii) combined at 20 marks). Answers were very mixed for this requirement. Some candidates clearly understood the meaning of a risk of material misstatement, and could apply their knowledge to the question requirement, resulting in sound explanations. However, despite this being a regularly examined topic and the cornerstone of audit planning under the Clarified ISAs, the majority of answers were unsatisfactory.

First, many candidates included a discussion about this being a first year audit which would result in a risk of material misstatement, but this was both incorrect and showed that the question had not been read carefully enough. Then, when attempting to explain a risk of material misstatement, many candidates could do little more than state a financial reporting rule, and then say the risk was that 'this would be incorrectly accounted for'. It was not clear if this type of vague statement was down to candidates being reluctant to come to a decision about whether a balance would be over or understated, or if they thought that their answer was specific enough. Very few answers were specific enough on the actual risk of misstatement to earn credit.

The matters that tended to be better explained were the risks of misstatement to do with inventory obsolescence, impairment of property plant and equipment, and the finance costs associated with the new loan.

On a general note, many candidates seemed confused between a business risk and a risk of material misstatement, and some answers mixed up the two. Candidates are reminded that it is an essential skill of an auditor to be able to identify both types of risk, and that they are related to each other, but they are not the same thing.

Requirement (a) (iii) was for 8 marks, and focused on ethical issues. The requirement was to discuss the ethical issues raised in the scenario and to recommend actions to be taken by the audit firm. There were two ethical issues of relevance to planning the audit – the contingent fee that had been requested by the audit client, and the matter of the previous audit manager potentially gaining employment at the client. Answers here were mixed, and generally the answers in relation to the contingent fee were better than those in relation to employment at a client company. On the contingent fee most candidates seemed confident in their knowledge, and correctly identified that a contingent fee is not allowed for an audit engagement, and recommended sensible actions such as ensuring a discussion of the matter with those charged with governance. The majority of candidates had the correct knowledge here, and could apply appropriately to the question. As usual, candidates appear reasonably comfortable with the ethics part of the syllabus, but are reminded that to score well on ethical requirements in P7, they must do more than just identify a threat.

On the matter of the previous audit manager going to work at the audit client answers were unsatisfactory. Most could identify that it was an ethical threat, and could suggest which threat(s) arose, but were less competent at explaining why the threat arose in the first place. Most answers suggested at least one safeguard, usually involving reviews of work performed and ensuring that the manager has no further involvement with the audit, which were fine, but many also made inappropriate suggestions along the lines of 'forbidding' the manager to work at the client, 'prohibiting' the audit client from taking on the manager, and 'disciplining' the manager himself. Very few answers considered the key ethical issue of considering whether the audit manager retained any connection with the audit firm. Some answers had incorrectly assumed that the manager was being loaned to the client on a temporary basis, rather than taking up a permanent position, and some thought that he would be involved in both the audit and the preparation of financial statements. It is important to read the scenario carefully and to take time to think through the information that has been given before starting to write an answer.

The requirements discussed so far attracted a maximum of four professional marks. Generally candidates presented their answer in a logical and appropriate manner, and a significant number of answers included both an introduction and an appropriate conclusion. Most answers used headings to separate their answer points and generally the presentation was improved from previous sittings.

Requirement (b) was for 8 marks and asked candidates to recommend the audit procedures that should be carried out in respect of an insurance claim that had been submitted by the client just before the year end. The wording of the requirement should have been familiar to candidates as it has been used in many previous exam questions. The scenario contained a brief description which should have made candidates sceptical of the claim being eligible to be recognised as a receivable – particularly the fact that the claim was highly material, and if recognised would have turned the company's loss into a profit, and also the fact that the amount being claimed seemed very unrealistic when compared to the annual revenue. Unfortunately very few candidates picked up on these matters, and did not question the amount of the claim or the timing of it, and very few answers specified the impact that it would have on the financial statements. Most answers included one materiality calculation but not the impact the adjustment would have on the reported loss for the year.

While some answers correctly discussed the accounting and disclosure requirements for a contingent asset, a number of answers incorrectly thought that the claim should result in some kind of provision or liability.

The audit procedures that were recommended were mixed in quality. Most candidates suggested a review of the terms and conditions of the insurance policy to see if the situation was covered, and most also recommended reviewing the actual claim and contacting the insurance provider. All of these are valid and appropriate procedures and generally were well described. Some answers tended to state that the matter should be 'discussed with management' with no further explanation, or that 'an expert should be consulted' but with no description of what evidence the expert should be asked to provide, or even who the expert should be. Too many candidates seemed to want to rely on representations and discussions about the possible outcome of the insurance claim when there were other stronger sources of audit evidence available.

ACCA marking scheme				Marks
(a)	(i)	Business risks		
		Up to 2 marks for each business risk evaluated (up to a maximum of 3 marks in total if risks identified but not evaluated):		
		– Exchange rate risk		
		– Imports – transportation costs and potential for disrupted supply		
		– Reliance on one supplier		
		– Quality control issues		
		– High-tech/competitive industry		
		– Reliance on key customer contracts		
		– Regulatory issues		
		– Liquidity/solvency issues		
		– Poor profitability		
		– Change in key management		
			Maximum	12

(ii) Risk of material misstatement
Up to 2 marks for each risk of material misstatement identified and explained to a maximum of four risks (up to a maximum of 2 marks in total for identification only):
– Initial translation of foreign exchange transactions
– Retranslation and exchange gains and losses –
– Obsolete inventory
– Refunds to customers
– Capitalisation of borrowing costs to new production line
– Impairment of old production line
– Loan classification, measurement and disclosure

Maximum	8

(iii) Ethical issues
Generally 1 mark per comment:
– Explain why familiarity threat arises
– Explain why intimidation threat arises
– Significant connections should be evaluated
– If significant connections remain, firm should resign
– If continue with audit, consider modifying audit approach and change audit team
– Review any work recently performed on Grohl Co audit by Bob Halen
– Consider firms policies and procedures
– Contingent fee not acceptable
– The basis for calculation of the audit fee must be agreed with client

Maximum	8

Professional marks:
Generally 1 mark for heading, 1 mark for introduction, 1 mark for use of headings within the briefing notes, 1 mark for clarity of comments made

Maximum	4

(b) Insurance claim
Generally 1 mark per matter/procedure:
Matters:
– Accounting treatment for contingent asset
– Claim may not be covered by insurance
– Amount of the claim seems unreasonable
– Materiality
– Potential risk of material misstatement and impact on report
Procedures:
– Inspect claim and supporting documentation
– Inspect insurance terms and conditions
– Review correspondence
– Communicate with insurance provider
– Enquiry with lawyers

Maximum	8

Total	**40**

6   JOVI GROUP *Walk in the footsteps of a top tutor*

Key answer tips

Part (a) (i) requires an explanation of why materiality should be reassessed as the audit progresses. This is a mainly knowledge based requirement.

(a) (ii) asks for an assessment of the key audit findings for the completion of the audit. The key audit findings are clearly identifiable with a subheading and are also numbered. Work your way through the 9 notes in turn explaining why each is significant. The requirement specifies that you consider if there is a risk of material misstatement and the adequacy of the evidence obtained. Do not give additional procedures as you have been specifically told not to do this.

Part (b) requires advantages and disadvantages of joint audits. This is rote-learned knowledge and should therefore be quite straightforward.

(a)   (i)   **Materiality**

Materiality is a matter of judgement, and is commonly determined using a numerical approach based on percentages calculated on revenue, profit before tax and total assets. ISA 320 *Materiality in Planning and Performing an Audit* requires that the auditor shall revise materiality for the financial statements as a whole in the event of becoming aware of information during the audit that would have caused the auditor to determine a different level of materiality initially.

It may be that during the audit, the auditor becomes aware of a matter which impacts on the auditor's understanding of the client's business and which leads the auditor to believe that the initial assessment of materiality was inappropriate and must be revised. For example, the actual results of the audit client may turn out to be quite different to the forecast results on which the initial level of materiality was based.

Or, a change in the client's circumstances may occur during the audit, for example, a decision to dispose of a major part of the business. This again would cause the auditor to consider if the previously determined level of materiality were still appropriate.

If adjustments are made to the financial statements subsequent to the initial assessment of materiality, then the materiality level would need to be adjusted accordingly.

The initial calculation of materiality for the Jovi Group was based on the client's listed status, and therefore on an assumption of it being high risk. It is therefore important that any events, such as those explained above, are taken into account in assessing a new level of materiality for this client to ensure that sufficient appropriate evidence is obtained to support the audit opinion.

(ii)   **Audit implications**

Property disposal

A material profit has been recognised on the disposal of a property, and the asset derecognised. This may not be the correct accounting treatment, as the sales agreement contains an option to repurchase, and the transaction may be a financing arrangement rather than a genuine sale. Further work needs to be carried out to determine the substance of the transaction. If it is in substance a loan secured on the value of the property, then the asset should be reinstated and a loan payable recognised on the statement of financial position, with finance charges accruing according to IFRS 9 *Financial Instruments*. Profit is overstated by a material amount if the disposal has been incorrectly accounted for.

Revaluation

The revaluation gain recognised of $800,000 is below the level of materiality set initially which was $900,000. However, the level of materiality has now been revised to $700,000, meaning that the gain now needs to be subject to audit procedures to ensure there is no material misstatement. Further audit work may be needed to ensure that this is the only property that should be revalued, given that all assets in the same class should be subject to revaluation.

Actuarial loss

The loss recognised is material to the financial statements, but only limited procedures have been conducted. Axle Co is a service organisation, and audit procedures should be carried out according to ISA 402 *Audit Considerations Relating to an Entity Using a Service Organisation*. Auditors are required to gain an understanding of the service organisation either from the user entity, which in this case is the Jovi Group (the Group), or by obtaining a report on the service organisation.

The procedures that have been conducted so far are not sufficient, as written confirmation and agreement to Axle Co's records do not provide evidence as to the basis of the valuation of the pension plan, which has a material impact on the Group financial statements. The audit team themselves should perform procedures to provide evidence as to the measurement of the plan and the actuarial loss, and not simply rely on the accounting records of the service organisation.

Goodwill impairment

Goodwill has remained at the same amount in the financial statements, but the goodwill may be overstated in value. One of the subsidiaries, Copeland Co, has suffered a 25% reduction in revenue. This is an indicator of impairment of goodwill, and a written representation and arithmetical check is not sufficient appropriate evidence for such a material and subjective matter. Further audit work should be conducted on management's assumptions used in the impairment review of goodwill relating to Copeland Co. As Sambora & Co performs the audit of Copeland Co, the firm should have sufficient business understanding to challenge management's assumptions on the impairment review of goodwill.

Goodwill classification

A trading division relating to one-third of a subsidiary's net assets is held for sale at the year end. Any goodwill relating to this trading division should be reclassified out of goodwill and into the disposal group of assets held for sale. It may be a subjective and complex process to determine how much of the subsidiary's goodwill should be allocated to the trading division which is held for sale. It may be that no goodwill is attached to this trading division, but this should be confirmed through further audit procedures.

The two matters explained above both indicate that the Group's goodwill figure could be materially overstated and that further audit procedures should be performed.

Associate

The statement of financial position recognises an associate at $4.23 million in both the current and prior periods. It is unusual to see no movement in this figure, especially given that the statement of profit or loss recognises a share of profit generated from the associate, which should normally result in an increase in the value of the associate recognised as an investment of the Group.

It is unacceptable not to obtain evidence in respect of the associate. The audit team should enquire as to the accounting entries that have been made in relation to the associate and confirm whether no movement in the investment is reasonable.

Assets held for sale

There seems to be incorrect and incomplete disclosure in relation to the disposal group of assets held for sale. As discussed above, it seems that no goodwill has been allocated to the disposal group, which needs further investigation. In addition, the disposal group of assets should not be disclosed under the non-current assets heading but should be disclosed in a separate category on the statement of financial position.

Also, any liabilities associated with the disposal group should be presented separately from other liabilities. It is not clear from the draft accounts whether the $7.8 million disclosed as assets held for sale is just non-current assets, or whether it is a net figure including both assets and liabilities. It is required by IFRS 5 *Non-Current Assets Held for Sale and Discontinued Operations* that the assets and liabilities of disposal groups should not be offset and must be presented separately within total assets and total liabilities. Therefore, procedures should be performed to determine how the $7.8 million has been calculated, and to ensure appropriate disclosure of any liabilities of the disposal group.

The assets of a disposal group should also be remeasured if necessary to fair value less cost to sell, if this is lower than carrying value. The audit team needs to determine whether management has conducted a review of the value of assets held in the disposal group. The amounts recognised may be overstated.

Finally, the sale of the trading division would seem to meet the definition of a discontinued operation according to IFRS 5, as its assets were held for sale at the year end, and it is likely to constitute a separate major line of business. IFRS 5 requires that the face of the statement of profit or loss discloses a single figure in respect of discontinued operations, comprising the post-tax profit or loss of the discontinued operation and the post-tax gain or loss recognised on any measurement of its assets to fair value, less cost to sell. The Group's statement of profit or loss does not include any figure in relation to the trading division which is being sold. Audit procedures should be performed to determine whether this is necessary.

Regarding evidence obtained, the external confirmation from the buyer is a reliable source of evidence. However, it was obtained a number of months ago, since when circumstances may have changed. The buyer should be contacted again to reconfirm at a date closer to the signing of the audit report their intention to purchase the trading division.

Non-controlling interest

The statement of financial position correctly discloses the non-controlling interest as a component of equity, as required by IAS *1 Presentation of Financial Statements.* However, the statement of profit or loss does not disclose the profit for the year or total comprehensive income for the year attributable to the non-controlling interest. Therefore the audit team must enquire as to whether this disclosure will be made by management.

Finance cost

A loan of $8 million was taken out in October 2011, carrying a 2% interest charge. This would mean finance costs of $120,000 ($8 million × 2% × 9/12) should be accrued for. However, the Group's finance cost has increased by $40,000 only. Therefore the finance cost may not have been recognised in full, overstating profit and understating liabilities. Work should be performed to understand the components of the finance charge recognised, as other finance costs may have ceased during the year. The notes to the financial statements should also be reviewed to ensure there is adequate disclosure of the loan taken out.

(b) In a joint audit, two or more audit firms are responsible for conducting the audit and for issuing the audit opinion. The main advantage of a joint audit of May Co is that the local audit firm's understanding and experience of May Co will be retained, and that will be a valuable input to the audit. At the same time, Sambora & Co can provide additional skills and resources where necessary.

The country in which May Co is located may have different regulations to the rest of the Group, for example, there may be a different financial reporting framework. It makes sense for the local auditors, therefore, to retain some input to the audit as they will have detailed knowledge of such regulations.

The fact that May Co is located in a distant location means that from a practical point of view it may be difficult for Sambora & Co to provide staff for performing the bulk of the audit work. It will be more cost effective for this to be carried out by local auditors.

Two audit firms can also stand together against aggressive accounting treatments. In this way, a joint audit works to enhance the quality of the audit. The benchmarking that takes place between the two firms raises the level of service quality.

The main disadvantage is that for the Group, having a joint audit is likely to be more expensive than appointing just one audit firm. However, the costs are likely to be less than if Sambora & Co took sole responsibility, as having the current auditors retain an involvement will at least cut down on travel expenses. And the small local firm will probably offer a cheaper audit service than Sambora & Co.

For the audit firms, there may be problems in deciding on responsibilities, allocating work, and they will need to work very closely together to ensure that no duties go underperformed, and that the quality of the audit is maintained.

Examiner's comments

This question was for 28 marks, and was split into three requirements. The scenario was based on the completion of a group audit, and candidates were given draft consolidated financial statements and a selection of key audit findings, based on the audit work that had already been performed.

Requirement (a) (i) was for four marks and asked for an explanation of why auditors need to reassess materiality as the audit progresses. This was linked to a part of the scenario where it was explained that the materiality level applied to the audit of the Group has been reduced. Answers were usually limited here to a definition of materiality and a suggestion of how an appropriate materiality figure is determined, and few answers actually answered the question requirement. Those that did tended to focus on risk assessment and the auditor uncovering new information about the client as the audit progresses. These points are both valid, but very few answers discussed them, or any other relevant points, in sufficient detail.

Requirement (a) (ii) was for 18 marks, and asked candidates to assess the implications of the key audit findings provided on the completion of the audit. Guidance was given on this requirement, instructing candidates that they needed to consider risk of material misstatement and the adequacy of the audit evidence obtained.

Candidates were also specifically instructed not to recommend further audit procedures. The scenario provided nine key audit findings to be assessed.

This is a good example of a question requirement where candidates were expected to think on their feet and not rely on rote learnt facts. The candidates that did as the question instructed and took time to think about the information in the scenario scored well, and there were some sound answers. However the majority of candidates could not apply their knowledge to this scenario, leading to unfocused answers that did not actually answer the question requirement. Answers were on the whole unsatisfactory. Candidates tended to approach the key audit findings in a logical way, working though them in the order presented in the question. However, for each key audit finding most answers simply stated that audit evidence was not adequate without explaining why, and then gave a list of audit procedures, which was specifically not asked for. As in Q1(a) (ii), answers were inadequate at explaining risks of material misstatement, and in fact were worse in this question, maybe because audit completion is less frequently examined than audit planning. Candidates made mistakes in calculating materiality, using the wrong basis for most calculations, and generally did not understand the part of the information provided that dealt with other comprehensive income and its components.

Some key audit findings were better answered, mainly because marks could be awarded for financial reporting issues which candidates seemed comfortable discussing, namely the property disposal that could have been a financing arrangement, and the potential impairment of goodwill. However, all other key audit findings were inadequately dealt with, with some in some cases not even warranting an attempt at an answer, even though the issues, when thought through, were not difficult. For example, the key issue in relation to the actuarial loss that has been suffered was that a written representation is not sufficient evidence for such a material figure, and that no work had been done to consider the competence of the service organisation which had provided the figures. In relation to the associate, candidates did not seem sceptical of the fact that there was no movement on the statement of financial position, which in itself indicates a potential misstatement. A significant number of answers thought that the auditor need not obtain audit evidence for a material balance if it had not moved during the year.

Requirement (b) was for six marks, and asked for a discussion of the advantages and disadvantages of a joint audit being performed on a newly acquired subsidiary. Most candidates could identify at least two advantages and two disadvantages, though often they were not discussed at all and the answer amounted to little more than a list of bullet points, which would not have attracted many marks. Some answers seemed to confuse a joint audit with an audit involving component auditors, and some used the fact that the foreign audit firm was a small firm to argue that it could not possibly be competent enough to perform an audit or have a good ethical standing.

Most answers identified the cost implications for the client, and the advantage of involving a local firm who would have knowledge of the local law and regulations.

ACCA marking scheme				Marks
(a)	(i)	Materiality		
		Up to 1 mark for each comment:		
		– Recognise materiality is subjective		
		– Auditor's business understanding may change during the audit, making some balances and transactions material		
		– Client's circumstances may change during the audit, making some balances and transactions more material		
		– Adjustments to the accounts mean materiality has to be revised		
		– Recognise the high-risk status of the client		
			Maximum	4
	(ii)	Audit completion issues		
		Up to 2 marks for each audit completion issue assessed:		
		– Property disposal/sale and leaseback		
		– Property revaluation		
		– Actuarial loss		
		– Goodwill impairment		
		– Goodwill classification into assets held for sale –		
		– Associate		
		– Presentation of assets held for sale (separate and not netted off)		
		– Measurement of assets held for sale		
		– Lack of disclosure of discontinued operation		
		– Non-controlling interest		
		– Finance cost and loan		
			Maximum	18
(b)		Joint audit		
		Up to 1 mark for each advantage/disadvantage discussed:		
		– Retain local auditors' knowledge of May Co		
		– Retain local auditors' knowledge of local regulations		
		– Sambora & Co can provide additional skills and resources		
		– Cost effective – reduce travel expenses, local firm likely to be cheaper		
		– Enhanced audit quality		
		– But employing two audit firms could be more expensive		
		– Problems in allocating work – could increase audit risk		
			Maximum	6

7   CROW *Walk in the footsteps of a top tutor*

Key answer tips

Part (a) (i) requires explanation of the implications of the acquisition of a subsidiary on the planning of the audit of CS Group. A good way to approach this requirement is to think about the planning aspects of a single company audit and apply them to the group situation e.g. risk assessment, materiality assessment, etc.

Part (a) (ii) asks for evaluation of the risks of material misstatement for both the individual financial statements of the parent and the consolidated financial statements. Risks of material misstatement are the risks to the financial statements. It is important to identify the balances or disclosures that could be wrong and to explain why this might be the case. Risks of material misstatement result from non-compliance with accounting standards so try to remember the relevant accounting standard and what the accounting treatment should be. Vague answers stating that there is a risk that the relevant accounting standard might not have been followed will not earn marks. State the requirements of the standards.

Part (a) (iii) asks for principal audit procedures to be performed in respect of goodwill. Procedures should be specific enough that another audit team member would know what to do if they were asked to perform the procedure. Be as specific as possible to ensure the marks are awarded.

Part (b) deals with the ethical implications of the audit partner attending board meetings, an audit manager being seconded to the client and assistance with recruiting a replacement finance director. There are only 6 marks to cover these three issues so be careful not to spend too much time on each.

(a)   (i)   Implications of the acquisition of Canary Co for audit planning Individual financial statement audit

Our firm has been appointed auditor of the new subsidiary which was acquired on 1 February 2012. This means that we must plan the audit of its individual financial statements, and then consider its implications for the audit of the consolidated financial statements.

First, we must plan to develop an understanding of the company, including its environment and internal control, as required by ISA 315 *Identifying and Assessing the Risks of Material Misstatement through Understanding the Entity and Its Environment. We* must obtain an understanding of the relevant industry, regulatory and other external factors, the nature of the company's operations, ownership and governance structures, its selection and application of accounting policies, its objectives and strategies, and the measurement and review of its financial performance. Without this knowledge of the business we will be unable to properly perform risk assessment.

From our audit of the CS Group we will already have knowledge of the pottery industry, however, Canary Co's operations are different in that it specialises in figurines and makes some sales online.

Second, ISA 315 requires that the auditor obtains an understanding of internal controls relevant to the audit. Therefore we must document our understanding of Canary Co's accounting systems and internal controls. This is important given that Canary Co has different IT systems to the rest of the group.

Canary Co makes sales online, and due to the likely complexity of the online sales system, consideration should be given as to whether the use of an expert is required, or whether computer-assisted audit techniques (CAATs) can be used to obtain sufficient evidence on revenue.

It will take time to gain this knowledge and to properly document it. Given that the company's year end is less than one month away, it is important that we plan to begin this work as soon as possible, to avoid any delay to the audit of either the individual or the consolidated financial statements. We need to arrange with the client for members of the audit team to have access to the necessary information, including the accounting system, and to hold the necessary discussions with management. Once we have gained a thorough understanding of Canary Co we will be in a position to develop an audit strategy and detailed audit plan.

We have been provided with the CS Group's forecast revenue and profit for the year, but need to perform a detailed preliminary analytical review on a full set of Canary Co's financial statements to fully understand the financial performance and position of the company, and to begin to form a view on materiality. This review will also highlight any significant transactions that have occurred this year.

As this is an initial audit engagement, we are required by ISA 300 *Planning an Audit of Financial Statements* to communicate with the predecessor auditor. If this has not yet occurred, we should contact the predecessor auditor and enquire regarding matters which may influence our audit strategy and plan. We may request access to their working papers, especially in respect of any matters which appear contentious or significant. We should also review the prior year audit opinion as this may include matters that impact on this year's audit.

As the opening balances were audited by another firm, we should plan to perform additional work on opening balances as required by ISA 510 *Initial Audit Engagements – Opening Balances.*

Consolidated financial statements audit

As Canary Co will form a component of the consolidated financial statements on which we are required to form an opinion, we must also consider the implications of its acquisition for the audit of the CS Group accounts. ISA 600 *Special Considerations – Audits of Group Financial Statements (Including the Work of Component Auditors)* requires that the group auditor must identify whether components of the group are significant components. Based on the forecast results Canary Co is a significant component, as it represents 11.9% of forecast consolidated revenue, and 23.5% of forecast consolidated profit before tax.

As our firm is auditing the individual financial statements of Canary Co, our risk assessment and planned response to risks identified at individual company level will also be relevant to the audit of the consolidated financial statements. However, we must also plan to obtain audit evidence in respect of balances and transactions which only become relevant on consolidation, such as any inter-company transactions that may occur.

A significant matter which must be addressed is that of the different financial year end of Canary Co. We will have audited Canary Co's figures to its year end of 30 June 2012, but an additional month will be consolidated to bring the accounts into line with the 31 July year end of the rest of the CS Group. Therefore, additional procedures will have to be planned to gain audit evidence on significant events and transactions of Canary Co which occur in July 2012. This may not entail much extra work, as we will be conducting a review of subsequent events anyway, as part of our audit of the individual financial statements.

It may be that Canary Co's year end will be changed to bring into line with the rest of the CS Group. If so, we need to obtain copies of the documentary evidence to demonstrate that this has been done.

When performing analytical procedures on the consolidated financial statements, we must be careful that when comparing this year's results with prior periods, we are making reasonable comparisons. This is because Canary Co's results are only included since the date of acquisition on 1 February 2012 and comparative figures are not restated. Calculations such as return on capital employed will also be distorted, as the consolidated statement of financial position at 31 July 2012 includes Canary Co's assets and liabilities in full, but the consolidated statement of profit or loss will only include six months' profit generated from those assets.

Materiality needs to be assessed based on the new, enlarged group structure. Materiality for the group financial statements as a whole shall be determined when establishing the overall group audit strategy. The addition of Canary Co to the group during the year is likely to cause materiality to be different from previous years, possibly affecting audit strategy and the extent of testing in some areas.

Finally, we must ensure that sufficient time and resource is allocated to the audit of the consolidated financial statements as there will be additional work to perform on auditing the acquisition itself, including the goodwill asset, the fair value of assets acquired, the cash outflows, the contingent consideration, and the notes to the financial statements. As this is a complex area we should consider allocating this work to a senior, experienced member of the audit team. Relevant risks of material misstatement and audit procedures in respect of goodwill are discussed later in these notes.

(ii) **Risks of material misstatement**

General matters

ISA 315 provides examples of conditions and events that may indicate risks of material misstatement. These include changes to corporate structure such as large acquisitions, moving into new lines of business and the installation of significant new IT systems related to financial reporting. The CS Group has been involved in all three of these during the financial year, so the audit generally should be approached as high risk.

Goodwill

The client has determined goodwill arising on the acquisition of Canary Co to be $45 million, which is material to the consolidated financial statements, representing 8.2% of total assets. The various components of goodwill have specific risks attached. For the consideration, the contingent element of the consideration is inherently risky, as its measurement involves a judgement as to the probability of the amount being paid.

Currently, the full amount of contingent consideration is recognised, indicating that the amount is certain to be paid. IFRS 3 (Revised) *Business Combinations* requires that contingent consideration is recognised at fair value at the time of the business combination, meaning that the probability of payment should be used in measuring the amount of consideration that is recognised at acquisition. This part of the consideration could therefore be overstated, if the assessment of probability of payment is incorrect.

Another risk is that the contingent consideration does not appear to have been discounted to present value as required by IFRS 3, again indicating that it is overstated.

The same risk factors apply to the individual financial statements of Crow Co, in which the cost of investment is recognised as a non-current asset.

The other component of the goodwill calculation is the value of identifiable assets acquired, which IFRS 3 requires to be measured at fair value at the date of acquisition. This again is inherently risky, as estimating fair value can involve uncertainty. Possibly the risk is reduced somewhat as the fair values have been determined by an external firm.

Goodwill should be tested for impairment annually according to IAS 36 *Impairment of Assets*, and a test should be performed in the year of acquisition, regardless of whether indicators of impairment exist. There is therefore a risk that goodwill may be overstated if management has not conducted an impairment test at the year end. If the impairment review were to indicate that goodwill is overstated, there would be implications for the cost of investment recognised in Crow Co's financial statements, which may also be overstated.

Loan stock

Crow Co has issued loan stock for $100 million, representing 18.2% of total assets, therefore this is material to the consolidated financial statements. The loan will be repaid at a significant premium of $20 million, which should be recognised as finance cost over the period of the loan using the amortised cost measurement method according to IFRS *9 Financial Instruments*. A risk of misstatement arises if the premium relating to this financial year has not been included in finance costs.

In addition, finance costs could be understated if interest payable has not been accrued. The loan carries 5% interest per annum, and six months should be accrued by the 31 July year end, amounting to $2.5 million. Financial liabilities and finance costs will be understated if this has not been accrued.

There is also a risk of inadequate disclosure regarding the loan in the notes to the financial statements. IFRS *7 Financial Instruments: Disclosures* requires narrative and numerical disclosures relating to financial instruments that give rise to risk exposure. Given the materiality of the loan, it is likely that disclosure would be required.

The risks described above are relevant to Crow Co's individual financial statements as well as the consolidated financial statements.

Online sales

There is a risk that revenue is not recognised at the correct time, as it can be difficult to establish with online sales when the revenue recognition criteria of IAS 18 *Revenue* have been met. This could mean that revenue and profits are at risk of over or understatement. This is a significant issue as 30% of Canary Co's sales are made online, which approximates to sales of $4.8 million or 3.6% of this year's consolidated revenue, and will be a higher percentage of total sales next year when a full year of Canary Co's revenue is consolidated.

Prior to the acquisition of Canary Co, the CS Group had no experience of online sales, which means that there will not yet be a group accounting policy for online revenue recognition.

There may also be risks arising from the system not operating effectively or that controls are deficient leading to inaccurate recording of sales.

Canary Co management

As this is the first time that Canary Co's management will be involved with group financial reporting, they will be unfamiliar with the processes used and information required by the CS Group in preparing the consolidated financial statements. There is a risk that information provided may be inaccurate or incomplete, for example in relation to inter-company transactions.

Financial performance

Looking at the consolidated revenue and profit figures, it appears that the group's results are encouraging, with an increase in revenue of 8% and in profit before tax of 1.2%.

However, this comparison is distorted, as the 2012 results include six months' revenue and profit from Canary Co, whereas the 2011 results are purely Crow Co and Starling Co. A more meaningful comparison is made by removing Canary Co's results from the 2012 figures, enabling a comparison of the results of Crow Co and Starling Co alone:

	$ million 2012 forecast Crow Co	$ million 2012 forecast Starling Co	$ million 2012 forecast Crow Co and Starling Co	$ million 2011 Actual Crow Co and Starling Co	% change
Revenue	69	50	119	125	(4.8%)
Profit before tax	3.5	3	6.5	8.4	(22.6%)

The analysis reveals that Crow Co and Starling Co combined have a significantly reduced profit for the year, with revenue also slightly reduced. The apparent increase in costs may be caused by one-off costs to do with the acquisition of Canary Co, such as due diligence and legal costs. However there remains a risk of misstatement as costs could be overstated or revenue understated.

Possible manipulation of financial statements

A risk of misstatement arises in relation to Canary Co as its financial statements have been prone to manipulation. In particular, its management may have felt pressure to overstate revenue and profits in order to secure a good sale price for the company. The existence of contingent consideration relating to the Group's post acquisition revenue is also a contributing factor to possible manipulation, as the Group will want to avoid paying the additional consideration.

Grant received

Starling Co has received a grant of $35 million in respect of environmentally friendly capital expenditure, of which $25 million has already been spent. There is a risk in the recognition of the grant received. According to IAS 20 *Accounting for Government Grants and Disclosure of Government Assistance* government grants shall be recognised as income over the periods necessary to match them with the related costs which they are intended to compensate. This means that the $35 million should not be recognised as income on receipt, but the income deferred and released to profit over the estimated useful life of the assets to which it relates. There is a risk that an inappropriate amount has been credited to profit this year.

A further risk arises in respect of the $10 million grant which has not yet been spent. Depending on the conditions of the grant, some or all of it may become repayable if it is not spent on qualifying assets within a certain time, and a provision may need to be recognised. $10 million represents 1.8% of consolidated assets, likely to be material to the CS Group financial statements. It is likely to form a much greater percentage of Starling Co's individual assets and therefore be more material in its individual financial statements.

New IT system

A new system relevant to financial reporting was introduced to Crow Co and Starling Co. ISA 315 indicates that the installation of significant new IT systems related to financial reporting is an event that may indicate a risk of material misstatement. Errors may have occurred in transferring data from the old to the new system, and the controls over the new system may not be operating effectively.

Further, if Canary Co is not using the same IT system, there may be problems in performing its consolidation into the CS Group, for example, in reconciling inter-company balances.

Starling Co finance director

One of the subsidiaries currently lacks a finance director. This means that there may be a lack of personnel with appropriate financial reporting and accounting skills, increasing the likelihood of error in Starling Co's individual financial statements, and meaning that inputs to the consolidated financial statements are also at risk of error. In addition, the reason for the finance director leaving should be ascertained, as it could indicate a risk of material misstatement, for example, if there was a disagreement over accounting policies.

(iii)   **Audit procedures relating to goodwill**

- Obtain the legal purchase agreement and confirm the date of the acquisition as being the date that control of Canary Co passed to Crow Co.

- From the legal purchase agreement, confirm the consideration paid, and the details of the contingent consideration, including its amount, date potentially payable, and the factors on which payment depends.

- Confirm that Canary Co is wholly owned by Crow Co through a review of its register of shareholders, and by agreement to legal documentation.

- Agree the cash payment of $125 million to cash book and bank statements.

- Review the board minutes for discussion regarding, and approval of, the purchase of Canary Co.

- Obtain the due diligence report prepared by the external provider and confirm the estimated fair value of net assets at acquisition.

- Discuss with management the reason for providing for the full amount of contingent consideration, and obtain written representation concerning the accounting treatment.

- Ask management to recalculate the contingent consideration on a discounted basis, and confirm goodwill is recognised on this basis in the consolidated financial statements.

Tutorial note

Procedures relating to impairment testing of the goodwill at the year end are not relevant to the requirement, which asks for procedures relating to the goodwill initially recognised on acquisition.

(b)   **Ethical matters regarding the CS Group**

Firstly, regarding the audit engagement partner attending board meetings, there is nothing to prohibit an auditor attending the board meetings of an audit client. Indeed it is common practice for this to occur, and there may be times when the auditor should attend in order to raise issues with management and/or those charged with governance pertaining to the audit.

However, the auditor attending the client's board meeting must be careful that they take no part in any management decisions made at the meeting. If matters not relevant to the audit are debated on which the auditor's opinion is sought, the auditor could be deemed to be involved with management decisions, or to be providing an additional service to the client which potentially creates a threat to objectivity.

IFAC's *Code of Ethics for Professional Accountants* and ACCA's *Code of Ethics and Conduct* both advise that if an auditor serves as a director or officer of an audit client, the self-review and self-interest threats created would be so significant that no safeguards could reduce the threats to an acceptable level. Accordingly, no partner or employee shall serve as a director or officer of an audit client. In summary, it is acceptable for the audit engagement partner to attend the board meetings, as long as he is not involved with making management decisions, and if he is not appointed to the board.

The second matter relates to an audit manager being seconded to Starling Co in a role as finance director. IFAC's Code refers to this situation as a temporary staff assignment, and states that the lending of staff by a firm to an audit client may create a self-review threat. Such assistance may be given, but only for a short period of time and the firm's personnel shall not be involved in providing non-assurance services or assuming management responsibilities.

It seems that in this case, the temporary staff assignment should not go ahead, as clearly the audit manager would be making management decisions involving the preparation of Starling Co's individual financial statements, and providing information for the consolidated financial statements. It is not likely that any safeguard could reduce the self-review threat created to an acceptable level.

Finally, our firm has been asked to help in the recruitment of a new finance director to Starling Co. IFAC's Code states that providing recruitment services to an audit client may create self-interest, familiarity or intimidation threats. The existence and significance of any threat will depend on factors such as the nature of the requested assistance, and the role of the person to be recruited.

The significance of any threat created shall be evaluated and safeguards applied when necessary to eliminate the threat or reduce it to an acceptable level. In all cases, the firm shall not assume management responsibilities, including acting as a negotiator on the client's behalf, and the hiring decision shall be left to the client.

The firm may generally provide such services as reviewing the professional qualifications of a number of applicants and providing advice on their suitability for the post. In addition, the firm may interview candidates and advise on a candidate's competence for financial accounting, administrative or control positions.

Therefore Magpie & Co may provide some assistance in the recruitment of the new finance director, but may wish to put safeguards in place such as obtaining written acknowledgement from the client that the ultimate decision will be made by them.

Examiner's comments

This 37-mark question was based on the planning of a group audit when there had been a change in the group structure during the year. A wholly-owned subsidiary had been acquired, and candidates were given descriptions of some significant transactions and events, as well as limited financial information.

It was obvious that the majority of candidates were familiar with this part of the syllabus. Candidates also seem comfortable with the style of the question and with the amount of information that had been given in the scenario.

Requirement (a) (i) for 8 marks asked candidates to identify and explain the implications of the acquisition of the new subsidiary for the audit planning of the individual and consolidated financial statements. Most answers to this requirement identified the main planning implications, such as the determination of component and group materiality levels, the audit firm's need to obtain business understanding and assess the control environment in relation to the new subsidiary, and practical aspects such as the timings and resources needed for the group audit. Weaker answers to this requirement tended to just list out financial reporting matters, for example, that in the group financial statements related party transactions would have to be disclosed, and inter-company balances eliminated, but failed to link these points sufficiently well to audit planning implications.

The next part of the question dealt with risk assessment, requiring in (a) (ii) that candidates evaluate the risk of material misstatement to be considered in planning the individual and consolidated financial statements. This was for 18 marks. The majority of answers focused on the correct type of risk (i.e. inherent and control risks), though some did discuss detection risks, which are irrelevant when evaluating the risk of material misstatement. Answers to (a) (ii) tended to cover a wide range of points but very often did not discuss the points in much depth.

For example, almost all candidates identified that accounting for goodwill can be complex, leading to risk of misstatement, but few candidates explained the specific issues that give rise to risk. Similarly, most identified that the grant that had been received by one of the subsidiaries posed risk to the auditor, but most answers just suggested (often incorrectly) an accounting treatment and said little or nothing about the specific risk of misstatement. Many answers also went into a lot of detail about how particular balances and transactions should be audited, recommending procedures to be performed by the auditor, which was not asked for. Weaker answers simply stated an issue, for example, that a grant had been received, and said the risk was that it would not be accounted for properly. Clearly this is not really an evaluation, as required, and will lead to minimal marks being awarded.

It was pleasing to see many candidates determining the materiality of the transactions and balances to the individual company concerned and to the group. However, candidates are reminded that materiality should be calculated in an appropriate manner. For example, the materiality of an asset or liability should usually be based on total assets and not on revenue.

Candidates' understanding of the relevant financial reporting issues varied greatly. Most understood the basics of accounting for grants received, the revenue recognition issues caused by online sales, and that contingent consideration should be discounted to present value. However, knowledge on accounting for loan stock that had been issued by the parent company was inadequate, and very few properly discussed how the probability of paying the contingent consideration would affect its measurement at the reporting date.

Candidates attempting the UK and IRL adapted papers are reminded that the syllabus is based on International Financial Reporting Standards. References to, and discussions of, accounting treatments under UK GAAP are not correct and cannot be given credit. For example, a significant minority of answers discussed the amortisation of goodwill, which is not permitted under IFRS (though it is correct under UK GAAP) and so could not be given any marks for this discussion.

The issues that were dealt with well included:

- The due diligence on Canary Co that had been provided by an external valuer
- The measurement of contingent consideration at present value
- Online sales creating risks to do with revenue recognition
- The control risks arising as a result of a new IT system
- The non-coterminous year end of Canary Co.

The issues that generally were inadequately evaluated included:

- The recognition and measurement of loan stock issued by Crow Co
- The classification and measurement of the grant received by Starling Co

The financial information provided in relation to the group – very few answers performed any analytical review on the performance of the group and its components

Requirement (a) (iii), for 5 marks, asked candidates to recommend the principal audit procedures to be performed in respect of goodwill initially recognised on the acquisition of Canary Co. Generally candidates did well on this requirement, with many providing well described, relevant procedures. This represented a definite improvement from previous sittings. Most answers considered the need to look at source documentation regarding the acquisition, the importance of assessing the fair values attributed to Canary Co at acquisition, and the need to assess the probability of the contingent consideration being paid.

The final part of Question One dealt with ethical issues. For 6 marks candidates were required to evaluate the ethical implications of the audit engagement partner attending the client's board meetings, the secondment of the audit manager to the client, and assistance in recruiting a new finance director for one of the subsidiaries. Most answers went through the issues in order and identified the ethical threats that arose. However, a lot of answers took a scattergun approach, and said that all of the issues would give rise to the same threats of familiarity, management, self-review and self-interest, but then did not go on to explain how, or why, the threats arose and whether it would be possible for safeguards to reduce the threats to an acceptable level. Candidates appear comfortable with this part of the syllabus, but are reminded that to score well on ethical requirements in P7, they must do more than just identify a threat.

ACCA marking scheme		
		Marks
(a) (i) **Audit implications of Canary Co acquisition** Up to 1½ marks for each implication explained (3 marks maximum for identification):		
– Develop understanding of Canary Co business environment		
– Document Canary Co accounting systems and controls		
– Perform detailed analytical procedures on Canary Co		
– Communicate with previous auditor		
– Review prior year audit opinion for relevant matters		
– Plan additional work on opening balances		
– Determine that Canary Co is a significant component of the Group		
– Plan for audit of intra-company transactions		
– Issues on auditing the one month difference in financial year ends		
– Impact of acquisition on analytical procedures at Group level		
– Additional experienced staff may be needed, e.g. to audit complex goodwill		
	Maximum	8
(ii) **Risk of material misstatement** Up to 1½ marks for each risk (unless a different maximum is indicated below):		
– General risks – diversification, change to group structure		
– Goodwill – contingent consideration – estimation uncertainty (probability of payment)		
– Goodwill – contingent consideration – measurement uncertainty (discounting)		
– Goodwill – fair value of net assets acquired		
– Goodwill – impairment		
– Identify that the issues in relation to cost of investment apply also in Crow Co's individual financial statements (1 mark)		
– Loan stock – premium on redemption		
– Loan stock – accrued interest		

- Loan stock – inadequate disclosure
- Identify that the issues in relation to loan stock apply to cost of investment in Crow Co's individual financial statements (1 mark)
- Online sales and risk relating to revenue recognition (additional 1 mark if calculation provided on online sales materiality to the Group)
- No group accounting policy for online sales
- Canary Co management have no experience regarding consolidation
- Financial performance of Crow Co and Starling Co deteriorating (up to 3 marks with calculations)
- Possible misstatement of Canary Co revenue and profit
- Grant received – capital expenditure
- Grant received – amount not yet spent
- New IT system
- Starling Co – no finance director in place at year end

Maximum	18

(iii) Goodwill
Generally 1 mark per specific procedure (examples shown below):
- Confirm acquisition date to legal documentation
- Confirm consideration details to legal documentation
- Agree 100% ownership, e.g. using Companies House search/register of significant shareholdings
- Vouch consideration paid to bank statements/cash book
- Review board minutes for discussion/approval of acquisition –
- Obtain due diligence report and agree net assets valuation
- Discuss probability of paying contingent consideration
- Obtain management representation regarding contingency
- Recalculate goodwill including contingency on a discounted basis

Maximum	5

(b) **Ethical matters**
Generally 1 mark per comment:
- Reasonable for partner to attend board meetings
- But must avoid perception of management involvement
- Partner must not be appointed to the board
- Seconded manager would cause management and self-review threat
- Safeguards could not reduce these threats to an acceptable level
- Some recruitment services may be provided – interviewing/CV selection
- But avoid making management decision and put safeguards in place

Maximum	6
Total	37

8   HAWK *Walk in the footsteps of a top tutor*

Key answer tips

Part (a) (i) asks for matters to be considered in agreeing the terms of engagement for an examination of a forecast. This is the matters that need to be included in the engagement letter for this assignment. A good approach to take for this question is to identify matters that could lead to misunderstandings in future that the firm would want clarifying in writing. Knowledge of audit engagement letters can also be used and tailored to this type of engagement.

Part (a) (ii) requires the procedures to be performed on the forecast. It is important to remember that these events and transactions have not yet happened and therefore cannot be agreed to supporting documentation in the same way as historical figures. You need to generate procedures which will help you assess whether the assumptions used in the forecast are reasonable.

Part (bi) deals with a different client and asks for audit procedures to be performed in respect of the closure of the factory. As a provision has been set up for the closure costs, procedures should focus on whether the provision is an obligation at the year end.

Part (b) (ii) asks for discussion of difficulties measuring and reporting on social and environmental performance. This is again rote-learned knowledge from the text book which can be applied to the specific KPI's mentioned in the scenario to make it relevant.

(a)   (i)   **Management's responsibilities**

The terms of the engagement should set out management's responsibilities for the preparation of the business plan and forecast financial statements, including all assumptions used, and for providing the auditor with all relevant information and source data used in developing the assumptions. This is to clarify the roles of management and of Lapwing & Co, and reduce the scope for any misunderstanding.

The intended use of the business plan and report

It should be confirmed that the report will be provided to the bank and that it will not be distributed or made available to other parties. This will establish the potential liability of Lapwing & Co to third parties, and help to determine the need and extent of any liability disclaimer that may be considered necessary. Lapwing & Co should also establish that the bank will use the report only in helping to reach a decision in respect of the additional finance being sought by Hawk Co.

The elements of the business plan to be included in the review and report

The extent of the review should be agreed. Lapwing & Co need to determine whether they are being asked to report just on the forecast financial statements, or on the whole business plan including any narrative descriptions or explanations of Hawk Co's intended future business activities. This will help to determine the scope of the work involved and its complexity.

The period covered by the forecasts

This should be confirmed when agreeing the terms of the engagement, as assumptions become more speculative as the length of the period covered increases, making it more difficult for Lapwing & Co to substantiate the acceptability of the figures, and increasing the risk of the engagement. It should also be confirmed that a 12-month forecast period is sufficient for the bank's purposes.

The nature of the assumptions used in the business plan

It is crucial that Lapwing & Co determine the nature of assumptions, especially whether the assumptions are based on best estimates or are hypothetical. This is important because ISAE 3400 *The Examination of Prospective Financial Information* states that the auditor should not accept, or should withdraw from, an engagement when the assumptions are clearly unrealistic or when the auditor believes that the prospective financial information will be inappropriate for its intended use.

The planned contents of the assurance report

The engagement letter should confirm the planned elements of the report to be issued, to avoid any misunderstanding with management. In particular, Lapwing & Co should clarify that their report will contain a statement of negative assurance as to whether the assumptions provide a reasonable basis for the prospective financial information, and an opinion as to whether the prospective financial information is properly prepared on the basis of the assumptions and is presented in accordance with the relevant financial reporting framework. The bank may require the report to be in a particular format and include specific wordings in order to make their lending decision.

(ii) **General procedures**

- Re-perform calculations to confirm the arithmetic accuracy of the forecast financial statements.

- Agree the unaudited figures for the period to 31 May 2012 to management accounts, and agree the cash figure to bank statement or bank reconciliation.

- Confirm the consistency of the accounting policies used in the preparation of the forecast financial statements with those used in the last audited financial statements.

- Consider the accuracy of forecasts prepared in prior periods by comparison with actual results and discuss with management the reasons for any significant variances.

- Perform analytical procedures to assess the reasonableness of the forecast financial statements. For example, finance charges should increase in line with the additional finance being sought.

- Discuss the extent to which the joint venture with Kestrel Co has been included in the forecast financial statements.

- Review any agreement with Kestrel Co, or minutes of meetings at which the joint venture has been discussed to understand the nature, scale, and timeframe of the proposed joint business arrangement.

- Review any projected financial information for the joint venture, and agree any components relating to it into the forecast financial statements.

Forecast statement of profit or loss

- Consider the reasonableness of forecast trends in the light of auditor's knowledge of Hawk Co's business and the current and forecast economic situation and any other relevant external factors.

- Discuss the reason for the anticipated 21.4% increase in revenue with management, to understand if the increase is due to the inclusion of figures relating to the joint venture with Kestrel Co, or other factors.

- Discuss the trend in operating profit with management – the operating margin is forecast to improve from 30% to 33.8%. This improvement may be due to the sale of the underperforming Beak Retail Park.

- Obtain a breakdown of items included in forecast operating expenses and perform an analytical review to compare to those included in the 2012 figures, to check for any omissions.

- Using the cost breakdown, consider whether depreciation charges have increased in line with the planned capital expenditure.

- Request confirmation from the bank of the potential terms of the $30 million loan being negotiated, to confirm the interest rate at 4%. Consider whether the finance charge in the forecast statement of profit or loss appears reasonable. (If the loan is advanced in August, it should increase the company's finance charge by $1 million ($30 million × 4% × 10/12).)

- Discuss the potential sale of Beak Retail with management and review relevant board minutes, to obtain understanding of the likelihood of the sale, and the main terms of the sale negotiation.

- Recalculate the profit on the planned disposal, agreeing the potential proceeds to any written documentation relating to the sale, vendor's due diligence report, or draft legal documentation if available.

- Agree the potential proceeds on disposal to management's cash flow forecast, and confirm that operating cash flows relevant to Beak Retail are not included from the anticipated date of its sale.

- Discuss the reason for not including current tax in the profit forecast.

Forecast statement of financial position

- Agree the increase in property, plant and equipment to an authorised capital expenditure budget, and to any plans for the joint development with Kestrel Co.

- Obtain and review a reconciliation of the movement in property, plant and equipment. Agree that all assets relating to Beak Retail are derecognised on its disposal, and that any assets relating to the joint development with Kestrel Co are recognised in accordance with capital expenditure forecasts, and are properly recognised per IFRS 11 Joint Arrangements.

- Discuss the planned increase in equity with management to understand the reason for any planned share issue, its date and the nature of the share issue (rights issue or issue at full market price being the most likely).

- Perform analytical procedures on working capital and discuss trends with management, for example, receivables days is forecast to reduce from 58 to 53 days, and the reason for this should be obtained.

Tutorial note

Credit will be awarded for other examples of ratios calculated on the figures provided such as inventory turnover and average payables payment period.

- Agree the increase in long-term borrowings to documentation relating to the new loan, and also to the forecast cash flow statement (where it should be included as a cash flow arising from financing activities).

- Discuss the deferred tax provision with management to understand why no movement on the balance is forecast, particularly given the planned capital expenditure.

- Obtain and review a forecast statement of changes in equity to ensure that movements in retained earnings appear reasonable. (Retained earnings are forecast to increase by $800,000, but the profit forecast for the period is $10.52 million – there must be other items taken through retained earnings such as a planned dividend.)

- Agree the movement in cash, and the forecast closing cash position to a cash flow forecast.

(b) **Briefing notes**

From: Audit manager

To: Audit partner Regarding: Osprey Co

Introduction

These briefing notes will firstly recommend the principal audit procedures to be performed in respect of the costs of closure of the factory involved in the environmental contamination. I will also discuss the difficulties in measuring and reporting on environmental and social performance.

(i) **Recommended audit procedures**

- Review board minutes for discussion of the closure and restructuring, noting the date the decision was made to restructure, which should be before the year end.

- Obtain any detailed and formal plan relating to the closure of the factory and relocation of its operations, noting the date the plan was approved, which should be before the year end.

- Discuss with management any indication that the company has started to implement the plan prior to the year end, e.g. the date of any public announcement, the date that plant began to be dismantled.

- Physically inspect the factory prior to the year end for evidence that dismantling has commenced.

Tutorial note

The procedures outlined above should establish whether a constructive obligation exists at the year end, in which case it is appropriate to recognise a provision according to IAS 37 Provisions, Contingent Liabilities and Contingent Assets. If there is no detailed formal plan in place, and no evidence that a valid expectation exists that the company will carry out the restructuring at the year end, then no provision should be recognised.

- Obtain a breakdown of the $1.25 million costs of closure and review to ensure that only relevant costs have been included, e.g. redundancy payments, lease cancellation fees. This is an important procedure for the potential overstatement of the provision.
- Cast the schedule for arithmetic accuracy.
- Agree a sample of relevant costs included in the provision to supporting documentation, e.g. redundancy payments to employees' contracts, lease cancellation fees (if any) to lease agreement.
- Enquire as to whether any gain is expected to be made on the sale of assets, and ensure that if so, the gain has not been taken into account when measuring the provision.

Tutorial note

IAS 37 prescribes that only costs necessarily entailed by the restructuring and not associated with the ongoing activities of the business may be included in the provision. In practice this means that very few costs can be included, and costs to do with relocation of employees, plant and equipment and inventories, retraining staff, investments in new infrastructure are not included as they are related to ongoing activities.

- Review the relevant disclosure note to the financial statements for accuracy and adequacy, where the provision should be treated as a separate numerical class and a description of it given.

Tutorial note

Credit will also be awarded for procedures relevant to ascertaining whether the factory closure constitutes a discontinued operation, and procedures relevant to any consequential disclosure requirements.

(ii)   **Measuring and reporting on social and environmental performance**

Many companies attempt to measure social and environmental performance by setting targets or key performance indicators (KPIs), and then evaluating whether they have been met. The results are often published to enable a comparison to be made year on year or between companies. But it can be difficult to measure social and environmental performance for a number of reasons.

First, targets and KPIs are not always precisely defined. For example, Osprey Co may state a target of reducing environmental damage caused by its operations, but this is very vague. It is difficult to measure and compare performance unless a target or KPI is made more specific, for example, a target of reducing electricity consumption by 5% per annum.

Second, targets and KPIs may be difficult or impossible to quantify, with Osprey Co's planned KPI on employee satisfaction being a good example. This is a very subjective matter, and while there are methods that can be used to gauge the levels of employee satisfaction, whether this can result in a meaningful statistic is questionable.

Third, systems and controls are often not established well enough to allow accurate measurement, and the measurement of socio-environmental matters may not be based on reliable evidence. In Osprey Co's case, it may not be possible to quantify how much toxic chemical has been leaked from the factory.

Finally, it is hard to compare these targets and KPIs between companies, as they are not strictly defined, so each company will set its own target. It will also be difficult to make year on year comparisons for the same company, as targets may change in response to business activities. For example, if Osprey Co were to expand its operating, its energy and water use would increase, making its performance on environmental matters look worse. Users would need to understand the context in order to properly appraise why a target had not been met.

Conclusion

These briefing notes have shown that the environmental incident at Osprey Co will have an impact on our audit in that detailed audit procedures will need to be conducted to gain evidence regarding whether or not a provision for costs of closure should be recognised, and if so, its measurement. In addition, Osprey Co's intention to publish socio-environmental targets and KPIs is commendable, but it will be difficult for management to measure and report on these matters due to their often subjective nature.

Examiner's comments

This 33 mark question was in two sections. Part (a), for 19 marks, dealt with an engagement to report on prospective financial information. Part (b), for 14 marks covered the audit of a factory closure, and the difficulties in measuring environmental and social performance. Generally candidates performed better on part (a) than part (b).

The first part of the question related to an audit client, Hawk Co that had requested its auditor to provide a report on forecast financial statements included in a business plan, which would be used to help secure a loan. The scenario contained extracts from a forecast statement of comprehensive income and a forecast statement of financial position.

Requirement (a) (i), for 6 marks, asked candidates to identify and explain the matters that should be considered in agreeing the terms of engagement. Candidates were specifically told not to consider ethical threats to objectivity. Answers varied greatly in quality for this requirement. The best answers focused on matters that should be discussed with the client, such as management's responsibilities, the nature of the assumptions used in the forecasts and the planned contents of the review report and explained why those matters should form part of the terms of the engagement. Most answers discussed that negative assurance should be given, and explained the importance of determining the intended user of the report including issues to do with the use of a liability disclaimer. A significant number of candidates achieved high marks on this requirement. Weaker answers discussed only matters such as fee arrangements and deadlines, which, while relevant, are not enough to score well. Some answers discussed ethical issues, which specifically were not required, and others explained matters that would be more relevant to the initial acceptance of the engagement rather than agreeing terms with the client, such as whether the firm had the competence to perform the work.

The second requirement, (a) (ii) was for 13 marks, and asked candidates to recommend the procedures that should be used to examine and report on the forecast financial statements to be included in the business plan. The best answers made good use of the forecast financial statements that had been provided, and gave procedures that were both well described and relevant to the specific content of the financial statements. Many candidates also performed analytical procedures to determine unusual trends and relationships in the figures and information provided, which helped to generate very exact procedures. Sound answers had a range of procedures, some general, some focused on income and expenses, some focused on assets, liabilities and equity.

Weaker answers tended to state simple enquiries, for example 'ask management who prepared the forecasts', or 'ask why sales has increased' without any further development. Another problem arose in answers that seemed not to realise that the figures were forecasts, so source documentation would not be available in the same way that it is for an audit of historical information. For example, many answers suggested agreeing assets purchased to invoices from suppliers, or the forecast increase in share capital to share certificates, but these items would not yet exist as they relate to future transactions. The one area that was missing from almost all answers was the need to ensure internal consistency in all forecast figures, so for example cross-checking from the forecast financial statements to a capital expenditure budget and to cash flow forecasts.

Another problem with weaker answers was that they tended not to always provide procedures. For example, some answers contained a lengthy discussion as to whether a part of the business that was planned to be sold should be accounted for as a held-for-sale group of assets, which is not very relevant to the question requirement. These answers seemed to be drifting into an assessment of potential material misstatements, which was not asked for.

The second part of this question was generally not well answered. This part of the question dealt with a client which had suffered an environmental accident resulting in the closure of a factory. The audit engagement partner had asked for briefing notes to be prepared in which the principal audit procedures to be performed in respect of the cost of closure of the factory were recommended. This first part of the briefing notes, requirement (bi), was for 6 marks.

Answers were often lacking in focus. Sound answers recommended a range of procedures specific to the types of cost that would normally be included in a cost of closure provision, such as redundancy costs. Very few candidates recognised that the date at which an obligation arose in relation to the closure of the factory was crucial, and many could recommend little more than asking for management representations. There was often discussion of the recognition criteria for provisions contained in IAS 37 Provisions, Contingent Liabilities and Contingent Assets, but little on the specific accounting requirements in relation to a restructuring, which could have prompted some specific procedures.

Requirement (b) (ii), for 4 marks, was a discussion on the difficulties in measuring and reporting on environmental and social performance. Candidates often struggled to write more than a few bullet points here, and sometimes wrote from the point of view of the auditor trying to obtain evidence on key performance indicators. However, most answers did identify difficulties in defining performance measures on what can be quite intangible matters, and many also discussed the problems in quantifying socio-environmental issues.

Requirement (b) also contained 4 professional marks in relation to the briefing notes requested by the audit partner. Most candidates attempted a correct format and structure for the briefing notes, and the use of paragraphs, headings and an introduction meant that many candidates scored well here.

		ACCA marking scheme	
			Marks
(a)	(i)	**Matters to be included in the terms of agreement** Up to 1½ marks for each matter identified and explained (2 marks maximum for identification): – Management's responsibilities – Intended use of the information and report – The contents of the business plan – The period covered by the forecasts – The nature of assumptions used in the forecasts – The format and planned content of the assurance report	
		Maximum	6

	(ii)	**Procedures on forecast financial information**
		Up to 1 mark for each procedure (brief examples below):
		– General procedures examples:
		  • Re-perform calculations
		  • Consistency of accounting policies used
		  • Discuss how joint venture has been included
		  • General analytical procedures
		– Procedures on statement of profit or loss:
		  • Discuss trends – allow up to 3 marks for calculations performed and linked to procedures
		  • Review and compare breakdown of costs
		  • Recalculate profit on disposal, agreement of components to supporting documentation
		– Procedures on statement of financial position:
		  • Agree increase in property, plant and equipment to capital expenditure budget
		  • Discuss working capital trends – allow 2 marks for calculations performed and linked to procedures
		  • Agree movement in long-term borrowings to new loan documentation
		  • Obtain and review forecast statement of changes in equity and confirm validity of reconciling items	

		Maximum	13

(b)	(i)	Audit procedures on costs of closure Generally 1 mark per specific procedure, examples given below: – Review board minutes for discussion and date of decision – Review detailed, formal plan and date of its approval – Review any public announcement and the date it was made – Physically inspect factory prior to year end for evidence of dismantling of assets – Consider whether costs included are relevant (redundancies and lease cancellation fees are the most common type of relevant costs included) – Agree relevant costs to supporting documentation – Review note to financial statements for accuracy and completeness		
			Maximum	6
	(ii)	**Problems in measuring and reporting on social and environmental performance Up to 1½ marks per comment discussed** – Difficulties in defining and measuring targets and KPIs – Problems in quantifying some measures, e.g. employee satisfaction – Inadequate systems and controls to accurately measure – Difficult to compare between companies or over time		
			Maximum	4
		Professional marks for the overall presentation of the notes, and the clarity of the explanation and assessment provided.		
			Maximum	4
Total				33

9   OAK   *Walk in the footsteps of a top tutor*

Key answer tips

Part (a) (i) requires analytical procedures to be performed to help identify audit risks. The mark allocation did not specify the split between analytical procedures and audit risks. Students who had practised lots of past papers would have been able to use their experience to judge the approximate split of marks. This demonstrates the importance of past paper practise as a key element of preparation for this exam.

Be careful not to spend too much time on the calculations to the detriment of talking about the numbers and explaining the audit risks. A good approach to take is to choose 5 or 6 key ratios or trends, calculate them and then move on to writing about the risks. Try to link the results of the calculations with the information in the scenario for a more rounded answer.

In particular, when calculating ratios such as receivables days, be careful not to go into auto-pilot and use a standard 365 day period. The information provided may not always be for a full year, therefore the calculation will need to be adapted accordingly.

Remember that audit risks are the risks of material misstatement and any detection risks.

Part (a) (ii) asks for principal audit procedures in respect of *recognition and measurement* of the share based payment plan and *classification* of the lease. It is important to keep your answers focused on these specific characteristics rather than giving audit procedures that deal generally with the balances.

Procedures should be specific enough that another audit team member would know what to do if they were asked to perform the procedure. Be as specific as possible to ensure the marks are awarded.

Part (b) covers practice management and quality control issues raised by the audit manager's suggestions to improve profitability. There are 3 issues mentioned for a 6 mark requirement. Be careful not to spend too much time going into great detail of the issues. Tailor the length of your answers to the mark allocation to avoid wasting valuable time.

(a) **Notes for inclusion in planning section of audit working papers**

Subject: Oak Co – audit planning

Introduction

These notes provide the results of a preliminary analytical review performed on the 11-month financial information of Oak Co as at 30 November 2011, and the principal audit risks are also identified and explained. The relevant calculations are shown in appendix 1. I also detail the principal audit procedures recommended in relation to a new lease, and the company's share-based payment plan.

(i) **Audit risks**

Profitability

The results of the preliminary analytical review indicate that Oak Co is suffering from declining profitability. Revenue has fallen by 12.3% and the gross margin has fallen from 45.7% to 40%. Operating profit has fallen by 27.8%, and the operating margin has fallen from 19.3% to 15.9%. The declining sales and gross profits may be linked to the company losing several customer contracts.

Return on capital employed (ROCE) as calculated based on the information provided shows a reduction from 7% to 4.4%. However, the capital employed figure is not comparable due to the revaluation that occurred during this year. When recalculated based on an adjusted capital employed figure, this year's ROCE is 4.9%. Whichever measure is used for capital employed, the trend shows a reduction in efficiency in generating profit.

The falling profitability indicates that going concern should be regarded as an audit risk, especially when the company's liquidity position is considered (see below).

The company's interest cover has fallen from 3.7 to 2.7, indicating that while there is sufficient profit to cover interest payments this year, any further debt raised will place additional strain on the company's ability to meet interest repayments.

In addition, there are several adjustments that may need to be made, which would further reduce the company's profitability. These adjustments are in relation to the share-based payment and lease expenses, which will need to be recognised depending on the outcome of our audit work in these areas.

Management bias

As Oak Co is renegotiating long-term finance, management could be biased to present as good a profit figure as possible. We should therefore be alert to the risk of accounting practices being used which overstate revenue and understate expenses. The statement of financial position is also at a risk of misstatement, as management may wish to overstate assets and understate liabilities to improve the appearance of the company's liquidity and solvency.

Operating expenses

Operating expenses have fallen by 20%. This is not in proportion with the fall in revenue of 12.3% or the fall in cost of sales of 3%, indicating that operating expenses could be understated. Given the costs involved in setting up a new trading division, operating expenses could be expected to increase this year, due to additional set-up and advertising costs. As the trend is not as expected we must extend our audit procedures on operating expenses.

There could also be a misallocation of expenses between cost of sales and operating expenses.

In addition, the revaluation of Oak Co's properties during the year by $10 million should have resulted in a higher depreciation charge. There is a risk that depreciation has not been re-measured as a result of the revaluations, leading to understated operating expenses and/or cost of sales.

Share-based payment plan

Equity-settled share-based payment plans are complicated to value and account for, and are inherently risky.

IFRS *2 Share-based Payment* requires that an expense should be recognised over the vesting period, calculated based on the fair value of the share options at the grant date. The condition relating to the 10% increase in share price is a market condition. Market conditions should be taken into account when determining the fair value of the share options at the grant date and are not to be taken into account for the purpose of estimating the number of equity instruments that will vest. This means where the target increase in share price has not been met, an expense should be recognised irrespective of whether that condition is satisfied, and an expense continues to be recognised over the remainder of the vesting period.

The issue here is that no expense has been recognised, and so operating expenses are understated. The corresponding entry to equity has not been made, so equity is also understated.

A further issue relating to the measurement of the expense is that it should be adjusted for the condition relating to executives and senior managers remaining in employment at the end of the vesting period. A risk of inaccurate measurement of the expense arises if no assessment of whether an adjustment being necessary is made, or if the assumptions relating to the continued service of the executives are unrealistic.

The share-based payment plan should also have a deferred tax consequence – a deferred tax asset arises due to the deductible temporary difference arising from the accounting treatment. There is a risk that assets are incomplete if this is not recognised in the statement of financial position.

Tutorial note

Credit will be awarded for comments relating to the use of option pricing models and the audit risks associated with them. In determining the expense to be recognised, Oak Co needs to use a valuation method for estimating the fair value of the share options at the grant date. Various models can be used, but all are based on inputs such as share price, exercise price, rate of return and estimated dividend yield. The risk is that inappropriate assumptions have been input to the valuation model, resulting in an unrealistic estimate of the fair value of share options at the grant date. Further, there is a risk that the wrong valuation model has been used.

Finance costs

The financial information shows that finance costs have remained static. This seems unrealistic given that the company has built up a significant overdraft over the year. Finance costs are likely to be understated.

Liquidity

Oak Co has moved from a positive cash position of $2.35 million to a negative net cash position of $1.2 million. This increases the going concern risk facing the company, and we must ensure our going concern audit procedures are extended to address this risk.

My preliminary analytical review indicates that the company is still solvent, but liquidity ratios reveal a deteriorating position. The current ratio has reduced from 2.5 to 1.4, and the quick ratio has reduced from 2.1 to 1. Any further deterioration could mean that the company cannot meet its current liabilities as they fall due.

Further indications of problems with operating cash flows are shown by the receivables collection period increasing from 55 to 64 days, and the inventory holding period increasing from 36 to 39 days. Oak Co is also taking longer to settle trade and other payables, with the average payment period increasing from 73 to 76 days.

Oak Co is clearly relying on its overdraft to fund operating cash flows. The fact that it is nearing the overdraft limit is another indication of the going concern risk facing the company this year end.

Revaluation

A material revaluation occurred mid-year. A revaluation surplus of $10 million, representing 10.2% of total assets, has been recognised. Despite the valuations being performed by an independent expert, we should be alert to the risk that non-current assets could be overstated in value. This is especially the case given that Oak Co is renegotiating finance, and will want to show a healthy asset position to the provider of finance. We should consider the additional procedures that may need to be conducted to assess the work of this expert.

As mentioned above, there is also a risk that depreciation was not re-measured at the point of the revaluation, leading to understated expenses.

The revaluation should also have a deferred tax consequence, as the revaluation gives rise to a taxable temporary difference. If a deferred tax liability is not recognised the statement of financial position is at risk of misstatement through understated liabilities.

Finally, a further audit risk is incorrect or inadequate disclosure in the notes to the financial statements. IAS 16 *Property, Plant and Equipment* requires extensive disclosure of matters such as the methods and significant assumptions used to estimate fair values, the effective date of the revaluation, and whether an independent valuer was used, as well as numerical disclosures.

Leased property

The lease taken out in July 2011 has been treated as a finance lease. However, there are indications that it is in fact an operating lease. Firstly, the lease is for only five years, which for a property lease is not likely to be for the major part of the economic life of the asset. According to IAS *17 Leases,* an indicator of a finance lease is that the lease term is for the major part of the economic life of an asset.

Secondly, the amount capitalised of $5 million represents only 25% of the fair value of the asset. Under IAS 17, for a lease to be classified as a finance lease, the present value of minimum lease payments (the amount capitalised) should amount to at least substantially all of the fair value of the asset. 25% is not substantially all of the fair value, indicating that this is actually an operating lease.

Therefore it appears that the accounting treatment is incorrect. The lease should have been treated as an operating lease. Currently, property, plant and equipment and non-current liabilities are overstated. The finance cost will be overstated if any interest accrued on the lease has been included. Operating expenses are understated as lease payments should have been included in this heading, and so profits are likely to be overstated. However, operating expenses will currently contain depreciation charges for the leased asset, which will need to be reversed. The overall impact on operating expenses could be minimal as the two adjustments will offset each other to an extent.

Intangible asset

The amount invested in the new website has been capitalised as an intangible asset. The risk is that amounts have been capitalised which do not meet the criteria for recognition as an asset, leading to an overstatement of non-current assets.

Only costs in respect of the development of a website should be capitalised, subject to meeting the recognition criteria of IAS 38 *Intangible Assets.* Any costs incurred in planning must be expensed, as should expenditure incurred once the website is operational. The risk is that the costs involved in setting up the website have not been categorised correctly, leading to incorrect accounting treatment.

In addition, the website should only be recognised as an asset at all if it can be demonstrated that it will generate probable future economic benefit to Oak Co. There is a risk that this is not the case, in which case all of the expenses should be written off.

Finally, there is a risk that the costs involved with the advertising campaign, and possibly other costs involved in setting up this seemingly significant business division, have been capitalised. Such costs should be expensed as incurred, hence there is a risk of overstated non-current assets and understated operating expenses.

Current assets

Inventory and receivables have both increased, whereas revenue has fallen. As mentioned above, the receivables collection period has increased from 55 to 64 days, and the inventory holding period increased from 36 to 39 days. This could indicate that both are overstated. The nature of the products being manufactured mean a high risk of obsolescence exists. Cut-off problems may also account for the increase in inventory. Receivables could be overstated if sufficient allowance has not been made for irrecoverable balances.

Long-term borrowings

The long-term borrowings are due for repayment in two equal instalments, one of which is within 12 months of the year end. The borrowings need to be split into two components of $12.5 million and disclosed separately in current liabilities and non-current liabilities. If this is not done the financial statements will be materially misstated, as the borrowings equate to 25.5% of total assets. Thus the disclosure of the loan is a significant audit risk.

Tutorial note

Credit will be awarded where candidates include the effect of reclassification of $12.5 million as a current liability into their ratio analysis.

Given the company's lack of cash, if the loans are not successfully renegotiated, it may not be possible for the repayments to be made, creating a going concern risk.

Provision

The provision for warranties has reduced by 20%, which is not in proportion to the reduction in revenue of 12.3%. Possibly the company has changed its policy on providing warranties, or is selling fewer products with warranties attached. However, we should be alert to the risk of the warranty provision being understated, especially given the incentive for the accounts to be subject to management bias.

It is questionable whether the warranty provisions should be classified as non-current liabilities. It is likely that some, if not all, of the provision will lead to an outflow of economic benefits within the next 12 months and it should be recognised within current liabilities. This potential misclassification affects analysis of liquidity.

(ii) **Principal audit procedures**

(1) **Share-based payment plan**

- Obtain the details of the share-based payment plan to ascertain the major terms of the plan including:
  - The grant date and vesting date
  - The number of executives and senior managers awarded options
  - The number of share options awarded to each individual
  - The required conditions attached to the options
  - The fair value of the share options at the grant date.
- Scrutinise the conditions attached to the options to confirm the 10% increase in share price as a market condition, and continued service as a non-market condition according to IFRS 2.
- Review the assumptions used, and inputs into the option pricing model used by management to estimate the fair value of the share options at the grant date.
- Consider the appropriateness of the model used to generate a fair value for the share options.
- Consider the use of an expert possessing specialist skills in share option pricing, such as a chartered financial analyst, to provide evidence as to the validity of the fair value of share options used in the calculations.
- Obtain and review a forecast of staffing levels or employee turnover rates relevant to executives and senior managers over the vesting period and consider whether assumptions used appear reasonable.
- Check the sensitivity of the calculations to a change in the assumptions used in the valuation.

(2) **Lease**

- Review the lease contract (using a signed copy of the lease obtained from the lessor) to ascertain the major clauses of the lease indicating whether risk and reward has transferred to Oak Co.
- Using the lease contract, confirm the length of the lease and compare it to the estimated life of the property.
- Ascertain from the lease contract whether Oak Co or the lessor is responsible for repairs and maintenance of the property – for the lease to be treated as a finance lease Oak Co should bear this responsibility, but if the lease stipulates that the lessor bears this responsibility then the lease in substance is an operating lease.
- Scrutinise the lease contract for indicators that the lease is a finance lease, e.g. the existence of a bargain purchase option, legal title passing to Oak Co at the end of the lease.
- Recalculate the present value of minimum lease payments and compare them with the fair value of the leased property at the inception of the lease (the fair value should be obtained from the lease contract).

- Agree amounts paid to the lessor (instalments and possibly a deposit) to the cash book and bank statement.

- Recalculate the finance charge expensed during the accounting period, and agree the rate of interest to the lease contract, to determine the value of any necessary adjustment.

Conclusion

These notes have explained that there are many significant audit risks to be considered in the planning of Oak Co's audit. In particular, we must ensure that adequate procedures are planned in relation to going concern, the valuation of assets and the new lease and share-based payment transactions. The principal audit procedures in relation to these transactions have been provided.

Appendix 1: Preliminary Analytical Review – Calculations

		2011	*2010*
Gross margin	Gross profit/revenue	10,280/25,700 = 40%	13,400/29,300 = 45.7%
Operating margin	Operating profit/revenue	4,080/25,700 = 15.9%	5,650/29,300 = 19.3%
ROCE	Operating profit/capital employed	4,080/62,278 + 31,000 = 4.4% Excluding revaluation surplus: 4,080/52,278 + 31,000 = 4.9%	5,650/54,895 + 26,250 = 7%
Current ratio	Current assets/current liabilities	6,828/4,800 = 1.4	8,880/3,485 = 2.5
Quick ratio	Receivables + cash/current liabilities	5,028/4,800 = 1	7,165/3,485 = 2.1
Inventory holding period	Inventory/(cost of sales × 12/11) × 365	1,800/16,822 × 365 =39 days	1,715/17,345 × 365 = 36 days
Receivables collection period	Receivables/(revenue × 12/11) × 365	4,928/28,036 × 365 =64 days	4,815/31,964 × 365 = 55 days
Payables period	Trade payables/(cost of sales × 12/11) × 365	3,500/16,822 × 365 =76 days	3,485/17,345 × 365 = 73 days
Gearing ratio	Long-term liabilities/equity	31,000/62,278 = 0.5 Excluding revaluation surplus: 31,000/52,278 = 0.6	26,250/54,895 = 0.5
Interest cover	Operating profit/finance cost	4,080/1,500 = 2.7	5,650/1,500 = 3.7

Tutorial note

Credit will be awarded for ratios calculated on an alternative basis, as long as relevant to the scenario. Credit will also be awarded for relevant trends calculated.

(b)   **Materiality**

Setting materiality at the maximum possible level would reduce the work conducted on an audit by reducing sample sizes, and raising the materiality threshold also means that more balances and transactions would be considered immaterial when compared to the threshold.

While materiality is recognised to be a judgemental matter, setting materiality at a high level may mean that some balances and transactions are ignored despite them containing a specific risk of material misstatement. This increases detection risk and impairs the quality of the audit. Materiality should be judged based on the specific circumstances of each client as is affected by factors such as misstatements identified in previous years' audits, the results of risk assessment procedures and the regulatory environment in which the client operates. Using the maximum materiality level possible will simply not be appropriate in all audits.

ISA 320 *Materiality in Planning and Performing an Audit* requires that materiality should be revised if necessary as the audit progresses. Fixing materiality at the planning stage is contrary to the ISA and could increase detection risk if insufficient audit work is performed on matters deemed to be immaterial when planning the audit.

Training

Many firms consider reducing the amount they spend on training as a response to difficult economic conditions. However, any prolonged reduction in training for all members of the audit department will have a long-term detrimental effect on audit quality.

ISQC 1 *Quality Control for Firms that Perform Audits and Reviews of Financial Statements, and Other Assurance and Related Services Engagements* requires that an audit firm shall establish policies and procedures designed to promote an internal culture recognising that quality is essential in performing engagements. Part of creating this internal culture includes training staff appropriately.

Training is essential in order for auditors to be kept up-to-date with developments in the profession. Many audit firms are currently applying the Clarified ISAs for the first time, and without the necessary training there is a risk that not all of the requirements will be met. Additionally, qualified members will need to verify that they have met Continuing Professional Development requirements, for which training on new developments in auditing will be essential.

Quicker audits

It is unprofessional to make a guarantee to clients that audits will be performed in a shorter time than previously. The audit firm cannot know how long an audit will take until they have completed the planning of that audit. The client's circumstances may have changed since the previous year, or there may be special considerations in this year's audit which mean that the audit will take longer than previously.

Trying to complete the audit as quickly as possible will have an implication for the quality of the work performed. Short-cuts may be taken which reduce the appropriateness or sufficiency of evidence obtained, leading to increased audit risk.

In summary, the audit manager's suggestions are not appropriate, as each would impair the short-term and long-term quality of audit work carried out by the firm.

Examiner's comments

This question was for 39 marks, and was based on an audit planning scenario, as is typical for question one. The audit client had provided financial information in the form of a statement of financial position and a statement of comprehensive income, extracted from management accounts, along with accompanying notes. Less written background information had been provided than in some previous audit planning questions, encouraging candidates to focus their answer on the financial information provided.

The first requirement, for 23 marks, was to perform preliminary analytical review, and then to identify and explain principal audit risks. A reasonable proportion of candidates responded quite well to the requirement regarding analytical review, with most at least calculating some simple trends, usually focusing on revenue and expenses. Sound answers calculated a range of trends and/or ratios, and used this analysis to explain a range of audit risks relevant to each of the elements of the financial statements. Some answers mainly ignored the analytical review, and just discussed audit risks. This certainly would generate some marks, but many of the audit risks could only be clearly identified and explained by reference to some analytical review. It was very common for some answers to calculate a trend but then just state the trend in words, e.g. calculating that revenue had decreased by 12% and then just stating that 'revenue has gone down' with no discussion of any risk at all. Some answers identified an audit risk but then failed to explain why it is an audit risk, e.g. many candidates calculated that the warranty provision had decreased by 20%, and went on to suggest a risk of understatement of the provision. This is correct, but it does not really explain the risk (an answer should link the movement in the provision to the movement in revenue and explain the risk on that basis). The weakest answers contained incorrectly calculated trends, little or no discussion of audit risk and very inadequate presentation.

Candidates also need to avoid repetition – many answers discussed going concern as an audit risk, which was correctly identified, but rather than discuss it as a discrete risk, it was just referred to as a risk at the end of every paragraph. This wastes time, and also detracts from the professionalism of the answer.

Many candidates also wasted time at the start of their answers by writing a page or more discussing irrelevant matters such as a definition of audit risk and its components, general descriptions of how to plan an audit, and describing how to calculate materiality in great depth. Candidates should note that such discussions do not earn marks and are not a suitable 'introduction' to an audit risk question. Another waste of time was to suggest audit procedures for each area being discussed. It was not uncommon for a candidate to calculate a trend, identify a risk, and then spend half a page discussing what they thought would be a good audit strategy for the risk identified, or to suggest a number of specific audit procedures. None of this is asked for, and so does not earn marks.

The other common problem were answers which focused on business risks rather than audit risks, leading to long discussions of operational or financial problems that the client was facing, but again failing to develop the point into a specific audit risk.

There were two risks specific to items which appeared to have been incorrectly accounted for – a share based payment scheme, and a leased asset. Many candidates produced reasonable answers, especially regarding the leased asset, explaining why the accounting treatment seemed incorrect, resulting in a clear conclusion as to the relevant audit risk. However, some answers focused entirely on explaining the accounting treatment and failed to develop the point into an audit risk. Looking at accounting issues in general, many candidates clearly have a sound knowledge of financial reporting standards, which is essential for this paper. But candidates should be aware that simply quoting financial reporting rules is not enough – they need to apply the rules to the scenario and to the specific question requirement in order to score marks. The share based payment scheme was a difficult issue, but relatively easy marks were available for discussing the inherent risk created by the complexity of the accounting treatment.

The second requirement, for 8 marks, related specifically to the share- based payment plan and the leased asset, asking candidates to recommend the principal audit procedures to be performed in respect of the two items. Specifically, procedures relating to the recognition and measurement of the share-based payment plan, and the classification of the lease were required. Unfortunately answers to this requirement were inadequate. Most candidates could do little more than repeat the necessary accounting treatment, and then request a management representation that the correct treatment has been carried out. Some answers recommended a wider range of procedures, but some were often irrelevant to the specific requirement, e.g. not focusing on the classification of the lease.

The procedures recommended were often too vague to score credit, e.g. many candidates recommended that the lease document should be obtained, but did not say what the auditor should do with it, other than sometimes suggesting a 'review'. **Candidates should note that obtaining a document is not in itself an audit procedure.**

There were 2 professional marks available in connection with requirement (a). Most candidates attempted an appropriate format by included an appropriate heading and introduction, and it was pleasing to see a reasonable proportion of answers including a conclusion as to the overall level of audit risk identified. When producing figures as for the required analytical review, it is good practice to present the trends and ratios calculated in a tabular format, which can then be referred to in the main body of the answer. Candidates are reminded that resources are available on ACCA's website providing guidance on the importance of professional marks.

The second task, in requirement (b), required candidates to comment on practice management and quality control issues raised by another audit manager's suggestions to help the audit firm's profitability, for 6 marks. Most candidates scored well on this requirement, working through the manager's suggestions and commented that each would impact on quality control in a detrimental way. There were fewer comments on practice management issues, but a lot of candidates at least mentioned that the suggestions could in fact lead to the audit firm losing audit clients rather than gaining new clients. Many answers correctly made the link between quality control and ethical issues, but some took this too far, and almost exclusively discussed general ethical issues rather than the specifics of the question scenario.

It was encouraging to see that many candidates allocated their time well while answering Q1. It was rare to see requirement (b) not attempted, which allowed candidates to obtain some of the more straight forward marks on this question.

			Marks
		ACCA marking scheme	
(a)	(i)	**Audit risks and preliminary analytical review**	
		Up to 2 marks for each audit risk/area from preliminary analytical review assessed and 1 mark for each ratio and comparative, and ½ mark for each relevant trend calculated:	
		– Profitability	
		– Liquidity	
		– Going concern	
		– Management bias	
		– Operating expenses	

– Share-based payment (up to 3 marks)		
– Lease		
– Revaluation		
– Intangible asset		
– Current assets		
– Long-term borrowings		
– Provision		
	Maximum	23

(ii) **Principal audit procedures**

Generally 1 mark per audit procedure:

(1) **Share-based payment plan:**

- Review and obtain understanding of the terms of the share-based payment plan
- Confirm 10% increase in share price and continued service as conditions
- Review assumptions used to determine fair value of share options
- Consider appropriateness of the model used
- Consider use of an auditor's expert for the valuation of share options
- Review assumptions relating to expected staff turnover
- Perform sensitivity analysis

(2) **Lease:**

- Obtain and review lessor signed copy of lease
- Confirm length of lease and estimated life of property and compare
- Ascertain responsibility for repairs and insurance
- Review lease for indicators of substance of lease
- Recalculate present value of minimum lease payments and compare to fair value
- Agree payments made to cash book and bank statement
- Recalculate finance charge

Maximum	8

Professional marks for the overall presentation of the notes, and the clarity of the explanation and assessment provided. One mark is specifically awarded for the presentation of the results of analytical procedures.

Maximum	2

(b) Practice management and quality control issues

Generally 1 mark per comment from ideas list:

- Raising materiality level increases detection/audit risk
- Materiality judgemental and should be specifically determined for each client
- Should not fix materiality at planning stage – against ISA 320
- Training promotes a culture of high quality auditing
- Cutting training is contrary to the principles of ISQC 1
- Audit teams will not be up to date on current developments
- Quicker audits cannot be guaranteed
- Short-cuts will reduce audit quality and increase detection risk
- The manager's suggestions are inappropriate

	6

| **Total** | **39** |

10   WILLOW CO   *Walk in the footsteps of a top tutor*

Key answer tips

Part (a) requires audit implications of the three issues related to the audit work raised by the audit senior. The requirement then goes on to explain what should be included in your answer – sufficiency of evidence, adjustments required, audit report implications and further audit procedures. By addressing each of these aspects the 15 marks available should be easy to obtain.

Part (b) asks for explanation of the other matters which should be brought to the attention of the audit committee. These issues are clearly identified as 'other issues for your attention' so it is easy to identify which part of the scenario relates to each part of the requirement. There are 4 issues to explain for 8 marks therefore assume 2 marks for each issue and write an answer of appropriate length for 2 marks.

Briefing notes

To: Jasmine Berry, Audit engagement partner

From: Audit manager

Subject: Willow Co – audit completion issues and matters to be brought to the attention of the audit committee Introduction

I have prepared briefing notes which contain, as requested, an assessment of matters raised by the audit senior, and an explanation of the issues that should be brought to the attention of the client's audit committee at your meeting with them. Our audit work is substantially complete, but there are some additional procedures to be performed, which I have recommended in the first section of these notes.

(a)   **Audit implications of matters raised by the audit senior**

(i)   **Audit work on inventory**

The potentially obsolete inventory is not material to either profit or assets. However, when combined with other potential adjustments there could be a material impact on profit for the year.

IAS 2 *Inventories* requires that items are measured at the lower of cost and net realisable value. If the items cannot be sold, the net realisable value is zero, so the items should be written off completely unless they can be recycled for future use. The adjustment to write off the inventory would reduce assets and reduce gross profit by $130,000.

If this adjustment were not made to the financial statements, it would in isolation be immaterial and have no impact on the auditor's opinion.

A written representation has been requested on this matter. According to ISA 580 Written Representations, written representations can provide necessary audit evidence, but they do not provide sufficient appropriate audit evidence on their own about any of the matters with which they deal. The fact that management provides reliable written representations does not affect the nature or extent of other audit evidence that the auditor obtains. Written representations should therefore support other evidence obtained by the auditor.

The written representation is insufficient audit evidence, and further audit procedures are necessary to determine whether the potentially obsolete items are made from material that can be recycled. I recommend the following:

- Physically inspect the items to see if some of the material could be recycled (e.g. the covers may be coated with plastic but the pages may not be and therefore are recyclable).

- Enquire of relevant personnel such as a production manager whether the plastic coating is unsuitable for recycling by the company.

- Consider if the items could be sold to a company specialising in recycling plastic material, in which case the items would have a realisable value.

- Review any invoices raised after the year end for evidence that the items have been sold, to determine whether a net realisable value exists.

(ii) **Audit work on provisions**

A provision should be recognised where a present obligation gives rise to a probable outflow of economic benefit, according to IAS 37 Provisions, Contingent Liabilities and Contingent Assets. The financial statements may need to be adjusted to include a provision in liabilities and increasing operating expenses.

The legal claim against the company of $125,000 is individually immaterial to profit and assets. However, when combined with the potential adjustment necessary to inventory discussed above, the total potential adjustment necessary to profit would be $255,000.

This total is material to profit and, if adjustments that we consider necessary after the completion of audit procedures are not made, we should consider the implication for the audit opinion as the financial statements would be materially misstated. In this case a qualified opinion would be appropriate.

In addition, we should ensure that any legal costs unpaid at the year end have been accrued for.

Audit evidence indicates that the amount is probable to be paid. However, our conclusion is based on a verbal confirmation from Willow Co's lawyers. According to ISA 500 Audit Evidence, audit evidence in documentary form, whether paper, electronic, or other medium, is more reliable than evidence obtained orally. We should therefore seek a more reliable source of evidence than a verbal confirmation.

Ideally we should ask for a written confirmation from the lawyers on their opinion of whether the amount is probable to be paid. The fact that Cherry has refused our request to ask for this evidence is a matter to be brought to the attention of the audit committee. We should consider the integrity of management and why they may be refusing to authorise us to seek written confirmation from their lawyers. It also constitutes a management-imposed limitation in scope, which could have consequences for the audit opinion if evidence cannot be obtained from other sources, or if the audit committee do not override Cherry and allow our request for written confirmation to go ahead.

Other evidence regarding the provision should be obtained by performing these additional procedures:

- Review correspondence between the lawyers and Willow Co for indications that the lawyers have stated in that correspondence their opinion on the outcome of the legal claim.
- Review board minutes for evidence that the outcome of the legal claim has been discussed.
- Discuss the matter with any internal legal expert of Willow Co.
- Inspect invoices received from the lawyers and confirm any amounts relating to the period ended 31 August 2011 are included in accruals if not yet paid.

(iii)   **Audit work on current assets**

The loan advanced to Cherry is immaterial in monetary terms. However, the loan is material by nature and meets the definition of a related party transaction, as Cherry's position as finance director means that she is a member of key management personnel, and as such is a related party of Willow Co.

According to IAS 24 *Related Party Disclosures* disclosure is required in the notes to the financial statements of the nature of the related party relationship and information about the transaction including the amount of the transaction and the amount outstanding, the terms and conditions and whether the balance is secured.

If this disclosure is not provided, the financial statements will be materially misstated as the requirements of IAS 24 have not been met. Accordingly, we should consider the implication for the audit opinion, which would be qualified as the misstatement is material but not pervasive.

An additional consideration is whether any interest has been accrued as receivable. The amount would be immaterial individually, as interest due of only $40 would have accrued by the year end ($6,000 × 4% × 2/12).

Many large companies prohibit loans to directors as part of their ethical code, so the audit committee should be informed about this matter to enable them to consider if the loan is in breach of any voluntary code established by the company.

Further recommended procedures:

- Obtain the written terms of the loan to confirm an interest rate of 4% and to review for any other terms and conditions.
- Review the loan account in the general ledger for other movements in the year, for example whether other loans were made and paid back prior to the advance of $6,000.
- Inspect the cash book for evidence that interest payments have been made by Cherry. If not, ensure the interest due is included in accrued income.

Summary of potential adjustments to the financial statements

DR	Cost of sales	130,000
CR	Inventory	130,000

Being adjustment in respect of obsolete inventory (assuming no proceeds will be received from recycling the items)

DR	Operating expenses	125,000
CR	Provisions	125,000

Being adjustment in respect of legal claim

DR	Director's Loan receivable	40
CR	Finance costs/interest receivable	40

Being interest receivable to be accrued

The overall impact is a reduction in profit of $254,960 which is material to the financial statements.

(b) **Issues to be brought to the attention of the audit committee**

Property revaluations

This planned change in accounting policy could have a significant impact on Willow Co's financial statements. ISA 260 *Communication with Those Charged with Governance* suggests that communication with those charged with governance may include a discussion of the qualitative aspects of accounting practices, including any changes in significant accounting policies. We may wish to explain to the audit committee the potential impact on earnings if such a policy were adopted, and provide information on the key aspects of the accounting policy, for example, the ways that fair value can be established, and the need for monitoring movements in fair value so that subsequent revaluation gains and losses can be properly identified and accounted for. We may also wish to discuss the practical implications of this policy, such as the cost of external valuations.

Non-current asset register

The audit committee should be made aware of the delay encountered in receiving the non-current asset register reconciliation. ISA 260 requires that those charged with governance are informed of significant difficulties encountered during the audit, including delays in management providing information and the unavailability of expected information. It seems that the non-current asset register reconciliation should have been prepared by the client and ready for the audit team but it had not been prepared as requested. The information was eventually received, but the delay will have meant that the audit did not run as efficiently as planned.

It is concerning that the same issue arose last year. We should query the audit committee as to why last year's discussion has not been acted upon.

Procurement issues

There are two issues to be raised with the audit committee on this matter. Firstly, there seems to be weak controls over procurement. Not matching invoices to goods received notes means that payments could be made to fictitious suppliers, or payments could be made to bona fide suppliers but for goods never received. We should highlight the potential fraud risk here, and recommend that controls are strengthened with immediate effect, such that invoices cannot be approved for payment without first being matched back to a goods received note.

Secondly, constantly switching suppliers to achieve best prices may be good from a cost control point of view. However, there may be issues with the quality and provenance of goods supplied. This is particularly important given that Willow Co promotes its use of recycled paper in its printing process. Using different suppliers could mean that paper being purchased is not always recycled, which is in breach of the company's stated operating policy.

Financial controller's actions

The offer of the use of a holiday home for three weeks, made to the audit team, is a threat to the auditors' objectivity, as it represents gifts and hospitality. The offer could be perceived as a bribe, and represents a self-interest threat.

The audit committee should be made aware of the situation, and they should take steps to ensure that all officers and employees of Willow Co, who are likely to have dealings with members of the audit team are made aware that offers of this kind should not happen.

The fact that the financial controller bought lunch for the audit team is less significant. It represents hospitality, and while this can also create a self-interest threat to objectivity, it is likely to be of an insignificant monetary amount, and so the audit team's objectivity is less likely to be impaired as a result of accepting this hospitality.

Conclusion

The audit senior has raised many issues, some of which require further audit procedures to be performed, and all of which need to be brought to the attention of the audit committee to some degree. In particular there are adjustments which may be necessary which, on a cumulative basis, are material to the financial statements.

Examiner's comments

This question was for 25 marks, and was based on audit completion issues. The candidate was placed in a role as audit manager of a client, with the first task in requirement (a) of reviewing the notes left by the audit senior in relation to three specific matters. Specifically, the requirement was to assess the audit implications of three matters (inventory valuation, provision for a legal case, and a loan made to a related party) – considering the adequacy of the evidence obtained, explaining any adjustments necessary to the financial statements, and describing the impact on the audit report if those adjustments were not made. Further audit procedures were also asked for. This was for 15 marks.

Candidates responded well to the practical nature of this question, and a proportion of answers scored very well. These answers went through each of the three issues, and logically answered each part of the requirement, starting with a consideration of materiality (the materiality level was given in the question), then commenting on the appropriateness of the audit evidence already obtained and suggesting further audit procedures, and finally discussing the impact of the issue on the financial statements and the audit report. There was a lot to do for the marks available, and students who realised this, made their answers succinct, but well explained, and avoided irrelevant matters. Good answers commented that the first two audit issues were immaterial by monetary value on an individual basis, but when aggregated the total adjustment to the financial statements would become material, therefore having an implication for the auditor's opinion.

However, there were several common weaknesses in answers. First, a sizeable proportion of candidates did not realise that a materiality level had already been determined and given in the question. They then incorrectly calculated materiality on the wrong basis, leading to irrelevant discussions of qualifications to the auditor's opinion for the first two issues in isolation. Second, many candidates did not answer the full set of requirements for each issue, with the most common problem being that no further audit procedures were recommended at all, limiting the marks available.

A further issue was that a significant number of candidates who had correctly identified that a matter such as the inventory valuation was immaterial in isolation then went on to state that the audit opinion should be modified because of that issue. This type of comment indicates that the candidate either does not understand when an audit opinion should be modified, or lacks the courage to base their comment on audit report implications on what they have already discussed. A number of candidates suggested that a breach of an accounting standard of any kind was 'material by nature'. This raises the concern that such candidates have no clear understanding of what is meant by materiality.

It is concerning that many candidates do not seem to have the fundamental knowledge needed on audit reports. Many answers confused qualified opinions with disclaimers, suggested adverse opinions for immaterial matters, and even more thought that an Emphasis of Matter or Other matter paragraph could be used to communicate just about any audit issue at all with shareholders. Candidates should be aware from reading past papers and examiner's reports that audit reports is a very important part of the paper P7 syllabus, and can be examined in the compulsory questions. There is therefore no excuse for a lack of knowledge in this area.

Candidates are also encouraged to take time to carefully read through the scenario. Reading too quickly and not stopping to think before starting to write their answer may have caused a lot of candidates to misunderstand the information given about materiality, as discussed above, and also about the loan made to the financial controller, which many candidates suggested should be reclassified as a current liability rather than a current asset.

Requirement (b) focused on matters to be reported to the audit committee, and was for 8 marks. A brief description of four matters that had arisen on the audit was given, and candidates were required to explain the matters that should be brought to the attention of the audit committee. Most candidates seemed comfortable with some of the issues in this requirement, especially the parts on ethical issues, and on control deficiencies. The main problem was that a lot of answers failed to really explain why the client's audit committee would need to be informed of such matters, and instead just discussed how the audit firm should react to the issues raised (e.g. the audit team need to be trained on ethical matters – not something of relevance to the client's audit committee). Some answers tended to repeat the information from the question with no further development, and then say 'the audit committee need to be told about this'. Regarding the issue to do with a potential change in accounting policy most answers just stated the accounting treatment they thought would be necessary (usually incorrectly) but did not view this as an issue that the audit client would need some advice on.

2 professional marks were available for the requested briefing notes, and the vast majority of candidates attempted to produce their answer in the required format. This is an improvement on previous sittings.

The UK and IRL adapted papers had slightly different wording in the question requirement, and the requirements were not split into (a) and (b). This less prescriptive requirement allowed for a potentially slightly wider range of matters to be discussed, and candidates responded very well to this.

	ACCA marking scheme	
		Marks
(a)	**Audit implications**	
	Generally up to 1½ marks for each implication assessed and 1 mark for each impact on the financial statements identified:	
	Inventory:	
	– Comment on individual materiality	
	– Value at lower of cost and NRV and impact on profit	
	– Written representation not sufficient evidence	
	– Recommend procedures (1 mark each)	
	Legal claim:	
	– Immaterial individually but material to profit when combined with inventory adjustment	
	– Financial statements materially misstated when two issues combined – implication for opinion	
	– Suitability of verbal representation as source of evidence	
	– Recommended procedures (1 mark each)	
	Current assets:	
	– Material by nature but not material in monetary terms	
	– Identification of related party transaction	
	– Disclosure in notes to financial statements inadequate	
	– implication for opinion	
	– Interest should have been accrued	
	– Recommended procedures (1 mark each)	
	Maximum	15
(b)	**Issues for attention of audit committee**	
	Generally up to 2 marks for each matter discussed:	
	– Property revaluations	
	– Delay in receiving non-current asset register affects audit efficiency	
	– Weak controls in procurement department	
	– Lack of approved supplier list on integrity of supply chain	
	– Threat to objectivity from financial controller's actions	
	Maximum	15
	Professional marks for the overall presentation of the briefing notes, and the clarity of the explanation and assessment provided	
	Maximum	2
Total		**25**

11   BILL   *Walk in the footsteps of a top tutor*

Key answer tips

Part (a) (i) requires the accounting treatment, risks of material misstatement and audit procedures to be performed in respect of two issues. Your answer should deal with each of the issues in turn, addressing the matters requested.

Part (a) (ii) requires a critical evaluation of the planning completed by the previous audit manager. You should identify the areas of the planning which have not been completed in accordance with the relevant ISA's. If possible, state which ISA has not been complied with. The requirement also asks for any ethical matters arising, i.e. threats to objectivity.

Part (b) asks for limitations which may mean the auditor does not identify related parties and related party transactions and then procedures in respect of a related party transaction mentioned in the scenario. This was a very similar requirement to a past paper question from the June 08 exam and demonstrates the importance of practising past paper questions as an important element of preparing for this exam.

(a)   **Briefing notes**

To: Audit partner

From: Audit manager

Regarding: Audit planning of Bill Co

Introduction

These briefing notes contain two sections. Firstly, risks of material misstatement and other matters that should be considered relevant to two recent issues that have arisen at Bill Co are explained. Audit procedures to address the risks identified will be recommended. The two events are the discovery of additional work, and costs, on a significant property development, and the planned sale of a material business division. Secondly, the audit planning performed so far will be evaluated.

(i)   **Bridgetown property development**

The property development at Bridgetown now appears to be a loss-making contract. According to IAS 11 *Construction Contracts*, when it is probable that contract costs will exceed total contract revenue, the expected loss should be recognised immediately as an expense. In this case, the additional costs of $350,000 cannot be passed onto the customer, and a loss of $150,000 is now expected to arise. The whole amount of the loss should be recognised immediately, regardless of the stage of completion of the development. The risk of material misstatement is that the loss is not recognised, or not recognised in full, resulting in overstated profit.

In addition, there may be late-completion penalties arising from the delayed completion of the contract. These should be accounted for in accordance with IAS 37 *Provisions, Contingent Liabilities and Contingent Assets*. The risk is that such penalties have not been provided for if necessary, overstating profit, and understating liabilities.

As Alex and Ben are planning to sell Bill Co within a few years, they may be reluctant to recognise the loss on this contract as it will lead to a reduction in profit for the year, which potentially could reduce any valuation placed on the company by a potential buyer. The loss on the contract of $150,000 represents 6% of the forecast profit before tax and is therefore material to the financial statements.

Tutorial note

IAS 11 (paragraph 5) states that contracts for the restoration of assets is specifically included in the scope of the standard. Bill Co's property developments meet the definition of construction contracts as the contracts are fixed-price in nature and have been specifically negotiated.

Planned audit procedures to address these risks would include:

- Obtain and recalculate the budget for the Bridgetown development to verify the accuracy of the schedule and confirm the expected loss of $150,000.

- Examine the customer-signed contract to verify the fixed price, and also to reveal any penalty clauses relating to late completion.

- Inspect the list of provisions included in the accounts at the year end, and review for inclusion of any relevant fines and penalties as required by customer-signed contracts.

- Inspect any report made by the architect regarding the structural improvements, which should include an estimate of the additional costs, and a basis for the estimation.

- Discuss the additional costs with contractors or relevant employees to assess if the estimate appears reasonable and if the timeframe for completion of the contract is feasible.

- Review Bill Co's cash flow forecast to ensure adequate funds to cover the additional costs.

- Enquire if any quote has been received regarding the additional costs, and if so verify the amount.

- Consider using an expert to obtain evidence regarding the completeness of the estimated additional costs.

- Recompute the forecast loss on the contract for accuracy, compare to management's forecast, and ensure the inclusion of the additional costs in the calculation.

'Treasured Homes'

'Treasured Homes' represents a disposal group according to IFRS 5 *Non-current Assets Held for Sale and Discontinued Operations*. The disposal group is material, representing 8% of total assets. A disposal group should be classified as held for sale where the assets are available for sale in their present condition, and the sale is highly probable, and these conditions are met before the year end. As a buyer is already interested in 'Treasured Homes', and negotiations are expected to commence shortly leading to a sale in August 2011, it seems that classification of the assets as held for sale is appropriate.

Under IFRS 5, the assets should be presented separately, measured at the lower of carrying amount and fair value less costs to sell, and the assets should no longer be depreciated.

The risk therefore is that if the classification as held for sale is not made, the financial statements will fail to correctly disclose the disposal group in the statement of financial position. In addition, the assets may be measured incorrectly, for example, if following the measurement rules of IFRS 5 would result in impairment of the assets, and if depreciation continues to be charged. The measurement and depreciation issues would also impact on the profit for the year, though any misstatement may not be material to profit.

A further consideration is that 'Treasured Homes' is also likely to meet the definition of a discontinued operation, because it operates as an independent business division, so it can be distinguished operationally and for financial reporting purposes. The division contributes 15% to total revenue, so arguably represents a major line of business. According to IFRS 5, once the discontinued operations definition is met, in this case due to 'Treasured Homes' being classified as held for sale, its results should be presented separately in the statement of profit or loss. This should apply to the results for the entire period, and not just the results since the operation became discontinued. Comparative figures should also be re-stated. The risk is that this separate presentation is not made, or that comparatives not restated. A further disclosure risk arises from IFRS 5's requirement for the net cash flows of the discontinued operation to be disclosed on the face of, or in the notes to the statement of cash flows.

Tutorial note

IFRS 5 defines a disposal group as 'a group of assets to be disposed of by sale or otherwise, together as a group in a single transaction'. IFRS 5 defines a discontinued operation as 'a component of an entity that has either been disposed of, or is held for sale, and represents a separate major line of business or geographical area of operations, and is part of a single co-ordinated plan to dispose...'

Planned audit procedures to address these risks would include:

- Review and file a copy of the board minutes for evidence that management are committed to the planned sale.

- Inspect any documents pertaining to the sale negotiations, e.g. copy of vendor's due diligence report, legal correspondence with potential buyer.

- Obtain management's calculations on the fair value less cost to sell of 'Treasured Homes' and assess the validity of any assumptions used.

- Inspect forecasts and budgets for the year ending 30 June 2012 to see that 'Treasured Homes' is not included from the intended date of sale.

- Confirm that separate disclosure as required by IFRS 5 has been made in the statement of financial position, statement of profit or loss, and statement of cash flows.

- Confirm that depreciation has not been charged as required by IFRS 5, and that comparatives have been restated for the statement of profit or loss.

Tutorial note

By the time the final audit work is carried out, sale negotiations should be at an advanced stage, so evidence should be easy to obtain.

(ii) **Critical evaluation of audit planning and risk assessment**

The notes made by the previously assigned audit manager Tara Lafayette indicate that the audit has not been planned in accordance with ISA requirements. The manager seems to have been more concerned with saving time and reducing costs, than following the requirements of the ISAs.

Firstly, only limited analytical procedures have been conducted. Analytical procedures help the auditor to assess risk and identify unusual transactions and events, and so form an essential part of the overall planning and risk assessment of an audit. The manager's notes indicate that some procedures have been performed, but none relating to assets or liabilities. The fact that the figures have not changed significantly could itself indicate a risk of misstatement, and further analytical procedures should be performed on the statement of financial position as soon as possible.

The auditor should also obtain an understanding of internal control relevant to the audit. The design of controls shall be evaluated, and the auditor shall determine whether the controls have been implemented. Inquiry alone is not sufficient, so further procedures should be carried out, for example, walk-through tests and inspection of documents and reports. It is important that our systems documentation is up to date, and walk-through tests will confirm that is the case. Without considering the effectiveness of controls in more detail, we will be unable to identify control deficiencies and respond accordingly.

The risk assessment process must be fully documented. ISA 315 *Identifying and Assessing the Risks of Material Misstatement through Understanding the Entity and Its Environment* requires that the auditor shall identify and assess the risk of material misstatement at the financial statement level, and at the assertion level for classes of transactions, account balances and disclosures. The identified and assessed risks and related controls shall then be included in audit documentation. The fact that the audit manager has simply said that the whole engagement is low risk implies that a much too superficial approach has been taken to risk assessment. Without considering business risks in detail it will be impossible for the audit plan to contain procedures specific enough to address risks of material misstatement. ISA 315 specifically requires that audit documentation shall include key elements of the understanding obtained regarding aspects of the entity such as the entity's objectives and strategies, and a measurement and review of financial performance. The audit documentation should therefore be expanded to include comments on business risk, and not just a comment that the whole engagement is 'low risk'.

It is right that our firm should make use of an expert to obtain evidence regarding the stage of completion, and therefore the valuation, of the development properties at the reporting date. This work requires specialist skills and experience beyond the expertise of the audit firm. ISA 620 *Using the Work of an Auditor's Expert,* requires that the auditor shall evaluate the competence, capability and objectivity of the auditor's expert. Clearly in this case, the architect being an employee of the audit client means that the work performed could not be considered to be objective audit evidence. Being a new recruit, the architect will want to create a favourable impression, and could be subject to considerable influence to inflate the property valuations, or accelerate the stage of completion. As Ben and Alex want to sell the company, there will be an incentive for figures to be manipulated to show the company in as positive a light as possible. Additionally, the architect is newly qualified, so may lack the experience required to carry out this work. It is crucial that the audit firm engages an independent expert to provide evidence for this significant area.

Finally, Bill Co has offered office space to our firm at a nominal rent of $100 per year, which, for a luxury office building, must be significantly below the market rate. This should be considered in light of IFAC's *Code of Ethics for Professional Accountants,* which states that an offer of gifts or hospitality may create a self-interest, familiarity or intimidation threat to objectivity and independence. The audit firm should consider the nature, value and intent of the offer. If the value were trivial and inconsequential, then the offer could be considered. However, with the rental charge being so small compared to the likely market value, this is unlikely to be the case. The firm should also consider the reason behind the offer. It could be seen as a bribe, in that Alex and Ben will be keen to have an unmodified audit opinion given the planned sale of the company. The audit firm should definitely decline the offer, and explain the reasons for this to the management of Bill Co.

In conclusion, this audit has been inadequately planned, and fails to meet the requirements of several ISAs. In addition, the ethical issue raised may give rise to suspicions of intimidation from the client. The planning should be re-performed, with much more detailed documentation placed on file. The deficiencies in the planning should be discussed with the previous manager, who should receive training if necessary to ensure future audits are planned and documented in adherence to ISA requirements.

(b) (i) Related parties, and related party transactions can be difficult to identify. Management may be unaware of the existence of all related party relationships and transactions, resulting in them not being revealed to the auditor on enquiry. Auditors of smaller companies can often find it difficult to identify related parties because management does not understand the disclosure requirements or the significance of the disclosures required.

It can also be difficult to decide if a related party relationship exists, as some of the definitions in IAS *24 Related Party Disclosures* are subjective, also resulting in non-disclosure to the auditor of potential related parties and transactions. Management of larger companies may have a better understanding of recording and disclosing related party transactions. However auditors of the larger companies have to deal with larger more complex transactions that can be more difficult to understand and follow.

There could also be a deliberate attempt by management to conceal related party relationships or transactions. Knowledge of related party relationships is largely confined to management, and in the absence of alternative procedures other than management enquiry, the auditor could not know of the existence of some related party relationships, especially the family members of key management personnel. ISA 550 *Related Parties* identifies that related party relationships may represent a greater opportunity for collusion, concealment or manipulation by management.

The accounting system may not be set up to identify related party transactions. For example, cash payments made to a related party may not be separately identified from payments to trade suppliers within the ledgers.

Finally, some related party transactions occur at minimal value, and sometimes at nil value. This makes the transaction almost impossible for the auditor to detect, other than relying on management to disclose the transaction on enquiry.

(ii) Audit procedures should include:

- Review invoices received from Lantern Co to verify the amount of the expense. Confirm cash payments to the cash book.

- Inspect Lantern Co's trade payables account to confirm any amount outstanding at the year end.

- Compare the cost of refurbishment carried out by Lantern Co to the cost of refurbishment carried out by other suppliers, to determine if the transaction is at arm's length.

- Discuss the informal lease with management, and obtain a written representation regarding the nature of the arrangement, and whether any amount is payable to Bill Co.

- Confirm through enquiry with management the date the lease arrangement commenced, and the expected period of the lease.

- Enquire if any written documentation exists regarding the lease arrangement, if so, review and place on file.

- Review the disclosure made (if any) regarding these transactions in the draft financial statements.

Examiner's comments

This question was for 37 marks and involved a property development company which was a long-standing audit client. The candidate was placed in the role of a newly assigned audit manager, whose first task in requirement (a) (i) was to explain the matters that needed to be considered, and the financial statement risks relating to two issues. The planned audit procedures in response to the risks identified were also required. This requirement was for 16 marks. The wording of the requirement should have been familiar as has been used in many past questions.

Most candidates recognised the loss-making nature of the contract described in the scenario, and correctly calculated the loss, and the majority then went on to discuss the financial statement risk that profit would be overstated if the loss were not recognised in full. However, having gone this far, many candidates then went on to consider other potential accounting issues and different financial reporting standards, leading to confused answers and often contradictory advice. The most common example here was where a candidate having stated that the loss should be recognised in full ('to be prudent'), they then went on to argue the opposite point in the next sentence - that according to revenue recognition principles only a part of the loss should now be recognised. No conclusion was provided and the contradictory comments clearly detract from the overall quality of an answer. Some candidates simply could not decide which financial reporting standard was most relevant, and applied several or all of the following to the contract in question: provisions (IAS 37), property, plant and equipment (IAS 16), development costs (IAS 38), inventories (IAS 2) and investment properties (IAS 40). It was common to see answers of this type stretching over many pages, when all that was needed was a succinct discussion of the loss making contract in the context of IAS 11, which could be done in a few short paragraphs.

The other common problem were answers which focused on business risks rather than risks of material misstatement, leading to long discussions of cash availability, the company's reputation, and inevitably going concern problems.

The procedures recommended for the loss making contract were often too vague to score credit, e.g. many candidates recommended that the architect's plans should be obtained, but did not say what the auditor should do with them. Similarly, it was often recommended that the auditor should obtain the forecast of the development, but then failed to say what should be done with it. Candidates should note that obtaining a document is not in itself an audit procedure.

The second issue in requirement (a) (i) dealt with a significant business segment which management planned to sell, which should have lead candidates to discuss whether the business segment should be classified as a discontinued operation/held-for-sale disposal group at the year end. Most candidates did correctly identify this issue and could properly apply the IFRS 5 criteria to justify their answer. However, the same problems as noted above for the loss making contract equally applied here – many candidates seemed unsure which was the relevant financial reporting standard, and went on to discuss disclosure as an event after the reporting date (IAS 10) and/or provisions (IAS 37). This wasted time and meant answers were overly long and largely irrelevant. Few candidates could recommend any procedures other than 'discuss with management' or 'review board minutes'- which are relevant but must be explained to earn a mark. Again, some candidates continued their obsession with going concern matters here, discussing at length whether it was the right decision to sell off the business segment, and advising management to reconsider.

The UK and IRL adapted papers contained a different second issue – an operating lease which had characteristics of an onerous contract. Many did identify the onerous contract but could say little more than that a provision should be made. Many also ignored the question and discussed the lease as if it were a finance lease, leading to irrelevant discussion as to whether the asset in question was impaired. Again, there were a lot of discussions of business risks (not asked for), plenty of criticism of management's decision to purchase a new warehouse, and advice to potentially minimise the losses incurred. Candidates really need to focus on audit issues.

On the whole, the answers to (a) (i) were unsatisfactory, with most lacking focus and containing a lot of irrelevant discussion. Candidates did not need to write a lot to score very well on this requirement, and it was a shame to see candidates wasting so much time on irrelevance. This shows how important it is to read the question carefully and to spend a little time thinking and clarifying the audit issues instead of rushing to put pen to paper as soon as possible.

The second task, in requirement (a) (ii) required candidates to critically evaluate the audit planning that had been prepared by the previous audit manager, for 11 marks. Most candidates scored well on this requirement, especially given the wholly applied nature of the question and requirement. The ethical issues in particular were usually well explained, the quality control issues less so. Some candidates tended to use a logical approach – working through the scenario to discuss each issue in turn. However some candidates talked generically about independence issues without really explaining the point, e.g. just stating 'familiarity is a problem', 'we must be independent', and there were many calls for the previous audit manager to be disciplined for her 'incompetence'. But on the whole this was one of the best answered requirements for many candidates.

There were 2 professional marks available in connection with requirement (a). Most candidates attempted the briefing notes format by including an appropriate heading and introduction. Candidates are reminded that resources are available on ACCA's website providing guidance on the importance of professional marks.

Requirement (b) was for 8 marks, and dealt with related parties. Requirement (bi) required candidates to explain the limitations which mean that auditors may not identify related parties and related party transactions, for 4 marks. On the whole answers were satisfactory, with most candidates able to explain that knowledge is confined to management, and that transactions at nil value are impossible to detect from accounting systems. Some answers found a variety of ways to say 'they are difficult to find out about' without actually explaining the limitations. Requirement (b) (ii) asked for audit procedures specific to related party transactions described in the scenario, for 4 marks. Answers were often unsatisfactory here, as many candidates ignored the question requirement and just provided a rote-learnt list of procedures to identify related party transactions in general, not focusing on the transactions in the scenario. Even those that did think about the scenario provided inadequate procedures e.g. 'check the lease is market rate'- but not explaining how the auditor should do this.

ACCA marking scheme			
			Marks
(a)	(i)	**Loss-making contract**	
		Generally 1 mark per comment on matter/risk of material misstatement/ evidence point:	
		– Identify loss-making status of contract (only ½ mark if no calculation of loss)	
		– Per IAS 11 the loss must be recognised in full	
		– FSR is overstated profit if loss not recognised	
		– Penalties for late completion may exist	
		– FSR is overstated profit/understated liabilities if not recognised	
		– Incentive for loss not to be recognised due to planned sale of company	
		– Consideration of materiality	
		Evidence:	
		– Obtain budget and recompute anticipated loss	
		– Agree fixed price to contract	
		– Review contract for late-completion penalty clauses	
		– Review internal architect's report	
		– Inspect quote or other supporting document for amount of additional costs	
		– Consider use of an expert regarding amount of additional costs	
		– Discuss estimate of additional costs and timeframe with contractors	
		– Review cash flow forecasts	

Held for sale disposal group		

Held for sale disposal group

Generally 1 mark per comment on matter/risk of material misstatement/ evidence point:

- Identify 'Treasured Homes' as a disposal group per IFRS 5
- Explain why meets criteria for treatment as a disposal group
- Assets should be presented separately and tested for impairment
- Risk is overvalued assets and incorrect presentation
- Identify 'Treasured Homes' as a discontinued operation per IFRS 5
- Risk is incorrect presentation of its results in SOCI and SOCF
Consideration of materiality

Evidence:

- Review board minutes to confirm management's commitment to the sale
- Inspect any documents relevant to the negotiation
- Inspect 2012 budgets to confirm 'Treasured Homes' not included
- Obtain and review management's impairment test on the disposal group
- Confirm disclosures made according to IFRS 5 in draft financial statements

Maximum (max 8 marks each issue)	16

(ii) Critical evaluation of planning

Up to 2 marks for each point evaluated from ideas list, plus 1 mark for overall conclusion:

- Insufficient analytical review performed
- No systems work or controls evaluation carried out
- Inadequate assessment and documentation of business risk
- Inappropriate to plan to use client employee as auditor's expert
- Ethical threats raised by offer to use office space
- Conclusion (1 mark)

Maximum	11

Professional marks for the overall presentation of the briefing notes, and the clarity of the explanation and assessment provided

Maximum	2

(b) (i) Limitation on identification of related party relationships and transactions

1 mark each point explained (to maximum 4 marks):

- Management not aware of relationship or transaction
- Subjectivity/complexity in deciding on who or what is a related party
- Deliberate concealment of relationship or transaction
- Accounting systems do not specifically identify related party transactions
- Transactions at nil value especially hard to detect

(ii) Audit procedures

1 mark each specific procedure (to maximum 4 marks):

- Review invoices/inspect cash book to confirm amount of cash paid
- Review payables ledger to confirm any amount outstanding
- Consider if transaction is arm's length by comparing value to non-related party transaction
- Discuss/obtain written representation on details of informal lease
- Review any written documentation that may exist regarding the lease
- Review disclosures on draft financial statements

Maximum	8

Total	**37**

12   BUTLER & CO *Walk in the footsteps of a top tutor*

Key answer tips

Part (a) (i) requires analytical procedures to be performed to help identify going concern issues. Be careful not to spend too much time on the calculations to the detriment of talking about the risks.

Part (a) (ii) asks for audit procedures to be performed on the cash flow forecast. Procedures should focus on obtaining evidence to support the assumptions which provide the basis for the forecast. It is important to remember that these events and transactions have not yet happened and therefore cannot be agreed to supporting documentation in the same way as historical figures.

Part (b) deals with audit reporting implications where there are material uncertainties regarding Butler's ability to continue as a going concern. Whilst this requirement is often covered in Q5 of the exam, students should be prepared for any syllabus area being tested in any question of the exam.

(a)   **Briefing notes**

To: Audit partner

From: Audit manager

Re: Initial going concern assessment – Butler Co

Introduction

Butler Co faces significant business risk due to declining sales and loss of customers and market share. These briefing notes contain an initial assessment of going concern, based on the draft statement of financial position, and a cash flow forecast prepared for the first three months of the next financial year. Audit procedures will also be recommended for the cash flow forecast.

(i)   **Assessment of draft statement of financial position.**

The most obvious issue is that Butler Co currently does not have a positive cash balance. The statement of financial position includes an overdraft of $25 million. This lack of cash will make it difficult for the company to manage its operating cycle and make necessary interest payments, unless further cash becomes available.

Butler Co is in a position of net liabilities, as indicated by the negative shareholders' funds figure. The company's retained earnings figure is now negative. Net liabilities and significant losses are both examples of financial conditions listed in ISA 570 *Going Concern,* which may cast doubt about the going concern assumption.

Note 3 indicates that Butler Co has been loss making for several years. Recurring losses are a further indication of going concern problems. Few companies can sustain many consecutive loss-making periods.

There are several items recognised in the statement of financial position, which, if adjusted, would make the net liabilities position worse. For example, a deferred tax asset is recognised at $235 million. This asset should only be recognised if Butler Co can demonstrate that future profits will be sufficient to enable the recoverability of the asset. As Butler Co has been loss-making for several years, it is arguable that this asset should not be recognised at all. Additionally, an intangible asset relating to development costs of $120 million is recognised. One of the criteria for the capitalisation of such costs is that adequate resources exist for completion of the development. Given Butler Co's lack of cash, this criteria may no longer be applicable. If adjustments were made to write off these assets, the net liabilities would become $580 million.

Note 2 indicates that fixed charges exist over assets valued at $25 million. If Butler Co fails to make repayments to the creditor holding the charge over assets, the assets could be seized, disrupting the operations of Butler Co.

There are significant short-term borrowings due for repayment – notably a bank loan of $715 million due for repayment in September 2011. It is hard to see how Butler Co will be able to repay this loan given its current lack of cash. The cash flow forecast does not indicate that sufficient cash is likely to be generated post year end to enable this loan to be repaid.

Provisions have been classified as non-current liabilities. Given that the provisions relate to customer warranties, it is likely that some of the provisions balance should be classified as a current liability. This potential incorrect presentation impacts on assessment of liquidity, as incorrect classification will impact on the cash flow required to meet the warranties obligation.

Butler Co's poor financial position means it is unlikely to be able to raise finance from a third party.

Assessment of cash flow forecast

From an overall point of view, the cash flow forecast indicates that by the end of August, Butler Co will still be in a negative cash position. As discussed above, this is particularly concerning given that a loan of $715 million is due to be repaid in September.

The assumption relating to cash receipts from customers seems optimistic. It is too simplistic to assume that anticipated economic recovery will lead to a sudden improvement in cash collection from customers, even if additional resources are being used for credit control.

$200 million of the cash receipts for this three-month period relate to loans and subsidies which are currently being negotiated and applied for. These cash inflows are not guaranteed, and if not received, the overall cash position at the end of the period will be much worse than currently projected.

The cash inflow for June 2011 includes the proceeds of a sale of financial assets of $50 million. It is questionable whether this amount of cash will be generated, given the financial assets are recognised on the statement of financial position at $25 million. The assumed sales value of $50 million may be overly optimistic.

In conclusion, the cash flow forecast may not be reliable, in that assumptions are optimistic, and the additional funding is not guaranteed. This means that three months into the next financial year, the company's cash position is likely to have worsened, and loans and trade payables which are due for payment are likely to remain unpaid. This casts significant doubt as to the ability of Butler Co to continue operating as a going concern.

Tutorial note

Credit will be awarded for calculation and explanation of appropriate ratios relevant to Butler Co's going concern status.

(ii) **Recommended audit procedures:**

- Discuss with management the reasons for assuming that cash collection from customers will improve due to 'anticipated improvement in economic conditions'. Consider the validity of the reasons in light of business understanding.

- Enquire as to the nature of the additional resources to be devoted to the credit control function, e.g. details of extra staff recruited.

- For the loan receipt, inspect written documentation relating to the request for finance from Rubery Co. Request written confirmation from Rubery Co regarding the amount of finance and the date it will be received, as well as any terms and conditions.

- Obtain and review the financial statements of Rubery Co, to consider if it has sufficient resources to provide the amount of loan requested.

- For the subsidy, inspect the application made to the subsidy awarding body and confirm the amount of the subsidy.

- Read any correspondence between Butler Co and the subsidy awarding body, specifically looking for confirmation that the subsidy will be granted.

- Regarding operating expenses, verify using previous months' management accounts, that operating cash outflows are approximately $200 million per month.

- Enquire as to the reason for the increase in operating cash outflows in August 2011.

- Verify, using previous months' management accounts, that interest payments of $40 million per month appear reasonable.

- Confirm, using the loan agreement, the amount of the loan being repaid in August 2011.

- Enquire whether any tax payments are due in the three month period, such as sales tax.

- Agree the opening cash position to cash book and bank statement/bank reconciliation, and cast the cash flow forecast.

- Ensure that a cash flow forecast for the full financial year is received as three months' forecast is inadequate for the purposes of the audit.

Tutorial note

Marks would also be awarded for the more general procedures required under ISA 570 in relation to audit procedures on a cash flow forecast, such as evaluation of the reliability of underlying data, and requesting a written representation regarding the feasibility of plans for future action.

Conclusion to briefing notes

The review of the draft statement of financial position and cash flow forecast shows that there are many factors indicating that Butler Co is experiencing going concern problems. In particular, the lack of cash, and the significant amounts due to be paid within a few months of the year end cast significant doubt over the use of the going concern assumption in the financial statements. The company has requested finance from its parent company, but even if this is forthcoming, cash flow remains a significant problem.

(b) When the use of the going concern assumption in the financial statements is appropriate, but a material uncertainty exists, the auditor must consider if adequate disclosure of the situation has been made in the financial statements.

IAS *1 Presentation of Financial Statements* requires that in this situation, the material uncertainty should be disclosed in the financial statements. ISA 570 *Going Concern* requires that the auditor shall determine whether the financial statements adequately describe the events or conditions that may cast doubt on the entity's ability to continue as a going concern. In determining the adequacy of this disclosure, the auditor would consider whether the disclosure explicitly draws the reader's attention to the possibility that the entity may be unable to continue realising its assets and discharging its liabilities in the normal course of business.

Where the amount of detail regarding going concern disclosed is considered adequate, the financial statements are fully compliant with the financial reporting framework. The auditor is therefore able to express an unmodified opinion (i.e. there is no material misstatement and there is no limitation on scope). ISA 570 requires that the auditor shall include an Emphasis of Matter paragraph in the audit report.

The Emphasis of Matter paragraph should highlight that a material uncertainty exists, and should describe the uncertainty, including any relevant financial information, such as the amount of net liabilities at the year end. The paragraph should clearly state the existence of a material uncertainty that may cast significant doubt over the company's ability to continue as a going concern.

The Emphasis of Matter paragraph should also state that the audit opinion is not qualified, and refer to the note to the financial statements where the material uncertainty is discussed.

In extremely rare cases, there may be multiple uncertainties that are significant to the financial statements as a whole. In this case the auditor may consider it appropriate to issue a disclaimer of opinion instead of adding an Emphasis of Matter paragraph to the audit report. A disclaimer is issued in these rare cases due to the number of uncertainties leaving the auditor unable to form an opinion as to the truth and fairness of the financial statements.

In some cases, the auditor may conclude that the disclosure regarding the going concern uncertainty is inadequate. In this case, the auditor considers the financial statements to be materially misstated, as they fail to comply with the requirements of IAS 1 as discussed above. Depending on the severity of the material uncertainties, the auditor shall issue either a qualified opinion, or an adverse opinion.

In either case, a paragraph should be included, headed either 'Basis for Qualified Opinion' or 'Basis for Adverse Opinion', as appropriate. The paragraph should explain the reason for the material misstatement, i.e. contain a description of the material uncertainty, and also state that the financial statements do not disclose the uncertainty.

Examiner's comments

This question was for 27 marks, and was largely based on going concern. The answers to this question were generally unsatisfactory.

The candidate was placed in a role as audit manager of a new client, with the first task in requirement (a) (i) being to review draft extracts from financial statements and a cash flow forecast to identify and explain matters which may cast significant doubt on the company's ability to continue as a going concern. The majority of candidates seemed to ignore this instruction, providing an answer that did little more than work down the statement of financial position, calculating the materiality of each balance, and discussing the accounting treatment of each item, saying nothing about going concern. Only when turning to the cash flow forecast did these answers say anything about going concern, and then the comments were usually restricted to the likelihood of the company receiving a loan and a subsidy. Some candidates tended to get confused when looking at the cash flow forecast and tried to apply financial reporting rules e.g. by arguing that the income from the government grant should be deferred.

However, there were some sound answers focusing entirely on going concern matters, providing relevant calculations, e.g. the total amount of debt due to be paid in 12 months, and discussing ratios such as the current and quick ratios to provide discussion points. Some answers saw that the parent company would be unlikely to provide a further loan to its loss making subsidiary when it already has a loan advanced which is unlikely to be paid back, and that on this basis surely the company could not continue in operations.

The second task, in requirement (a) (ii) was to recommend audit procedures to be carried out on the cash flow forecast. Most candidates could provide at least a few well explained procedures – the most common focusing on the loan from the parent company and the government grant. Some procedures were not well explained e.g. 'check the price of the financial asset' without saying how this could be done. Some answers provided procedures for the assets and liabilities on the draft statement of financial position, which was not asked for. Most candidates identified the extreme optimism of the cash flow forecast and that the closing cash position was negative, but not many candidates could recommend sound procedures to verify the claims of management regarding cash receipts from customers, which was a key issue.

Finally, there were 2 professional marks available for requirement (a). The majority of candidates attempted to achieve these marks by using an appropriate format but often no conclusion was provided.

Requirement (b) dealt with the impact of multiple going concern uncertainties on the auditor's report, for 7 marks. Although some candidates scored well on this requirement, the majority again failed to answer the question as set, and discussed every conceivable auditor's report that could be issued for a client with going concern problems. The question

---

stated that 'the use of the going concern assumption is appropriate', yet many candidates ignored this and spent a lot of time discussing what should happen if the use of the going concern assumption were NOT appropriate. Most candidates earned a few marks by discussing the use of emphasis of matter paragraphs, but often the description of the paragraph was brief. Only a minority correctly focused their answers on the requirement for management to disclose significant uncertainties in the notes to the financial statements, and that the adequacy of these disclosures would drive the auditor's opinion on the financial statements. Overall answers were very inadequate.

ACCA marking scheme

			Marks
(a)	(i)	**Going concern matters**	
		Up to 1½ marks per matter identified and explained (maximum 3 marks for identification):	
		– Negative cash position	
		– Net liabilities position	
		– Recurring losses	
		– Possible adjustment to deferred tax and development intangible asset exacerbate net liabilities position (allow 3 marks max)	
		– Fixed charge over assets	
		– Significant short term liabilities	
		– Potential misclassified provisions	
		– Forecast to remain in negative cash position	
		– Assumptions re sales optimistic	
		– Receipt of loan and subsidy not guaranteed	
		– Assumption of sale value of financial assets could be optimistic	
		Maximum	10
	(ii)	**Procedures on cash flow forecast**	
		Generally 1 mark per specific procedure:	
		– Enquire regarding and consider validity of assumption re cash sales	
		– Inspect any supporting documentation re additional resources for credit control	
		– Seek written confirmation from Rubery Co re loan	
		– Review financial statements of Rubery Co re adequacy of resources	
		– Inspect subsidy application	
		– Seek third party confirmation that subsidy will be awarded	
		– Confirm cash outflows for operating expenses and interest appear reasonable	
		– Enquire about potentially missing cash outflows	
		– Agree date and amount of short term loan repayment to loan documentation	
		– Agree opening cash to cash book and bank statements	
		Maximum	8
		Professional marks for presentation and clarity of explanations	2
(b)		Matters to be considered and potential impacts on auditor's report	
		1 mark each point explained:	
		– Disclosure of material uncertainty required by IAS 1	
		– Auditor considers adequacy of disclosure	
		– If disclosure adequate – no qualification	
		– If disclosure adequate – include EOM paragraph	
		– If disclosure inadequate – material misstatement leading to qualification or adverse opinion	
		– If disclosure inadequate – basis of opinion paragraph explains material uncertainty	
		– If multiple uncertainties – opinion may be disclaimed in rare circumstances	
		Maximum	7
Total			**27**

13   JOLIE CO *Walk in the footsteps of a top tutor*

Key answer tips

Part (a) requires you to evaluate business risk, i.e. the unique events, conditions, circumstances, actions or inactions that could adversely affect Jolie Co's ability to achieve its objectives and execute its strategies. It is important that your answer is specific to the information in the scenario, and that you **evaluate** the risks identified. You should therefore introduce examples from the scenario into your answer and then explain the potential business consequence(s) of each example you have introduced.

There are two professional marks available in part (a) **for the format of the answer and the clarity of the evaluation.** Your answer should be labelled 'briefing note'. It should identify the intended purpose of the briefing note by including a subject line. For the introduction use the words from the requirement. The briefing notes should have a clear structure including headings and a conclusion summarising the key points identified.

Part (b) is about the risk of material misstatement. You are required to identify and explain **five** risks, i.e. you should state what the risk is, and then explain the potential impact on the financial statements.

Part (c) requires audit procedures for the **valuation** of a **purchased** brand name. It is important that you address the specific requirements (highlighted in bold) otherwise you are not answering the question set.

The highlighted words are key phrases that markers are looking for.

(a)   **Briefing notes**

Subject: Business risks facing Jolie Co

Introduction

These briefing notes evaluate the business risks facing our firm's new audit client, Jolie Co, which operates in the retail industry, and has a year ended 30 November 2010.

Ability to produce fashion items

The company is reliant on staff with the skill to produce high fashion clothes ranges, and also with the ability to respond quickly to changes in fashion. If Jolie Co fails to attract and retain skilled designers then the clothing ranges may not be desirable enough to attract customers in the competitive retail market. The high staff turnover in the design team indicates that Jolie Co struggles to maintain consistency in the design team. This could result in deterioration of the brand name deterioration of the brand name and, ultimately, reduced sales.

There would be a high cost associated with frequently recruiting – this would have an impact on operating margins.

Inventory obsolescence and margins

There is a high operational risk that product lines will go out of fashion quickly, because new ranges are introduced so quickly to the stores (every eight weeks), leading to potentially large volumes of obsolete inventory. These product lines may be marked down to sell at a reduced margin. The draft results show that operating margins have already reduced from 17.9% in 2009 to 16.8% in 2010. Any significant mark down of product lines will cause further reductions in margins.

Wide geographical spread of business operations

Jolie Co operates a large number of stores, many distribution centres, and has an outsourced function which is located overseas. This type of business model could be hard to control, increasing the likelihood of inefficiencies, system deficiencies, and theft of inventories or cash.

E-commerce – volume of sales

On-line sales now account for $255 million ($250 per order × 1,020,000 orders). In the previous year, on-line sales accounted for $158 million ($300 per order × 526,667 orders). This represents an increase of 61.4% (255 − 158/158 × 100%). One of the risks associated with the on-line sales is the scale of the increase in the volume of transactions, especially when combined with a new system introduced recently. There is a risk that the system will be unable to cope with the volume of transactions, leading possibly to unfilled orders and dissatisfied customers. This would harm the reputation of the company and the JLC brand.

The company has recently upgraded its computer system to integrate sales into the general ledger. A disaster plan should have been put into place, for use in the event of a system shutdown or failure. The risk is that no plan is in place and the business could lose a substantial amount of revenue in the event of the system failure.

E-commerce – security of systems

It is crucial that the on-line sales system is secure as customers are providing their credit card details to the site. Any breach of security could result in credit card details being stolen, and Jolie Co may be liable for losses suffered by customers if their credit card details were used fraudulently. There would clearly be severe reputational issues in this case. Additionally, the system must be secure from virus infiltration, which could cause system failure, interrupted sales, and loss of customer goodwill.

E-commerce – tax and regulatory issues

There are several compliance risks, which arise due to on-line sales. Overseas sales expose Jolie Co to potential sales tax complications, such as extra tax to be paid on the export of goods to abroad, and additional documentation on overseas sales that may be needed to comply with regulations. Another important regulatory issue is that of data protection. Jolie Co faces the risk of non-compliance with any data protection regulation relevant to customers providing personal details to the on-line sales system.

Jolie Co is now making sales overseas. If these sales are made in a different currency to Jolie Co's currency, the business will be exposed to exchange rate fluctuations which will have an impact on the company's profit margin.

Tutorial note

Credit will be awarded for other e-commerce related risks, such as the risk of obsolescence (leading to the need to continually update the website and system), and associated costs; and the risk of not having enough staff skilled in IT and e-commerce issues.

Outsourcing of phone ordering system

The fact that Jolie Co engaged the outsource provider offering the least cost could lead to business risks. Staff at the call centre may not be properly motivated, due to low wages being paid, and *may fail to provide a quality service* to Jolie Co's customers, leading to *loss of customer goodwill.* As the call centre is overseas, the *staff may have a different first language to Jolie Co's customers, leading to customer frustration* if they are not understood, and *incorrect orders* possibly being made. In addition, there may be *staff shortages* due to the low wage offered, leading to delay in answering calls and *lost sales.*

Overseas call centres are not always popular with customers, so Jolie Co may find that fewer customers use this method of purchase. However, the on-line system is there as an alternative for customers, and is proving popular, so this may not be a significant risk for the company.

The fact that Jolie Co opted for the lowest cost provider for the phone ordering system could pose a potential problem in that the provider may not be sustainable in the long term. If the provider fails to generate sufficient profit or cash, it may shut down, leaving Jolie Co without a crucial part of the sales generating system.

Ethical Trading Initiative

Jolie Co has aligned itself to an initiative supporting social and environmental well-being, presumably to promote its corporate social responsibility. The risk associated with this is that the claims that products have been produced in a responsible way can easily be undermined if the supply chain is not closely managed and monitored. Such claims are often closely scrutinised by the public and pressure groups, and any indication that Jolie Co's products have not been sourced responsibly will lead to loss of customer goodwill and waste of expenditure on the advertising campaign.

Distribution centres

There is a risk of non-compliance with the operating licence issued by the local government authority. The authority will monitor the operating hours of the distribution centres, and also the noise levels created by them. Breaches of the terms of the licence could lead to further revocations of licences, causing huge operational problems for Jolie Co if the centres are forced to close for any period of time. Fines and penalties may also be imposed due to the breach of the licence.

Financial performance

Total revenue has decreased by $80 million, or 5.2% (80/1,535 × 100). Operating profit has also fallen, by $30 million, or 10.9% (30/275 × 100). The information also shows that the average spend per order has fallen from $300 to $250. These facts may signify cause for concern, but operating expenses for 2010 are likely to include one-off items, such as the costs of the new on-line sales system, and the advertising of the 'fair-trade' initiative. The fall in spend per customer could be a symptom of general economic difficulties. The company has increased the volume of on-line transactions significantly; so on balance the overall reduction in profit and margins is unlikely to be a significant risk at this year-end, though if the trend were to continue it may become a more pressing issue.

Jolie Co's finance costs have increased by $3 million, contributing to a fall in profit before tax of 13%. The company has sufficient interest cover to mean that this is not an immediate concern, but the company should ensure that finance costs do not escalate.

Conclusion

Jolie Co faces a number of operational and compliance risks, the most significant of which relate to the need for constant updating of the product lines and the potential for obsolete inventory. The new on-line sales system also raises risks in terms of security, systems reliability and the sheer volume of transactions. Jolie Co must also carefully manage the risk of non-compliance with local government authority regulations. The trend in financial performance should be carefully monitored, as further reductions in revenue and margins could indicate that a change in business strategy is needed.

(b) **Risks of material misstatement**

Valuation of inventory

High fashion product lines are likely to become out-of-date and obsolete very quickly. Jolie Co aims to have new lines in store every eight weeks, so product lines have only a short shelf life. Per IAS 2 Inventories, inventory should be valued at the lower of cost and net realisable value, and could be easily overvalued at the year-end if there is not close monitoring of sales trends, and necessary mark downs to reflect any slow movement of product lines. The decline in revenue could indicate that the JLC brand is becoming less fashionable, leading to a higher risk of obsolete product lines.

Orders made over the phone or by the internet are prone to higher levels of returns than items purchased in a store, as the customer may find that the item is not the correct size, or they do not like the item when it arrives. The risk is insufficient provision has been made in the financial statements for pre year-end sales being returned post year-end.

Completeness/existence of inventory

Jolie Co has 210 stores and numerous distribution centres. It may be hard to ensure that inventory counting is accurate in this situation. There may be large quantities of inventory in-transit at the year-end, which may be missed from counting procedures, meaning that the inventory quantities are incomplete. Equally, it may be difficult for the auditor to verify the existence of inventory if it cannot be physically verified due to being in-transit at the year-end. Inventory could be the subject of fraudulent financial reporting, as it would be relatively easy for management to 'inflate' quantities of inventory to increase the amount recognised on the statement of financial position. The clothing items could also be at risk of theft, making inventory records inaccurate.

Unrecorded revenue

The on-line and phone sales systems could contribute to a risk of misstated revenue figures. Firstly, the on-line sales system is integrated with the general ledger, so sales made through the system should automatically be recorded in the accounting system. However, the system is new, and it is possible that the integration is not functioning as expected. The scenario does not state whether the phone sales system is integrated, but it is unlikely given that the function is outsourced, so a similar risk of unrecorded transactions may arise here.

Sales made in store will include a proportion of cash sales. The risk is that the cash could be misappropriated, and the revenue unrecorded.

Over-capitalisation of IT/website costs

The on-line sales system has been upgraded at significant cost. There is a risk that costs have been incorrectly capitalised.

SIC 32 Intangible Assets – *Website Costs* states that only costs relating to the development phase of the project should be capitalised, but costs of planning, and all costs when the website is operational should be expensed. Software development costs follow similar accounting principles. Hence there is a risk of overvalued assets and unrecognised expenses.

Overvaluation of the brand name

The JLC brand name is recognised as an intangible asset, which is the correct accounting treatment for a purchased brand.

The risk is that the asset is overvalued, for two reasons. Firstly, if no amortisation is being charged on the asset, management are assuming that there is no end to the period in which the brand will generate an economic benefit. This may be optimistic, and there is a risk that the brand is overvalued, and operating expenses incomplete if there is no annual write-off. An intangible asset which is not being amortised should be subject to an annual impairment review according to IAS 38 Intangible Assets.

If no such review has been conducted, the asset could be overvalued. The falling revenue figures could indicate that the asset is overvalued.

Secondly, a significant amount has been spent on promoting the brand name during the year. This amount should be expensed, and if any has been capitalised, the brand is overvalued, and operating expenses incomplete.

Overvaluation of properties

There are two indications from the scenario that properties may need to be tested for impairment, and so could be overvalued.

The first is the potential for distribution centres' operating licences to be revoked. If this were to occur, the asset would cease to provide economic benefit, triggering the need for an impairment review. Secondly, the average revenue per store has fallen.

IAS 36 Impairment of Assets suggests that worse economic performance than expected is an indicator that an asset could be impaired. For these reasons, both stores and distribution centres have the potential to be overvalued.

Unrecognised provision/undisclosed contingency

The revocation of an operating licence could lead to a fine or penalty being paid to the local authority. Two licences have been revoked during the year. The risk is that Jolie Co has not either provided for any amount payable, or disclosed the existence of a contingent liability in accordance with IAS 37 Provisions, Contingent Liabilities and Contingent Assets.

Opening balances and comparative figures

As this is our first year auditing Jolie Co, extra care should be taken with opening balances and comparative figures, as they were not audited by our firm. Additional audit procedures will need to be planned.

Tutorial note

More than the required number of risks of material misstatement have been described in the answer above. Credit may be awarded for the discussion of other, relevant risks to a maximum of five risks of material misstatement.

(c)   **Principal audit procedures in respect of the JLC brand**

- Agree the cost of the brand to supporting documentation provided by management. A purchase invoice may not be available depending on the length of time since the acquisition of the brand name.

- Agree the cost of the brand to prior year audited financial statements.

- Review the monthly income streams generated by the JLC brand, for indication of any decline in sales.

- Review the results of impairment reviews performed by management, establishing the validity of any assumptions used in the review, such as the discount rate used to discount future cash flows, and any growth rates used to predict the cash inflows from revenue.

- Perform an independent impairment review on the brand, and compare to management's impairment review.

- Review the level of planned expenditure on marketing and advertising to support the brand name, and consider its adequacy to maintain the image of the brand.

- Inquire as to the results of any customer satisfaction or marketing surveys, to gain an understanding as to the public perception of the JLC brand as a high fashion brand.

- Consider whether non-amortisation of brand names is a generally accepted accounting practice in the fashion retail industry by reviewing the published financial statements of competitors.

- Discuss with management the reasons why they feel that non-amortisation is a justifiable accounting treatment.

Tutorial note

As this is a first year audit, no marks will be awarded for procedures relating to prior year working papers of the audit firm.

Examiner's comments

Requirement (a) asked for an evaluation of business risks, for 15 marks. The audit client operated in the retail industry and had recently initiated several strategies aimed at expansion, including e-commerce.

It was clear that most candidates were prepared for this type of requirement, and on the whole performed well. Answers tended to display reasonable application skills, with some candidates prioritising the risks identified, and reaching an overall conclusion. There was much less evidence here of 'knowledge-dumping' than in answers to other requirements. Some answers worked through the scenario, and for each risk identified explained the potential impact on the business. Some answers also made connections between different aspects of the client's business, for example, that joining the Fair Trade Initiative would have cost repercussions at a time when profit margins were reducing.

However, answers still left a lot of room for improvement. Common weaknesses in answers to the requirement included:

Repeating large chunks of text from the scenario with no explanation provided

Not actually explaining or evaluating a risk identified – just saying 'this is a risk'

Providing detailed definitions of business risk, which was not asked for

Providing audit procedures for risks, again not asked for

Providing recommendations for mitigating the risk, not asked for

There was far too much emphasis on going concern risk, often raised indiscriminately for every risk area identified. In addition, it is worth noting that very few candidates used the figures provided in the scenario to identify risk exposure. The client's revenue and profit had fallen from the previous year, and some simple financial analysis could have revealed falling profit margins and worsening interest cover. This type of analysis is not difficult or time consuming, and is something that demonstrates mark-generating application skills.

Finally, some candidates simply failed to answer the question requirement. A minority of candidates took the opportunity to provide many pages of answer which just described how you would plan an audit in general, including descriptions of contacting the previous auditor, determining materiality levels, and meeting the client to discuss the engagement. All of this was totally irrelevant, and failed to generate any marks. Candidates are reminded that they must answer the specific question requirement, and not the requirement they would like to have been asked.

There were 2 professional marks available in connection with requirement (a). Most candidates attempted the briefing notes format by including an appropriate heading and introduction. It seemed that by the end of their answer however, candidates had forgotten about the professional marks, as it was rare to see a conclusion provided on the business risk evaluation. Candidates are reminded that resources are available on ACCA's website providing guidance on the importance of professional marks.

Requirement (b) was for 10 marks, and asked candidates to identify and explain five risks of material misstatement from the scenario. The quality of answers to this requirement was unsatisfactory. The minority of candidates who scored well on this requirement provided a succinct explanation of the risk of material misstatement, clearly stating the potential impact of the risk identified on the financial statements. Some answers, which were by far the majority, tended to just outline an accounting treatment with no mention of the actual risk itself. Another common weakness was to discuss the detection risk which may arise with a new audit client, which is not a risk of material misstatement. Given that risks of material misstatement have featured in several previous examinations it was somewhat surprising that the majority of candidates could not provide a satisfactory answer, especially when requirement (a) had asked for a business risk evaluation, which should then lead into the identification of risks of material misstatement as part of audit methodology.

Some candidates used the financial information provided to identify risks of material misstatement, rarely with any success. Common statements of this type were along the lines of 'revenue is reduced, so there is a risk of understatement'.

Finally, there was a tendency for candidates to provide more than the required number of risks of material misstatement, which is clearly a waste of time.

Requirement (c) asked candidates to recommend principal audit procedures in relation to the valuation of a purchased brand name, which was recognised at cost in the financial statements. Some candidates scored well here, providing well written procedures specific to the valuation of an intangible asset. Some answers recognised that procedures should focus on determining whether or not the brand was impaired and whether the non-amortisation policy was appropriate. The most common errors here included:

Mis-reading the scenario and thinking the brand was internally generated (the scenario clearly stated that the brand had been purchased several years ago).

Mis-reading the scenario and thinking the brand was amortised (the scenario clearly states it is not amortised).

Providing detailed explanations of the requirements of IAS 38 *Intangible Assets* (not asked for).

ACCA marking scheme		*Marks*
(a)	**Briefing note evaluating business risks** ½ mark for each risk identified (to max 4 marks) and up to 1½ further marks for explanation:	
	• High fashion items/high staff turnover in design team	
	• Obsolete inventory and pressure on margins	
	• Widespread geographical business model hard to control	
	• Volume of e-commerce sales – ability of systems to cope	
	• Security of e-commerce operations	
	• Tax and regulatory issues on e-commerce	
	• Foreign exchange risk on new overseas transactions	
	• Outsourcing of phone operations – quality issues	
	• Outsourcing of phone operations – unpopular with customers	
	• Long-term sustainability of outsourced function	
	• Ethical Trading Initiative – supply chain issues	
	• Potential restrictions on operation of distribution centres	
	• Financial performance – general comments on revenue/ profitability/margins	
	Up to 2 marks for calculation of margins, trends, etc	15
	Professional marks: 1 for presentation, 1 for quality of evaluation	2
	Maximum marks	17

(b)	**Risks of material misstatement**		
	½ mark for identification, up to 1½ further marks for explanation, FIVE matters only		
	• Inventory valuation (IAS 2)		
	• Inventory existence (IAS 2)		
	• Unrecorded revenue		
	• Capitalisation of IT/website costs (SIC 32)		
	• Valuation of brand name (IAS 38)		
	• Valuation of properties (IAS 36)		
	• Recognition of provision/contingent liability (IAS 37)		
	• Opening balances and comparatives (1 mark only)		
	Maximum marks		10
(c)	**Audit procedures: brand name**		
	1 mark per specific procedure		
	• Agree cost to supporting documentation/prior year accounts		
	• Review assumptions used in management impairment review		
	• Perform independent impairment review		
	• Review planned level of expenditure to support the brand		
	• Review results of any marketing/customer satisfaction surveys		
	• Consider if non-amortisation is GAAP for this industry		
	• Discuss reasons for non-amortisation with management		
	Maximum marks		5
Total			**32**

14 NEWMAN & CO *Walk in the footsteps of a top tutor*

Key answer tips

Part (a) and (b) of this question require knowledge of some core topics, i.e. professional and ethical matters and gathering evidence, and the ability to apply the knowledge to the specific, and slightly more unusual scenarios described.

You should take a methodical approach in applying your knowledge to the scenario in part (a), and work through the list of **professional and ethical** matters that apply to the consideration of accepting any assurance engagement.

In part (b), although these are not figures presented within the financial statements, in generating audit procedures to try to verify the figures you should treat them in the same way, i.e. think about the documentation Newman & Co might have which could be used to verify the information; think about all of the different types of evidence available to an auditor; and generate procedures that are relevant for the organisation described and the KPIs being verified.

Part (c) of the question tested an aspect of audit reporting, specifically ISA 720 *The Auditor's Responsibilities in Relation to Other Information in Documents Containing Audited Financial Statements*. This question highlights the importance of breadth of knowledge across the syllabus; this includes modifications to the audit report that do not affect the audit opinion.

There are two professional marks available in part (c) **for the format and the clarity of your answer.** The question asks you to prepare briefing notes for the trainee accountant – your answer should be labelled 'briefing note'; it should state who the audience of the notes is e.g. 'To: Trainee Accountant'; it should identify the intended purpose of the briefing note by including a subject line and an introduction – use the words from the requirement in the introduction; and your briefing note should have a clear structure including headings and a conclusion summarising the key points identified.

The highlighted words are key phrases that markers are looking for.

(a)   **Matters that should be considered in making acceptance decision**

Objectivity

The proposed assurance engagement represents a non-audit service. IFAC's *Code of Ethics for Professional Accountants* does not prohibit the provision of additional assurance services to an audit client, however, the audit firm must carefully consider whether the provision of the additional service creates a threat to objectivity and independence of the firm or members of the audit team.

For example, when the total fees generated by a client represent a large proportion of a firm's total fees, the perceived dependence on the client for fee income creates a self-interest threat. Due to the nature of the proposed engagement, self-review and advocacy threats may also be created, as the Sustainability Report is published with the audited financial statements, and the audit firm could be perceived to be promoting the interests of its client by providing an assurance report on the key performance indicators (KPI)s.

Newman & Co should only accept the invitation to provide the assurance engagement after careful consideration of objectivity, and a review as to whether safeguards can reduce any threat to objectivity to an acceptable level. As Eastwood Co is a 'major client', the fee level from providing both the audit and the assurance services could breach the permitted level of recurring fees allowed from one client. The fact that the company is listed means that the assessment of objectivity is particularly important, and a second partner review of the objectivity of the situation may be considered necessary.

(UK SYLLABUS: Ethical Standard 5 (Revised) Non-audit services provided to audit clients suggests that the audit engagement partner should assess the significance of any threat to objectivity created by the potential provision of the non-audit service and should consider whether there are safeguards that could be applied and which would be effective to eliminate the threat or reduce it to an acceptable level. If such safeguards can be identified and are applied, the non-audit service may be provided. However, where no such safeguards are applied, the only course is for the audit firm either not to undertake the engagement to provide the non-audit service in question or not to accept (or to withdraw from) the audit engagement.)

The fact that a separate team, with no involvement with the audit, will be working on the KPIs strengthens the objectivity of the assignment.

Eastwood Co's requirements

Assurance engagements can vary in terms of the level of work that is expected, and the level of assurance that is required. This will clearly impact on the scale of the assignment. For example, Eastwood Co may require specific procedures to be performed on certain KPIs to provide a high level of assurance, whereas a lower level of assurance may be acceptable for other KPIs.

Newman & Co should also clarify the expected form and content and expected wording of the assurance report itself, and whether any specific third party will be using the Sustainability Report for a particular purpose, as this may create risk exposure for the firm.

Competence

The audit firm's sustainability reporting assurance team has only been recently established, and the firm may not have sufficient experienced staff to perform the assurance engagement. The fundamental principle of professional competence and due care requires that members of an engagement team should possess sufficient skill and knowledge to be able to perform the assignment, and be able to apply their skill and knowledge appropriately in the circumstances of the engagement.

Some of Eastwood Co's KPIs appear quite specialised – verification of CO_2 emissions for example, may require specialist knowledge and expertise. Newman & Co could bring in experts to perform this work, if necessary, but this would have cost implications and would reduce the recoverability of the assignment.

Scale of the engagement

The Sustainability Report contains 75 KPIs, and presumably a lot of written content in addition. All of these KPIs will need to be verified, and the written content of the report reviewed for accuracy and consistency, meaning that this is a relatively large engagement. Newman & Co should consider whether the newly established sustainability reporting assurance team has enough resources to perform the engagement within the required time scale, bearing in mind the time pressure which is further discussed below.

Time pressure

Given that the financial statements are scheduled to be published in four weeks, it is doubtful whether the assurance assignment could be completed, and a report issued, in time for it to be included in the annual report, particularly given the global nature of the assignment. Newman & Co may wish to clarify with Eastwood Co's management whether they intend to publish the assurance report within the annual report, as they have done previously, or whether a separate report will be issued at a later point in time, which would allow more time for the assurance engagement to be conducted.

Fee level and profitability

Such a potentially large scale assignment should attract a large fee. Costs will have to be carefully managed to ensure the profitability of the engagement, especially considering that overseas travel will be involved, as presumably much of the field work will be performed at Eastwood Co's Sustainability Department in Fartown. The fee level would need to be negotiated bearing in mind the specialist nature of the work, and the urgency of the assignment, both of which mean that a high fee could be commanded.

Global engagement

The firm's sustainability reporting team is situated in a different country to Eastwood Co's Sustainability Department. Although this does not on its own mean that the assignment should not be taken on, it makes the assignment logistically difficult.

Members of the assurance department must be willing to travel overseas to conduct at least some of their work, as it would be difficult to perform the engagement without visiting the department responsible for providing the KPIs. Other locations may also need to be visited. There are also cost implications of the travel, which will need to be built into the proposed fee for the engagement. Language may also present a barrier to accepting the engagement, depending on the language used in Fartown's location.

Risk

Eastwood Co is a large company with a global presence. It is listed on several stock exchanges, and so it appears to have a high public profile. In addition, pressure groups are keen to see the added credibility of an assurance report issued in relation to the KPIs disclosed. For all of these reasons, there will be scrutiny of the Sustainability Report and the assurance report.

Newman & Co should bear in mind that this creates a risk exposure for the firm. If the assignment were taken, the firm would have to carefully manage this risk exposure through thorough planning of the engagement and applying strong quality control measures. The firm would also need to ensure that the fee is commensurate with the level of risk exposure. Given the inconsistency that has come to light regarding one of the draft KPIs, which appears to overstate charitable donations made by the company, we may need to consider that management are trying to show the company's KPIs in a favourable way, which adds to the risk of the engagement.

Commercial consideration

If Newman & Co does not accept the assurance engagement, the firm risks losing the audit client in future years to another firm that would be willing to provide both services. As Eastwood Co is a prestigious client, this commercial consideration will be important, but should not override any ethical considerations.

(b) (i) **Procedures to verify the number of serious accidents in the workplace**

- Review records held by human resources, which summarise the number and type of accidents reported in the workplace.
- Review the accident log book from a sample of locations.
- Discuss the definition of a 'serious' accident (as opposed to a 'minor' accident) and establish the nature of criteria applied to an accident to determine whether it is serious.
- Review correspondence with legal advisors which may indicate legal action being taken against Eastwood Co in respect of serious accidents in the workplace.
- Review minutes of board meetings for discussions of any serious accidents and associated repercussions for the company.
- Ascertain through discussion with management and/or legal advisors, if Eastwood Co has any convictions for health and safety offences during the year (which could indicate that serious accidents have occurred).
- Enquire as to whether the company has received any health and safety visits (the regulatory authority would usually perform one if an employee has a serious accident). Review documentation from any health and safety visits for evidence of any serious accidents.
- Consider talking to employees to identify if any accidents have not been recorded in the accident book.

(ii)   **Procedures to verify the annual training spend per employee**

- Review Eastwood Co's approved training budget in comparison to previous years to ascertain the overall level of planned spending on training.

- Obtain a breakdown of the total training spend and review for any items mis-classified as training costs.

- Agree significant components of the total training spend to supporting documentation such as contracts with training providers and to invoices received from those providers.

- Agree the total amount spent on significant training programmes to cash book and/or bank statements.

- Using data on total number of employees provided by the payroll department, recalculate the annual training spend per employee.

(c)   **Briefing notes**

To: Trainee Accountant

Subject: Other information – auditor's responsibilities

Introduction

These briefing notes explain the auditor's responsibility in relation to other information published with the financial statements. The notes then consider the situation in respect of Eastwood Co, where there is currently a discrepancy between a disclosure in the financial statements, and the other information.

(i)   **Auditor's responsibility**

Guidance is found in ISA 720 *The Auditor's Responsibilities Relating to Other Information in Documents Containing Audited Financial Statements*. Other information is defined as financial and non-financial information included in a document containing audited financial statements and the auditor's report. Examples include a Chairman's Statement, Directors' Report, and in Eastwood Co's case a Sustainability Report.

The requirement of ISA 720 is that the auditor shall read the other information, in order to identify material inconsistencies with the audited financial statements. A material inconsistency arises where the other information contradicts information in the audited financial statements, and may possibly raise doubt about the audit opinion. Effectively, a material inconsistency undermines the credibility of the audit opinion.

(UK SYLLABUS: ISA 720A (UK & Ireland) The Auditor's Responsibilities Relating to Other Information in Documents Containing Audited Financial Statements requires the auditor to identify any information contained within any of the financial or non-financial information in the annual report that is apparently materially incorrect based on, or materially inconsistent with, the knowledge acquired by the auditor in the course of performing the audit. If on reading the other information, the auditor becomes aware of a material misstatement of fact that management refuses to correct, they may include a description of this misstatement of fact in an Opinion on Other Matters paragraph).

ISA 720 also requires that in the event of a material inconsistency being discovered, the auditor shall determine whether the financial statements or the other information needs to be revised, so that the inconsistency is removed.

If the inconsistency is not resolved, the auditor's responsibilities depend on whether it is the other information, or the financial statements that have not been corrected. If the financial statements have not been revised, and therefore contain an item which the auditor believes to be materially misstated, then the audit opinion should be modified.

If it is the other information which has not been revised, and so the financial statements are correct, the audit report should contain an Other Matter paragraph which describes the material inconsistency. In extreme situations, where a material inconsistency remains uncorrected by management, it may be necessary for the audit firm to withdraw from the audit. In such cases legal advice should be sought, to protect the interests of the audit firm.

(UK SYLLABUS: Where the auditor concludes that the other information contains inconsistencies which are not resolved, the auditor should consider requesting those charged with governance to consult a qualified third party, such as the entity's legal counsel.)

Finally, on reading the other information, the auditor may become aware of a material misstatement of fact. This is where a matter unrelated to the financial statements is incorrectly stated or presented in the other information. This has no implication for the audit report, as there is nothing to suggest that the financial statements are misstated. The auditor should communicate the details of any apparent material misstatement of fact to those charged with governance.

(ii) **Action to be taken**

Eastwood Co's Sustainability Report contains a material inconsistency, as the figure disclosed for charitable donations of $10.5 million is different from that disclosed in a note to the financial statements of $9 million.

Audit procedures indicate that the figure in the note is correctly stated at $9 million. The audit work performed on this figure should be reviewed to ensure that sufficient and appropriate evidence has been gained to support the conclusion that $9 million is correct.

The matter should be discussed with management, who should be asked to amend the disclosure in the Sustainability Report and the Chairman's Statement to the correct figure of $9 million. Management should be presented with the results of our audit work, to justify if necessary that the figure of $9 million is correct. The inclusion of the wrong figure in the draft information could be a genuine mistake, in which case management should be happy to make the change.

If management refuse to change the disclosure in the other information, then the audit report should contain an Other Matter paragraph. This should be presented immediately after the opinion paragraph, and should describe the inconsistency clearly. The matter should also be communicated to those charged with governance.

(UK SYLLABUS: The audit firm should carefully review the content of the director's report for reference to the charitable donations (required under the Companies Act 2006). The director's report should be consistent with the figure disclosed in the note to the financial statements. The auditor must state in the audit report whether the information given in the directors' report is consistent with the information in the accounts. Any inconsistency would therefore be highlighted in the audit report.)

As Eastwood Co is listed on several stock exchanges, the auditor should consider whether any additional responsibilities exist in relation to the other information issued in the annual report, as required by Listing Requirements. For example, some jurisdictions may require the auditor to apply specific procedures, or in the case of a misstatement, refer to the matter in the auditor's report.

If management refuse to change the other information, the audit team may wish to consider why this is the case, as it hints that management may lack integrity. Areas of the audit where evidence was dependent on management representations may need to be reviewed.

Conclusion

Auditors do have specific responsibilities with regard to other information, and in the case of Eastwood Co, our firm needs to carefully consider the requirements of ISA 720 to ensure that we have met those responsibilities.

Examiner's comments

Requirement (a) for 12 marks, asked candidates to identify and explain the matters that should be considered in evaluating whether the audit firm should perform an assurance engagement on the client's Sustainability Report.

It was clear that most candidates knew the matters that should be considered (ethical constraints, resources, knowledge, timescale, fees etc), and most candidates took the right approach to the question, by working through the various 'matters' and applying them to the question. The fact that this was not an audit engagement did not seem to faze candidates, and there were many sound answers to this requirement.

Some answers evaluated the many ethical problems with taking on the assurance engagement as well as providing the audit for 'a major client', and appreciated that with only four weeks to complete the work, it would probably be impossible to ensure quality work could be performed on a global scale to such a tight deadline by an inexperienced team.

Some answers also picked up on the fact that the client's listed status would probably prevent the audit firm from conducting the assurance engagement, and certainly the situation would need to be discussed with, and approved by the audit committee.

However, some answers were much too brief for the 12 marks available, amounting to little more than a bullet point list of matters to be considered but with no application to the scenario. Without application it was not possible to pass this requirement. Other common mistakes included:

Ignoring the fact that the client was already an existing audit client, so discussing the need to contact its auditors for information.

Not reading the question and thinking that you had been approached to perform the audit.

Only discussing the potential problems and not identifying the benefits of providing the service (e.g. it would provide experience for the newly established assurance team).

Ignoring information given in the question (e.g. saying that the firm would need to ask about the use of the assurance report – when the question clearly states that it would be published in the annual report with the financial statements).

Requirement (b) asked for procedures that could be used to verify two Key Performance Indicators (KPIs) – the number of serious accidents in the workplace, and the average annual spend on training per employee. A fair proportion of answers were sound, with precise procedures recommended.

But, many recommended procedures relied too much on observation and enquiry, and ignored the fact that the client was a global company with 300,000 employees which led to some bizarre and meaningless procedures being given, such as 'observe a serious accident', 'inspect the location of a serious accident', 'ask how much is spent on training', and 'look at the training room to see how many chairs are there'. None of these could verify the KPIs and are pointless.

Requirement (c) focused on other information published with financial statements. In the scenario an inconsistency had been discovered between a figure relating to charitable donations which had been stated at $9 million in a note to the financial statements, and $10.5 million in the Chairman's Statement and Sustainability Report. The requirement, for 8 marks, was to explain the auditor's responsibility, and to recommend actions to be taken.

This requirement was inadequately attempted overall. Answers were usually extremely brief, and it was clear that most candidates did not know the requirements of ISA 720 *The Auditor's Responsibilities in Relation to Other Information in Documents Containing Audited Financial Statements.* Most answers took a guess that the matter would need to be discussed with management, and that if unresolved there would be some kind of impact on the auditor's report (an 'except for' opinion was the usual recommendation). But few could say more than this about the issue. Some candidates assumed that some kind of money laundering was taking place, leading to irrelevant discussions of reporting the situation to outside authorities. Very few candidates recognised that if uncorrected, the issue should be included in an Other Matter paragraph, as required by ISA 720. This could imply a lack of knowledge, or that some candidates are studying from out of date learning materials.

Finally, there were 2 professional marks available for requirement (c). The majority of candidates attempted to achieve these marks by using an appropriate format. However a significant minority incorrectly thought that the professional marks were attached to requirement (a).

ACCA marking scheme

		Marks
(a)	**Identify and explain acceptance matters** ½ mark for each matter identified (to max 4 marks) and up to 1½ further marks for explanation • Objectivity (up to 3 marks allowed) • Client's specific requirements • Competence • Large scale engagement • Fee level and profitability • Time pressure • Global engagement • Risk • Commercial consideration	
	Maximum marks	12

(b) **(i)** **Procedures on number of serious accidents**

1 mark per specific procedure

- HR records review
- Accident book review
- Determine criteria for serious accident
- Review legal correspondence
- Review board minutes
- Review documentation of health and safety inspections
- Ascertain any convictions for breach of health and safety rules

(ii) **Procedures on average training spend**

1 mark per specific procedure

- Review approved training budget
- Review components of total spend for mis-classified items
- Agree sample of invoices/contracts with training providers
- Agree sample to cash book/bank statement (½ only)
- Recalculate average

	Maximum marks	6

(c) **(i)** **Auditor's responsibilities regarding other information**

1 mark per comment

- Definition/examples of other information
- Auditor reads to look for material inconsistency
- Implication if inconsistency in financial statements not resolved (qualification)
- Implication if inconsistency in other information (Other Matter paragraph)
- Material misstatements of fact

(ii) **Action by Newman & Co**

1 mark per comment

- Review audit work on charitable donations
- Discuss inconsistency with management/those charged with governance
- If refuse to change the figure, reconsider reliance on management representations
- Implication for audit report

Professional marks: 1 for presentation, 1 for quality of explanation

		8
		2
	Maximum marks	10

Total 28

15 GRISSOM GROUP *Walk in the footsteps of a top tutor*

Key answer tips

The focus of part (a) is audit risk, i.e. the unique risks that the financial statements of Grissom Group are materially misstated and Vegas & Co fail to detect this. It is important that your answer is specific the information in the scenario. Therefore introduce examples from the scenario into your answer to support your explanations/justifications of audit risk.

Part (b) is a reasonably straightforward question about reliance on the work of a component auditor. Most of this can be answered with reference to relevant group auditing standards.

Part (c) requires audit tests for the **classification** of non-controlling interests and the **conditions** attached to the grant. It is important that you address the specific requirements (highlighted in bold) otherwise you are not answering the question. It is therefore vital that you take time to understand the meaning of each question and focus your response on this.

The highlighted words are key phases that markers are looking for.

(a) **Briefing notes**

To: Audit team

Regarding: Principal audit risks relating to the consolidated financial statements of Grissom Co, for the year ending 30 June 2010.

Introduction

These briefing notes summarise the principal audit issues for the consolidated financial statements of the group. There are three subsidiaries in the group and several other investments. The notes consider the audit issues company by company, and other issues which are relevant to the whole group.

Grissom Co

Non-controlling interests

The first risk is an inherent risk that the investments have been inappropriately classified as associates. According to IAS *28 Investments in Associates,* an investment should only be classified and accounted for as an associate if there is power to participate in financial and operating policy decisions, in which case equity accounting should be used to measure the investments in the group statement of financial position. The risk is that the investments have been classified and accounted for incorrectly. If Grissom Co cannot demonstrate the ability to exercise significant influence, then the investments should be treated as trade investments, and would not be consolidated. Alternatively, the substance of the interest in these companies could be a joint venture, if control is shared between Grissom Co and the other investors.

A second issue raised by the diversification away from the group's normal activities is that the group's finance team may not have sufficient experience in these two new areas, for example, there may be a risk that they have insufficient knowledge to know how to correctly recognise and defer the revenue for a travel agent.

In addition, a detection risk arises from the activities of the non-controlling interests. They represent a departure from the other activities of the group, and our firm may have little experience or knowledge of travel agencies and pet shops. This means that we may fail to identify risks of material misstatement relating to the amounts included from these investments in the consolidated financial statements.

Bonus and changes to accounting estimates

The directors receive a bonus based on group profit before tax. This leads to inherent risks of overstatement of income and/or understatement of expenses. The directors will want to maximise profits due to their financial interest in the group's results, which could lead to the manipulation of profits to achieve a desired bonus. The fact that the finance director left following a disagreement could indicate that the changes to accounting estimates were inappropriate. The estimates could have been changed as part of an earnings management strategy.

Changes to accounting estimates can represent a high risk of material misstatement. IAS *8 Accounting Policies, Changes in Accounting Estimates and Errors* requires that changes to estimates are accounted for prospectively rather than retrospectively. There is a risk that management has confused changes to estimates with changes in policies, which require a retrospective accounting treatment.

No group finance director

The lack of a group finance director increases inherent risk and control risk. A group finance director should be in place, in order to ensure that group accounting policies are adhered to throughout the production of the consolidated financial statements. It is much more likely that a material misstatement could occur during the consolidation process if there is no one overseeing it. Errors are more likely to occur, and to remain undetected, as the group finance director should exercise a supervisory control over the whole consolidation process.

Willows Co

Dismantling costs

According to IAS 16 Property, *Plant and Equipment,* the cost of an asset should include the estimated costs of dismantling and removing the asset (also known as decommissioning costs) if there is an obligation to incur the cost at the end of the life of the asset. A provision should also be recognised as a non-current liability. IAS *37 Provisions, Contingent Liabilities and Contingent Assets* contains criteria that must be met in order to recognise a provision. The requirement contained in the planning permission creates an obligation leading to a probable outflow of economic benefit, and the construction of the factory is a past event.

The risk is that the decommissioning cost has not been capitalised as part of the asset, in which case the asset is understated, and the other side of the entry will be missing, leading to incomplete provisions. In addition, the depreciation expense would be understated.

Even if the costs have been recognised, there are specific rules regarding the measurement of the amount recognised, which should be discounted to present value. There is risk that the calculation has not been carried out correctly, for example, using the incorrect discount factor. Furthermore, a finance charge should be recognised each year to reflect the unwinding of the discounted provision. The risk is that the charge has not been made, or has been measured incorrectly.

Hodges Co

Grant received

IAS *20 Accounting for Government Grants and Disclosure of Government Assistance* requires that grants should be recognised as income over the periods necessary to match them with the related costs that they are intended to compensate. This means that the income should be deferred, and recognised as income over the estimated useful life of the packing lines, beginning in February 2010. The risk is that the income has been immediately recognised in full, overstating profit for the year, which would help the directors to maximise their bonus.

Tutorial note

Under IAS 20, the grant should be presented on the statement of financial position either as deferred income, or by deducting the grant in arriving at the asset's *carrying value. Credit will be given for answers referring to either accounting treatment.*

Secondly, there is a condition attached to the grant. If Hodges Co fails to meet the environmental targets, the grant may have to be repaid, partly or in full. If this is the case, a provision should be recognised for the potential repayment (or a note should disclose a contingent liability in the case of a possible repayment). The risk is a potential understatement of provisions if the target has not been met.

Identifying whether the company has defaulted from the conditions of the grant poses a risk in itself, as it may be difficult for the audit firm to obtain sufficient evidence on this matter, other than a written management representation or reliance on third party reports.

Brass Co

Mid-year acquisition

Brass Co was acquired part way through the accounting period. Its results should be consolidated into the group statement of profit or loss from the date that control passed to Grissom Co. The risk is that results have been consolidated from the wrong point in time. Given the directors' incentive to maximise group profit, the results may have been consolidated from too early a point in time if Brass Co is profitable.

Goodwill on acquisition

The goodwill on acquisition should be calculated according to IFRS 3 (Revised) *Business Combinations.* The calculation is inherently risky due to the need for significant judgements over the fair value of assets and liabilities acquired. There is also risk that not all acquired assets and liabilities have been separately identified, measured and disclosed. Risks are heightened due to the overseas location of the company, meaning that estimations of fair value may be more complex and subjective.

Retranslation of Brass Co's financial statements

The company's functional and presentational currency is local, and different to the rest of the group. Prior to consolidation, the financial statements must be retranslated, using the rules in IAS 21 *The Effects of Changes in Foreign Exchange Rates.* The assets and liabilities should be retranslated using the closing exchange rate, income and expenses at the average exchange rate, and exchange gains or losses on the retranslation should be recognised in group equity. This is a complex procedure, therefore inherently risky, and the determination of the average rate for the year can be subjective.

The goodwill intangible asset must also be calculated using the closing exchange rate, which is effectively treated as a revaluation. The risk is that this retranslation has not occurred, and that goodwill remains at historic cost.

Adjustments necessary to bring in line with group accounting policies

Brass Co does not use the same financial reporting framework as the rest of the group. The company's financial statements must be adjusted to align them with group accounting policies. This will require considerable expertise and skill, and combined with the absence of a group finance director, the risk of errors is high.

Intra-group transactions

The trading transactions between Brass Co and Willows Co must be eliminated on consolidation. The risk is that the intra-group elimination is not performed, resulting in overstated revenue and operating expenses at group level (and receivables and payables if any amounts are outstanding at the yearend).

In addition, for any items remaining in inventory which contain unrealised profit, a provision for unrealised profit must be made. If this adjustment is not carried out, inventory and group profit will be overstated.

Conclusion

Due to the many factors described in these notes the audit of several material components of the consolidated financial statements is relatively high risk. However, the consolidation of Grissom Co, Willows Co and Hodges Co is relatively low risk, as our firm has audited the consolidated financial statements for several years, and those companies all use the same reporting framework, report in the same currency, and have the same year end.

(b)   ISA 600 *Special Considerations – Audits of Group Financial Statements (Including the Work of Component Auditors)* provides guidance on the factors that should be considered in relation to the work of component auditors. Sidle & Co audit a significant component of the group. ISA 600 requires that the group engagement team obtains an understanding of the component auditor when it plans to request the component auditor to perform work on the financial information of a component for the group audit.

Tutorial note

'Component' is defined as an entity or business activity for which financial information is included in the group financial statements. In this scenario, Brass Co is a wholly owned subsidiary, so meets the definition of a component. Sidle & Co, the auditors of Brass Co, are component auditors using the ISA 600 terminology.

Ethical status

The first factor to be considered is the ethical status of the firm, particularly independence. According to ISA 600, the component auditors are subject to the same ethical requirements that are relevant to the group audit. This means that because Vegas & Co, the group audit firm, is bound by IFAC's *Code of Ethics for Professional Accountants,* and ACCA's *Code of Ethics and Conduct, (UK SYLLABUS: and the FRC Ethical Standards)* then Sidle & Co is bound by the same ethical rules, irrespective of the ethical code that exists in Chocland.

If the ethical rules and principles are found to be less stringent in Chocland, then less reliance can be placed on the work of Sidle & Co. This is because there may be doubts over the objectivity and integrity of the audit firm, and also over its competence to conduct the audit.

Qualifications and professional competence

The professional competence of Sidle & Co must be considered. The auditors' qualifications may not be of the same standard as those of Vegas & Co. The quality of their work could therefore be questionable.

In addition, the auditors at Sidle & Co may not have the necessary skills or resources to be involved in a group audit. For example, the group audit team may instruct Sidle & Co to perform work necessary for the group audit, such as verification of related parties, or fair value measurements. The firm may not have previous experience in these matters, and indeed may not have been involved in a group audit before.

ISAs are not followed in Chocland, meaning that the audit work conducted may be less rigorous than expected. This means that audit evidence gathered may not be sufficient to support the group audit opinion.

Monitoring

There should be consideration of whether Sidle & Co operates in a regulatory environment that actively oversees and monitors auditors. This would enhance not only the firm's ethical status, but also adds credibility to its competence.

Audit Evidence

There should be an evaluation as to whether the group engagement team will be able to be involved in the work of the component auditor to the extent necessary to obtain sufficient appropriate audit evidence on material matters.

Procedures could include:

* Obtaining and reviewing the ethical code followed by audit firms in Chocland, and comparing it to codes used by Vegas & Co.

* Obtaining a statement from Sidle & Co that the firm has adhered to any local ethical code and the IFAC Code.

* Establishing through discussion or questionnaire whether Sidle & Co is a member of an auditing regulatory body, and the professional qualifications issued by that body.

* Obtaining confirmations from the professional body to which Sidle & Co belong, or the authorities by which it is licensed.

* Determining through discussion or questionnaire whether Sidle & Co is a member of an affiliation or network of audit firms.

- Discussion of the audit methodology used by Sidle & Co in the audit of Brass Co, and compare it to those used under ISAs (e.g. how the risk of material misstatement is assessed, how materiality is calculated, the type of sampling procedures used).

- A questionnaire or checklist could be used to provide a summary of audit procedures used.

- Ascertaining the quality control policies and procedures used by Sidle & Co, both firm-wide and those applied to individual audit engagements.

- Requesting any results of monitoring or inspection visits conducted by the regulatory authority under which Sidle & Co operates.

- Communicating to Sidle & Co an understanding of the assurances that our firm will expect to receive, to avoid any subsequent misunderstandings.

(c) (i) Audit procedures on classification of non-controlling interests:

- Determine the percentage shareholding acquired, using purchase documentation, legal agreements, etc.

- Confirm that the percentage shareholding is within the normal range for an associate i.e. between 20 and 50% of equity shares.

- Obtain a list of directors (using published financial statements or an internet search) for the companies to confirm whether Grissom Co has appointed director(s) to the boards.

- Discuss with the directors of Grissom Co their level of involvement in policy decisions made at the companies.

- Obtain a written representation detailing the nature of involvement and influence exerted over the companies (for example, a letter from the investee's board of directors confirming the voting power of Grissom Co).

- Consider the identity of the other shareholders and the relationship between them and Grissom Co. This may reveal that the situation is in substance a joint venture and would need to be accounted for as such.

Tutorial note

As the non-controlling interests are not audited by your firm, it is not appropriate to expect to see books and records maintained by those companies, such as minutes of directors' meetings.

(ii) Audit procedures on the condition attached to the grant received by Hodges Co:

- Obtain the grant document and review the terms, to verify that a 25% reduction is stated in the document.

- Determine over what period the 25% reduction must be demonstrated e.g. must it be achieved by a certain point in time and sustained for a certain period.

- Review the terms to establish the financial repercussions of breaching the condition – would the grant be repayable in full or in part, and when would repayment be made.

- Obtain documentation from management showing the monitoring procedures that have been put in place regarding energy use.
- Identify how the energy efficiency is monitored – internally, or through third party inspection and confirmation.
- Review the results and adequacy of any monitoring that has taken place before the yearend to see if the condition has been breached (for example, compare electricity meter readings pre and post installation of the packing line to confirm reduced levels of electricity are being used).
- Discuss the energy efficiency of the packing lines with an appropriate employee to obtain their views on how well the assets are performing.

Examiner's comments

This question was for 36 marks, and focussed on the planning of a group audit engagement. Requirements related to an evaluation of audit risk, reliance on the work of a component auditor, and audit procedures with respect to investments in associates and a grant received. Overall performance on this question varied considerably. Candidates who answered the specific question requirements scored well. However, despite the requirements of (a) and (c) covering familiar issues seen in many previous papers, a significant proportion of candidates did not answer the specific question requirements, leading to largely irrelevant answers scoring very few marks.

Requirement (a) asked for an evaluation of principal audit risks, for 18 marks. Two professional marks were also available for the briefing notes required. The scenario provided plenty of indicators of potential audit risks, and many candidates produced sound answers which identified the risk and explained it in sufficient detail. Most candidates dealt well with the more obvious risks such as a profit-related bonus, a provision for decommissioning costs and the realignment of a foreign subsidiary's accounting policies. The majority of candidates managed to identify at least some of the audit risks specific to a group which acquired a foreign subsidiary during the year, and it was pleasing to see so many answers referring to goodwill, fair values, retranslation to group currency and alignment to group accounting policies. However, some of the explanations of audit risks identified were weak, amounting to little more than a statement of the correct accounting treatment, and not the risk to the auditor. Many scripts contained the following errors:

Discussion of business risk without linking the business risk to financial statement risk (e.g. 'there is a risk of failing to comply with relevant laws and regulations', or 'there is a risk that inventories are obsolete').

Including audit procedures (which were not asked for).

Long description of the components of audit risk (inherent, control and detection risks) with no application to the scenario.

Explanations too vague to earn marks (e.g. 'the risk is it is not accounted for properly' or 'the risk is that the accounting standard is not followed').

Discussing reliance on the component auditor (which the requirement explicitly said should not be considered).

Many candidates included the inevitable references to going concern problems, even though there was no hint in the scenario that the group faced operational or financial difficulties. Also, some candidates misread the scenario, leading to inappropriate comments. The most commonly seen example of this appeared in answers explaining that a change in accounting policy had occurred (the question stated 'changes in accounting estimates'). Candidates must read the scenario carefully to avoid this type of error. Candidates who structured their answers under three heading of inherent risk, control risk and detection risk tended not to score very well. Those who worked through the scenario and discussed the audit risks associated with each of the group companies in turn, and then the audit risk of the consolidation process performed well. A significant minority of candidates did not attempt to earn the 2 professional marks available for this requirement. Candidates are reminded that resources are available on ACCA's website providing guidance on the importance of professional marks.

	ACCA marking scheme	
		Marks
(a)	**Evaluation of audit risks and other matters to be considered** ½ mark for identification (to a maximum of 5 marks) and up to 1½ further marks for evaluation	
	• Classification of non-controlling interests (IAS 28)	
	• Auditors lack knowledge of activities of non-controlling interests	
	• Bonus and potential earnings management	
	• Change of accounting estimates (IAS 8)	
	• Lack of group finance director	
	• Capitalisation of dismantling costs (IAS 16)	
	• Provision – discounting and finance charge (IAS 37)	
	• Deferral of grant income (IAS 20)	
	• Potential provision or contingent liability (IAS 37)	
	• Mid-year acquisition	
	• Goodwill on acquisition – subjective (IFRS 3)	
	• Retranslation of Brass Co financial statements (IAS 21)	
	• Retranslation of goodwill	
	• Adjustments necessary to bring in line with group accounting policies	
	• Intra-group transactions	
	Maximum	18
	Professional marks for presentation of answer, clarity of explanations	2
(b)	**Matters to be considered and procedures – reliance on component auditor** 1 mark per comment on matters/procedure	
	• Ethics	
	• Competence/qualifications	
	• Skills/resources	
	• Quality control	
	• Monitoring activities	
	Maximum	8
(c) (i)	Principal audit procedures for non-controlling interests Generally 1 mark per procedure	
	• Confirm % shareholding acquired	
	• Confirm if Grissom Co appointed any board members	
	• Consider relationship with other shareholders	
	• Discussion of involvement	
	• Written representation re involvement	
	Maximum	4
(ii)	Principal audit procedures for condition attached to grant Generally 1 mark per procedure	
	• Confirm 25% to terms of grant	
	• Ascertain from grant document:	
	• The period required to demonstrate reduction	
	• The amount that would be repaid if condition breached	
	• Review results of monitoring performed	
	Maximum	4
Total		**36**

16   PAPAYA CO   *Walk in the footsteps of a top tutor*

Key answer tips

Part (a) & (b) require little more than pre-learnt knowledge about two fundamental auditing concepts: analytical procedures and audit strategy/audit plans.

Parts (c) & (d) are more typical of P7 and require application of fundamental concepts to a specific scenario. Therefore you must ensure that all your responses can be illustrated through discussion of matters in the material in the question.

Remember: the risks of material misstatement are those matters that could lead to fraud or error in the year end accounts.

The highlighted words are key phases that markers are looking for.

(a)   (i)   It is mandatory to perform analytical procedures as part of risk assessment. Analytical procedures can help the auditor to develop an understanding of the entity, and highlight matters of which the auditor was previously unaware. Procedures are therefore invaluable in terms of developing knowledge about the operations and performance of the entity. For example, this may be particularly important in the case of a new audit client, when analytical procedures such as a comparison of margins made by the entity with those made by its competitors will provide the auditor with some degree of knowledge about the relative performance of the entity within its business environment.

In addition, performing analytical procedures at the planning stage may indicate aspects of the financial statements which appear to carry a high risk of material misstatement. This would happen when unexpected trends and unusual relationships between pieces of financial data were revealed by the analytical procedures. For example, procedures may reveal that revenue has increased by 20% compared to the previous year, but that the budgeted increase was only 5% and the industry average increase was only 8%. These results could indicate the possible overstatement of revenue, and thus the auditor has been alerted to a possible material misstatement in the financial statements.

For these reasons, performing analytical procedures can help the auditor to identify and to prioritise potential areas of risk, and to develop an appropriate audit strategy to minimise detection risk.

(ii)   Analytical procedures are usually performed before the financial year end, and will therefore be based on draft projected figures up to the year end, or interim financial information, budgets and management accounts. This may make the analysis problematic for the following reasons.

Firstly, the information will not cover the entire accounting period. Extrapolating figures to cover a 12 month period is not always easy to do, especially for a seasonal business where income and expenses do not accrue evenly throughout the year. Care must be taken when performing the procedures to take account of this, and it should not be assumed that income and expense figures should simply be grossed up on a monthly basis to enable annual comparisons.

Secondly, yearend close down procedures will not have occurred. For example, many entities will only account for items such as asset impairments or revisions to estimated figures such as provisions at the financial year end. Thus comparisons to figures derived from prior year published accounts may not be valid.

Thirdly, information may be produced differently during the year, controls may be weaker, and the internal management accounts may not be produced in compliance with the same reporting framework as the yearend financial statements. Measurement, recognition and presentation of financial information may be very different, so care should be taken when extracting figures from management accounts to be used in comparisons with published financial information.

Finally, some entities, especially smaller companies, may not have a complete or formal reporting system during the year, making analytical procedures before the yearend accounts have been produced difficult. It may be possible to perform some limited analysis on the information that is available before the year end, but the use of this analysis will be limited due to its incomplete nature. This means that it may be impossible to base expectations on the data, as it is incomplete at the time of the preliminary analytical review.

(b)   The definitions of 'overall audit strategy' and 'audit plan' are found in ISA 300 (Redrafted) *Planning an Audit of Financial Statements*.

The overall audit strategy sets the scope, timing and direction of the audit. Scope involves determining the characteristics of the audit client, such as its locations, and the relevant financial reporting framework, as these factors will help to establish the scale of the assignment. Timing refers to establishing deadlines for completion of work and key dates for expected communications. Establishing the overall audit strategy also includes the consideration of preliminary materiality, and initial identification of high risk areas within the financial statements. All of these matters contribute to the assessment of the nature, timing and extent of resources necessary to perform the engagement.

The overall audit strategy should then lead to the development of the audit plan.

The audit plan is more detailed than the audit strategy and includes a description of the risk assessment procedures, and the further planned audit procedures necessary at the assertion level for gathering evidence on the material transactions and balances in the financial statements. The general purpose of developing the audit plan is to design audit procedures which will reduce audit risk to an acceptably low level.

The difference between the audit strategy and the audit plan is therefore that the strategy is the initial planning to ensure there will be adequate resources allocated to the audit assignment in response to an initial evaluation of the entity's characteristics, whereas the audit plan is a detailed programme of audit procedures.

The strategy will therefore usually be developed before the plan; however, the two activities should be seen as inter-related, as changes in one may result in changes to the other. Both the strategy and the plan should be fully documented as this represents the record of proper planning of the audit assignment.

(c) Financial information is needed in order to calculate operating and net margins and to compare to prior period(s). If possible, separate information from the statement of profit or loss, and asset and liability information should be obtained for each segment of the business.

It is important that the information is disaggregated as Papaya Co operates in different business segments and different geographical locations. Information would be needed at a minimum level of disaggregation as follows:

- Financial information for the Papaya Mart chain of supermarkets
- Financial information for the operations in Farland
- Financial information for the Papaya Express chain of supermarkets
- Financial information for the new financial services division.

The information should be separated out as above to enable analytical procedures to be performed on each separate component of the business, as each component is likely to achieve different margins and returns on capital. Calculating ratios and making comparisons for the company as a whole would be relatively meaningless. For example, the margins made by the two different supermarket chains are likely to be different, as the Papaya Express stores are in city centres where overheads are likely to be much higher than in the out of town locations used by the Papaya Mart stores. The two types of supermarket also sell a different range of goods, which will also make the overall margins different.

Analytical procedures should be performed on the operations in Farland as a separate exercise if possible. This division is likely to have a different cost base, and revenue may be based on a different pricing structure due to the overseas locations of the stores. There may also be distortions to the figures caused by retranslation into the currency of Papaya Co.

The financial services division will have a completely different profit structure, cost base and return on investment than the retail divisions and so must be analysed separately. It is likely to be much less capital intensive, which will mean that returns on investment and asset utilisation ratios will be very different to the retail divisions.

Information about any significant non-recurring items of income and expense for each division should also be requested as these would cause fluctuations in profit and make comparisons difficult if not taken into account. For example, the heavy advertising costs of the new overseas operations will reduce the margin of that division of supermarkets compared to the local stores.

Budgeted information should also be requested. This will be important for the two new divisions – the foreign stores, and the financial services division. As these are start-up activities during the year, there will be no possible comparisons to prior year information. Therefore the main analytical procedures to be performed will be comparisons of actual to budgeted performance. The auditor should bear in mind the reliability of the budgeted information when performing these procedures.

The auditor should also request any information about new accounting policies or estimation techniques which have been used this year. New accounting treatments may distort comparisons, so full understanding of the impact of any new policies is important when evaluating the results of analytical procedures. For example, the new forward exchange contracts entered into during the year will have caused the introduction of a new accounting policy which may cause fluctuations in profit.

It is also useful to make comparisons to similar companies in the same industry. There should be financial information which is readily available for Papaya Co's competitors in the supermarket retail sector, and also for financial services companies. This is a useful source of information, as the auditor will be able to gauge the relative performance of Papaya Co, and assess if margins and returns are similar to industry comparisons or averages. Care should be taken however when comparing the new divisions to industry competitors, as there may be one-off start-up costs included in the statement of profit or loss for this year, which will reduce profitability.

(d)   **Briefing notes to be used at audit planning meeting**

Subject: Risks of material misstatement identified at planning meeting

Introduction

At a recent planning meeting held with the finance director of Papaya Co, several issues were discussed which could lead to risks of material misstatement. All of these issues relate to matters which are potentially material to the financial statements.

Alleged collusion and price fixing

It appears that several companies are under investigation for breaching regulations, and Papaya Co could face potentially material financial penalties if found guilty. The situation needs to be assessed by reference to IAS 37 *Provisions, Contingent Liabilities and Contingent Assets.* The risk is that the financial statements do not reflect the situation as either a provision or a contingent liability, depending on the evaluation of the potential outcome of the case. If it is considered that the company faces a probable cash outflow, then a provision and associated expense should be recognised. If the outflow is considered possible, then a note to the financial statements should describe the contingent liability and show an estimate of the potential financial effect. Therefore the risk of material misstatement is both understated liabilities and overstated profit, if the cash outflow is considered probable but no provision is made. Alternatively, the risk is incomplete disclosure if the outflow is considered possible and no note is provided.

Convertible debentures

According to IFRS 7 *Financial Instruments: Disclosures*, convertible debt instruments should be presented in the statement of financial position split into two separate components. This is because the company does not know if it has an obligation to pay cash on the redemption of the debt in 2015, or whether the debt will be settled by an equity distribution. Therefore, on the receipt of cash proceeds, the credit entry is split between debt and equity. The debt is valued by discounting the potential cash outflows to present value, with the credit entry to equity a residual balancing figure. The risk of material misstatement is firstly that split accounting has not been applied, so the whole of the credit has been recognised as either debt or equity, and therefore incorrectly recognised in the statement of financial position. This would then have a further consequence for the statement of profit or loss, as any finance charge calculated on the basis of an incorrect debt component would then also be incorrectly measured.

Forward exchange contracts

These contracts are derivative financial instruments. As such, they must be recognised in the statement of financial position at the year end, as a financial asset or a financial liability, depending on whether the terms of the derivative contract are favourable or unfavourable at the reporting date. The risk of material misstatement is that the derivatives have not been recognised at all, particularly because the contracts were acquired at no cost, so there is no accounting entry when the contract is taken out. A second risk relates to the valuation of the derivative asset or liability. This could be complex to calculate, and if not performed by an experienced specialist, could cause the over or understatement of the financial instrument recognised, and an associated incorrect entry recognised in profit. Finally, IFRS 7 *Financial Instruments: Disclosures* imposes potentially onerous disclosure requirements in relation to derivative instruments. The risk is that disclosures made in the notes to the financial statements are incomplete.

Land held for development potential

There are indicators that the land could be impaired at the year end. Some land was sold at a loss during the year, and it seems that planning permission for the development of the sites is becoming harder to obtain, meaning that the value of the land has fallen. Following IAS 36 *Impairment of Assets*, an impairment review must be carried out if there are indicators of impairment to an asset. It is likely that land will be overstated in the statement of financial position, and expenses understated, unless an impairment review is conducted and any resulting loss fully recognised. In addition, the losses made on the disposal of land during the year should be separately disclosed in the statement of profit or loss or a note to the financial statements per IAS 1 (Revised) *Presentation of Financial Statements*, so there is a risk of inadequate disclosure if this is not done.

Inspection of warehouses

A new regulatory requirement has resulted in an inspection of all of the warehouses operated by Papaya Co. Under IAS 16 *Property, Plant and Equipment*, costs of a major inspection should be capitalised and then depreciated over the period to the next inspection. The risk is that the cost has been expensed, in other words, treated as an operating expense. This would result in understated profit and understated non-current assets.

Other risks of material misstatement (not arising from notes made at the planning meeting) include the following:

Disclosure of operating segments

IFRS 8 *Operating Segments* requires listed companies to disclose in a note to the financial statements information about the performance of the various different operating segments of the business. Papaya Co has two potential new disclosures this year end. The first is the new financial services division, which is likely to be a separate reportable segment under IFRS 8. The second new disclosure relates to the overseas expansion of the company, as IFRS 8 requires disclosure of limited geographical analysis of revenue and non-current assets. The risk of material misstatement is the non-disclosure of information relating to these new operating and geographical segments.

Internally generated brand names

Papaya Mart and Papaya Express are internally generated brand names. IAS 38 Intangible Assets prohibits the recognition of internally generated brands. The risk arises from significant expenditure on the launch of the brand in Farland. If any of the associated expense has been capitalised as a brand name, this would mean that non-current assets are overstated, and profit for the year would be overstated.

Conclusion

There are several risks of material misstatement identified at the planning meeting, resulting from the company operating in a regulated industry, changed market conditions, and new business activities for the company. Now that the risks have been identified, an appropriate audit strategy will be devised to minimise the risk of material misstatement in relation to these matters.

Tutorial note

Credit will be awarded for other risks of material misstatement identified from the question scenario, such as potential over-valuation of inventory, incorrect timing of recognition of revenue from financial services products, and potential impairment of loans made to financial services customers.

Examiner's comments

Requirement (a) asked candidates to explain the reasons for performing analytical procedures as part of risk assessment, and to discuss the limitations of performing analytical procedures at the planning stage of the audit. For the first part of the requirement, most candidates could suggest that analytical procedures should help to identify risks, a point suggested in the question, but fewer identified that such procedures would help the auditor to develop business understanding. Most candidates used examples to illustrate their comments, as required, but on the whole the examples were weak and did not help to explain why the procedure was being carried out. The answers to the second part of the requirement were extremely disappointing. The vast majority of candidates seemed not to have read the last eight words of the requirement, so failing to discuss the limitations of analytical procedures at the planning stage of the audit. This lead to answers discussing the problems of analytical procedures in general terms, and many answers focussed on the limitations of analytical procedures as a substantive procedure.

A final comment on (a) – many answers seemed disproportionately long given the marks available. This usually meant that the answers to the other requirements were rushed and not detailed enough to score well. Candidates are reminded of the need to carefully allocate time between question requirements.

Requirement (b) asked candidates to explain and differentiate the terms 'audit strategy' and 'audit plan'. Some candidates performed well here, but some candidates mixed up the two terms or failed to differentiate between them. Many also re-used wording from the question requirement, for example 'the audit strategy is the strategy for the audit, 'the audit plan is the plan for the audit'. Clearly such comments add no value and cannot be awarded credit.

Requirements (a) and (b) were fairly brief in terms of mark allocation and were not based on the question scenario. Requirement (c) was based on the scenario, and asked candidates to explain the information required in order to perform analytical procedures during the planning of the audit of Papaya Co. For this requirement, candidates performed well if they applied their knowledge to the question scenario. However, the majority of candidates failed to do this, and instead produced a list of vague bullet points, referring to information that would be required for the planning of any audit. Most candidates listed prior year accounts, management accounts, a cash flow statement, and little else. Some candidates explained the need for segmental information, and the importance of budgets and industry comparisons for the newly established financial services division. Some candidates gave procedures rather than information required.

Requirement (d) asked for an assessment of the risks of material misstatement, produced in the form of briefing notes. Some candidates performed well for this requirement, by producing briefing notes that identified and explained the specific risks for Papaya Co, and by prioritising these risks to reach an overall conclusion to the risk assessment. The risks created by brand names, segmental reporting, land impairment, and provisions for penalties were identified by most candidates, but not always well explained. Some candidates identified the risk, but gave no further comment other than 'it should be treated in accordance with the relevant accounting standard'. Candidate's understanding of the relevant accounting standard was sound for some issues – namely the provision, impairment, intangible assets and foreign exchange issues from the overseas division. However, some of the issues were not well understood – namely the inspection costs, and the forward exchange contract.

As ever, when asked for risks of material misstatement, some candidates incorrectly focussed on business risks. Irrelevant comments included comments on Papaya Co's business strategy ('can they afford the inspection costs', 'will the overseas expansion work'), or pure speculation ('they may have bribed officials overseas to set up the business in a foreign land').

Some candidates wrote at great length in answering requirement (d), but unfortunately quantity does not equate to quality. It was at times frustrating to see pages of writing scoring few marks, because points made were either irrelevant, technically incorrect, or not actually explaining the risk to the auditor. Many candidates provided numerous examples of substantive procedures or audit impacts ('we must discuss the court case with lawyers', 'we must see who can audit the overseas division'), again not relevant to the requirement.

Regarding professional marks, candidates' approach was extremely varied. The best candidates used a proper format, separated their notes into sections, each with a clear heading, and provided a conclusion which summarised the assessment of risk. However, many candidates made no attempt at a format, and simply produced a list of bullet points as their answer.

Candidates need to bear in mind that professional marks are awarded partly for the quality of language used. This requirement asked for briefing notes to be used at a meeting with your audit team. So comments such as 'the company might be going down the drain' (sic), 'we're gona have to go to the stocktaking', (sic) would not be used in a professional document and will detract from the quality of the answer provided.

	ACCA marking scheme	
		Marks

(a)	(i)	**Reasons for performing analytical procedures during risk assessment** Up to 1 mark for each reason, and 1 mark for relevant example: • Develop business understanding + example • Identify risks + example	
	(ii)	**Limitations of analytical procedures at planning** 1 mark each point explained (limit to ½ mark if just identified): • Does not cover whole period • Year end procedures not yet carried out • Weaker controls/different reporting framework • Small entities may lack interim financial data	
		Maximum marks allocated 3 to (a) (i) and 3 to (a) (ii)	6
(b)		**Explain and differentiate between the terms 'audit plan' and 'overall audit strategy'** • Up to 2 marks for each explanation • 1 mark for each point of comparison or comment on timing	
		Maximum	4
(c)		**Identify with reasons, information needed for analytical procedures** Generally ½ mark for identification, 1 further mark for reasons, from ideas list. • Disaggregation by business segment i.e. supermarkets v financial services • Separate out the different brands of supermarket • Separate out the foreign division • Information regarding one-off items • Information regarding new accounting policies/treatments • Budget information • Industry/competitor comparisons	
		Maximum	6
(d)		**Risks of material misstatement** Professional marks to be awarded for format (heading, introduction, conclusion) – 1 mark, and clarity of explanation – 1 mark Generally ½ mark for identifying risk of material misstatement, up to further 2 marks for explanation (credit may be awarded for other risks not shown on the list below, as long as the risk is specific to the question scenario). • Lack of disclosure of contingent liability/understatement of provision (IAS 37) • Incorrect recognition and measurement of separate components of convertible debenture (IFRS 7) • No recognition of financial asset or liability regarding derivative/incorrect measurement/lack of disclosure (IFRS 7) • Impairment of land (IAS 36) • Undervaluation of PPE if inspection cost not capitalised (IAS 16) • Operating segments – risk of non-disclosure (IFRS 8) • Risk of capitalisation of internally generated brand (IAS 38)	
		Maximum – technical	16
		Maximum professional marks	2
Total			34

17   BLUEBELL CO   *Walk in the footsteps of a top tutor*

Key answer tips

The main element of the question focuses on risk of material misstatement, i.e. the risk that the accounts contain errors, and the procedures that would be employed to gather evidence on the final audit. This question marks a significant step up in the complexity of financial reporting matters covered. Therefore knowledge retained from P2 is vital. In this case the question focuses on share options and deferred tax. That said, there are many simple areas of this question, such as: revenue recognition, provisions and impairments.

For part (a) students must focus their discussion on issues referred to in the scenario. General discussion of problems facing the hotel industry will not score.

For part (b) students must focus on the *specific* wording of the question, i.e. *measuring* the share based expense and *recoverability* of the deferred tax asset. Discussions of authorisation of the share options and the calculation of deferred tax are irrelevant.

Part (c) requires little more than business common sense. The question asks for some social and environmental KPIs. These must be *measurable*, i.e. targets in $ or %. Simply stating 'environmentally friendly' is not a KPI. Evidence should (preferably) be written and external.

Part (c) has 2 professional marks attached. Pay close attention to format and presentation.

The highlighted words are key phases that markers are looking for.

(a)   **Risks of material misstatement**

Revenue Recognition

Bluebell Co has an accounting policy of recognising revenue when a room is occupied. The deposits (and possibly sometimes even full payment) are received when the room is booked. Revenue will be overstated if it is recognised too early. On receipt of a deposit prior to the occupation of the room, the revenue should be deferred and disclosed as a liability, per IAS 18 *Revenue*. Liabilities may therefore be understated and profit overstated.

Further indication of possible overstatement of revenue is shown by Bluebell Co's 24.8% increase in revenue compared to industry average of only 20%.

Share-based payment

The expense could be overstated if the assumption regarding all of the shares vesting is incorrect. The expense should be calculated by considering whether performance conditions attached to the share options will be met. It is unlikely that every single employee granted an option will meet the required performance criteria and therefore a more realistic, lower estimate should be made of the expense. The expense should be adjusted each year end to account for staff turnover. If the expense is overstated due to an incorrect assumption, then the corresponding credit to equity is also overstated.

In addition, the calculation of the total cost of the share-based payment is complex, and if any of the components of the calculation are incorrect, then the expense will be over or understated. For example, the fair value used to calculate the expense should be the fair value of the granted share options calculated at the grant date, the use of fair value at any other date is incorrect. The model used to calculate fair value (e.g. the Black-Scholes Model) must comply with IFRS 2 *Share-based Payment*.

It is also important for the measurement of the expense that it has been calculated based on the share options being granted mid way through the accounting period.

Provisions

The provisions for repairing flood damage should only be recognised if Bluebell Co has an obligation to perform the repairs at the year end. There is unlikely to be any legal or constructive obligation attached to this situation so a provision should not have been recognised in this accounting period. Operating expenses (and property, plant and equipment if the portion of the provision relating to refurbishment has been capitalised) and liabilities are therefore overstated.

Disclosure should be made in a note to the financial statements for any capital commitment entered into before the year end.

In addition, it is important to consider that the buildings are covered by an insurance policy, which will pay out for repair and refurbishment costs to the assets. The fact that Bluebell Co has recognised a repair expense of $100 million indicates that either the buildings were not covered by adequate insurance (a business risk), or that the accounting implication of the reimbursement has been ignored.

Impairment of flood damaged properties

The carrying value of the properties will be overstated if the carrying value has not been fully written down to recoverable amount. It is not stated whether or not the damaged properties have been tested for impairment, but it would seem likely that given the amount of damage caused by flooding, that some impairment loss should have been recognised this year.

Potential understatement of operating expenses

A comparison of operating expenses for the two years reveals an unusual trend. The operating expenses for 2008 include two new items – the share-based payment expense of $138 million, and the repairs of $100 million. Once these have been eliminated to enable a meaningful comparison to the previous year, the 2008 operating expenses is $597 million ($835 – 138 – 100). This is a reduction in operating expenses compared to the prior year of $93 million i.e. 13.5% (93/690 × 100).

Given that revenue has increased by 24.8% (as discussed above), it would appear likely that operating expenses for the current year are understated.

Property disposals

It is correct that profit on asset disposals should be recognised within other operating income, or alternatively, if material, be disclosed separately on the face of the statement of profit or loss. However, it appears that the substance of this transaction is more a financing arrangement than a genuine sale. Bluebell Co has retained operational control of the assets and is still exposed to the risk and the reward associated with the properties, as shown by the financial return received each year based on the performance of the hotels. In addition, the option to repurchase in 15 years time indicates that at that time Bluebell Co will be repaying the long term finance secured on the properties 'sold'.

Therefore the assets should remain on the statement of financial position, with the proceeds received on the 'sale' recognised as a liability. There should be no profit recorded on the transaction. Currently other operating income is overstated by the 'profit' of $125 million. Property plant and equipment are understated by the value of the properties 'sold', and liabilities understated by the amount of finance raised.

In addition, Bluebell Co will need to continue to depreciate the properties. Operating expenses are currently understated due to the lack of depreciation on the disposed properties since the date of disposal.

Finally, as the 'sale' is in reality a finance arrangement, it is likely that Bluebell Co should accrue finance charges. The total finance charge associated with the sale and repurchase arrangement should be allocated over the period of the finance. It is likely that finance charges are understated due to the lack of inclusion of finance cost in relation to the sale and repurchase arrangement.

Property revaluations

Property, plant and equipment is a highly material figure, representing 44% of total assets (2007 – 51%). The revaluation during the year introduces risk of material misstatement to the carrying value of the assets given the subjective nature of establishing the fair value of properties. As Bluebell Co is trying to raise finance in order to improve liquidity, there is a definite incentive for overvaluation of the properties, as this will strengthen the statement of financial position and make Bluebell Co more attractive to potential providers of finance.

Under IAS 12 Income Taxes, a deferred tax provision must be recognised on the revaluation of a property, with the debit recorded within equity. If the properties have been overvalued in the financial statements then the corresponding deferred tax liability and equity entry will be similarly misstated.

Tutorial note

Note 6 shows a deferred tax entry of $88 million charged to equity during the year, representing 35.2% of the $250 million revaluation gain recognised (note 4). Therefore the risk of material misstatement is not that the deferred tax has not been recognised, but that its value will be incorrect if the revaluation itself is misstated.

Deferred tax asset

IAS 12 states that a deferred tax asset can only be recognised where the recoverability of the asset can be demonstrated. Unutilised tax losses can be carried forward for offset against future taxable profits, so Bluebell Co must demonstrate using budgets and forecasts, that future tax profits will be available for the losses to be fully utilised. If this cannot be demonstrated then the deferred tax asset recognised should be restricted to the level of future profits that can be measured with reasonable certainty.

The financial statements currently show a profit before tax of $145 million, indicating healthy performance. However, when the profit on asset disposal is removed from profit before tax, if adjustments are necessary in respect of the impaired properties (as discussed above), and if finance costs and depreciation charges need to be expensed in respect of the sale and repurchase agreement, then it could be that Bluebell Co's profitability has actually substantially decreased from last year, and is likely to be a loss.

Tutorial note

Credit will be awarded where candidates calculate a new profit before tax figure based on the adjustments suggested in their answer.

Given this detrimental underlying trend in profitability, and given the past losses generated by the company, it could be difficult to demonstrate that the tax losses are recoverable against future profits. If this is the case then the deferred tax asset is overstated.

Going concern

Given poor liquidity, and an underlying trend of falling profits, the company could face going concern problems. Disclosure regarding the availability of long-term finance may be necessary for the financial statements to show a true and fair view.

(b) (i) **Principal audit procedures – measurement of share-based payment expense**

– Obtain management calculation of the expense and agree the following from the calculation to the contractual terms of the scheme:

– Number of employees and executives granted options

– Number of options granted per employee

– The official grant date of the share options

– Vesting period for the scheme

– Required performance conditions attached to the options.

– Recalculate the expense and check that the fair value has been correctly spread over the stated vesting period.

– Agree fair value of share options to specialist's report and calculation, and evaluate whether the specialist report is a reliable source of evidence.

– Agree that the fair value calculated is at the grant date.

Tutorial note

A specialist such as a chartered financial analyst would commonly be used to calculate the fair value of non-traded share options at the grant date, using models such as the Black-Scholes Model

– Obtain and review a forecast of staffing levels or employee turnover rates for the duration of the vesting period, and scrutinise the assumptions used to predict level of staff turnover.

– Discuss previous levels of staff turnover with a representative of the human resources department and query why 0% staff turnover has been predicted for the next three years.

– Check the sensitivity of the calculations to a change in the assumptions used in the valuation, focusing on the assumption of 0% staff turnover.

– Obtain written representation from management confirming that the assumptions used in measuring the expense are reasonable.

Tutorial note

A high degree of scepticism must be used by the auditor when conducting the final three procedures due to the management assumption of 0% staff turnover during the vesting period.

(ii)   **Principal audit procedures – recoverability of deferred tax asset**

–   Obtain a copy of Bluebell Co's current tax computation and deferred tax calculations and agree figures to any relevant tax correspondence and/or underlying accounting records.

–   Develop an independent expectation of the estimate to corroborate the reasonableness of management's estimate.

–   Obtain forecasts of profitability and agree that there is sufficient forecast taxable profit available for the losses to be offset against. Evaluate the assumptions used in the forecast against business understanding. In particular consider assumptions regarding the growth rate of taxable profit in light of the underlying detrimental trend in profit before tax.

–   Assess the time period it will take to generate sufficient profits to utilise the tax losses. If it is going to take a number of years to generate such profits, it may be that the recognition of the asset should be restricted.

–   Using tax correspondence, verify that there is no restriction on the ability of Bluebell Co to carry the losses forward and to use the losses against future taxable profits.

Tutorial note

In many tax jurisdictions losses can only be carried forward to be utilised against profits generated from the same trade. Although in the scenario there is no evidence of such a change in trade, or indeed any kind of restriction on the use of losses, it is still a valid audit procedure to verify that this is the case.

(c)   **Briefing notes Guidance on the establishment of social and environmental Key Performance Indicators (KPIs) within Bluebell Co For discussion with Daisy Rosepetal, internal auditor of Bluebell Co**

Introduction

Many companies use social and environmental KPIs as a means of establishing performance targets and measuring actual results against the performance target set. Social KPIs involve performance relating to employees, customers, and the wider community. Environmental KPIs are focused on the environmental impact of the company's activities.

The following table recommends some KPIs and suggests the evidence that should be available in relation to each KPI:

KPI	Nature of evidence
Social – employees	
% female employees, % ethnic minority employees.	Personnel files, starters and leavers documentation.
Staff absentee rates – number of days of absenteeism compared to total labour days per year.	Payroll records, medical certificates, supporting sick leave.
Employee satisfaction/engagement index.	Internal audit could prepare a questionnaire/survey of Bluebell Co's staff. Alternatively, summaries of staff appraisal records could provide evidence.
Monetary value of staff training and development.	Cash book to verify amount. Also documents authorising the training and outlining the need for the training.
Staff turnover	Personnel files, leavers' documentation from payroll records, exit interview records.
Social – customers	
Customer satisfaction rates – % satisfaction with service provided, cleanliness of room, quality of food, etc.	Surveys or questionnaires completed by customers after staying at a hotel or using a room for an event.
Level of repeat bookings – repeat bookings as % of total bookings.	Customer account details from the sales system would indicate multiple bookings. Bluebell Co may operate a loyalty reward scheme to attract multiple bookings – this would provide detailed evidence.
Level of complaints – number of customers who have demanded refunds or have made a formal written complaint.	Management log book of complaints received. Sales system could provide evidence of refunds via credit notes issued.
Number of customers reporting accidents while on Bluebell Co premises (this point could also be made in relation to staff).	Accident log book describing the nature of the injury, seriousness, whether emergency services called.
Social – wider community	
Monetary value of any donations made to local or other charities, could be expressed as % profit.	Cash book will show value of any donations. Board minutes should contain evidence of authorisation.
Number of times Bluebell Co has made its hotels available for use free of charge for local community or charity events.	Register of events – Bluebell Co will have some kind of diary or timetable indicating date and reason for use of facilities. Approval by manager of free use.

KPI	Nature of evidence
Environmental	
% change in water use, electricity use, etc compared to prior year.	Comparison of utilities costs using suppliers bills received. Review of actual to budgeted consumption of water, electricity, etc.
Monetary amount of investment in or purchase of environmentally friendly items, e.g. energy efficient light bulbs, recycled paper, water efficient dishwashers.	List of preferred suppliers and products. Observation by internal auditor or products used in the hotels.
Quantification of carbon footprint, and % change from to prior years.	Review energy supplier contracts for evidence that energy used is from renewable source. Board authorisation of any payments made for carbon offsetting.
% waste recycled compared to non-recycled.	Cash book should show amounts invested in recycling facilities at each hotel. Observation of the use of recycling facilities.

Conclusion

The specific KPIs set by Bluebell Co should reflect the priorities of the company. There is an extremely wide range of measures that could be used – **the important thing is to make each measure quantifiable** and to ensure that evidence will be readily available to support the stated KPI. In the absence of this, the KPIs may lack credibility if disclosed in the future as part of Bluebell Co's annual report or in any publicly available information.

Tutorial note

The answer states more than the required number of KPIs to illustrate the wide variety of points that could have been made in answering the question. As indicated in the conclusion to the briefing notes, there are many alternative KPIs which could have been suggested for use by Bluebell Co. Credit will be awarded for any suitable KPI and associated evidence.

Examiner's comments

Requirement (a) asked the candidate to 'identify and explain risks of material misstatement to be addressed when planning the final audit'. This requirement should not have been a surprise, as risk of material misstatement had appeared in the previous exam, and a recent examiner's article had discussed how financial reporting issues impacted on the auditor at the planning stage of the audit. However, some common failings in answers to requirement (a) are noted below:

- Describing a financial reporting issue but then failing to develop the point to provide a risk of material misstatement. For example, most candidates appreciated that the property sale was some kind of financing arrangement. However, too few candidates discussed the risk of non-current assets being understated due to the properties being incorrectly removed from the statement of financial position, or the risk of finance charges being understated.

- Clutching at straws – many candidates seemed not to know what the exact risk of material misstatement was, and so put that the risk was 'over or understatement' of a balance.

- Vague answers – many candidates simply explained a risk as 'risk of incorrect accounting treatment' or 'risk that accounting standard not followed'. These answers unfortunately highlight to markers a lack of knowledge rather than an application of knowledge.

- A propensity for asking questions was apparent in many scripts. For example a risk explained by asking 'is the accounting treatment for the provision correct?' or 'has the property been valued correctly?' These are not risks of material misstatement and are definitely not explanations of such risks.

- Failure to think about the figures provided. Very few candidates looked at the trends shown by the draft financial statements. For example; only a small minority recognised that after removing the share-based payment and property repair expenses, the company's underlying operating expenses had decreased by 13.5%, whereas revenue had increased by 24.8%. This should have prompted a discussion that either revenue was overstated, expenses understated, or both.

- Lack of basic accounting knowledge. One of the more worrying features of many answers to Q1(a) was a display of inadequate basic accounting knowledge. For example, many claimed that 'the repairs should be a provision not an expense' or that 'the revaluation should be a reserve, not on the statement of financial position'.

Requirement (b) asked candidates to describe principal audit procedures in respect of specific assertions relevant to the share-based payment expense, and deferred tax asset. Unfortunately, candidates still fail to answer the specific requirement. Requirement (bi) focused on the measurement of the expense, (b) (ii) on the recoverability of the asset. The majority of candidates ignored these assertions and instead provided procedures irrelevant to the requirement, for example, on the calculation of tax rather than the likelihood of it providing a future benefit to the company.

The second problem was that many so-called procedures provided were not actually audit procedures at all, but a vague hint as to what the auditor might do. For example, 'check calculation of share-based payment expense' – yes, the auditor would need to do this, but how? The 'how' is the audit procedure. Other examples of inadequate answers include 'ensure appropriate disclosure' and 'check last year's figure' – both are too vague and not relevant to the assertions required.

Finally, many candidates seemed not to understand the nature of the items in question. Some seemed to think that the deferred tax asset was a tangible asset, with many claims that it should be 'physically verified to ensure existence', and for the share-based payment, the auditor should 'count the share certificates' even though the question is about share options rather than shares. Candidates must take a little time to stop and think about whether their answer is logical before putting pen to paper.

Requirement (c) tended to be either extremely well answered, or extremely inadequately answered. Inadequate answers usually attempted to recommend KPIs relevant to hotels, but they usually described the policies that a company should have in place rather than the KPI that would measure the success of such a policy. For example, there were many calls for the company to be environmentally friendly, for example by recycling waste. This is a policy. A relevant KPI might be to increase the proportion of waste recycled by 30% in the next 12 months.

A significant minority of candidates failed to give even one KPI, and many provided no specific sources of evidence at all. For example, a candidate may have identified a staff turnover rate as a KPI, which is fine, but then went on to say that evidence would be to 'check with human resources'. This is much too vague to gain credit.

ACCA marking scheme		Marks
(a) **Risks of material misstatement** Generally ½ mark each risk/matter identified. Maximum 2 marks for materiality calculations.		
– Share-based payment (3 marks) *IFRS 2*		
– Revenue recognition (2 marks + 1 mark for trend/calc) *IAS 18*		
– Provision for repairs (2 marks) *IAS 37*		
– Insurance reimbursement (1 mark)		
– Understatement of operating expenses (2 marks)		
– Impairment of properties (1 mark) *IAS 36*		
– Property disposals (3½ marks)		
– Property revaluation (1½ marks) *IAS 16*		
– Deferred tax on property revaluation (1½ marks) IAS 12		
– Deferred tax asset (2 marks + 1 mark for recalculating) *IAS 12*		
– Going concern (1 mark)		
	Maximum marks	14
(b) (i) **Audit Procedures – share options** Generally 1 mark per procedure		
– Agree components of calculation to scheme documentation (½ mark per item agreed, max 2)		
– Recalculate + check vesting period		
– Agreement of grant date, fair values, etc to specialist report		
– Review of forecast staffing levels		
– Management representation		
– Discussion with HR re assumptions used		
	Maximum marks	6
(ii) **Audit Procedures – deferred tax** Generally 1 mark per procedure		
– Obtain client tax comp + deferred tax schedules, recalculate		
– Form independent estimate of amount		
– Profitability forecasts – assumptions		
– Profitability forecast – time period for losses to be utilised		
– Tax authority agreement on c/f of losses		
	Maximum marks	4

(c)	**Social and environmental KPIs**		
	Up to 2 professional marks for format, logical structure and use of language appropriate to internal auditor i.e. free from jargon, all comments clearly explained. Tabular format not required. **Specifically: ½ heading, ½ introduction, 1 for whether KPIs are specific to hotels, easy to quantify, sensible etc.**		
	Generally ½ mark per KPI, ½ mark per evidence point. Can increase to 1 mark (for either) if the point is very specific to a hotel business.		
	Ideas list		
	Employees:		
	– Training spend		
	– Absenteeism rates		
	– Employee engagement index		
	Customers		
	– Customer satisfaction rate		
	– Number of complaints		
	– Number of accidents		
	– Repeat business rates		
	Community		
	– Charitable donations		
	– Free use of hotel facilities		
	Environment		
	– Waste recycling		
	– Energy efficient items purchased		
	– Carbon footprint		
		Maximum marks	10
Total			34

18   ROSIE CO *Walk in the footsteps of a top tutor*

Key answer tips

The question features an expanding group of companies. The question followed an examiner's article entitled 'Group Audit Issues,' published in March 2008 and well prepared students who have read the article should not find this question too challenging. Group audit is an important part of the syllabus and candidates should expect to see it examined on a regular basis. The question also combines discussion of due diligence. This should be considered in the context of non-audit review engagements or agreed upon procedures and is linked closely to engagements reporting on prospective financial information.

The highlighted words are key phases that markers are looking for.

(a) **Report to Leo Sabat outlining the purpose and scope of a due diligence assignment.**

Introduction

Before purchasing a company, it is crucial that the purchaser undertake a comprehensive survey of the business in order to avoid any operational or financial surprises post-acquisition. Due diligence can simply be seen as 'fact finding', and as a way to minimise the risk of making a bad investment. This report provides a summary of the purpose of due diligence and also contrasts the scope of a due diligence assignment with the scope of an audit of financial statements.

Purpose of due diligence

Information gathering

Investigative due diligence is the process by which information is gathered about a target company, for the purpose of ensuring that the acquirer has full knowledge of the operations, financial performance and position, legal and tax situation, as well as general commercial background. Essentially the aim is to uncover any 'skeletons in the closet' and therefore to reveal any potential problem areas before a decision regarding the acquisition is made.

For example, Maxwell Co may have taken out debt finance. It is crucial for the acquirer to understand the terms of any debt covenant attached to such finance, and to know if there is a history of Maxwell Co defaulting on payment to the provider of that finance. This information is unlikely to be available unless a detailed due diligence investigation is carried out.

Verification of specific management representations

Additionally, the vendor may make representations to the potential acquirer which it is essential to verify. For example, the vendor of Maxwell Co may state that the company has never been the subject of a tax investigation, or that the company fully complies with all relevant health and safety regulations. Due diligence work should substantiate such claims.

Identification of assets and liabilities

From an accounting perspective it is crucial that all of the assets of the target company are identified. This is important because internally generated intangibles such as customer databases, trademarks, and brand names are unlikely to be recognised in the individual company statement of financial position, but should be identified and valued for the purpose of calculating goodwill on acquisition. As these assets are, by definition, without physical substance, only a detailed due diligence investigation will uncover them.

As well as being important for the goodwill calculation, it is crucial to identify these assets as they represent 'hidden wealth' within the target company, and should be taken into account when negotiating the acquisition price.

Contingent liabilities must also be identified, as the acquirer will need to understand the likelihood of the liability crystallising, and the potential financial consequence. Intangible assets and contingent liabilities are notoriously difficult to value, and the directors of Rosie Co could choose to have the valuation performed as part of the due diligence exercise, as they themselves are likely to lack this expertise.

Operational issues

As discussed above, one of the key benefits of due diligence is to discover problems or risks within the entity. These risks may not necessarily arise in the context of a contingent liability, but could instead be operational issues such as high staff turnover, or the need to renegotiate contract terms with suppliers or customers. The directors of the acquiring company will need to carefully consider whether such matters constitute deal breakers, in which case the investment would be considered too risky and so would not go ahead. Alternatively, the risks uncovered could be useful in negotiation to reduce the consideration paid, or the target company could be asked to provide assurance that these problems will be resolved pre-acquisition.

Acquisition planning

The due diligence investigation will also **assess** the commercial benefits, and potential drawbacks, of the acquisition. On the positive side, it will highlight matters such as expected operational synergies to be created post acquisition, and potential economies of scale to be exploited. On the downside there will be acquisition expenses to pay, costs in terms of reorganisation and possible redundancies, as well as the important but hard to quantify issue of change management. The due diligence provider may be able to offer recommendations as to the best way to integrate the new company into the group.

Management involvement

Due diligence investigations can be performed internally, by the directors of the acquiring company. However, this can be time consuming, and the directors may lack sufficient specialist knowledge to perform the investigation. Therefore one of the purposes of an externally provided due diligence service is to reduce time spent by the directors on fact finding, leaving more time to focus on strategic matters to do with the acquisition and on running the existing group.

Credibility

An external investigation will also provide an independent, impartial view on the situation, enhancing the credibility of the investment decision, and the amount paid for the investment.

Rosie Co has only recently acquired Dylan Co, with a cash outflow of $2.5 million in January 2008. The group may already be short of liquid resources, and may be stretched financially and in terms of change management coping with this new addition to the group. Acquiring Maxwell Co in July 2008 would potentially worsen any cash flow problems and operational issues arising from additions to the group. For this reason it is important for the directors of Rosie Co to carefully consider the benefits and timing of the proposed acquisition of Maxwell Co so soon after the acquisition of Dylan Co. It may be that senior management should concentrate in the short term on the successful integration of Dylan Co into the existing group structure, and leave the due diligence investigation to external providers, or even postpone the investigation and potential acquisition.

Scope of a due diligence assignment compared to an audit

When conducting a due diligence assignment, the scope is focused, as discussed above, primarily on fact finding. This means that although the most recent set of financial statements will form a crucial source of information, the investigation will draw on a much wider range of sources of information, including:

- Several years prior financial statements
- Management accounts
- Profit and cash flow forecasts
- Any business plans recently prepared
- Discussions with management, employees and third parties.

The aim of due diligence, in contrast to an audit, is **NOT** to provide assurance that financial data is free from material misstatement, but rather to provide the acquirer with a set of information that has been reviewed. Consequently no detailed audit procedures will be performed unless there are specific issues which either cause concern, or have been specifically selected for further verification. For example, the acquirer may specifically request that the due diligence exercise provides an estimate of the valuation of acquired intangible assets, as discussed above.

The type of work performed will therefore be quite different, as a due diligence investigation will primarily use analytical procedures as a means of gathering information. Very few, if any substantive procedures would be carried out, unless they had been specifically requested by the client.

Due diligence is much more 'forward looking' than an audit. Much of the time during a due diligence investigation will be spent assessing forecasts and predictions. In comparison audit procedures only tend to cover future events if they are directly relevant to the year end financial statements, for example, contingencies, or going concern problems.

In contrast to an audit, when it is essential to evaluate systems and controls, the due diligence investigation will not conduct detailed testing of the accounting and internal control systems, unless specifically requested to do so.

Conclusion

To summarise, it can be seen that due diligence provides necessary information for the directors of an acquiring company to decide whether to go ahead with an acquisition, the timing of the acquisition, the value of consideration to be paid, and to assess the operational impact of the acquisition. Due diligence should be viewed as a risk management tool, which is crucial when a significant acquisition is being considered. That a due diligence exercise has taken place will increase stakeholder confidence in the acquisition decision.

(b) (i) **Cost of investment on acquisition of Dylan Co**

Matters to consider

According to the schedule provided by the client, the cost of investment comprises three elements. One matter to consider is whether the cost of investment is complete.

Acquisition-related costs such as legal fees must be expensed in the period in which the costs are incurred. These costs cannot be capitalised per IFRS 3 *Business Combinations*, and there is a risk that these costs have been capitalised in error, leading to overstatement of the investment. It appears that no legal or professional fees have been included in the cost of investment (unless included within the heading 'cash consideration'), but this will need to be confirmed.

The cash consideration of $2.5 million is the least problematical component. The only matter to consider is whether the cash has actually been paid. Given that Dylan Co was acquired in the last month of the financial year it is possible that the amount had not been paid before the year end, in which case the amount should be recognised as a current liability on the statement of financial position. However, this seems unlikely given that normally control of an acquired company only passes to the acquirer on cash payment.

IFRS 3 states that the cost of investment should be recognised at fair value, which means that deferred consideration should be discounted to present value at the date of acquisition. If the consideration payable on 31 January 2009 has not been discounted, the cost of investment, and the corresponding liability, will be overstated. It is possible that the impact of discounting the $1.5 million payable one year after acquisition would be immaterial to the financial statements, in which case it would be acceptable to leave the consideration at face value within the cost of investment.

IFRS 3 requires the fair value of any contingent consideration to be accrued. There is a risk that the contingent consideration has not been recognised at all, resulting in the understatement of the investment and corresponding liability (particularly as there is some uncertainty regarding whether this element of the consideration will eventually be paid or not).

Audit evidence

– Agreement of the monetary value and payment dates of the consideration per the client schedule to legal documentation signed by vendor and acquirer.

– Agreement of $2.5 million paid to Rosie Co's bank statement and cash book prior to year end. If payment occurs after year end confirm that a current liability is recognised on the individual company and consolidated statement of financial position.

– Board minutes approving the payment.

– Recomputation of discounting calculations applied to deferred and contingent consideration.

– Agreement that the discount rate used is pre-tax, and reflects current market assessment of the time value of money (e.g. by comparison to Rosie Co's weighted average cost of capital).

– Revenue and profit projections for the period until January 2012, checked for arithmetic accuracy.

– A review of assumptions used in the projections, and agreement that the assumptions are comparable with the auditor's understanding of Dylan Co's business.

Tutorial note

As the scenario states that Chien & Co has audited Dylan Co for several years, it is reasonable to rely on their cumulative knowledge and understanding of the business in auditing the revenue projections.

(ii) Audit procedures on the consolidation schedule of the Rosie Group:

– Agree correct extraction of individual company figures by reference to individual company audited financial statements.

– Cast and cross cast all consolidation schedules.

– Recalculate all consolidation adjustments, including goodwill, elimination of pre acquisition reserves, cancellation of intercompany balances, fair value adjustments and accounting policy adjustments.

– By reference to prior year audited consolidated accounts, agree accounting policies have been consistently applied.

– Agree brought down figures to prior year audited consolidated accounts and audit working papers (e.g. goodwill figures for Timber Co and Ben Co, consolidated reserves).

– Agree that any post acquisition profits consolidated for Dylan Co arose since the date of acquisition by reference to date of control passing per the purchase agreement.

– Reconcile opening and closing group reserves and agree reconciling items to group financial statements.

(c)   A joint audit is when two or more audit firms are jointly responsible for giving the audit opinion. This is very common in a group situation where the principal auditor is appointed jointly with the auditor of a subsidiary to provide a joint opinion on the subsidiary's financial statements. There are several advantages and disadvantages in a joint audit being performed.

Advantages

It can be beneficial in terms of audit efficiency for a joint audit to be conducted, especially in the case of a new subsidiary. In this case, Lead & Co will have built up an understanding of Maxwell Co's business, systems and controls, and financial statement issues. It will be time efficient for the two firms of auditors to work together in order for Chien & Co to build up knowledge of the new subsidiary. This is a key issue, as Chien & Co need to acquire a thorough understanding of the subsidiary in order to assess any risks inherent in the company which could impact on the overall assessment of risk within the group. Lead & Co will be able to provide a good insight into the company, and advise Chien & Co of the key risk areas they have previously identified.

On the practical side, it seems that Maxwell Co is a significant addition to the group, as it is expected to increase operating facilities by 40%. If Chien & Co were appointed as sole auditors to Maxwell Co it may be difficult for the audit firm to provide adequate resources to conduct the audit at the same time as auditing the other group companies. A joint audit will allow sufficient resources to be allocated to the audit of Maxwell Co, assuring the quality of the opinion provided.

If there is a tight deadline, as is common with the audit of subsidiaries, which should be completed before the group audit commences, then having access to two firms' resources should enable the audit to be completed in good time.

The audit should also benefit from an improvement in quality. The two audit firms may have different points of view, and would be able to discuss contentious issues throughout the audit process. In particular, the newly appointed audit team will have a 'fresh pair of eyes' and be able to offer new insight to matters identified. It should be easier to challenge management and therefore ensure that the auditors' position is taken seriously.

Tutorial note

Candidates may have referred to the recent debate over whether joint audits increase competition in the profession. In particular, joint audits have been proposed as a way for 'mid tier' audit firms to break into the market of auditing large companies and groups, which at the moment is monopolised by the 'Big 4'. Although this does not answer the specific question set, credit will be awarded for demonstration of awareness of this topical issue.

Disadvantages

For the client, it is likely to be more expensive to engage two audit firms than to have the audit opinion provided by one firm. From a cost/benefit point of view there is clearly no point in paying twice for one opinion to be provided. Despite the audit workload being shared, both firms will have a high cost for being involved in the audit in terms of senior manager and partner time. These costs will be passed on to the client within the audit fee.

The two audit firms may use very different audit approaches and terminology. This could make it difficult for the audit firms to work closely together, negating some of the efficiency and cost benefits discussed above. Problems could arise in deciding which firm's method to use, for example, to calculate materiality, design and pick samples for audit procedures, or evaluate controls within the accounting system. It may be impossible to reconcile two different methods and one firm's methods may end up dominating the audit process, which then eliminates the benefit of a joint audit being conducted. It could be time consuming to develop a 'joint' audit approach, based on elements of each of the two firms' methodologies, time which obviously would not have been spent if a single firm was providing the audit.

There may be problems for the two audit firms to work together harmoniously. Lead & Co may feel that ultimately they will be replaced by Chien & Co as audit provider, and therefore could be unwilling to offer assistance and help.

Potentially, problems could arise in terms of liability. In the event of litigation, because both firms have provided the audit opinion, it follows that the firms would be jointly liable. The firms could blame each other for any negligence which was discovered, making the litigation process more complex than if a single audit firm had provided the opinion. However, it could be argued that joint liability is not necessarily a drawback, as the firms should both be covered by professional indemnity insurance.

Examiner's comments

Requirement (a) focused on due diligence. Some candidates seemed not to know what a due diligence investigation involves. Although most answers picked up on the fact that due diligence is carried out in a potential business combination (a fact which was itself given in the question scenario), very few answers discussed the fact-finding nature of the investigation, and that the result of the investigation can help the management make a decision about whether or not to go ahead with the acquisition (which again is given in the scenario).

Comparison of the scope with that of an audit was poorly attempted. Most candidates simply discussed 'negative assurance' compared with 'true and fair view', and hardly any answers mentioned the fact that due diligence is forward looking, and makes use of a wide range of information about the company being investigated.

Some answers were extremely disparaging in their attitude towards due diligence investigations, many claiming that it would be 'very expensive and not as good as an audit' and that 'you don't even get an opinion' or 'you can't place any reliance on due diligence'. These comments display a lack of commercial awareness. The tone of the report should have been more positive towards the benefits of such investigations – ultimately the directors in the scenario should be provided with a report which encourages them to initiate due diligence on the target company Maxwell, but many answers would have persuaded the directors even more against it.

Requirement (b) was probably the worst answered section of the whole paper. Most candidates were completely unable to restrict their answer to the cost of investment as shown in the scenario, and most launched into a discussion of the accounting treatment of goodwill. This was NOT asked for. Candidates at this level in their examinations should be able to distinguish between the cost of an investment in the parent company's financial statements, and the goodwill which arises on consolidation. The requirement clearly referred to the financial statements of the parent company and no marks were awarded for irrelevant discussions of net assets acquired or goodwill impairment or amortisation, as these balances only arise in the group consolidated financial statements.

The majority of candidates seemed not to know the contents of a consolidation schedule, or how to audit it. However, those candidates who had read the relevant article in student accountant tended to score well on this requirement. However even these answers were not always tailored to the scenario. For example, some answers described an audit procedure to determine the accuracy of the calculation of the minority interest in the group, despite the scenario clearly stating 'all subsidiaries are wholly owned.' Making irrelevant comments not only wastes time in the exam, but also detracts from the overall quality of an answer.

Thankfully, **requirement (c)** was well attempted by the majority of candidates. This requirement differentiated clearly between strong and weak candidates.

		ACCA marking scheme	Marks
(a)	(i)	**Report on due diligence – purpose and benefit of investigation** Award up to 2 professional marks for good style of report with clear explanations and logical flow 1–1½ marks per point from ideas list: Introduction Fact finding Verify specific representations Identify and value assets, especially intangibles, and contingencies Tool to aid negotiation of consideration Operational issues identified – staff, suppliers, customers, contracts Consideration of commercial impact – synergies and drawbacks Benefit of external provision – free up management time, independent investigation Enhanced credibility Maximum	10
	(ii)	**Report on due diligence – scope compared to audit of financial statements** ½ mark for identification and 1 mark for explanation: Wider scope – more information sources No detailed testing of transactions/balances – unless specifically agreed No detailed evaluation of internal systems and controls Greater use of analytical procedures, reduced scope for substantive procedures Forward looking Maximum	4
(b)	(i)	**Matters and evidence for cost of investment on acquisition of Dylan Co:** Generally 1 mark per matter and specific audit procedure: Completeness – missing professional fees Agree consideration to legal documentation Agree cash consideration to bank statement Deferred consideration – discounted per IFRS 3 Recalculate (1/2 mark only) Agree reasonable discount factor used Contingent consideration –accrue per IFRS 3 NB: no marks to be awarded for discussion of materiality as scenario states that all figures are material no marks for discussion of goodwill – this is not asked for Maximum	7

(ii)	**Principal audit procedures on consolidation schedule:**		
	Generally 1 mark per specific audit procedure:		
	Agree figures to individual co financial statements		
	Cast and cross cast schedule		
	Agree brought down figures		
	Recalculate consolidation adjustments – award ½ mark for each adjustment clearly identified, max 2 marks		
	Reconcile opening and closing reserves		
	Agree post acquisition reserves consolidated for Dylan Co		
	Maximum	4	

(c)	**Joint audit**		
	1 mark for definition		
	1 mark for each ad and disad – cap at max 3 for each		
	Advantages:		
	Knowledge sharing		
	Increase resource availability		
	Easier to meet tight deadline		
	Improve audit quality		
	New insight of new auditor		
	Current issue – increase competition		
	Disadvantages:		
	Higher cost for client		
	Bureaucracy		
	Difference in audit approach		
	Problems in working together		
	Joint liability		
	Maximum	7	
Total		**32**	

Section 4

ANSWERS TO PRACTICE QUESTIONS – SECTION B

PROFESSIONAL/ETHICAL CONSIDERATIONS AND PRACTICE MANAGEMENT

19   CHESTER & CO   *Walk in the footsteps of a top tutor*

Key answer tips

This was a straightforward ethical and professional issues question and should not pose too many problems. There are three clients to deal with and the mark allocation for each is clearly shown. Make enough points for the marks available and remember to consider the significance of the issues as well as identifying them and explaining them. Safeguards should also be included in your answer.

(a)   **Tetbury Co**

Chester & Co needs to conduct customer due diligence (know your client) procedures to ensure that anti-money laundering requirements are adhered to. This is especially important given the highly regulated nature of Tetbury Co's business. Background checks will need to be made on Juan Stanton and other members of management, and the nature of the business including the sources of income must be fully understood before deciding on accepting the audit appointment.

The competence of the audit firm in relation to the audit of a financial services firm should be evaluated, as it is a relatively specialised area. This is an ethical matter, with IESBA's (IFAC) *Code of Ethics for Professional Accountants* Code stating that a self-interest threat to professional competence and due care is created if the engagement team does not possess, or cannot acquire, the competencies necessary to properly carry out the engagement.

Chester & Co should consider whether it is appropriate to be appointed as auditor to Tetbury Co from an ethical point of view. The IESBA Code states that before accepting a new client relationship, a professional accountant in public practice shall determine whether acceptance would create any threats to compliance with the fundamental principles. Threats to integrity may arise from questionable activities by management of the company or from inappropriate financial reporting.

It appears that Tetbury Co's management may lack integrity due to its past investigation by the financial services authority. Chester & Co should find out more about this matter, for example, reading press reports or contacting the financial services authority for more information.

In addition, the resignation of the previous auditors over a disagreement indicates a possible problem with management's integrity. There may also be ethical issues, for example, management may have intimidated the previous auditors over the financial reporting issue which prompted their resignation.

Chester & Co should request permission to contact the previous audit firm to obtain further information on the reasons behind the resignation, and if there are any other matters which should be considered in deciding whether to take on the audit appointment. It is important that all relevant facts are known before an acceptance decision is made. A threat to professional competence and due care arises where the appointment is accepted without full knowledge of relevant information.

Juan's comment about deficient controls is also a cause for concern, as it indicates that the audit would be high risk. While this alone does not mean that the audit should not be taken on, Chester & Co should consider whether the audit risk can be reduced to an acceptable level, for example, by using an experienced audit team and a substantive audit approach. As part of its client acceptance decision, Chester & Co should consider whether the fee for the audit outweighs the risk involved.

The audit firm could apply a safeguard such as securing Juan's commitment to improve the company's control environment before accepting the client.

Tetbury Co is owner-managed. This means that management comes to rely on the auditor for advice and recommendations and the audit firm could be perceived to be taking on the responsibilities of management. This is especially relevant to Juan's suggestion that the audit firm can provide business advice.

According to the IESBA Code, this situation gives rise to potential self-review and self-interest threats to objectivity. If the audit firm were to assume management responsibilities, then no safeguards can reduce the threat to an acceptable level. However, providing advice and recommendations to assist management in discharging its responsibilities is not assuming a management responsibility.

If the audit appointment is accepted, Chester & Co may wish to obtain written confirmation from management that it acknowledges responsibility for business decisions taken.

(b) **Stratford Co**

The request to attend a meeting with the company's bank can give rise to an advocacy threat to objectivity. IESBA's Code defines an advocacy threat as the threat that a professional accountant will promote a client's or employer's position to the point that the professional accountant's objectivity is compromised. In this case, the managing director may want the audit engagement partner to support a view that Stratford Co will be able to continue as a going concern and that the loan ultimately will be repaid. This means that the audit partner is promoting the client which leads to the creation of an advocacy threat.

In addition, from a legal perspective, the audit firm must be careful not to create the impression that they are in any way guaranteeing the future existence of the company or providing assurance on the draft financial statements. In legal terms, attending the meeting and promoting the interests of the client could create legal 'proximity', which increases the risk of legal action against the auditor in the event of Stratford Co defaulting on any loan provided by the bank.

It may be possible for a partner other than the audit engagement partner to attend the meeting with the bank, which would be a form of safeguard against the ethical threat. Chester & Co's partner responsible for ethics should consider the severity of the threat and whether this, or another safeguard, could reduce the threat to an acceptable level.

There is also an intimidation threat to objectivity caused by the managing director's hint at putting the audit out to tender. IESBA's Code states that an audit firm being threatened with dismissal from a client engagement represents an intimidation threat. The managing director's actions should also lead to questions over his integrity, and the audit firm may wish to consider resigning from the audit if the threat becomes too severe.

Overdue audit fees are a self-interest threat, according to IESBA's Code, which states that a self-interest threat may be created if fees due from an audit client remain unpaid for a long time, especially if a significant part is not paid before the issue of the audit report for the following year. The audit firm should determine the amount of fee that is unpaid, and whether it could be perceived to be a loan made to the client. It may be a relatively insignificant amount, and it may not be long overdue as it relates to work performed less than four months ago, in which case the threat to objectivity is not significant.

(c)   **Banbury Co**

Providing an actuarial valuation service is an example of providing a non-assurance service. According to IESBA's Code, the provision of such services can create threats to objectivity of self-review and self-interest. The self-review threat arises because the defined benefit pension plan on which Chester & Co has been asked to provide a valuation service is included in the statement of financial position, and the audit firm would need to audit the figure which has been generated by a member of the firm. The self-interest threat arises from the fee which would be paid to the firm.

Chester & Co needs to evaluate the significance of the threats and whether safeguards could be used to reduce the threats to an acceptable level. In assessing the self-review threat the following factors should be considered:

- Whether the valuation will have a material effect on the financial statements.
- The extent of the client's involvement in determining and approving the valuation methodology and other significant matters of judgement.
- The availability of established methodologies and professional guidelines.
- For valuations involving standard or established methodologies, the degree of subjectivity inherent in the item. –The reliability and extent of the underlying data.
- The degree of dependence on future events of a nature that could create significant volatility inherent in the amounts involved.
- The extent and clarity of the disclosures in the financial statements.

A key matter to be considered is the materiality of the pension plan to Banbury Co's financial statements. Banbury Co is a listed company, and therefore a public interest entity. The Code states that an audit firm shall not provide valuation services to an audit client which is a public interest entity if the valuations would have a material effect, separately or in the aggregate, on the financial statements on which the firm will express an opinion.

Based on the 2012 financial statements, the pension liability at the year end represented only 0.3% of total assets and was immaterial. Chester & Co should consider whether there are any indications that the pension deficit may have become more significant during the year, which may have caused the balance to become material. In which case the audit firm should not provide the valuation service to Banbury Co.

An actuarial valuation involves significant subjectivity, for example, in determining the appropriate discount rate, and in estimating key variables to be used in the calculations. It is also unlikely that Banbury Co's management will possess sufficient knowledge and experience to have much involvement, if any, in the valuation. However, it may be possible to use safeguards to reduce the threats to an acceptable level.

Examples of such safeguards include:

- Having a professional who was not involved in providing the valuation service review the audit or valuation work performed; or
- Making arrangements so that personnel providing such services do not participate in the audit engagement.

Examiner's comments

This was the most popular of the Section B questions, and was generally well attempted. Three short scenarios were provided, describing a range of situations giving rise to ethical threats and other issues, with the requirement to identify and discuss the ethical and other professional issues raised, and to recommend any actions to be taken by the audit firm for each of the scenarios given. This is a fairly standard type of question for P7, and many candidates performed well, obviously having practiced some past exam questions.

Requirement (a) was for 8 marks, and described a potential new audit client, a small owner-managed company providing financial services. There were several issues that candidates should have spotted in the scenario including a potential lack of integrity of the company's managing director, potential self-interest and self-review threats arising from the provision of non-audit services, threats arising from non-compliance with the regulatory body, and a potential for audit pre-conditions not to be met. The majority of candidates picked up on most of these issues and explained the ethical threats well. There has been a definite improvement in the way that candidates tackle this type of question, and in many cases close to the maximum marks were awarded.

Requirement (b) was for 6 marks, and outlined the situation of an existing client facing going concern problems.

The audit engagement partner had been asked to accompany the managing director to a meeting with the bank where additional finance would be sought, and there were intimidation threats in that the client had threatened to put the audit out for tender, and there were also outstanding fees. Again, candidates generally did well on this requirement, identifying and explaining the correct ethical threats, and on the whole recommending appropriate courses of action. The only problem in some scripts was a focus on the lack of integrity of the managing director, rather than discussing specific ethical threats raised.

Requirement (c) was for 6 marks, and described the situation in which a listed client company had asked the audit firm to perform an actuarial valuation of its pension plan. The audit firm had an appropriately qualified person to perform the work, and as with the other requirements of this question, on the whole this was well attempted. Some answers failed to correctly calculate the materiality of the pension plan to the financial statements, and in some answers the fact that the client was a listed entity was not considered. However most candidates suggested an appropriate course of action in response to the ethical matters identified.

ACCA marking scheme		Marks
(a)	Generally 1 mark for each point identified and discussed: Tetbury Co – Customer due diligence/know your client procedures to be performed – Audit firm's competence to audit a financial services client – Acceptance decision should also include consideration of ethical threats – Management integrity threatened by past investigation by financial services authority – Integrity also threatened by possible inappropriate financial reporting – Management may have intimidated the previous auditors – Contact previous auditors for further information – Controls appear weak leading to high audit risk – Responses to high risk should be considered, e.g. use of experienced audit team – Confirm client's intention to improve controls – Threats to objectivity arise from giving business advice –– perceived as assuming management responsibility – Self-review and self-interest threats created – Safeguard to be put in place, e.g. management acknowledge responsibility for business decisions	
	Maximum	8
(b)	Stratford Co – Advocacy threat created by attending meeting – Legal proximity may be created by attending meeting – Intimidation threat from threat of removal from office – Consider appropriate safeguards – Integrity of the managing director questionable – Overdue fees may represent self-interest threat – But amount may be insignificant and not long overdue	
	Maximum	6
(c)	Banbury Co – Provision of valuation service creates self-review and self-interest threats to objectivity – Service cannot be provided if the pension deficit is material – Calculate and comment on materiality in 2013 financial statements – Other matters to consider including level of subjectivity, lack of informed management (1 mark each) – Safeguards may be used to reduce threat to acceptable level (1 mark each)	
	Maximum	6
Total		20

20 WELLER & CO *Walk in the footsteps of a top tutor*

Key answer tips

This question is split into two parts, with ethical and professional issues being part (b) and part (a) dealing with tendering.

For the tender document you need to identify ways in which you can sell your firm to the client. Try and match the firm with the prospective client from the information in the scenario. Don't just give rote learnt knowledge without applying it to the scenario.

The ethical requirement is split into two parts so take each in turn explaining the issues that would be created by the suggestions and evaluating the significance of them, as well as suggesting any safeguards that could be applied.

(a) **Matters to be included in tender document**

Outline of Weller & Co

A brief outline of the audit firm, including a description of different services offered, and the firm's membership of an international network of audit firms. This should provide comfort to the Plant Group's audit committee that Weller & Co has the capability to audit its overseas subsidiary, and that the audit firm has sufficient resources to conduct the Plant Group audit now and in the future, given the Plant Group's rapid expansion.

Specialisms of Weller & Co

A description of areas of particular audit expertise, focusing on those areas of relevance to the Plant Group, namely the audit firm's telecoms audit department. The tender document should emphasise the audit firm's specialism in auditing this industry sector, which highlights that an experienced audit team can be assembled to provide a high quality audit.

Identify the audit requirements of the Plant Group

An outline of the requirements of the client, including confirmation that Weller & Co would be providing the audit service to each subsidiary, as well as to the parent company, and to the Plant Group. Weller & Co may also wish to include a clarification of the purpose and legal requirements of an audit in the jurisdictions of the components of the Plant Group, as requirements may differ according to geographical location.

Identify any audit-related services that may be required

Due to the Plant Group's listed status, there may be additional work to be performed. For example, depending on the regulatory requirements of the stock exchange on which the Plant Group is listed, there may be additional reporting requirements relevant to corporate governance and internal controls. This should be clarified and included in the tender document to ensure that the audit committee understands any such requirements, and that Weller & Co can provide an all-encompassing service.

Audit approach

A description of the proposed audit approach, outlining the stages of the audit process and the audit methodology used by the firm. Weller & Co may wish to emphasise any aspects of the proposed audit methodology which would be likely to meet the audit committee's requirement of a cost effective audit. The proposed audit approach could involve reliance to some extent on the Plant Group's controls, which are suggested to be good, and the tender document should explain that the audit firm will have to gauge the strength of controls before deciding whether to place any reliance on them.

Deadlines

The audit firm should clarify the timescale to be used for the audit. This is very important, given the audit committee's hope for a quick audit. It would be time pressured for the audit of all components of the Plant Group and of the consolidated financial statements to be completed in two months, especially given the geographical spread of the Plant Group. The audit firm may wish to propose a later deadline, emphasising that it may be impossible to conduct a quality audit in such a short timeframe.

Quality control and ethics

Weller & Co should clarify its adherence to IFAC's *Code of Ethics for Professional Accountants,* and to International Standards on Quality Control. This should provide assurance that the audit firm will provide an unbiased and credible audit report. This may be particularly important, given the recent listing obtained by the Plant Group, and consequential scrutiny of the financial statements and audit report by investors and potential investors.

Fees

The proposed audit fee should be stated, with a breakdown of the main components of the fee. The audit firm may wish to explain that the audit fee is likely to be higher in the first year of auditing the Plant Group, as the firm will need to spend time obtaining business understanding and ensuring there is appropriate documentation of systems and controls. The tender document could explain that the audit is likely to become more cost effective in subsequent years, when the audit firm has gone through a learning curve.

Tutorial note

Credit will also be awarded for alternative comments regarding fees, for example, candidates may suggest that the audit fee will be relatively constant year on year (the reason being that initial costs are not passed on to the client in the first year of providing the audit service).

Additional non-audit services

The audit firm should describe any non-audit services that it may be able to provide, such as tax services or restructuring services, which may be relevant given the rapid expansion of the Plant Group. The provision of such services would have to be considered carefully by the audit firm due to the threat to objectivity that may be created, so the tender document should outline any safeguards that may be used to reduce risks to an acceptable level. This is particularly important, given the listed status of the Plant Group. This part of the tender document may remind the audit committee members that corporate governance requirements may prohibit the audit firm from offering certain non-audit services.

Tutorial note

Credit will be awarded for discussion of other matters that may be included in the tender document, if made relevant to the Plant Group.

(b) **Ethical issues**

Weller & Co must ensure that any efforts to increase the firm's revenue do not create any threats to objectivity and independence.

The suggestion to remunerate partners with a bonus on successful sale of a non-audit service to an audit client creates a potential self-interest threat to objectivity. IFAC's *Code of Ethics for Professional Accountants* states that a self-interest threat is created when a member of the audit team is evaluated on or compensated (remunerated) for selling non-assurance services to that audit client.

The significance of the threat depends on factors such as:

- The proportion of the individual's compensation or performance evaluation that is based on the sale of such services
- The role of the individual on the audit team; and
- Whether promotion decisions are influenced by the sale of such services.

In this case, the fact that the remuneration will be paid to the partner creates a significant threat to objectivity due to their influential position in the audit team. IFAC's Code states that a key audit partner shall not be evaluated on or compensated (remunerated) based on that partner's success in selling non-assurance services to the partner's audit client. Therefore the bonus scheme should not be offered to partners as it creates an unacceptable threat to objectivity.

IFAC's Code does not specifically state that managers should not be evaluated or remunerated for selling services to audit clients. It may be possible in the case of an audit manager having been remunerated for such a sale for safeguards to be put in place to reduce the threat to objectivity to an acceptable level, for example by having a review of the work of the manager in relation to the client. However, it would be more prudent for Weller & Co not to offer the remuneration scheme at all.

The second suggestion, regarding offering an 'extended audit' service to clients, also creates ethical problems. The issue is that providing an internal audit service to an audit client creates a self-review threat to independence, if the firm uses the internal audit work in the course of a subsequent external audit. The self-review threat arises because of the possibility that the audit team will use the results of the internal audit service, without appropriately evaluating those results or exercising the same level of professional skepticism as would be exercised when the internal audit work is performed by individuals who are not members of the firm. An acceptable safeguard would be for the internal audit engagement to be performed by a separate team.

IFAC's Code also states that performing a significant part of the client's internal audit activities increases the possibility that firm personnel providing internal audit services will assume a management responsibility. This threat cannot be reduced to an acceptable level, and IFAC's Code requires that audit personnel shall not assume a management responsibility when providing internal audit services to an audit client. Management responsibility may include, for example, performing procedures that are part of the internal control and taking responsibility for designing, implementing and maintaining internal control.

Accordingly, an audit firm may only provide internal audit services to an audit client where:

- The client designates an appropriate and competent resource, preferably within senior management, to be responsible at all times for internal audit activities and to acknowledge responsibility for designing, implementing, and maintaining internal control
- The client's management or those charged with governance reviews, assesses and approves the scope, risk and frequency of the internal audit services
- The client's management evaluates the adequacy of the internal audit services and the findings resulting from their performance
- The client's management evaluates and determines which recommendations resulting from internal audit services to implement and manages the implementation process; and
- The client's management reports to those charged with governance detail the significant findings and recommendations resulting from the internal audit services.

In the case of an audit client that is a public interest entity, an audit firm shall not provide internal audit services that relate to:

- A significant part of the internal controls over financial reporting
- Financial accounting systems that generate information that is, separately or in the aggregate, significant to the client's accounting records or financial statements on which the firm will express an opinion; or
- Amounts or disclosures that are, separately or in the aggregate, material to the financial statements on which the firm will express an opinion.

Where internal audit services are supplied to an audit client, they should be the subject of a separate engagement letter and billing arrangement, and should also be pre-approved by those charged with governance of the audited entity.

Examiner's comments

This question was marginally the most popular of the optional questions. Requirement (a) focussed on tendering, and provided information in relation to a potential new audit client – a multinational, newly listed group requiring a cost effective audit to a tight deadline. The requirement, for eight marks, was to identify and explain the matters to be included in the tender document.

This was generally well attempted, with a significant minority of answers achieving close to full marks. The best answers went through each of the typical contents of a tender document and related them specifically to the Group in the question, resulting in focussed and well explained answer points. Interestingly these answers were often relatively brief, but still managed to attract a high mark through application of knowledge to the question scenario. The more common areas discussed were the international network, audit specialism, fees and deadline, and the introduction of key members of the potential audit team.

Some answers tended to either be much too brief - sometimes little more than a list of bullet points, or did not answer the question requirement, and instead of explaining matters to be included in a tender document, discussed the matters that may impact client acceptance, such as whether the audit firm has sufficient resources, and whether a fee dependency would be created. Candidates are advised to read question requirements carefully and not to make assumptions about what is being asked for.

Requirement (b) was also for eight marks, and focussed on ethics. Two suggestions had been made to help an audit firm increase its revenue – one was to give managers and partners a financial reward for selling non-audit services to clients, and the other to provide an external audit service to clients. The requirement was to comment on the ethical and professional issues raised by the two suggestions. Answers tended to discuss one of the suggestions reasonably well, but then repeat almost identical points in relation to the second suggestion. There was some overlap given that both involved the provision of a non-audit service to an audit client, but there were enough separate points that could be made to avoid repetition. In relation to the financial incentives for partners and manager selling services to audit clients, hardly any candidates discussed the issue of the significance of the ethical threat depending on seniority and that partners couldn't have the arrangement. Many also discussed the self-interest threat in relation to the audit firm rather than its personnel.

In relation to the extended audit, most answers explained the self-review threat and suggested appropriate safeguards, usually that of separate teams. Fewer discussed the need for extended review procedures or for separate engagement letters and billing arrangements were the internal audit service provided to an audit client.

Fewer still knew the position of the ethical codes in relation to this matter, and there was very little in the way of discussion of the topic as a current issue.

The UK and IRL adapted papers were slightly different in this requirement, as they focussed solely on the extended audit situation and asked for discussion of the how the Auditing Practices Board (APB) has responded to ethical issues raised. Answers on the whole were satisfactory, with candidates appreciating the revision made to APB Ethical Standards in relation to the provision of non-audit services generally, and that robust safeguards are needed in the situations where a non-audit service is provided to an audited entity. Candidates seemed aware that this is a very topical issue and were largely ready to discuss the issue in some detail.

ACCA marking scheme		
		Marks
(a) **Matters to be included in tender document** Up to 1½ marks for each matter identified and explained with relevance to the maximum of 2 marks in total for matters identified only): – Outline of the audit firm including international network – Audit firm specialism in telecoms – Client audit requirements – Outline of audit firm's audit methodology – Deadlines – Discuss provision of audit-related services – Quality control and ethics – Fees – Discuss provision of non-audit services		
	Maximum	6

(b) **Ethical matters**
Up to 1 mark for each relevant comment:
– Explain self-interest threat arising on bonus suggestion
– Significance depends on seniority of person, materiality of compensation
– Partners may not have this arrangement
– Safeguard could be put in place for other audit team members
– Explain self-review threat arising on internal audit service
– Identify impact on professional scepticism
– Explain management threat arising in internal audit service
– Safeguards (1 mark each), e.g. separate team
– Not allowed for public interest clients
– Separate engagement letter/billing arrangements
– Approval of those charged with governance

Maximum | 8

Total | 16

21 RAVEN *Walk in the footsteps of a top tutor*

Key answer tips

There are two clients to deal with in this question with two different issues. The first is a straightforward ethical issue. For the second, there are a range of issues to cover dealing with ethical and professional issues. Take note of the mark allocation and write enough for the marks but no more as this will waste valuable time.

(a) The business venture proposed by Grouse Co's managing director, while potentially lucrative for the audit firm, would create significant threats to objectivity. A financial interest in a joint venture such as the one being proposed is an example of a close business arrangement given in IFAC's *Code of Ethics for Professional Accountants.*

According to the *Code,* a close business relationship between an audit firm and the audit client or its management, which arises from a commercial relationship or common financial interest, may create self-interest or intimidation threats. The audit firm must maintain independence, and the perception of independence will be affected where the audit firm and client are seen to be working together for mutual financial gain.

Unless the financial interest is immaterial and the business relationship is insignificant to the firm and the client or its management, the threat created by the joint venture would be so significant that no safeguards could reduce the threat to objectivity to an acceptable level. Therefore, unless the financial interest is immaterial and the business relationship is insignificant, the business relationship should not be entered into.

There would also be ethical issues raised if Raven & Co were to sell the software packages to audit clients. First, there would be a self-interest threat, as the audit firm would benefit financially from the revenues generated from such sales. Full disclosure would have to be made to clients in order for them to be made aware of the financial benefit that Raven & Co would receive on the sale.

Second, there would be a self-review threat, as when performing the audit, the audit team would be evaluating the accounting software which itself had sold to the audit client, and auditing tax figures generated by the software. It is difficult to see how this threat could be reduced to an acceptable level as the accounting and tax software would be fundamental to the preparation of the financial statements.

Third, by recommending the software to audit clients, it could be perceived that the audit firm is providing a non-audit service by being involved with tax calculations, and providing IT systems services. The provision of non-audit services creates several threats to objectivity, including a perception of taking on management's responsibilities. Risks are heightened for audit clients that are public interest entities, for example, the audit firm should not be involved with tax calculations for such clients according to IFAC's *Code*.

If having considered the ethical threats discussed above, Raven & Co still wishes to pursue the business arrangement, they must cease to act as Grouse Co's auditors with immediate effect. The lost income from the audit fee of Grouse Co should also be taken into account, as it is a 'significant' client of the firm.

The potential commercial benefits of the business venture should be considered carefully, as there may be little demand for the suggested product, especially as many software packages of this type are already on the market. Also, the quality of the software developed should be looked into, as if Raven & Co recommends inferior products they will lose customers and could face bad publicity.

Finally, if Raven & Co decides to go ahead with the joint venture, the partners would need to consider if such a diversification away from the firm's core activity would be advisable. The partners may have little experience in such a business, and it may be better for the firm to concentrate on providing audit and assurance services.

(b)   It appears that a surgeon is carrying out medical procedures without the necessary qualifications. This could clearly lead to serious damage being caused to a patient while undergoing laser eye surgery, and indeed this seems to have already occurred. The medical profession is highly regulated, and it is important for the auditor to consider obligations in the event of any serious breach of laws and regulations relevant to Plover Co.

It is management's responsibility that laws and regulations are followed, and auditors are not expected to prevent or detect non-compliance, especially non-compliances which have limited impact on the financial statements.

ISA 250 *Consideration of Laws and Regulations in an Audit of Financial Statements* provides relevant guidance. It is required that if the auditor becomes aware of a suspected non-compliance, an understanding of the nature of the act and the circumstances in which it occurred should be obtained.

Therefore the auditor should establish whether it is the case that the surgeon is not qualified, possibly through reviewing the personnel file of the surgeon or discussing with the person responsible for recruitment.

The auditor should also discuss the matter with management and/or those charged with governance. It may be that they are unaware of the surgeon's apparent lack of qualifications, or possibly there is an alternative explanation in that the surgeon is qualified to perform laser eye surgery but does not possess a full medical qualification.

The potential impact of the apparent non-compliance should be evaluated. In this case, Plover Co could face further legal action from dissatisfied or injured patients, fines and penalties from the regulatory authorities and its going concern may be in jeopardy if that authority has the power to revoke its operating licence. If these potential effects are considered to be material to the financial statements, legal advice may need to be obtained.

In the event that the surgeon's work is in breach of relevant laws and regulations, management should be encouraged to report the non-compliance to the relevant authority.

If management fail to make such a disclosure, the auditor should consider making the necessary disclosure. However, due to the professional duty to maintain the confidentiality of client information, it is generally not acceptable to disclose client-related matters to external parties.

ACCA's *Code of Ethics and Conduct* provides additional guidance, stating that a member may disclose information which would otherwise be confidential if disclosure can be justified in the public interest. There is no definition of public interest which places members in a difficult position as to whether or not disclosure is justified. Matters such as the gravity of the situation, whether members of the public may be affected, and the possibility and likelihood of repeated non-compliance should be considered.

Determination of where the balance of public interest lies will require very careful consideration and it will often be appropriate to take legal advice before making a decision. The reasons underlying any decision whether or not to disclose should be fully documented.

The fact that a legal claim has been filed against Plover Co means that the audit work on provisions and contingent liabilities should be extended. Further evidence should be obtained regarding the legal correspondence, in particular the amount of the compensation claim. The date of the claim and the date of the medical incident to which it relates should also be ascertained in order to determine whether a provision for the claim should be recognised in accordance with IAS 37 *Provisions, Contingent Liabilities and Contingent Assets,* or whether a note to the financial statements regarding the non-adjusting event should be made.

Tutorial note

Per IAS 37 commencing major litigation arising solely out of events that occurred after the year end is an example of a non-adjusting event after the reporting period.

The audit firm may wish to consider the integrity of the audit client. If the management of Plover Co knowingly allowed an unqualified person to carry out medical procedures then its integrity is questionable, in which case Raven & Co may wish to resign from the audit appointment as soon as possible. This is especially important given the legal claim recently filed against the client, which could result in bad publicity for Plover Co, and possibly by association for Raven & Co.

Examiner's comments

This question provided two short scenarios both of which described an ethical dilemma that had arisen at an audit firm. Candidates were required to identify and discuss the ethical, commercial and other professional issues raised, and to recommend any actions that should take place. This was the most popular of the optional questions.

Part (a) was for 8 marks. The scenario described a situation in which an audit client has approached the audit firm with a business opportunity involving the development and sale of accounting and tax software, with the audit firm's client base being a potential customer base. The audit firm had been invited to jointly develop the business with the audit client. Sound answers here used a logical approach, being prompted by the question requirement to discuss in turn the ethical issues, then commercial issues, then professional issues and leading to a set of recommended actions. There were some sound answers in which the ethical threats to objectivity had been fully evaluated, especially the self-interest and self-review threats. Commercial issues were explored in the better answers, where typically the audit firm's level of skill to develop software was questioned, as well as the issue as to whether the audit firm would want to diversify into this type of business as it may detract from the quality of audit and accounting services they offer to clients.

Weaker answers tended to just list in bullet point format all of the possible threats to objectivity without any real discussion or development of the threats specific to the scenario. Candidates are reminded that the IESBA's Code of Ethics for Professional Accountants provides a framework for the evaluation of threats to objectivity, including the identification of threats, the evaluation of the significance of threats identified, and the use of professional judgement in deciding whether the application of safeguards can reduce threats identified to an acceptable level. The use of this framework is recommended in answering questions of this type.

Part (b) was for 7 marks, and described a situation that had arisen at an audit client whose business involved medical procedures at a private hospital. The audit senior had overheard a comment made by an employee of the hospital which insinuated that the employee was not qualified to perform medical procedures. Most candidates identified that the main issues for the audit firm to consider related to a potential breach of law and regulations by the hospital, and that the audit firm should consider disclosure in the public interest. Most answers identified that confidentiality was in issue, and that the matter should be firstly discussed with those charged with governance.

Some candidates focussed on disciplinary action to be taken against the employee of the hospital, and on the possibility that the hospital's management were somehow colluding with the employee to deliberately breach law and regulations and commit some type of fraud, which missed the point. Weaker answers also failed to consider the financial statement and therefore audit implications of a letter claiming negligence, which could lead to the recognition of a provision or disclosure of a contingent liability, and could potentially have going concern implications. These matters were relevant as the audit was ongoing.

ACCA marking scheme		
		Marks
	For each requirement, generally 1 mark for each matter discussed:	
(a)	**Grouse Co**	
	– Situation is a close business arrangement giving rise to threat to objectivity	
	– Explain self-interest threat	
	– Explain intimidation threat	
	– Only acceptable if financial interest immaterial and relationship insignificant	
	– Sale of software to audit clients would require full disclosure of financial benefit	
	– Sale of software to audit clients creates self-review threat	
	– Sale of software perceived as providing non-audit service	
	– Risks heightened for listed/public interest entities	
	– If enter business arrangement must withdraw from audit of Grouse Co	
	– Commercial consideration – demand for product	
	– Commercial consideration – experience of partners	
	Maximum	8
(b)	**Plover Co**	
	– Potential breach of law and regulations	
	– Further understanding to be obtained	
	– Consider potential impact on financial statements	
	– Discuss with those charged with governance	
	– Management should disclose to relevant regulatory body	
	– Auditor could disclose in public interest	
	– Issues with confidentiality	
	– Take legal advice	
	– Extend audit work in relation to the legal claim	
	– Risk of material misstatement	
	– Consider integrity of audit client	
	Maximum	7
Total		**15**

22 WEXFORD *Walk in the footsteps of a top tutor*

Key answer tips

This question requires consideration of the matters affecting the firm's acceptance decision for a prospective client. The issues are quite easy to see but don't be tempted to just identify points in a bullet point style. Each point will need to be explained as to why the audit firm must consider them.

Part (b) asks for procedures to be performed on opening balance of inventory for a new audit client.

(a)   **Initial audit engagement**

The prior year financial statements have not been audited, and have been prepared by a part-qualified accountant. This leads to a risk of misstatement in the opening balances. If the audit engagement is accepted, procedures should be planned to ensure that the opening balances have been brought forward correctly, and reflect the application of appropriate accounting policies.

Lack of internal controls

The small size of the company and the fact that there is only one person preparing management information relating to the accounts would indicate that internal controls are likely to be weak. For example, there is limited scope for segregation of duties or for authorisation and approval controls. Additionally it seems that Ravi and Rita do not exercise a managerial control over the financial reporting process, as they do not perform a detailed review of the accounts. The lack of internal control procedures may not necessarily mean an increased risk of fraud or error but the auditor should assess the suitability of the systems in place for each specific client's purposes when establishing a client's risk profile.

Preparation of financial statements

The audit firm has been approached to prepare the financial statements as well as provide the audit service. Providing an audit client with bookkeeping or accounting services, including the preparation of the financial statements, provides a self-review threat to objectivity and independence when the firm subsequently audits the financial statements. According to IFAC's *Code of Ethics for Professional Accountants,* for an audit client which is not a public interest client, such as Wexford Co, it is acceptable to provide the bookkeeping or accounting service if appropriate safeguards can reduce the threat to an acceptable level, for example, if the service were provided by individuals who are not part of the audit team. The audit firm must therefore consider if it has sufficient resources to enable this safeguard to be put into place.

The bookkeeping service provided should be of a routine and mechanical nature, to avoid the auditor making judgements about the amounts included in the financial statements. For example, the client should pre-approve journal entries made to the trial balance.

Small businesses may have the problem of very informal accounting systems and completeness of records may be a specific audit risk as the auditors may find it impossible to be sure that they have been given full information.

Statement of cash flows

The client has suggested that a statement of cash flows should not be prepared. This indicates the lack of knowledge and experience that the directors have with regard to financial reporting matters. The fundamental principle of IAS *7 Statement of Cash Flows* is that all entities that prepare financial statements in conformity with IFRS are required to present a statement of cash flows. One of the preconditions for an audit referred to in ISA 210 *Agreeing the Terms of Audit Engagements* that should be present is that management acknowledges and understands its responsibility for the preparation of the financial statements. The matter should be discussed with Ravi and Rita, and only once they have accepted their responsibility for the preparation of the statement of cash flows should the engagement be accepted.

Conflict of interest

The audit firm already provides the audit service to a competitor of Wexford Co, leading to a potential conflict of interest if the audit engagement were accepted. The *Code* identifies a conflict of interest such as providing the audit service to competing entities as a potential threat to objectivity. The significance of the threat should be evaluated, and appropriate safeguards considered, such as disclosing the conflict to all relevant parties, requesting the consent of the two entities involved, and the use of separate engagement teams (also known as the use of Chinese Walls). Other relevant procedures could include the use of confidentiality agreements signed by partners and staff of both audit engagements, and procedures to limit access to information.

Potential limitation on scope

Ravi states that he does not want to allow the auditor access to the board minutes, as they contain confidential information. The auditor has the right of access to all information that is relevant to the preparation of the financial statements, and ISA 210 requires that the auditor shall obtain the agreement of management to provide such information as one of the preconditions affecting audit engagement acceptance. The matter should be discussed with Ravi and Rita. It may be that they are unaware that the auditor should have unrestricted access to company books and records, including the minutes of meetings. They may also be unaware of the auditor's principle of confidentiality. Once these matters have been discussed, the client should be happy to allow access to the board minutes. If, however, there remains a potential limitation on the scope of the auditor's work, the audit engagement should not be accepted.

(b)   ISA 510 *Initial Audit Engagements – Opening Balances* requires certain audit procedures to be carried out in an initial engagement where the prior year financial statements were not audited.

Firstly, it is required that the auditor shall read the most recent financial statements for information relevant to opening balances, including disclosures.

Then the auditor shall obtain sufficient appropriate evidence about whether the opening balances contain misstatements that materially affect the current year's financial statements. This evidence is obtained by firstly determining whether the prior period's closing balances have been correctly brought forward.

The auditor shall also determine whether the opening balances reflect the application of appropriate accounting policies.

Depending on the nature of the opening balances, specific audit procedures are performed to gain specific evidence on those opening balances. Additional procedures would be required if it appears that the opening balances contain misstatements that could materially affect the current period's financial statements.

Finally, the auditor shall obtain sufficient appropriate evidence about whether the accounting policies reflected in the opening balances have been consistently applied in the current period's financial statements, and that any changes in accounting policies have been accounted for and disclosed in accordance with IAS *8 Accounting Policies, Changes in Accounting Estimates and Errors*.

In relation to the opening balance of inventory, the following procedures are recommended:

- Inspection of records of any inventory counts held at the prior period year end, 31 July 2010, to confirm the quantity of items held in inventory agrees to accounting records.

- Observation of an inventory count at the current period year end, 31 July 2011, and reconciliation of closing inventory quantities back to opening inventory quantities.

- Analytical procedures on gross profit margins, comparing the opening and closing gross profit margins year on year for the various types of items held in inventory.

- Verifying the sales value in the current financial year of items held in inventory at 31 July 2010, and comparing the sales value with cost. This should provide evidence that inventory is correctly valued at the lower of cost and net realisable value.

- Inspection of management accounts for evidence of any inventory items written off in the current financial period – this is important for inventory of calendars and diaries which are likely to be obsolete.

- Discussion with management regarding any slow moving items of inventory which were included in opening inventory.

- Analytical procedures such as inventory turnover calculations to highlight slow moving inventory from the opening balance.

Examiner's comments

This was the most popular of the optional Section B questions, probably because 10 of the 18 marks available were related to audit acceptance and ethical issues – both of which are topics which candidates seem to be comfortable with. However, the remaining 8 marks dealt with the requirements of ISA 510 on opening balances, and unfortunately candidates' obvious lack of knowledge of this syllabus area meant that for many this was actually an inadequate choice of question.

Requirement (a) involved a new potential new audit client, and candidates were asked to identify and explain the matters that should be considered in deciding whether to accept the audit appointment. Candidates who had practised previous similar exam questions would have been well prepared, and there were many sound answers. Candidates were comfortable in discussing the specific ethical issues relevant to the scenario including self-review, confidentiality and conflicts of interest, and it was good to see a good number of answers refer to the requirements of ISA 210 on audit preconditions, which had been the subject of a recent Examiner's article.

Some answers were not made specific to the scenario, and discussed general matters such as resourcing, fees and engagement letters. It was interesting to see so many candidates being overly critical of the client's part-qualified accountant, who was often accused of incompetence, lack of integrity, and even fraudulent activities. As all candidates taking this paper are themselves part-qualified accountants maybe a little more insight into this person's role in the client's accounting function would be appropriate.

Requirement (b) dealt with opening balances and was inadequately answered by the majority. Some candidates could explain the audit procedures required by ISA 510, but **few** could recommend more than a couple of specific procedures in relation to the opening balance of inventory as specified in the requirement. Many answers gave procedures for non-current assets, receivables and cash which were not asked for, and many forgot that the company in the question had not been audited before, leading to irrelevant discussion of 'previous auditor's working papers'. Many suggested impossible procedures e.g. 'reperform last year's inventory count' and very few picked up on the major issue of obsolescence given the company's inventory comprise calendars and diaries.

ACCA marking scheme		
		Marks
(a)	**Acceptance issues**	
	Up to 2 marks per matter identified and explained (max 3 marks for identification):	
	– Initial engagement – higher risk	
	– Lack of internal control – higher risk	
	– Non-audit service – ethical issue	
	– Cashflow statement – management lack understanding of responsibility	
	– Conflict of interest – ethical issue	
	– Limitation on scope – precondition not met	
	Maximum	10
(b)	**ISA 510 requirements**	
	1 mark per principal audit procedure (to max 2):	
	– Read prior year financial statements	
	– Determine whether brought forward correctly	
	– Determine whether appropriate accounting policies applied to opening balances	
	– Specific procedures on certain items e.g. if risk of material misstatement	
	– Review for consistency of accounting policies in current period	
	1 mark per procedure specific to opening inventory (to max 6):	
	– Review records of prior year inventory count	
	– Reconcile results of current year inventory count back to opening balances	
	– Analytical procedures on gross profit	
	– Sales value confirmation for items in opening inventory	
	– Discussion with management re any inventory write offs relevant to opening balances	
	– Review of management accounts for any inventory write offs relevant to opening balances	
	– Analytical procedures such as inventory turnover periods	
	Maximum	8
Total		18

23   NEESON & CO   *Walk in the footsteps of a top tutor*

Key answer tips

This question examines a core subject, that of ethical and professional matters. This is a really interesting question, and so it is no wonder it proved a popular choice in the exam. The question includes some more unusual areas of the ethics topic, including obtaining professional work by advertising, and a current issue; compulsory rotation of audit firms.

The key to success in this question is to not just state what the issues are, but explain the issues, i.e. not to just state *what* the unprofessional aspects of the advertisement are in part (a), but explain *why* these aspects of the advertisement are unprofessional. Equally, it is not enough to state whether or not the use of contingent fee is appropriate, you need to explain why this is the case.

Part (b) requires some the application of core knowledge regarding the impact on objectivity of long association with audit clients, and a more topical question regarding compulsory rotation. Although wider reading of current issues will help your understanding of the current issue, a common sense evaluation of the practical implications of compulsory rotation will score well. Approaching the question from a number of different angles, by considering the point of view of the audit client, the auditor, and the users of the financial statements, will help you to develop the required number of points. Make sure you provide sufficient detail in your evaluation.

The highlighted words are key phrases that markers are looking for.

(a)   (i)   Advertising is not prohibited by IFAC's *Code of Ethics for Professional Accountants* or by ACCA's *Code of Ethics and Conduct*. However, the Code states that a professional accountant in public practice should not bring the profession into disrepute when marketing professional services. The professional accountant in public practice should be honest and truthful when advertising services and should not:

- Make exaggerated claims for services offered, qualifications possessed or experience gained.

- Be misleading, either directly or by implication.

- Make disparaging references or unsubstantiated comparisons to the work of another.

In addition to consideration of the above, firms of accountants should also ensure that any advertisements comply with local regulations, such as Advertising Standards Regulations.

Neeson & Co's advertisement begins by claiming that the firm is the largest in the country. The firm has only three offices and 12 partners, and it may be misleading to claim that the firm is the largest in the country. It is also claimed that Neeson & Co is the 'most professional' firm. This claim is impossible to substantiate, and could be misleading, as members of the public may be led to believe that the firm can demonstrate that it is 'better' than its competitors.

The advertisement claims that the firm's services guarantee improved business efficiency. This cannot be guaranteed, so the advertisement is not honest in this respect. In addition, there is a guarantee that the firm will save tax for the client. This also cannot be guaranteed, as each individual client will have different tax issues, and it will only be on detailed investigation of the exact tax affairs of the individual client that tax planning methods leading to savings could be suggested.

In addition, the claims increase the risk that the firm is exposed to litigation claims, as clients that engage Neeson & Co and do not see improvements in business efficiency or reduction in tax may take action against the firm on the grounds of false claims being made in the advertisement.

Second opinions are not prohibited, but it is unusual for clients to seek a second opinion, and extremely uncommon to advertise this service. The advertisement implies that Neeson & Co can offer a 'better' audit opinion than other firms, which is unprofessional and lacking in integrity. The advertisement could also imply that it is common practice for a second opinion to be sought, which is not the case, and is misleading to the public.

Offering an introductory fee would not in itself be prohibited. However, fees should be calculated based on the time that would need to be devoted to an assignment to ensure a quality service was provided. Offering a fee 25% lower than the current auditor is effectively lowballing. Cutting fees by 25% could result in poor quality work being conducted.

(UK SYLLABUS: Ethical Standard 4 (Revised) Fees, remuneration and evaluation policies, litigation, gifts and hospitality does not prescribe that a particular method of calculating audit fees must be used, but the audit fee should be sufficient to allow sufficient staff with an appropriate skill level being assigned to the audit.)

It is also unwise for the firm to offer a reduction in fee when both audit and tax services are provided, as the provision of a non-audit service such as tax planning can create a threat to objectivity of self-review and advocacy, which means that both services cannot be offered to the client without the use of safeguards to reduce the threat to an acceptable level. *(UK SYLLABUS: ES4 requires that audit fees are not influenced or determined by the provision of non-audit services to the audited entity.)*

The advertisement claims that the firm's rates are approved by ACCA. This is a false claim, as ACCA does not monitor or approve the rates charged by firms for their services. The statement implies that ACCA endorses the firm's activities, and takes advantage of using 'ACCA' as a brand, which is unprofessional. This could lead to disciplinary action against the firm or individual partners by ACCA.

(ii)   Although the new partner has experience in the banking sector, and therefore appears to be competent to provide this corporate finance service, there are several problems raised by the suggested service.

The first problem is that by negotiating finance arrangements on behalf of an audit client, Neeson & Co is exposed to an advocacy and self-review threat to objectivity. This threat occurs when the audit firm takes a position on behalf of the client, and promotes the client's interests to a third party. The audit firm could be perceived as taking on a management role, thus compromising independence.

The significance of any threat to objectivity should be evaluated and safeguards applied when necessary to eliminate the threat or reduce it to an acceptable level. Examples of such safeguards include:

- Ensuring that the new partner is not involved in the audit of any clients for which he has provided a corporate finance service.

- Using a professional who was not involved in providing the corporate finance service to advise the audit team on the service and review the accounting treatment, and any financial statement treatment.

The second issue is the contingent fee. A contingent fee arises where the audit firm receives a fee which is dependent on a certain outcome, in this case the outcome being securing finance at a favourable cost of borrowing.

Contingent fees are not allowed for audit engagements, according to IFAC's *Code of Ethics* because of the self-interest threat to objectivity created. The Code argues that for an audit engagement, no safeguards could reduce the threats to an acceptable level.

For non-assurance work performed for an audit client, contingent fees may still create such a significant self-interest threat that safeguards could not reduce the threat to an acceptable level. This would be the case where the contingent fee is material to the provider of the service, or the fee is related to a matter which is material to the financial statements. It is usually inappropriate to accept a contingent fee for non-assurance work that is carried out for an audit client. Neeson & Co should not offer the finance negotiation service to audit clients for these reasons unless the fee received is clearly immaterial to the firm, and the matter is immaterial in the context of the client's financial statements. *(UK SYLLABUS: ES5 (Revised) Non-audit services provided to audit clients states that the audit firm should not provide corporate finance services for an audit client where the fees are on a contingent basis, and the engagement fees are material to the audit firm.)*

However, contingent fees could be used for corporate finance services offered to Neeson & Co's non-audit clients. A self-interest threat may still arise, and the firm should consider the significance of any threat by reference to the nature of the engagement, the range of possible fees and the basis for determining the fee.

If Neeson & Co goes ahead with offering this service to non-audit clients, safeguards should be considered, such as:

- An advance written agreement with the client as to the basis of remuneration.

- Ensuring that the partner providing the corporate finance service is not involved with other work for the same client.

(b) (i) It is not uncommon for firms to act as auditor for a client for a number of years. However, the *Code (UK SYLLABUS: and ES 3 (Revised) Long association with the audit engagement)* argues that using the same senior personnel on an assurance engagement over a long period of time may create a familiarity and self-interest threat. The significance of the threat will depend upon factors such as:

- The length of time that the individual has been a member of the assurance team.

- The role of the individual on the assurance team.

- The structure of the firm.
- The nature of the assurance engagement.
- Whether the client's management team has changed.
- Whether the nature, complexity of the client's accounting and reporting issues have changed.

The problem of long association is that a familiarity threat to objectivity is created. The senior personnel risk losing their professional scepticism, and may cease to challenge the client on significant matters. A close relationship will be built up between the senior audit personnel and senior members of the client's management team, so the auditors become too sympathetic to the interests of the client.

The Code requires that for public interest clients, the key audit partner should be rotated after a pre-determined period of seven years, as a means to safeguard against the familiarity threat. After such time, the key audit partner shall not be a member of the engagement team or be a key audit partner for the client for two years. During that period, the individual shall not participate in the audit of the entity, provide quality control for the engagement, consult with the engagement team or the client regarding technical or industry-specific issues, transactions or events or otherwise directly influence the outcome of the engagement.

(UK SYLLABUS: In the UK, ES 3 contains similar guidance on the period of time for which the audit engagement partner may act for the client. However, ES 3's rules are more stringent, in that an audit engagement partner may only act for five years before rotation for a listed client. For a non-listed client, after an engagement partner has acted for ten years, careful consideration should be given as to whether there is any impairment of objectivity and independence.)

(ii)   The main argument in favour of compulsory rotation of audit firms is that it should work to eliminate the familiarity threat. By not only rotating the key partner, but the entire audit firm, it is argued that the auditor's independence is not compromised, and that this adds credibility to auditors' reports and to the profession as a whole.

It can also be argued that clients would benefit from a 'fresh pair of eyes' after a number of years. A new audit firm can offer different insights from a fresh point of view.

However, there are significant disadvantages to compulsory rotation of the audit firm. Firstly, from the audit firm's perspective, there will be a loss of fee income when forced to resign as auditor. Also, the firm may be unwilling to make investments that may increase the quality or efficiency of a particular audit (for example, investing in bespoke audit software for a client), as the rewards would only be in the short-term.

Audit effectiveness depends upon the audit firm's accumulated knowledge of, and long-term experience with, the client's operations and financial reporting issues. Compulsory rotation undermines this accumulation of knowledge and experience. Audit problems are more likely to occur when the audit firm lacks this base. In the first few years auditors will know less about the client company and its management, and will be in a weaker position in making judgements about reporting issues. This severely detracts from the quality of the audit, and creates higher levels of risk exposure for the firm.

Compulsory rotation of audit firms increases audit costs and creates significant practical problems. With each rotation, a new audit team must be brought up to speed on the client's operations and reporting issues, involving significant management time. Systems will need to be documented and evaluated. The increase in costs is likely to be passed onto the client in the form of a higher audit fee.

Finally, from the client's perspective, as well as facing increased audit fees and a potential loss of audit quality, the periodic rotation of audit provider could be disruptive to the business.

On balance, it would seem that the disadvantages to both the audit firm and the client would outweigh the perceived benefits of compulsory rotation. The best safeguard to reduce familiarity threat is partner rotation, which allows the audit firm to continue in office, but avoids close relationships being built up.

[Postscript: New regulations require compulsory tendering of audits rather than compulsory rotation of audit firms.]

Examiner's comments

Requirement (a) (i) asked candidates to critically evaluate a proposed advertisement to be placed in a national newspaper, for 8 marks. This was probably the best answered requirement of the whole paper, with many achieving a clear pass, and quite a few maximum marks were awarded. The few unsatisfactory answers tended to simply repeat extracts from the advertisement and say 'this is unprofessional'.

Requirement (a) (ii) asked candidates to evaluate whether a corporate finance service could be offered to clients, for 5 marks. This was not well answered. While most candidates could state obvious issues, like whether one person would be enough to provide the service, unfortunately very few clearly distinguished between audit and non-audit clients, which was a key issue, as the scenario clearly stated that only one third of the audit firm's clients were audit clients. Few dealt with the issue of the contingent fee in enough detail, with answers usually saying that it was 'unprofessional' but not elaborating further.

Requirement (b) dealt with the ethical problems raised by long association of audit firms and their clients. For 7 marks, candidates were asked to explain the ethical threats, and to evaluate the advantages and disadvantages of compulsory firm rotation. On the whole, this was well answered. Most candidates could identify and explain to some extent the various ethical threats posed by long association, with the familiarity threat being the most common to be discussed. The advantages and disadvantages were often dealt with reasonably well, though a lot of answers were just bullet point lists with no real evaluation provided at all. For many candidates this was the last requirement attempted, so the brevity of answers was probably linked to time management in the exam.

		ACCA marking scheme		
				Marks
(a)	(i)	**Evaluation of advertisement**		
		Generally 1 mark per comment		
		• Advertising not prohibited but must follow ACCA guidelines		
		• Cannot be misleading/exaggerated claims		
		• Exaggerated claim re size		
		• Unprofessional claim re 'most professional'		
		• Cannot guarantee improvements/tax saving		
		• Second opinions		
		• Introductory fee		
		• Audit and non-audit services		8
		• Fees not approved by ACCA		
		• Improper reference to ACCA		
	(ii)	**Corporate finance**		
		Generally 1 mark per comment explained:		
		• Partner is competent		
		• Advocacy threat		
		• Self-review threat		5
		• Identify contingent fee		
		• Contingent fee not appropriate for audit clients		
		• Contingent fee allowed for non-audit client with safeguards		
		• Safeguards should be in place (examples)		
			Maximum	13
(b)	(i)	**Long association threat**		3
		Generally 1 mark per comment		
		• Familiarity threat (½ mark only)		
		• Threat more significant for senior personnel		
		• Level of threat depends on various factors		
		• Lose scepticism		
		• Code requires partner rotation for listed clients		
	(ii)	**Compulsory firm rotation**		
		Generally 1 mark per comment		
		• Eliminates familiarity threat		
		• Fresh pair of eyes for audit client		
		• Loss of fee income		
		• Unwilling to invest – lower quality audit		
		• Loss of cumulative knowledge – lower quality audit		4
		• Increase in cost and audit fee		
		• Disruption to client		
			Maximum	7
Total				**20**

24   CARTER & CO *Walk in the footsteps of a top tutor*

Key answer tips

This question is a typical 'ethics/professional issues' question. To plan your answer remember that such questions can be subdivided into the following categories:

– Ethics (code of ethics + threats): use the standard language, e.g. familiarity, self-interest etc.

– Quality control: ISQC 1 e.g. leadership, human resources. This also includes engagement planning (i.e. risk assessment).

– Practice management: e.g. staffing.

– Legal issues: e.g. money laundering, negligence, ISA 250, ISA 240.

By considering all of these areas when planning your answer (rather than the typical response that goes no further than ethics) you should be able to draft a suitable, relevant response.

The highlighted words are key phases that markers are looking for.

(a)   The provision of a valuation service is an example of providing a non-audit service. *(UK SYLLABUS: Guidance on this type of situation is provided in Ethical Standard 5 (Revised) Non-audit Services Provided to Audit Clients.)* The key issue is that if an audit firm provides a valuation service for an item which will be included in the financial statements, a self-review threat arises. The self review threat exists because the audit firm will be auditing a balance on which they have themselves placed a valuation.

The significance of the risk depends on the level of materiality of the item in the financial statements. According to IFAC's *Code of Ethics for Professional Accountants*, if the valuation service involves the valuation of matters material to the financial statements, and the valuation involves a significant degree of subjectivity, the self-review threat created could not be reduced to an acceptable level by the application of any safeguards. If this were the case, the audit firm should not provide the valuation service. Alternatively, if the valuation service were provided, the firm should resign from providing the audit service.

Carter & Co must assess the degree of risk in valuing Fernwood Co's pension liability. If the amount is immaterial to the financial statements, or does not involve a significant degree of subjectivity, the valuation service can be provided, as long as safeguards are put in place, for example:

• Using separate personnel for the valuation service and the audit.

• Performing a second partner review.

• Confirming that the client understands the valuation method and the assumptions used.

The valuation of the pension balance recognised is likely to involve many judgments and assumptions, and so is likely to be a subjective exercise. It is, therefore, most likely that Carter & Co will assess the situation as creating a significant self-review threat which safeguards cannot reduce to an acceptable level, in which case the valuation service should not be provided as well as carrying out the audit.

If Carter & Co were to provide the valuation service, either because the self-review threat is assessed as low, or if they were to resign as auditor, then the firm should carefully consider whether it possesses sufficient skills and expertise to perform the valuation. This is a specialist area, and the firm would have to ensure that it could perform the work competently.

(b) Allocation of staff to an audit team should be the decision of the audit firm, and should not be influenced by the wishes of the client. This point should be made clear to the finance director of Hall Co.

Staff should be allocated to an audit team based on the needs of the audit. The team should comprise staff with a mix of skills, experience and technical knowledge as appropriate to the size and complexity of the audit, as well as logistical issues such as location and deadlines. Introducing an audit senior with no previous experience of the client may lead to ineffective leadership of the team, and could jeopardise the quality of the audit.

On the other hand, working on a new audit client will provide Kia with more experience and broaden her knowledge and expertise.

A further issue is that Kia is a relative of the financial controller of Hall Co. A family or personal relationship between a member of the audit team, and an officer or employee of the audit client can create threats to objectivity. *(UK SYLLABUS: Guidance on how the audit firm should consider the impact of close relationships on the audit is provided in Ethical Standard 2 (Revised) Financial, Business, Employment and Personal Relationships.)* The threats that arise are as follows:

- Familiarity – Kia may fail to approach the audit with professional scepticism.
- Intimidation – the financial controller may be able to exert influence on Kia, for example, influence her conclusions on work performed.
- Self-interest – Kia may be unwilling to challenge the financial controller about accounting matters for fear of causing problems for her relative.

The degree of threat depends on the level of seniority of the close family member. Where they are in a position to exert direct and significant influence over the financial statements then the threat is significant. In this case, Kia's relative is the financial controller, so is clearly in an influential position. Kia herself is also in a position of some influence over the audit, as she would take the position of audit senior, therefore responsible for the day-to-day supervision and direction of the junior members of the audit team.

The most appropriate course of action would be that Kia is not assigned to the audit of Hall Co, and the reasons for this should be explained to the client.

(c) Usually documents such as title deeds or insurance certificates are held by the audit client or their legal advisors, but sometimes the service is provided by the accountant.

IFAC's *Code of Ethics* states that before agreeing to provide custodial services the audit firm must ensure that there is no legal restriction on holding assets (documents or tangible assets). A self-interest threat could be created as the firm receives a financial benefit from the fee charged for the service. There could also be a perception of a close relationship between the audit firm and the client, if one is holding documents on behalf of the other.

Appropriate safeguards to be used in the provision of a custodial service could include:

- Keeping the assets physically separate from the firm's assets.
- Keep orderly documentation regarding the assets and be ready to account for them to the client when requested.
- Establishing strict controls over the physical access to the assets.
- Comply with all relevant laws and regulations in respect of holding the assets.

Confidentiality is also a key issue – the firm must ensure that documentation is only ever given to the client who has entrusted it to the firm. The reasons for this should be explained to the client.

In addition Carter & Co should be vigilant in respect of money laundering regulations. The tangible assets could be purchased using the proceeds of crime and as such the firm in custody of such assets would be deemed to be involved with money laundering. The firm would have to be careful to ascertain the true origin of the assets in its custody.

A further issue is whether Carter & Co has sufficient security to offer such a service. Employment of extra security methods such as alarm systems, CCTV, security personnel could be costly, and might outweigh the revenue to be derived from offering the service.

In order to maximise the revenue from this source of income, Carter & Co could be tempted to concentrate on holding high value assets, as these would attract the highest fees. This would compound the security issues discussed above, especially the cost of extra insurance.

If there were ever a problem such as documents held in custody being lost or damaged, or assets being stolen, then Carter & Co would face major reputational risk. This risk, along with the extra costs discussed above, may outweigh the relatively small revenue stream that the custodial service would provide.

(d)   Referral fees are not prohibited by IFAC's *Code of Ethics*. However, a self-interest threat can arise, as the audit firm gains a financial benefit for each audit client referred to Gates Co. The referrals and payments to Carter & Co can continue, provided that safeguards are put in place. Safeguards could include:

- Disclosing to the audit clients that a referral fee arrangement exists, and the details of the arrangement.
- Receiving confirmation from the audit clients that they are aware of the referral arrangement.
- Receiving confirmation from all employees of Carter & Co that they have no interest in Gates Co.

Carter & Co may also wish to consider the quality of the training provided by Gates Co. Any problems with the training provided could cause damage to the reputation of Carter & Co.

		Marks
ACCA marking scheme		

ACCA marking scheme

		Marks
(a)	**Fernwood Co**	
	Up to 1 mark each point explained:	
	• Self-review threat (restrict to ½ mark if not explained)	
	• Provision of non-audit service	
	• Threat depends on materiality of balance	
	• Threat depends on degree of subjectivity	
	• Can only perform if low threat and safeguards used	
	• Pension very subjective so unlikely to be able to reduce threat to acceptable level	
	• If service provided assess skills and competence	
	Maximum	6
(b)	**Hall Co**	
	Up to 1 mark each point explained:	
	• Client should not influence selection of audit team members	
	• Kia has no experience of the client	
	• Family relationship creates 3 objectivity threats (1 mark each explained)	
	• Degree of threat depends on level of influence	
	• Do not assign Kia to the team	
	• Explain to client why Kia has not been assigned	
	Maximum	6
(c)	**Collier Co**	
	Up to 1 mark each point explained:	
	• Custodial service creates self-interest threat (½ mark if not explained)	
	• Safeguards to be applied (1 mark each)	
	• Money laundering consideration	
	• Consider security of offices/availability of space	
	• Extra costs e.g. insurance, more security measures	
	• Reputational risk in event of theft/loss of documents	
	• Confidentiality issues	
	Maximum	5
(d)	**Gates Co**	
	Up to 1 mark each point explained:	
	• Referral fee creates self-interest threat	
	• Allowed if safeguards in place (1 mark for each safeguard)	
	• Consider quality of service provided	
	Maximum	3
Total		**20**

25   CLIFDEN & CO *Walk in the footsteps of a top tutor*

Key answer tips

This question is a typical 'ethics/professional issues' question. To plan your answer remember that such questions can be subdivided into the following categories:

– Ethics (code of ethics + threats): use the standard language, e.g. familiarity, self-interest etc.

– Quality control: ISQC 1 e.g. leadership, human resources.

– Practice management: e.g. staffing.

– Legal issues: e.g. money laundering, negligence, ISA 250.

By considering all of these areas when planning your answer (rather than the typical response that goes no further than ethics) you should be able to draft a suitable, relevant response.

The highlighted words are key phases that markers are looking for.

(a)   'Professional competence and due care' is one of the fundamental ethical principles explained as part of the Code's conceptual framework. It can be broken down into two parts.

Professional competence

This is the concept that a professional accountant must firstly achieve, and subsequently maintain, professional knowledge and skill at the level required to ensure that clients and employers receive competent professional service.

Attaining professional knowledge is achieved through a mixture of formal professional qualifications, informal 'on the job' training, and gaining experience of a range of professional work.

Maintaining professional knowledge is achieved through continuing professional development. Professional accountants must ensure that they are aware of changes in technical fields such as tax, auditing and financial reporting regulations where relevant to the services they offer to clients. Professional accountants should also be aware of general business developments, such as the use of information technology and e-commerce.

Due care

This is about acting diligently in accordance with applicable technical and professional standards when providing professional services. This means applying knowledge to a specific situation with careful consideration, minimising the chance of mistakes being made. It may also include wider issues such as making sure that there is enough time to complete work with due care, and ensuring that staff fully understand the objectives of the work they are being asked to perform.

Compliance with the principle

Attaining and maintaining professional knowledge:

Firms can offer training on specific technical matters, such as changes to tax rules or new auditing guidelines, which could be provided by senior members of the firm or by external consultants.

Due care

Adherence to quality control guidelines will help ensure that due care has been exercised. Particularly the supervision and review of work by more senior members of the firm should act as a preventative and detective control to pick up any errors made in the work.

In addition, formal and informal staff appraisals will enable members of staff to raise issues with more senior members of staff, e.g. if they felt under too much time pressure to properly perform their work.

Reviews carried out as part of the normal audit cycle (i.e. hot and cold reviews) can also help to identify where the firm may need to organise more training for staff.

(i) **Contaminated plastic**

It appears that Headford Co has manufactured items which potentially could cause serious injury or even death to a consumer. Management has decided not to recall any products, which indicates a lack of integrity. Even though the risk of this happening has been assessed by management as low, it would still be ethically appropriate to announce the problem, allowing customers to return potentially harmful products. As the contaminated products were made in the last few months of the year, it is likely that some items are still held within the company as finished goods inventory, in which case the company is putting its own staff and assets in danger. The assertion by management that the risk of injury is 'remote' should be treated with scepticism.

Firstly, Clifden & Co should encourage the management of Headford Co to make the problem with the products public. There will obviously be reluctance to do this due to the bad publicity which would follow, especially in the competitive industry in which the company operates. However, the auditors should try to explain to management the reasons why they should disclose, and hopefully convince management that this would be the ethically correct way to proceed.

If management still refuse to make a disclosure, Clifden & Co should consider their duty of confidentiality. Both IFAC and ACCA recognise that information discovered while performing a professional engagement must not be disclosed without proper and specific authority to do so, or unless there is a legal or professional right or duty to disclose. Clifden & Co may wish to disclose the problem with the products in order to protect consumers from potential harm, but the firm must be very careful to consider whether it has a right or duty to disclose.

ISA 250 *Consideration of Laws and Regulations in an Audit of Financial Statements* may provide relevant guidance in this situation. It is likely that children's toys have to be tested in accordance with industry regulations for health and safety. If this is the case, and the use of contaminated ingredients constitutes a non-compliance with law and regulations, the auditor may have a statutory right or duty to report the situation to the appropriate authority.

In the absence of any industry regulation, Clifden & Co should consider if there is a necessary disclosure in the public interest. This is a difficult and subjective decision, as there is little guidance on what is meant by 'public interest', and it would be hard to decide who exactly the recipient of any disclosure should be. In deciding whether to disclose in the public interest, the auditors should consider the reasons for the client's unwillingness to disclose, the seriousness of the matter i.e. the likelihood of harm being caused, and the relevant laws and regulations.

Before making any disclosure, Clifden & Co should obtain information and evidence regarding the contamination, e.g. how the contamination was discovered (did a toy actually explode?) and whether anyone has been injured. If this is the case there could be legal claims already in progress against the company.

As a last resort, Clifden & Co could consider resigning from the audit. The firm could then circularise a 'statement of circumstances' which would describe the reason for the resignation, including details of the faulty products and the lack of management integrity.

In addition Clifden & Co should establish whether the supplier of the plastic raw material has been contacted, the number of products sold which are contaminated and the number still held as inventory (if any). There could be a counter-claim against the supplier in which case the likelihood of the claim's success should be evaluated.

Finally, the situation also impacts on the audit procedures that are currently being planned. Any contaminated inventory still held by Headford Co should be written off, and provisions may be necessary for refunds of returned products, if the matter becomes known. The financial statements may need to contain disclosures relating to contingent liabilities, or provisions may need to be recognised in respect of damages claimed by customers in the event of any injuries occurring and legal action being taken against Headford Co. The audit should be planned to devote sufficient time to these matters.

Careful consideration should be made relating to the year end inventory count. Assuming that some finished goods containing the contaminated ingredient are still held by the company, audit staff may be in danger of injury when they attend the inventory count. Headford Co must take action to make the items safe or to keep them in safe conditions i.e. at low temperatures, in order to prevent any injuries to its own staff and members of the audit team.

(ii)   The invitation to audit Cong Co gives rise to a potential conflict of interest between the interests of different clients. There is nothing ethically wrong in having clients operating in the same industry, in fact it is normal for firms of auditors to specialise in the provision of services to companies in a particular industry or market sector, some of whom are likely to be competitors. However, acting for two competing companies can give rise to ethical threats, particularly objectivity and confidentiality. It could be perceived that impartial, objective services and advice cannot be offered to a company where the audit firm also audits a competitor, and the client companies may be concerned that commercially sensitive information may become known to its competitor if the same audit firm is used by both companies.

The main safeguard in this situation is disclosure of the potential conflict to all parties concerned. Therefore, the audit of Cong Co should only be accepted if both companies have been informed of the services provided by Clifden & Co which could be perceived to create a conflict of interest, and if both companies give their consent to act.

If the audit of both companies goes ahead, then the following extra safeguards should be considered:

- The use of separate engagement teams.
- Issuing clear guidelines to the teams on issues of security and confidentiality.
- The use of confidentiality agreements by audit team members.
- Regular review of the safeguards by an independent partner.

In addition, as Cong Co is a large company, an evaluation as to whether Clifden & Co has sufficient resources to carry out both audits using totally separate teams should take place.

It is quite likely that one or both of the companies do not give consent, in which case Clifden & Co will have to decide which company to act for. As Cong Co is a larger company, it is probable that a higher audit fee would be charged. In addition the provision of non-audit services can be lucrative, indicating that it may be commercially advantageous to take on Cong Co as a client, and to resign from the audit of Headford Co.

Examiner's comments

Requirement (a): A proportion of candidates achieved maximum marks for this requirement. However, some candidates could not provide a definition other than 'professional competence is when you are competent to take on a professional engagement,' which does not add anything to what is given in the question. Due care was sometimes badly defined as just 'being careful' or 'acting professionally'.

Requirement (bi): Answers were often limited to brief comments relating to the client's lack of integrity, and the need to recall the products. Many candidates missed the main point of the requirement, which was the auditor's duty to maintain confidentiality, and whether that duty should be breached in this case in the public interest. Only the better answers considered the potential impact of the events on the financial statements, or the risk to the audit firm's reputation if the situation is not handled appropriately. A significant proportion of candidates focused entirely on what the client should do in this situation, (better quality control, sack the production manager, put a notice in newspapers, etc), and hardly mentioned the ethical and professional issues relating to the audit firm at all.

Requirement (b) (ii): Although the mark allocation for (b) (ii) was lower than that of (bi), most candidates wrote the same, or more, for (b) (ii). Answers here tended to be adequate, with the majority of answers identifying the problems of conflict of interest, and client confidentiality, and most were able to recommend appropriate actions such as full disclosure of the situation, and the use of separate teams for the two clients if the audit appointment were to go ahead.

ACCA marking scheme			
			Marks
(a)		**Competence and due care** Generally 1 mark per comment from ideas list: – Definition of competence, including for example: – Competence – attain knowledge/skills – Competence – maintain knowledge/skills – Definition of due care – To ensure compliance: training, study support, QC, appraisals etc Max 2 marks for definition/explanation of term and 2 marks for compliance comments		
		Maximum marks	4
(b)	(i)	**Plastic ingredients** Generally 1 mark per comment/specific action to be taken: – Management lack integrity – Encourage management to disclose – Auditors' duty of confidentiality – Consider law and regs – Consider disclosure in public interest – Legal advice – Consider resignation – Seek evidence/information re matter – Impact on financial statements and planned audit procedures – Safety of staff attending inventory count		
		Maximum marks	8
	(ii)	**Audit of Cong Co** Generally 1 mark per comment/specific action to be taken: – Conflict of interest – explain why – Disclosure to both parties – Other safeguards (1 mark each max 3) – Commercial considerations		
		Maximum marks	5
Total			17

ASSIGNMENTS

26 DASSET *Walk in the footsteps of a top tutor*

Key answer tips

This question is a typical 'matters and evidence' question. First, consider the materiality of the issue. Next discuss the appropriate accounting treatment and give the risks of material misstatement that would arise if the appropriate treatment is not followed. Finally, the evidence is what you would expect to be recorded on the audit file when you come to review it. Be specific about the evidence, don't say 'supporting documentation', suggest what that documentation would be and what it would show.

Part (b) tests your knowledge of the auditor responsibilities in respect of laws and regulations.

(a) (i) **Matters which should be considered**

Impairment of assets

The mine is recognised at $10 million, representing 5.7% of Dasset Co's total assets, and therefore material to the statement of financial position.

The accident has caused part of the mine to be unusable, which indicates that it has become impaired. IAS 36 *Impairment of Assets* requires that an impairment review should be conducted when there is an indicator of potential impairment, and therefore management should have performed a review to determine the recoverable amount of the mine.

If an impairment review has not been performed, and no adjustment made to the carrying value of the mine, then assets will be overstated and profit overstated. One-third of the mine has become unusable, so presumably no future economic benefit can be derived. Therefore one-third of the mine's carrying value may need to be written off. This amounts to $3.33 million, which represents 18.5% of profit for the year. The impairment write off is therefore potentially material to Dasset Co's profit.

A worst case scenario is that more than one-third of the mine is unusable. It could be that all of the mine is unsafe and should be shut down, or possibly the National Coal Mining Authority may withdraw its licence to operate the Ledge Hill mine completely. In either case, the impairment loss would then be extended to the full value of the mine, increasing the materiality of the matter in the financial statements.

Another consideration is there is likely to be some equipment which is contained in the tunnels which can no longer be used. It is possible that some of the equipment may be recovered, but it is likely that a large proportion of it will have to be abandoned and written off, increasing the impairment loss to be recognised.

IAS 1 *Presentation of Financial Statements* requires that an individual item of income or expense which is material should be disclosed separately, and gives impairment of assets as an example of a circumstance which may warrant separate disclosure.

The costs which have been incurred and are yet to be incurred to ensure the safety of the mine in the future should be treated as capital expenditure at the time when the costs are incurred. There may also be costs to be incurred in making the unusable tunnels safe, for example, entrances may need to be blocked up. These costs should be expensed as they do not relate to future economic benefit and so do not meet the definition of an asset. There is a risk that capital and revenue expenses have not been appropriately classified.

Provisions and liabilities

There has also been damage caused to some properties situated above the mine. Dasset Co may need to recognise a provision in relation to any costs it will suffer in relation to repairing or demolishing the properties. According to IAS 37 *Provisions, Contingent Liabilities and Contingent Assets*, a provision should be recognised if there is a present obligation as a result of a past event, a probable outflow of economic benefits, and a reliable estimate can be made.

It seems that the criteria have been met, as the accident happened before the year end and gives rise to an obligating event. Dasset Co is meeting all expenses of the residents who have been relocated, so the company appears to be acknowledging responsibility for the accident and its impact on the residential properties. The damage to the properties will result in a cash outflow for the company whether they have to be demolished or repaired, and the expert should be able to provide a reliable estimate of the amount. Therefore a provision should be recognised.

The company may suffer further cash outflows as a result of the accident, and consideration needs to be made as to whether a provision or a contingent liability should be recognised in respect of them. The residents may claim further damages against the company, for example, for stress caused by the accident, and compensation for expenses such as damaged fixtures in the properties.

There may also be a clause in the National Coal Mining Authority's operating licence that imposes a fine on Dasset Co in the event of any non-compliance with health and safety regulations. Any such fines may need to be recognised as provisions or contingent liabilities.

There is a risk that provisions have not been appropriately recognised, leading to overstated profit and understated liabilities, or that contingent liabilities have not been disclosed accurately and completely.

Going concern

Finally, there may be going concern implications as a result of the accident. Given the relatively small size of the Ledge Hill mine in relation to the company's total operations, it is unlikely that the closure of part, or even all, of the mine alone would create a risk to going concern. However, bad publicity may create difficult trading conditions, and a claim for high compensation from the group of local residents could place the company's cash flow under strain. If these factors cast significant doubt on going concern, then disclosures should be made in the note to the financial statements.

The very worst case scenario is that the National Coal Mining Authority could withdraw the company's operating licence completely, which would cause it to cease operational existence. This may be very unlikely; however, it would mean that the financial statements should be prepared on the break up basis.

(ii) **Evidence**

- A copy of the operating license, reviewed for conditions relating to health and safety and for potential fines and penalties which may be imposed in the event of non-compliance.

- A written representation from management on their intention (or not) to bring the non-compliance to the attention of the National Coal Mining Authority.

- A copy of board minutes where the accident has been discussed to identify the rationale behind the non-disclosure.

- A copy of reports issued by engineers or other mining specialists confirming the extent of the damage caused to the mine by the accident.

- Any quotes obtained for work to be performed to make the mine safe and for blocking off entrances to abandoned tunnels.

- Confirmation that the undamaged portion of the mine is operational, e.g. from reviewing a specialist's report.

- A copy of the surveyor's report on the residential properties, reviewed for the expert's opinion as to whether they should be demolished.

- A review of correspondence entered into with the local residents who have been relocated, to confirm the obligation the company has committed to in respect of their relocation.

- Copies of legal correspondence, reviewed for any further claims made by local residents.

- A review of the Ledge Hill Mine accident book, for confirmation that no one was injured in the accident.

- A copy of management's impairment review, if any, evaluated to ensure that assumptions are reasonable and in line with auditor's understanding of the situation.

- Confirmation that impairment losses have been recognised as an operating expense.

- A review of draft disclosure notes to the financial statements where provisions and contingent liabilities have been discussed.

- A review of cash flow and profit forecasts, forming a view on the overall going concern status of the company.

(b) **Responsibilities to report the accident to the National Coal Mining Authority**

Dasset Co operates in a highly regulated industry, and Burton & Co must consider the requirements of ISA 250 *Consideration of Laws and Regulations in an Audit of Financial Statements*. ISA 250 states that it is management's responsibility to ensure that operations are conducted in accordance with relevant law and regulations. The auditor is expected to obtain a general understanding of the applicable legal and regulatory framework and how the entity is complying with that framework.

In this case, there is a suspected non-compliance with the National Coal Mining Authority's health and safety requirements. The accident may have been caused by using unsafe equipment or mining methods which failed to meet the authority's strict requirements. Management has not informed the authority, which may be for a genuine belief that there is no need to make a report concerning the accident, or it could be because management has something to hide and does not wish to come under the scrutiny of the authority.

ISA 250 states that if the auditor becomes aware of information concerning an instance of non-compliance or suspected non-compliance with laws and regulations, the auditor shall obtain an understanding of the nature of the act and the circumstances in which it has occurred; and further information to evaluate the possible effect on the financial statements. Further audit procedures will therefore be necessary.

The matter should be discussed with those charged with governance, as required by ISA 250. Management should be asked to confirm the reason why the authority has not been notified of the accident, and a written representation should be obtained. Burton & Co may wish to encourage management to disclose the accident to the authority.

ISA 250 also requires that the auditor shall determine whether the auditor has a responsibility to report the identified or suspected non-compliance to parties outside the entity. Burton & Co needs to carefully evaluate their legal responsibility to report suspected non-compliance to the National Coal Mining Authority, and legal advice should be obtained to determine the appropriate course of action.

Confidentiality is an issue, as usually auditors cannot disclose information obtained during the audit to external parties without the prior consent of the client. However, this may be overridden in some cases by legislation or court order. In certain cases, disclosure in the public interest may warrant disclosure without client consent. Again, legal advice would be helpful here, to determine whether confidentiality can or should be breached and a report made to the National Coal Mining Authority if management fail to do so.

Examiner's comments

This question was in the style of a typical paper P7 question, set in the completion stage of an audit, and asking candidates to comment on the matters to be considered, and he audit evidence that should be expected to be found during the review of the audit files by the audit manager. Candidates were well prepared for this type of question, and it was quite well attempted by many of the candidates that chose to attempt it.

The scenario involved a coal mining company operating in a highly regulated environment. An accident had caused significant damage to one of the coal mines, and to residential properties located in its vicinity.

Management had agreed to meet some expenses relating to the relocation of the residents of these properties, which may need to be demolished in the future. Management had not reported the accident to the relevant regulatory body.

Requirement (a) contained standard wording for a P7 requirement, asking candidates to comment on the matters to consider and the evidence that should be found in undertaking a review of the audit file and financial statements of the company. This was for 14 marks. There were some sound answers, and most candidates correctly identified impairment, provisions or contingent liabilities and going concern as the main financial reporting issues

---

that would need to be considered, and in many cases a range of appropriate evidence was described. The impairment issue tended to be the best dealt with, and as usual in this type of question, many candidates demonstrated a sound understanding of the financial reporting matter and linked this to its audit implication.

Where candidates performed less well on this requirement, it tended to be due to focussing on just one issue, and dealing only very briefly with other matters. For example, in some scripts almost all of the answer discussed the impairment issue, and only touched on provisions in a couple of sentences at the end. In other scripts the answer focussed on going concern, almost to the exclusion of any other matters. Some answers displayed a lack of basic financial accounting knowledge, suggesting that lost revenue should be provided for. Audit evidence points were often not well described, sometimes too vague to be awarded any credit, for example 'discuss with management' or 'check properly disclosed' – these comments are pretty meaningless as they have no context.

Requirement (b) was for 6 marks and focussed on management's decision not to report the accident to the regulatory authority, asking candidates to discuss the auditor's responsibilities and recommend the actions to be taken by the auditor in respect of this. Most candidates had some basic knowledge of the auditor's responsibilities in relation to law and regulations, but not many could capitalise on this knowledge through proper application to the scenario. Many answers focussed on the lack of integrity of management, suggesting that the audit firm should 'discipline' the company's directors. Other answers were too vague and brief, simply suggesting without any real explanation that the auditor should report to the regulatory authority, and failing to justify this as an appropriate course of action. The best answers applied the requirements of the relevant ISA to the scenario and recommended an appropriate course of action.

ACCA marking scheme		
		Marks
(a) (i) **Matters to consider**		
Generally 1 mark for each point made:		
– Materiality of the mine to total assets		
– Impairment review should have been performed		
– Materiality of the potential write off to profit		
– No impairment write off means overstated assets and profit		
– Potentially all of the mine may be closed down and therefore impaired		
– Equipment which cannot be recovered also needs to be written off		
– Improvements to health and safety should be capitalised		
– Costs of abandoning/sealing up collapsed tunnels should be expensed		
– Separate presentation of material impairment costs in financial statements		
– Provision to be recognised for damaged properties/relocation costs of local residents		
– Further claims may be made leading to provisions or contingent liabilities		
– The authority may impose fine/penalty – provision or contingent liability		
– Going concern disclosure if accident creates significant doubt		
– Break up basis if authority withdraw company's operating licence		

(ii) **Evidence**

- Operating licence, reviewed for conditions relating to health and safety and for potential fines and penalties
- A written representation from management on their intention (or not) to bring the non-compliance to the attention of the National Coal Mining Authority
- A copy of board minutes where the accident has been discussed to identify the rationale behind the non-disclosure
- A copy of reports issued by engineers or other mining specialists confirming the extent of the damage caused to the mine by the accident
- Any quotes obtained for work to be performed to make the mine safe and for blocking off entrances to abandoned tunnel
- Confirmation, possibly by physical inspection, that the undamaged portion of the mine is operational
- A copy of the surveyor's report on the residential properties, reviewed for the expert's opinion as to whether they should be demolished
- A review of correspondence entered into with the local residents who have been relocated, to confirm the obligation the company has committed to in respect of their relocation
- Copies of legal correspondence, reviewed for any further claims made by local residents
- A review of the Ledge Hill Mine accident book, for confirmation that no one was injured in the accident
- A copy of management's impairment review, if any, evaluated to ensure that assumptions are reasonable and in line with auditor's understanding of the situation
- Confirmation that impairment losses have been recognised as an operating expense
- A review of draft disclosure notes to the financial statements where provisions and contingent liabilities have been discussed
- A review of cash flow and profit forecasts, forming a view on the overall going concern status of the company

| | Maximum | 14 |

(b) Responsibilities, actions and reporting

Generally 1 mark for each point discussed:

- Management responsible for compliance with laws and regulations
- Auditor responsible for understanding applicable laws and regulations
- There is suspected non-compliance with laws and regulations and further procedures are necessary
- Matter should be discussed with those charged with governance
- Need to understand reason for non-disclosure/encourage management to disclose
- The need for external reporting should be evaluated
- Legal advice may be sought
- Confidentiality may be overridden in some circumstances

| | Maximum | 6 |

| Total | | 20 |

27   SETTER STORES *Walk in the footsteps of a top tutor*

Key answer tips

This question is a typical 'matters and evidence' question. First, consider the materiality of the issue. Next discuss the appropriate accounting treatment and give the risks of material misstatement that would arise if the appropriate treatment is not followed. Finally, the evidence is what you would expect to be recorded on the audit file when you come to review it. Be specific about the evidence, don't say 'supporting documentation', suggest what that documentation would be and what it would show.

There are three issues to deal with and each has its own mark allocation therefore deal with both matters and evidence for the assets held for sale, then the sale and leaseback, and finally the licence. Don't deal with matters for all three then evidence for all three as the structure of the requirements and the mark allocations indicates that this is not appropriate presentation.

(a)   **Matters**

The properties classified as assets held for sale are material to the financial statements as the year-end carrying value of $24 million represent 8% of total assets. The amount written off the assets' value at the date of classification as held for sale of $2 million represents less than 1% of revenue and 4.2% of profit before tax, which on both measures is immaterial to the statement of profit or loss and other comprehensive income.

Assets can only be classified as held for sale if the conditions referred to in IFRS 5 *Non-current Assets Held for Sale and Discontinued Operations* are met. The conditions include the following:

- Management is committed to a plan to sell
- The assets are available for immediate sale
- An active programme to locate a buyer is initiated
- The sale is highly probable, within 12 months of classification as held for sale (subject to limited exceptions)
- The asset is being actively marketed for sale at a sales price reasonable in relation to its fair value
- Actions required to complete the plan indicate that it is unlikely that the plan will be significantly changed or withdrawn.

There is a risk that the assets have been inappropriately classified if the above conditions have not been met.

IFRS 5 requires that at classification as held for sale, assets are measured at the lower of carrying value and fair value less costs to sell. This appears to have been correctly accounted for when classification occurred in October 2012. Though not specifically required by IFRS 5, an impairment review should take place at 31 January 2013, to ensure that there is no further impairment of the properties to be recognised at the year end. If an impairment review has not taken place, the assets may be misstated in value.

The assets should not be depreciated after being classified as held for sale, therefore audit procedures should confirm that depreciation has ceased from October 2012.

Disclosure is needed in the notes to the financial statements to include a description of the non-current assets classified as held for sale, a description of the facts and circumstances of the sale and its expected timing, and a quantification of the impairment loss and where in the statement of profit or loss and other comprehensive income it is recognised.

Evidence

- A copy of the board minute at which the disposal of the properties was agreed by management.
- Details of the active programme in place to locate a buyer, for example, instructions given to real estate agency, marketing literature.
- A copy of any minutes of meetings held with prospective purchasers of any of the properties, or copies of correspondence with them.
- Written representation from management on the opinion that the assets will be sold before October 2013.
- Subsequent events review, including a review of post year-end board minutes and a review of significant cash transactions, to confirm if any properties are sold in the period after the year end.
- Details of any impairment review conducted by management on the properties at 31 January 2013.
- A copy of the client's depreciation calculations, to confirm that depreciation was charged up to October 2012 but not subsequent to the reclassification of the assets as held for sale.

(b) **Matters**

The sale and leaseback arrangement relates to an asset with a carrying value of $27 million, which represents 9% of total assets and is material to the statement of financial position. The fair value of the asset (cash proceeds) is also material at 12.3% of total assets.

It appears appropriate to classify the leaseback as a finance lease, as Setter Stores Co retains the risk exposure of the asset and the economic benefit of using the asset for the remainder of its useful life.

The accounting treatment for a sale and leaseback transaction should follow the requirements of IAS 17 *Leases*. Where the leaseback is a finance lease, the substance of the transaction is a financing arrangement in which the lessee, in this case Setter Stores Co, never disposes of the risks and rewards of the asset, and so should not recognise a profit or loss on the disposal and should continue to recognise the asset in the statement of financial position. Any apparent profit, being the difference between the fair value of the asset and its carrying value, should be deferred and amortised over the lease term. The asset should be re-measured to fair value.

Setter Stores Co appears to have incorrectly accounted for the transaction. The following entry should have been made on the disposal and leaseback of the property complex:

DR Cash	$37 million
CR Property, plant and equipment	$27 million
CR Deferred income	$10 million

And the asset and finance lease liability should be recognised at fair value:

DR Property, plant and equipment $37 million
CR Obligations under finance lease $37 million

Therefore property, plant and equipment is understated by $10 million and deferred income also understated by $10 million. $10 million represents 3.3% of total assets and is material. An adjustment should be made and, if not, the audit firm should consider the implication for the auditor's opinion, which may be qualified on the grounds of material misstatement.

In forthcoming accounting periods, depreciation should be calculated based on the $37 million carrying value of the asset allocated over the remaining life of the property of 20 years, and the deferred income should be amortised over the same period.

Evidence

- A copy of the lease, signed by the lessor, and a review of its major clauses to confirm that risk and reward remains with Setter Stores Co, and that the arrangement is a finance leaseback.

- A copy of insurance documents stating that Setter Stores Co is responsible for insuring the asset.

- Physical inspection of the property complex to confirm it is being used by Setter Stores Co.

- Confirmation of the fair value of the property complex, possibly using an auditor's expert.

- Agreement of the $37 million cash proceeds to bank statement and cash book.

- A schedule showing the adjustment required in the financial statements.

- Minutes of a discussion with management regarding the accounting treatment and including an auditor's request to amend the financial statements.

(c)   **Matters**

The amount capitalised as an intangible asset is material to the statement of financial position, representing 5% of total assets.

According to IAS 38 *Intangible Assets*, an intangible asset is recognised in the financial statements if it meets the definition of an intangible asset, if it is probable that future economic benefits will flow to the reporting entity, and if its cost can be reliably measured. It would seem appropriate that the licence is recognised as an intangible asset as it has been purchased as a separable asset without physical substance and has a reliable cost. Management should be able to demonstrate the economic benefit that has been, or is expected to be, derived from the licence.

As the licence has a fixed term of five years, it should be amortised over that period. However, it appears that amortisation has not been charged, as the amount recognised at the year end is the original cost of the licence. Amortisation of $1.25 million (15 million/5 years × 5/12) should have been charged from 1 September to the year end. This amount represents less than 1% of revenue and only 2.6% of profit before tax, and is not considered material to profit.

Evidence

- A copy of the distribution licence, confirming the five-year period of the licence, and the cost of $15 million.

- Agreement of the cash paid to the bank statement and the cash book.

- Minutes of a discussion with management regarding the apparent non-amortisation of the licence, including any reasons given for the non-amortisation.

- Sales records in relation to the soft drink and also forecast sales, to determine the future economic benefit to be derived from the licence.

Examiner's comments

This question was in the style of a typical paper P7 question, set in the completion stage of an audit, and asking candidates to comment on the matters to be considered, and the audit evidence that should be expected to be found during the review of the audit files by the audit manager. Candidates were well prepared for this type of question, and as one of the optional questions, it was attempted by the majority of candidates.

Requirement (a) was for 8 marks, and described a number of properties that had been classified as held for sale.

Information was given on the carrying value and fair value less cost to sell of the properties. Most answers were satisfactory, largely because candidates were confident in explaining the relevant financial reporting requirements and applying them to the brief scenario. The audit evidence points were sometimes a little vague, for example 'discuss with management', 'get management representation', 'review board minutes', and only a limited amount of credit could be awarded for such comments. However generally there has been an improvement in how well audit evidence is described, and in many cases the answer points were sufficiently precise and detailed.

Requirement (b) was for 7 marks, and described how a sale and leaseback arrangement had been accounted for.

Answers to this requirement varied greatly in quality. Some were excellent, covering all of the financial reporting issues and correctly concluding that the treatment was wrong and if not corrected could have implications for the auditor's opinion. In these cases, evidence points also tended to be adequate, focussing on the classification of the lease as a finance lease, and on the adjustment necessary in the financial statements. Inadequate answers discussed the points in a vague manner, seeming uncertain as to whether the accounting treatment was correct or not, resulting in the suggestion of a few unclear audit evidence points.

Requirement (c) was for 5 marks. This concerned a distribution licence that had been purchased and capitalised as an intangible asset and held at cost. Candidates seemed more comfortable with this requirement than the preceding one, and many discussed all of the relevant financial reporting concerns, particularly in relation to amortisation and/or impairment of the asset. Audit evidence points were usually provided and reasonably well explained.

Overall this was a well attempted question by many. I would however point out that candidates need to think carefully when calculating and commenting on materiality. Most candidates calculated the materiality of every figure given in the question in relation to each of revenue, profit before tax and assets. By this stage in their studies candidates should appreciate that often this is not necessary, for example there is little relevance in calculating an item of expense in relation to assets. Performing all of these calculations must take some time, and the irrelevant calculations will not generate marks.

		Marks
	ACCA marking scheme	

(a) **Assets held for sale**
Generally 1 mark for each matter considered/evidence point explained:
Matters:
- Assets held for sale are material (calculation)
- Amount written off is not material (calculation)
- Conditions required to classify assets as held for sale (up to 2 marks)
- Re-measurement at classification appears correct
- Further impairment review may be needed at year end
- Depreciation should not be charged after reclassification
- Disclosure in notes to financial statements

Evidence:
- Board minute at which the disposal of the properties was agreed by management
- Details of the active programme in place to locate a buyer
- A copy of any minutes of meetings held with prospective purchasers of any of the properties
- Written representation from management that the assets will be sold before October 2013
- Subsequent events review
- Confirm depreciation ceased on reclassification
- Details of any impairment review conducted by management

Maximum   8

(b) **Sale and leaseback**
Generally 1 mark for each matter considered/evidence point explained:
Matters:
- Asset is material (calculation)
- On disposal the asset should be re-measured to fair value
- Apparent profit should be deferred and amortised
- Accounting treatment currently not correct
- Discuss materiality of adjustments needed
- Implication for auditor's opinion
- Treatment as a finance lease appears correct

Evidence:
- A copy of the lease to confirm that the arrangement is a finance lease
- Physical inspection of the property complex
- A copy of insurance documents
- Confirmation of the fair value of the property complex, possibly using an auditor's expert
- Agreement of the $37 million cash proceeds to bank statement and cash book
- A schedule showing the adjustment required in the financial statements
- Minutes of a discussion with management regarding the accounting treatment and including an auditor's request to amend the financial statements

Maximum   7

(c)	**Distribution licence**		
	Generally 1 mark for each matter considered/evidence point explained:		
	Matters:		
	• Materiality of the asset (calculation)		
	• Identify event as intangible asset that should be capitalised		
	• Identify that no amortisation has been charged		
	• The non-amortisation is not material		
	Evidence:		
	• A copy of the licence		
	• Agreement of cost to bank statement and cash book		
	• Discussion with management regarding the non-amortisation		
	• Sales records of the soft drink since 1 September 2012		
		Maximum	5
Total			**20**

28 SPANIEL   *Walk in the footsteps of a top tutor*

Key answer tips

Part (a) addresses the issue of auditor liability and whether the audit firm has been negligent due to failure to detect a fraud. Knowledge of the conditions for a negligence claim to succeed and discussion of each of these conditions in turn should help to score the 12 marks.

Part (b) is a discussion question regarding the difficulties auditing financial instruments and the matters to be considered when planning the audit of forward exchange contracts. For the first part, think about the risks associated with financial instruments. For the planning aspects, think about what the auditor does at the planning stage of an audit and why, and apply it to the specific area of financial instruments.

(a) It is not the auditor's primary responsibility to detect fraud. According to ISA 240 *The Auditor's Responsibilities Relating to Fraud in an Audit of Financial Statements*, management is primarily responsible for preventing and detecting fraud. The auditor is required to obtain reasonable assurance that the financial statements are free from material misstatement whether caused by fraud or error.

The total amount estimated to have been stolen in the payroll fraud represents 5.6% of Spaniel Co's assets. If the amount has been stolen consistently over a 12-month period, then $3 million (8/12 × 4.5 million) had been stolen prior to the year end of 31 December 2012. $3 million is material, representing 3.8% of total assets at the year end. Therefore the fraud was material and it could be reasonably expected that it should have been discovered.

However, material misstatements arising due to fraud can be difficult for the auditor to detect. This is because fraud is deliberately hidden by the perpetrators using sophisticated accounting techniques established to conceal the fraudulent activity. False statements may be made to the auditors and documents may have been forged. This means that material frauds could go undetected, even if appropriate procedures have been carried out.

ISA 240 requires that an audit is performed with an attitude of professional scepticism. This may not have been the case. Spaniel Co is a long-standing client, and the audit team may have lost their sceptical attitude. Necessary tests of control on payroll were not carried out because in previous years it had been possible to rely on the client's controls.

It seems that ISAs may not have been adhered to during the audit of Spaniel Co. ISA 330 *The Auditor's Responses to Assessed Risks* requires that the auditor shall design and perform tests of controls to obtain sufficient appropriate audit evidence as to the operating effectiveness of relevant controls if the auditor's assessment of risks of material misstatement at the assertion level includes an expectation that the controls are operating effectively. It can be acceptable for the auditor to use audit evidence from a previous audit about the operating effectiveness of specific controls but only if the auditor confirms that no changes have taken place. The audit partner should explain whether this was the case.

Substantive procedures have not been performed on payroll either. This effectively means that payroll has not been audited.

This leads to a conclusion that the audit firm may have been negligent in conducting the audit. Negligence is a common law concept in which an injured party must prove three things in order to prove that negligence has occurred:

- That the auditor owes a duty of care
- That the duty of care has been breached
- That financial loss has been caused by the negligence.

Looking at these points in turn, Groom & Co owes a duty of care to Spaniel Co, because a contract exists between the two parties. The company represents all the shareholders as a body, and there is an automatic duty of care owed to the shareholders as a body by the auditor.

A breach of duty of care must be proved for a negligence claim against the audit firm to be successful. Duty of care generally means that the audit firm must perform the audit work to a good standard and that relevant legal and professional requirements and principles have been followed. For an audit firm, it is important to be able to demonstrate that ISAs have been adhered to. Unfortunately, it seems that ISAs have been breached and so the audit firm is likely to have been negligent in the audit of payroll.

Tutorial note

Credit will be awarded for references to legal cases as examples of situations where audit firms have been found to have been negligent in performing an audit, such as Re Kingston Cotton Mill.

Finally, a financial loss has been suffered by the audit client, being the amount stolen while the fraud was operating.

In conclusion, Spaniel Co is likely to be able to successfully prove that the audit firm has been negligent in the audit of payroll, and that Groom & Co is liable for some or all of the financial loss suffered.

(b)   **The audit of financial instruments**

There are many reasons why financial instruments are challenging to audit. The instruments themselves, the transactions to which they relate, and the associated risk exposures can be difficult for both management and auditors to understand. If the auditor does not fully understand the financial instrument and its impact on the financial statements, it will be difficult to assess the risk of material misstatement and to detect errors in the accounting treatment and associated disclosures. Even relatively simple financial instruments can be complex to account for.

The specialist nature of many financial instruments means that the auditor may need to rely on an auditor's expert as a source of evidence. In using an expert, the auditor must ensure the objectivity and competence of that expert, and then must evaluate the adequacy of the expert's work, which can be very difficult to do where the focus of the work is so specialist and difficult to understand.

The auditor may also find that there is a lack of evidence in relation to financial instruments, or that evidence tends to come from management. For example, many of the financial reporting requirements in relation to the valuation of financial instruments are based on fair values. Fair values are often based on models which depend on management judgement. Valuations are therefore often subjective and derived from management assumptions which increase the risk of material misstatement.

It is imperative that the auditor retains professional scepticism in the audit of financial instruments, but this may be difficult to do when faced with a complex and subjective transaction or balance for which there is little evidence other than management's judgement.

There may also be control issues relating to financial instruments. Often financial instruments are dealt with by a specialist department and it may be a few individuals who exert significant influence over the financial instruments that are entered into. This specialist department may not be fully integrated into the finance function, leading to the accounting treatment being dealt with outside the normal accounting system. Internal controls may be deficient and there may not be the opportunity for much segregation of duty. However, some companies will have established strong internal controls around financial instruments, leading to a lower risk of material misstatement.

In planning the audit of Bulldog Co's financial instruments, the auditor must first gain an understanding of the relevant accounting and disclosure requirements. For example, the applicable financial reporting standards should be clarified, which are likely to be IFRS 9 *Financial Instruments* and IFRS 7 *Financial Instruments: Disclosures*. These standards can be complex to apply, and the auditor should develop a thorough understanding of how they relate to Bulldog Co's financial instruments.

The auditor must also obtain an understanding of the instruments in which Bulldog Co has invested or to which it is exposed, including the characteristics of the instruments, and gain an understanding of Bulldog Co's reasons for entering into the financial instruments and its policy towards them.

It is important that the resources needed to audit the financial instruments are carefully considered. The competence of members of the audit firm to audit these transactions should be assessed, and it may be that an auditor's expert needs to be engaged. If so, this should be explained to the client. Instructions will have to be drawn up and given to the expert to ensure that the work performed is in line with audit objectives and follows the relevant financial reporting requirements, for example, in relation to valuing the financial instruments.

The audit planning should include obtaining an understanding of the internal control relevant to Bulldog Co's financial instruments, including the involvement, if any, of internal audit. An understanding of how financial instruments are monitored and controlled assists the auditor in determining the nature, timing and extent of audit procedures, for example, whether to perform tests on controls.

Specific consideration should be given to understanding management's method for valuing financial instruments for recognition in the year-end financial statements. The valuation is likely to involve some form of estimate, and ISA 540 *Auditing Accounting Estimates, Including Fair Value Accounting Estimates and Related Disclosures* requires the auditor to obtain an understanding of how management makes accounting estimates and the data on which accounting estimates are based.

Finally, the materiality of the financial instruments should be determined and the significance of the risk exposure associated with them should be assessed.

Examiner's comments

This was the least popular of the section B questions, though for UK and IRL candidates this was less the case.

The question was divided into separate requirements – requirement (a) was for 12 marks and concerned auditor liability, and requirement (b) for 8 marks, focussed on the audit of financial instruments.

Requirement (a) provided a scenario which described that an audit firm had given an unmodified audit opinion on Spaniel Co's financial statements, and that subsequent to the audit report being issued a fraud had been discovered that had been operating during the period covered by the audit report. The scenario also pointed out that the audit firm had not performed audit procedures in relation to the area in which the fraud was occurring, namely payroll. The requirement asked candidates to explain the matters to be considered in determining the audit firm's liability to Spaniel Co in respect of the fraud.

There were some excellent answers to this requirement. The best ones clearly outlined the factors that have to be proven to determine negligence, and applied them methodically to the scenario. The materiality of the fraud was considered, the duty of care owed to the audit client, and the fact that the auditor may not have been exercising professional scepticism during the audit due to the long-standing nature of the audit appointment. It was also appropriate to discuss the responsibilities of management and auditors in relation to fraud, and whether it is appropriate for auditors to rely on the conclusions reached in previous year's audit.

Some answers tended to only provide a rote-learnt description of responsibilities in relation to fraud, and usually failed to reach an appropriate conclusion. With little application to the scenario there is limited scope for marks to be awarded.

Requirement (b) described a different audit client, Bulldog Co, which had expanded overseas and set up a treasury management function dealing with forward exchange contracts. The requirement was to discuss why the audit of financial statements is challenging and explain the matters to be considered in planning the audit of the forward exchange contracts. Answers here were extremely mixed in quality. Satisfactory answers focused on why financial instruments generally are difficult to audit, discussing their complex nature, the changing landscape of financial reporting requirements, the potential for both client and auditor to lack appropriate knowledge and skills, and the frequent need to rely on an expert. In terms of planning the audit, adequate answers focussed on simple matters such as managing resources, obtaining an understanding of the nature of the contracts and the controls in relation to them, and assessing how management value the financial instruments.

Inadequate answers did not include much reference to audit at all, and simply listed out financial reporting rules, with no consideration of audit implications other than saying that financial instruments are complex and subjective.

There were very few references to relevant ISA requirements, and little evidence that the audit of complex matters such as financial instruments had been studied at all, even though it is a topical current issue.

ACCA marking scheme

		Marks
(a)	**Fraud and auditor's liability** Generally up to 2 marks for each point explained:	
	• Not auditor's primary responsibility to detect fraud unless it is material in impact on financial statements	
	• Determine that the payroll fraud would have been material (include calculation)	
	• Reasons why fraud is hard to detect	
	• Audit firm may not have been sufficiently sceptical	
	• Non-adherence to ISAs on controls assessment and evidence obtained	
	• Discuss whether duty of care owed to client	
	• Discuss breach of duty of care	
	• Identify financial loss suffered and firm likely to have been negligent	——
	Maximum	12
(b)	**Audit of financial instruments** Generally up to 1½ marks for each point explained: **Why is audit of financial instruments challenging?**	——
	• Financial reporting requirements complex	
	• Transactions themselves difficult to understand	
	• Lack of evidence and need to rely on management judgement	
	• Auditor may need to rely on expert	
	• May be hard to maintain attitude of scepticism	
	• Internal controls may be deficient	
	Planning implications	
	• Obtain understanding of accounting and disclosure requirements	
	• Obtain understanding of client's financial instruments	
	• Determine resources, i.e. skills needed and need for an auditor's expert	
	• Consider internal controls including internal audit	
	• Determine materiality of financial instruments	
	• Understand management's method for valuing financial instruments	——
	Maximum	8
		——
Total		**20**
		——

29   KOBAIN   *Walk in the footsteps of a top tutor*

Key answer tips

Part (a) provides a statement for discussion. An approach to take for discussion questions such as this is to think of reasons why you agree with the statement and reasons why you might disagree with it. Different circumstances might mean that you agree in some cases but not in others. This helps to provide a balanced view point

Part (b) is a typical 'matters and evidence' question. First, consider the materiality of the issue. Next discuss the appropriate accounting treatment and give the risks of material misstatement that would arise if the appropriate treatment is not followed. Finally, the evidence is what you would expect to be recorded on the audit file when you come to review it. Be specific about the evidence, don't say 'supporting documentation', suggest what that documentation would be and what it would show.

Part (c) is becoming a common question covering forensic investigations. Apply your auditing skills for gathering evidence to the circumstances of the fraud to quantify the amount.

(a)   **Revenue recognition**

A high risk area of the audit is one where a risk of material misstatement is considered likely to occur. A factor giving rise to a risk of material misstatement is subjectivity, and in many companies revenue recognition is a subjective matter. For example, a company which provides services to customers over a long period of time will need to gauge the proportion of a service that has been provided during the financial year in order to determine the amount of revenue that may be recognised, possibly on a percentage basis. This determination involves judgement, therefore increasing the risk of material misstatement.

Revenue recognition can also be a complex issue. For example, companies that engage in multiple-element sales transactions need to carefully consider when revenue can be recognised, for instance if selling a tangible item such as a computer, and selling as part of the transaction a two-year warranty, the company needs to separate the sale of the goods and the sale of the services and recognise the revenue on each element of the transaction separately.

Tutorial note

Credit will be awarded for any relevant examples of situations where revenue recognition is subjective or complex, for example, when accounting for long-term contracts, linked transactions, sale and leaseback or bill and hold arrangements.

The method of sale and the absence of appropriate internal controls can also mean that revenue has a high risk of material misstatement. For example, when sales are made over a company's website, there is a risk that the website is not fully integrated into the accounting system, creating a risk that sales go unrecorded.

A further issue relevant to revenue recognition is that of fraud. ISA 240 *The Auditor's Responsibilities Relating to Fraud in an Audit of Financial Statements* states that the auditor should use a presumption that there are risks of fraud in revenue recognition. Revenue recognition is regarded as an accounting area at risk of fraudulent financial reporting, as it is susceptible to management bias and earnings management techniques. Revenue can be overstated through premature revenue recognition or recording fictitious revenues, or revenue can be understated by improperly shifting revenues to a later period.

There may be issues particular to the company, which mean that deliberate manipulation of revenue is more likely, for example, in a listed company where performance is measured in terms of year-on-year revenue or profit growth.

In a company where a substantial proportion of revenues are generated through cash sales, there is a high risk of unrecorded sales transactions. There is a high risk of theft of cash received from customers which would then lead to unrecorded sales and understated revenue in the financial statements.

However, it is not the case that all companies' revenue recognition is complex, subjective or at particular risk of fraud. Smaller companies with a single source of revenue based on simple transactions do not have a particularly high risk of material misstatement in relation to revenue. ISA 240 requires that where the presumption of a risk of material misstatement due to fraud relating to revenue is not applicable in the circumstances of an audit, the reasons must be fully documented.

(b)   **Matters**

The accounting treatment of the revenue and inventory in respect of the consignment stock arrangement with vendors must be carefully considered, as there is a risk that Kobain Co is recognising revenue too early. According to IAS 18 *Revenue,* the sale of goods criteria should be applied to a transaction to determine whether the company has the right to recognise revenue. Crucially, revenue may only be recognised when the entity has transferred to the buyer the significant risks and rewards of ownership of the goods and where the entity does not retain managerial involvement or control over the goods.

Kobain Co's accounting policy is to recognise revenue at the point of delivery of goods to the external vendors. But it seems that Kobain Co retains managerial involvement, as Kobain Co retains the ability to change the selling price of the jewellery. Also Kobain Co retains risk exposure, as any goods unsold after nine months, i.e. goods which are slow moving and potentially obsolete, are returned.

Therefore revenue is being recognised too early, and is overstated by $4 million. Profit is overstated by $1 million; this is material to profit at 6.7% of profit before tax. Inventory is understated by $3 million as it should remain recognised in the statement of financial position, until such time as risk and reward have passed. The inventory held at external vendors is material to the statement of financial position at 5.5% of assets.

If an adjustment is not made to the financial statements, the auditor should consider the implication for the auditor's opinion, which would be qualified due to material misstatement.

There may also be adjustments necessary to the opening balances, which were not audited by Beck & Co. Any correction to opening balances should be accounted for retrospectively according to IAS *8 Accounting Policies, Changes in Accounting Estimates and Errors.*

Evidence

- Copies of sales contracts with key external vendors and confirmation of the terms of the contract.

- A review of the terms of the contract and conclusion whether the terms indicate that Kobain Co retains risk exposure and managerial involvement with the goods.

- Results of a direct circularisation to selected external vendors for inventory balances at the year end to ensure the accuracy of the records.

- Enquiries as to the proportion of goods which are usually returned from the external vendors to form an understanding of potential levels of obsolete goods.

- Results of auditor's test counts of inventory at a selection of vendors' premises to ensure the existence of goods held on consignment.

- Client's working papers from the previous year end, such as analysis of receivables and external vendors' inventory reports at 31 July 2011, reviewed to determine the potential adjustment required to opening balances.

(c)   **Recommended forensic investigation procedures:**

- Obtain all of the claims for sales commission submitted by the sales representative since January 2012 and total the amount of these claims.

- Reconcile the sales per the sales commission claims to the sales ledger control account.

- Agree all sales per the sales commission claims to customer-signed orders and to other supporting documentation confirming that window installation took place, for example, customer-signed agreement of work carried out.

- Obtain external confirmations from customers of the amount they paid for the work carried out.

- Perform analytical procedures to compare the weekly or monthly sales generated by the sales representative committing the fraud to other sales representatives.

Examiner's comments

This question looked at revenue recognition from the auditor's point of view, beginning with a short discussion requirement, and moving onto two requirements based on short scenarios. This was marginally the least popular of the optional questions in Section B.

Requirement (a) was for six marks, and asked candidates to discuss the statement 'Revenue recognition should always be approached as a high risk area of the audit'. Answers here were mixed. There were some sound answers, which often used simple examples to illustrate the type of situation where revenue recognition is complex or subjective, with construction contracts, hotel deposits and the provision of services being common and pertinent examples. Many answers also referred to the problems of manipulation of revenue, and again sound answers illustrated the point with a simple example, the most common being pressure on management to maximise revenue or profit. It was however unsatisfactory that so few answers referred to ISA 240 *The Auditor's Responsibilities Relating to Fraud in an Audit of Financial Statements*, specifically the fact that ISA 240 requires the auditor to use a presumption that there are risks of fraud in revenue recognition.

Most answers focussed exclusively on the risk factors. Only a minority of answers tried to provide a counter argument that some companies with good controls and simple revenue generating streams as being low risk. It is important in a discussion question to consider both sides of an argument.

Requirement (b) was for six marks and asked candidates to comment on the matters that should be considered and the evidence they should expect to find when reviewing the audit file in respect of a consignment stock arrangement, which was described in the scenario. This was generally well attempted, with most candidates discussing that the accounting treatment adopted for the consignment stock arrangement was not compliant with IAS 18 Revenue, and correctly determining the impact on profit, and the overall materiality of the transactions to the financial statements. It is perhaps odd that while this requirement did not ask for risks of material misstatement, most answers were competent at explaining exactly what the risk of misstatement was and also quantifying its impact, in contrast with Q1(a) (ii) and Q2(a) (ii), when risks of material misstatement was asked for, but not answered well. Candidates were less competent at explaining the audit evidence they would expect to find, and the answers here were usually limited to a review of the terms of the consignment stock arrangement, and evidence of an inventory count.

Requirement (c) took a different slant on revenue, this time providing a brief scenario in which a fraud had been discovered whereby a sales representative had been submitting false claims for commission earned on sales generated. The requirement, which was for four marks, asked for procedures that should be used to determine the amount of the fraud. Only a minority of candidates realised that procedures should focus on testing the validity of the sales that the sales representative had claimed to have generated – and these candidates then usually recommended some specific, valid procedures. Other answers were inadequate, and relied on evidence from 'discussing with management' or 'interviewing the suspect' – but without actually recommending the questions they would ask. Some answers simply did not answer the question, and instead of providing procedures gave an explanation of the steps involved in a forensic investigation or focussed on how they would 'catch' the culprit and punish them.

ACCA marking scheme		
		Marks
(a) **Revenue recognition**		
Up to 1½ marks for each matter discussed:		
– Revenue often a subjective area		
– Revenue often a complex area		
– Adequacy of internal controls		
– Link to fraudulent financial reporting/earnings management		
– Example of deliberate manipulation of revenue		
– Cash-based business particularly high risk		
– Small/simple entities not high risk		
	Maximum	6
(b) **Kobain Co**		
Up to 1 mark for each matter/evidence:		
Matters		
– Risk and reward not transferred to external vendor		
– Kobain Co retains managerial involvement		
– Revenue recognised too early		
– Materiality		
– Implication for auditor's opinion		
– Opening balances could be misstated		

Evidence		
– Confirm terms of arrangement by review of signed contract		
– Consider whether terms of contract mean that revenue should be recognised		
– Confirmation of inventories held by external vendors		
– Determine amount of returns normally made under the contract		
– Attendance at external vendors inventory count		
– Supporting documentation on opening balances		
	Maximum	6
(c) Investigative procedures on false revenue claims Generally 1 mark per procedure:		
– Obtain all claims made by the sales representative		
– Agree all sales to supporting documentation		
– Conduct external confirmation of sales made		
– Reconcile claims to sales ledger/control accounts		
– Conduct analytical procedures		
	Maximum	4
Total		**16**

30 HERON *Walk in the footsteps of a top tutor*

Key answer tips

Part (a) requires knowledge of the auditor's responsibilities when suspicious transactions are identified. Money laundering is a topic regularly examined and this requirement should be quite straightforward.

Part (b) covers professional scepticism and how to apply it. In this scenario the auditor has been given contradictory evidence from the client and the requirement asks for the further actions that should be taken by the auditor. You should think of ways in which to obtain further evidence to reach a conclusion as to which evidence can be relied on.

(a) (i) The circumstances described by the audit senior indicate that Jack Heron may be using his company to carry out money laundering. Money laundering is defined as the process by which criminals attempt to conceal the origin and ownership of the proceeds of their criminal activity, allowing them to maintain control over the proceeds and, ultimately, providing a legitimate cover for the sources of their income. Money laundering activity may range from a single act, such as being in possession of the proceeds of one's own crime, to complex and sophisticated schemes involving multiple parties, and multiple methods of handling and transferring criminal property as well as concealing it and entering into arrangements to assist others to do so.

Heron Co's business is cash-based, making it an ideal environment for cash acquired through illegal activities to be legitimised by adding it to the cash paid genuinely by customers and posting it through the accounts. It appears that $2 million additional cash has been added to the genuine cash receipts from customers. This introduction of cash acquired through illegal activities into the business is known as 'placement'.

The fact that the owner himself posts transactions relating to revenue and cash is strange and therefore raises suspicions as to the legitimacy of the transactions he is posting through the accounts. Suspicions are heightened due to Jack Heron's refusal to explain the nature and reason for the journal entries he is making in the accounts.

The $2 million paid by electronic transfer is the same amount as the additional cash posted through the accounts. This indicates that the cash is being laundered and the transfer is known as the 'layering' stage, which is done to disguise the source and ownership of the funds by creating complex layers of transactions. Money launderers often move cash overseas as quickly as possible in order to distance the cash from its original source, and to make tracing the transaction more difficult. The 'integration' stage of money laundering occurs when upon successful completion of the layering process, the laundered cash is reintroduced into the financial system, for example, as payment for services rendered.

The secrecy over the reason for the cash transfer and lack of any supporting documentation is another indicator that this is a suspicious transaction.

Jack Heron's reaction to being questioned over the source of the cash and the electronic transfer point to the fact that he has something to hide. His behaviour is certainly lacking in integrity, and even if there is a genuine reason for the journals and electronic transfer his unhelpful and aggressive attitude may cast doubts as to whether the audit firm wish to continue to retain Heron Co as a client.

The audit senior was correct to be alarmed by the situation. However, by questioning Jack Heron about it, the senior may have alerted him to the fact that the audit team is suspicious that money laundering is taking place. There is a potential risk that the senior has tipped off the client, which may prejudice any investigation into the situation.

Tipping off is itself an offence, though this can be defended against if the person did not know or suspect that the disclosure was likely to prejudice any investigation that followed.

The amount involved is clearly highly material to the financial statements and will therefore have an implication for the audit. The whole engagement should be approached as high risk and with a high degree of professional skepticism.

The firm may wish to consider whether it is appropriate to withdraw from the engagement (if this is possible under applicable law and regulation). However, this could result in a tipping off offence being committed, as on withdrawal the reasons should be discussed with those charged with governance.

If Lark & Co continue to act as auditor, the audit opinion must be considered very carefully and the whole audit subject to second partner review, as the firm faces increased liability exposure. Legal advice should be sought.

(ii)   The audit senior should report the situation in an internal report to Lark & Co's Money Laundering Reporting Officer (MLRO). The MLRO is a nominated officer who is responsible for receiving and evaluating reports of suspected money laundering from colleagues within the firm, and making a decision as to whether further enquiries are required and if necessary making reports to the appropriate external body.

Lark & Co will probably have a standard form that should be used to report suspicions of money laundering to the MLRO.

Tutorial note

According to ACCA's Technical Factsheet 145 Anti-Money Laundering Guidance for the Accountancy Sector, there are no external requirements for the format of an internal report and the report can be made verbally or in writing.

The typical content of an internal report on suspected money laundering may include the name of the suspect, the amounts potentially involved, and the reasons for the suspicions with supporting evidence if possible, and the whereabouts of the laundered cash.

The report must be done as soon as possible, as failure to report suspicions of money laundering to the MLRO as soon as practicable can itself be an offence under the money laundering regulations.

The audit senior may wish to discuss their concerns with the audit manager in more detail before making the report, especially if the senior is relatively inexperienced and wants to hear a more senior auditor's view on the matter. However, the senior is responsible for reporting the suspicious circumstances at Heron Co to the MLRO.

Tutorial note

ACCA's Technical Factsheet 145 states that: 'An individual may discuss his suspicion with managers or other colleagues to assure himself of the reasonableness of his conclusions but, other than in group reporting circumstances, the responsibility for reporting to the MLRO remains with him. It cannot be transferred to anyone else, however junior or senior they are.'

(b)   The term professional skepticism is defined in ISA 200 *Overall Objectives of the Independent Auditor and the Conduct of an Audit in Accordance with ISAs* as follows: 'An attitude that includes a questioning mind, being alert to conditions which may indicate possible misstatement due to error or fraud, and a critical assessment of audit evidence'.

Professional skepticism means for example, being alert to contradictory or unreliable audit evidence, and conditions that may indicate the existence of fraud. If professional skepticism is not maintained, the auditor may overlook unusual circumstances, use unsuitable audit procedures, or reach inappropriate conclusions when evaluating the results of audit work. In summary, maintaining an attitude of professional skepticism is important in reducing audit risk.

IFAC's *Code of Ethics for Professional Accountants* also refers to professional skepticism when discussing the importance of the auditor's independence of mind. It can therefore be seen as an ethical as well as a professional issue.

In the case of the audit of Coot Co, the audit junior has not exercised a sufficient degree of professional skepticism when obtaining audit evidence. Firstly, the reliability of the payroll supervisor's response to the junior's enquiry should be questioned. Additional and corroborating evidence should be sought for the assertion that the new employees are indeed temporary.

The absence of authorisation should also be further investigated. Authorisation is a control that should be in place for any additions to payroll, so it seems unusual that the control would not be in place even for temporary members of staff.

If it is proved correct that no authorisation is required for temporary employees the audit junior should have identified this as a control deficiency and made a management letter point to be reported to those charged with governance.

The contradictory evidence from comments made by management also should be explored further. ISA 500 *Audit Evidence* states that 'if audit evidence obtained from one source is inconsistent with that obtained from another... the auditor shall determine what modifications or additions to audit procedures are necessary to resolve the matter'.

Additional procedures should therefore be carried out to determine which source of evidence is reliable. Further discussions should be held with management to clarify whether any additional employees have been recruited during the year.

The amendment of payroll could indicate that a fraud ('ghost employee') is being carried out by the payroll supervisor. Additional procedures should be conducted to determine whether the supervisor has made any other amendments to payroll to determine the possible scope of any fraud. Verification should be sought as to the existence of the new employees. The bank accounts into which their salaries are being paid should also be examined, to see if the payments are being made into the same account.

Finally, the audit junior should be made aware that it is not acceptable to just put a note on the file when matters such as the lack of authorisation come to light during the course of the audit. The audit junior should have discussed their findings with the audit senior or manager to seek guidance and proper supervision on whether further testing should be carried out.

Examiner's comments

This 15 mark question focussed on money laundering and fraud. Two short scenarios relating to two audit clients were presented.

Part (a)'s scenario described a cash-based business whose owner manager was acting suspiciously in relation to the accounting for cash sales. A large sum of cash had been transferred to an overseas bank account and the transaction had no supporting evidence. The first requirement, (a)(i) for 6 marks, was to discuss the implications of these circumstances. This open requirement allowed for discussion of many different implications for the audit firm, included suspected fraud and/or money laundering, a poor control environment, the ethical implications of the owners intimidating behaviour, and problems for the audit firm in obtaining evidence. Most candidates covered a range of points and the majority correctly discussed fraud and/or money laundering.

Weaker answers tended to focus on the materiality of the cash transferred to overseas, and seemed not to notice the client's suspicious behaviour. Candidates are reminded that they will often be expected to identify a key issue in a question scenario and that in a question of this type it is important to stop and think about what is happening in the scenario before rushing to start to write an answer. This question is a good example of one where a relatively short answer could generate a lot of marks – if the scenario has been properly thought through before writing the answer.

Requirement (a) (ii) was for 3 marks and asked for an explanation of any reporting that should take place by the audit senior. Candidates who had identified money laundering as an issue in (a) (i) usually scored well here, describing the need to report to the audit firm's Money Laundering Reporting Officer, and what should be reported to them. Weaker answers discussed the audit report or that the fraud/money laundering should be reported to the client's management - this is not good advice given that the owner- manager was the person acting suspiciously and would have resulted in him being tipped off.

Part (b) was for 6 marks, and described a client where unauthorised additions had been made to payroll, and contradictory audit evidence had been obtained. Candidates were asked to explain the term 'professional skepticism' and to recommend further actions to be taken by the auditor. Answers here were reasonably good, with most candidates able to attempt an explanation of the term, and most identifying poor controls leading to a possible fraud involving the payroll supervisor. Some very specific further procedures were often recommended, and candidates often scored better on part (b) than part (a) for this question.

ACCA marking scheme				Marks
(a)	(i)	Implications of the audit senior's note		
		Generally 1 mark for each matter discussed relevant to money laundering:		
		– Definition of money laundering		
		– Placement – cash-based business		
		– Owner posting transactions		
		– Layering – electronic transfer to overseas		
		– Secrecy and aggressive attitude		
		– Audit to be considered very high risk		
		– Senior may have tipped off the client		
		– Firm may consider withdrawal from audit		
		– But this may have tipping off consequences		
			Maximum	6
	(ii)	Reporting that should take place		
		Generally 1 mark for each comment:		
		– Report suspicions immediately to MLRO		
		– Failure to report is itself an offence		
		– Examples of matters to be reported (identity of suspect, etc)		
		– Audit senior may discuss matters with audit manager but senior responsible for the report		
			Maximum	3

(b)	Professional scepticism Generally 1 mark for each comment: – Definition of professional scepticism – Explain – alert to contradictory evidence/unusual events/fraud indicator (up to 2 marks) – Part of ethical codes – Coot Co – evidence is unreliable and contradictory – Absence of authorisation is fraud indicator – Additional substantive procedures needed – Management's comments should be corroborated – Control deficiency to be reported to management/those charged with governance – Audit junior needs better supervision/training on how to deal with deficiencies identified		
		Maximum	6
Total			15

31   FIR   *Walk in the footsteps of a top tutor*

Key answer tips

Part (a) is a typical 'matters and evidence' question. First, consider the materiality of the issue. Next discuss the appropriate accounting treatment and give the risks of material misstatement that would arise if the appropriate treatment is not followed. Finally, the evidence is what you would expect to be recorded on the audit file when you come to review it. Be specific about the evidence, don't say 'supporting documentation', suggest what that documentation would be and what it would show.

Part (b) is a typical requirement asking for procedures to evaluate the work of an auditor's expert. This is quite knowledge based and you should refer to the requirements of ISA 620.

Part (c) requires the audit reporting implications where the client has dealt incorrectly with a change of accounting estimate. Whilst reporting is normally examined in Q5 of the exam, you should be prepared for any syllabus area being tested in any requirement.

(a)   **Fir Co**

Matters to consider

According to IAS 16 *Property, Plant and Equipment*, the cost of an asset should include the estimated costs of dismantling and removing the asset (also known as decommissioning costs) if there is an obligation to incur the cost at the end of the life of the asset. The first matter to consider is whether Fir Co has an obligation to decommission the nuclear power stations at the end of their useful life. According to IAS 37 *Provisions, Contingent Liabilities and Contingent Assets*, a provision should only be recognised if there is a present obligation as a result of a past event, giving rise to a probable outflow of economic benefit. If Fir Co only 'intends' to decommission the power stations, but has no legal or constructive obligation to do so, then a provision should not be recognised. However, it is common practice that authorities would require decommissioning, and the obligation would normally be part of the consent given to Fir Co to operate the power stations.

The measurement of the provision is inherently subjective and complex, as it involves estimations of the expected decommissioning cost, the estimated life of the power stations, and the application of an appropriate discount factor to calculate the present value of the expected costs. There is risk that inappropriate assumptions have been used in determining these estimates.

The auditor should consider whether it seems reasonable for the value of the provision to have reduced since last year. It would normally be expected to see the value of the provision increase over time, as the provision is unwound each year to increase its present value. The fact that the provision has decreased in value could indicate that management has changed one or more of the assumptions used in the measurement of the provision (e.g. using a higher interest rate to calculate the present value of the provision), the reasons for which would need to be investigated.

It should be considered whether sufficient disclosure has been made in the notes to the financial statements. IAS 37 requires that the notes should contain narrative information including a brief description of the nature of the obligation and the expected timing of any outflows of economic benefits, and an indication of the uncertainties about the amount or timing of those outflows. In addition, the notes should disclose the major assumptions made concerning future events. The notes should also contain numerical disclosures, namely a reconciliation of the opening and closing provision, analysing the movement in the year.

In addition, IAS 1 *Presentation of Financial Statements* requires that the notes disclose information about the assumptions made about the future, and sources of estimation uncertainty at the end of the reporting period, that have a significant risk of resulting in a material adjustment to the carrying amounts of assets and liabilities within the next financial year.

There is a risk that sufficient information is not provided in the notes regarding these matters. If the disclosures are not expanded to meet the requirements of IAS 37 and IAS 1, there may be implications for the auditor's report, which may need to contain a qualified opinion on the basis of material misstatement.

Audit evidence

- A review of any agreement issued by authorities pertaining to Fir Co's operation of the power stations, and confirmation that there is an obligation to decommission.

- A copy of management's calculations used to measure the provision, and confirmation that the calculation is based on assumptions in line with our understanding of the entity, and which are consistent with other audit evidence obtained (e.g. that the remaining life of the assets is 20 years, that the discount rate used to determine the present value of the provision is appropriate).

- A review of documentation used to support management's assumptions (e.g. any documentation to verify that the power stations must be shut down in 20 years' time, possibly in an operating licence; and documentation to support the estimated cost of decommissioning).

- A discussion with management as to whether there has been, or ought to have been, a change from the prior year in the methods for making the estimates or assumptions used in the measurement of the provision.

- An assessment of the controls in place over the estimate of the provision (e.g. are there controls to ensure that the circumstances giving rise to the provision, and the assumptions used in calculations are periodically reviewed, and whether there is review and approval of the calculations).

- A written representation from management indicating that management consider that significant assumptions used in making the accounting estimate are reasonable.

- A review of the notes to the draft financial statements to confirm sufficiency of narrative and numerical disclosures provided in compliance with IAS 37 and IAS 1.

(b) **Spruce Co**

Written instructions should have been provided by the auditor to the expert prior to them carrying out the work. The instructions should include matters such as the scope of the work, the applicable financial reporting framework and any specific matters to be addressed. As a first step, the auditor should consider if these instructions have been followed by the expert.

ISA 620 *Using the Work of an Auditor's Expert* contains requirements and guidance in evaluating the adequacy of the auditor's expert's work.

The procedures that should be performed may include:

- Review the auditor's expert's working papers and reports to ensure that:
  - the work meets the objectives of the audit
  - the evidence contained in the report is consistent with other evidence obtained by the auditor
  - the work is based on the correct period and takes into account events after the reporting date where necessary.

- Evaluate the appropriateness of models used by the expert to determine fair value.

- Compare the findings of the expert with results produced by management, e.g. compare the fair values determined by the expert with those determined by management.

- Reperform any calculations contained in the expert's working papers, e.g. recalculate movements in fair value on the derivatives.

- Evaluate the assumptions used by the expert, including:
  - whether the assumptions are consistent with the requirements of the relevant financial reporting framework
  - if the assumptions are consistent with the auditor's knowledge and understanding of Spruce Co's operations and environment.

- Verify the origin of source data used in the expert's work, e.g. agree figures used in calculations to the general ledger and documentation maintained by the trading division.

- Agree figures used in calculations to supporting documentation, e.g. contracts relating to derivative financial instruments.

(c) **Pine Co**

The revision to the estimated useful life of properties is a change in accounting estimates, governed by IAS 8 *Accounting Policies, Changes in Accounting Estimates and Errors*. The effect of a change in accounting estimates should be accounted for prospectively, and included in profit or loss from the date of the change in estimate. In other words, it is only current and future periods which are affected by the change in estimate.

The current accounting treatment is therefore incorrect, as the financial statements recognise the effect of the change in estimate retrospectively. No adjustment should have been made to opening non-current assets and equity. Management seem to have treated the revision to estimated useful life as a change in accounting policy, which is incorrect. The financial statements are materially misstated, due to an overstatement of non-current assets and equity.

In addition, IAS 8 requires a note to the financial statements to disclose the nature and amount of a change in an accounting estimate that has an effect in the current period or is expected to have an effect in future periods. As a note has not been provided, the disclosure requirements of IAS 8 have not been met, leading to material misstatement of the financial statements.

The audit firm should discuss the accounting treatment and disclosure with management, and explain that the current treatment is incorrect, and disclosure is inadequate. If management agree to make the necessary amendments the material misstatement will be resolved and an unmodified opinion can be given.

However, if the financial statements are not amended, the auditor's opinion should be qualified on the grounds of material misstatement. This would be an 'except for' opinion as the matter is material to the financial statements but not pervasive. The opinion paragraph should be headed 'Qualified Opinion', and the report should include a 'Basis for Qualified Opinion' paragraph which describes the matter giving rise to the modification, including a description and quantification of the financial effects of the misstatement, and an explanation of how the disclosures in the notes to the financial statements are misstated. This paragraph should be presented immediately before the opinion paragraph.

The auditor should also discuss the reason for the change in accounting estimate with management, to form an opinion as to the validity of the change.

Examiner's comments

This question focussed on the audit issues pertaining to fair values and estimates, and contained three short scenarios. Unfortunately for many candidates it was an inadequate choice of question, as answers to at least two of the three parts of the question were generally unsatisfactory.

The first scenario, for 8 marks, described an audit client involved in energy production, and the accounting issue was a provision for decommissioning of its nuclear power stations. The requirement (a) was to comment on the matters that should be considered, and to explain the audit evidence that should be found in a file review in respect of the decommissioning provision. This is standard wording for a requirement and should have been familiar to candidates.

Candidates performed best on this requirement of question three, but answers were still lacking in substance. Many answers discussed the appropriate accounting treatment for the provision correctly, including the issue of measuring the provision at present value. But few identified that the reduction in the provision was a key issue, or that estimates generally give rise to audit risk due to their subjective nature, especially when dealing with a provision that will not give rise to a cash outflow for another 20 years. Most of the evidence that was suggested should be on file focussed on an expert's report and the inevitable written representation from management that the provision had been correctly accounted for. Very few answers used the approach of ISA 540 Auditing Accounting Estimates, Including Fair Value Accounting Estimates, and Related Disclosures in challenging the assumptions used by management in developing the estimate of decommissioning costs. Few answers considered the lack of disclosure of the provision, or that a provision may not even be needed at all.

Requirement (b) focussed on the use of an auditor's expert in obtaining evidence in respect of the fair value of a portfolio of financial instruments. Unfortunately very few answers performed satisfactorily on this requirement, which was to explain the procedures that should be performed in evaluating the adequacy of the auditor's expert's work, for 5 marks.

Most answers ignored the requirement as given in the question and instead discussed how the audit firm should evaluate the independence and competence of the expert – though the question stated that this had already been confirmed by the audit firm. This is a classic example of candidates answering the question they would like to have been asked, rather than what was actually asked for, and meant that many answers scored no marks at all on this requirement.

The few who answered this requirement appropriately tended to score highly, with answers mirroring the requirements of ISA 620 Using the Work of an Auditor's Expert, discussing e.g. the need to evaluate the assumptions used by the expert, to confirm the work accords with instructions given by the auditor, and to verify the reliability of the source data used by the expert.

Requirement (c) dealt with changes in accounting policies and estimates. The scenario described an adjustment put through a client's financial statements as a result of a change in accounting estimate – the extension of the useful life of 120 properties. For 5 marks the candidates were required to explain the impact on the auditor's report of the accounting treatment of the change in the accounting estimate. However, most candidates instead of focussing on whether the accounting treatment was correct (it was not) and the implications for the audit report, focussed on whether the client should have been 'allowed' to change the estimate of useful lives and whether this amounted to some kind of fraud. This led to irrelevant discussions that failed to answer the question requirement. Few candidates understood that the accounting treatment was incorrect, but those that did tended to explain their point well and link it to a potential qualification of the audit opinion. Some candidates described how this qualification would impact on the auditor's report, as asked for, by describing the paragraphs used to explain the reason for the qualification. As in Q2 however, many answers displayed a lack of understanding of auditor's reports, with many claiming that an Emphasis of Matter or Other Matter paragraph should be used to highlight the 'lack of integrity' or 'fraudulent reporting' that they alleged was occurring.

				Marks
	ACCA marking scheme			

ACCA marking scheme

			Marks
(a)	**Fir Co**		
	Generally 1 mark per matter/evidence point explained:		
	Matters:		
	– Whether a present obligation exists		
	– Assumptions used in estimate are complex/subjective		
	– Investigate why provision fallen in value		
	– IAS 37 disclosure requirements not met		
	– IAS 1 disclosure requirements not met		
	– Potential misstatement due to insufficient disclosure		
	Evidence:		
	– Supporting documentation regarding existence of obligation		
	– Assess whether assumptions in line with business understanding/other evidence		
	– Discuss assumptions and estimation method with management		
	– Review supporting documentation (operating licence/government agreement)		
	– Assess controls in place		
	– Written representation		
	– Review of draft notes to financial statements		
	Maximum		8
(b)	**Spruce Co**		
	Generally 1 mark for each procedure:		
	– Consider whether expert has followed auditor's written instructions		
	– Ensure expert's findings consistent with other evidence obtained		
	– Ensure expert's work considers events after the year end where necessary		
	– Compare expert's results with those determined by management		
	– Reperform calculations		
	– Consider suitability of models used in the expert's work		
	– Evaluate assumptions and ensure in line with auditor's understanding		
	– Verify source data		
	– Agree figures and terms to supporting documentation		
	Maximum		5
(c)	**Pine Co**		
	Generally 1 mark per matter explained:		
	– Consider whether change in estimate is valid		
	– Incorrect accounting treatment used (up to 2 marks for detailed explanation)		
	– Insufficient notes to the financial statements		
	– Discuss with management and encourage amendments		
	– Opinion to be qualified 'except for' due to material misstatement		
	– Description of reason for qualification to be provided in auditor's report		
	Maximum		5
	Total		18

32 CHESTNUT *Walk in the footsteps of a top tutor*

Key answer tips

Part (a) covers the syllabus area of forensic accounting and asks for ethical and professional issues if your firm investigates the fraudulent activity. Think about the threats that could arise and how they could be safeguarded. Remember to explain and evaluate the significance of the threats.

Part (b) requires the matters to be considered when planning the fraud investigation. Forensic accounting was the subject of a technical article in 2008 and this provides guidance on how to plan and perform such engagements.

Part (c) is a current issues question asking for arguments for and against the prohibition of auditors providing non-audit services to audit clients. Remember to deal with both sides of the argument and set these answers out under two subheadings to make it clear you are dealing with both aspects.

(a)   An investigation into the alleged fraudulent activity is a forensic investigation. If Cedar & Co were to conduct the forensic investigation, this would be a non-audit service performed for an audit client. Specifically, this investigation would be deemed a litigation support service.

Tutorial note

Litigation support services may include activities such as acting as an expert witness, calculating estimated damages or other amounts that might become receivable or payable as the result of litigation or other legal dispute, and assistance with document management and retrieval.

According to IFAC's *Code of Ethics for Professional Accountants*, before a firm accepts an engagement to provide a non-audit service to an audit client, a determination should be made as to whether providing such a service would create a threat to independence. Self-review, self-interest and advocacy threats to independence may arise.

The self-review threat exists because the forensic investigation will determine the monetary amount of the fraud, and the amount which Chestnut Co will attempt to recover from the fraudsters. Given the potential scale of the fraud, it could be that the amounts involved are material to the financial statements and therefore the audit team would be reviewing figures determined by members of the audit firm.

In addition, the forensic investigation team will, as part of their work, review systems and controls over expenses claimed by Chestnut Co's employees. This means that the forensic investigation team are also exposed to a self-review threat, as they will be reviewing systems and controls which have been considered during the audit of Chestnut Co's financial statements.

The advocacy threat arises because going to court and speaking as an expert witness in relation to the fraud would be seen as the audit firm promoting the interests of its client and supporting a position taken by management in an adversarial context.

A self-interest threat could also arise, as the forensic investigation may be a lucrative source of income for Cedar & Co. This could create the perception that Cedar & Co is reliant on Chestnut Co for income and impairs the objectivity of the firm.

The firm should evaluate the significance of these threats. In particular, the firm should consider the potential materiality of the amounts involved in the fraud, and the degree of subjectivity that may be involved in determining the amounts involved. If the matter is material, and would involve significant judgements, then no safeguards would reduce the threat to an acceptable level and the forensic investigation should not be conducted by the audit firm.

It is likely, however, that the investigation would not involve a significant degree of judgement and the investigation could be performed as long as safeguards were used, such as:

- Having a senior member of the audit firm, who was not involved in the forensic investigation, review the results of the investigation and the impact on the financial statements

- Performing a second partner review on the audit of Chestnut Co; and

- Ensuring that the forensic investigation is not performed by anyone involved in the audit engagement. Possibly the investigation could be performed by a different office of the firm.

The ethical situation must be discussed with those charged with governance of Chestnut Co. Depending on any relevant regulation in Chestnut Co's jurisdiction, it may not be possible for the audit firm to carry out this non-audit assignment, or it may be permitted with the approval of those charged with governance (or an audit committee, if one exists).

Furthermore, the IFAC Code's fundamental ethical principles apply to all professional assignments, including a forensic investigation. One of the fundamental principles is that of professional competence and due care. Forensic investigations are specialist assignments and may require very specific skills, which will not be possessed by individuals unless they have undergone specific training. Cedar & Co must consider whether there are any members of the firm who possess the necessary skills before accepting the assignment.

It is likely that relatively senior staff will need to be assigned to the investigation, which will bring necessary authority and experience to the investigation team. It should be considered whether Cedar & Co is able to divert senior staff from other assignments at short notice. Resourcing the team could be a problem.

In addition, confidentiality is a crucial issue in such investigations as members of the investigation team will have access to sensitive information which will be used as evidence in court. Any breach of confidentiality could jeopardise the integrity of the legal proceedings against the fraudsters. Anyone involved with the investigation must be made aware of these issues and confidentiality agreements should be signed.

(b) Discuss the purpose, nature and scope of the investigation. In particular, confirm whether evidence gathered will be used in criminal proceedings and in support of an insurance claim.

Confirm that Chestnut Co's objectives are to identify those involved with the fraud, and to quantify the amount of the fraud. This will help to clarify the terms of the engagement, which will be detailed in an engagement letter.

Determine the time-scale involved, whether Jack Privet needs the investigation to commence as soon as possible and the deadline for completing the investigation. This is necessary to determine the resources needed to perform the investigation, and whether resources need to be diverted from other assignments.

Enquire as to how many sales representatives have been suspended (i.e. are suspected of involvement in the fraud). This will help the firm to determine the potential scale of the investigation.

Gain an understanding as to how the fraud came to light (e.g. was it uncovered by internal audit or a member of the sales department) and who reported their suspicions to Jack Privet. This information will indicate how the investigation should commence (e.g. by interviewing the whistle-blower).

Determine whether Chestnut Co will provide resources to help with the investigation, e.g. members of the internal audit team could provide assistance in obtaining evidence.

Ask for Jack Privet's opinion as to why the fraud had not been prevented or detected by the company's internal controls. In particular, enquire if there has been a breakdown in controls over authorisation of expenses.

Determine whether recommendations to improve controls are required as an output of the investigative work.

Discuss the investigative techniques which may be used (e.g. interviewing the alleged fraudsters, detailed review of all expense claims made by sales representatives, analytical review of expenses) and ensure that investigators will have unrestricted access to individuals and documentation.

Enquire as to whether the police have been informed, and if so, the name and contact details of the person informed. It is likely that a criminal investigation by the police will take place as well as Cedar & Co's own investigation.

Confirm that Chestnut Co grants permission to Cedar & Co's investigation team to communicate with third parties such as the police and the company's lawyers regarding the investigation.

(c) The issue of auditors providing non-audit services to audit clients has been topical for many years, and there are many arguments for and against their outright prohibition.

Those arguing in favour of outright prohibition suggest that this would be a simple way to eliminate the threats to objectivity, which the provision of non-audit services to audit clients creates. Typically, management, self-interest and self-review threats arise, which result in the perception that the auditor cannot be objective when performing the audit service.

In particular, non-audit services can be very lucrative, leading potentially to a self-interest threat. The greater the volume and financial significance of the non-audit services provided, the greater the risk that the auditor will have relationship and economic reasons not to challenge management's views and positions with the necessary degree of professional scepticism.

It has also been argued that outright prohibition would benefit the market, allowing smaller audit firms to provide the services which larger firms would no longer be able to offer to their audit clients.

Tutorial note

Credit will be awarded for appropriate examples of regimes in which there is tight regulation on the provision of non-audit services, such as the US Sarbanes-Oxley legislation.

However, there are also many arguments against outright prohibition. By having the same firm provide the audit and the non-audit service, the client benefits in two ways. The audit firm will already possess a good knowledge and understanding of the client and its operating environment, resulting in deeper insight and a better quality service being provided. This will then lead to cost benefits, as the non-audit service will be provided in a more efficient way.

Audit firms would also argue that participation in services such as due diligence reviews and forensic investigations, allows the audit firm to understand their clients' business and risks better and to obtain insights into management's objectives and capabilities which are useful in an audit context.

Finally, non-audit services can be safely provided as long as steps are taken to assess potential threats to objectivity, and to adequately address those risks, for example, by the use of separate teams to provide audit and non-audit services.

The UK Corporate Governance Code requires the audit committee to review and monitor the external auditor's independence and objectivity. This includes the audit committee evaluating approving the provision of non-audit services by the audit firm.

To conclude, a principles-based approach to the provision of non-audit services, in which such services can be provided as long as risks are assessed and managed, appears to benefit both audit firms and their clients.

Examiner's comments

This was the most popular of the optional questions, and focussed on a forensic investigation into a fraud that had been uncovered at an audit client. One of the requirements focussed on ethical issues, probably explaining the popularity of this question.

Requirement (a), for 6 marks, required an assessment of the ethical and professional issues raised by the request from the audit client to investigate the fraudulent activity. Most answers were satisfactory, identifying the main ethical threats (advocacy, self-review etc) raised by the scenario and explaining them to an extent. Some answers also discussed whether the audit firm would have the necessary skills and resources to perform such a specialist piece of work. Some answers however tended to focus on why the audit firm had not discovered the fraud during the previous audit, and the possibility of the audit firm being sued for negligence or the need to 'discipline' the audit manager. Some answers also contained irrelevant discussions of the responsibilities of management and auditors in relation to fraud, and other answers used the fundamental principles as a framework for their answer, probably as this had been set on a previous exam paper, but with a completely different question requirement.

Requirement (b), also for 6 marks, asked candidates to explain the matters that should be discussed in a meeting with the client, in terms of planning the forensic investigation. Some answers were very satisfactory, covering a wide range of matters including the timeframe, the required output of the investigation, access to the client's accounting systems amongst others. Some answers however tended to simply list out the procedures that would be performed in conducting the investigation, or explain to the client's management the controls that should have been in place to stop the fraud in the first place.

Requirement (c), also for 6 marks, focussed more theoretically on the debate over whether audit firms should be prohibited from providing non-audit services to their audit client. Although most candidates seemed prepared for a question of this type, most approached the question by discussing the pros and cons of audit firms offering non-audit services to their clients, rather than discussing whether prohibition would be desirable. There is some overlap between the two approaches, but the way that candidates tackled this requirement indicated that a rote-learnt answer had been provided, rather than evidence of candidates thinking on their feet and coming up with their own opinion on the matter. A lot of answers simply explained several ethical threats and concluded that because threats may exist auditors should not provide non-audit services to their clients. This is not a broad enough response to the question requirement.

ACCA marking scheme		Marks
(a)	Ethical and professional issues	
	Generally 1 mark per issue assessed:	
	– Non-audit service creates self-review threat	
	– Non-audit service creates advocacy threat	
	– Significance of threat to be evaluated	
	– Significance depends on materiality and subjectivity	
	– Examples of safeguards (1 mark each)	
	– Competence to provide service	
	– Resources to provide service	
	– Confidentiality agreements	
	Maximum	6
(b)	Matters to be discussed	
	Generally 1 mark for each matter explained:	
	– Purpose, nature and scope of investigation	
	– Confirm objectives of investigation	
	– Time-scale and deadline	
	– Potential scale of the fraud	
	– How fraud reported to finance director	
	– Possible reasons for fraud not being detected by internal controls	
	– Resources to be made available to investigation team	
	– Whether matter reported to police	
	Maximum	6

(c)	Provision of non-audit services		
	Generally 1 mark per comment discussed and 1 mark for conclusion:		
	– Simple way to eliminate threats to objectivity		
	– Examples of threats e.g. lucrative nature of non-audit services		
	– Benefit to audit market of outright prohibition		
	– Benefits to client of auditor providing non-audit services		
	– Benefits to audit firm of providing non-audit services		
	– Safeguards should be used to reduce threats arising		
	– Principles-based approach versus prescriptive approach		
		Maximum	6
Total			18

33 **JACOB** *Walk in the footsteps of a top tutor*

Key answer tips

This was an unusual question to see on Q4 of the paper. This emphasises the need to be prepared for any syllabus area being tested in any part of the paper.

Part (a) asks for benefits of externally provided due diligence prior to the acquisition of a company. Try and think of reasons why the client might not be able to do the due diligence for themselves.

Part (b) requires the information you would require for your due diligence review. Think about the information that would help you identify whether there were any financial, operational, tax or legal issues with the company being acquired. Is there anything happening that would deter the client from purchasing the company? Is there anything that would impact the price that they would be prepared to pay for the company?

(a) There are many potential benefits to the potential purchaser of a company in having a due diligence review.

One benefit is that by conducting a due diligence review, the assets and liabilities of Locke Co can be identified and a potential value placed on them. Without a due diligence review it will be difficult for management to negotiate a fair price for Locke Co, as the price paid should include consideration of assets and liabilities not necessarily shown in the accounts, for example, any contingent liabilities which may exist in connection with warranties provided to customers of Locke Co.

A second benefit is that the due diligence review should uncover more information about operational issues, which may then help Jacob Co's directors in deciding whether to go ahead with the acquisition. For example, Locke Co may need to relocate its head office, as it is currently located on the owners' family estate. If this is the case, significant expense could be involved in building or purchasing new premises, or the head office function could be merged with that of Jacob Co. Either way, it is a practical operational issue that will need to be planned for, if the acquisition were to go ahead.

A third benefit is that an externally provided due diligence review, as opposed to a review conducted by management of Jacob Co, is likely to provide information in a time-efficient, impartial manner. The audit firm has the financial and business understanding and expertise to provide a quality due diligence review. The management of Jacob Co can focus their attention on operational issues, for example, considering how best to merge the acquired business into existing operations, leaving the detailed due diligence review to be performed by independent experts.

Tutorial note

The answer above includes three benefits (as required). Credit will be awarded for explanation of any three benefits which are specific to the scenario. Other benefits could include an assessment of the significance of the court case against the company, and its potential impact on the valuation of the business; enhanced credibility provided by an external due diligence review; and a review of the terms and conditions of the significant bank loan, and its potential impact on the future liquidity profile of Locke Co.

(b)   Further information to be requested could include:

Directors, and any other key management personnel's contracts of employment – these will be needed to see if there are any contractual settlement terms if the contract of employment is terminated after the acquisition. The family members who founded the company may be looking for an exit route and may not wish to be involved with the company after acquisition, so sizeable amounts could be payable to them on termination of their contracts.

An organisational structure should be obtained, in order to identify the members of management and key personnel and their roles within Locke Co. After acquisition, Jacob Co may wish to retain the services of some members of key management, while others may be made redundant as activities with Jacob Co are streamlined.

Details of any legal arrangement, such as a lease, covering the use of the family owned property by the company. Jacob Co's management may wish to relocate and/or merge Locke Co's head office function. If there is a formal lease arrangement currently in place, there could be early termination penalties to be paid on early termination of the lease.

Purchase documentation regarding the land obtained for the purpose of building a new head office. This will provide information on the location and size of the land. Jacob Co may wish to consider an alternative use for this land, or its sale, or possibly not including the land in the acquisition deal, if it does not wish to go ahead with the construction of the new premises. A copy of planning permission, if any has been sought, regarding the planned construction of a new head office should also be obtained.

Prior-year audited financial statements, and management accounts for this financial year – this information can be used to verify the assertion that Locke Co has enjoyed rapid growth. The financial statements will also provide useful information regarding contingent liabilities, the liquidity position of the company, accounting policies, and the value of assets. Further information should be sought regarding the market value of assets if the financial statements have been prepared using the historical cost convention.

The most recent management accounts for the current year should be analysed. They will reveal any significant change in the company's position or performance since the last audited accounts, for example, if revenue has decreased significantly, or further finance taken out.

Forecasts and budgets for future periods will enable an analysis of the future prospects of the company. Attention should be paid to the cash flow forecast in particular, given that the company has seasonal cash inflows, and uses an overdraft for several months of the year. Expansion in the past should not lead to an assumption that expansion will continue, and the assumptions underpinning the forecasts and budgets should be carefully considered for validity.

The signed loan agreement should be reviewed. Jacob Co will need to know the exact amount and terms of the loan, including the interest rate, any other finance charges, whether the loan is secured on company assets, the repayment terms, and any covenants attached to the loan. The amount is described as significant, and Jacob Co should be wary of taking on this amount of debt without a clear understanding of its associated risk exposure.

Details should also be obtained regarding the overdraft facility, such as the maximum facility that is extended to the company, the interest rate, when the facility is due for renewal or review, and how many months on average the facility is used in a financial year. If the acquisition were to go ahead, Locke Co could prove to be a cash drain on the group. Jacob Co may plan to alleviate this by an inter-company loan of cash during the winter months, but the seasonality of the cash flows must be clearly understood before an acquisition decision is made.

Legal correspondence pertaining to the court case should be obtained. This should show the amount of damages claimed against the company, and the timescale as to when the case should go to court. The correspondence should also show the amount of legal fees incurred so far, and give an indication as to the future amount of fees likely to be paid. A review of the board minutes of Locke Co may indicate the likelihood of the court case going against the company. Jacob Co will need a detailed understanding of the financial consequences of this legal matter if they are to acquire the company.

Information should also be sought regarding the bad publicity caused by the court case. A copy of any press statements made by company representatives would be useful background information.

It is stated that Locke Co enjoys a 'good reputation'. Information to substantiate this claim should be sought, such as the results of customer satisfaction surveys, or data showing the level of repeat customers. Any exaggeration of the claim regarding the company's reputation could mean that Jacob Co can negotiate a lower purchase price, and will need to consider the impact of Locke Co's reputation on its own operations.

Details of warranties offered to customers should be obtained, including the length of period covered by the warranty, and any limits on the amount that can be claimed under warranty, to consider the level of contingent liability they may represent. If significant potential warranty claims exist, this should be reflected in the price offered to acquire Locke Co.

The contract between Locke Co and Austin Co should be obtained and scrutinised. It is essential to understand exactly what services are performed by the service organisation – which could include bookkeeping, payroll, preparation of management accounts and dealing with tax issues. The cost of the outsourcing should also be considered, as well as the reputation of Austin Co. These are important considerations, as Jacob Co may wish to bring the accounting function back in-house, most likely to streamline Locke Co's accounting systems with that of Jacob Co.

Examiner's comments

This was the second most popular of the optional questions, and focussed on due diligence. The scenario described a potential acquisition being planned by an audit client of your firm.

Requirement (a), for 6 marks, required an explanation of three benefits of an externally provided due diligence review to the audit client. This was reasonably well answered, though many answers were not made very specific to the scenario and tended to discuss the benefits of any due diligence review rather than an externally provided one. Also, a significant number of candidates provided more than three benefits, which was a waste of time.

Requirement (b), for 12 marks asked for additional information to be made available for the firm's due diligence review. Answers were satisfactory, and the majority of candidates did not struggle to apply their knowledge to the scenario, usually providing some very focussed answers dealing well with the specifics of the question scenario.

Most answers seemed to use a logical approach – working through the information provided to generate answer points, and this meant that on the whole most of the key issues from the scenario were covered in the answer. A small proportion of answers also included irrelevant discussions of the type of report that would be provided to the client, or a discussion of ethical issues which were not asked for

---

ACCA marking scheme		Marks
(a) **Benefits of due diligence**		
Up to 2 marks for each benefit explained (only three benefits required):		
– Identify and value assets and liabilities to be acquired		
– Identify and allow planning for operational issues		
– Provision by external experts – technically competent and time efficient		
– Assessment of potential impact of court case		
– Evaluation of the liquidity position of Locke Co		
– Enhanced credibility provided by an independent review		
	Maximum	6

(b)	**Information required**		
	Generally ½ mark for identification and up to 1 further mark for explanation (maximum 3 marks for identification):		
	– Service contracts of directors		
	– Organisational structure		
	– Lease/arrangement regarding head office		
	– Details of land purchased		
	– Planning permission for new head office		
	– Prior year accounts and management accounts		
	– Forecasts and budgets		
	– Loan agreement		
	– Overdraft facility details		
	– Legal correspondence		
	– Customer satisfaction surveys		
	– Details of warranty agreements		
	– Outsourcing agreement		
		Maximum	12
Total			18

34 CLOONEY CO *Walk in the footsteps of a top tutor*

Key answer tips

This question requires you to consider your answer from the perspective of the manager responsible for the audit, undertaking a review of the audit working papers. However, it is a 'traditional' audit question requiring explanation of the matters to be considered, and evidence required, in relation to three specific areas of significance to the audit.

This question demonstrates the importance of assumed knowledge for the paper, requiring a sound understanding of the relevant accounting standards and requirements, specifically: *IAS 37 Provisions, Contingent Liabilities and Contingent Assets; IAS 36 Impairment of Assets*; and *IAS 10 Events After the Reporting Period*.

The question also highlights the need to read and consider the information provided carefully. For example, in order to identify the relevant accounting standards, it is important to note the airline company went into liquidation before the year end but the acquisition of the subsidiary took place after the year-end.

A methodical and logical approach will help you succeed in this question. Start your answer for each area with a calculation of the materiality of the amounts. Keep your answers focused to the core issue described, and ensure you include specific and detailed audit procedures/evidence and matters to consider, in order to score a good mark.

The highlighted words are key phrases that markers are looking for.

(a)   **Compensation claim**

Matters to consider

The claim for compensation is material to profit as it represents 13.3% of profit before tax (20/150 × 100%). It is not material to the statement of financial position as it represents only 0.49% of total assets (20/4,100 × 100%).

Management may want to ignore the provision, as its recognition would reduce profit before tax by a material amount, therefore reducing their bonus payment. This issue is also inherently risky as it is based on reaching a judgement about the probability of the amount becoming payable.

However the claim cannot be ignored. A proper assessment should be made as to whether the amount claimed should be treated as a provision or a contingent liability. According to IAS 37 Provisions, Contingent Liabilities and Contingent Assets, a provision should be recognised where there is a present obligation as a result of a past event, a probable outflow of economic benefit, and a reliable estimate can be made of the amount. In the event that there is a possible outflow of economic benefit, a note to the financial statements describing the nature and estimated potential financial effect of contingent liability should be provided.

The fact that the compensation, if paid, would be covered by insurance does not mean that the matter should be ignored. Any amount potentially recoverable from the insurers should be assessed as to whether it is virtually certain to be received, in which case a receivable should be recognised, or if the recoverability is less than virtually certain, a note to the financial statements describing the contingent asset should be provided. An assessment should be carried out on the recoverability of the amount claimed.

Further liabilities may also need to be recognised in respect of legal costs. This would further reduce the year-end profit figure.

In the event that the claim results in the recognition of a provision, and the insurance reimbursement results in the recognition of a receivable, the two items should be separately presented in the statement of financial position, and not netted off.

Evidence

- A copy of the claim made by the group of holiday-makers, detailing the $20 million claimed and the basis of the claim.

- A review of correspondence between the 'claim group' and the company.

- Correspondence from Clooney Co's legal representatives, showing their opinion on the most likely outcome of the claim.

- A copy of any press releases made by Clooney Co concerning the stranded holiday-makers – this could help to establish whether a constructive obligation exists.

- A review of press coverage and internet stories about the situation, to assess any comments made in public by company representatives regarding the claim.

- A review of the standard terms and conditions that holiday-makers agree to on booking a holiday – this could help to establish any legal obligation, e.g. to cover the cost of accommodation before being returned home.

- Details of any helpline or other means by which the stranded holiday-makers were given advice at the time of the incident (e.g. if the company advised them to book alternative accommodation this may imply that the company is liable for the cost).

- A review of invoices received pre and post year-end in respect of legal costs, to ensure adequately included in expenses and accrued for if necessary.

- A copy of the business insurance contract detailing the level of cover, if any, provided for this situation, and any amount that will not be covered (an excess on the policy).

- Correspondence between the insurance company and Clooney Co establishing whether a claim on the insurance has been made.

- A written management representation stating management's opinion on the outcome of the court case, and the likelihood of reimbursement from the insurance cover.

(b) **Shelly's Cruises**

Matters to consider

The Shelly's Cruises operation is clearly a significant part of Clooney Co's activities, contributing 20% to revenue (640/3,200 × 100%). This revenue stream is material to the financial statements. The identifiable assets of the business segment represent 5.7% of total assets (235/4,100 × 100%), so they are material to the statement of financial position.

The fact that the brand has performed badly is an indicator of impairment according to IAS 36 Impairment of Assets. Although the brand itself is not recognised, the assets identifiable with the brand should be assessed for impairment by management, to determine their recoverable amount.

The assets represent a cash generating unit, as the cash flows generated by the assets identifiable with Shelly's Cruises are independent of cash flows generated by other assets of the company. Management should conduct an impairment test by calculating the value-in-use of the cash generating unit, and also calculate the fair value less cost to sell, to determine the recoverable amount of the assets collectively. Any impairment loss should be expensed. Management will want to avoid recognising an impairment loss in profit due to the detrimental impact on their bonus payment.

The calculations involved in the impairment test contain subjective elements, such as determining the appropriate discount rate for discounting cash flows to present value, and assumptions over the projected cash flows of the brand. Management's assumptions may need to be approached with scepticism due to the bonus based on profit.

Evidence:

- A review of management's impairment test (if conducted), including:
  - assessment that an appropriate discount rate has been used.
  - agreement that the assumptions to determine future cash flows are reasonable and in line with business understanding.
  - agreement that the correct carrying value of assets has been used for comparison of recoverable amount.
  - agreement that all identifiable assets have been included in the cash generating unit.
  - recalculation of all figures.

- Discussion with management over the expected future performance of Shelly's Cruises including any strategies to be put in place to combat the declining performance.

- A review of post year-end management accounts for the performance of Shelly's Cruises after the reporting date.

- A review of the level of bookings made in advance for cruises to be taken in the future.

(c) **Craig Co**

Matters

According to IAS 10 Events After the Reporting Period, the acquisition of a subsidiary after the year-end is a non-adjusting event, as it is unrelated to a condition existing at the year-end. If non-adjusting events after the reporting date are material, non-disclosure could influence the economic decisions of users taken on the basis of the financial statements.

A note to the financial statements should disclose for each material category of non-adjusting event the nature of the event and an estimate of its financial effect, or a statement that such an estimate cannot be made.

As a note has not been provided, and Craig Co represents a significant acquisition, there is currently a breach of the disclosure requirements of IAS 10. If a note is not provided, the audit opinion should be qualified 'except for' due to material misstatement caused by a lack of disclosure required by accounting standards.

Evidence:

- A copy of the press release announcing the acquisition, including the date of the announcement.

- A copy of any legal agreement pertaining to the acquisition, including the date that control passes to Clooney Co.

- A review of any due diligence report received pertaining to the acquisition, detailing the value of assets purchased, and the consideration paid.

- A review of the financial statements of Craig Co, to determine that it represents a significant acquisition for the group, therefore warranting a disclosure note.

- A review of any note provided by management to be included in the financial statements.

Examiner's comments

Requirement (a) for 8 marks, described a legal claim which had been made against the client by a group of customers. No provision had been made, and the client's management justified this on the grounds that the amount would be covered by insurance. Almost all candidates were able to generate marks by calculating the materiality of the amount, and describing the basic accounting treatment for provisions. Fewer went on to discuss the potential impact of the insurance cover, and some answers drifted into a discussion of going concern and other business risks.

Some candidates mistakenly thought that the event happened after the year-end, and others thought that the airline 'belonged' to the client. Surprisingly, only a minority of candidates picked up on the fact that management would not want to recognise the provision due to a bonus being based on profit before tax of the company.

Audit procedures were often inadequately focused, with no regard to the scale of the issue. Although most suggested looking at legal documents, candidates rarely mentioned looking at the group claim document. Some candidates proposed lots of very detailed tests on the validity of individual claims, such as checking hotel bills and airline tickets.

Requirement (b) for 7 marks, dealt with a business segment which had seen significant reductions in revenue and profit. This part of the question was not dealt with well. Very few candidates recognised that the business segment represented a cash generating unit that required an impairment test. Most picked up a mark by calculating materiality, but then could only discuss the fact that the internally generated brand name was correctly not recognised in the financial statements. Even those candidates that did pick up on the impairment issue could rarely provide evidence points other than 'check the value of the assets' (too vague) or 'inspect the assets' (irrelevant, and ignoring the fact that the assets in question are cruise liners in operation so very unlikely to be conveniently located near the auditor). Many candidates could only provide evidence points on the brand name, even though this was not recognised in the financial statements at all, leading to pointless procedures such as 'inspect the brand name in the register', 'observe the operation of the brand name' and 'check the value of the brand name'.

Requirement (c) for 5 marks, concerned a post year-end acquisition, which should have been disclosed in the notes to the financial statements. Many candidates correctly discussed the issue, and provided sensible evidence points concerning the verification of the date that control of the new subsidiary passed to the client, and the scale of its operations.

Unfortunately, many candidates wanted to see the new subsidiary consolidated, even though it had clearly been purchased after the end of the reporting period. At the other end of the spectrum, some candidates suggested that as the event happened after the year end, the auditor need not perform any procedures at all. Both of these approaches totally missed the point of the scenario, and indicate that candidates must take time to think about the information that has been presented to them before rushing to write their answer.

ACCA marking scheme		
		Marks
(a)	**Compensation claim**	
	1 mark per matter, 1 mark per specific procedure	
	Matters:	
	• Materiality	
	• Provision/contingent liability	
	• Recoverability under insurance	
	• Management reluctant to provide	
	Evidence:	
	• Copy of legal claim	
	• Legal correspondence	
	• Press releases/news stories to establish constructive obligation	
	• Booking conditions to verify legal obligation	
	• Advice given by the company at the time of the incident	
	• Copy of insurance contract	
	• Copy of claim made on insurance	
	• Written representation on outcome	
	Maximum marks	8

(b)	**Shelly's Cruises**		
	1 mark per matter, 1 mark per specific procedure		
	Matters:		
	• Materiality		
	• Impairment of assets (NOT brand)		
	• Cash generating unit		
	• Subjective elements in impairment calculations		
	Evidence:		
	• Review management impairment test (max 2 marks if detailed)		
	• Discuss future strategy re Shelly's Cruises		
	• Review post year-end performance/bookings in advance		
		Maximum marks	7
(c)	**Acquisition of Craig Co**		
	1 mark per matter, 1 mark per specific procedure		
	Matters:		
	• Non-adjusting event		
	• Note to disclose		
	• Implication for audit report if not disclosed		
	Evidence:		
	• Copy of press release announcing acquisition		
	• Copy of legal agreement or due diligence report on acquisition		
	• Review of financial statements to determine significance of acquisition		
	• Review of any note disclosed		
		Maximum marks	5
Total			**20**

35   BANANA CO   *Walk in the footsteps of a top tutor*

Key answer tips

This question combines a number of syllabus areas:

- audit procedures
- quality control
- money laundering.

As mentioned in previous questions, this highlights the need to revise the syllabus broadly. A goal that can be achieved by attempting a range of questions from this kit.

As with all matters/evidence style questions it is vital to identify exactly what you are being asked to consider. Don't just skim read the question and identify certain words: understand the **WHOLE** requirement. In (a) you need to identify matters/evidence relevant to 'training costs that have been **capitalised into the cost of the new machinery**' and 'trade receivables recognised in relation to **Cherry Co.**' If your answer is not specific to these matters you will not score. In this instance you are reviewing the audit files. Consider the 'matters' that are relevant to this stage of an audit.

Part (b) is really asking you to identify deficiencies in the audit with regard to quality control. Make sure you relate your knowledge of quality control and ISQC1/ISA 220 to the details in the scenario.

Part (c) requires little more than pre-learnt knowledge about money laundering.

The highlighted words are key phases that markers are looking for.

(a) (i) **Training costs**

Matters to consider

Materiality – the relevant materiality calculations are:

Based on revenue: 500,000/12.5 million × 100 = 4%

Based on net profit: 500,000/400,000 × 100 = 125%

Based on total assets: 500,000/78 million × 100 = <1%

Based on the above, the training costs are immaterial to the statement of financial position, but material to the statement of profit or loss and therefore to revenue and profit. It is important to note that any adjustment made to recognise the costs as an expense will have the effect of turning the profit of $400,000 currently recognised into a loss of $100,000.

Accounting treatment

The finance director's argument is based on the idea that the training costs are directly related to the assets concerned and therefore should be capitalised. IAS 16 *Property, Plant and Equipment* (paragraph 19 c) does not permit the capitalisation of these costs as they are operating costs rather than costs directly attributable to the item of plant. The concept behind this is that assets should only be recognised if they are controlled by the entity. It is unlikely that Banana Co can exercise control over the skills of its staff which have been developed by the training programme, as staff may decide to leave employment with the company. In addition, IAS 38 *Intangible Assets* also argues against the recognition of training costs as an intangible asset. Therefore there are no grounds for recognising the training costs as a non-current asset, and the $500,000 cost of the training programme should be expensed in the financial statements.

Audit opinion

If the financial statements are not amended, the audit opinion should be modified due to a material misstatement. This would most likely be a qualified 'except for' opinion due to the material but not pervasive nature of the matter.

Evidence

- A schedule detailing the major categories of expenses which make up the total $500,000 costs of the training programme.
- Agreement of a sample of the costs per the schedule to supporting documentation such as invoices provided from the external training firm.
- Agreement of a sample of the costs to the cash book and/or the bank statement.
- Confirmation that the training programme was completed before the yearend (i.e. that none of the $500,000 represents a prepayment of costs).
- Confirmation that the $500,000 is complete, and that no further invoices received after the year end in respect of training carried out before the yearend should have been accrued.
- Clarification that Banana Co does not exercise specific control over the skills of its staff, by a review of standard terms of employment.

- Confirmation that the amount spent on the training programme agrees to an authorised budget or an approved expenditure programme relating to the new machinery, and that the amount incurred is in line with expectations.

(ii) **Trade receivable**

Matters to consider

Materiality – the relevant calculations for the total value of the trade receivable are as follows:

Based on revenue: 300,000/12.5 million × 100 = 2.4%

Based on net profit: 300,000/400,000 × 100 = 75%

Based on total assets: 300,000/78 million × 100 = <1%

Therefore the total receivable is not material to the statement of financial position, however, it is material to the statement of profit or loss and therefore to profit for the year, which is relevant given that it appears that an impairment loss should be recognised in respect of this amount.

Accounting treatment

IFRS 9 *Financial Instruments* requires that impaired trade receivables are recognised at fair value, which is the present value of estimated cash inflows. According to the information provided by Cherry Co's administrators, it is likely that 25% of the amount outstanding will be paid. Therefore, it seems that 75% of the $300,000 trade receivable is irrecoverable, and so an impairment loss of $225,000 should be recognised. This is material to the statement of profit or loss, illustrated by the following materiality calculations:

Based on revenue: 225,000/12.5 million × 100 = 18%

Based on net profit: 225,000/400,000 × 100 = 56%

The potential expense to be recognised is highly material to net profit.

A further issue is that there may be inventory in relation to Cherry Co within current assets. As Banana Co has several contracts with Cherry Co, there may be raw materials purchased specifically for use in a contract agreed with Cherry Co, or items of work-in-progress. As Cherry Co is in insolvency, all activity on such contracts will cease with immediate effect. Any such inventory should be reviewed to see if it can be re-allocated to different contracts or back into general inventory. If not, the inventory should be written down to the lower of cost and fair value less costs to sell, with the associated loss recognised in profit for the year.

Audit opinion

If the impairment loss on the trade receivable is not recognised, the audit opinion should be modified due to a material misstatement. This would most likely be a qualified 'except for' opinion due to the material but not pervasive nature of the matter.

Looking at the two issues together, it appears that with the adjustments needed in respect of the training costs, and the impairment to be recognised for the receivable, the statement of profit or loss should show a loss for the year of $325,000 (400 – 500 – 225). If the adjustments are not made, the auditor may come to the opinion that the statement of profit or loss is rendered meaningless, and may issue an adverse opinion, stating that the financial statements are not fairly presented.

Tutorial note

Credit will be awarded for discussion of going concern issues arising from the loss of a major customer.

Audit evidence

- The initial correspondence from the administrators of Cherry Co confirming that the company is insolvent and that only 25% of amounts outstanding is likely to be paid.
- A written confirmation from the administrators of Cherry Co stating the amount that is likely to be paid, and an anticipated payment date.
- Agreement of the amount owed by Cherry Co to the receivables ledger, and to confirmation from the administrators.
- Recalculations of the impairment losses.
- A review of inventory documentation for the value of inventory relating to contracts with Cherry Co.

(b) **Evaluation of the management of the audit of Banana Co**. The comments made by the junior indicate that the audit has not been properly planned or supervised. Both ISQC1 *Quality Control for Firms that Perform Audits and Reviews of Historical Financial Information* and Other Assurance and Related Services Engagements, and ISA 220 *Quality Control for Audits of Historical Financial Information* provide guidance in this area. There are many indicators of poor quality control which are evaluated below.

No audit planning meeting was held at the start of the audit. A meeting is important as this is where the audit partner should direct the audit assignment by explaining to the members of the audit team their responsibilities, the nature of the client's business, and significant risk or fraud indicators identified, and the detailed approach to the audit. If no meeting is held at the start of the audit, then it is unlikely that members of the audit team will understand the audit strategy, the objectives of the work they have been asked to perform or how tasks have been allocated amongst members of the team. The audit partner should lead the meeting, as it is their responsibility to ensure that the audit is directed, supervised and performed in accordance with professional and regulatory standards.

Audit manager and supervisor are not always available. All audit assignments should be properly supervised. In the absence of a manager and supervisor, the more junior members of the audit team will not be able to resolve problems which arise, and the longer there is a lack of supervision, the more problems will accumulate. Without supervision, the audit plan may not be properly followed, and inappropriate modifications may be made to audit programmes.

Junior was given the tasks of auditing goodwill and inventory. It seems that audit work has not been properly delegated amongst members of the audit team. An inexperienced audit junior should not be given relatively complex procedures to perform. Both goodwill and work-in-progress can be challenging to audit, and involve the use of judgement (e.g. the evaluation of the stage of completion of work-in-progress), and it is unlikely that a junior who has only been on two audits will have enough knowledge and experience to fully understand the complexities of the accounting and audit issues involved. Tasks associated with goodwill and work-in-progress should be allocated to a more experienced member of the team, leaving more straightforward tasks for the junior.

Junior helped with the count procedures during the inventory count. The junior did not understand the objectives of the inventory count. Test counts should have been performed by the junior, in order to gather audit evidence for the completeness and existence of inventory items, but members of the audit team should not 'help out' the client's staff with counting. Instead, the junior should have observed the client's staff and assessed whether the count was being performed in accordance with count instructions.

Junior asked to challenge the finance director. It is inappropriate for an inexperienced junior to challenge a senior member of client's management. Contentious issues should be discussed with the client by the audit manager or partner, as they have a more appropriate level of authority and will be in a better position to explain why the provision is considered to be inadequate. This is an inappropriate delegation of tasks within the audit team.

Inadequate time to complete necessary audit procedures. It seems that either not enough time has been allowed to complete the necessary audit procedures, or that in the absence of much direction and supervision, the audit procedures have been performed inefficiently. One of the key aspects of supervision is to keep track on the progress of the audit engagement. The audit plan should initially determine appropriate timescales and deadlines, and if it transpires that more time is needed, this should be discussed with the client.

Modification to planned audit procedures. The audit procedures have been changed in response to lack of time. It is not acceptable to cut corners by reducing sample sizes or changing the items selected for the sample. Modifications should be discussed by senior members of the audit team, and should only occur for genuine reasons. The danger is that reduced sample sizes or changing the items selected for testing will not provide sufficient, reliable audit evidence as the sample selected may no longer be representative of the population as a whole.

Conclusion

Poor quality control means that this audit engagement has not had appropriate direction and supervision. The evidence gathered may be inappropriate and inadequate for the purposes of issuing an audit opinion. This could result in an incorrect opinion being issued. A detailed hot and cold review should be performed to determine if any areas need extra audit work performed, and to consider what measures the firm should take to improve its quality control monitoring procedures.

(c)   **Briefing notes to be used at training session**

Subject: Money laundering policies and procedures

(i)   **Introduction**

In recent years accountants and auditors have become subject to anti-money laundering regulations. This is largely due to the work of the inter-governmental body the Financial Task Force on Money-Laundering (FATF). A firm of Chartered Certified Accountants must establish sound policies and procedures to ensure that the firm meets its responsibilities under the relevant regulation in which the firm is operating *(UK SYLLABUS: this includes the Proceeds of Crime Act and the Money Laundering Regulations)*. It is important that everyone who is a member of an audit engagement team is aware of the regulations, the firm's policies and procedures, and their own responsibilities regarding money laundering activities.

Definition of money laundering

Money laundering is a process by which criminals attempt to conceal the true origin and ownership of the proceeds of criminal activities. It is a way in which money earned from criminal activities ('dirty money') is transferred and transformed so it appears to have come from a legitimate source ('clean money'). Money laundering includes a wide range of potential crimes including possessing, dealing with, or concealing the proceeds of crime.

Illustrations

Money laundering activities could include:

*   Acquiring, using or possessing the proceeds of criminal activities such as drug trafficking and terrorist activities, or retaining control over the proceeds of tax evasion.
*   Benefits obtained through bribery or corruption.
*   Inciting, aiding, counselling or concealing such activities.

The three stages of the money laundering process are placement, layering and integration:

*   Placement is putting money into financial products or instruments, including life policies, pension arrangements, unit trusts, travellers' cheques, and bank deposits.
*   Layering is creating a series of transactions so that the original source of funds is obscured and difficult to trace.
*   Integration is converting the proceeds of money laundering into a legitimate form.

For accountants there are specific ways that they could commit offences relating to money laundering. These could include:

*   Handling the proceeds of criminal activity, or advising on the use of such proceeds.
*   Failure to report knowledge or suspicion of money laundering activities to the appropriate authority.
*   Making a disclosure which is likely to prejudice an investigation into money laundering (known as 'tipping off').

- Failure to comply with the specific regulatory requirements in relation to money laundering in the jurisdiction in which the accountant is operating.

(ii) **Policies and procedures**

Appointment of a Money Laundering Reporting Officer (MLRO). The MLRO is a nominated officer who is responsible for receiving and evaluating reports of suspected money laundering from colleagues within the firm, and making a decision as to whether further enquiry is required and if necessary making reports to the appropriate external body *(UK SYLLABUS: the National Crime Agency)*. The MLRO should have an appropriate level of seniority and experience and would usually be a senior partner.

Customer identification procedures. This is often referred to as customer due diligence, or 'know your client' procedures. The point of these procedures is to ensure that the firm has verified the identity of clients (whether the client is an individual or an entity), and has obtained evidence of that identity. For an individual, typical evidence of identity would be a passport, driving licence, and evidence of address such as a utility bill. For an entity evidence may include a certificate of incorporation. The identification process for an entity would also involve identification of key management personnel and those people in control of the entity, and an assessment as to whether any connected individuals are politically exposed people.

Enhanced record keeping. Records must be kept of clients' identity, the firm's business relationship with them, and details of transactions with the client. All records should be kept for five years after the end of the business relationship or completion of the transactions. Internal and external reports made in connection to money laundering should also be securely kept for five years.

Communication and training. All relevant employees should receive training so that they are aware of the main provisions of money laundering regulations, and so that they know how to recognise and deal with activities which may be money laundering. The training programme should be offered to all members of the firm with an involvement in audit engagements. Training should also be provided on the firm's internal policies and procedures with relation to money laundering. In particular all staff should be aware of appropriate lines of communication, and who they should report suspicions of money laundering activities to. Training should be considered for all staff, including support staff who do not carry out an advisory role.

Internal controls, risk assessment, management and monitoring. The firm should establish systems and controls to effectively manage the risk that the firm is exposed to in terms of money laundering activities. This could include:

- Client screening procedures to minimise the risk of taking on a new client with a high risk of money laundering activities
- Systems and controls to ensure that training is taken/attended and understood by all relevant employees
- Systems that allow periodic testing that the firms' policies and procedures comply with legislative and regulatory requirements.

All of the above contribute to the acceptance and following of firm-wide practices by all relevant individuals and can be seen as quality control measures.

Conclusion

It can be seen that the firm needs to have in place appropriate measures to ensure that complex anti-money laundering regulation is adhered to. It is the responsibility of all relevant staff to be alert for suspicious activities and to understand their own responsibility to report the activity. Failing to do so places the individual and the firm at risk of a breach of regulation.

ACCA marking scheme			
			Marks
(a)	(i)	**Training Costs** Generally 1 mark per matter/evidence Matters: • Correct calculation and assessment of materiality • Cannot capitalise training costs • Expenditure does not create an asset which the entity controls • Potential modification re material misstatement Evidence: • Schedule of costs (½ only) • Agree costs to supporting documentation • Agree costs to cash book/bank *statement* (½ mark only) • Cut-off procedure • Compare to budgeted cost • Confirm cost to approved plan/budget	6
	(ii)	**Trade receivable** Generally 1 mark per matter/evidence point: Matters: • Correct calculation and assessment of materiality • Receivable impaired • Consider any inventory in relation to Cherry Co • Potential modification re material misstatement • Impact of two issues together on the audit opinion Evidence: • Initial correspondence with administrators of Cherry Co • Confirmation with the administrators • Agreement to receivables ledger • Recalculations of impairment losses • Review of inventory schedules	6 ――― 12 ―――
(b)		**Quality control matters** Up to 1½ marks per point evaluated, plus 1 mark for overall conclusion • No audit planning meeting – lack of direction • Absence of manager and senior – lack of supervision • Junior assigned difficult audit work (goodwill and WIP) • Junior helped out with inventory count – lack of understanding/supervision • Junior asked to challenge FD – inappropriate delegation • Audit running out of time – poor planning? • Changed sample size – inappropriate response to time pressure • Changed item selected in sample – inappropriate response	
		Maximum	10 ―――

(c) **Money laundering briefing notes**

Professional marks to be awarded for format (heading, introduction, conclusion) – 1 mark, and clarity

of explanation – 1 mark

Generally up to 3 marks for each explanation from list below:

- Definition of money laundering (1 mark)
- Examples of money laundering activities (max 3 marks)
- Procedures – appoint MLRO
- Procedures – enhanced record keeping systems
- Procedures – know your client
- Procedures – staff training
- Procedures – internal controls, monitoring and management of compliance

Maximum – technical	10
Professional marks	2
Total	**34**

36 APRICOT CO *Walk in the footsteps of a top tutor*

Key answer tips

This is an excellent example of an audit related assignment to report on PFI, in this case a cash flow forecast. The most important consideration here is recommending procedures that are relevant to this unique engagement. You are given information about the nature and circumstances of the company and imminent changes to it. You must therefore design procedures that reflect this understanding. Also consider who is requesting the assignment and what they would hope to get out of it.

Part (b) is more general and simply asks what the contents of a typical PFI assurance report are. This requires little more than pre-learnt knowledge.

The highlighted words are key phases that markers are looking for.

(a) Recommended procedures to be performed on the cash flow forecast include:

Accuracy checks:

- Agree the opening cash position to cash book and bank statement/bank reconciliation.
- Cast the forecast.

Cash receipts:

- Assess whether the assumption regarding the split of revenue between cash and credit sales is accurate by considering whether it is in line with knowledge of the business.
- Agree the forecast cash receipts from cash sales to the forecast revenue figures in the profit forecast for January, February and March 2010.
- Verify the 10% discount has been accounted for in calculating the cash sales by recalculation.

- Agree the 10% discount to a small sample of invoices raised.
- Recalculate the pattern of receipts from credit customers by applying the stated average credit terms to actual sales in October, November and December 2009, and the forecast sales for January, February and March 2010.
- Review the latest aged receivables analysis available for confirmation of the pattern of payment from credit customers.

Purchases:

- Recalculate the pattern of cash flows relating to purchases by applying the stated credit terms to the forecast purchases figures in the profit forecast.
- Using the latest available information, calculate a suppliers payment ratio to compare with the stated usual credit terms applied to purchases of 30 days.
- Agree the 12% discount to invoices received, supplier statement reconciliations, or signed contracts with suppliers.

Other operating cash outflows:

- Discuss with the management of Apricot Co the relationship between sales and operating cash outflows. It appears that outflows could be understated, as salaries and expenses are static, whereas cash receipts from sales are increasing over the period.
- Agree the monthly salary cash outflow to latest available payroll records, and to the profit forecast.
- Obtain a breakdown of the contents of the overheads cash outflow category and review the schedule for any non-cash items which should not be included, e.g. depreciation and amortisation, bad debt expenses.
- Compare the components of the overhead cash outflow to a breakdown of operating expenses included in the profit forecast, looking for omissions.

Non-recurring cash flows:

- Agree the cost of the licence to supporting documentation, e.g. any correspondence already received from the issuing body, and compare the cost of $35,000 to the cost of the previous year's licence.
- Confirm that the 2009 licence expires in December and that the new licence will be required in January 2010 by reviewing the terms of the licence.
- Discuss the inspections required for the new licence to be granted, and ascertain if the inspections have yet taken place, and if so, the results of the inspection.
- Review the board minutes, and minutes of shareholder meetings for approval of the dividend payment in February 2010.

Cash flows associated with the new premises:

- For the new fixtures, agree the estimated cost to supplier price lists, or to any quotations received.
- Discuss the timing of the cash outflow in relation to fixtures with management. Presumably the fixtures can only be put into place once the premises have been acquired, which is planned for the end of March. It seems likely that the fixtures will not be purchased until April, in which case the cash payment is recognised too early in the forecast.
- For the premises, agree the potential purchase price to correspondence with the vendor and solicitors.

- Obtain a breakdown of the potential cost of $500,000 and review to ensure the cost is complete, i.e. have legal fees, stamp duty and other associated costs been included.

- Review board minutes for approval of the purchase, and approval that the finance will be raised from Pik Choi.

General enquiries:

Enquire with the preparer of the forecast regarding the following:

- Enquire as to the competence and experience of the preparer of the forecast.

- No finance costs or tax payments appear to have been included – have they been omitted or are there no finance or tax payments in the three-month period?

- Are there any other costs to be incurred in relation to the new premises in the three-month period? e.g. recruitment costs for new staff, any additional working capital requirements, installation of plant and fixtures to the new premises.

- Discuss the reason for the acquisition of the new premises.

- Enquire whether any payments in advance or deposits will need to be made; currently the full amount is forecasted to be paid on the date of acquisition.

- Enquire about any other potential sources of finance in case Pik Choi fails to provide the full amount required, or in case the new premises cost more than the estimated amount.

(b) Main contents of an assurance report:

ISAE 3400 *The Examination of Prospective Financial Information* provides guidance on the content of an assurance report given when a professional accountant has examined forecasts or projections.

- Title and addressee.

- Identification of the prospective financial information (PFI); this should be by reference to a page number, or to the titles of the statements which have been evaluated. There should also be a reference to the period that the PFI covers.

- A reference to ISAE 3400 or relevant national standards applicable to the examination of PFI. This adds credibility to the report because it has been prepared according to a recognised regulatory statement.

- A statement that management is responsible for the PFI including the assumptions on which it is based. There should be a page reference for the assumptions, as these are a key component of the PFI.

- Where applicable, a reference to the purpose and/or restricted distribution of the prospective financial information. The report should caution readers that because the PFI is based on hypothetical assumptions, the events and figures contained in the PFI may not necessarily occur as expected. There should also be a caution as to the potential use of the PFI.

- A statement of negative assurance as to whether the assumptions provide a reasonable basis for the PFI. This would be stated as follows: 'nothing has come to our attention which causes us to believe that the assumptions do not provide a reasonable basis for the projection...'.

- An opinion as to whether the PFI is properly prepared on the basis of the assumptions and is presented in accordance with the relevant financial reporting framework.

- Appropriate caveats concerning the achievability of the results indicated by the PFI.
- The date, name of the audit firm, and a signature.

The following points are not specifically referred to in ISAE 3400, but would commonly be included by firms providing assurance reports on PFI:

- A reference to the engagement letter and to the specific procedures that were requested, and have been carried out.
- A statement that the procedures carried out were those specified by the company and the third party to whom the report is issued.
- Details of any errors and exceptions found.

If the auditor believes that the presentation and disclosure of the PFI is not adequate, the auditor should express a qualified or adverse opinion. If one or more significant assumptions do not provide a reasonable basis for the PFI, the auditor should express an adverse opinion on the report. A modified opinion due to lack of sufficient appropriate evidence should be expressed if conditions preclude application of one or more procedures considered necessary in the circumstances.

	ACCA marking scheme	
		Marks
(a)	**Procedures on cash flow forecast**	
	Generally 1 mark per specific procedure from ideas list:	
	• Accuracy checks – recalculation	
	• Agree opening cash position	
	• Recalculate patterns of cash in and out for credit sales and purchases	
	• Agree patterns using aged receivables analysis/working capital ratios	
	• Agree discounts received and allowed to invoices/contracts/ correspondences	
	• Agree derivation of figures from profit forecast	
	• Agree monthly salary expense to payroll	
	• Review content of overheads – check non-cash expenses not included	
	• Review for missing outflows e.g. tax and finance charges	
	• Agree premises costs e.g. to legal documents	
	• Discuss timing of fixtures cash flow	
	• General enquiries with the preparer of the forecast	
	Maximum	11
(b)	**Content of an assurance report**	
	Up to 1 mark per point if explained:	
	• Title/addressee (½ mark)	
	• Identification of PFI	
	• Management responsibility	
	• Purpose of PFI	
	• Restricted use of PFI	
	• Negative assurance opinion re assumptions	
	• Opinion on presentation	
	• When may modifications be necessary/explanation of errors found	
	• Reference to engagement letter (½ mark)	
	• Statement/reference to procedures carried out (½ mark)	
		5
Total		16

37 ROBSTER CO *Walk in the footsteps of a top tutor*

Key answer tips

This is a relatively straightforward matters/evidence question, albeit concerning two complex, technical accounting areas. It should be noted that the examiner has chosen two areas of financial reporting that she described as 'likely to be examined in detail' in her article 'The Importance of Financial Reporting Standards to Auditors.'

Matters to consider at the review stage include: whether potential areas of contention are material; relevant accounting guidance; indications of potential errors; and impacts on the audit report. The audit procedures recommended in part a(ii) should link directly to your discussion of possible concerns in a(i).

The highlighted words are key phases that markers are looking for.

(a)   (i)   **Leases**

Matters to consider

Materiality

The amounts recognised in the statement of financial position in relation to the leases are material to the financial statements. The amount recognised in non-current assets amounts to 8% of total assets, and the total finance lease payable recognised amounts to 7.1% of total assets.

Accounting treatment

IAS 17 *Leases* contains detailed guidance on the classification and recognition of leased assets. There are several matters to consider:

- Whether the leases are correctly categorised as finance leases or operating leases. This depends on whether the risk and reward of ownership have passed to Robster Co (the lessee) from the lessor. The leases should only be recognised on the statement of financial position if Robster Co has the risk and reward of ownership.

- Indicators of risk and reward passing to Robster Co would include:
    - Robster Co is responsible for repairs and maintenance of the assets.
    - A bargain purchase option exists.
    - The lease period is for most of the expected useful life of the assets.
    - The present value of the minimum lease payments is substantially all of the fair value of the asset.

- Whether the amounts capitalised are solely in respect of the buildings element of the leases. Leases of land and buildings should be 'unbundled' and the two elements accounted for separately (unless the land element is immaterial).

- The impact of the leases on the statement of profit or loss must be considered. A finance charge should be calculated and expensed each accounting period, using the actuarial method of calculation (or the sum of digits method as an approximation). In addition, leased assets should be depreciated over the shorter of the lease term and the economic useful life of the asset.

Presentation and disclosure

The finance lease payable recognised of $3.2 million should be split between current and non-current liabilities in the statement of financial position.

IAS 17 requires extensive disclosure relating to leases in the notes to the financial statements, including an analysis showing the amounts outstanding under the lease, and the timing of the cash outflows.

Audit evidence

- A review of the lease contract (using a copy of the lease obtained from the lessor) including consideration of the major clauses of the lease which indicate whether risk and reward has passed to Robster Co.

- A calculation of the present value of minimum lease payments and comparison with the fair value of the assets at the inception of the lease (the fair value should be obtained from the lease contract).

- A recalculation of the finance charge expensed during the accounting period, and agreement of the interest rate used in the lease contract.

- Agreement to the cash book of amounts paid to the lessor i.e. deposit and instalments paid before the year end.

- A recalculation of the depreciation charged, and agreement that the period used in the calculation is the shorter of the lease term and the useful life of the assets.

- Confirmation using the lease contract that the amounts capitalised relate only to the buildings element of the lease.

- For the land elements which should be treated as operating leases, a recalculation of the lease expense recognised in the statement of profit or loss (this should be calculated on a straight-line basis over the lease term).

- A recalculation and confirmation of the split of the total finance lease payable between current and non-current liabilities.

- A confirmation of the adequacy of the disclosure made in the notes to the financial statements, and agreement of the future payments disclosed to the lease contract.

(ii) **Financial assets**

Matters to consider

Materiality

The financial assets are material to the statement of financial position as the amount recognised in non-current assets amounts to 2.8% of total assets. The gain recognised is material to the statement of profit or loss, representing 10.9% of profit before tax, and 3.3% of revenue.

Accounting treatment

Robster Co has classified financial assets as 'financial assets at fair value through profit or loss' as they are considered to be 'held for trading' investments. IFRS 9 *Financial Instruments* states that all financial assets are measured at fair value at initial recognition. Fair value at initial recognition is normally cost incurred excluding transaction costs.

Subsequent measurement depends on whether the financial asset is a debt instrument or an equity instrument, although both are normally measured at fair value through profit or loss.

Robster Co could choose to measure a debt instrument at amortised cost, if certain criteria were met, i.e. the asset must be held to collect contractual cash flows associated with the asset and these cash flows must consist solely of payment of interest and capital. As the assets are 'held for trading' measuring at amortised cost appears inappropriate.

If an equity instrument is not held for trading, an irrecoverable election can be made to designate the equity instrument as fair value through other comprehensive income. This election would not be appropriate as Robster Co considers the assets to be 'held for trading' investments.

It would appear that Robster Co has correctly classified the financial assets.

Investments classified in this way must be measured at fair value each year end, with gains and losses taken into the statement of profit or loss as part of net profit for the year.

Disclosure

IFRS 7 *Financial Instruments: Disclosures* contains extensive disclosure requirements in relation to financial assets, including for example, a narrative description of how the risks in relation to the investments are managed and monitored, and quantitative disclosures including sensitivity analysis relating to the market risk associated with the valuation of investments.

Audit evidence

- A schedule showing all the investments held in the category, their purchase price and their year-end valuation.
- Agreement of the purchase prices of investments to supporting documentation, e.g. stockbrokers' statements.
- Agreement of the year end valuation for each investment to external sources of information, e.g. stock exchange website, financial press.
- Recalculation, and confirmation of the gain recognised in the statement of profit or loss.
- A review of the internal function which has been set up to manage the investments, to confirm that investments are generally short-term in nature, that the investments are managed as a portfolio, and that there is evidence of frequent transactions.
- Confirmation that the other information published with the financial statements, e.g. the operating and financial review, describes Robster Co's investment activities in line with the classification of investments as held for trading, and refers to the valuation and gain made during the year.

- A review of the proposed note to the financial statements confirming adherence to the disclosure requirements of IFRS 7, and recalculations of numerical disclosures.

(b) Guidance on reviews of interim financial statements is provided in ISRE 2410 *Review of Interim Financial Information Performed by the Independent Auditor of the Entity*. The standard states that the auditor should plan their work to gather evidence using analytical procedures and enquiry.

The auditor should perform analytical procedures in order to discover unusual trends and relationships, or individual figures in the interim financial information, which may indicate a material misstatement. Procedures should include the following:

- Comparing the interim financial information with anticipated results, budgets and targets as set by the management of the company.
- Comparing the interim financial information with:
  - comparable information for the immediately preceding interim period,
  - the corresponding interim period in the previous year, and
  - the most recent audited financial statements.
- Comparing ratios and indicators for the current interim period with those of entities in the same industry.
- Considering relationships among financial and non-financial information. The auditor also may wish to consider information developed and used by the entity, for example, information in monthly financial reports provided to the senior management or press releases issued by the company relevant to the interim financial information.
- Comparing recorded amounts or ratios developed from recorded amounts, to expectations developed by the auditor. The auditor develops such expectations by identifying and using plausible relationships that are reasonably expected to exist based on the accountant's understanding of the entity and the industry in which the entity operates.
- Comparing disaggregated data, for example, comparing revenue reported by month and by product line or operating segment during the current interim period with that of comparable prior periods.

As with analytical procedures performed in an audit, any unusual relationships, trends or individual amounts discovered which may indicate a material misstatement should be discussed with management. However, unlike an audit, further corroboration using substantive procedures is not necessary in a review engagement.

Examiner's comments

The first part of this question was a standard audit evidence question of the type seen in numerous previous examinations. Nearly all candidates correctly calculated and concluded on the materiality of both items, and considered the financial reporting implications of the information provided.

In terms of the finance leases, most candidates indentified the correct financial reporting standard, and discussed the classification of the lease as finance or operating lease. Some candidates could provide nothing further, but better answers continued on to describe the factors that should be considered in lease classification, referring not just to 'substance over form', but to the specific indicators that risk and reward had passed to the lessee. Only a small minority of candidates discussed whether the lease should be unbundled into the separate land and buildings elements.

The evidence points tended to be quite brief for this requirement, usually limited to 'check the lease document', 'check lease approved by management' and the inevitable 'get management representation that it is a finance lease'. Such comments are much too vague, and better answers provided more specific pieces of evidence that should be sought, such as a recalculation of minimum lease payments, and a review of the clauses of the lease in terms of responsibility for insurance and repairs to the assets.

(a) (ii) was generally unsatisfactorily answered, and the information given in the question was often misinterpreted. Candidates tended to know the number of the relevant financial reporting standard for financial assets, but not the technical content of that standard. Despite the question clearly stating that the assets are all investments in listed companies, a significant proportion of candidates chose to base their answer around investment properties, and others seemed to think the assets were some kind of inventory, to be valued at the lower of cost and net realisable value. Even those candidates who appreciated that the assets were investments were confused by terminology, frequently stating that 'fair value through profit and loss' and 'held for trading' are contradictory, which is not the case. Most candidates thought that the revaluation gain should not be recognised in profit for the year, which again is not the case.

The evidence points were also inadequate for this requirement. Even a candidate lacking knowledge of the financial reporting issues for investments in listed companies should be able to suggest confirming the year end share price to an external source of information on share prices, such as the financial times, but unfortunately few candidates could even provide this as a piece of evidence.

Requirement (b) was unsatisfactorily answered by almost all candidates. This asked for the principal analytical procedures that should be used to gather evidence in a review of interim financial information. Candidates are repeatedly reminded that non-audit engagements are part of the syllabus, and likely to feature regularly in the examination. However, few candidates seemed to know the purpose of a review of interim financial information, which meant that their answers lacked clarity. Most answers could only suggest a comparison with the prior period, and hardly any answers mentioned the disaggregation of data, or comparison with budget. Only a handful of candidates seemed aware of the existence of ISRE 2410, *Review of Interim Financial Information Performed by the Independent Auditor of the entity,* on which the requirement is based.

Some candidates confused a 'review of interim financial information' with an 'interim audit', despite the short scenario describing a review of interim financial information for the avoidance of any such confusion.

		ACCA marking scheme		
				Marks
(a)	(i)	**Leases**		
		Generally 1 mark per matter/evidence point:		
		Matters:		
		– Correct calculation and assessment of materiality		
		– Classification of lease		
		– IAS 17 indicators of finance lease		
		– Split between land and buildings		
		– Finance charge		
		– Depreciation		
		– Disclosure		
		Evidence		
		– Lease clauses re risk and reward		
		– Recalculate PV of MLP v FV		
		– Recalculate depn and finance charge		
		– Cash book for payments		
		– Review of disclosures		
		– Split current/non-current payable		
			Maximum marks	8
	(ii)	**Financial Assets**		
		Generally 1 mark per matter/evidence point:		
		Matters:		
		– Correct calculation and assessment of materiality		
		– Classification as held for trading		
		– Assets shown at fair value – could be subjective		
		– Disclosure		
		Evidence		
		– Agree purchase price		
		– Agree fair value		
		– Recalculate gain		
		– Review of disclosures in notes		
		– Review of disclosures in OFR/other information published with financial statements		
			Maximum marks	5
(b)		**Interim Financial Information**		
		Generally 1 mark per procedure:		
		– Comparisons with past data e.g. to preceding period, to corresponding interim last year, to last audited accounts		
		– Comparisons to anticipated results		
		– Comparisons to non financial data/ratios		
		– Comparisons to similar entities		
		– Disaggregation of data		
			Maximum marks	4
Total				**17**

38 DRAGON GROUP *Walk in the footsteps of a top tutor*

Key answer tips

This question based upon the principles of appointing an auditor.

Part (a) requires little more than common sense regarding why auditors may not wish to continue auditing a particular client.

Part (b) requires a basic knowledge of the contents of a tender document. You then need to flesh this out by applying this knowledge to the specific information given. For ten marks you need to make at least 7 explained points.

Part (c) asks you to consider what professional issues you need to consider before accepting a new client. This could include any aspect of audit quality control, ethics or general practice management/administration.

Part (d) required some basic knowledge and then some common sense suggestions about the difficulty of cross-border audit.

The highlighted words are key phases that markers are looking for.

(a)   **Reasons why a firm of auditors may decide not to seek re-election – any FOUR of the following:**

Disagreement with the client

The audit firm may have disagreed with the client for a number of reasons, for example, over accounting treatments used in the financial statements. A disagreement over a significant matter is likely to cause a breakdown in the professional relationship between auditor and client, meaning that the audit firm could lose faith in the competence of management. The auditor would be reluctant to seek re-election if the disagreement were not resolved.

Lack of integrity of client

The audit firm may feel that management is not acting with integrity, for example, the financial statements may be subject to creative accounting, or dubious business ethics decisions could be made by management, such as the exploitation of child labour. The auditor would be likely not to seek re-election (or to resign) in this case to avoid being associated with the client's poor decisions.

Fee level

The audit firm could be unable to demand a high enough audit fee from the client to cover the costs of the audit. In this situation the audit firm may choose not to offer itself for re-election, to avoid continuing with a loss making audit engagement, and consequently to use resources in a more commercially advantageous way.

Fee payments

The audit firm could have outstanding fees which may not be fully recovered due to a client's poor cash flow position. Or, the client could be slow paying, causing the audit firm to chase for payment and possibly affecting the relationship between the two businesses. In such cases the audit firm may make the commercial decision not to act for the client any longer.

Resources

The audit firm may find that it lacks the resources to continue to provide the audit service to a client. This could happen if the client company grows rapidly, financially or operationally, meaning that a larger audit team is necessary. The audit firm may simply lack the necessary skilled staff to expand the audit team.

Competence

The audit firm could feel that it is no longer competent to perform an audit service. This could happen for example if a client company diversified into a new and specialised business operation of which the audit firm had little or no experience. The audit firm would not be able to provide a high quality audit without building up or buying in the necessary knowledge and skills, and so may decide not to be considered for re-election.

Overseas expansion

A client could acquire one or several material overseas subsidiaries. If the audit firm does not have an associate office in the overseas location, the firm may feel that the risk and resources involved in relying on the work of other auditors is too great, and so decide not to act for the client any longer.

Independence

There are many ethical guidelines in relation to independence which must be adhered to by auditors, and in the event of a potential breach of the guidelines, the audit firm may decide not to seek re-election. For example, an audit firm may need to increase the audit fee if a client company grows in size. This could have the effect of increasing the fee received from the client above the allowed thresholds. As there would be no ethical safeguard strong enough to preserve the perception of independence, in this case the audit firm would not be able to continue to provide the audit service.

Tutorial note

Other examples may be used to explain why the issue of independence could cause an audit firm not to seek re-election, e.g. audit firm takes on a financial interest in the client, close personal relationships develop between the firm and the client.

Conflicts of interest

An audit firm may become involved in a situation where a conflict of interest arises between an existing audit client and another client of the firm. For example, an audit firm could take on a new audit client which is a competitor of an existing audit client. Although with the use of appropriate safeguards this situation could be successfully managed, the audit firm may decide that stepping down as auditor of the existing firm is the best course of action.

(b)   **Matters to be included in tender document**

Brief outline of Unicorn & Co

This should include a short history of the firm, a description of its organisational structure, the different services offered by the firm (such as audit, tax, corporate finance, etc), and the locations in which the firm operates. The document should also state whether it is a member of any international audit firm network. The geographical locations in which Unicorn & Co operates will be important given the multi-national structure of the Dragon Group.

Specialisms of the firm

Unicorn & Co should describe the areas in which the firm has particular experience of relevance to the Dragon Group. It would be advantageous to stress that the firm has an audit department dedicated to the audit of clients in the retail industry, as this emphasises the experience that the firm has relevant to the specific operations of the group.

Identification of the needs of the Dragon Group

The tender document should outline the requirements of the client, in this case, that each subsidiary is required to have an individual audit on its financial statements, and that the consolidated financial statements also need to be audited. Unicorn & Co may choose to include here a brief clarification of the purpose and legal requirements of an audit. The potential provision of non-audit services should be discussed, either here, or in a separate section of the tender document (see below).

Outline of the proposed audit approach

This is likely to be the most detailed part of the tender document. Here the firm will describe how the audit would be conducted, ensuring that the needs of the Dragon Group (as discussed above) have been met. Typically contained in this section would be a description of the audit methodology used by the firm, and an outline of the audit cycle including the key deliverables at each phase of work. For example:

*   How the firm would intend to gain business understanding at group and subsidiary level.
*   Methods used to assess risk and to plan the audits.
*   Procedures used to assess the control environment and accounting systems.
*   Techniques used to gather evidence, e.g. the use of audit software.

How the firm would structure the audit of the consolidation of the group financial statements and how they would liaise with subsidiary audit teams.

The firm should clarify its adherence to International Standards on Auditing, ethical guidelines and any other relevant laws and regulations operating in the various jurisdictions relevant to the Dragon Group. The various financial reporting frameworks used within the group should be clarified.

Quality control

Unicorn & Co should emphasise the importance of quality control and therefore should explain the procedures that are used within the firm to monitor the quality of the audit services provided. This should include a description of firm-wide quality control policies, and the procedures applied to individual audits. The firm may wish to clarify its adherence to International Standards on Quality Control.

Communication with management

The firm should outline the various reports and other communication that will be made to management as part of the audit process. The purpose and main content of the reports, and the timing of them, should be outlined. Unicorn & Co may provide some 'added value' bi-products of the audit process. For example, the business risks identified as part of the audit planning may be fed back to management in a written report.

Timing

Unicorn & Co should outline the timeframe that would be used. For example, the audits of the subsidiaries' financial statements should be conducted before the audit of the consolidated financial statements. The firm may wish to include an approximate date by which the group audit opinion would be completed, which should fit in, if possible, with the requirements of the group. If Unicorn & Co feel that the deadline requested by the client is unrealistic, a more appropriate deadline should be suggested, with the reasons for this clearly explained.

Key staff and resources

The document should name the key members of staff to be assigned to the audit, in particular the proposed engagement partner. In addition, the firm should clarify the approximate number of staff to be used in the audit team and the relevant experience of the key members of the audit team. If the firm considers that external specialists could be needed, then this should be explained in this section of the document.

Fees

The proposed fee for the audit of the group should be stated, and the calculation of the fee should be explained, i.e. broken down by grade of staff and hourly/daily rates per grade. In addition, invoicing and payment terms should be described, e.g. if the audit fee is payable in instalments, the stages when each instalment will fall due.

Extra services

Unicorn & Co should ensure that any non-audit services that it may be able to offer to the Dragon Group are described. For example, subject to ethical safeguards, the firm may be able to offer corporate finance services in relation to the stock exchange listing that the group is seeking, although the provision of this non-audit service would need to be carefully considered in relation to independence issues.

(c)   **Evaluation of matters to be considered:**

Size and location of the group companies

The Dragon Group is a large multi-national group of companies. It is extremely important that Unicorn & Co assesses the availability of resources that can be allocated to the audit team. The assignment would comprise the audit of the financial statements of all 20 current subsidiaries, the audit of the parent company's and the group's financial statements. This is a significant engagement which will demand a great deal of time.

The location of half of the group's subsidiaries in other countries means that the overseas offices of Unicorn & Co would be called upon to perform some or all of the audit of those subsidiaries. In this case the resource base of the relevant overseas offices should be considered to ensure there is enough staff with appropriate skills and experience available to perform the necessary audit work.

Unicorn & Co must consider if they have offices in all of the countries in which the Dragon Group has a subsidiary.

Depending on the materiality of the overseas subsidiaries to the group financial statements, it is likely that some overseas visits would be required to evaluate the work of the overseas audit teams. Unicorn & Co should consider who will conduct the visits (presumably a senior member of the audit team), and whether that person has the necessary skills and experience in evaluating the work of overseas audit teams.

Planned expansion of the group

In light of the comments above, Unicorn & Co should consider that the planned further significant expansion of the group will mean more audit staff will be needed in future years, and if any subsidiaries are acquired in other countries, the audit is likely to be performed by overseas offices. The firm should therefore consider not only its current resource base in the local and overseas offices, but whether additional staff will be available in the future if the group's expansion goes ahead as planned.

Relevant skills and experience

Unicorn & Co has an audit department specialising in the audit of retail companies, so it should not be a problem to find audit staff with relevant experience in this country.

On consolidation, the financial statements of the subsidiaries will be restated in line with group accounting policies and financial reporting framework, and will also be retranslated into local presentational currency. All of this work will be performed by the management of the Dragon Group. Unicorn & Co must evaluate the availability of staff experienced in the audit of a consolidation including foreign subsidiaries.

Timing

It is important to consider the timeframe when conducting a group audit. The audit of each subsidiary's financial statements should be carried out prior to the audit of the consolidated financial statements. Unicorn & Co should consider the expectation of the Dragon Group in relation to the reporting deadline, and ensure that enough time is allowed for the completion of all audits. The deadline proposed by management of 31 December is only three months after the year end, which may be unrealistic given the size of the group and the multi-national location of the subsidiaries. The first year auditing a new client is likely to take longer, as the audit team will need to familiarise themselves with the business, the accounting systems and controls, etc.

Mermaid Co – prior year modification

If Unicorn & Co accepts the engagement, the firm will take on the audit of Mermaid Co, whose financial statements in the prior year were in breach of financial reporting standards. This adds an element of risk to the engagement. Unicorn & Co should gather as much information as possible about the contingent liability, and the reason why the management of Mermaid Co did not amend the financial statements last year end. This could hint at a lack of integrity on the part of the management of the company.

The firm should also consider whether this matter could be significant to the consolidated financial statements, by assessing the materiality of the contingent liability at group level.

Further discussions should be held with the management of the Dragon Group in order to understand their thoughts on the contingency and whether it should be disclosed in the individual financial statements of Mermaid Co, and at group level. Contacting the incumbent auditors (after seeking relevant permission from the Dragon Group) would also be an important procedure to gather information about the modification.

Minotaur Co – different business activity

The acquisition of Minotaur Co represents a new business activity for the group. The retail business audit department may not currently have much, if any, experience of auditing a distribution company. This should be easily overcome, either by bringing in staff from a different department more experienced in clients with distribution operations, or by ensuring adequate training for staff in the retail business audit department.

Highly regulated/reliance on financial statements and audit report

The Group is listed on several stock exchanges, and is therefore subject to a high degree of regulation. This adds an element of risk to the engagement, as the management will be under pressure to publish favourable results. This risk is increased by the fact that a new listing is being sought, meaning that the financial statements and audit report of the group will be subject to close scrutiny by the stock exchange regulators.

There may be extra work required by the auditors due to the listings, for example, the group may have to prepare reconciliations of financial data, or additional narrative reports on which the auditors have to express an opinion under the rulings of the stock exchange. The firm must consider the availability of staff skilled in regulatory and reporting listing rules to perform such work.

Previous auditors of Dragon Group

Unicorn & Co should consider the reason why the previous audit firm is not seeking re-appointment, and whether the reason would impact on their acceptance decision. After seeking permission from the Dragon Group, contact should be made with the previous auditors to obtain confirmation of the reason for them vacating office (amongst other matters).

In conclusion, this is a large scale, multi-national group, which carries a fairly high level of risk. Unicorn & Co must be extremely careful to only commit to the group audit if it has the necessary resources, can manage the client's expectation in relation to the reporting deadline, is convinced of the integrity of management, and is confident to take on a potentially high profile client.

Tutorial note

Credit will be awarded in this requirement for discussion of ethical matters which would be considered prior to accepting the appointment as auditor of the Dragon Group. However, as the scenario does not contain any reference to specific ethical matters, marks will be limited to a maximum of 2 for a general discussion of ethical matters on acceptance.

(d) (i) **Definition:** A transnational audit means an audit of financial statements which are or may be relied upon outside the audited entity's home jurisdiction for the purpose of significant lending, investment or regulatory decisions.

Relevance: The Dragon Group is listed on the stock exchange of several countries, (and is planning to raise more finance by a further listing). This means that the group is subject to the regulations of all stock exchanges on which it is listed, and so is bound by listing rules outside of its home jurisdiction. The group also contains many foreign subsidiaries, meaning that it operates in a global business and financial environment.

(ii) **Transnational audit and audit risk** – any TWO of the following:

Application of auditing standards

Although many countries of the world have adopted International Standards on Auditing (ISAs), not all have done so, choosing instead to use locally developed auditing regulations. In addition, some countries use modified versions of ISAs. This means that in a transnational audit, some components of the group financial statements will have been audited using a different auditing framework, resulting in inconsistent audit processes within the group, and potentially reducing the quality of the audit as a whole.

Regulation and oversight of auditors

Similar to the previous comments on the use of ISAs, across the world there are many different ways in which the activities of auditors are regulated and monitored. In some countries the audit profession is self-regulatory, whereas in other countries a more legislative approach is used. This also can impact on the quality of audit work in a transnational situation.

Financial reporting framework

Some countries use International Financial Reporting Standards, whereas some use locally developed accounting standards. Within a transnational group it is likely that adjustments, reconciliations or restatements may be required in order to comply with the requirements of the jurisdictions relevant to the group financial statements (i.e. the jurisdiction of the parent company in most cases). Such reconciliations can be complex and require a high level of technical expertise of the preparer and the auditor.

Corporate governance requirements and consequent control risk

In some countries there are very prescriptive corporate governance requirements, which the auditor must consider as part of the audit process. In this case the auditor may need to carry out extra work over and above local requirements in order to ensure group wide compliance with the requirements of the jurisdictions relevant to the financial statements. However, in some countries there is very little corporate governance regulation at all and controls are likely to be weaker than in other components of the group. Control risk is therefore likely to differ between the various subsidiaries making up the group.

Examiner's comments

Requirement (a) was a short factual requirement, not related to the detail of the question scenario, which asked candidates to explain four reasons why a firm of auditors may decide not to seek re-election as auditor. There were two main problems with answers to this requirement. Firstly, too few candidates actually provided an **explanation of the reasons** they gave. For example, an answer stated that the auditor had a disagreement with the client over something in the financial statements. While this is indeed a reason why the auditor may chose not to seek re-election, it is not an explanation, which would entail going on to say that the disagreement had caused a breakdown in the working relationship between the auditor and client, and that the auditor had lost faith in the competence and/or integrity of management.

Secondly, the requirement asked for **FOUR** reasons. It is a waste of time and effort to provide more than the required number of reasons.

The **second requirement** focussed on the audit tendering process, and asked for matters to be included in a tender document to be presented to the Dragon Group. This requirement seemed to polarise candidates. Those candidates who tailored their answer to the question scenario tended to do well, with a significant proportion achieving close to the maximum marks available. However, candidates who provided a list of points to be included in ANY tender, regardless of the information provided about the prospective client, and about your audit firm, scored inadequately. In other words, it is important to **apply knowledge** to score well, as is true for any scenario-based question.

Sound answers to (b) appreciated that the point of the tender document is to sell your audit firm's services to the client, and recommended points to include such as the global positioning of both audit firm and prospective client, the specialism of the audit firm in retail, and the firm's ability to potentially provide services relating to the expansion plans of the group, such as due diligence.

Weak answers simply stated vague comments: 'we should discuss fees', 'we should set a deadline,' etc. Some answers confused a tender document with an engagement letter, and included points more suited to that document, such as a statement of responsibilities or a legal disclaimer.

Inadequate answers to (b) were those that seemed to confuse the requirements with those of (c). Candidates are reminded that it is important to **read ALL of the requirements** of a question before beginning their answer, to avoid such confusion. Examples of statements commonly seen in answers to (b) which are more relevant to (c) are:

- 'are we competent to audit the group'
- 'can we audit the goodwill and foreign exchange transactions which are complex'
- 'will any of our audit staff want to go abroad to work'
- 'do any of our partners hold shares in Dragon Group'.

These comments definitely do not belong in a tender document, which should highlight the audit firm's capabilities to service the prospective client, rather than question the firm's competence or ability to take on the assignment. Such comments indicate a failure to read and understand the question requirement, as well as a lack of commercial awareness.

Requirement (c) asked candidates to evaluate the matters that should be considered before accepting the audit engagement. Answers here were weak, despite this being a **regularly examined syllabus area**. Most answers were not tailored to the question, and just provided a list of questions or actions, such as 'get permission to contact previous auditor', or 'check the integrity of management', and 'do we have the skill to audit foreign currencies'.

Providing a list of such comments will not generate enough marks to pass the question requirement. Better answers discussed, amongst other points:

- the risk posed by the numerous stock exchange listings of the potential client, and whether the audit fee would be enough to compensate for that risk
- the practical difficulties entailed in co-ordinating an audit of more than 20 companies across many different countries
- the tight deadline imposed by the potential client, especially in light of this being a first year audit, and the learning curve that the audit firm would need to go through.

Some candidates appeared to think that the audit would be too much trouble – a sizeable number of scripts contained comments such as 'auditing a company far from our main office would be tedious and inconvenient'. I would suggest that most audit firms, on being successful in a tender for an audit as significant as this, would consider the inconvenience worthwhile.

Requirement (c) had 2 professional marks associated, awarded for the clarity and presentation of the evaluation provided. It was not necessary to present the answer in a particular format, the presentation mark was awarded to candidates who used headings and a logical structure. An evaluation should contain prioritisation, and a conclusion, but very few candidates suggested that some of the matters they had considered were more important than others, and even fewer concluded as to whether the firm should accept the appointment as group auditor.

Requirement (d) was the worst answered on the paper. Clearly, very few candidates had studied the issue of transnational audits, and answers displayed a lack of knowledge. (di) asked for a definition of transnational audit, and an explanation as to why the term was applicable to the Dragon Group audit. Only a small minority of candidates could provide the correct definition, the rest guessing from the scenario that it was 'an audit covering many countries', or 'an audit performed by several audit firms from different countries', neither of which is true. (d) (ii) asked for two features of a transnational audit that contribute to a high level of audit risk. Answers again appeared to be based mainly on guesswork, with common suggestions being 'language difficulties' and 'communication barriers'. However, some candidates could identify variations in auditing standards and financial reporting frameworks as issues contributing to high risk, but these points were rarely developed to their full potential.

ACCA marking scheme		Marks
(a) **Identify and explain using examples why an audit firm may not seek re-election** Generally ½ mark for identification, 1 for explanation/example, any FOUR: – Disagreement – Lack of integrity – Fee level – Late payment of fees – Resources – Overseas expansion – Competence – Independence – Conflict of interest		
	Maximum marks	6

(b)	**Contents of tender document**		
	Up to 1½ marks per matter described:		
	– Outline of firm		
	– Specialisms		
	– Audit requirement of Dragon Group		
	– Outline audit approach (max 3 marks if detailed)		
	– QC		
	– Communication with management		
	– Timing		
	– Key staff/resources		
	– Fees		
	– Extra services		—
	Maximum marks		10
(c)	**Matters to consider re. acceptance**		—
	Professional marks to be awarded for clarity of evaluation, use of headings and conclusion based on points discussed		2
	Generally ½ mark for identification, 1 further mark for explanation, from ideas list:		
	– Large and expanding group – availability of staff now and in the future		
	– Use of overseas offices		
	– Visits to overseas audit teams		
	– Skills/experience in retail/foreign subsidiaries consolidation		
	– Timing – tight deadline		
	– Mermaid Co – implication of prior year modification		
	– Minotaur Co – implication of different business activity		
	– Highly regulated – risk/additional reporting requirements		
	– Reason for previous auditors leaving office		—
	Maximum marks		7
(d) (i)	**Define transnational audit and relevance to Dragon Group**		—
	1 mark for definition		
	2 marks for relevance to Dragon Group		—
	Maximum marks		3
(ii)	**Audit risk factors in a transnational audit**		—
	2 marks per point explained		
	– Auditing standards		
	– Regulation of auditors		
	– Financial reporting standards		
	– Corporate governance/control risk		—
	Maximum marks		4
			—
Total			32
			—

39 POPPY CO (A) *Walk in the footsteps of a top tutor*

Key answer tips

Question 3 begins with a discussion of audit risk and fair values. The first thing to note is that much of this is basic common sense: why do estimates increase audit risk? Secondly, the question asks you to *discuss* the statement. You must therefore produce a balanced argument, i.e. discuss why fair value accounting may also lead to a reduction of audit risk. The marking guide does cap one-sided arguments below the maximum attainable marks.

Part b(i) requires a discussion of how auditors assess the reliability and objectivity of external valuers and part b(ii) requires little more than a basic knowledge of how to audit the value of property, which should have been covered at F8 level.

The highlighted words are key phases that markers are looking for.

(a) Balances held at fair value are frequently recognised as material items in the statement of financial position. Sometimes it is required by the financial reporting framework that the measurement of an asset or liability is at fair value, e.g. certain categories of financial instruments, whereas it is sometimes the entity's choice to measure an item using a fair value model rather than a cost model, e.g. properties. It is certainly the case that many of these balances will be material, meaning that the auditor must obtain sufficient appropriate evidence that the fair value measurement is in accordance with the requirements of financial reporting standards. ISA 540 *Auditing Accounting Estimates Including Fair Value Accounting Estimates and Related Disclosures* contains guidance in this area.

As part of the understanding of the entity and its environment, the auditor should gain an insight into balances that are stated at fair value, and then assess the impact of this on the audit strategy. This will include an evaluation of the risk associated with the balance(s) recognised at fair value.

Audit risk comprises three elements, each is discussed below in the context of whether material balances shown at fair value will lead to increased risk for the auditor.

Inherent Risk

Many measurements based on estimates, including fair value measurements, are inherently imprecise and subjective in nature. The fair value assessment is likely to involve significant judgments, e.g. regarding market conditions, the timing of cash flows, or the future intentions of the entity. In addition, there may be a deliberate attempt by management to manipulate the fair value to achieve a desired aim within the financial statements, in other words to attempt some kind of window dressing.

Many fair value estimation models are complicated, e.g. discounted cash flow techniques, or the actuarial calculations used to determine the value of a pension fund. Any complicated calculations are relatively high risk, as difficult valuation techniques are simply more likely to contain errors than simple valuation techniques. However, there will be some items shown at fair value which have a low inherent risk, because the measurement of fair value may be relatively straightforward, e.g. assets that are regularly bought and sold on open markets that provide readily available and reliable information on the market prices at which actual exchanges occur.

In addition to the complexities discussed above, some fair value measurement techniques will contain significant assumptions, e.g. the most appropriate discount factor to use, or judgments over the future use of an asset. Management may not always have sufficient experience and knowledge in making these judgments.

Thus the auditor should approach some balances recognised at fair value as having a relatively high inherent risk, as their subjective and complex nature means that the balance is prone to contain an error. However, the auditor should not just assume that all fair value items contain high inherent risk – each balance recognised at fair value should be assessed for its individual level of risk.

Control risk

The risk that the entity's internal monitoring system fails to prevent and detect valuation errors needs to be assessed as part of overall audit risk assessment. One problem is that the fair value assessment is likely to be performed once a year, outside the normal accounting and management systems, especially where the valuation is performed by an external specialist. Therefore, as a non-routine event, the assessment of fair value is likely not to have the same level of monitoring or controls as a day-to-day business transaction.

However, due to the material impact of fair values on the statement of financial position, and in some circumstances on profit, management may have made great effort to ensure that the assessment is highly monitored and controlled. It therefore could be the case that there is extremely low control risk associated with the recognition of fair values.

Detection risk

The auditor should minimise detection risk via thorough planning and execution of audit procedures. The audit team may lack experience in dealing with the fair value in question, and so would be unlikely to detect errors in the valuation techniques used. Over-reliance on an external specialist could also lead to errors not being found.

Conclusion

It is true that the increasing recognition of items measured at fair value will in many cases cause the auditor to assess the audit risk associated with the balance as high. However, it should not be assumed that every fair value item will be likely to contain a material misstatement. The auditor must be careful to identify and respond to the level of risk for fair value items on an individual basis to ensure that sufficient and appropriate evidence is gathered, thus reducing the audit risk to an acceptable level.

(b)   (i)   **Enquiries in respect of the external valuer**

Enquiries would need to be made for two main reasons, firstly to determine the competence, and secondly the objectivity of the valuer. ISA 620 *Using the Work of an Auditor's Expert* contains guidance in this area.

Competence

Enquiries could include:

–   Is the valuer a member of a recognised professional body, for example a nationally or internationally recognised institute of registered surveyors?

–   Does the valuer possess any necessary licence to carry out valuations for companies?

–   How long has the valuer been a member of the recognised body, or how long has the valuer been licensed under that body?

–   How much experience does the valuer have in providing valuations of the particular type of investment properties held by Poppy Co?

–   Does the valuer have specific experience of evaluating properties for the purpose of including their fair value within the financial statements?

–   Is there any evidence of the reputation of the valuer, e.g. professional references, recommendations from other companies for which a valuation service has been provided?

–   How much experience, if any, does the valuer have with Poppy Co?

Using the above enquiries, the auditor is trying to form an opinion as the relevance and reliability of the valuation provided. ISA 500 *Audit Evidence* requires that the auditor gathers evidence that is both sufficient and appropriate. The auditor needs to ensure that the fair values provided by the valuer for inclusion in the financial statements have been arrived at using appropriate knowledge and skill which should be evidenced by the valuer being a member of a professional body, and, if necessary, holding a licence under that body.

It is important that the fair values have been arrived at using methods allowed under IAS 40 *Investment Property*. If any other valuation method has been used then the value recognised in the statement of financial position may not be in accordance with financial reporting standards. Thus it is important to understand whether the valuer has experience specifically in providing valuations that comply with IAS 40, and how many times the valuer has appraised properties similar to those owned by Poppy Co.

In gauging the reliability of the fair value, the auditor may wish to consider how Poppy Co decided in appointing this particular valuer, e.g. on the basis of a recommendation or after receiving references from companies for which valuations had previously been provided.

It will also be important to consider how familiar the valuer is with Poppy Co's business and environment, as a way to assess the reliability and appropriateness of any assumptions used in the valuation technique.

Objectivity

Enquiries could include:

– Does the valuer have any financial interest in Poppy Co, e.g. shares held directly or indirectly in the company?

– Does the valuer have any personal relationship with any director or employee of Poppy Co?

– Is the fee paid for the valuation service reasonable and a fair, market based price?

With these enquiries, the auditor is gaining assurance that the valuer will perform the valuation from an independent point of view. If the valuer had a financial interest in Poppy Co, there would be incentive to manipulate the valuation in a way best suited to the financial statements of the company. Equally if the valuer had a personal relationship with a senior member of staff at Poppy Co, they may feel pressured to give a favourable opinion on the valuation of the properties.

The level of fee paid is important. It should be commensurate with the market rate paid for this type of valuation. If the valuer was paid in excess of what might be considered a normal fee, it could indicate that the valuer was encouraged, or even bribed, to provide a favourable valuation.

(ii)   **Additional audit procedures**

Audit procedures should focus on the appraisal of the work of the expert valuer. Procedures could include the following:

–   Inspection of the written instructions provided by Poppy Co to the valuer, which should include matters such as the objective and scope of the valuer's work, the extent of the valuer's access to relevant records and files, and clarification of the intended use by the auditor of their work.

–   Evaluation, using the valuation report, that any assumptions used by the valuer are in line with the auditor's knowledge and understanding of Poppy Co. Any documentation supporting assumptions used by the valuer should be reviewed for consistency with the auditor's business understanding, and also for consistency with any other audit evidence.

–   Assessment of the methodology used to arrive at the fair value and confirmation that the method is consistent with that required by IAS 40.

–   The auditor should confirm, using the valuation report, that a consistent method has been used to value each property.

–   It should also be confirmed that the date of the valuation report is reasonably close to the year-end of Poppy Co.

–   Physical inspection of the investment properties to determine the physical condition of the properties supports the valuation.

–   Inspect the purchase documentation of each investment property to ascertain the cost of each building. As the properties were acquired during this accounting period, it would be reasonable to expect that the fair value at the year end is not substantially different to the purchase price. Any significant increase or decrease in value should alert the auditor to possible misstatement, and lead to further audit procedures.

–   Subsequent events should be monitored for any additional evidence provided on the valuation of the properties. For example, the sale of an investment property shortly after the year end many provide additional evidence relating to the fair value measurement.

–   Obtain a management representation regarding the reasonableness of any significant assumptions, where relevant, to fair value measurements or disclosures.

Examiner's comments

This was the least popular of the optional questions, though it was attempted by approximately half of the candidates. The question dealt with a high profile topical issue – the recognition of items in financial statements at fair value, and the auditing implications of this.

Requirement (a) was a discussion as to whether having items recognised at fair value would lead to an increase in audit risk. A small minority of answers were sound, referring to the current trend in financial reporting for fair value accounting, and linking this to the various elements of audit risk. Some answers used examples to illustrate their comments, and some referred to the current economic climate and inactive markets which make determining a fair value difficult. Such answers display not only technical knowledge, but also commercial awareness of an important issue.

However, many answers to (a) focussed incorrectly on materiality, and while many were strong on the financial reporting issues, this was not often successfully linked to audit risk implications. The recent examiner's article on financial reporting issues for the auditor had clearly not been read by many candidates.

Requirement (b) provided a brief scenario setting the scene of an audit client which has revalued several investment properties. **Requirement (bi)** asked for a recommendation and explanation of enquiries that should be made before relying on the work of an external valuer. Most candidates successfully recommended enquiries, but a number then failed to explain the reason for the enquiries. Candidates should take care to follow the question requirement carefully, as failing to provide an explanation when one is asked for will severely restrict the marks that can be awarded.

Requirement (b) (ii) asked the candidate to 'identify and explain principal audit procedures to be performed on the valuation of the investment properties'. Answers here were unsatisfactory. This requirement was the most mis-read of all on the paper. Many answers repeated the points made in (bi). Most ignored the fact that procedures relevant to valuation had been asked for, and instead provided a list of general procedures covering other assertions, in particular existence, and rights and obligations. Some scripts provided a heading for every single assertion and one procedure for each assertion. Candidates must follow the instructions given in the requirement, in order to give a focussed answer. Unfortunately many candidates wasted a lot of time here on writing completely irrelevant answers.

ACCA marking scheme		
(a)	**Fair values and audit risk**	*Marks*
	Generally 1 mark per point:	
	– Introduction referring to need to recognise fair values	
	– Example of item recognised at fair value	
	– Discussion of inherent risk – subjectivity	
	– Discussion of inherent risk – deliberate manipulation	
	– Discussion of inherent risk – complexity	
	– Discussion of control risk – non routine transactions	
	– BUT may lead to increased level of monitoring	
	– Discussion of detection risk	
	– Conclusion	
	Allow 1 mark for definition of fair value	
	Cap marks at 5 if no attempt is made to produce a rounded discussion (i.e. should not assume that fair value automatically increases audit risk)	
	Maximum	7
(b) (i)	**Enquiries of valuer**	
	Generally ½ mark per enquiry and 1 mark per point of explanation from ideas list:	
	– Membership of professional body	
	– Whether a license is held	
	– Reputation – references, etc	
	– Experience with Poppy Co's type of property	
	– Experience with preparing valuations under IAS 40	
	– Financial interest	
	– Personal interest	
	Up to 4 marks for assessment of reliability, up to 2 marks for assessment of objectivity.	
	Maximum marks	7

(ii)	**Audit procedures**		
	Generally 1 mark per procedure from ideas list:		
	– Review written instructions		
	– Evaluate assumptions		
	– Check consistent method used		
	– Check date of report close to year end		
	– Method to follow IAS 40 fair value framework		
	– Physical inspection		
	– Review of purchase documentation		
	– Subsequent events		
	– Management representation		
		Maximum marks	6
Total			20

40 CROCUS CO *Walk in the footsteps of a top tutor*

Key answer tips

Prior to attempting this question students may find it helpful to read the examiner's article 'Forensic Auditing' from September 2008 as the question followed its publication.

Firstly, it is important to note that the question contains 3 professional marks. Once again students must take care to present their work accordingly to secure these valuable marks. The question asks you to respond directly to a client who suspects a fraud at her work place. You are asked to discuss the objectives of an investigation and the steps involved. The objectives require little more than repetition of basic knowledge. The steps involved require the student to apply themselves more to the scenario by tailoring their answer to the style of fraud being committed. It should be noted that part b (ii) requires *examples of procedures as a sub-element* to the question. Simply discussing tests you would perform would not obtain a good mark. The question requires you to consider the whole investigation from the planning stage all the way through to the ultimate court case.

The highlighted words are key phases that markers are looking for.

(a) (i) Forensic accounting utilises accounting, auditing, and investigative skills to conduct an examination into a company's financial statements. The aim of forensic accounting is to provide an accounting analysis that is potentially suitable for use in court. Forensic accounting is an umbrella term encompassing both forensic investigations and forensic audits. It includes the audit of financial information to prove or disprove a fraud, the interview process used during an investigation, and the act of serving as an expert witness.

Tutorial note

Forensic accounting can be used in a very wide range of situations, e.g. settling monetary disputes in relation to a business closure, marriage break up, insurance claim, etc. Credit will be awarded for any reasonable examples provided

(ii)   A forensic investigation is a process whereby a forensic accountant carries out procedures to gather evidence, which could ultimately be used in legal proceedings or to settle disputes. This could include, for example an investigation into money laundering. A forensic investigation involves many stages (similar to an audit), including planning, evidence gathering, quality control reviews, and finally results in the production of a report.

(iii) Forensic auditing is the specific use of audit procedures within a forensic investigation to find facts and gather evidence, usually focused on the quantification of a financial loss. This could include, for example, the use of analytical procedures, and substantive procedures to determine the amount of an insurance claim.

(b) **Report to Gita Thrales**

Subject: Forensic investigation into alleged payroll fraud

Introduction

This report has been requested in order to outline and explain the operation of a forensic investigation into an alleged payroll fraud. The report will outline the steps taken in such an investigation and provide an explanation of the expected output of the work performed.

Objectives of a forensic investigation

The first objective is to decide if a deliberate fraud with the intention of stealing cash from the company has actually taken place. There is a possibility that the employees made redundant have remained on the payroll records by error rather than fraud. The investigation should uncover whether the situation has arisen through mistake or through deliberate criminal action.

Secondly, the investigation will aim to discover the perpetrator(s) of the fraud, and ultimately to assist in their prosecution. The investigation will gather evidence, which may include an interview with the suspected fraudster, which can then be used in criminal procedures against the individual(s) concerned. In this case there is an individual suspected of involvement in the alleged fraud. It will be an important part of the investigation to discover if there were other people involved, as frauds often involve collusion between several individuals.

Thirdly, the investigation should quantify the financial loss suffered by Crocus Co as a result of the fraud. The evidence gathered will determine the amount which has been stolen from the company as a result of the fraud. It is important for the loss to be quantified; as legally a crime has only been committed if a victim (i.e. Crocus Co) has suffered a financial loss.

Steps in investigating a suspected fraud

The first step will be to determine the type of fraud that has taken place. The fact that employees no longer employed by the company have not been removed from the payroll indicates a fraud known as a 'ghost employee' scheme, whereby the fraudster diverts the payroll of the non-existent employees into their own possession.

Then the investigator will need to consider how the fraud could have taken place. This would normally be due to the fraudster(s) circumventing internal controls and concealing their actions from their colleagues and supervisors. For example, there should be a control in place to ensure that any amendments made to payroll data (in this case an amendment appears to have been made to re-route the ex-employees pay into the bank account of the fraudster) must be approved by a senior manager, and should be flagged by an exception report.

The investigator will also need to establish how long the fraud has been operating – in this case it is likely that the fraud began at the same time as the factory closure, but this will need to be clarified.

The next step would be to gather evidence – this is a crucial part of the investigation as it should determine both the identity of the perpetrator(s) and the monetary value of the fraud. Gathering evidence could include an examination of accounting records and other documentation, the use of computer-assisted auditing techniques (CAATs), interviewing employees of the company, and discussions with management. A key issue here is to ensure that the evidence will be sufficient to prove three matters:

- That a fraud has taken place,
- The identity of the fraudster, and
- The amount of the loss to the company.

This is essential because the legal framework will require clear evidence in order for a prosecution to be instigated against the perpetrator(s) of the fraud.

Evidence must be sufficient and relevant to the accusations being made. For example, the legal framework is likely to require evidence of the following:

- The motive for the fraud,
- The ability of the alleged fraudster to conduct the fraud,
- Any attempt made by the alleged to conceal the crime.

Investigative procedures could include, for example:

- Review of authorisation of monthly payroll.
- Use of CAATs to determine any alteration of payroll details.
- Use of CAATs to determine:
  - Any individual on the payroll who has no contact details.
  - Any bank account receiving the pay of more than one individual.
  - Employees who have not taken holiday or sick leave.
- Reconciliation of employees in the payroll database with employees in the human resources database.

The purpose of the above is to establish how the controls that should have been operating in the payroll system were circumvented. It would seem that authorisations to alter payroll details, i.e. altering payments so that they all go into one bank account, have not taken place.

The investigation should also involve an interview with the suspect(s), with the aim of extracting a confession. This would form a key part of the evidence to be ultimately presented at court.

The investigator will produce a report for the attention of the management of Crocus Co, summarising all findings and concluding on the identity of the fraudster(s) and the amount of financial loss suffered. This report is also likely to be presented as part of evidence during court proceedings.

Though not strictly part of the investigation, which ends on the production of the report described above, it is worth mentioning that the investigator would be likely to be called as an expert witness during the legal process, whereby the evidence gathered and report produced as part of the investigation would be explained to those involved in the legal proceedings, and the investigator may be asked questions regarding the investigation performed.

Finally, advice can be provided to management, as to how to prevent this kind of fraud from occurring again. Recommendations would be likely to focus on improvements in internal systems and controls in the specific part of the business where the fraud occurred.

Conclusion

This report has explained that the objective of a forensic investigation is to clarify whether a fraud has taken place, to discover the identity of the fraudster, and to quantify the financial loss suffered. The specialist skills of the investigation team will produce evidence which is sufficient and relevant enough to be used to assist legal proceedings against those involved with the fraud.

(c) **Application of ethical principles to a fraud investigation**

IFAC's *Code of Ethics for Professional Accountants* applies to all ACCA members involved in professional assignments, including forensic investigations. There are specific considerations in the application of each of the principles in providing such a service.

Integrity

The forensic investigator is likely to deal frequently with individuals who lack integrity, are dishonest, and attempt to conceal the true facts from the investigator. It is imperative that the investigator recognises this, and acts with impeccable integrity throughout the whole investigation.

Objectivity

As in an audit engagement, the investigator's objectivity must be beyond question. The report that is the outcome of the forensic investigation must be perceived as independent, as it forms part of the legal evidence presented at court. The investigator must adhere to the concept that the overriding objective of court proceedings is to deal with cases fairly and justly. Any real or perceived threats to objectivity could undermine the credibility of the evidence provided by the investigator.

This issue poses a particular problem where an audit client requests its auditors to conduct a forensic investigation. In this situation, the audit firm would be exposed to threats to objectivity in terms of advocacy, management involvement and self-review. The advocacy threat arises because the audit firm may feel pressured into promoting the interests and point of view of their client, which would breach the overriding issue of objectivity in court proceedings. Secondly, the investigators could be perceived to be involved in management decisions regarding the implications of the fraud, especially where the investigator acts as an expert witness. It is however the self-review threat that would be the most significant threat to objectivity. The self-review threat arises because the investigation is likely to involve the estimation of an amount (i.e. the loss), which could be material to the financial statements.

For the reasons outlined above, The Code states that the firm should evaluate threats and put appropriate safeguards in place, and if safeguards cannot reduce the threats to an acceptable level, then the firm cannot provide both the audit service and the forensic investigation.

Professional competence and due care

Forensic investigations will involve very specialist skills, which accountants are unlikely to possess without extensive training. Such skills would include:

–   Detailed knowledge of the relevant legal framework surrounding fraud,

–   An understanding of how to gather specialist evidence,

–   Skills in the safe custody of evidence, including maintaining a clear 'chain' of evidence,

–   Strong personal skills in, for example, interview techniques, presentation of material at court, and tactful dealing with difficult and stressful situations.

It is therefore essential that forensic work is only ever undertaken by highly skilled individuals, under the direction and supervision of an experienced fraud investigator. Any doubt over the competence of the investigation team could severely undermine the credibility of the evidence presented at court.

Confidentiality

Normally accountants should not disclose information without the explicit consent of their client. However, during legal proceedings arising from a fraud investigation, the court will require the investigator to reveal information discovered during the investigation. There is an overriding requirement for the investigator to disclose all of the information deemed necessary by the court.

Outside of the court, the investigator must ensure faultless confidentiality, especially because much of the information they have access to will be highly sensitive.

Professional behaviour

Fraud investigations can become a matter of public interest, and much media attention is often focused on the work of the forensic investigator. A highly professional attitude must be displayed at all times, in order to avoid damage to the reputation of the firm, and of the profession. Any lapse in professional behaviour could also undermine the integrity of the forensic evidence, and of the credibility of the investigator, especially when acting in the capacity of expert witness.

During legal proceedings, the forensic investigator may be involved in discussions with both sides in the court case, and here it is essential that a courteous and considerate attitude is presented to all parties.

Examiner's comments

Requirement (a) asked for definitions of forensic accounting, forensic investigation, and forensic auditing. There were many sound displays of this factual knowledge, though some candidates who did not know the difference between the three tended to write the same thing for each one.

Requirement (b) was the core of the question. A scenario was provided in which a potential fraud had been discovered, and a report was required, describing the objectives of a forensic investigation, and explaining the steps involved. Encouragingly, the vast majority of candidates produced their answer in an appropriate format and included an introduction and conclusion, enabling at least some of the professional marks available to be awarded.

The majority of answers successfully described the objectives of a forensic investigation, and most adequately explained the steps involved in such an investigation. It was clear that most candidates appreciated that this is a very different engagement to an audit, with many mentioning the potential role as an expert witness, and the importance of evidence being admissible in court. However two common problems detracted from the quality of many answers for this requirement:

Firstly, providing tactless and unnecessary comments regarding whether the assignment should be accepted. For example, discussing whether the firm had sufficient competence to perform the work (presumably this is the case, as the question stated that 'you are a manager in the forensic investigation department of your firm', or considering whether there were any ethical issues to consider prior to acceptance (presumably not given that the question stated that Crocus Co is not an audit client)). Such comments show that candidates had failed to read and understand the scenario. However the more significant issue is that such comments would not be made in a report to a potential client, they are internal issues, inappropriate for an external communication.

Secondly, the procedures suggested where often too vague, or not even procedures at all. It was common to see 'procedures' suggested such as 'obtain a list of the current payroll' or 'use CAATs to get payroll data on those made redundant'. What the investigator should do with this information was not discussed. Some candidates recognised that information about the system in use and the ownership of the bank account should be gathered before the suspect was interviewed, but few recognised this as a priority.

As in Q1(c), some candidates got a little carried away with the scenario, providing some far-fetched discussions of getting DNA evidence and blood samples, and using the police to 'hunt and capture' the suspect. Such comments are clearly based more on popular TV shows than the scenario provided, and can detract from an otherwise professional answer.

Requirement (c) was not often well answered. This requirement asked for the application of the fundamental ethical principles to the provision of a forensic investigation service. The best answers went through each ethical principle in turn, explaining its specific application to this type of service. Some candidates recognised the vital importance of confidentiality in the context of a fraud investigation, and others realised the significance of acting with utmost integrity when dealing with criminal activity.

However, many answers were just not applied in any way, making little or no reference to forensics. A significant number of candidates simply wrote the principles down with a brief definition of each, not answering the question requirement at all.

A lot of candidates were unable to identify the fundamental ethical principles, and focussed purely on independence.

	ACCA marking scheme		
			Marks
(a)	**Definitions**		
	2 marks per definition (general principle rather than exact wording. Examples can be used to illustrate definition – **give ½ mark per example**)		
		Maximum marks	6
(b)	**Report**		
	Up to 3 marks for use of professional business English, language appropriate to client and to finance director (i.e. not patronising), tactful (i.e. does not criticise client). **Specifically ½ for headings, 1 for introduction, then up to 1½ for remainder.**		
	Up to 1½ marks per comment:		
	– Intro ref. reason for report and to clarify contents (1 mark)		
	– Aim – clarify fraud taken place		
	– Aim – discover the perpetrator(s)		
	– Aim – prosecute the perpetrator(s)		
	– Aim – quantify losses		
	– Method – consider type of fraud – ghost employee		
	– Method – identify opportunity – controls override		
	– Method – collect evidence – + up to 2 for examples		
	– Method – interview suspect		
	– Method – produce reports		
	– Expert witness		
	– Advice and recommendations to prevent another fraud		
		Maximum marks	14
(c)	**Ethics**		
	Up to 1½ marks per comment		
	– Integrity (max 1 mark)		
	– Objectivity (max 3 marks)		
	– Professional competence and due care		
	– Confidentiality		
	– Professional behaviour		
	1 mark for recognition that principles apply to all professional engagements		
		Maximum marks	6
Total			26

41 SEYMOUR

Key answer tips

(i) 'Matters' will often encompass considerations of, materiality, accounting treatment, and risk.

(ii) 'Evidence' (ISA 500) – consider sufficiency and appropriateness for the three issues. Consider what evidence you would have obtained had you performed the testing over this area.

You will need to consider the relevant accounting standards/principles to deal with the three issues properly.

(a) **Costs of Tournose**

(i) **Matters**

- Development costs at 30 September 2005 have a carrying value of $3 million (i.e. $4 million less 5 years' amortisation at 5% p.a.) that represents 7.4% of total assets at that date (5.6% of total assets at 30 September 2006) and are therefore material.

- Straight line annual amortisation based on 20 year estimate of useful life ($200,000) represents 1.5% of 2006 profit before tax (PBT) and is not material. The patent cost, $11,600 is very immaterial.

- Management must review the useful life of the development costs at 30 September 2006 (IAS 38 *Intangible Assets*).

- The competitor's announcement during the current year (to 30 September 2006) may provide evidence that:

    - the useful life of the development costs is substantially less than the remaining period covered by the patent.

    - there has been a change in the expected pattern of consumption of future economic benefits.

    - development costs are impaired (i.e. recoverable amount is less than carrying value).

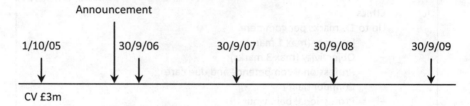

Remaining useful life 15 years ⇒ £200,000 amortisation p.a.?

Or just 3 years ⇒ £1 million amortisation p.a.?

- A change in the estimated useful life should be accounted for as a change in accounting estimate in accordance with IAS 8 *Accounting Policies, Changes in Accounting Estimates and Errors*. For example, if the development costs have little, if any, useful life after the introduction of the alternative drug ('worst case' scenario), the carrying value ($3 million) should be written off over the current and remaining years, i.e. $1 million p.a. The increase in amortisation/decrease in carrying value ($800,000) is material to PBT (6%) and total assets (1.5%).

- Similarly a change in the expected pattern of consumption of the future economic benefits should be accounted for as a change in accounting estimate (IAS 8). For example, it may be that the useful life is still to 2020 but that the economic benefits may reduce significantly in two years time.

- After adjusting the carrying amount to take account of the change in accounting estimate(s) management should have tested it for impairment and any impairment loss recognised in profit or loss.

(ii) **Audit evidence**

- $3 million carrying amount of development costs brought forward agreed to prior year working papers and financial statements.

- A copy of the press release announcing the competitor's alternative drug.

- Management's projections of future cash flows from Tournose-related sales as evidence of the useful life of the development costs and pattern of consumption.

- Reperformance of management's impairment test on the development costs: Recalculation of management's calculation of the carrying amount after revising estimates of useful life and/or consumption of benefits compared with management's calculation of value in use.

- Sensitivity analysis on management's key assumptions (e.g. estimates of useful life, discount rate).

- Written management representation on the key assumptions concerning the future that have a significant risk of causing material adjustment to the carrying amount of the development costs. (These assumptions should be disclosed in accordance with IAS 1 *Presentation of Financial Statements*.)

(b) **Goodwill**

(i) **Matters**

- Cost of goodwill, $1.8 million, represents 3.4% consolidated total assets and is therefore material.

- It is correct that the goodwill is not being amortised (IFRS 3 *Business Combinations*). However, it should be tested at least annually for impairment, by management.

- Aragon has incurred losses amounting to $1.1 million since it was acquired (two years ago). The write-off of this amount against goodwill in the consolidated financial statements would be material (being 61% cost of goodwill, 8.3% PBT and 2.1% total assets).

- The cost of the investment ($4.5 million) in Seymour's separate financial statements will also be material and should be tested for impairment.

- The fair value of net assets acquired was only $2.7 million ($4.5 million less $1.8 million). Therefore the fair value less costs to sell Aragon will be less than the carrying amount of the investment (i.e. the investment is impaired by at least the amount of goodwill recognised on acquisition).

- In assessing recoverable amount, value in use (rather than fair value less costs to sell) is only relevant if the going concern assumption is appropriate for Aragon.

- Supporting Aragon financially may result in Seymour being exposed to actual and/or contingent liabilities that should be provided for/disclosed in Seymour's financial statements in accordance with IAS 37 *Provisions, Contingent Liabilities and Contingent Assets*.

(ii) **Audit evidence**

- Carrying values of cost of investment and goodwill arising on acquisition to prior year audit working papers and financial statements.

- A copy of Aragon's draft financial statements for the year ended 30 September 2006 showing loss for year.

- Management's impairment test of Seymour's investment in Aragon and of the goodwill arising on consolidation at 30 September 2006. That is a comparison of the present value of the future cash flows expected to be generated by Aragon (a cash-generating unit) compared with the cost of the investment (in Seymour's separate financial statements).

- Results of any impairment tests on Aragon's assets extracted from Aragon's working paper files.

- Analytical procedures on future cash flows to confirm their reasonableness (e.g. by comparison with cash flows for the last two years).

- Bank report for audit purposes for any guarantees supporting Aragon's loan facilities.

- A copy of Seymour's 'comfort letter' confirming continuing financial support of Aragon for the foreseeable future.

(c) **Discontinued operation**

(i) **Matters**

- Petcare product revenue represents 12% consolidated revenue and is therefore very material. Consolidated PBT would be 10% higher if the loss on the petcare products was excluded – so also material in relation to Seymour's results.

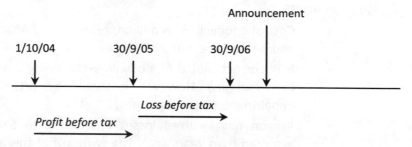

- Under IFRS 5 the 'petcare' operation should only be treated as a discontinued operation if either it was discontinued before the yearend or is held for sale as at the year end, neither of which seem to be the case here.

- It should not, therefore, be treated as discontinued in the current year's financial statements.

- However the discontinuation of the product line after the statement of financial position date provides additional evidence that, as at the statement of financial position date, it was of poor quality. Therefore, as at the statement of financial position date:

  - an allowance ('provision') may be required for credit notes for returns of products after the year end that were sold before the year-end.

  - goods returned to inventory should be written down to net realisable value (may be nil).

  - any plant and equipment used exclusively in the production of the petcare range of products should be tested for impairment.

  - any material contingent liabilities arising from legal claims should be disclosed.

(ii)   **Audit evidence**

- A copy of Seymour's announcement (external 'press release' and any internal memorandum).

- Credit notes raised/refunds paid after the year end for faulty products returned.

- Condition of products returned as inspected during physical attendance of inventory count.

- Correspondence from customers claiming reimbursement/compensation for poor quality.

- Direct confirmation from legal adviser (solicitor) regarding any claims for customers including estimates of possible payouts.

42   RBG

Key answer tips

This question should be fairly straightforward with the possible exception of Part (b) which links into practice management and requires a bit more thought.

(a)   **Potential advantages and disadvantages to RBG of outsourcing internal audit services**

Advantages

- Affordability as there should be a cost benefit (budget savings) of replacing fixed cost full-time employees with a variable cost service.

- Further, if reliance on internal audit by the external auditors is substantially increased, the external audit fee may be reduced.

- Even if there are some changes in staff within the audit firm providing the internal audit services, there should be greater continuity than currently (as RBG has high employee turnover in this department).

- A wider range of industry-related expertise might be available to RBG from contracted-in auditors that would be too expensive to maintain internally. This may be particularly beneficial for ad hoc needs such as due diligence reviews for acquisitions or business continuity plans in the event of fire or flood.

- Experienced internal auditors will be available as and when needed (as typically the audit firm's staff will be experienced) whereas RBG is currently losing its experienced employees to other departments. Outsourcing also offers flexibility to provide more staff at busy times.

- Outsourcing to an audit firm can provide geographic coverage and more advanced technology.

- Independent evaluation (e.g. of organizational risk) by the audit firm may provide new ideas for improvements (e.g. enhancing risk management).

- Better recommendations for improvements as the audit firm can suggest practical, tried and tested solutions and not just theoretical ones.

- Greater assistance to management in the evaluation of the performance of the external auditors (because the outsourced internal audit firm should be more experienced to make this assessment).

- Earlier assessment of the impact of changes in financial reporting requirements (because the outsourced internal audit firm should be technically up-to-date).

- Better utilization of core competencies, for example, management will have more time to focus on strategic objectives.

- The audit firm may provide a customer-focused service that could be lacking in an in-house department.

Disadvantages

- Over time the audit firm may command a greater premium for internal audit services as RBG becomes dependent on the audit firm's knowledge of the group (i.e. cost savings may be only short term).

- An out-sourced department may not be as effective as an in-house department if, for example, the audit firm's staff assigned to RBG are changed regularly.

- The audit firm's staff may not understand RBG's business as well as employed staff if, for example, they work only part-time on the RBG assignment. Employed staff are more likely to have a broader perspective of the group from having worked in other parts of it.

- The internal audit staff's principle allegiance will be to the audit firm, not RBG. If the services provided by the audit firm are not seen to be an integral part of management, the company may not buy-in to their suggestions.

- If the audit firm plans to schedule internal audit services to RBG in its 'quiet periods', they may not always be available when needed.

- RBG will lose a valuable management training ground that provides a source of future managers. The internal audit department's current loss of high performing employees to other departments is a gain to the other departments.

(b) **Principal matters to be included in submission to provide internal audit services**

- Introduction/background – details about York including its organization (of functions), offices (locations) and number of internal auditors working within each office. The office that would be responsible for managing the contract should be stated.

- A description of York's services most relevant to RBG's needs (e.g. in the areas of risk management, IT audits, value for money (VFM) and corporate governance).

- Client-specific issues identified. For example, revenue audits will be required routinely for control purposes and to substantiate the contingent rents due. Other areas of expertise that RBG may be interested in taking advantage of, for example, special projects such as acquisitions and mergers.

- York's approach to assessing audit needs including the key stages and who will be involved. For example:

  (1) Preliminary – review of business, industry and the entity's operating characteristics

  (2) Planning – including needs analysis and co-ordination with external audit plan

  (3) Post-Audit – assurance that activities were effectively and efficiently executed

  (4) Review – of services provided, reports issued and management's responses.

- A description of internal audit tools used and methodologies/approach to audit fieldwork including use of embedded audit software and programs developed by York.

- A description of York's systems-based audit, the IT issues to be addressed and the technological support that can be provided.

- Any training that will be offered to RBG's managers and staff, for example, in a risk management approach.

- A description and quantity of resources, in particular the number of full-time staff, to be deployed in providing services to RBG. An outline of RBG's track record in human resource retention and development.

- Relevant experience – e.g. in internal and external audit in the retail industry. The relative qualifications and skills of each grade of audit staff and the contract manager in particular.

- Insurance certifications covering, for example, public liability and professional indemnity insurance.

- Work ethic policies relating to health and safety, equal opportunities' and race relations.

- How York ensures quality throughout the internal audit process including standards to be followed (e.g. Institute of Internal Auditors' standards).

- Sample report templates – e.g. for reporting the results of risk analysis, audit plans and quarterly reporting of findings to the Audit and Risk Management Committee.

- Current clients to whom internal audit services are provided from whom RBG will be able to take up references, by arrangement, if York is short-listed.

- Any work currently carried out/competed for that could cause a conflict of interest (and the measures to avoid such conflicts).

- Fees (daily rates) for each grade of staff and travel and other expenses to be reimbursed. An indication of price increases, if any, over the three-year contract period. Invoicing terms (e.g. on presentation of reports) and payment terms (e.g. the end of the month following receipt of the invoice).

- Performance targets to be met such as deadlines for completing work and submitting and issuing reports.

(c) **Impact on the audit of the financial statements**

Tutorial note

The answer to this part should reflect that it is not the external auditor who is providing the internal audit services. Thus comments regarding objectivity impairment are not relevant.

- As Grey & Co is likely to be placing some reliance on RBG's internal audit department in accordance with ISA 610 (Revised) *Using the Work of Internal Auditors* the degree of reliance should be reassessed.

- The appointment will include an evaluation of organizational risk. The results of this will provide Grey with evidence, for example:

  – supporting the appropriateness of the going concern assumption

  – of indicators of obsolescence of goods or impairment of other assets.

- As the quality of internal audit services should be higher than previously, providing a stronger control environment, the extent to which Grey may rely on internal audit work could be increased. This would increase the efficiency of the external audit of the financial statements as the need for substantive procedures should be reduced.

- However, if internal audit services are performed on a part-time basis (e.g. fitting into the provider's less busy months) Grey must evaluate the impact of this on the prevention, detection and control of fraud and error.

- The internal auditors will provide a body of expertise within RBG with whom Grey can consult on contentious matters.

COMPLETION AND REPORTING

43   BURFORD   *Walk in the footsteps of a top tutor*

Key answer tips

This question focuses on going concern and the audit reporting implications.

Part (a) asks for indicators of going concern issues in the scenario. This is a straightforward requirement and could just as easily be tested at the F paper level so should not cause any issues.

Part (b) asks for procedures to be performed on the forecast as part of your going concern review. The same approach can be used here as for PFI engagements. You need to assess whether the assumptions used as the basis of the forecast are reasonable. If not, the forecast can't be relied upon to justify whether the company is likely to be able to continue to trade.

Part (c) is a straightforward reporting requirement where the client does not wish to make disclosure of going concern issues. Again, this requirement could be tested at the F paper level and should be straightforward at this stage of the qualification.

(a)   (i)   **Going concern**

The information available in respect of Burford Co indicates many events or conditions which individually or collectively may cast doubt on the use of the going concern assumption in its financial statements.

Profitability – Burford Co's performance has deteriorated dramatically in the year, and despite being profitable in the previous year, it is reporting a loss of $500,000 for the year to 31 July 2013. It is likely that profitability will suffer even more in the next financial year due to the obsolescence of the QuickFire product which accounted for 45% of revenue. Substantial operating losses are an indicator of going concern problems.

Current and quick ratios show that Burford Co's current liabilities exceed its current assets, meaning that the company is unlikely to be able to pay debts as they fall due. If suppliers go unpaid they may restrict supply, causing further working capital problems. There may be insufficient cash to pay wages or other overheads, or to pay finance charges.

In addition, the company's **cash inflows** are likely to be very much reduced by the obsolescence of its major product, the QuickFire. The development of the replacement GreenFire product will have put severe strain on cash resources and given the company's cash position, there may be insufficient funds to complete the development. Hopefully there is enough cash to complete the development of GreenFire, and to keep the company afloat prior to its launch next year. Even then, it will take time for the new product to generate a cash inflow.

Loan covenant – given the further deterioration in the company's liquidity since the year end, it is likely that the current ratio now breaches the terms of the loan covenant. If this is the case, the loan provider may recall the loan, which Burford Co does not seem to be in a position to repay. It may be forced to sell assets in order to raise cash for the loan repayment, which may not raise the amount required, and would put operations in jeopardy.

(ii) **Audit evidence**

- Agreement of the opening cash position to the audited financial statements and general ledger or bank reconciliation, to ensure accuracy of extracted figures.

- Confirmation that casting of the cash flow forecast has been reperformed to check arithmetical accuracy.

- A review of the results of any market research which has been conducted on the GreenFire product, to ensure the assumption regarding its successful launch is appropriate.

- Discussion of the progress made on GreenFire's development with a technical expert or engineer, to gauge the likelihood of a successful launch in February 2014 .

- A review of any correspondence with existing customers to gauge the level of interest in GreenFire and confirm if any orders have yet been placed.

- A review of any sales documentation relating to the planned sale of plant and equipment to confirm that $50,000 is achievable.

- Physical inspection of the plant and equipment to be sold, to gauge its condition and the likelihood of sale.

- A review of any announcement made regarding the redundancies, to confirm the number of employees affected and the timing of the planned redundancies.

- Sample testing of a selection of those being made redundant, agreeing the amount they are to be paid to human resource department records, to ensure accuracy of figures in the forecast.

- A review of the application made to the government to confirm the amount of the grant applied for.

- Confirmation to correspondence from the government department of the $30,000 grant to be received.

- Depending on the timing of audit procedures, the $30,000 may be received prior to completion of the audit, in which case it should be agreed to cash book and bank statement.

- Agreement that the cash flow forecast is consistent with profit and other financial forecasts which have been prepared by management.

- Confirmation that any other assumptions used in the cash flow forecast are consistent with auditor's knowledge of the business and with management's intentions regarding the future of the company.

- Comparison of the cash flow forecast for the period August–November 2013 with management accounts for the same period, to ensure accuracy of the forecast.

- Analytical review of the items included in the cash flow forecast, for example, categories of expenses, to look for items which may have been omitted.

(b) **Going concern impact on audit report**

The note on going concern should be reviewed by the auditors to ensure that the disclosure regarding going concern is sufficiently detailed, and that it includes all relevant matters and is understandable.

In evaluating the adequacy of the disclosure in the note, the auditor should consider whether the disclosure explicitly draws the reader's attention to the possibility that the entity may not be able to continue as a going concern in the foreseeable future. The note should include a description of conditions giving rise to the significant doubt, and the directors' plans to deal with the conditions. This is a requirement of IAS 1 *Presentation of Financial Statements*.

Note adequately describes going concern issues

If the note contains adequate information on going concern issues, then there is no breach of financial reporting standards, and therefore no material misstatement has occurred. The audit opinion should not be modified and should state that the financial statements show a true and fair view, or are fairly presented.

However, in accordance with ISA 570 *Going Concern*, the auditors should modify the auditor's report by adding an Emphasis of Matter paragraph to highlight the existence of the material uncertainties over Burford Co's going concern status, and to draw users' attention to the note to the financial statements where the uncertainties are disclosed. The Emphasis of Matter paragraph should contain a brief description of the uncertainties, and also refer explicitly to the note to the financial statements where the situation has been fully described.

ISA 706 *Emphasis of Matter Paragraphs and Other Matter Paragraphs in the Independent Auditor's Report* states that the Emphasis of Matter paragraph should be placed immediately below the auditor's opinion, and it should re-iterate that the audit opinion is not qualified.

ISA 570 requires that going concern matters, including the adequacy of related notes to the financial statements, should be discussed with those charged with governance. ISA 706 also requires that those charged with governance should be informed by the auditor of the expected inclusion of an Emphasis of Matter paragraph in the auditor's report, and the proposed wording of the paragraph.

Note does not contain adequate information on going concern

It could be the case that a note has been given in the financial statements, but that the details are inadequate and do not fully explain the significant uncertainties affecting the going concern status of the company. In this situation the auditors should express a qualified opinion, as the disclosure requirements of IAS 1 have not been followed, leading to material misstatement. The auditor would need to use judgement to decide whether a qualified or an adverse opinion should be given.

ISA 570 requires that in this case the auditor shall state in the auditor's report that there is a material uncertainty which may cast significant doubt about the entity's ability to continue as a going concern.

ISA 705 *Modifications to the Opinion in the Independent Auditor's Report* provides guidance on the presentation of the audit report in the case of a modification of the audit opinion. The audit report should include a paragraph entitled 'Basis for Qualified Opinion' or 'Basis for Adverse Opinion', which contains specific reference to the matter giving rise to material or pervasive misstatement. The paragraph should include a clear description of the uncertainties and should be presented immediately before the opinion paragraph.

The situation must be discussed with those charged with governance, who should be given opportunity to amend the financial statements by amending the note. ISA 705 states that when the auditor expects to modify the opinion in the auditor's report, the auditor shall communicate with those charged with governance the circumstances which led to the expected modification and the proposed wording of the modification.

Examiner's comments

This question combined the topics of going concern and audit reports. The scenario gave some detailed information about an audit client, Burford Co, facing various financial and operating difficulties, due in part to the obsolescence of its main product. A new product was being developed as a replacement being due to launch in the next financial year. A cash flow forecast had been prepared by management, and the key assumptions used in the forecast were provided.

Requirment (a) (i) asked candidates to identify and explain the matters which cast doubt on the going concern status of Burford Co. This was for 6 marks. Some candidates provided sound explanations. However, as seen in other questions, many candidates did not provide explanations for the matters that they had identified.

Candidates should be aware that by this stage in their professional studies simply repeating information from the given scenario is not enough to secure a pass mark for an individual requirement.

Requirement (a) (ii) required candidates to explain the audit evidence they should expect to find when performing a file review in respect of the cash flow forecast. Again, answers were mixed in quality, with some answers providing well explained, specific evidence points, while other answers were too vague to score well. Typically weak evidence points would include 'discuss cash flows with management' or 'agree figures to supporting documentation' which are simply too vague. Some candidates also seemed to forget that they were commenting on a cash flow forecast, suggesting that all of the figures in the forecast should be agreed to the company's bank statement even though some of the transactions included in the forecast were due to occur a few months in the future. Another problem in some scripts was that the evidence points provided did not focus on the cash flow forecast as requested, but instead were evidence points on going concern generally.

Requirement (c) focused on the audit report. The scenario described that the Burford Co's audit committee would include a brief note on going concern in the company's financial statements, but that a detailed note would not be provided. The requirement asked candidates to discuss the implications of this for the auditor's report and to recommend further actions to be taken. This was for 6 marks. This was generally answered in a satisfactory way, with most answers correctly discussing the use of the Emphasis of Matter paragraph where the note provided by the client is deemed sufficiently detailed, and that the audit opinion would be modified if it were not sufficiently detailed. Many answers explained these issues well, and provided the appropriate actions to be taken by the auditor.

Requirement (c), was often the best answered requirement of this question.

ACCA marking scheme			Marks
(a)	(i)	Going concern indicators Up to 1½ marks for each going concern indicator discussed, for example: – Declining profitability and implication – Poor liquidity – inability to pay suppliers/employees/overheads – Poor liquidity – breach of loan covenant and implication – Development of new product is a further drain on cash – Success of new product is not guaranteed	
		Maximum	6
	(ii)	Procedures on cash flow forecast Generally 1 mark for each well described procedure: – Agreement of the opening cash position to the audited financial statements and general ledger or bank reconciliation – Confirmation that casting of the cash flow forecast has been reperformed – Review of the results of any market research which has been conducted on the GreenFire product – Discussion of the progress made on GreenFire's development with a technical expert or engineer – Review of correspondence with existing customers to gauge the level of interest in GreenFire and confirm if any orders have yet been placed – A review of any sales documentation relating to the planned sale of plant and equipment – Physical inspection of the plant and equipment to be sold, to gauge its condition and the likelihood of sale – Review of any announcement made regarding the redundancies – Sample testing of a selection of those being made redundant, agreeing the amount they are to be paid to HR records – Correspondence from the government department of the $30,000 grant to be received – If the grant of $30,000 has been received, agree to cash book and bank statement – Agreement that the cash flow forecast is consistent with profit and other financial forecasts which have been prepared by management – Confirmation that any other assumptions used in the cash flow forecast are consistent with auditor's knowledge of the business and with management's intentions regarding the future of the company – Comparison of the cash flow forecast for the period August–November 2013 with management accounts for the same period – Analytical review of the items included in the cash flow forecast, for example, categories of expenses, to look for items which may have been omitted	
		Maximum	8

(b) Implications for auditor's report and audit completion

Generally up to 1½ marks for each point discussed:

- Review adequacy of note
- Evaluate its compliance with applicable financial reporting requirements

If note is adequate:

- No modification of auditor's opinion
- Emphasis of Matter paragraph to be included (up to 3 marks for discussion of its contents and positioning)
- Discuss use of EOM with those charged with governance

If note is not adequate:

- Non-compliance with financial reporting requirements therefore material misstatement
- Auditor's judgement as to whether misstatement is material or pervasive
- Content of Basis of Opinion paragraph
- Discuss modification of opinion with those charged with governance

Maximum   6

Total   20

---

44 POODLE *Walk in the footsteps of a top tutor*

Key answer tips

This question focuses on audit reporting implications in a group context but also required explanation of any adjustments and further audit procedures necessary.

There are three issues which need to be discussed, first of all in isolation i.e. one issue at a time. However, remember that the aggregate effects of misstatements should also be considered so finish off your answer by doing this.

When considering the implications for the audit report, remember to consider not just the opinion but any other paragraphs that may need to be added. To earn the marks you will need to justify your answer, e.g. say whether the issue is material; justify why it is material but not pervasive.

(a) **Toy Co**

The amount claimed against Toy Co is material to consolidated profit, representing 25% of consolidated profit before tax. The amount is not material to consolidated total assets, representing less than 1% of that amount.

The same accounting policies should be applied across the Group in the consolidated financial statements. Therefore in accordance with IAS 37 *Provisions, Contingent Liabilities and Contingent Assets*, a provision should be recognised in the consolidated financial statements if the amount is probable to be paid. The adjustment needed is:

DR Operating expenses $500,000

CR Current liabilities – provisions $500,000

The audit evidence obtained by the component auditors is insufficient. Verbal evidence is not a reliable source of evidence. Further audit procedures should be performed, including:

- Obtain written evidence from Toy Co's legal advisors including a statement that in their opinion the damages are probable to be paid, and the basis of that opinion

- Review the claim itself to confirm that $500,000 is the amount claimed by the ex-employee

- Inspect the board minutes of Toy Co for evidence of discussion of the claim, to obtain an understanding as to the reason for the claim and whether it has been disputed by Toy Co.

These further audit procedures may be performed by the component auditor, or by the Group audit team.

If, having obtained evidence to confirm that the damages are probable to be paid, the consolidated financial statements are not adjusted to include the provision, the consolidated statement of profit or loss and other comprehensive income will be materially misstated. This would result in a qualified 'except for' opinion due to the material, but not pervasive, nature of the material misstatement. In accordance with ISA 705 *Modifications to the Opinion in the Independent Auditor's Report*, the report should contain a paragraph entitled 'Basis for Qualified Opinion' describing the matter giving rise to the qualification. A quantification of the financial effect of the misstatement should also be given.

The auditor should discuss the need for the adjustment with the client (including those charged with governance), and explain that a qualified opinion will result from the material misstatement.

(b)   **Trade receivable**

The trade receivable is material to the consolidated financial statements, representing 2.8% of total assets and 80% of profit before tax. The amount that is potentially irrecoverable is 90% of the total balance outstanding, i.e. $1.44 million. This amount is also material, representing 2.5% of total assets and 72% of profit before tax.

IFRS 9 *Financial Instruments* requires that impaired trade receivables are recognised at fair value, which is the present value of estimated cash inflows. According to the information provided by Terrier Co's administrators, it is likely that 10% of the amount outstanding will be paid and the remaining 90% should be written off. The adjustment needed is:

DR Operating expenses (irrecoverable debts expense) $1,440,000

CR Trade receivables $1,440,000

The amount should be adjusted in the financial statements for the year ended 31 March 2013, even though notice was not received until May 2013. This is because according to IAS 10 *Events After the Reporting Period*, an adjusting event is one that provides additional information about conditions existing at the year end.

If the financial statements are not adjusted for the impaired receivable, current assets will be overstated and profits overstated by $1.44 million. This is a very significant matter as the adjustment to profit is highly material.

Tutorial note

Credit will be awarded for comments relating to whether separate disclosure on the face of the statement of profit or loss and other comprehensive income is appropriate, due to the material and unusual nature of the item.

The auditor should perform additional procedures as follows:

- Obtain the notice from Terrier Co's administrators confirming that the company is insolvent and that only 10% of amounts outstanding is likely to be paid

- Obtain a written confirmation from the administrators stating the expected timing of the payment

- Check post year-end cash receipts to see if any of the amount outstanding has been received from Terrier Co

- Recalculate the impairment losses and trace the posting of the impairment into the general ledger and the financial statements.

If the consolidated financial statements are not adjusted for the irrecoverable amount, both the statement of financial position and the statement of profit or loss and other comprehensive income will be materially misstated. This would result in a qualified 'except for' opinion due to the material, but not pervasive, nature of the material misstatement.

Aggregate impact on the financial statements

The materiality and overall significance of the two matters discussed above should be considered in aggregate. When combined, the adjustment needed to net assets and to operating expenses is $1.94 million. This adjustment would reduce the draft consolidated profit before tax to only $60,000.

The combined misstatement could be considered both material and pervasive to the financial statements as the profit figure is so impacted by the adjustments necessary. In this case, the auditor should express an adverse opinion, stating that the financial statements do not show a true and fair view. A paragraph should be included above the opinion, entitled 'Basis for Adverse Opinion', which describes the reason for the adverse opinion and provides quantification.

The auditor should discuss the need for the adjustment with the client (including those charged with governance), and explain that a qualified or adverse opinion will result from the material misstatements. This communication is required by ISA 705.

(c)   **Chairman's statement**

ISA 720 *The Auditor's Responsibilities Relating to Other Information in Documents Containing Audited Financial Statements* requires the auditor to read other information, defined as financial and non-financial information, included in a document containing audited financial statements and the auditor's report.

The purpose of reading the other information is to identify material inconsistencies with the audited financial statements. A material inconsistency arises where the other information contradicts information in the audited financial statements, and may possibly raise doubt about the audit opinion. A material inconsistency undermines the credibility of the audit opinion.

ISA 720 requires that in the event of a material inconsistency being discovered, the auditor shall determine whether the financial statements or the other information needs to be revised, so that the inconsistency is removed. If the inconsistency is not resolved, the auditor's responsibilities depend on whether it is the other information, or the financial statements that have not been corrected.

In the Group's case, the chairman's statement contains an inconsistency, as according to the consolidated financial statements, revenue has increased by 5.9%, but the chairman states that revenue has increased by 20%.

The audit work performed on revenue should be reviewed to ensure that sufficient and appropriate evidence has been gained to support the figures in the financial statements.

The matter should be discussed with management, who should be asked to amend the disclosure in the chairman's statement. Management should be presented with the results of the audit work, to justify, if necessary, that the amendment needs to be made. The inclusion of the incorrect figure in the draft chairman's statement could be a genuine mistake, in which case management should be happy to make the change.

If management refuse to change the disclosure in the other information, then the audit report should contain an Other Matter paragraph. This should be presented immediately after the opinion paragraph and should describe the inconsistency clearly. The matter should also be communicated to those charged with governance.

If the inconsistency remains, the audit firm may wish to speak at a meeting of shareholders of the Poodle Group to explain the additional paragraph that has been included in the audit report.

Examiner's comments

Many candidates chose to attempt Question 5, which focussed on audit completion and audit reports, despite clearly having very little knowledge and understanding of audit reports. Performance tended to be weak on this question overall.

The question was based in a Group audit scenario, in which three matters pertaining to the completion of the audit were described. The scenario made it clear that management was reluctant to adjust the consolidated financial statements in respect of the matters described.

Requirement (a) was for 7 marks and described the situation in relation to Toy Co, an overseas subsidiary of the Group that was audited by local auditors and reported under the local financial reporting framework, not IFRS.

The main issue was that under the local financial reporting rules a claim against the company would not result in the recognition of a provision, but under IFRS the provision should be recognised. The amount was correctly identified by almost all as material to the Group financial statements, and answers were generally satisfactory, despite the slightly complex scenario. Most candidates explained how an adjustment should be made at Group level and that if not made, the audit opinion should be qualified due to material misstatement. Some answers insisted, incorrectly, that the adjustment should be made in the subsidiary's individual financial statements. The fact that the audit evidence so far obtained was insufficient was not always identified, and only a minority of answers suggested the further audit procedures that should be conducted. Some answers were confused about the impact on the opinion and suggested various options including adverse, disclaimer or in some cases, both.

Requirement (b) was also for 7 marks and provided a short description relating to a receivables balance outstanding in the parent company's financial statements for which payment was unlikely to be received due to the insolvency of the company owing the amount. Many candidates correctly identified this as an adjusting event after the reporting period, and determined that the amount was highly material. Some answers tended to focus on the going concern status of both companies, or suggested that the matter should be disclosed in both sets of financial statements but not adjusted for. Comments on the audit opinion were also mixed here, with many incorrectly stating that the issue should be highlighted in an emphasis of matter paragraph if not adjusted by Group management.

Before moving on to look at requirement (c) there are two other comments to make in relation to how candidates dealt with the audit report implications of requirements (a) and (b). The first point is that very few candidates considered the issues of (a) and (b) in aggregate. This was important because in aggregate the potential adjustments had a significant impact on Group results, and a discussion of whether this would result in an adverse opinion was relevant. Candidates are encouraged to always look at the bigger picture and even though the scenarios are described separately, they should at some point in the answer be considered collectively.

The second issue is that very few answers went beyond discussing the impact on the audit opinion. However the question asked for impact on the audit report, so marks were available for describing the structure and content of the basis of opinion paragraph as well as the opinion itself.

Turning to requirement (c), this was for 6 marks and briefly described how the chairman's statement to be published in the Group's annual report, contained a statement that the Group's revenue had increased by 20%.

The vast majority of answers correctly determined that this was incorrect, revenue had actually increased by 5.9% and that this constituted a misstatement of fact. While there were some sound answers here from candidates who clearly understood the implications, unfortunately in many answers there was little else to be said, indicating a lack of knowledge of the auditor's responsibilities in relation to other information published with the financial statements, or the impact of such a misstatement on the auditor's report. Many answers suggested the use, incorrectly, of an emphasis of matter paragraph, but more suggested that there would be no impact at all on the auditor's report, and that the chairman's statement was nothing to do with the auditor's responsibilities.

ACCA marking scheme		
		Marks
Audit completion, adjustments necessary, additional audit procedures, implications for auditor's report Generally up to 1 mark for each point assessed/procedure recommended:		
(a) **Toy Co** • Potential provision is material to Group accounts (calculation) • Group accounting policy should be applied • Adjustment needed to operating profit and current liabilities • Recommend additional procedures (1 mark each) • Material misstatement if not adjusted and qualified opinion • Describe 'Basis for Qualified Opinion' paragraph Maximum		7
(b) **Trade receivable** • Potential impairment of receivables is material to Group accounts (calculation) • Account for as an adjusting event • Adjustment needed to operating profit and current assets • Recommend additional procedures (1 mark each) • Material misstatement if not adjusted and qualified opinion **Potential adjustments in aggregate (marks can be awarded either in answer to (a) or (b))** • In aggregate, the two matters almost wipe out profit before tax • Could be considered to be pervasive to financial statements leading to adverse opinion • Must be discussed with those charged with governance Maximum		7
(c) **Chairman's statement** • Auditor required to read other information which includes the draft chairman's statement • Other information should be consistent with financial statements • Inconsistencies undermine the audit opinion • The draft chairman's statement contains a misstatement of fact regarding revenue • Review audit work performed on revenue • Request draft chairman's statement to be amended • If inconsistency remains, the auditor's report to include an Other Matter paragraph • Consider speaking at meeting of shareholders regarding the inconsistency Maximum		6
Total		20

45   HENDRIX *Walk in the footsteps of a top tutor*

Key answer tips

This is a slightly more unusual question style.

Part (a) (i) asks for actions to be taken by the auditor and the implications for the audit report. Here, you need to consider if there is anything further that can be done to obtain the evidence required. Implications for the audit report should consider not just the opinion but any other modifications that may be necessary.

Part (a) (ii) requires quality control procedures to be undertaken before issuing the report. Draw on your knowledge from the quality control chapter and specifically the engagement performance section of ISQC 1 and the requirements for listed clients.

Part (b) requires matters to be considered in forming a conclusion on the interim financial statements. Even though this is not an audit engagement, the same approach can be taken as for other 'matters' questions. Refer to the materiality of the warranty provision made in the previous year, discuss the appropriate accounting treatment and what should be done. In terms of the opinion, remember that limited assurance will be given so the wording needs to reflect this.

(a)   (i)   There is a clear lack of audit evidence in respect of payroll, receivables and revenue. The written statement from Hendrix Co is not sufficient appropriate evidence on which to reach a conclusion regarding these balances and transactions which are material to the financial statements of Dylan Co.

The auditor should consider whether audit procedures alternative to those planned could be used to gather sufficient appropriate evidence. For example, procedures could be performed on the manual reconstruction of accounting records which has been performed by Hendrix Co, and receivables could still be contacted to confirm the balances outstanding at the year end. This would rely on the cooperation of Hendrix Co, who would have to allow the audit firm access to its accounting records and the reconstruction that has taken place.

The audit firm could request an extension to the agreed deadline for the completion of the audit to perform such additional work. This may be seen as a favourable option to the client, who presumably would want to avoid a modified audit opinion in the event that insufficient audit evidence was obtained.

Given that Hendrix Co's accounting systems were affected in August, only one month before the financial year end, it may be possible to obtain sufficient appropriate evidence for the majority of transactions that occurred during the year, and that it is only a small proportion of transactions that cannot be confirmed, which may be immaterial to the financial statements. In this case, an unmodified opinion would be issued.

If further evidence cannot be obtained, the auditor should consider a modification to the auditor's opinion in accordance with ISA *705 Modifications to the Opinion in the Independent* Auditor's *Report.* If the auditor is unable to obtain sufficient appropriate audit evidence on which to base the opinion, but the auditor concludes that the possible effects on the financial statements of undetected misstatements, if any, could be material but not pervasive, then a qualified opinion should be given. In this opinion, the auditor states that except for the possible effects of the potential misstatements of payroll, receivables and revenue, the financial statements give a true and fair view.

The auditor may conclude that the possible effects on the financial statements of undetected misstatements, if any, could be both material and pervasive, in which case the auditor should disclaim an opinion. In this case, the auditor states that sufficient appropriate evidence has not been obtained to provide a basis for an audit opinion, and accordingly the auditor does not express an opinion on the financial statements.

In any modified audit report, a basis for modification paragraph should describe the matters giving rise to the modification. This should be placed immediately before the opinion paragraph.

It is required that potential modifications are communicated to those charged with governance. The reasons for the modification should be explained, and those charged with governance may be able to provide the auditor with further information and explanations. Given that Dylan Co is listed, the communication is likely to be with its audit committee.

(ii) **Quality control**

ISA *220 Quality Control for an Audit of Financial Statements* requires that for audits of financial statements of listed entities, an engagement quality control reviewer shall be appointed. The audit engagement partner shall then discuss significant matters arising during the audit engagement with the engagement quality control reviewer.

In the case of Dylan Co's audit, clearly the lack of evidence in respect of significant financial statement balances and transactions, and its impact on the auditor's report should be discussed. The engagement quality control reviewer must review the financial statements and the proposed auditor's report, in particular focusing on the conclusions reached in formulating the auditor's report and consideration of whether the proposed auditor's opinion is appropriate. The audit documentation relating to payroll, receivables and revenue will be carefully reviewed, and the reviewer is likely to consider whether there are any alternative means of confirming the balances and transactions.

Given the listed status of Dylan Co, any modification to the auditor's report will be scrutinised, and the firm must be sure of any decision to modify the report, and the type of modification made. Once the engagement quality control reviewer has considered the necessity of a modification, they should consider whether a qualified or disclaimer of opinion is appropriate. This is an important issue, given that it is a matter of judgement whether the matters would be material or pervasive to the financial statements.

The engagement quality control reviewer should ensure that there is adequate documentation regarding the judgements used in forming the audit opinion, and that all necessary matters have been brought to the attention of those charged with governance.

The auditor's report may not be signed and dated until the completion of the engagement quality control review.

(b) **Review of interim financial statements**

Reviews of interim financial statements are governed by ISRE 2410 *Review of Interim Financial Information Performed by the Independent Auditor of the Entity*. Reviews are based on enquiries and analytical procedures, and having determined that Squire Co has changed its accounting treatment regarding the warranty provision, management must be asked to explain the reason for the change.

Interim financial statements should be prepared under the same financial reporting framework as annual financial statements. Therefore IAS *37 Provisions, Contingent Liabilities and Contingent Assets* should be applied.

It would appear correct that a warranty provision is not recognised for cars sold since 1 July 2012, as Squire Co has no obligation relating to those sales. However, cars sold previous to that date are subject to a three-year warranty, so a warranty provision should continue to be recognised for the obligation arising in respect of those sales. Therefore Squire Co's interim financial statements understate liabilities and overstate profits.

The warranty provision as at 30 April represented 5.5% of total assets, therefore material to the financial statements. If the same warranty provision still needs to be recognised at 31 October, it would represent 5% of total assets, therefore material to the interim financial statements.

ISRE 2410 requires that when a matter comes to the auditor's attention that leads the auditor to question whether a material adjustment should be made to the interim financial information, additional inquiries should be made, or other procedures performed. In this case, the auditor may wish to inspect sales documentation to ensure that warranties are no longer offered on sales after 1 July. The auditor should also review customer correspondence to ensure that warranties on sales prior to 1 July are still in place.

If as a result of performing the necessary procedures, the auditor believes that a material adjustment is needed in the interim financial information, the matter must be communicated to the appropriate level of management, and if management fail to respond appropriately within a reasonable period of time, to those charged with governance. In order to avoid a modification of the report, it is likely that adjustment would be made by management to the interim financial statements.

If the amount remains unadjusted, meaning that in the auditor's opinion the interim financial statements contain a material departure from the applicable financial reporting framework, the report on the review of interim financial information should contain a qualified or adverse conclusion. This is a modification of the report, and the auditor must describe the reason for the modification, which is provided in a paragraph entitled 'Basis for Qualified Conclusion', presented immediately before the qualified conclusion.

The qualified conclusion would be worded as follows: 'Based on our review, with the exception of the matter described in the preceding paragraph, nothing has come to our attention that causes us to believe that the accompanying interim financial information does not give a true and fair view...'

Finally, the audit firm should consider whether it is possible to withdraw from the review engagement and resigning from the audit appointment.

Examiner's comments

This question, as is typical for question five in paper P7, focussed on reporting. The scenario for requirement (a) described the loss of accounting records that had occurred one month before the year end of a listed audit client.

The records had been held by a service organisation, which had provided reconstructed records in respect of those that had been lost. Requirement (a) (i) was for seven marks, and asked candidates to comment on the actions that should be taken by the auditor, and the implication for the auditor's report. Most candidates correctly discussed that fact that the auditor was unable to obtain sufficient, appropriate audit evidence based on the reconstructed records, leading them to explain that the audit opinion should be disclaimed. Fewer candidates suggested that alternative procedures could be used to obtain evidence, and fewer still recognised that as the accounting records were available for eleven months of the year, the audit report may not necessarily be subject to a disclaimer of opinion, or even qualified at all if alternative procedures could take place. A small minority of answers discussed the fact that due to the client being a listed entity, it would most likely have back up records of its own and not be totally reliant on the service organisation in any case.

Some answers demonstrated a lack of knowledge on audit reports, stating incorrectly that an adverse opinion would be most appropriate, and few answers described the need for discussing the potential modification with those charged with governance, instead opting for resignation in the face of such 'incompetent' management.

Requirement (a) (ii) for three marks asked for a discussion of quality control procedures that should be carried out by the audit firm prior to the audit report being issued. Sound answers appreciated that because the client in the scenario was listed, an Engagement Quality Control review would be required, and the answers that described what such a review would entail achieved the maximum marks. Most answers were too general however, simply describing the quality control procedures that would be relevant to any audit. Many answers were extremely brief, with little more than a sentence or two provided.

Requirement (b) was for six marks, and was based on a scenario which described a review engagement that was taking place on the interim financial statements of another listed company. An accounting policy in relation to warranty provisions had been changed in the interim financial statements, and based on the information provided, candidates should have appreciated that the accounting treatment was incorrect. Figures were provided to enable materiality to be calculated. The requirement was to assess the matters that should be considered in forming an opinion on the interim financial statements, and the implications for the review report. Most answers were good at discussing the accounting treatment for the warranty provision, that the non-recognition was not appropriate, and the majority correctly assessed the materiality of the issue. Answers were inadequate in discussing the impact of this on the review report, being mostly unable to say much more than the auditor would need to mention it in the review report. There seemed to be a lack of knowledge on anything other than the standard wording for a review report, with many answers stating that the wording should be 'nothing has come to our attention' followed by a discussion that there actually was something to bring to shareholders' attention but with no recommendation as to how this should be done.

		ACCA marking scheme	
			Marks
(a)	(i)	**Actions and implications in respect of the auditor's report on Dylan Co**	
		– Up to 1½ marks for each action/implication	
		– Insufficient appropriate audit evidence so far obtained	
		– Possible to extend audit procedures on reconstructed figures/other procedures	
		– Majority of transactions during the year likely to have sufficient evidence	
		– If no further evidence available, consider modification to opinion	
		– Discuss whether material or pervasive	
		– Description of audit report contents if opinion modified	
		– Communicate with those charged with governance	
		Maximum	7
	(ii)	**Quality control procedures**	
		Up to 1 mark for each comment:	
		– EQCR required as Dylan Co is listed	
		– EQCR to review sufficiency and appropriateness of evidence obtained	
		– EQCR to consider judgement used in forming audit opinion	
		– EQCR to ensure matters communicated to those charged with governance	
		Maximum	3
(b)		**Interim financial statement review**	
		Up to 1½ marks for each matter to be considered in forming conclusion/implication for report:	
		– Interim financial information should use applicable financial reporting framework	
		– Identify and explain unrecognised provision	
		– Correct calculation of materiality (1 mark)	
		– Communicate necessary adjustment to management/those charged with governance	
		– If amount unadjusted, the conclusion will be qualified	
		– Reason for qualified conclusion to be explained in the report	
		– Consider withdrawing from engagement/resign from audit appointment	
		Maximum	6
Total			**16**

46 SNIPE *Walk in the footsteps of a top tutor*

Key answer tips

Part (a) This question is a typical 'matters and evidence' question. First, consider the materiality of the issue. Next discuss the appropriate accounting treatment and give the risks of material misstatement that would arise if the appropriate treatment is not followed. Finally, the evidence is what you would expect to be recorded on the audit file when you come to review it. Be specific about the evidence, don't say 'supporting documentation', suggest what that documentation would be and what it would show.

Part (b) asks for a critical appraisal of the draft audit report extracts. Don't just focus on whether the opinion is appropriate. You should also think about the titles of the paragraphs included and whether the names are correct, the order they appear in, whether the required information that should be included has been included and whether the wording used is professional and appropriate.

(a) **Matters to consider**

The total cost of the new processing area of $5 million represents 2·9% of total assets and is material to the statement of financial position. The borrowing costs are not material to the statement of financial position, representing less than 1% of total assets; however, the costs are material to profit representing 10% of profit before tax.

The directly attributable costs, including borrowing costs, relating to the new processing area should be capitalised as property, plant and equipment. According to IAS 23 *Borrowing Costs,* borrowing costs that are directly attributable to the acquisition, construction or production of a qualifying asset should be capitalised as part of the cost of that asset. The borrowing costs should be capitalised only during the period of construction, with capitalisation ceasing when substantially all the activities necessary to prepare the qualifying asset for its intended use or sale are complete.

In this case, the new processing area was ready for use on 1 September, so capitalisation of borrowing costs should have ceased at that point. It seems that the borrowing costs have been appropriately capitalised at $100,000, which represents six months' interest on the loan ($4m × 5% × 6/12).

The new processing area should be depreciated from 1 September, as according to IAS 16 Property, *Plant and Equipment,* depreciation of an asset begins when it is in the location and condition necessary for it to be capable of operating in the manner intended by management.

There should therefore be five months' depreciation included in profit for the year ended 31 January 2012, amounting to $138,889 ($5m/15 years × 5/12).

Evidence

- A breakdown of the components of the $4·9 million capitalised costs (excluding $100,000 borrowing costs) reviewed to ensure all items are eligible for capitalisation.

- Agreement of a sample of the capitalised costs to supporting documentation (e.g. invoices for tangible items such as cement, payroll records for internal labour costs).

- A copy of the approved budget or capital expenditure plan for the extension.

- An original copy of the loan agreement, confirming the amount borrowed, the date of the cash receipt, the interest rate and whether the loan is secured on any assets.

- Documentation to verify that the extension was complete and ready for use on 1 September, such as a building completion certificate.

- Recalculation of the borrowing cost, depreciation charge and carrying value of the extension at the year end, and agreement of all figures to the draft financial statements.

- Confirmation that the additions to property, plant and equipment are disclosed in the required note to the financial statements.

(b) The titles and positioning of the two paragraphs included in the extract are not appropriate. According to ISA 705 *Modifications to the Opinion in the Independent Auditor's Report,* when the auditor modifies the opinion, a paragraph should be placed immediately before the opinion paragraph entitled 'Basis for Adverse Opinion', which describes the matter giving rise to the modification. This should then be followed by the opinion paragraph, which should be entitled 'Adverse Opinion'. In this case, the titles are incorrect, and the paragraphs should be switched round, so that the basis for modification is provided before the opinion.

The description and explanation provided for the adverse opinion is not sufficient, for a number of reasons. Firstly, the matter is not quantified. The paragraph should clearly state the amount of $10.5 million, and state that this is material to the financial statements.

The paragraph does not say whether the pension plan is in surplus or deficit, i.e. whether it is an asset or a liability which is omitted from the financial statements.

There is no description of the impact of this omission on the financial statements. Wording such as 'if the deficit had been recognised, total liabilities would increase by $10.5 million, and shareholders' equity would reduce by the same amount' should be included.

It is not clear whether any accounting for the pension plan has taken place at all. As well as recognising the plan surplus or deficit in the statement of financial position, accounting entries are also required to deal with other items such as the current service cost of the plan, and any actuarial gains or losses which have arisen during the year. Whether these have been omitted as well, and their potential impact on profit or equity is not mentioned.

No reference is made to the relevant accounting standard IAS 19 *Employee Benefits.* Reference should be made in order to help users' understanding of the breach of accounting standards that has been made.

The use of the word 'deliberate' when describing the omission of the pension plan is not professional, sounds accusatory and may not be correct. The plan may have been omitted in error and an adjustment to the financial statements may have been suggested by the audit firm and is being considered by management.

Finally, it is unlikely that this issue alone would be sufficient to give rise to an adverse opinion. ISA 705 states that an adverse opinion should be given when misstatements are both material and pervasive to the financial statements. The amount of the deficit, and therefore the liability that should be recognised, is $10.5 million, which represents 6% of total assets. The amount is definitely material, but would not be considered pervasive to the financial statements.

Tutorial note

According to ISA 705 if a misstatement is confined to specific elements of the financial statements, it would only be considered pervasive if it represents a substantial proportion of the financial statements.

Examiner's comments

This question was in two parts. Part (a) was for 8 marks and described the self-construction of new property, plant and equipment at a client. A loan had been taken out to help finance the construction, and financial information was provided in relation to the asset and the loan. Candidates were asked to comment on the matters that should be considered, and the evidence that should be found when conducting a file review of non-current assets.

Candidates should have been familiar with this type of question requirement, as it commonly features in P7. Sound answers contained a calculation and explanation of the materiality of the asset and of the borrowing costs that had been capitalised, followed by a discussion of the appropriate accounting treatment, including whether the borrowing cost should be capitalised, and when depreciation in relation to the asset should commence. There were some sound answers here, with candidates demonstrating sound knowledge of the relevant financial reporting standard requirements, and going on to provide some very well described and relevant audit procedures.

Weaker answers said that it was not possible to capitalise borrowing costs, or incorrectly thought that the construction should be accounted for as some kind of long-term construction contract. Procedures in the weaker answers tended to rely on management representations and recalculations of every figure provided in the question.

Part (b) was for 7 marks and involved the critique of an extract from an audit report. The report contained an adverse opinion, which most candidates spotted, in relation to the non-recognition of a defined benefit pension deficit on the company's statement of financial position. There were some sound answers here, and candidates' performance in questions of this type has shown a definite improvement. Some answers not only identified but also provided an explanation of the problems with the audit report. The majority of answers suggested that an 'except for' qualification may be more suitable than an adverse opinion, and correctly calculated the materiality of the pension plan deficit to support their discussion. A significant proportion of answers picked up on the incorrect order of the paragraphs in the report and on the incorrect wording used in the headings, and on the lack of explanation that had been provided in the report regarding the material misstatement. Fewer answers discussed the inappropriate use of the phrase 'deliberate omission'.

The weaker answers tended to just list out bullet points with no explanation, limiting the amount of marks that could be awarded. Other weaker answers attempted to discuss the appropriate accounting treatment for the pension, often incorrectly.

	ACCA marking scheme	
		Marks
(a)	**New processing area** Generally 1 mark for each matter/specific audit procedure: **Matters:** – Materiality calculation – Borrowing costs are directly attributable to the asset – Borrowing costs should be capitalised during period of construction – Amounts are correctly capitalised – Depreciate from September 2011 – Additions to non-current assets should be disclosed in note **Evidence:** – Review of costs capitalised for eligibility – Agreement of sample of costs to supporting documentation – Copy of approved capital expenditure budget/discuss significant variances – Agreement of loan details to loan documentation – Recalculation of borrowing costs, depreciation, asset carrying value – Confirmation of completeness of disclosure in notes to financial statements	
	Maximum	8
(b)	**Audit report** Generally 1 mark per comment: – Inappropriate headings – Paragraphs wrong way round – Amounts not quantified – Impact on financial statements not described – Unclear from audit report if any accounting taken place for the – No reference made to relevant accounting standard – Use of word 'deliberate' not professional – Materiality calculation – Discuss whether adverse opinion appropriate (up to 2 marks)	
	Maximum	7
Total		15

47 **YEW** *Walk in the footsteps of a top tutor*

Key answer tips

Part (a) focuses on completion of the audit and how to resolve an accounting issue prior to issuing the audit report. A methodical approach should be taken. Consider the materiality of the issue, discuss the accounting treatment required and finally the audit reporting implications if it is not resolved.

Part (b) asks for advice dealing with two issues whether verbal representations are acceptable and whether a prior year modification requires mentioning in this year's audit report if the issue giving rise to the modification has been resolved. Each of these issues is worth 3 marks so be careful not to spend too much time on each.

(a) The intangible asset measured at $12.5 million is material to the statement of financial position, representing 6% of total assets. The amount is also material to profit, representing 54% of profit before tax.

It appears that the criteria for capitalisation of development costs contained in IAS 38 *Intangible Assets* have not been met, for two reasons. First, IAS 38 requires that the entity must be able to demonstrate how the intangible asset will generate probable future economic benefits.

Among other things, the entity should demonstrate the existence of a market for the output of the intangible asset, or if it is to be used internally, the usefulness of the intangible asset.

The market research conducted by Yew Co indicates that there may not be a foreseeable economic benefit to be derived from the development, which was confirmed through written representation. This indicates that the audit work should conclude that the recognition criteria have not been met and that therefore the intangible asset should be derecognised.

A further criterion in IAS 38 is that the entity should be able to demonstrate the availability of adequate technical, financial and other resources to complete the development and to use or sell the intangible asset. As Yew Co appears to be short of finance, it is questionable whether sufficient funds would be available to complete the development and take the product to market. This further indicates that the intangible asset should be derecognised, with all research and development costs treated as operating expenses.

Based on the above, the draft financial statements contain a material misstatement, as non-current assets are overstated, and profits overstated, by a material amount. The auditor should discuss this matter with management and those charged with governance, explaining the problem with the accounting treatment, and requesting that the financial statements be amended.

If no amendment is made, the auditor must consider the implications for the auditor's report, which would be qualified due to a material, but not pervasive, misstatement. This should also be explained to management and those charged with governance.

The audit firm could consider whether any further evidence should be obtained to support the conclusions reached over the accounting treatment. The matter should be discussed with the chairman who, given the comments in the chairman's statement, may have contradictory evidence that actually the development is likely to be successful.

The firm should consider extending the work conducted on going concern, in particular to validate the concerns expressed by members of management that the company is struggling to raise finance. If there is significant doubt over the company's going concern status, disclosures should be made by management in the notes to the financial statements. The audit working papers should clearly document the assessment of Yew Co's going concern status, and whether any doubt over it is significant.

The audit firm should also consider whether the treatment of the development costs as an intangible asset represents fraudulent financial reporting. If the company is struggling to raise finance, there may be an incentive for the financial statements to present a healthy statement of financial position, which would be helped by the inclusion of these material costs as an asset.

Given the significance of the intangible asset in the financial statements, and the potential qualification of the auditor's opinion, it is crucial that the audit work is carefully reviewed, possibly by a second partner with no involvement in the audit of Yew Co, to ensure that the audit work conducted was of high quality and supports the auditor's conclusions.

The annual report is scheduled to be issued next week. The audit engagement partner could discuss whether there is any scope for delaying this until further information becomes available in respect of the new products and the going concern status of the company, e.g. if a customer is about to sign a contract for the supply of the new products this will provide further confirmation of the economic benefit to be derived from the research and development.

The other issue to be addressed is the apparent inconsistency between the discussion of the development of the new aircraft engines in the chairman's statement, and the evidence obtained by the auditors which should result in the amendment of the financial statements. The chairman's statement implies that the products are going to be successful in the short-term, yet audit evidence, and the financial statements if amended, contradict this.

The inconsistency should be discussed with management, and the audit engagement partner should encourage the wording of the chairman's statement to be revised. According to ISA 720 *The Auditor's Responsibilities Relating to Other Information in Documents Containing Audited Financial Statements,* if management refuse to make the necessary revision to the chairman's statement, such that an inconsistency exists between the chairman's statement and the amended financial statements, an Other Matter paragraph should be included in the auditor's report to describe the material inconsistency. The auditor's opinion is not modified in respect of the material inconsistency.

All of these matters should be brought to the attention of those charged with governance as soon as possible, in the hope that they can be persuaded to make the necessary amendment to the financial statements and to the chairman's statement, thus avoiding the need for qualification of the audit opinion and the inclusion of an Other Matter paragraph in the auditor's report.

The audit firm may wish to speak at a meeting of shareholders to explain the additional paragraph(s) included in the auditor's report.

(b) (i) **Date of signing the auditor's report**

ISA 700 *Forming an Opinion and Reporting on Financial Statements* requires that the auditor shall not sign and date the auditor's report earlier than the date on which the auditor has considered all necessary sufficient appropriate available evidence.

The auditor cannot reach an opinion until all evidence has been assessed, including written representations from management. Even though the content of the representations have been discussed with management, the audit partner should not sign the audit report until the written representations have been received.

Written representations are a necessary piece of audit evidence. In particular, written representations are made concerning events after the year end. If a significant event were to occur after the partner had issued the auditor's report, the financial statements may need to be amended and the original auditor's report would be inappropriate.

In summary, it is contrary to ISA 700 for the audit partner to sign the auditor's report prior to obtaining and concluding on the evidence obtained in the written representation.

(ii) **Prior year auditor's opinion**

The general rule is that the auditor has sole responsibility for expressing an opinion on the financial statements, and should not refer to third parties (such as auditor's experts or service organisation's auditors) as this may imply that some responsibility has been delegated to those parties.

However, ISA 710 *Comparative Information – Corresponding Figures and Comparative Financial Statements* states that it is acceptable to refer to the predecessor auditor's report on corresponding figures, as long as this is not prohibited by law or regulation. ISA 710 makes it clear that it is the auditor's choice to refer to the predecessor's auditor's report.

If such reference were made, it would be included in an Other Matter paragraph, placed directly below the auditor's opinion. The Other Matter paragraph should contain a statement that the financial statements of the prior period were audited by the predecessor auditor, the type of opinion expressed, and the date of that report.

In this case, because the opinion expressed on the prior year financial statements was modified, the Other Matter paragraph should also explain the reasons for that modification.

Examiner's comments

The final question was in two parts. Requirement (a) for 12 marks was based on a scenario which described matters arising as an audit was drawing to a close. There were essentially three matters to deal with – a potentially incorrect accounting treatment, a going concern issue, and an inconsistency in the chairman's statement (director's report for UK and IRL adapted papers). The requirement was to consider the implications of these issues on the completion of the audit and for the auditor's report, and to recommend any further actions to be taken by the auditor. Answers on the whole were satisfactory. Most answers successfully identified and explained the three issues, with most answers focussing more on the accounting treatment of research and development costs, which potentially needed an adjustment. In answering this requirement candidates tended to be more comfortable with the audit report implications than in Q2, usually correctly identifying the use of an Other Matter paragraph regarding the inconsistency, and an Emphasis of Matter paragraph regarding the going concern issue. The only area which many answers failed to deal with was the further audit procedures needed regarding the development costs and the going concern issues.

Requirement (b), for 6 marks contained two short requirements concerning the auditor's report. The first issue concerned whether the auditor's report should be issued prior to receiving written representations from management, and the second dealt with whether an auditor's report should refer to a matter in the previous year's financial statements, which caused a modification of the previous year's auditor's opinion, but which had since been resolved. Candidates were more comfortable with the first issue, usually correctly identifying that the written representation is a necessary piece of audit evidence, and that a verbal confirmation is not sufficient. On the second issue many answers were just too brief – often little more than a few words – usually saying that no reference need be made. These requirements were fairly knowledge based, and it was apparent that a lot of candidates who chose to attempt question 5 did so on the basis of requirement (a) and not requirement (b).

The UK adapted paper had a different second scenario in requirement (b), focussing on the pros and cons of audit reports cross-referencing to the Auditing Practices Board's website. Answers were satisfactory, with candidates providing a proper evaluation and sometimes a conclusion to the matter

ACCA marking scheme			Marks

(a) Yew Co

Generally up to 1½ marks for each matter discussed/recommended:

- Calculate and comment on materiality
- No probable economic benefit – IAS 38 recognition criteria not met
- Lack of finance – IAS 38 recognition criteria not met
- Consider whether sufficient appropriate evidence obtained
- Financial statements contain material misstatement and implication for auditor's report
- Could indicate fraudulent financial reporting
- Lack of cash may indicate going concern problems – extend audit procedures
- Audit work should be subject to 2nd partner review
- Consider asking for a delay in issuing financial statements if necessary for further evidence to be sought
- Discuss apparent inconsistency in chairman's statement wording
- Discuss accounting treatment, potential qualification and chairman's statement wording with those charged with governance
- Include Other Matter paragraph in report if material inconsistency remains

Maximum **12**

(b) (i) Signing of audit report

Generally 1 mark per point:

- Date report when all necessary evidence received, including written representations
- Especially important with regard to subsequent events
- Contrary to ISA 700 to sign report prior to receiving written representations

Maximum **3**

(ii) Prior year auditor's opinion

Generally 1 mark per point:

- Generally auditors do not refer to third parties in their report
- But optional to refer to predecessor auditor unless prohibited by law and regulations
- If reference made, should be in Other Matter paragraph
- Describe contents of reference made to predecessor auditor
- If prior year modified, explain this in Other Matter paragraph

Maximum **3**

Total **18**

48 NASSAU GROUP *Walk in the footsteps of a top tutor*

Key answer tips

Part (a) deals with matters to consider and actions to be taken before issuing the report for a group. Here, there is a modification of opinion in one of the subsidiaries which requires consideration of whether it has a material impact on the group financial statements in order to be able to determine the group audit opinion.

Part (b) asks for the procedures to be performed on the consolidation process. This is rote learnt knowledge from the text book.

(a) **Significant component**

A significant component is defined in ISA 600 *Special Considerations – Audits of Group Financial Statements (Including the Work of Component Auditors)* as a component identified by the group audit engagement team that is of individual significance to the group. Exuma Co meets the definition of a significant component because it contributes 20% of group profit before tax, and 23.5% of group total assets. Exuma Co is therefore material to the group financial statements.

Materiality of accounting issue

The legal case against Exuma Co involves a claim against the company of $2 million. This is material to the individual financial statements of Exuma Co as it represents 50% of profit before tax, and 10% of total assets. The matter is also material to the group financial statements, representing 10% of group profit before tax, and 2.4% of group total assets.

Qualified Opinion – Exuma Co financial statements

Jalousie & Co has expressed a qualified opinion due to a material misstatement regarding the accounting treatment of the court case. Management has treated the matter as a contingent liability, as they believe that it is possible, but not probable, that the court case will go against the company, but the auditors believe that it should have been recognised as a provision according to IAS 37 *Provisions, Contingent Liabilities and Contingent Assets*. Given the materiality of the matter to the individual financial statements, this opinion seems appropriate (rather than an adverse opinion), as long as the audit evidence concludes that a provision is necessary. In other words, the audit evidence should indicate that it is probable that the legal claim will give rise to an outflow of cash.

Review and discussion of audit work relating to the court case

Due to the significance of this matter, the audit work performed by Jalousie & Co should be subject to review by the group audit engagement team. Specifically, the evidence leading to the conclusion that a probable outflow of cash will occur should be reviewed, and the matter should be discussed with the audit partner responsible for the opinion on Exuma Co's financial statements. Evidence should include copies of legal correspondence, a copy of the actual claim showing the $2 million claimed against the company, and a written representation from management detailing management's reason for believing that there is no probable cash outflow.

Further audit procedures

According to ISA 600, when a risk of material misstatement has been identified in a component in which a component auditor has performed the audit work, the group engagement team shall evaluate the appropriateness of any further audit procedures being performed, and shall determine whether it is necessary to be involved in the further audit procedures. Given the subjective nature of this matter, the group engagement partner may consider engaging an external expert to provide an opinion as to the probability of the court case going against Exuma Co.

Discussion with Nassau Group management

The matter should be discussed with the Group management team, and the views of Group management as to whether a provision is necessary should be sought and documented in a written representation. There should also be discussion with management, and communication with those charged with governance regarding the potential impact of the matter on the group audit opinion. The impact depends on whether an adjustment is made in the individual accounts of Exuma Co, on consolidation, or not made at all, as explained below:

Adjustment to Exuma Co financial statements

Exuma Co is a subsidiary of Nassau, and by definition is under the control of the parent company. Therefore, management of Exuma Co can be asked to adjust the financial statements to recognise a provision. If this happens, Jalousie & Co's audit report can be redrafted as unqualified, and the group audit opinion will also be unqualified.

Adjustment on consolidation

Even if Exuma Co's financial statements are not amended, an adjustment could be made on consolidation of the group financial statements to include the provision. In this case, the opinion on Exuma Co's financial statements would remain qualified, but the group audit opinion would not be qualified as the matter causing the material misstatement has been rectified.

No adjustment made

If no adjustment is made, either to Exuma Co's individual financial statements, or as a consolidation adjustment in the group financial statements, and if the group engagement partner disagrees with this accounting treatment, then the group audit opinion should be qualified due to a material misstatement. In this case, a paragraph entitled Basis for Qualified Opinion should explain the reason for the qualification, i.e. non-compliance with IAS 37, and should also quantify the financial effect on the consolidated financial statements. Reference to the work performed by a component auditor should not be made.

Tutorial note

The answer assumes that none of the other subsidiary's audit opinions are modified. Credit will be awarded for recognition of this as an issue, and for recommending that the reports of all subsidiaries should be reviewed by the group audit partner.

(b)   ISA 600 firstly requires that the auditor shall obtain an understanding of the group-wide controls and the consolidation process. This includes an evaluation of instructions given by group management to components of the group. The operating effectiveness of controls over the consolidation process will be tested.

The audit procedures will mainly focus on adjustments made on consolidation. For example, significant adjustments such as goodwill calculations and impairments are recalculated, underlying assumptions checked for validity, and the authorisation of the adjustment should be checked. Adjustments should be agreed to underlying documentation, and where relevant, to prior year audited financial statements or audit working papers.

The elimination of inter-company transactions is usually a key feature of the consolidation process. Reconciliations of intercompany balances should be arithmetically checked, and unrealised profits should be recalculated for accuracy.

Figures included in the consolidation schedules should be agreed back to audited financial statements of all components. Disclosures made in the notes to the group financial statements should also be agreed back to the individual component's financial statements where relevant, for example disclosures on related parties.

Audit procedures will be needed to verify that subsidiary balances have been included where relevant at fair value in the consolidated financial statements. For example, properties may be held at cost in the individual financial statements of the component, but should be consolidated at fair value. The auditor may consider the need to engage an expert to provide evidence on fair values, especially if the amounts involved are material. The audit of fair values is crucial as it forms the basis of the goodwill calculation.

The accounting policies of all components of the group should be checked for consistency, as additional adjustments may be necessary to bring the components into line with group accounting policies.

The deferred tax consequences of consolidation and fair value adjustments should be reviewed for completeness, and calculations re-performed for accuracy.

Where the group has investments in non-controlling interests, additional procedures will be necessary to check the validity of treating the investments as associates and/or joint ventures, such as verification of the percentage shareholding by a review of purchase documentation or obtaining copies of the register of significant investors from the investee companies.

The consolidation schedule should be arithmetically checked by casting and cross-casting.

Examiner's comments

This was the least popular of the optional questions, focussing on audit reports and group audit issues. The scenario described a group audit in which the component auditors suggested a qualified audit opinion on a subsidiary's financial statements due to an alleged material misstatement concerning a provision.

Requirement (a), for 10 marks, asked candidates to identify and explain the matters that should be considered and the actions that should be taken by the group audit engagement team in forming an opinion on the consolidated financial statements. Most candidates gained marks by calculating the materiality of the provision to the group and to the individual financial statements of the subsidiary. However, few determined the materiality of the component itself to the group.

Candidates are usually happy to be critical of auditors in question scenarios, but in this case when it was actually appropriate to raise concerns over the evidence (or lack of it) obtained to support the qualified opinion, very few answers tackled this issue. However, some candidates did waste time criticising the extract audit report that had been provided – this was not asked for – and implied that candidates had not read the question requirement at all. Only some candidates picked up on the fact that an adjustment could be made at group level to avoid any qualification in the consolidated financial statements, and that pressure could be put on the subsidiary's management to adjust in the individual financial statements as well.

Few candidates provided any 'actions' at all, which was unsatisfactory as some relatively easy marks could have been gained by suggesting a detailed review of the component auditors working papers, requesting evidence from the subsidiary's management to support their accounting treatment, or discussing the matter with those charged with governance.

Requirement (b) asked candidates to explain the principle audit procedures that should be performed on the consolidation process, for 8 marks. Many candidates clearly knew the consolidation process very well, but had trouble expressing this knowledge in terms of audit procedures. Many answers simply described what should happen in a consolidation, and thought that by including the words 'check' or 'ensure' every so often that would be enough e.g. 'check goodwill calculation', 'ensure all subsidiaries included' but didn't actually say how these things should be done. However, despite these problems most answers were satisfactory. Taking a step back to consider the effectiveness of controls over the whole process was rarely considered.

The UK and IRL requirement (b) was different, and concerned a subsidiary that had been disposed of during the year. The requirement was to comment on the matters that should be considered and the evidence that should be found in a review of audit working papers. Candidates responded well to this, and most earned marks by calculating materiality, discussing the appropriate accounting treatment in the consolidated financial statements, and could provide several examples of relevant evidence.

Repeating a comment made in the previous Examiner's report, answers to question 5 (a) were unsatisfactory, given that audit reports is a regularly examined syllabus area.

ACCA marking scheme		Marks

(a) **Matters/actions**
Up to 2 marks for each matter/action identified and explained (max 3 marks for identification):
– Exuma Co is a significant component
– Matter is material to individual and group financial statements
– Accounting treatment/qualification for Exuma Co's financial statements
– Review of audit work performed
– Consideration of further audit work
– Discuss with group management and those charged with governance
– Request that Exuma Co's management adjust financial statements
– Adjustment could be made on consolidation
– Impact on group opinion if no adjustment made

Maximum   **10**

(b) **Principal procedures on consolidation**
Generally 1 mark per procedure explained:
– Test controls
– Review group instructions
– Recalculate adjustments
– Reconcile inter-company balances
– Review fair values/consider need for expert
– Consider consistency of accounting policies
– Recalculate deferred tax implications
– Agreement to component financial statements
– Consider treatment of non-controlling interests
– Arithmetical accuracy of consolidation schedule

Maximum   **8**

Total   **18**

49 WILLIS CO *Walk in the footsteps of a top tutor*

Key answer tips

This question requires sound knowledge of the technical aspects of audit reporting, and the ability to apply the knowledge to critically appraise an audit report given in the scenario. The best approach to this question is to work through the audit report line by line, identifying and explaining deficiencies in the report as you go. In order to answer questions like this in the exam, you need to be able to recognise the type of modification to an audit report used and understand when it is appropriate to use each modification – in this case a Disclaimer of opinion. You also need to have an awareness of the wording that would be used for each type of modification. Reporting is a core topic in this syllabus, and sound knowledge of this area is key to passing the exam.

Part (b) tests the requirements of ISA 265, and in order to answer this question you need to be able to distinguish significant deficiencies from deficiencies and know how the auditor's responsibilities differ with respect to each.

This question highlights the need for students to ensure breadth and depth of knowledge across the syllabus, as well as the need to practice applying knowledge to a variety of scenarios.

The highlighted words are key phrases that markers are looking for.

(a) (i)   The draft audit report contains a disclaimer of audit opinion. According to ISA 705 *Modifications to the Opinion in the Independent Auditor's Report*, a disclaimer should be used when the auditor is unable to obtain sufficient appropriate audit evidence on which to base the opinion, and where the possible effect on the financial statements of undetected misstatements could be both material and pervasive.

The audit senior has produced this report as a result of management restricting access to necessary evidence, resulting in a lack of evidence to support the capitalisation of research and development costs as an intangible asset. The senior is correct to identify that a management-imposed limitation on scope has been imposed. The results of trials on the new drugs would be a crucial element of necessary audit work, and without the results to demonstrate that the development costs will lead to future economic benefit, it is not possible to conclude that the accounting treatment is correct.

However, the management-imposed limitation has not been explained in the audit report. ISA 705 requires that when the auditor modifies the audit opinion, a paragraph should be included in the audit report which describes the matter giving rise to the modification. In this case the report should describe that management did not allow access to the results of drug trials, and as a result of this, the audit firm is unable to determine whether any adjustments are necessary to the carrying value of the intangible asset.

The terms used in the Basis for Opinion (*UK SYLLABUS: Basis for Opinion on Financial Statements*) paragraph are a little vague to fully explain the situation. Development costs should be referred to rather than just 'intangible assets' in order to specifically identify the type of asset concerned.

Reference could also be made to IAS 38 *Intangible Assets* as the relevant financial reporting standard.

In addition, the potential impact on the financial statements has not been quantified. The paragraph should state that the asset is recognised on the statement of financial position at $4.4 million. Also, reference to the materiality of the item should be made, for example by stating that the asset equates to 8% of the total assets of Willis Co.

It is debatable whether a disclaimer of opinion is too harsh. It is clear from the information that the intangible asset is material to the statement of financial position, representing 8% of total assets. So the audit opinion should at least be qualified with an 'except for' opinion. A disclaimer should only be used where the auditor is unable to reach an opinion on the financial statements as a whole. Possibly the audit senior has concluded that a disclaimer should be given due to the materiality of the item in relation to Willis Co's profit. If any adjustment were found to be necessary in terms of writing off the development costs instead of capitalising them, the profit for the year of $3.1 million would become a loss for the year of $1.3 million. So the uncertainty over the treatment of the development costs is extremely significant and is fundamental to users' understanding of the financial statements as a whole.

The headings used in the report are not appropriately worded. ISA 705 requires that the paragraph used to explain the reason for the modification should be headed 'Basis for Disclaimer of Opinion' (*UK SYLLABUS: 'Basis for Disclaimer of Opinion on Financial Statements*) and should be presented immediately above the opinion paragraph.

The opinion paragraph should be headed 'Disclaimer of Opinion'(*UK SYLLABUS: 'Disclaimer of Opinion on Financial Statements*). The audit opinion is not correctly worded. According to ISA 705, the opinion paragraph should state:

(i)   Because of the significance of the matter(s) described in the Basis for Disclaimer of Opinion paragraph, the auditor has not been able to obtain sufficient appropriate audit evidence to provide a basis for an audit opinion; and, accordingly,

(ii)   The auditor does not express an opinion on the financial statements.

Finally, some of the wording used is not professional. It is inappropriate to refer to management lacking integrity. Although this may be a valid concern of the audit firm, it is not professional to mention this in the audit report. Also using the phrase 'we are worried that...' is not professional.

(ii)   The audit firm must communicate with those charged with governance for two reasons. Firstly, the fact that management has imposed a limitation on the work of the audit firm should be brought to their attention. It is a specific requirement of

ISA 260 *Communication with Those Charged with Governance*, that significant difficulties encountered during the audit be reported to those charged with governance, of which a management-imposed limitation on scope is an example.

Secondly, whenever the auditor expects to modify the audit opinion, the circumstances leading to the expected modification, and the expected wording of the modification should be communicated to those charged with governance.

The firm should consider if alternative audit procedures may be available to gain evidence as to the capitalisation of the development cost. However, for drugs being developed, the results of scientific tests and trials are crucial, and without this evidence it is difficult to see how capitalisation can be confirmed as the correct accounting treatment.

The audit firm should also consider the integrity of management. It is extremely unusual for management to impose a limitation on the work of auditors, as one of the rights of the auditor is to have access to all necessary books and records.

The audit firm may wish to revisit representations made by management in light of this apparent lack of integrity. The firm could also perform an engagement quality review on the audit, due to the higher risk now attached to the engagement.

Finally, the firm should consider withdrawing from the audit engagement as soon as possible, in order to protect the integrity of the firm. A further consideration is that according to ISA 210 *Agreeing the Terms of Audit Engagements*, one of the pre-conditions that should be present in order to accept or continue an audit engagement is that management acknowledges and understands its responsibility to provide the auditor with access to all information relevant to the preparation of the financial statements. Even if the audit firm completes the current audit engagement, it should not be continued for the next financial year.

In the event of withdrawing from the audit engagement, the audit firm should consider if the withdrawal, and the circumstances prompting the withdrawal, need to be communicated with any regulatory authority. (*UK SYLLABUS: The audit firm must comply with the requirements of the Companies Act 2006 regarding the statement to be made by auditors in relation to ceasing to hold office.*) The audit firm may wish to take legal advice to protect its position.

(b) Further audit work should be conducted on the trade payables to see if the errors identified already are relatively isolated, or whether the errors have occurred repeatedly throughout the year. One reason for extending this testing is to identify whether adjustments are necessary to the financial statements, and the materiality of any such adjustments.

The audit firm should consider its reporting responsibilities under ISA 265 *Communicating Deficiencies in Internal Control to Those Charged with Governance and Management*. Moore Co has a deficiency in internal control, as audit work has identified that errors have occurred in the trade payables figure. A deficiency in internal control is defined by ISA 265 as a control designed, implemented or operated in such a way that it is unable to prevent, or detect and correct, misstatements on a timely basis, or a control necessary to prevent, or detect and correct, misstatements in financial statements on a timely basis is missing.

After completing further audit procedures, the audit firm must decide if the control deficiencies identified constitute deficiencies, or significant deficiencies in internal control. This is an important distinction because significant deficiencies should be communicated in writing to those charged with governance on a timely basis during the audit. This implies that the control deficiency, being significant, should be communicated as soon as possible, so that corrective action can be taken quickly by the company. Management should also be made aware of significant deficiencies on a timely basis.

The written communication of significant deficiencies should include a description of the deficiencies and an explanation of their potential effects. This need not include a quantification of the effect of the control deficiency. Recommendations may also be made as to how management should correct the deficiency identified.

For control deficiencies that are not evaluated as being significant, the audit firm should consider whether the deficiency is of sufficient importance to be brought to the attention of management.

Examiner's comments

Requirement (a) (i) for 10 marks, asked for a critical appraisal of a draft audit report, in which a disclaimer of opinion had been given, following a management imposed limitation in scope resulting in a lack of evidence with regard to research and development costs. Some answers were sound, and worked through the audit report, explaining its deficiencies in a logical manner. Some answers appreciated that the disclaimer of opinion may be an over-reaction, and that a qualification may be more suitable. Other points raised in some answers concerned the inappropriate wording of the audit report, the reference to management lack of integrity, and the fact that the matter had not been quantified, making it difficult for users of the report to gauge the significance of the matter. Almost all candidates correctly determined the materiality of the matter.

Unsatisfactory answers, which were by far the majority, tended not to appraise the audit report at all, and instead provided lengthy explanations of the accounting treatment for research and development, but completely missed the point that the auditor was unable to verify if the correct accounting treatment had been applied. Some blamed the audit team, rather than the client, for the lack of evidence, and suggested that the whole audit be re-performed.

Requirement (a) (ii) continued the theme of (a)(i), asking for matters that should be considered and further actions that should be taken by the auditor, in light of the limitation in scope. Most candidates suggested that the limitation in scope and its potential impact on the audit report be taken to audit committee or those charged with governance for discussion, and many also raised management integrity as an issue. Some candidates tended to repeat what they had written for (a) (i) without further development.

Requirement (b) focussed on the new requirements of ISA 265 in relation to reporting internal control deficiencies to management and those charged with governance. A brief scenario was provided, outlining internal control deficiencies discovered during the audit of trade payables, and candidates were asked the further actions they would take, and to outline any reporting requirements. This was reasonably well attempted, with most answers referring to management letter points, and making recommendations for improving controls to the client. However, there were very few references to ISA 265, and only a handful of answers discussed the importance of determining whether a deficiency is significant or not.

Overall, answers to question 5 were unsatisfactory, given that audit reports is a regularly examined syllabus area.

		ACCA marking scheme	
			Marks
(a)	(i)	**Critical appraisal of audit report**	
		Up to 1½ marks per comment applied to the scenario	
		• No explanation of imposed limitation	
		• Development costs not specifically referred to	
		• No quantification of the asset	
		• No reference to potential impact on profit	
		• ½ mark calculation materiality	
		• Disclaimer or qualification more appropriate (2 marks max)	
		• Incorrect headings used	
		• Incorrect wording of opinion	
		• Unprofessional to refer to management integrity	10
		• 'We are worried' not professional	
	(ii)	**Further consequences**	
		Generally 1 mark per comment	
		• Communicate limitation imposed to those charged with governance	5
		• Communicate proposed modification to those charged with governance	
		• Consider alternative procedures for development costs	
		• Consider integrity of management	
		• Consider withdrawal from audit/resignation	
		• Audit pre-condition (ISA 210)	
		Maximum marks	15
(b)		**Actions/implications of control deficiency identified**	
		Generally 1 mark per comment	
		– Extend audit testing	
		– Determine if deficiency is a deficiency or significant deficiency	
		– If significant report in writing to those charged with governance	
		– Communication to include description and recommendation	
		– Communication on a timely basis	
		– Insignificant deficiency need not be reported – depends on auditor judgement	
		Maximum marks	5
Total			20

 KAPLAN PUBLISHING

50   GRIMES CO (A) *Walk in the footsteps of a top tutor*

Key answer tips

Part (a) requires pre-learnt knowledge. However, this is a potentially confusing area and is rarely dealt with well by candidates. It is therefore advised that you consult your texts thoroughly before attempting the question and ensure you review the answer in detail. This is an area that will continue to be heavily examined.

Part (b) is a more peripheral topic: liability limitation. This highlights the importance of a broad knowledge of the syllabus. The second part of the question is a little bit more difficult so the application of a little bit of common sense and judgement is recommended. Take your time to consider what a liability limitation agreement is and what this provides both the employer and the client. On this basis it should be simple to achieve at least half marks.

The highlighted words are key phases that markers are looking for.

(a)   (i)   The Emphasis of Matter (EOM) paragraph is a paragraph included in the auditor's report that refers to a matter appropriately presented or disclosed within the financial statements, that in the auditor's judgement, is of such importance that it is fundamental to the users' understanding of the financial statements. ISA 706 *Emphasis of Matter Paragraphs and Other Matter Paragraphs in the Independent* Auditor's *Report,* states that the paragraph must only be used provided the auditor has sufficient appropriate audit evidence that the matter is not materially misstated in the financial statements. Such a paragraph should refer only to information presented or disclosed in the financial statements.

The paragraph is therefore used to highlight a fundamental issue to the users of the financial statements. It does not relate to a modified opinion, and therefore is not in any way a modification of the audit opinion. The EOM paragraph should clearly state that the auditor's opinion is not modified in respect of the matter emphasised. The EOM paragraph should include a clear reference to the matter being emphasised, and to where relevant disclosures that fully describe the matter can be found in the financial statements.

Examples are provided in ISA 706 of the potential situations in which an EOM paragraph may be used:

- An uncertainty relating to the future outcome of exceptional litigation or regulatory action.
- Early application (where permitted) of a new accounting standard that has a pervasive effect on the financial statements in advance of its effective date.
- A major catastrophe that has had, or continues to have, a significant effect on the entity's financial position.
- Significant going concern issues.

(ii)   The Other Matter paragraph should be included in the auditor's report to refer to a matter other than those presented or disclosed in the financial statements that, in the auditor's judgement, is relevant to users' understanding of the audit, the auditor's responsibilities, or the auditor's report.

Examples of such matters could include:

- Law, regulation or generally accepted practice may require or permit the auditor to elaborate on matters that provide further explanation of the auditor's responsibilities or report.

- The auditor may be reporting on more than one set of financial statements (e.g. a set of statements prepared under national reporting framework, and a set of statements prepared under International Financial Reporting Standards).

- Any restrictions on the distribution of the auditor's report.

The paragraph is therefore used as means by which the auditor can communicate a matter to the users of the financial statements. The content of the paragraph should clearly reflect that the matter is not required to be presented or disclosed in the financial statements.

For both EOM and Other Matter paragraphs, there should be communication with those charged with governance, who should be made aware of the nature of any specific items that the auditor intends to highlight.

(b)   (i)   All audit firms want to avoid litigation, due to the bad publicity that is likely to follow, the financial consequences, and the potential collapse of the audit firm. There are several ways that an audit firm can reduce its exposure to claims.

Client acceptance procedures

Firms should carefully assess the risk associated with potential audit clients. Screening procedures should be used to identify matters that create potential exposure for the audit firm. For example, it would be unwise to take on a new client with significant going concern problems. The issue is that a client should only be accepted if the associated risk can be managed to an acceptably low level given the skills and resources of the audit firm.

Proper use of engagement letters

The engagement letter should be used to clearly state the responsibilities of the auditor, and of management. As it forms a contract between the audit firm and the client, it should be updated on an annual basis, with care being taken to ensure the client is fully aware of any changes in the scope of the audit, or the reporting responsibilities of the audit firm.

Performance and documentation of audit work

Audit firms should ensure that professional standards are maintained, and that International Standards on Auditing (ISAs) are adhered to. It is crucial that full documentation is maintained for all aspects of the audit, including planning, evaluation of evidence, and consideration of ethical issues. A claim of negligence is unlikely to be successful if the audit firm has documentary evidence that ISAs have been followed.

Quality control

Firms must ensure they have implemented firm-wide quality control procedures, as well as procedures applicable to the individual audit engagement. Quality control acts as an internal control for the audit firm, helping to ensure that ISAs and internal audit methods have been followed at all times.

External consultations

Firms should make use of external specialists when the need arises, for example obtaining legal advice where appropriate, to ensure that the auditor's actions are acceptable within the legal and regulatory framework.

Disclaimers

In recent years it has become common in some jurisdictions for audit firms to include a disclaimer paragraph in the audit report. This is an attempt to restrict the duty of care of the audit firm to the shareholders of the company, thereby attempting to restrict legal liability to that class of shareholders. Disclaimers, however, may not always be effective.

Tutorial note

More than the required number of points have been covered in the answer. Credit would be awarded for discussions of other, relevant means of limiting exposure to liability, such as the need for adequate Professional Indemnity Insurance.

(ii)   A liability limitation agreement is a contractual limitation of the auditor's liability to a company. There are several possible implications for the audit profession which are discussed below.

Audit quality

One of the main arguments against the use of such agreements is that audit quality could suffer as a result. The argument is that auditors could become less concerned with the quality of their work, in the knowledge that if there was a claim against them, the financial consequences are limited.

Value of the audit opinion

As a consequence of the point above, many argue that users of the financial statements will place less reliance on the audit opinion, resulting in less credible financial statements.

Pressure on audit fees

It is considered that firms may be under pressure from clients to reduce their audit fees. This is a response to the fact that if the audit firm has reduced its risk exposure, then the fee for providing the audit service should be reduced.

Competition in the audit market

The ability to set a cap on auditor's liability could distort the audit market. Bigger audit firms may have the ability to set a high cap, which creates a disadvantage to smaller audit firms. However, it can be argued that the ability to set a cap actually helps the audit market, by protecting firms and making collapse less likely, and can promote competition between the larger firms.

		ACCA marking scheme	
			Marks
(a)	(i)	**EOM paragraph**	
		1 mark each point made – maximum of 2 marks for definition:	
		• Highlights a fundamental matter	
		• Audit opinion not qualified	
		• Sufficient evidence obtained	
		• EOM to refer to place matter discussed in financial statements	
		1 mark each example:	
		• Uncertainty/going concern, new accounting standard adopted, catastrophe	
		Maximum	6
	(ii)	**Other matter paragraph**	
		1 mark each point made – maximum of 2 marks for definition:	
		• Communicate a matter not presented in the financial statements	
		• Matter relevant to users understanding of audit	
		• Matter relevant to other reporting responsibilities of the auditor	
		1 mark each example:	
		• Regulatory need, reporting on more than one set of accounts, restriction of use of audit report	
		Maximum	4
(b)	(i)	Methods of reducing exposure	
		Up to 1 mark for each method	
		• Client screening	
		• Engagement letter	
		• Adherence to ISAs and other regulation	
		• Quality control	
		• Disclaimer paragraphs	
		Maximum	4
	(ii)	Implications of liability limitation agreements	
		Up to 1½ marks each:	
		• Audit quality	
		• Less confidence in financial statements	
		• Pressure to reduce fees	
		• Distort audit market	
		Maximum	6
Total			20

51 LYCHEE CO (A) *Walk in the footsteps of a top tutor*

> **Key answer tips**
>
> Lychee is a typical reporting style question in that it focuses on a specifically challenging area of auditing, in this case, subsequent events. You are then asked to identify relevant aspects of the auditor's responsibility in relation to ISA's before considered the implications on the audit report of a specific client scenario.
>
> Remember with part (b) that the audit report can be modified either by modifying the audit opinion **or** by including an Emphasis of Matter or Other Matter paragraph.
>
> If the opinion is to be modified this can only be justified for one of two reasons:
>
> - the financial statements are materially misstated, or
> - the auditor has been unable to obtain sufficient appropriate evidence.
>
> The wording of the opinion then depends upon whether the matter is simply material **or** material and pervasive.
>
> The highlighted words are key phases that markers are looking for.

(a) **Auditor's responsibilities in relation to subsequent events.**

Subsequent events are defined as those events occurring between the date of the financial statements and the date of the auditor's report, and also facts discovered after the date of the auditor's report.

ISA 560 (Redrafted) Subsequent Events differentiates the auditor's responsibilities in relation to subsequent events depending on when the subsequent event occurs.

Events occurring up to the date of the auditor's report. The auditor has an active duty to perform audit procedures designed to identify, and to obtain sufficient appropriate evidence of all events up to the date of the auditor's report that may require adjustment of, or disclosure in, the financial statements. These procedures should be performed as close as possible to the date of the auditor's report, and in addition, representations would be sought on the date that the report was signed.

Procedures would include reviewing management procedures for ensuring that subsequent events are identified, reading minutes of meetings of shareholders and management, reviewing the latest interim financial statements, and making appropriate enquiries of management.

Where a material subsequent event is discovered, the auditor should consider whether management have properly accounted for and disclosed the event in the financial statements in accordance with IAS 10 Events After the Reporting Period.

Facts discovered after the date of the auditor's report but before the date the financial statements are issued. The auditor does not have any responsibility to perform audit procedures or make any enquiry regarding the financial statements or subsequent events after the date of the auditor's report. In this period, it is the responsibility of management to inform the auditor of facts which may affect the financial statements.

When the auditor becomes aware of a fact which may materially affect the financial statements, the matter should be discussed with management. If the financial statements are appropriately amended then a new audit report should be issued, and procedures relating to subsequent events should be extended to the date of the new audit report. If management do not amend the financial statements to reflect the subsequent event, in circumstances where the auditor believes they should be amended, a qualified or adverse opinion should be issued.

Facts discovered after the financial statements have been issued. After the financial statements have been issued, the auditor has no obligation to make any enquiry regarding the financial statements. However, the auditor may become aware of a fact which existed at the date of the audit report, which if known at the date may have caused a modification to the auditor's report. In this case, the matter should be discussed with management. This could result in the revision of the financial statements, in which case the auditor should issue a new audit report on the revised financial statements. This report should include an emphasis of matter paragraph referring to a note to the financial statements in which the reason for the revision is fully discussed. If management do not revise the financial statements, the auditor should take legal advice with the objective of trying to prevent further reliance on the auditor's report.

(b) (i) The announcement of a restructuring after the reporting date is a non-adjusting event after the reporting date, according to IAS 10 *Events After the Reporting Period*. This is because the event does not provide evidence in relation to a condition that existed at the year end.

Materiality calculations in respect of the potential cost of closure are as follows:

Based on revenue: $250,000/15 million = 1.67%

Based on profit: $250,000/3 million = 8.3%

Based on assets: $250,000/80 million = <1%

Therefore this amount is material to the statement of profit or loss.

Per IAS 10, a note should be provided to the financial statements, which describes the nature of the event, and provides an estimate of the financial effect.

Tutorial note

Credit will also be awarded for discussion of whether a provision for the restructuring costs is required under IAS 37 Provisions, Contingent Liabilities and Contingent Assets.

Audit procedures could include:

- Review any potential note to financial statements which should disclose the non-adjusting event, providing a brief description of the event, and an estimate of the financial effect.

- Discuss the reason for the restructuring with a member of key management personnel, and read minutes of board meetings where the plan was discussed, in order to gain an understanding about the reason for the restructuring.
- Verify the approval of the plan itself, and the approval of the announcement of the plan, which can be performed through a review of board minutes.
- Confirm the date on which the plan was approved, and also the date of the announcement, using supporting documentation such as press release, letters sent to employees, internal meetings held with employees, etc.
- Obtain a copy of the announcement and review for details, particularly a description of the exact nature of the restructuring, including the number of employees to be affected.
- Agree the $250,000 potential cost of closure to supporting documentation, including a schedule showing the number and grade of staff to be made redundant, which should be supported by payroll/contract details.
- Using the results of the discussion with management, assess the planned restructuring in the context of the auditor's knowledge of the business, considering whether any further costs are likely to be incurred.

(ii) **Actions to be taken by the auditor:**

If no note is provided to the financial statements, then there is a breach of IAS 10. In this case there is insufficient disclosure provided in the notes to the financial statements regarding a material non-adjusting event after the reporting date.

According to ISA 705 Modifications to the Opinion in the Independent Auditor's Report, in cases where the auditor is in disagreement with management regarding the application of a financial reporting standard and where the consequent misstatement is material to the financial statements, the auditor should express a qualified or an adverse opinion. Here, the matter is material (as discussed in (b)(i) above) but is not pervasive to the financial statements, so a qualified opinion should be given.

The audit report should contain a paragraph which explains the reason for the modification, specifying the breach of accounting standards, and stating the relevant financial amount. It would also be best practice for the auditor to clarify that the profit for the year is not affected by the breach of accounting standards, and that the misstatement is solely due to inadequate disclosure in the notes to the financial statements.

The auditors should ensure that the matter, and the potential consequence for the audit report, has been made known to those charged with governance. This will allow the highest level of management (including executive and non-executive directors) the opportunity to discuss the matter, having reference to all relevant facts of the misstatement and implications thereof.

Finally, the auditors could choose to raise this issue at the annual general meeting, where the matter leading to the qualified audit opinion should be explained to the shareholders of the company.

		ACCA marking scheme	
			Marks
(a)		**Auditor's responsibility in relation to subsequent events**	
		1 mark per comment explained:	
		• Definition of subsequent events	
		• Responsibility divided into three distinct periods	
		• Active duty up-to-date audit report issued	
		• Examples of procedures up-to-date of audit report	
		• Procedures to be as near to date of report as possible	
		• No active duty after date report issued	
		• Facts discovered before financial statements issued – discuss with management/reissue audit report if financial statements revised	
		• Facts discovered after financial statements issued – discuss with management/issue new audit report/need emphasis of matter/take legal advice	
		Maximum	6
(b)	(i)	**Audit procedures in respect of announcement of restructuring**	
		1 mark per specific procedure provided:	
		• Non-adjusting event after the reporting date	
		• 1 mark for calculation/consideration of materiality which can be awarded in either (b)(i) or (b)(ii)	
		• IAS 10 requires note to financial statements	
		• Obtain copy of announcement and review for details	
		• Confirm date of approval and announcement of restructuring	
		• Read minutes of board meetings where the restructuring was discussed	
		• Agree numerical disclosures to supporting documentation	
		• Consider completeness of the amount disclosed	
		• Discuss/review potential note to financial statements	
		Maximum	6
	(ii)	**Action to be taken if amendments not made**	
		Marks to be awarded as follows:	
		• 1 mark for each comment:	
		• Material misstatement	
		• Qualified opinion	
		• Description of reason for modification	
		• Report to those charged with governance	
		• Raise at AGM	
		Maximum	4
Total			16

52   PLUTO CO (A) *Walk in the footsteps of a top tutor*

Key answer tips

Part (a) of the question follows on from two fraud based articles written by both the F8 and the P7 exam team. Therefore prior to answering this question it would be worth reviewing these on the ACCA website.

The majority of the question asks you to consider the wording of an audit report. In order to answer these questions think of the following structure:

–   is there any relevant guidance? (i.e. standards)

–   what should have been done and what has been done?

–   does it lead to a misstatement or a lack of sufficient appropriate evidence?

–   is it material or pervasive?

–   in the circumstances what audit report should be issued?

The highlighted words are key phases that markers are looking for.

(a)   Fraudulent financial reporting is a type of fraud that causes a material misstatement in the financial statements.

The term is defined in ISA 240 *The Auditor's Responsibilities Relating to Fraud in an Audit of Financial Statements*. Fraudulent financial reporting is a deliberate act, i.e. an intentional misstatement, and can include omissions. The aim of the activity is to deceive the users of the financial statements. Fraudulent financial reporting tends to fall into three categories, described below:

Manipulation, falsification (including forgery), or alteration of accounting records or supporting documentation from which the financial statements are prepared. An example would be where the management deliberately change the trial balance which is then used as the basis of preparation of the financial statements. Fictitious journal entries could be used to 'window dress' the year-end figures.

Misrepresentation in, or deliberate omission from, the financial statements of events, transactions or other significant information. An example would be where management knowingly fail to account for a transaction, so that the financial statements are incomplete. Revenue or costs could be omitted or delayed until the next accounting period. Failure to provide information about going concern problems is a deliberate omission of significant information.

Intentional misapplication of accounting principles relating to amounts, classification, presentation or disclosure within the financial statements. An example would be the deliberate breach of a financial reporting standard. This could mean that balances are recognised inappropriately, necessary disclosures are not made, or the presentation is not correct.

Such actions are often carried out to manage earnings in order to influence the perceptions of the company's performance. This is commonly referred to as 'earnings management' and is prone to occur due to pressure on management to achieve a certain performance target. Alternatively, the statement of financial position of the company could be manipulated with the aim of securing finance.

(b) **Adverse opinion paragraph**

The title of the opinion paragraph clearly states that it is an adverse opinion. For the sake of clarity it may be better just to state that the opinion is adverse rather than go into the reason for the opinion in the title, i.e. remove wording 'arising from disagreement about application of IAS 37'.

Normally the reason for any modification to the audit report affecting the opinion is explained in a separate paragraph immediately preceding the opinion paragraph. Here the reason for the modification is explained within the opinion paragraph which could be confusing for the readers.

ISA 705 *Modifications to the Opinion in the Independent Auditor's Report* states that a clear description of all of the substantive reasons for any modification to the opinion should be included in the report, including, where practicable, an estimate of the financial effect. The proposed audit report partially explains the material misstatement but does not go into sufficient detail. Specifically no estimate of the financial effect has been provided. Quantification of the amount of the omitted provision must be available. Other detail of the provision should also be provided, such as the timing of the probable cash outflow.

To aid the readers' understanding of the breach of financial reporting standards that has occurred, it would be useful to fully state the title of IAS 37 *Provisions, Contingent Liabilities and Contingent Assets*.

The paragraph refers to a note to the financial statements where 'the matter is more fully explained'. This is ambiguous. Does the note explain the reason why the directors feel unable to quantify the value of the provision? Does the note describe the situation in terms of a contingent liability (which appears to be how the directors are treating the item)? The paragraph should be more precise in referring to what the note actually contains. A page reference should also be given to help the readers to find the note.

The paragraph ends with an observation that profits are overstated as a result of the non-recognition of the provision. There should also be a comment on the impact on the statement of financial position, in which liabilities are understated. The effect should be quantified, as discussed above.

Finally, and most importantly, whether this issue should give rise to an adverse opinion is debatable. An adverse opinion should be given when the effect of a misstatement is so material and pervasive that the financial statements are rendered meaningless. Without any figures being provided it is not possible to comment on materiality, however, the provision would have to be extremely significant for its omission to make the financial statements meaningless.

The report itself could appear to be contradictory, as it states that the omission has caused a 'material misstatement', implying a material but not a pervasive impact on the financial statements. It is likely in this case that a qualified 'except for' opinion would be sufficient.

Emphasis of matter paragraph

The paragraph appears to be describing a breach of financial reporting standards. IAS 33 *Earnings per Share* requires that listed companies must disclose basic and diluted earnings per share figures, including comparatives, on the face of the financial statements. The fact that the directors have decided not to disclose is a clear misapplication of the standard. Earnings per share is material by nature, so its omission represents a material misstatement in the financial statements.

The audit opinion should be qualified 'except for' due to a material misstatement. Therefore a paragraph discussing the misstatement should be inserted above the opinion paragraph, including an estimate of the financial effect, and a reference to a note to the financial statements if this has been provided.

The emphasis of matter paragraph does not state whether the prior year's earnings per share figure has been disclosed or not. A comparative is required by IAS 33.

The emphasis of matter paragraph should not be used to highlight situations where the directors have decided not to include a matter in the financial statements. The paragraph is reserved for use to explain significant uncertainties or going concern issues, and its use in this situation is entirely inappropriate.

(c) ISQC 1 *Quality Control for Firms that Perform Audits and Reviews of Historical Financial Information, and Other Assurance and Related Services Engagements* outlines how a firm decides on the eligibility of a person to perform an engagement review.

Firstly, the reviewer must have a high standard of technical knowledge, encompassing a thorough understanding of auditing and financial reporting standards, as well as any specific regulatory issues (such as stock exchange listing rules) which may be relevant to the client.

In addition, the reviewer should be an experienced auditor, preferably with specific practical experience of auditing companies operating in a similar industry or business sector as the client.

The reviewer should possess a level of authority within the firm. This will allow the reviewer to challenge the decisions made by other members of the firm, including senior managers and partners. It is important that the reviewer is not intimidated by the senior members of the audit team who could feel criticised by any negative comments that the reviewer may have on their work and decisions. ISQC 1 recommends that a reviewer of listed client's audits should normally be at partner level within the firm.

Finally, the reviewer must be independent of the audit team. This allows a totally objective review to take place. The engagement partner therefore should not be involved in deciding who should review the audit. Consultations between the engagement partner and the reviewer can take place during the audit, but care should be taken to preserve the reviewer's objectivity.

Examiner's comments

Requirement (a) Answers on the whole were reasonable, and in terms of illustration, a range of examples were usually provided.

Requirement (b) Answers were on the whole unsatisfactory. As noted in previous examiners' reports, candidates seem not to understand the concepts underpinning the modification of an audit report, and have even less comprehension of the use of an emphasis of matter paragraph.

Looking initially at the adverse opinion, most candidates correctly suggested that a misstatement had indeed occurred, and that an adverse opinion may be too harsh, meaning that a qualified 'except for' opinion would be more suitable. Fewer went on to criticise the audit report for its lack of quantification of the amount of the material misstatement.

Most candidates did not appraise the wording of the extract, but there were easy marks to be gained here, for example, for suggesting that the title of the financial reporting standard should be written in full, and the lack of reference to note or page numbers where more information about the redundancy costs could be found in the financial statements. Few candidates suggested that the description of the misstatement was inadequate, though it was deliberately so. The best answers rightly criticised the use of the word 'feel' in an audit report, as well as it being inappropriate to put forward the views of the directors in the report.

Regarding the emphasis of matter paragraph, a significant proportion of candidates did not attempt this part of the requirement. Those that did gained credit for briefly explaining the correct use of such a paragraph, but fewer went on to say why its use in this situation was inappropriate. Many candidates did not appreciate that the company in the question was listed, so disclosure of the earnings per share figure would be required.

Finally, many candidates were extremely concerned about the audit report containing both an adverse opinion and an emphasis of matter paragraph, missing the point that the opinion and the emphasis of matter paragraph dealt with two completely separate issues.

Requirement (c) Answers tended to be very brief, often in a bullet point format. The majority of answers mentioned that it should be a partner with experience who should perform the review. Though most candidates could suggest that the reviewer should be independent of both the audit team, and the audit client, few could suggest why.

ACCA marking scheme		Marks
(a) **Fraudulent financial reporting**		
Generally 1 mark per comment/example:		
– Material misstatement		
– Deliberate/intentional		
– Manipulation of underlying accounting records		
– Misrepresentation/omission in financial statements		
– Misapplication of IFRS		
– Earnings management		
	Maximum marks	4
(b) **Critical appraisal of audit report**		
Up to 1½ marks per issue explained:		
– Adverse opinion		
– Inadequate explanation of misstatement		
– No financial impact given		
– Clearer title needed		
– Better to refer to IAS 37 in full		
– Clearer reference to note needed		
– Explanation of misstatement should be in separate paragraph		
– Except for rather than adverse?		
– Emphasis of matter		
– EOM not used for this situation		
	Maximum marks	9
(c) **Eligibility to perform an engagement quality control review**		
Generally 1 mark per comment:		
– Technical expertise		
– Experience		
– Authority		
– Independence from audit team		
	Maximum marks	4
Total		17

53 DEXTER CO (A) *Walk in the footsteps of a top tutor*

Key answer tips

This question focuses on going concern. Students are required to discuss who is responsible for assessing the going concern status of a business and how disclosures relating to going concern (or a lack of them) affect the audit opinion.

Part (a) requires a little basic knowledge regarding who prepares the accounts and IAS 1. It also requires students to suggest specific procedures used to support going concern assessments.

Part (b) requires some common sense regarding why directors may not want to publish accounts that indicate going concern problems.

Part (c) requires students to consider whether the lack of disclosure contravenes any financial reporting standards and the consequent affect on the opinion. It is important that students use the language of audit reports, i.e. modified/unmodified, material misstatement/ lack of sufficient appropriate evidence, qualified/adverse/disclaimer. It should also be noted that the scenario states *'working papers conclude that the going concern assumption is appropriate.'* Therefore the going concern status is not under dispute, merely the lack of disclosure regarding a material uncertainty.

The highlighted words are key phases that markers are looking for.

(a)   **Responsibilities of management and auditors**

Basic responsibilities

ISA 570 Going Concern provides a clear framework for the assessment of the going concern status of an entity, and differentiates between the responsibilities of management and of auditors. Management should assess going concern in order to decide on the most appropriate basis for the preparation of the financial statements. IAS 1 *Presentation of Financial Statements (revised)* requires that where there is significant doubt over an entity's ability to continue as a going concern, the uncertainties should be disclosed in a note to the financial statements. Where the directors intend to cease trading, or have no realistic alternative but to do so, the financial statements should be prepared on a 'break up' basis.

Thus the main focus of the management's assessment of going concern is to ensure that relevant disclosures are made where necessary, and that the correct basis of preparation is used.

The auditor's responsibility is to consider the appropriateness of the management's use of the going concern assumption in the preparation of the financial statements and to consider whether there are material uncertainties about the entity's ability to continue as a going concern that need to be disclosed in a note.

The auditor should also consider the length of the time period that management have looked at in their assessment of going concern.

The auditor will therefore need to come to an opinion as to the going concern status of an entity but the focus of the auditor's evaluation of going concern is to see whether they agree with the assessment made by the management. Therefore whether they agree with the basis of preparation of the financial statements, or the inclusion in a note to the financial statements, as required by IAS 1, of any material uncertainty.

Evaluation techniques

In carrying out the going concern assessment, management will evaluate a wide variety of indicators, including operational and financial. An entity employing good principles of corporate governance should be carrying out such an assessment as part of the on-going management of the business.

Auditors will use a similar assessment technique in order to come to their own opinion as to the going concern status of an entity. They will carry out an operational review of the business in order to confirm business understanding, and will conduct a financial review as part of analytical procedures. Thus both management and auditors will use similar business risk assessment techniques to discover any threats to the going concern status of the business.

Auditors should not see going concern as a 'completion issue', but be alert to issues affecting going concern throughout the audit. In the same way that management should continually be managing risk (therefore minimising going concern risk), auditors should be continually be alert to going concern problems throughout the duration of the audit.

However, one difference is that when going concern problems are discovered, the auditor is required by IAS 570 to carry out additional procedures. Examples of such procedures would include:

–   Analysing and discussing cash flow, profit and other relevant forecasts with management.

–   Analysing and discussing the entity's latest available interim financial statements.

–   Reviewing events after the period end to identify those that either mitigate or otherwise affect the entity's ability to continue as a going concern.

–   Reading minutes of meetings of shareholders, those charged with governance and relevant committees for reference to financing difficulties.

Management are not explicitly required to gather specific evidence about going concern, but as part of good governance would be likely to investigate and react to problems discovered.

(b)   **Directors reluctance to disclose**

The directors are likely to have several reasons behind their reluctance to disclose the note as recommended by the audit manager. The first is that the disclosure of Dexter Co's poor cash flow position and perilous going concern status may reflect badly on the directors themselves. The company's shareholders and other stakeholders will be displeased to see the company in such a poor position, and the directors will be held accountable for the problems. Of course it may not be the case that the directors have exercised poor management of the company – the problems could be caused by external influences outside the control of the directors. However, it is natural that the directors will not want to highlight the situation in order to protect their own position.

Secondly, the note could itself trigger further financial distress for the company. Dexter Co is trying to raise finance, and it is probable that the availability of further finance will be detrimentally affected by the disclosure of the company's financial problems. In particular, if the cash flow difficulties are highlighted, providers of finance will consider the company too risky an investment, and are not likely to make funds available for fear of non-repayment. Existing lenders may seek repayment of their funds in fear that the company may be unable in the future to meet repayments.

In addition, the disclosures could cause operational problems, for example, suppliers may curtail trading relationships as they become concerned that they will not be paid, or customers may be deterred from purchasing from the company if they feel that there is no long-term future for the business. Unfortunately the mere disclosure of financial problems can be self-fulfilling, and cause such further problems for the company that it is pushed into non-going concern status.

The directors may also be concerned that if staff were to hear of this they may worry about the future of the company and seek alternative employment, which could lead in turn to the loss of key members of staff. This would be detrimental to the business and trigger further operational problems.

Finally, the reluctance to disclose may be caused by an entirely different reason. The directors genuinely feel that the cash flow and operational problems faced by the company do not constitute factors affecting the going concern status. They may be confident that although a final decision has not been made regarding financing, the finance is likely to be forthcoming, and therefore there is no long-term material uncertainty over the future of the company. However audit working papers conclude that there is a significant level of doubt over the going concern status of Dexter Co, and therefore it seems that the directors may be over optimistic if they feel that there is no significant doubt to be disclosed in the financial statements.

(c)   (i)   **Audit report implications**

Audit procedures have shown that there is a significant level of doubt over Dexter Co's going concern status. IAS 1 requires that disclosure is made in the financial statements regarding material uncertainties, which may cast significant doubt on the ability of the entity to continue as a going concern. If the directors refuse to disclose the note to the financial statements, there is a clear breach of financial reporting standards.

In this case the significant uncertainty is caused by not knowing the extent of the future availability of finance needed to fund operating activities. If the note describing this uncertainty is not provided, the financial statements are not fairly presented.

The audit report should contain a qualified or an adverse opinion due to the material misstatement. The auditors need to make a decision as to the significance of the non-disclosure. If it is decided that without the note the financial statements are not fairly presented, and could be considered misleading, an adverse opinion should be expressed. However, it could be decided that the lack of the note is material, but not pervasive to the financial statements, then a qualified 'except for' opinion should be expressed.

ISA 570 *Going Concern* and ISA 705 *Modifications to the Opinion in the Independent Auditor's Report* provides guidance on the presentation of the audit report in the case of a modification. The audit report should include a paragraph which contains specific reference to the fact that there is a material uncertainty that may cast significant doubt about the entity's ability to continue as a going concern. The paragraph should include a clear description of the uncertainties and would normally be presented immediately before the opinion paragraph.

(ii) If the directors agree to disclose the note, it should be reviewed by the auditors to ensure that it is sufficiently detailed. In evaluating the adequacy of the disclosure in the note, the auditor should consider whether the disclosure explicitly draws the reader's attention to the possibility that the entity may not be able to continue as a going concern in the foreseeable future. The note should include a description of conditions giving rise to significant doubt, and the directors' plans to deal with the conditions. If the note provided contains adequate information then there is no breach of financial reporting standards, and so no misstatement in the financial statements.

If the disclosure is considered adequate, then the opinion should not be modified. The auditors should consider a modification by adding an emphasis of matter paragraph to highlight the existence of the material uncertainties, and to draw attention to the note to the financial statements. The emphasis of matter paragraph should firstly contain a brief description of the uncertainties, and also refer explicitly to the note to the financial statements where the situation has been fully described. The emphasis of matter paragraph should re-iterate that the audit opinion is not qualified.

However, it could be the case that a note has been given in the financial statements, but that the details are inadequate and do not fully explain the significant uncertainties affecting the going concern status of the company. In this situation the auditors should express a qualified opinion due to a material misstatement in the financial statements, as the disclosure requirements of IAS 1 have not been followed.

Examiner's comments

Requirement (a)

The main deficiency in answers to this requirement was the lack of any kind of comparison of the responsibilities of management and auditors, despite the fact that the requirement began with 'compare and contrast'. The other problem was that many candidates did not restrict their answer, as requested, to the assessment of going concern, but digressed into issues such as corporate governance and maintaining shareholder value.

Requirement (b)

Many answers were provided here. However, some candidates failed to provide more than a couple of reasons, which is not enough for the mark allocation.

Requirement (c)

This question was rarely well answered, and many candidates obviously do not understand the different types of modifications to audit reports at all, let alone the implication for the audit report of non-disclosure of going concern issues. There was a tendency in (c) (i) to go straight for an adverse opinion, without any discussion of the level of significance of the non-disclosure. There was also confusion over the use of an adverse opinion and a disclaimer of opinion. Some candidates put down all possible types of audit opinion as their answer in the hope that one of them would be correct.

In (c) (ii) very few candidates suggested that the auditor should consider the adequacy of the note if the directors agree to provide one. For (c) (ii) most candidates did mention the emphasis of matter paragraph, but seemed unclear as to whether the inclusion of the paragraph in an audit report resulted in a modification. Some candidates confused an emphasis of matter paragraph with an 'except for' opinion, and seemed to provide the same answer for (c) (i) and (c) (ii).

In this advanced audit paper it is inexcusable that students do not know these basic facts about the audit report. It is strange that most candidates elected to answer this question on audit reports when clearly they did not have the technical knowledge to answer such a question. Candidates should also remember that writing one or two sentences is unlikely to be sufficient to answer an eight mark question requirement.

ACCA marking scheme		

		Marks
(a)	**Compare and contrast management and auditors' responsibilities regarding going concern**	

Management	Auditors
Focus is to follow IAS 1 requirements regarding disclosure of going concern problems or to prepare on break up basis.	Focus is to form independent opinion on going concern status and to see if IAS 1 requirements adhered to.
Range of indicators assessed	Range of indicators assessed
No requirement to perform specific procedures	ISA 570 requires specific procedures and assessment of period reviewed by management
Should be part of ongoing management of the business	Going concern should be considered throughout the audit

Generally 1 mark per explained point. **Maximum 3 marks for procedures.**
Maximum capped at 4 if no attempt to explain similarities or differences.
Allow ½ mark for definition of going concern.

		Maximum marks	**7**

(b) **Reluctance to disclose note**
Generally 1 mark per comment:
– Directors fear they will be held accountable for problems
– Trigger further financial distress as necessary finance is withheld
– Trigger operational distress due to reactions of suppliers and customers
– Trigger operational problems if key members of staff leave
– Directors may feel the problems do not impact on going concern status

		Maximum marks	**5**

(c) (i) **Audit report – note not provided**
Generally 1 mark per comment:
– Breach of IAS 1 leading to misstatement
– Opinion could be qualified or adverse
– Judgement needed
– Report to refer to material uncertainty

		Maximum marks	**4**

(ii) **Audit report – note provided**
Generally 1 mark per comment
– Review adequacy of disclosure
– If note is sufficient – unmodified opinion
– Emphasis of matter paragraph to highlight uncertainties
– If note inadequate – modified, qualified 'except for' opinion

		Maximum marks	**4**

Total			**20**

54   BLOD CO (A)   *Walk in the footsteps of a top tutor*

Key answer tips

This question requires a broader consideration of reporting issues, other than just 'what audit opinion would you make?' Instead the question requires consideration of the other main product of the audit: the management letter (of deficiencies). Auditors communicate with directors, primarily via an audit committee, about issues such as: deficiencies in internal controls; areas where accounting standards have not been followed; errors identified in the draft accounts; updates to or newly introduced standards; potential modifications, to name a few.

The question followed an article entitled 'auditors reports to those charged with governance' published in April 2008. It may be useful to review this article prior to reading the model answer.

The highlighted words are key phases that markers are looking for.

(a)   (i)   A report to those charged with governance is produced to communicate matters relating to the external audit to those who are ultimately responsible for the financial statements. ISA 260 *Communication with Those Charged With Governance* and ISA 265 *Communicating Deficiencies in Internal Control to Those Charged with Governance* require the auditor to communicate many matters, including independence and other ethical issues, the audit approach and scope, the details of management representations, and the findings of the audit. The findings of the audit are commonly referred to as management letter points. By communicating these matters, the auditor is confident that there is written documentation outlining all significant matters raised during the audit process, and that such matters have been formally notified to the highest level of management of the client. For the management, the report should ensure that they fully understand the scope and results of the audit service which has been provided, and is likely to provide constructive comments to help them to fulfil their duties in relation to the financial statements and accounting systems and controls more effectively. The report should also include, where relevant, any actions that management has indicated they will take in relation to recommendations made by the auditors.

      (ii)   **Control Deficiencies**

            ISA 265 contains guidance on the type of issues that should be communicated. One of the matters identified is a control deficiency in the capital expenditure transaction cycle. The assets for which no authorisation was obtained amount to 0.3% of total assets (225,000/78 million × 100%), which is clearly immaterial. However, regardless of materiality, the auditor should ensure that the deficiency is brought to the attention of the management, with a clear indication of the implication of the deficiency, and recommendations as to how the control deficiency should be eliminated.

The auditor is providing information to help those charged with governance improve the internal systems and controls and ultimately reduce business risk. In this case there is a high risk of fraud, as the lack of authorisation for purchase of office equipment could allow expenditure on assets not used for bona fide business purposes.

Material Misstatement of Intangible Brand Assets

Audit procedures have revealed a breach of IAS 38 *Intangible Assets*, in which internally generated brand names are specifically prohibited from being recognised. Blod Co has recognised an internally generated brand name which is material to the statement of financial position as it represents 12.8% of total assets ($10/78 \times 100\%$). The statement of financial position therefore contains a material misstatement.

The report to those charged with governance should clearly explain the rules on recognition of internally generated brand names, to ensure that the management has all relevant technical facts available. In the report the auditors should request that the financial statements be corrected, and clarify that if the brand is not derecognised, then the audit opinion will be modified on the grounds of a material misstatement – a qualified 'except for' opinion would be provided. Once the breach of IAS 38 is made clear to the management in the report, they then have the opportunity to discuss the matter and decide whether to amend the financial statements, thereby avoiding a qualified audit opinion.

Audit inefficiencies

Documentation relating to inventories was not always made readily available to the auditors. This seems to be due to poor administration by the client rather than a deliberate attempt to conceal information. The report should contain a brief description of the problems encountered by the audit team. The management should be made aware that significant delay to the receipt of necessary paperwork can cause inefficiencies in the audit process. This may seem a relatively trivial issue, but it could lead to an increase in audit fee. Management should react to these comments by ensuring as far as possible that all requested documentation is made available to the auditors in a timely fashion.

(b)   It is not uncommon for audit firms to word process and typeset the financial statements of their clients, especially where the client is a relatively small entity, which may lack the resources and skills to perform this task. It is not prohibited by ethical standards.

However, there could be a perceived threat to independence, with risk magnified in the case of Blod Co, which is a listed company. The auditors could be perceived to be involved with the preparation of the financial statements of a listed client company, which is prohibited by ethical standards. IFAC's *Code of Ethics for Professional Accountants* states that for a listed client, the audit firm should not be involved with the preparation of financial statements, which would create a self-review threat so severe that safeguards could not reduce the threat to an acceptable level. *(UK SYLLABUS: Ethical Standard 5 Non-audit services provided to audit clients states that for a listed client, the audit firm should not undertake an engagement to provide accounting services.)* Although the typing of financial statements itself is not prohibited by ethical guidance, the risk is that providing such a service could be perceived to be an element of the preparation of the financial statements.

It is possible that during the process of typing the financial statements, decisions and judgments would be made. This could be perceived as making management decisions in relation to the financial statements, a clear breach of independence.

Therefore to eliminate any risk exposure, the prudent decision would be not to type the financial statements, ensuring that Blod Co appreciates the ethical problems that this would cause.

Tutorial note

This is an area not specifically covered by ethical guides, where different audit firms may have different views on whether it is acceptable to provide a typing service for the financial statements of their clients. Credit will be awarded for sensible discussion of the issues raised bearing in mind other options for the audit firm, for example, it could be argued that it is acceptable to offer the typing service provided that it is performed by people independent of the audit team, and that the matter has been discussed with the audit committee/those charged with governance.

(c)   It has become increasingly common for audit firms to include a disclaimer paragraph within the audit report. However, it is not a requirement of auditing standards and individual audit firms need to assess the advantages and disadvantages of the use of a disclaimer paragraph.

The wording is used to state the fact that the auditor's report is intended solely for the use of the company's members as a body, and that no responsibility is accepted or assumed to anyone other than the company and the company's members as a body.

The main perceived advantage is that the disclaimer should help to reduce the exposure of the audit firm to liability claims from anyone other than the company or the company's body of shareholders. The disclaimer makes it clear that the audit firm reports only to those who appointed the firm, i.e. the members of the company, and this may make it more difficult for the audit firm to be sued by a third party.

It is also argued that the use of a disclaimer could help to bridge the 'expectation gap' by providing a clearer indication of the responsibility of the auditor.

In this way the audit firm can manage its risk exposure in an increasingly litigious environment. High profile legal cases against audit firms, such as the Bannerman case in Scotland, illustrate that an audit firm's duty of care can extend beyond the company and its shareholders, and that audit firms should consider how to protect themselves against liability claims.

Tutorial note

It is appropriate here to quote cases such as the Bannerman case to illustrate the reason why audit firms face increased potential exposure to claims from third parties. However, knowledge of specific legal cases is not required to gain full marks for this requirement.

However, it can be argued that a disclaimer does not necessarily work to protect an audit firm. Each legal case has individual circumstances, and while a disclaimer might protect the audit firm in one situation, equally it may not offer any protection where the facts of the case are different.

In addition, it is often argued that if an audit firm conducts an audit using full due care and diligence, there is no need for a disclaimer, as a high quality audit would be very unlikely to lead to any claims against the audit firm. Consequently, it could be argued that the use of disclaimers as a means to limit liability could permit low quality audits to be performed, the auditors being confident that legal cases against them are restricted due to the presence of a disclaimer within the audit report.

Examiner's comments

Candidates should be aware that the syllabus section on 'Reporting' is not confined to the audit report, but includes other outputs from the audit, as well as reports given for non-audit engagements. Therefore it should not be assumed that every P7 exam will include a question specifically on audit reports.

Requirement (a): Some candidates simply repeated facts from the scenario and provided very little comment of their own as to why the matters they identified should be included.

The first matter dealt with in the scenario involved a deterioration of internal controls with regard to capital expenditure. Most candidates calculated the materiality of the breakdown in controls in question, but an alarming minority calculated this incorrectly, which led them to believe that the control deficiency had led to a material mis-statement in the financial statements, which was technically incorrect, especially as the scenario stated that there were no material errors found during audit procedures on property, plant and equipment. The second matter, a material breach of financial reporting standards was generally well dealt with, although again there were a surprisingly large number of mistakes in the calculation of materiality.

It was the final matter in the scenario, which dealt with inefficient responses by the client to requests for information from the audit firm, which prompted the weakest answers to requirement (a). The most common mistake made by candidates was to assume that the client had caused a limitation in the scope of the audit, leading to speculation that the client was 'trying to hide something' or that a fraud was being perpetrated, and developed into a call for a disclaimer of audit opinion. Only a handful of candidates appreciated the importance of co-operation between internal and external auditors, and that failure to provide information to the external audit team not only delays the audit process, but also casts doubt on the efficiency and effectiveness of the internal audit team, and could potentially result in an increased audit fee. This is a crucial matter to raise with those charged with governance, who ultimately are responsible for the actions of the internal auditors who report to them.

Requirement (b): This requirement asked candidates to comment on a request made by the client, a listed company, for the audit firm to type the financial statements. This is not specifically prohibited by ethical guidelines, and the point of the requirement was to test the candidates' ability to think on their feet about a relatively common request. The issue is that the auditor could be perceived to be involved with the preparation of the financial statements or to be taking management decisions; however, with appropriate safeguards a typing service could be provided. As the client in this case was a listed company, some candidates suggested that even with safeguards, it may be a safer decision to explain to the client the threats and decline to provide the service.

Requirement (c): Auditor's liability is a topical issue and it was disappointing to see that roughly half of the candidates who chose to attempt this question had no comprehension of the concept of the liability disclaimer. Most of these answers instead discussed an opinion modified due to lack of sufficient appropriate evidence, while others made much of a paragraph which explains the responsibilities of auditors compared to managers. Those candidates who correctly identified the liability disclaimer (a paragraph used to clarify that the auditor's report is intended to be used by the shareholders of the company as a whole, and thus the auditors accept no responsibility towards third parties) tended to do very well, with clear arguments for and against the use of such paragraphs discussed. Many strong answers referred to the Bannerman case which prompted the widespread use of these paragraphs, and some even mentioned ACCA's views on the use of the paragraph (though this was not necessary to score full marks).

		ACCA marking scheme		
				Marks
(a)	(i)	**Purpose of including audit findings in a report to those charged with governance**		
		1 mark per comment:		
		– Formal communication of key audit matters		
		– Recommendations made to management		
			Maximum	2
	(ii)	**Identification and explanation of matters**		
		½ mark for identification, up to 2 marks for explanation:		
		Identification *Reason for inclusion*		
		Control deficiency – Not material to financial statements		
		– But indicates significant deficiency which could allow fraud to occur		
		– Recommendations to help management reduce business risk		
		Standards breach – Financial statements materially misstated		
		– Give technical detail to non-financial directors		
		– Report to state opinion will be modified unless brand derecognised		
		– Management have full facts and can decide whether to amend		
		Delay in receiving – Audit inefficiencies and possible increased audit paperwork fee		
		– Management to realise problems caused and react		
			Maximum	7
(b)		**Provision of typing service**		
		1 mark per comment from ideas list:		
		– Typing service not prohibited		
		– Could be seen as preparation of financial statements		
		– For listed client risk is increased		
		– Safest option to refuse/service		
		– Could be provided if significant safeguards in place		
			Maximum	3

(c)	**Disclaimer content and advantages and disadvantages**	
	1 mark per point:	
	Content of disclaimer:	
	– Report intended for use by company's members as a whole	
	– No responsibility accepted to third parties	
	– Commonly used but not required by standards	
	Advantages:	
	– Potential to limit liability exposure	
	– Clarifies extent of auditor's responsibility	
	– Reduces expectation gap	
	– Manages audit firm's risk exposure	
	Disadvantages:	
	– Each legal case assessed individually – no evidence that a disclaimer would offer protection in all cases	
	– May lead to reduction in audit quality	
	Maximum marks	5
Total		**17**

UK SYLLABUS ONLY

55   COXON *Walk in the footsteps of a top tutor*

Key answer tips

This question requires knowledge of the difference between fraudulent and wrongful trading. You then need to apply that knowledge to the scenario to assess whether the directors are guilty of either offence.

The question also asks you to describe the impact of the compulsory liquidation for the employees and creditors. Make sure you identify all aspects of the requirement when the requirement is embedded within the scenario like this to avoid missing out on vital marks.

Personal liability of company directors

Normally, the directors of a company which is placed in liquidation do not have a personal liability for the debts of the company. However, the liquidator who is appointed to wind up the company will investigate the reasons for the insolvency, which includes an assessment of whether fraudulent or wrongful trading has taken place, in which case the directors may become liable to repay all or some of the company's debts.

Wrongful trading is defined under s.214 Insolvency Act 1986, and is the less serious of the two offences. Wrongful trading applies when:

- the company has gone into insolvent liquidation

- at some time before the commencement of the winding up of the company, the directors knew, or ought to have known, that there was no reasonable prospect that the company would avoid going into insolvent liquidation

- the directors did not take sufficient steps to minimise the potential loss to creditors.

In deciding whether or not a director of a company ought to have known or ascertained the company was insolvent, the liquidator will consider the general knowledge, skill and experience which may reasonably be expected of a reasonable diligent person carrying out the same functions as are carried out by that director. If a director has greater than usual skill, they would be judged by reference to their own capacity.

The liquidator needs to apply to the court to proceed with an action against a director for wrongful trading. If found guilty, the director faces a civil liability and can be ordered to make a contribution to the company's assets. A director is not likely to be found guilty if they can demonstrate that they took every step with a view to minimising the potential loss to the company's creditors which they ought to have taken.

Fraudulent trading is the more serious offence. Here, a director faces a criminal charge as well as a civil charge under the Insolvency Act. The definition of fraudulent trading is if in the course of the winding up of a company, it appears that any business of the company has been carried on with intent to defraud creditors of the company, or for any fraudulent purpose. Carrying on a business can include a single transaction.

It is harder to prove fraudulent trading than wrongful trading. Only those directors who took the decision to carry on the business, or played an active role are liable. If found guilty, directors may have to make personal contributions to the company's assets and the court can also impose fines or imprisonment on guilty directors.

In the case of Coxon Ltd's directors, it seems that there was a decision to continue to trade even when there were clear signs of the company's financial distress. The company continued to purchase goods even though the directors were aware of severe cash shortages and difficult trading conditions. Therefore the liquidator is likely to conclude that there is evidence of at least wrongful trading, especially on the part of the finance director, who should have known that the company was insolvent, and did not take all steps necessary to protect creditors.

Impact of compulsory liquidation for employees and creditors

In a compulsory liquidation the employees are automatically dismissed. The liquidator effectively takes over control of the company, assuming management responsibility. The liquidator can require directors and other staff to assist with matters such as preparing and submitting the statement of affairs.

With regard to creditors, they have no involvement with the actual liquidation process, other than having the right to hold a meeting at which they appoint their choice of insolvency practitioner to act as liquidator.

The main impact of liquidation for both employees and creditors is the allocation of company assets at the end of the winding up. There is a prescribed order of priority for allocating company assets. Employees' salaries in arrears (subject to a maximum amount), pension contributions and holiday pay are all preferential creditors. This means that these amounts will be paid after liquidator's costs and fixed charge holders but before all other creditors.

Unsecured creditors and floating charge holders are paid next, followed by preference shareholders and finally members (equity shareholders). Trade creditors are likely to be unsecured creditors, so rank after employees for payment. They are protected to an extent by the 'prescribed part' which is a proportion of assets which is set aside for unsecured creditors. This means that they may not receive the full amount owed to them, but should receive a percentage of what is owed.

ACCA marking scheme	
	Marks
Wrongful and fraudulent trading	
Up to 1.5 marks for each matter explained:	
• Liquidator assesses reason for insolvency including director's actions	
• Definition of wrongful trading	
• Elements which must be proven for wrongful trading (up to 2 marks)	
• Matters looked at by court to determine liability – skill and experience	
• Implication of being found guilty of wrongful trading	
• Definition of fraudulent trading	
• Comment on or application of the above to Coxon Ltd's situation	
• Employees automatically dismissed but may assist liquidator if required	
• Creditors have limited role in liquidation other than ability to appoint liquidator	
• Employees rank as preferential creditors	
• Creditors can be secured, or unsecured and paid from prescribed part	
• Details of any impairment review conducted by management	
Total	**13**

56 HAWK (A) *Walk in the footsteps of a top tutor*

Key answer tips

Part (a) (i) asks for matters to be considered in agreeing the terms of engagement for an examination of a forecast. This is the matters that need to be included in the engagement letter for this assignment. A good approach to take for this question is to identify matters that could lead to misunderstandings in future that the firm would want clarifying in writing. Knowledge of audit engagement letters can also be used and tailored to this type of engagement.

Part (a) (ii) requires the procedures to be performed on the forecast. It is important to remember that these events and transactions have not yet happened and therefore cannot be agreed to supporting documentation in the same way as historical figures. You need to generate procedures which will help you assess whether the assumptions used in the forecast are reasonable.

Part (bi) asks you to examine the information to determine whether the company is insolvent i.e. does it have more liabilities than assets. This should be relatively straightforward.

Part (b) (ii) asks you to set out the options available to the directors for the future of the company. This requires rote learned knowledge from the text book about the key aspects of liquidation and administration. The requirement specifically asks you to provide a recommendation so you must reach a conclusion as to the best way forward for the company.

(a) (i)   The terms of the engagement to review and report on Hawk Ltd's business plan and forecast financial statements should be agreed in an engagement letter, separate from the audit engagement letter. The following matters should be included in the terms of agreement:

Management's responsibilities

The terms of the engagement should set out management's responsibilities for the preparation of the business plan and forecast financial statements, including all assumptions used, and for providing the auditor with all relevant information and source data used in developing the assumptions. This is to clarify the roles of management and of Lapwing & Co, and reduce the scope for any misunderstanding.

The intended use of the business plan and report

It should be confirmed that the report will be provided to the bank and that it will not be distributed or made available to other parties. This will establish the potential liability of Lapwing & Co to third parties, and help to determine the need and extent of any liability disclaimer that may be considered necessary. Lapwing & Co should also establish that the bank will use the report only in helping to reach a decision in respect of the additional finance being sought by Hawk Ltd.

The elements of the business plan to be included in the review and report

The extent of the review should be agreed. Lapwing & Co need to determine whether they are being asked to report just on the forecast financial statements, or on the whole business plan including any narrative descriptions or explanations of Hawk Ltd's intended future business activities. This will help to determine the scope of the work involved and its complexity.

The period covered by the forecasts

This should be confirmed when agreeing the terms of the engagement, as assumptions become more speculative as the length of the period covered increases, making it more difficult for Lapwing & Co to substantiate the acceptability of the figures, and increasing the risk of the engagement. It should also be confirmed that a 12-month forecast period is sufficient for the bank's purposes.

The nature of the assumptions used in the business plan

It is crucial that Lapwing & Co determine the nature of assumptions, especially whether the assumptions are based on best estimates or are hypothetical. This is important because the auditor should not accept, or should withdraw from, an engagement when the assumptions are clearly unrealistic or when the auditor believes that the prospective financial information will be inappropriate for its intended use.

The planned contents of the assurance report

The engagement letter should confirm the planned elements of the report to be issued, to avoid any misunderstanding with management. In particular, Lapwing & Co should clarify that their report will contain a statement of negative assurance as to whether the assumptions provide a reasonable basis for the prospective financial information, and an opinion as to whether the prospective financial information is properly prepared on the basis of the assumptions and is presented in accordance with the relevant financial reporting framework. The bank may require the report to be in a particular format and include specific wordings in order to make their lending decision.

(ii) **General procedures**

- Re-perform calculations to confirm the arithmetic accuracy of the forecast financial statements.

- Agree the unaudited figures for the period to 31 May 2012 to management accounts, and agree the cash figure to bank statement or bank reconciliation.

- Confirm the consistency of the accounting policies used in the preparation of the forecast financial statements with those used in the last audited financial statements.

- Consider the accuracy of forecasts prepared in prior periods by comparison with actual results and discuss with management the reasons for any significant variances.

- Perform analytical procedures to assess the reasonableness of the forecast financial statements. For example, finance charges should increase in line with the additional finance being sought.

- Discuss the extent to which the joint venture with Kestrel Ltd has been included in the forecast financial statements.

- Review any agreement with Kestrel Ltd, or minutes of meetings at which the joint venture has been discussed to understand the nature, scale, and timeframe of the proposed joint business arrangement.

- Review any projected financial information for the joint venture, and agree any components relating to it into the forecast financial statements.

Forecast income statement

- Consider the reasonableness of forecast trends in the light of auditor's knowledge of Hawk Ltd's business and the current and forecast economic situation and any other relevant external factors.

- Discuss the reason for the anticipated 21.4% increase in revenue with management, to understand if the increase is due to the inclusion of figures relating to the joint venture with Kestrel Ltd, or other factors.

- Discuss the trend in operating profit with management – the operating margin is forecast to improve from 30% to 33.8%. This improvement may be due to the sale of the underperforming Beak Retail park.

- Obtain a breakdown of items included in forecast operating expenses and perform an analytical review to compare to those included in the 2012 figures, to check for any omissions.

- Using the cost breakdown, consider whether depreciation charges have increased in line with the planned capital expenditure.

- Request confirmation from the bank of the potential terms of the £30 million loan being negotiated, to confirm the interest rate at 4%. Consider whether the finance charge in the forecast income statement appears reasonable. (If the loan is advanced in August, it should increase the company's finance charge by £1 million (£30 million × 4% × 10/12).)

- Discuss the potential sale of Beak Retail with management and review relevant board minutes, to obtain understanding of the likelihood of the sale, and the main terms of the sale negotiation.

- Recalculate the profit on the planned disposal, agreeing the potential proceeds to any written documentation relating to the sale, vendor's due diligence report, or draft legal documentation if available.

- Agree the potential proceeds on disposal to management's cash flow forecast, and confirm that operating cash flows relevant to Beak Retail are not included from the anticipated date of its sale.

- Discuss the reason for not including current tax in the profit forecast.

Forecast statement of financial position

- Agree the increase in property, plant and equipment to an authorised capital expenditure budget, and to any plans for the joint development with Kestrel Ltd.

- Obtain and review a reconciliation of the movement in property, plant and equipment. Agree that all assets relating to Beak Retail are derecognised on its disposal, and that any assets relating to the joint development with Kestrel Ltd are recognised in accordance with capital expenditure forecasts, and are properly recognised per IFRS 11 *Joint Arrangements*.

- Discuss the planned increase in equity with management to understand the reason for any planned share issue, its date and the nature of the share issue (rights issue or issue at full market price being the most likely).

- Perform analytical procedures on working capital and discuss trends with management, for example, receivables days is forecast to reduce from 58 to 53 days, and the reason for this should be obtained.

Tutorial note

Credit will be awarded for other examples of ratios calculated on the figures provided such as inventory turnover and average payables payment period.

- Agree the increase in long-term borrowings to documentation relating to the new loan, and also to the forecast cash flow statement (where it should be included as a cash flow arising from financing activities).

- Discuss the deferred tax provision with management to understand why no movement on the balance is forecast, particularly given the planned capital expenditure.

- Obtain and review a forecast statement of changes in equity to ensure that movements in retained earnings appear reasonable. (Retained earnings are forecast to increase by £800,000, but the profit forecast for the period is £10.52 million – there must be other items taken through retained earnings such as a planned dividend.)

- Agree the movement in cash, and the forecast closing cash position to a cash flow forecast.

(b) **Briefing notes**

To: Audit partner

From: Audit manager

Subject: Jay Ltd – financial results and the future of the company

Introduction

These briefing notes will examine the current financial position of Jay Ltd using the most recent available management accounts. The notes then go on to look at the future of the company, explaining the options available to the directors.

(i) **Financial position of Jay Ltd**

The company is clearly suffering from a shortage of cash and is reliant on a bank overdraft to manage its working capital. It is unlikely that this situation can be sustained in the long run. However, there is a difference between a company suffering from a cash shortage and a company which is insolvent. Insolvency exists when a company is unable to pay its payables even if it sold all of its assets, in other words the company is in a position of net liabilities.

In order to determine whether Jay Ltd is insolvent it is necessary to look at its net asset or net liability position, using figures from the latest management accounts:

	£000
Property, plant and equipment	12,800
Inventory	500
Trade receivables	400
Cash	0
Long-term borrowings	(12,000)
Trade payables	(1,250)
Bank overdraft	(1,400)
	———
Net liabilities	(950)
	———

Jay Ltd appears to be insolvent, as it is in a position of net liabilities at 31 May 2012.

Tutorial note

Credit will be awarded where candidates discuss further issues to do with the company being in a position of net liabilities, such as the directors needing to take care to avoid conducting wrongful trading, and the implications of it.

The management accounts show the very different results of 'Jay Sport' (JS) and 'Jay Plus' (JP). JS has clearly been badly affected by the revelation regarding one of its ingredients, with only a small amount of sales being made in the current financial year, and this business segment is loss-making overall. However, there seems to be continued demand for JP, which remains profitable. This indicates that the JP business segment may still be able to make a return for shareholders and creditors.

(ii)   **The future of the company – option 1: liquidation**

It may be decided that liquidation or 'winding up' is the best course of action. In this case the company's assets will be sold and a distribution made to its creditors with the proceeds. There is an order of priority for allocating the proceeds raised. Using the information available for Jay Ltd, and ignoring liquidator's costs, the long-term borrowings are secured by a fixed charge over property and rank high in the order of priority and would be paid before the other payables. The employees' wages of £300,000 rank as a preferential creditor and are paid next. Any proceeds remaining would be paid to unsecured creditors, then any residual amount to the shareholders. It is unlikely that the shareholders would receive anything in this case.

The directors cannot themselves begin liquidation proceedings. If they decide that this would be the best course of action for Jay Ltd, they can recommend that a creditor's voluntary winding up should be instigated. In this case a liquidator is appointed by the company's creditors, and a liquidation committee comprising both shareholders and creditors is established, so that the creditors have input to the conduct of the liquidation. A member's voluntary liquidation is not an option, as this form of liquidation can only be used for a solvent company.

If the directors take no action, then a creditor may end up applying to the court for a compulsory winding up order. Any creditor who is owed more than £750 can apply for this action to take place. The directors may wish to avoid the company being placed into compulsory liquidation as this means that employees are automatically dismissed.

In any liquidation the directors will have to stand down to be replaced by the liquidator, unless the liquidator decides to retain them.

The future of the company – option 2: administration

Administration is a very different course of action. It aims to save the company, and an insolvency practitioner is appointed to take control of the company and to attempt to rescue it as a going concern. Administration protects the company from the actions of creditors while a restructuring plan is prepared.

Administration can commence without a court order. The directors themselves may be able to appoint an administrator where a company is unable to pay its debts, though this depends on the company's articles of association.

Alternatively, a majority of shareholders, the directors or one or more creditors can apply for administration through the court. It is likely to be more expensive and time consuming to apply to the court.

The administrator takes on the role of the directors, and within eight weeks of appointment must send a document to the company's shareholders and creditors in which they state their proposals for rescuing the company, or states that the company cannot be saved. In Jay Ltd's case, it is likely that the JS business segment would be discontinued, and further finance may need to be raised to support the JP segment.

Conclusions and recommendation

From the information available, it seems that the JP range is still profitable, and could represent a way for the company to remain a going concern. The damage to the JS range does not seem to have tarnished the JP products, and therefore a rescue plan for the company may be feasible.

However, further information is needed before a definite decision is made. In particular, there may be costs that the company would be committed to continue to pay in relation to JS even if that part of the business were to cease to operate, for example, non-cancellable leases. From the information provided, and assuming that no large commitments are included in the overheads of JS, I would recommend that the directors consider an administration order for the company, which will give some breathing space for an appropriate strategy to be devised.

Administration may also benefit Jay Ltd's shareholders, who will continue to own their shares in what may become more profitable and solvent business. It may also be preferential for the creditors for the company to continue to trade, as they may be more likely to receive the amounts owed to them through the continued operation of the company compared to a forced sale of its assets.

ACCA marking scheme		
		Marks

(a)   (i)   **Matters to be included in the terms of agreement**
Up to 1½ marks for each matter identified and explained (2 marks maximum for identification):
–   Management's responsibilities
–   Intended use of the information and report
–   The contents of the business plan
–   The period covered by the forecasts
–   The nature of assumptions used in the forecasts
–   The format and planned content of the assurance report

Maximum   6

(ii)   **Procedures on forecast financial information**
Up to 1 mark for each procedure (brief examples below):
–   General procedures examples:
  •   Re-perform calculations
  •   Consistency of accounting policies used
  •   Discuss how joint venture has been included
  •   General analytical procedures
–   Procedures on income statement:
  •   Discuss trends – allow up to 3 marks for calculations performed and linked to procedures
  •   Review and compare breakdown of costs
  •   Recalculate profit on disposal, agreement of components to supporting documentation
–   Procedures on statement of financial position:
  •   Agree increase in property, plant and equipment to capital expenditure budget
  •   Discuss working capital trends – allow 2 marks for calculations performed and linked to procedures
  •   Agree movement in long-term borrowings to new loan documentation
  •   Obtain and review forecast statement of changes in equity and confirm validity of reconciling items

Maximum   10

(b)   (i)   **Examine financial position and determine whether the company is insolvent**
Generally 1 mark per comment:
–   Calculation of net liabilities position of Jay Ltd
–   Determination that Jay Ltd is insolvent
–   Explanation of meaning of insolvency
–   Discussion of different results of JS and JP business segments

Maximum   4

(ii)   **Evaluate the option available to the directors**
Up to 1½ marks per comment:
–   Explanation of meaning of liquidation
–   Application of order of priority in allocating proceeds of liquidation
–   Discussion of means of appointing an administrator
–   Benefits of administration over liquidation
–   Identify that a definite decision depends on further information
–   Overall recommendation

Maximum   9

Professional marks for the overall presentation of the notes, and the clarity of the explanation and assessment provided.

Maximum   4

Total

33

57   BUTLER (A) *Walk in the footsteps of a top tutor*

Key answer tips

Part (a) (i) requires analytical procedures to be performed to help identify going concern issues. Be careful not to spend too much time on the calculations to the detriment of talking about the risks.

Part (a) (ii) asks for audit procedures to be performed on the cash flow forecast. Procedures should focus on obtaining evidence to support the assumptions which provide the basis for the forecast. It is important to remember that these events and transactions have not yet happened and therefore cannot be agreed to supporting documentation in the same way as historical figures.

Part (b) requires the procedures involved with placing a company into compulsory liquidation and the consequences to the key stakeholder groups of doing this. This requires rote learned knowledge from the text book.

(a)   **Briefing notes**

> **To:**   Audit partner
>
> **From:**   Audit manager
>
> **Re:**   Initial going concern assessment – Butler Ltd

Introduction

Butler Ltd faces significant business risk due to declining sales and loss of customers and market share. These briefing notes contain an initial assessment of going concern, based on the draft statement of financial position, and a cash flow forecast prepared for the first three months of the next financial year. Audit procedures will also be recommended for the cash flow forecast.

(i)   **Assessment of draft statement of financial position.**

The most obvious issue is that Butler Ltd currently does not have a positive cash balance. The statement of financial position includes an overdraft of £25 million. This lack of cash will make it difficult for the company to manage its operating cycle and make necessary interest payments, unless further cash becomes available.

Butler Ltd is in a position of net liabilities, as indicated by the negative shareholders' funds figure. The company's retained earnings figure is now negative. Net liabilities and significant losses are both examples of financial conditions listed in ISA 570 (UK and Ireland) *Going concern,* which may cast doubt about the going concern assumption.

Note 3 indicates that Butler Ltd has been loss-making for several years. Recurring losses are a further indication of going concern problems. Few companies can sustain many consecutive loss-making periods.

There are several items recognised in the statement of financial position, which, if adjusted, would make the net liabilities position worse. For example, a deferred tax asset is recognised at £235 million. This asset should only be recognised if Butler Ltd can demonstrate that future profits will be sufficient to enable the recoverability of the asset. As Butler Ltd has been loss-making for several years, it is arguable that this asset should not be recognised at all. Additionally, an intangible asset relating to development costs of £120 million is recognised. One of the criteria for the capitalisation of such costs is that adequate resources exist for completion of the development. Given Butler Ltd's lack of cash, this criteria may no longer be applicable. If adjustments were made to write off these assets, the net liabilities would become £580 million.

Note 2 indicates that fixed charges exist over assets valued at £25 million. If Butler Ltd fails to make repayments to the creditor holding the charge over assets, the assets could be seized, disrupting the operations of Butler Ltd.

There are significant short-term borrowings due for repayment – notably a bank loan of £715 million due for repayment in September 2011. It is hard to see how Butler Ltd will be able to repay this loan given its current lack of cash. The cash flow forecast does not indicate that sufficient cash is likely to be generated post year end to enable this loan to be repaid.

Provisions have been classified as non-current liabilities. Given that the provisions relate to customer warranties, it is likely that some of the provisions balance should be classified as a current liability. This potential incorrect presentation impacts on assessment of liquidity, as incorrect classification will impact on the cash flow required to meet the warranties obligation.

Butler Ltd's poor financial position means it is unlikely to be able to raise finance from a third party.

Assessment of cash flow forecast

From an overall point of view, the cash flow forecast indicates that by the end of August, Butler Ltd will still be in a negative cash position. As discussed above, this is particularly concerning given that a loan of £715 million is due to be repaid in September.

The assumption relating to cash receipts from customers seems optimistic. It is too simplistic to assume that anticipated economic recovery will lead to a sudden improvement in cash collection from customers, even if additional resources are being used for credit control.

£200 million of the cash receipts for this three-month period relate to loans and subsidies which are currently being negotiated and applied for. These cash inflows are not guaranteed, and if not received, the overall cash position at the end of the period will be much worse than currently projected.

The cash inflow for June 2011 includes the proceeds of a sale of financial assets of £50 million. It is questionable whether this amount of cash will be generated, given the financial assets are recognised on the statement of financial position at £25 million. The assumed sales value of £50 million may be overly optimistic.

In conclusion, the cash flow forecast may not be reliable, in that assumptions are optimistic, and the additional funding is not guaranteed. This means that three months into the next financial year, the company's cash position is likely to have worsened, and loans and trade payables which are due for payment are likely to remain unpaid. This casts significant doubt as to the ability of Butler Ltd to continue operating as a going concern.

Tutorial note

Credit will be awarded for calculation and explanation of appropriate ratios relevant to Butler Ltd's going concern status.

(ii) **Recommended audit procedures:**

- Discuss with management the reasons for assuming that cash collection from customers will improve due to 'anticipated improvement in economic conditions'. Consider the validity of the reasons in light of business understanding.

- Enquire as to the nature of the additional resources to be devoted to the credit control function, e.g. details of extra staff recruited.

- For the loan receipt, inspect written documentation relating to the request for finance from Rubery Ltd. Request written confirmation from Rubery Ltd regarding the amount of finance and the date it will be received, as well as any terms and conditions.

- Obtain and review the financial statements of Rubery Ltd, to consider if it has sufficient resources to provide the amount of loan requested.

- For the subsidy, inspect the application made to the subsidy awarding body and confirm the amount of the subsidy.

- Read any correspondence between Butler Ltd and the subsidy awarding body, specifically looking for confirmation that the subsidy will be granted.

- Regarding operating expenses, verify using previous months' management accounts, that operating cash outflows are approximately £200 million per month.

- Enquire as to the reason for the increase in operating cash outflows in August 2011.

- Verify, using previous months' management accounts, that interest payments of £40 million per month appear reasonable.

- Confirm, using the loan agreement, the amount of the loan being repaid in August 2011.

- Enquire whether any tax payments are due in the three month period, such as VAT.

- Agree the opening cash position to cash book and bank statement/bank reconciliation, and cast the cash flow forecast.

- Ensure that a cash flow forecast for the full financial year is received as three months' forecast is inadequate for the purposes of the audit.

- Enquire if those charged with governance have assessed the going concern assumption for a period of 12 months from the date of approval of the financial statements.

Tutorial note

Marks would also be awarded for the more general procedures required under ISA 570 in relation to audit procedures on a cash flow forecast, such as evaluation of the reliability of underlying data, and requesting a written representation regarding the feasibility of plans for future action.

Conclusion to briefing notes

The review of the draft statement of financial position and cash flow forecast shows that there are many factors indicating that Butler Ltd is experiencing going concern problems. In particular, the lack of cash, and the significant amounts due to be paid within a few months of the year end cast significant doubt over the use of the going concern assumption in the financial statements. The company has requested finance from its parent company, but even if this is forthcoming, cash flow remains a significant problem.

(b)   (i)   A company is usually placed in compulsory liquidation by a payable (creditor), who uses compulsory liquidation as a means to recover monies owed by the company. The payable (creditor) must petition the court and the petition is advertised in the *London Gazette. There* are various grounds for a petition to be made for compulsory liquidation. The most common ground is that the company is unable to pay its debts. In this case the payable (creditor) must show that he or she is owed more than £750 by the company and has served on the company at its registered office a written demand for payment. This is called a statutory demand. If the company fails to pay the statutory demand in 21 days and does not dispute the debt, then the payable (creditor) may present a winding up petition at court.

The application for a winding up order will be granted at a court hearing where it can be proven to the court's satisfaction that the debt is undisputed, attempts to recover have been undertaken and the company has neglected to pay the amount owed.

On a compulsory winding up the court will appoint an Official Receiver, who is an officer of the court. Within a few days of the winding up order being granted by the court, the Official Receiver must inform the company directors of the situation. The court order is also advertised in the *London Gazette.*

The Official Receiver takes over the control of the company and usually begins to close it down. The company's directors are asked to prepare a statement of affairs. The Official Receiver must also investigate the causes of the failure of the company.

The liquidation is deemed to have started at the date of the presentation of the winding up petition.

At the end of the winding up of the company, a final meeting with payables (creditors) is held, and a final return is filed with the court and the Registrar. At this point the company is dissolved.

Tutorial note

Credit will be awarded to candidates who explain other, less common, means by which a company may face a compulsory liquidation:

A shareholder may serve a petition for compulsory liquidation. The grounds for doing so would normally be based on the fact that that the shareholder is dissatisfied with the management of the company, and that it is therefore just and equitable to wind up the company. This action by the shareholder is only allowed if the company is solvent and if the shareholder has been a shareholder for at least six months prior to the petition.

Very occasionally, if the Crown believes that a company is contravening legislation such as the Trading Standards legislation or is acting against the public or government interest, it is possible for the company to be liquidated compulsorily. This is very serious action to take and is not used very regularly.

    (ii)   Payables (creditors) – The role of the Official Receiver (or Insolvency Practitioner, if appointed), is to realise the company's assets, and to distribute the proceeds in a prescribed order. Depending on the amount of cash available for distribution, and whether the debt is secured or unsecured, payables (creditors) may receive some, all, or none of the amount owed to them.

           Employees – All employees of the company are automatically dismissed. A prescribed amount of unpaid employee's wages, accrued holiday pay, and contributions to an occupational pension fund rank as preferential debts, and will be paid before payables (creditors) of the company.

           Shareholders – Any surplus that remains after the payment of all other amounts owed by the company is distributed to the shareholders. In most liquidations the shareholders receive nothing.

ACCA marking scheme			
			Marks
(a)	(i)	**Going concern matters**	
		Up to 1½ marks per matter identified and explained (maximum 3 marks for identification):	
		– Negative cash position	
		– Net liabilities position	
		– Recurring losses	
		– Possible adjustment to deferred tax and development intangible asset exacerbate net liabilities position (allow 3 marks max)	
		– Fixed charge over assets	
		– Significant short term liabilities	
		– Potential misclassified provisions	
		– Forecast to remain in negative cash position	
		– Assumptions re sales optimistic	
		– Receipt of loan and subsidy not guaranteed	
		– Assumption of sale value of financial assets could be optimistic	——
		Maximum	10
			——

	(ii)	**Procedures on cash flow forecast**			
		Generally 1 mark per specific procedure:			
		–	Enquire regarding and consider validity of assumption re cash sales		
		–	Inspect any supporting documentation re additional resources for credit control		
		–	Seek written confirmation from Rubery Ltd re loan		
		–	Review financial statements of Rubery Ltd re adequacy of resources		
		–	Inspect subsidy application		
		–	Seek third party confirmation that subsidy will be awarded		
		–	Confirm cash outflows for operating expenses and interest appear reasonable		
		–	Enquire about potentially missing cash outflows		
		–	Agree date and amount of short term loan repayment to loan documentation		
		–	Agree opening cash to cash book and bank statements		
			Maximum	8	
		Professional marks for presentation and clarity of explanations		2	
(b)	(i)	**Procedures for compulsory liquidation**			
		Generally 1 mark each point explained:			
		–	Creditors petition court for winding-up order		
		–	Grounds for the petition must be demonstrated – usually an unpaid statutory demand		
		–	Court appoints an Official receiver		
		–	Official Receiver informs company directors and takes control of company		
		–	Shareholders can apply for compulsory liquidation (rare)		
		–	The Crown can apply for compulsory liquidation (very rare)		
			Maximum	7	
	(ii)	**Consequences for stakeholders**			
		Generally 1 mark each consequence explained:			
		–	Payables (Creditors)		
		–	Employees		
		–	Shareholders		
			Maximum	3	
Total				**27**	

58 ASPECTS OF INSOLVENCY *Walk in the footsteps of a top tutor*

Key answer tips

This question is not taken from a previous exam, but has been added to the bank to give you the opportunity to practise requirements relating to the UK syllabus area of insolvency.

Insolvency will not be examined in every sitting, and it will be a small requirement that forms part of a larger question, rather than a whole question solely covering the topic of insolvency.

(a) **Fraudulent trading**

Fraudulent trading is where a company carries on a business with the intention of defrauding creditors or for any other fraudulent purposes.

This would include a situation where the director(s) of a company continue to trade whilst insolvent, and enter into debts knowing that the company will not be in a position to repay those debts.

The Insolvency Act 1986 governs situations where, in the course of a winding up, it appears that the business has been carried on with the intent to defraud creditors, or for any other fraudulent purpose.

Fraudulent trading is also a criminal offence under the Companies Act 2006.

A director who is found guilty of fraudulent trading can be made personally liable for the debts of the company (a civil liability under the Insolvency Act); be disqualified as a director for between two and 15 years, and can be imprisoned for up to ten years.

Wrongful trading

Wrongful trading is when the director(s)of a company have continued to trade when they: 'knew, or ought to have concluded that there was no reasonable prospect of avoiding insolvent liquidation'.

A director can defend an action of wrongful trading if they can prove that they have taken sufficient steps to minimise the potential loss to creditors.

Wrongful trading is an action that can be taken only by a company's liquidator, once it has gone into insolvent liquidation (either voluntary or compulsory liquidation).

Unlike fraudulent trading, wrongful trading needs no finding of 'intent to defraud'. In addition, because wrongful trading is a civil offence (fraudulent trading is a criminal offence), it only needs to be proven 'on the balance of probabilities' (i.e. it is more likely than not that the director(s) are guilty of wrongful trading). Fraudulent trading needs to be proven 'beyond reasonable doubt' (i.e. it is almost certain that the director(s) are guilty of fraudulent trading).

For these reasons, wrongful trading is more common than fraudulent trading.

A director who is found guilty of wrongful trading can be made personally liable for the debts of the company; and be disqualified as a director for between two and 15 years.

(b) An auditor would examine the financial position of a company in order to determine whether it is insolvent.

There are two tests for insolvency defined in the Insolvency Act 1986.

(i) if assets are exceeded by liabilities, or

(ii) if a company is failing to discharge its debts as and when they fall due.

If a company meets either criteria then it is technically insolvent.

(c) **Compulsory liquidation**

Companies may be obliged to liquidate if a winding up order is presented to a court, usually by a creditor or member. Such a petition may be made for a number of reasons, which include (Insolvency Act 1986):

- the company being unable to pay its debts; and
- it is just and equitable to wind up the company.

(d)   **Consequences of liquidation**

If successful the court will appoint an official receiver (an officer of the courts) as liquidator. They may be replaced by a practitioner at a later date. The receiver investigates the company's affairs and the cause of its failure. The petition also has the following effects:

- all actions for the recovery of debt against the company are stopped.

- any floating charges crystallise.

- all legal proceedings against the company are halted and none may start unless the courts grant permission.

- the company must cease trading activity, unless it is necessary to complete the liquidation, e.g. completing work-in-progress the directors relinquish power and authority to the liquidator, although they may remain in office; and employees are automatically made redundant. The liquidator may choose to re-employ them to help complete the liquidation process.

(e)   **Explanation of Member's Voluntary Liquidation**

Liquidation is the process of terminating a company, thus ending its life. The assets of the company are physically liquidated, i.e. they are sold, so that cash can be used to pay off company creditors and equity holders.

Members' Voluntary Liquidation is used when a company is solvent.

In order to facilitate this the members must pass one of two resolutions:

- an ordinary resolution, where the articles provide for liquidation on the expiry of a fixed date or a specific event

- a special resolution, for any other reason.

Once this has been passed the directors must make a **declaration of solvency** stating that they are of the opinion that the company will be able to pay its debts within twelve months. A false declaration would constitute a criminal offence.

The company will then appoint a named insolvency practitioner to act as the liquidator. They will realise the company's assets and distribute the proceeds accordingly.

Once the liquidation process is complete the liquidator presents a report at the final meeting of the members, which is then submitted to the registrar of companies. The company will be dissolved three months later.

INT SYLLABUS ONLY

59   PUBLIC SECTOR ORGANISATIONS *Walk in the footsteps of a top tutor*

Key answer tips

This question is not taken from a previous exam, but has been added to the bank to give you the opportunity to practise requirements relating to the INT syllabus area of public sector performance information.

(a)   **Performance audits** aim to provide management with assurance and advice regarding the effective functioning of its operational activities.

Performance information is information published by public sector bodies regarding their objectives and the achievement of those objectives.

(b)   **Performance targets**

   (i)   Local police department

   - Reduce the number of crimes by x%
   - Reduce the number of offenders re-offending by x%
   - Reduce the number of deaths caused by dangerous driving x%
   - Increase public satisfaction to x%

   (ii)   Local hospital

   - Reduce emergency department waiting times to a maximum of x hours
   - Reduce the maximum waiting time for an operation to x weeks
   - Reduce the number of infections contracted in the hospital by x%
   - Reduce the number of re-admissions to hospital by x%

   (iii)   Local council

   - Increase public satisfaction to x%
   - To build x number of council houses in the next 5 years
   - To spend $x on road maintenance and improvements each year
   - To increase council tax by a maximum of the rate of inflation

Tutorial note

Credit will be awarded for any other relevant examples.

A target does not have to be SMART. Targets are typically more generalised than an objective.

(c)   **Stakeholder groups**

(i)   **Police department**

Stakeholder	Use
Government e.g. Home Office	To ensure that police departments are achieving the targets set by the government.
	To report to taxpayers on how government money in this area is being used to achieve the stated objectives.
Local residents	Residents may wish to know the level of crime in their area to assess the performance of their local police department.
Prospective residents	Prospective residents may use such information to decide whether to move to a particular town/city. If the crime rate is high they may decide not to move there.

(ii)   **Local hospital**

Stakeholder	Use
Local residents	To assess the performance of their local hospital as this will be on importance if they were ever to be admitted to hospital.
Patients awaiting treatment	Patients awaiting treatment may have a choice of hospital from which to receive treatment. In this case, patients are likely to choose the option with the lowest infection rates, highest success rates for a particular operation/procedure, or the quickest treatment time.
Government e.g. Department for Health	To ensure that hospitals are achieving the targets set by the government.
	To report to taxpayers on how government money in this area is being used to achieve the stated objectives.

(iii)   **Local council**

Stakeholder	Use
Local residents	To assess the performance of their local council and how their taxes are being used.
Suppliers/contractors	Suppliers/contractors will be interested to see the plans for the future to assess if there will be additional work being tendered. For example if the council has set a target to build an additional 1000 houses in the coming year, local building firms may be able to bid for the work.
Government e.g. Department for Communities and Local Government	To ensure that councils are achieving the targets set by the government.
	To report to taxpayers on how government money in this area is being used to achieve the stated objectives.

Tutorial note

Credit will be awarded for any other relevant examples e.g. employees to assess whether there is the possibility of redundancies if the target is to reduce costs significantly.

(d)   **Difficulties**

All relevant information may not be reported (e.g. number of crimes or number of hospital infections) therefore it may appear as though there has been improvement when problems may not have been recorded completely.

Where information is completely recorded, accuracy of the information may be an issue. The public sector organisation needs to have good internal controls in place in respect of this information in the same way as internal controls would be expected to be in place in respect of financial information.

Definitions of certain targets and measures may be ambiguous resulting in matters going un-recorded due to public sector employees recording the information in a different way. Information may be classified as something different by different members of staff unless thorough training is given.

Even so, information may not be comparable between different police departments/ hospitals/councils if each interpret the definitions in a different way.

There is also the risk that public sector departments will falsify the figures that have been reported if they are failing to meet the targets set by the government. This may be difficult for the auditor to detect as it is unlikely there will be alternative forms of corroborative evidence to highlight discrepancies.

Marking scheme		Marks
(a)	**Definitions**	
	Up to 1 for each definition	
	– Performance audit	
	– Performance information	——
	Maximum	2
(b)	**Performance targets**	——
	½ mark per performance target. Max of 2 per public sector body.	
	Maximum	6
(c)	**Stakeholder groups**	——
	½ mark per stakeholder group and ½ mark per reason for using the performance information. Max of 2 marks per public sector body	
	Maximum	6
(d)	**Difficulties**	——
	Up to 1 ½ per point made.	
	• Completeness	
	• Accuracy	
	• Ambiguity of targets	
	• Comparability	
	• Risk of falsification	——
	Maximum	6
Total		20
		——

Advanced Audit and Assurance (International)

Paper P7 (INT)

Time allowed

Reading and planning: 15 minutes

Writing: 3 hours

This paper is divided into two sections:

Section A – BOTH questions are compulsory and MUST be attempted

Section B – TWO questions ONLY to be attempted

**Do NOT open this paper until instructed by the supervisor.
During reading and planning time only the question paper may
be annotated. You must NOT write in your answer booklet until
instructed by the supervisor.
This question paper must not be removed from the examination hall.**

The Association of Chartered Certified Accountants

Note to attribute past questions and answers to the pilot paper

A selection of past scenarios, requirements, and parts thereof, have been used in presenting this Pilot Paper. Answers have been rewritten, technically updated or otherwise amended as necessary.

1   (a) and (b) J02 Q1
     (c)   D02 Q4 (a)
     (d)   D05 Q6 (c)

3   (a)–(d) D01 Q2 (a)–(c) and (e)
     (e)   D04 Q5 (c)

4   (d)   D05 Q4 (b) (ii)

5   (a)   J05 Q6 (b)
     (b)–(d) D05 Q5

2

1   You are an audit manager in Ribi & Co, a firm of Chartered Certified Accountants. One of your audit clients Beeski Co provides satellite broadcasting services in a rapidly growing market.

In November 2005 Beeski purchased Xstatic Co, a competitor group of companies. Significant revenue, cost and capital expenditure synergies are expected as the operations of Beeski and Xstatic are being combined into one group of companies.

The following financial and operating information consolidates the results of the enlarged Beeski group:

	Year end 30 September	
	2006 (Estimated)	2005 (Actual)
	$m	$m
Revenue	6,827	4,404
Cost of sales	(3,109)	(1,991)
Distribution costs and administrative expenses	(2,866)	(1,700)
Research and development costs	(25)	(22)
Depreciation and amortisation	(927)	(661)
Interest expense	(266)	(202)
Loss before taxation	(366)	(172)
Customers	14·9m	7·6m
Average revenue per customer (ARPC)	$437	$556

In August 2006 Beeski purchased MTbox Co, a large cable communications provider in India, where your firm has no representation. The financial statements of MTbox for the year ending 30 September 2006 will continue to be audited by a local firm of Chartered Certified Accountants. MTbox's activities have not been reflected in the above estimated results of the group. Beeski is committed to introducing its corporate image into India.

In order to sustain growth, significant costs are expected to be incurred as operations are expanded, networks upgraded and new products and services introduced.

Required:

(a) **Identify and describe the principal business risks for the Beeski group.**   (9 marks)

(b) **Explain what effect the acquisitions will have on the planning of Ribi & Co's audit of the consolidated financial statements of Beeski Co for the year ending 30 September 2006.**   (10 marks)

(c) **Explain the role of 'support letters' (also called 'comfort letters') as evidence in the audit of financial statements.**   (6 marks)

(d) **Discuss how 'horizontal groups' (ie non-consolidated entities under common control) affect the scope of an audit and the audit work undertaken.**   (5 marks)

(30 marks)

2 You have been asked to carry out an investigation by the management of Xzibit Co. One of the company's subsidiaries, Efex Engineering Co, has been making losses for the past year. Xzibit's management is concerned about the accuracy of Efex Engineering's most recent quarter's management accounts.

The summarised income statements for the last three quarters are as follows:

Quarter to	30 June 2006 $000	31 March 2006 $000	31 December 2005 $000
Revenue	429	334	343
Opening inventory	180	163	203
Materials	318	251	200
Direct wages	62	54	74
	560	468	477
Less: Closing inventory	(162)	(180)	(163)
Cost of goods sold	398	288	314
Gross profit	31	46	29
Less: Overheads	(63)	(75)	(82)
Net loss	(32)	(29)	(53)
Gross profit (%)	7·2%	13·8%	8·5%
Materials (% of revenue)	78·3%	70·0%	70·0%
Labour (% of revenue)	14·5%	16·2%	21·6%

Xzibit's management board believes that the high material consumption as a percentage of revenue for the quarter to 30 June 2006 is due to one or more of the following factors:
(1) under-counting or under-valuation of closing inventory;
(2) excessive consumption or wastage of materials;
(3) material being stolen by employees or other individuals.

Efex Engineering has a small number of large customers and manufactures its products to each customer's specification. The selling price of the product is determined by:
(1) estimating the cost of materials;
(2) estimating the labour cost;
(3) adding a mark-up to cover overheads and provide a normal profit.

The estimated costs are not compared with actual costs. Although it is possible to analyse purchase invoices for materials between customers' orders this analysis has not been done.

A physical inventory count is carried out at the end of each quarter. Items of inventory are entered on stocksheets and valued manually. The company does not maintain perpetual inventory records and a full physical count is to be carried out at the financial year end, 30 September 2006.

The direct labour cost included in the inventory valuation is small and should be assumed to be constant at the end of each quarter. Historically, the cost of materials consumed has been about 70% of revenue.

The management accounts to 31 March 2006 are to be assumed to be correct.

Required:

(a) Define 'forensic auditing' and describe its application to fraud investigations.   (5 marks)

(b) Identify and describe the matters that you should consider and the procedures you should carry out in order to plan an investigation of Efex Engineering Co's losses.   (10 marks)

(c) (i) Explain the matters you should consider to determine whether closing inventory at 30 June 2006 is undervalued; and

   (ii) Describe the tests you should plan to perform to quantify the amount of any undervaluation.   (8 marks)

(d) (i) Identify and explain the possible reasons for the apparent high materials consumption in the quarter ended 30 June 2006; and

   (ii) Describe the tests you should plan to perform to determine whether materials consumption, as shown in the management accounts, is correct.   (7 marks)

(30 marks)

3   You are a manager in Ingot & Co, a firm of Chartered Certified Accountants, with specific responsibility for the quality of audits. Ingot was appointed auditor of Argenta Co, a provider of waste management services, in July 2006. You have just visited the audit team at Argenta's head office. The audit team is comprised of an accountant in charge (AIC), an audit senior and two trainees.

Argenta's draft accounts for the year ended 30 June 2006 show revenue of $11·6 million (2005 – $8·1 million) and total assets of $3·6 million (2005 – $2·5 million). During your visit, a review of the audit working papers revealed the following:

(a)   On the audit planning checklist, the audit senior has crossed through the analytical procedures section and written 'not applicable – new client'. The audit planning checklist has not been signed off as having been reviewed.
(4 marks)

(b)   The AIC last visited Argenta's office when the final audit commenced two weeks ago on 1 August. The senior has since completed the audit of tangible non-current assets (including property and service equipment) which amount to $0·6 million as at 30 June 2006 (2005 – $0·6 million). The AIC spends most of his time working from Ingot's office and is currently allocated to three other assignments as well as Argenta's audit.   *(4 marks)*

(c)   At 30 June 2006 trade receivables amounted to $2·1 million (2005 – $0·9 million). One of the trainees has just finished sending out first requests for direct confirmation of customers' balances as at the balance sheet date.
(4 marks)

(d)   The other trainee has been assigned to the audit of the consumable supplies that comprise inventory amounting to $88,000 (2005 – $53,000). The trainee has carried out tests of controls over the perpetual inventory records and confirmed the 'roll-back' of a sample of current quantities to book quantities as at the year end.   *(3 marks)*

(e)   The AIC has noted the following matter for your attention. The financial statements to 30 June 2005 disclosed, as unquantifiable, a contingent liability for pending litigation. However, the AIC has seen a letter confirming that the matter was settled out of court for $0.45 million on 14 September 2005. The auditor's report on the financial statements for the year ended 30 June 2005 was unmodified and signed on 19 September 2005. The AIC believes that Argenta's management is not aware of the error and has not brought it to their attention.   *(5 marks)*

Required:

Identify and comment on the implications of these findings for Ingot & Co's quality control policies and procedures.

Note: The mark allocation is shown against each of the five issues.

(20 marks)

4 You are the manager responsible for four audit clients of Axis & Co, a firm of Chartered Certified Accountants. The year end in each case is 30 June 2006.

You are currently reviewing the audit working paper files and the audit seniors' recommendations for the auditors' reports. Details are as follows:

(a) Mantis Co is a subsidiary of Cube Co. Serious going concern problems have been noted during this year's audit. Mantis will be unable to trade for the foreseeable future unless it continues to receive financial support from the parent company. Mantis has received a letter of support ('comfort letter') from Cube Co.

The audit senior has suggested that, due to the seriousness of the situation, the audit opinion must at least be qualified 'except for'. (5 marks)

(b) Lorenze Co has changed its accounting policy for goodwill during the year from amortisation over its estimated useful life to annual impairment testing. No disclosure of this change has been given in the financial statements. The carrying amount of goodwill in the balance sheet as at 30 June 2006 is the same as at 30 June 2005 as management's impairment test show that it is not impaired.

The audit senior has concluded that a qualification is not required but suggests that attention can be drawn to the change by way of an emphasis of matter paragraph. (6 marks)

(c) The directors' report of Abrupt Co states that investment property rental forms a major part of revenue. However, a note to the financial statements shows that property rental represents only 1·6% of total revenue for the year. The audit senior is satisfied that the revenue figures are correct.

The audit senior has noted that an unqualified opinion should be given as the audit opinion does not extend to the directors' report. (4 marks)

(d) Audit work on the after-date bank transactions of Jingle Co has identified a transfer of cash from Bell Co. The audit senior assigned to the audit of Jingle has documented that Jingle's finance director explained that Bell commenced trading on 7 July 2006, after being set up as a wholly-owned foreign subsidiary of Jingle.

The audit senior has noted that although no other evidence has been obtained an unmodified opinion is appropriate because the matter does not impact on the current year's financial statements. (5 marks)

Required:

For each situation, comment on the suitability or otherwise of the audit senior's proposals for the auditors' reports. Where you disagree, indicate what audit modification (if any) should be given instead.

Note: The mark allocation is shown against each of the four issues.

(20 marks)

5 **(a)** Comment on the need for ethical guidance for accountants on money laundering. (5 marks)

(b) You are senior manager in Dedza & Co, a firm of Chartered Certified Accountants. Recently, you have been assigned specific responsibility for undertaking annual reviews of existing clients. The following situations have arisen in connection with three clients:

(i) Dedza was appointed auditor and tax advisor to Kora Co last year and has recently issued an unmodified opinion on the financial statements for the year ended 31 March 2006. To your surprise, the tax authority has just launched an investigation into the affairs of Kora on suspicion of underdeclaring income. (7 marks)

(ii) The chief executive of Xalam Co, an exporter of specialist equipment, has asked for advice on the accounting treatment and disclosure of payments being made for security consultancy services. The payments, which aim to ensure that consignments are not impounded in the destination country of a major customer, may be material to the financial statements for the year ending 31 December 2006. Xalam does not treat these payments as tax deductible. (4 marks)

(iii) Your firm has provided financial advice to the Pholey family for many years and this has sometimes involved your firm in carrying out transactions on their behalf. The eldest son, Esau, is to take up a position as a senior government official to a foreign country next month. (4 marks)

Required:

Identify and comment on the ethical and other professional issues raised by each of these matters and state what action, if any, Dedza & Co should now take. (15 marks)

Note: The mark allocation is shown against each of the three situations.

(20 marks)

End of Question Paper

7

Answers

Tutorial note: These model answers are considerably longer and more detailed than would be expected from any candidate in the examination. They should be used as a guide to the form, style and technical standard (but not length) of answer which candidates should aim to achieve. However, these answers may not include all valid points mentioned by a candidate – credit will be given to candidates mentioning such points.

1   Beeski Co

(a)   Principal business risks

Tutorial note: *The requirement to 'identify and describe' suggests that although marks will be awarded for the mere identification of risks from the scenario, those risks must be described (as illustrated below).*

Communications industry
- Rapid and new technological developments in the industry, providing faster data transmission and increasingly interactive capabilities, will render certain existing products and services obsolete.
- Beeski cannot predict how emerging and future technologies (eg 'Bluetooth') will affect demand for its services.

Competition
- Although Beeski may have reduced competition in the short-term (by having acquired a competitor), the communications market is still expanding. Increasing competition from other existing and new competitors offering new technologies could:
    - affect Beeski's ability to attract and retain customers
    - reduce Beeski's share of new and existing customers
    - force Beeski to reduce prices.
- The cost (and revenue-generating capabilities) of new technologies tends to fall significantly and relatively quickly (eg mobile phone technology is available in disposable form).

Integration
- Combining two groups which have previously operated independently (and competitively against each other) is likely to result in disruption.
- Potential difficulties may be encountered in seeking to retain customers and key personnel.
- The anticipated 'significant synergies' (in revenue, cost and capital expenditure) may have been optimistic. If they do not materialise to the extent predicted, Beeski's operational activities, financial condition and future prospects are likely to be adversely affected.
- Beeski may have difficulty in adapting its corporate image to the culture of the Indian network.

Operating losses
- Loss before taxation has more than doubled (increased by 113%). If Xstatic was making significant losses before it was acquired by Beeski those losses may have been expected to continue in the short-term. Although the groups operations are being combined and synergies are expected, recurring losses will clearly threaten the new group's operational existence as a going concern.

Falling ARPC
- ARPC, a key performance indicator, has fallen by more than 20% ((437-556/556 = 21.4%). This is likely to reflect falling tariffs in a competitive market.
- Although the number of customers has nearly doubled (increased by 96%), revenue has increased by only 55%. It seems unlikely that such a growth in customer base can be maintained, therefore the reduction in tariffs could result in falling revenues.
- Some (if not all) of the growth, is due to the acquisition of Xstatic. The fall in ARPC may indicate that Xstatic's ARPC (now absorbed into the enlarged Beeski group) is substantially less than that of Beeski. If Xstatic's tariffs were lower than Beeski's because it was offering a lower level of service it may be difficult for Beeski to increase them albeit for an enhanced service.

Sustaining growth
- Growth may not be sustainable as further expansion will incur significant costs and investment which must be financed.
- The significant costs expected to be incurred in upgrading networks may not be recouped if additional revenues are insufficient. Failure to maintain existing networks is likely to result in a loss of customers and market share.
- If Beeski's financial resources are insufficient to meet the operating losses it may need to issue equity and/or increase its debt. Possible adverse consequences of increasing indebtedness include:
    - high debt-service costs;
    - operating and financial restrictions being imposed by lenders;
    - difficulty in obtaining further finance in the future;
    - being unable to take advantage of business opportunities;
    - reduction in credit ratings.

Tutorial note: *Although there are relatively explicit pointers to the above business risks in the scenario, marks will also be awarded for other risks which are perhaps more implicit (as illustrated below).*

Countries of operation
- Operations have been expanded from European countries to India. Beeski's inexperience of economic and legal developments in India may impair the investment in MTbox.

Foreign exchange rates
- Beeski transacts business in several countries and foreign exchange rate fluctuations could have a material adverse affect on operating results.

Highly regulated market
- Network operations could be adversely affected by changes in the laws, regulations or government policies which regulate the industry.
- Difficulties in obtaining approvals for the erection and operation of transmitters could have an adverse effect on the extent, quality and capacity of Beeski's network coverage.
- Allegations of health risks (eg associated with radio waves from transmitter masts and mobile handsets) could reduce customer demand and increase exposure to potential litigation.

Tutorial note: *Candidates are not expected to have knowledge of industry-related complexities (eg of licensing, subsidies and network recharging) – however, appropriate marks would be awarded for comments on such business risks arising.*

(b)   Impact of acquisition on planning

Tutorial note: *Note that the context here is that of the principal auditor's planning of a group audit.*

Group structure
The new group structure must be ascertained to identify the entities that should be consolidated into the group financial statements of Beeski for the year ending 30 September 2006.

Materiality assessment
Preliminary materiality will be much higher, in monetary terms, than in the prior year. For example, if a % of revenue is a determinant of preliminary materiality, it will increase by 55% (based on estimate).

Tutorial note: *'Profit' is not a suitable criterion as group is loss-making.*

The materiality of each subsidiary should be assessed, in terms of the enlarged group as at the planning stage. For example, any subsidiary contributing more than 10% of the group's assets and revenue (but not result) is material and less than 5% (say) is not. This will identify, for example:
- those entities requiring an audit visit by the principal auditor; and
- those for which analytical procedures may suffice.

If MTbox is particularly material to the group, Ribi may plan (provisionally) to visit MTbox's auditors to discuss any problems shown to arise in their audit work summary (see group instructions below).

Goodwill arising
The audit plan should draw attention to the need to audit the amount of goodwill arising on the acquisitions and management's impairment test at the balance sheet date.

The assets and liabilities of Xstatic and MTbox, at fair value to the group, will be combined on a line-by-line basis and any goodwill arising recognised.

The calculation of the amount attributed to goodwill must be agreed to be the excess of the cost of the acquisition over the fair value of the identifiable assets and liabilities existing at the date of acquisition (Xstatic – November 2005, MTbox – August 2006).

Significant non-current assets such as properties are likely to have been independently valued prior to the acquisition. It may be appropriate to plan to place reliance on the work of quantity surveyors or other property valuers.

Group (related party) transactions and balances
A list of all the companies in the group (including any associated companies) should be included in group audit instructions to ensure that intra-group transactions and balances (and any unrealised profits and losses on transactions with associated companies) are identified for elimination on consolidation.

It should be confirmed at the planning stage that inter-company transactions are identified as such in the accounting systems of all Beeski companies and that inter-company balances are regularly reconciled. (Problems are likely to arise if new inter-company balances are not identified/reconciled. In particular, exchange differences are to be expected.)

On analytical procedures
Having brought in the operations of a group of companies (Xstatic) with similar activities may extend the scope of analytical procedures available. This could have the effect of increasing audit efficiency.

MTbox – on income statement
The effective date of the acquisition of MTbox may be so late in the financial year (only four to eight weeks, say, before the year end) that it is possible that its post-acquisition results are not material to the consolidated income statement.

Other auditors

Other auditors will include:
- any affiliates of Ribi in any of the countries in which Beeski (as combined with Xstatic) operates; and
- unrelated auditors (including those of MTbox).

Ribi will plan to use the work of MTbox's auditors who are Chartered Certified Accountants. Their competence and independence should be assessed (eg through information obtained from a questionnaire and evidence of their work).

A letter of introduction should be sent to the unrelated auditors, with Beeski's permission, as soon as possible (if not already done) requesting their co-operation in providing specified information within a given timescale.

Group instructions will need to be sent to affiliated and unrelated auditors containing:
- proforma statements;
- a list of group and associated companies;
- a statement of group accounting policies (see below);
- the timetable for the preparation of the group accounts (see below);
- a request for copies of management letters;
- an audit work summary questionnaire or checklist;
- contact details (of senior members of Ribi's audit team).

Accounting policies (Xstatic & MTbox)

Whilst it is likely that Xstatic has the same accounting policies as Beeski (because, as a competitor, it operates in the same jurisdictions) MTbox may have material accounting policies which do not comply with the rest of the group. Ribi may request that MTbox's auditors calculate the effect of any non-compliance with a group accounting policy for adjustment on consolidation.

Timetable

The timetable for the preparation of Beeski's consolidated financial statements should be agreed with management as soon as possible. Key dates should be planned for:
- agreement of inter-company balances and transactions;
- submission of proforma statements to Ribi;
- completion of the consolidation package;
- tax review of group accounts;
- completion of audit fieldwork by other auditors ;
- subsequent events review;
- final clearance on accounts of subsidiaries;
- Ribi's final clearance of consolidated financial statements.

Tutorial note: *The order of dates is illustrative rather than prescriptive.*

(c) 'Support letters'

Tutorial note: Although there are different types and uses of such letters (eg for registering a prospectus), the only reference to them in the P7 Syllabus and Study Guide is in the context of group audits.

Consolidated financial statements are prepared on a going concern basis when a group, as a single entity, is considered to be a going concern. However, the going concern basis may only be appropriate for certain separate legal entities (eg subsidiaries) because the parent undertaking (or a fellow subsidiary) is able and willing to provide support. Many banks routinely require a letter of reassurance from a parent company stating that the parent would financially or otherwise support a subsidiary with cashflow or other operational problems.

As audit evidence:
- Formal confirmation of the support will be sought in the form of a letter of support or 'comfort letter' confirming the parent company's intention to keep the subsidiary in operational existence (or otherwise meet its obligations as they fall due).
- The letter of support should normally be approved by a board minute of the parent company (or by an individual with authority granted by a board minute).
- The ability of the parent to support the company should also be confirmed, for example, by examining the group's cash flow forecast.
- The period of support may be limited (eg to one year from the date of the letter or until the date of disposal of the subsidiary). Sufficient other evidence concerning the appropriateness of the going concern assumption must therefore be obtained where a later repayment of material debts is foreseen.
- The fact of support and the period to which it is restricted should be noted in the financial statements of the subsidiary.

(d) 'Horizontal groups'

In general, the scope of a statutory audit should be as necessary to form an audit opinion (ie unlimited) and the nature, timing and extent of audit procedures (ie the audit work undertaken) should be as necessary to implement the overall audit plan.

Horizontal groups of entities under common control were a significant feature of the Enron and Parmalat business empires. Such business empires increase audit risk as fraud is often disguised through labyrinthine group structures. Hence auditors need to understand and confirm the economic purpose of entities within business empires (as well as special purpose entities (SPEs) and non-trading entities).

Horizontal groups fall outside the requirement for the preparation of group accounts so it is not only finance that is off-balance sheet when controlled entities are excluded from consolidated financial statements.

In the absence of consolidated financial statements, users of accounts of entities in horizontal groups have to rely on the disclosure of related party transactions and control relationships for information about transactions and arrangements with other group entities. Difficulties faced by auditors include:

- failing to detect related party transactions and control relationships;
- not understanding the substance of transactions with entities under common control;
- excessively creative tax planning;
- the implications of transfer pricing (eg failure to identify profits unrealised at the business empire level);
- a lack of access to relevant confidential information held by others;
- relying on representations made in good faith by those whom the auditors believe manage the company when control rests elsewhere.

Audit work is inevitably increased if an auditor is put upon inquiry to investigate dubious transactions and arrangements. However, the complexity of business empires across multiple jurisdictions with different auditors may deter auditors from liaising with other auditors (especially where legal or professional confidentiality considerations prevent this).

2   Efex Engineering Co

(a)   'Forensic auditing'

Definition
The process of gathering, analysing and reporting on data, in a pre-defined context, for the purpose of finding facts and/or evidence in the context of financial/legal disputes and/or irregularities and giving preventative advice in this area.

Tutorial note: *Credit will be awarded for any definition that covers the key components: An 'audit' is an examination (eg of financial statements) and 'forensic' means used in connection with courts of law. Forensic auditing may be defined as 'applying auditing skills to situations that have legal consequences'.*

Application to fraud investigation
As a fraud is an example of an irregularity, a fraud investigation is just one of many applications of forensic auditing, where evidence about a suspected fraud is gathered that could be presented in a court of law. The pre-defined objective of a fraud audit is:

- to prove or disprove the suspicions;
  and, if proven,
- to identify the persons involved;
- to provide evidence for appropriate action, possibly criminal proceedings.

As well as being 'reactive', forensic auditing can be 'proactive' by being preventative. That is, the techniques of forensic auditing can be used to identify risks of fraud with a view to managing those risks to an acceptable level.

(b)   Prior to commencement of the investigation

Tutorial note: *The phrase 'matters … and … procedures' is used to encourage candidates to think more widely than just 'considerations' or just 'actions. A possible structure for this answer could be under two separate headings: 'matters' and 'procedures'. However, many matters could be phrased as procedures (and vice versa). For example, a matter would be 'the terms of reference' and the procedure 'to obtain and clarify the TOR'. Candidates should note that a tabular/columnar answer is NOT appropriate as any attempt to match matters and procedures is likely to result in repetition of the same point (differently phrased).*

- Discuss the assignment with Xzibit's management to determine the purpose, nature and scope of the investigation. In particular, discuss whether any irregularity (theft/fraud) is suspected and, if so, whether evidence gathered will be used:
  - in criminal proceedings;
  - in support of an insurance claim.
- Obtain clarification of terms of reference (TOR) in writing from Xzibit's management.
- The TOR should give the investigating team full access to any aspect of Efex Engineering's operations relevant to their investigation.
- Investigation will involve consideration of:
  - possible understatement of inventory value at 30 June 2006;
  - high material consumption for the quarter ended 30 June 2006.
- Determine the level of experience of staff required for the investigation and the number of staff of each grade.
- The availability of suitable staff may affect the proposed start of the investigation. Alternatively, the timing of other assignments may have to be rescheduled to allow this investigation to be started immediately.
- Xzibit's management will presumably want the investigation completed before the next inventory count (at 30 September 2006) to know if the findings have any implications for the conduct of the count and the determination of year-end inventory.
- The investigation may have been commissioned to give credence to the period-end's accounts. The investigation may therefore be of the nature of a limited audit.

- Produce a budget of expected hours, grades of staff and costs. Agree the anticipated investigative fee with Xzibit's management.
- The depth of the investigation will depend on matters such as:
  - the extent of reliance expected to be placed on the investigation report;
  - whether the report is for Xzibit's internal use only or is it likely to be circulated to bankers and/or shareholders.
- The type of assurance (eg 'negative', reasonable) is likely to have a bearing on:
  - any caveats in the report;
  - the level of risk/potential liability for any errors in conclusions given in the final report;
  - the level of necessary detailed testing required (even if an audit is not requested).
- An engagement letter must be drafted and Xzibit's management must agree to its terms in writing before any investigative work can begin. The letter of engagement should include:
  - details of work to be carried out;
  - likely timescale;
  - basis of determining fee;
  - the reliance that can be placed on the final report and results of the investigation;
  - the extent of responsibilities agreed;
  - any indemnity agreed;
  - the information to be supplied as a basis for the investigation; and
  - any areas specifically excluded.
- Assess the appropriateness of an exclusion clause; for example: 'CONFIDENTIAL – this report has been prepared for the private use of Xzibit only and on condition that it must not be disclosed to any other person without the written consent of the preparing accountant'.

(c) (i) Inventory undervaluation – matters to consider

Physical inventory count
- Inventory will be undervalued at 30 June 2006 if all inventory is not counted. The investigation should consider the adequacy of quarterly physical count procedures. For example, whether or not:
  - all items are marked when counted;
  - management carries out test checks;
  - stocksheets are pre-numbered and prepared in ink;
  - a complete set of stocksheets is available covering all categories of inventory;
  - Efex Engineering's management uses the stocksheets to produce the inventory value.

Tutorial note: *Inventory will not be undervalued if it does not exist (eg because it has been stolen). Theft would be reflected in higher than normal materials consumption (see (d)).*

Cutoff
- Inventory will be undervalued at 30 June 2006 if:
  - any goods set aside for sale in July were excluded from the count;
  - a liability was recognised at 30 June 2006 for goods that were excluded from inventory (eg in transit from the supplier);
  - production did not cease during the physical count and raw materials being transferred between warehouse and production were omitted from inventory.

Scrap materials
- Inventory will be undervalued if any scrap from materials used in production that has a value (eg because it can be recycled) is excluded. Inventory may be undervalued compared with the previous quarter if there is any change in Efex's scrap/wastage policy (eg if previously it was valued in inventory but now it is excluded).
- If production problems increased wastage in the last period this would account for the lower value of inventory and higher materials consumption.

(ii) Tests to quantify the amount of any undervaluation

Tutorial note: *Any tests directed at quantifying an overstatement and/or instead of understatement will not be awarded credit.*

Physical count
- Inspect the warehouse/factory areas to identify high value inventory items and confirm their inclusion on the stocksheets at 30 June 2006 (or otherwise vouch to a delivery note raised after that date).
- Recast all additions and recalculate all extensions on the stocksheets to confirm that there have been no omissions, transposition errors or other computational discrepancies that would account for an undervaluation.

Cutoff
- Ascertain the last delivery notes and despatch notes recorded prior to counting and trace to purchase/sales invoices to confirm that an accurate cutoff has been applied in determining the results for the quarter to 30 June 2006 and the inventory balance at that date.
- Trace any large value purchases in June to the 30 June stocksheets. If not on the stocksheets inquire of management whether they are included in production (or sold). Verify by tracing to production records, goods despatch notes, etc.

Analytical procedures

- Compare large volume/high value items on stocksheets at 31 March with those at 30 June to identify any that might have been omitted (or substantially decreased). Inquire of management if any items so identified have been completely used in production (but not replaced), scrapped or excluded from the count (eg if obsolete). Any inventory excluded should be counted and quantified.
- Compare inventory categories for 30 June against previous quarters. Inventory value at 30 June is 10% less than at 31 March, though revenue is 28% higher. An increase in inventory might have been expected to support increased revenue if there is a general increase in trading activity. (Alternatively, a decrease in inventory may reflect difficulties in obtaining supplies/maintaining inventory levels if demand has increased).

Scrap materials

- Make inquiries of Efex Engineering's warehouse and production officials regarding the company's scrap/wastage policy and any records that are kept.
- Review production records on a month-on-month basis and discuss with the factory manager whether any production problems have increased wastage in the quarter to 30 June 2006.

Pricing test

- Raw materials – select a sample of high value items from the 31 March 2006 inventory valuation and confirm that any unit price reductions as shown by the 30 June 2006 valuation are appropriate (eg vouch lower unit price to recent purchase invoices or write down to net realisable value).
- WIP and finished goods – agree a sample of unit prices to costing records (eg batch costings). Recalculate unit prices on a sample basis and vouch make-up to invoices/payroll records, etc.

(d) (i) High materials consumption – matters to consider

Tutorial note: *Materials consumption has increased from 70% of revenue to 78%. There could be valid business reasons for this (eg there could be an abnormally high level of wastage) or accounting errors that result in overstatement of materials.*

Cutoff

- Raw material purchases: Materials consumption will be overstated if goods delivered after the quarter-end have been included (incorrectly) in purchases to 30 June 2006 although excluded (correctly) from the June count.
- Revenue: Materials consumption will be overstated as a percentage of revenue if revenue is understated (eg if goods sold before 30 June 2006 are recorded in the next quarter).

Losses

- Materials consumption will be higher than normal if there is an abnormally high level of raw materials scrapped or wasted during the production process. This could be due to inferior quality raw materials or technical problems with the manufacturing process.
- Materials consumption will also be overstated if raw materials recorded as being used in production are stolen.

Obsolete or redundant inventory

- Materials consumption will appear higher if inventory at 30 June 2006 is lower. For example, if slow-moving, damaged or obsolete inventory identified at the count was excluded or written-down (although included in the previous quarter's inventory valuation).

Individual contracts

- Materials consumption will be higher if the increase in revenue is attributable to a small number of large contracts for which substantial discounts have been negotiated.
- Materials consumption will be higher if the cost of materials on customers' specifications has been underestimated in the determination of selling prices.

Purchasing

- Materials consumed will increase if Efex Engineering has changed to a more expensive supplier in the quarter to 30 June 2006.

(ii) High materials consumption – tests

Cutoff

- Purchases: Select a sample of invoices included in purchases to 30 June 2006 and match to goods received notes to confirm receipt at 30 June 2006 and hence inclusion in inventory at that date.
- Revenue: Inspect despatch notes raised on or shortly before 30 June 2006 and trace goods sold to invoices raised on or before 30 June 2006.

Scrap

- Inquire of production/factory and warehouse officials the reasons for scrap and wastage and how normal levels are determined.
- Inspect records of materials wastage and confirm the authorisation for scrapping materials and/or reissuing replacement materials to the production process.
- Physically inspect scrap, if any, to confirm that its condition renders it unsuitable for manufacture (and hence confirm its exclusion from inventory at 30 June 2006).
- Review credit notes received after 30 June 2006 to identify materials returned (eg of inferior quality).

Obsolete or redundant inventory
- Inspect the stocksheets at 30 June 2006 for goods identified as obsolete, damaged, etc and compare with the level (and value) of the same items identified at the previous quarter's count.

Individual contracts
- Compare discounts given on new contracts with normal discount levels and confirm the authority of the person approving discounts.
- Calculate actual material cost as a percentage of revenue on individual major contracts and compare with the 70% benchmark.

Tests of controls
- Purchases: Inspect goods received notes to confirm that raw materials are being checked for quality and quantity upon receipt. Inspect invoices recorded to confirm that goods have been received (as evidenced by a goods received note).
    - Review goods returns recorded on pre-numbered goods return notes and confirm matched to subsequent credit notes received.
    - Observe gate controls and other physical security over inventory and review the segregation of duties that seek to prevent or detect theft of inventory.
- Sales: Review goods despatch notes and confirm matching to sales invoices that have been raised promptly and recorded on a timely basis.
- Sales returns: Review credit notes for authorisation and matching to goods returns notes.

3   Ingot & Co

Tutorial note: *Note that as well as the 20 marks for addressing five matters, there are also 'pervasive' issues which can be brought out as overall conclusions on QC policies and procedures at the level of the audit firm. Remember, it is a professional skill to recognise causes and effects or other linkages between the findings.*

(a)   Analytical procedures

Applying analytical procedures at the planning stage, to assist in understanding the business and in identifying areas of potential risk, is an auditing standard and therefore mandatory. Analytical procedures should have been performed (eg comparing the draft accounts to 30 June 2006 with prior year financial statements).

The audit senior may have insufficient knowledge of the waste management service industry to assess potential risks. In particular, Argenta may be exposed to risks resulting in unrecorded liabilities (both actual and contingent) if claims are made against the company in respect of breaches of health and safety legislation or its licence to operate.

The audit has been inadequately planned and audit work has commenced before the audit plan has been reviewed by the AIC. The audit may not be carried out effectively and efficiently.

Tutorial note: *An alternative stance might be that the audit senior did in fact perform the analytical procedures but was careless in completion of the audit planning checklist. This would have quality control implications in that the checklists cannot be relied on by the reviewer.*

(b)   AIC's assignments

The senior has performed work on tangible non-current assets which is a less material (17% of total assets) audit area than trade receivables (58% of total assets) which has been assigned to an audit trainee. Non-current assets also appear to be a lower risk audit area than trade receivables because the carrying amount of non-current assets is comparable with the prior year ($0.6m at both year ends), whereas trade receivables have more than doubled (from $0.9m to $2.1m). This corroborates the implications of (a).

The audit is being inadequately supervised as work has been delegated inappropriately. It appears that Ingot & Co does not have sufficient audit staff with relevant competencies to meet its supervisory needs.

(c)   Direct confirmation

It is usual for direct confirmation of customers' balances to be obtained where trade receivables are material and it is reasonable to expect customers to respond. However, it is already six weeks after the balance sheet date and, although trade receivables are clearly material (58% of total assets), an alternative approach may be more efficient (and cost effective). For example, monitoring of after-date cash will provide evidence about the collectibility of receivables (as well as corroborate their existence).

Tutorial note: *Ingot was only appointed in July and the audit started two weeks ago on 1 August.*

This may be a further consequence of the audit having been inadequately planned.

Alternatively, supervision and monitoring of the audit may be inadequate. For example, if the audit trainee did not understand the alternative approach but mechanically followed circularisation procedures.

(d) Inventory

Inventory is relatively immaterial from an auditing perspective, being less than 2.4% of total assets (2005 – 2.1%). Although it therefore seems appropriate that a trainee should be auditing it, the audit approach appears highly inefficient. Such in-depth testing (of controls and details) on an immaterial area provides further evidence that the audit has been inadequately planned.

Again, it may be due to a lack of monitoring of a mechanical approach being adopted by a trainee.

This also demonstrates a lack of knowledge and understanding about Argenta's business – the company has no stock-in-trade, only consumables used in the supply of services.

(e) Prior period error

It appears that the subsequent events review was inadequate in that an adjusting event (the out-of-court settlement) was not taken account of. This resulted in material error in the financial statements to 30 June 2005 as the provision for $0.45 million which should have been made represented 12.5% of total assets at that date.

The AIC has not taken any account of the implications of this evidence for the conduct of the audit as the overall audit strategy and audit plan should have been reconsidered. For example:
- the oversight in the subsequent events review may not have been isolated and there could be other errors in opening balances (eg if an impairment was not recognised);
- there may be doubts about the reliability of managements' representations if it confirmed the litigation to be pending and/or asserted that there were no post balance sheet events to be taken account of.

The error has implications for the quality of the prior period's audit that may now require that additional work be carried out on opening balances and comparatives.

As the matter is material it warrants a prior period adjustment (IAS 8 *Accounting Policies, Changes in Accounting Estimates and Errors*). If this is not made Argenta's financial statements for the year ended 30 June 2006 will be materially misstated with respect to the current year and comparatives – because the expense of the out-of-court settlement should be attributed to the prior period and not to the current year's net profit or loss.

The need for additional work may have a consequential effect on the current year's time/fee/staff budgets.

The error should have been brought to the attention of Argenta's management when it was discovered, so that a prior year adjustment could be made. If the AIC did not feel competent to raise the matter with the client he should have discussed it immediately with the audit manager and not merely left it as a file note.

QC policies procedures at audit firm level/Conclusions

That the audit is not being conducted in accordance with ISAs (eg 300 *Planning an Audit of Financial Statements*, 315 *Understanding the Entity and Its Environment and Assessing the Risks of Material Misstatement* and 520 *Analytical Procedures*) means that Ingot's quality control policies and procedures are not established and/or are not being communicated to personnel.

That audit work is being assigned to personnel with insufficient technical training and proficiency indicates weaknesses in procedures for hiring and/or training of personnel.

That there is insufficient direction, supervision and review of work at all levels to provide reasonable assurance that audit work is of an acceptable standard suggests a lack of resources.

Procedures for the acceptance of clients appear to be inadequate as the audit is being conducted so inefficiently (ie audit work is inappropriate and/or not cost-effective). In deciding whether or not to accept the audit of Argenta, Ingot should have considered whether it had the ability to serve the client properly. The partner responsible for accepting the engagement does not appear to have evaluated the firm's (lack of) knowledge of the industry.

The staffing of the audit of Argenta should be reviewed and a more experienced person assigned to its completion and overall review.

4 Axis & Co

(a) Mantis Co

If a letter of support had **not** been received, then a qualified opinion on the grounds of **disagreement** (about the appropriateness of the going concern presumption) would be required. As the matter is likely to be pervasive an adverse opinion would be appropriate (ISA 570 *Going Concern*).

However, the company has received a letter of support from its parent company to the effect that it will enable Mantis to continue trading. If this evidence (together with other evidence such as management's representations) is considered to be **sufficient** to support the appropriateness of the going concern presumption, a qualified opinion will not be necessary provided that the support is **adequately** disclosed in a note to the financial statements. If the evidence is sufficient, but the disclosure **inadequate**, an 'except for' opinion would be required.

If the letter of support does not provide sufficient evidence (eg if there are doubts about Cube's ability to provide the required finance), the significant uncertainty arising should be disclosed in an emphasis of matter paragraph in the auditor's report. This would not result in a qualified opinion (unless the disclosure relating to it were considered inadequate).

Conclusion
The audit senior's proposal is unsuitable. The auditor's report should be unmodified (assuming that disclosures are adequate).

(b)   Lorenze Co

In order to show fair presentation, in all material respects, the financial statements of an entity should contain not only accurate figures, but also sufficient disclosure in relation to those figures in order to allow the user to understand them. As required by IAS 1 *Presentation of Financial Statements*, items should be treated on a consistent basis from year to year. If this is not the case, then any change, together with the financial impact of this change, will need to be disclosed in a note to the financial statements.

Failure to disclose the reasons for change in policy (ie to comply with IFRS 3 *Business Combinations*) and its effects (eg the lack of annual amortisation) means that the financial statements do not comply with IAS 8 *Accounting Policies, Changes in Accounting Estimates and Errors*. A qualified opinion is therefore required on the grounds of disagreement on disclosure (IAS 1 and IAS 8). Assuming the matter to be material (but clearly not pervasive), an 'except for' opinion should be expressed.

The main purpose of an emphasis of matter paragraph is to describe a matter of significant uncertainty which has been taken into account in forming the audit opinion – it does not qualify that opinion. Such a paragraph highlights a note in the financial statements that more extensively discusses the matter. An emphasis of matter paragraph cannot therefore be used to 'make good' a lack of disclosure.

IFRS 3 also requires disclosure of a reconciliation of the carrying amount of goodwill at the beginning and end of the year. This should show no movement for the year ended 30 June 2006.

Conclusion
The audit senior's proposal is unsuitable. Unless all aspects of the change (including reason and effect) are adequately disclosed an 'except for' qualification will be required on the grounds of disagreement.

(c)   Abrupt Co

The audit opinion states whether the financial statements:
-   are presented fairly, in all material respects (or give a true and fair view) in accordance with the financial reporting framework; and
-   comply with statutory requirements (where appropriate).

The directors' report is not a part of financial statements prepared under International Financial Reporting Standards (IFRS). However, auditors have a professional responsibility to read other information in documents containing audited financial statements (eg the directors' report in an annual report) to identify material inconsistencies with the audited financial statements (or material misstatements of fact).

A material inconsistency exists when other information contradicts information contained in the audited financial statements. Clearly, 'major' is inconsistent with 1.6%.

If the inconsistency is resolved (eg because the directors' report is corrected to state '... major part of **other** income...') an unmodified auditor's report will be given.

If the inconsistency is not resolved, the audit opinion on the financial statements cannot be qualified (because the inconsistency is in the directors' report). In this case, an emphasis of matter paragraph may be used to report on this matter that does not affect the financial statements (ISA 700 *The Independent Auditor's Report on a Complete Set of General Purpose Financial Statements*).

Conclusion
An unqualified opinion on the financial statements is appropriate. If, however, the inconsistency is not resolved, it should be reported in a separate emphasis of matter paragraph, after the opinion paragraph.

(d)   Jingle Co

The cash transfer is a non-adjusting post balance sheet event. It indicates that Bell was trading after the balance sheet date. However, that does not preclude Bell having commenced trading before the year end.

The finance director's oral representation is wholly insufficient evidence with regard to the existence (or otherwise) of Bell at 30 June 2006. If it existed at the balance sheet date its financial statements should have been consolidated (unless immaterial).

The lack of evidence that might reasonably be expected to be available (eg legal papers, registration payments, etc) suggests a limitation on the scope of the audit. If such evidence has been sought but not obtained then the limitation is imposed by the entity (rather than by circumstances).

Whilst the transaction itself may be immaterial, the information concerning the existence of Bell may be material to users and should therefore be disclosed (as a non-adjusting event). The absence of such disclosure, if the auditor considered necessary, would result in a qualified 'except for', opinion.

Tutorial note: Any matter that is considered sufficiently material to be worthy of disclosure as a non-adjusting event must result in such a qualified opinion if the disclosure is not made.

If Bell existed at the balance sheet date and had material assets and liabilities then its non-consolidation would have a pervasive effect. This would warrant an adverse opinion.

Also, the nature of the limitation (being imposed by the entity) could have a pervasive effect if the auditor is suspicious that other audit evidence has been withheld. In this case the auditor should disclaim an opinion.

Conclusion
Additional evidence is required to support an unqualified opinion. If this were not forthcoming a disclaimer may be appropriate.

5   Dedza & Co

(a)   Need for ethical guidance

- Accountants (firms and individuals) working in a country that criminalises money laundering are required to comply with anti-money laundering legislation and failure to do so can lead to severe penalties. Guidance is needed because:
    - legal requirements are onerous;
    - money laundering is widely defined; and
    - accountants may otherwise be used, unwittingly, to launder criminal funds.
- Accountants need ethical guidance on matters where there is conflict between legal responsibilities and professional responsibilities. In particular, professional accountants are bound by a duty of confidentiality to their clients. Guidance is needed to explain:
    - how statutory provisions give protection against criminal action for members in respect of their confidentiality requirements;
    - when client confidentiality over-ride provisions are available.
- Further guidance is needed to explain the interaction between accountants responsibilities to report money laundering offences and other reporting responsibilities, for example:
    - reporting to regulators;
    - auditor's reports on financial statements (ISA 700);
    - reports to those charged with governance (ISA 260);
    - reporting misconduct by members of the same body.
- Professional accountants are required to communicate with each other when there is a change in professional appointment (ie 'professional etiquette'). Additional ethical guidance is needed on how to respond to a 'clearance' letter where a report of suspicion has been made (or is being contemplated) in respect of the client in question.

    Tutorial note: Although the term 'professional clearance' is widely used, remember that there is no 'clearance' that the incumbent accountant can give or withhold.

- Ethical guidance is needed to make accountants working in countries that do not criminalise money laundering aware of how anti-money laundering legislation may nevertheless affect them. Such accountants may commit an offence if, for example, they conduct limited assignments or have meetings in a country having anti-money laundering legislation (eg UK, Ireland, Singapore, Australia and the United States).

(b)   Annual reviews of existing clients

(i)   Tax investigation
- Kora is a relatively new client. Before accepting the assignment(s) Dedza should have carried out customer due diligence (CDD). Dedza should therefore have a sufficient knowledge and understanding of Kora to be aware of any suspicions that the tax authority might have.
- As the investigation has come as a surprise it is possible that, for example:
    - the tax authorities suspicions are unfounded;
    - Dedza has failed to recognise suspicious circumstances.

Tutorial note: In either case, Dedza should now review relevant procedures.

- Dedza should review any communication from the predecessor auditor obtained in response to its 'professional inquiry' (for any professional reasons why the appointment should not be accepted).
- A quality control for new audits is that the audit opinion should be subject to a second partner review before it is issued. It should be considered now whether or not such a review took place. If it did, then it should be sufficiently well documented to evidence that the review was thorough and not a mere formality.
- Criminal property includes the proceeds of tax evasion. If Kora is found to be guilty of under-declaring income that is a money laundering offence.
- Dedza's reputational risk will be increased if implicated because it knew (or ought to have known) about Kora's activities. (Dedza may also be liable if found to have been negligent in failing to detect any material misstatement arising in the 31 March 2006 financial statements.)
- Kora's audit working paper files and tax returns should be reviewed for any suspicion of fraud being committed by Kora or error overlooked by Dedza. Tax advisory work should have been undertaken and/or reviewed by a manager/partner not involved in the audit work.

- As tax advisor, Dedza could soon be making disclosures of misstatements to the tax authorities on behalf of Kora. Dedza should encourage Kora to make necessary disclosure voluntarily.
- If Dedza finds reasonable grounds to know or suspect that potential disclosures to the tax authorities relate to criminal conduct, then a suspicious transaction report (STR) should be made to the financial intelligence unit (FIU) also.

Tutorial note: *Though not the main issue credit will be awarded for other ethical issues such as the potential self-interest/ self-review threat arising from the provision of other services.*

(ii) Advice on payments
- As compared with (i) there is no obvious tax issue. Xalam is not overstating expenditure for tax purposes.
- Dedza should consider its knowledge of import duties, etc in the destination country before recommending a course of action to Xalam.
- The payments being made for security consultancy services may amount to a bribe. Corruption and bribery (and extortion) are designated categories of money laundering offence under The Forty Recommendations of the Financial Action Task Force on Money Laundering (FATF).

If this is a bribe:
- Xalam clearly benefits from the payments as it receives income from the contract with the major customer. This is criminal property and possession of it is a money laundering offence
- Dedza should consider the seriousness of the disclosure made by the chief executive in the context of domestic law.
- Dedza may be guilty of a money laundering offence if the matter is not reported. If a report to the FIU is considered necessary Dedza should encourage Xalam to make voluntary disclosure. If Xalam does not, Dedza will not be in breach of client confidentiality for reporting knowledge of a suspicious transaction.

Tutorial note: *Making a report takes precedence over client confidentiality.*

(iii) Financial advisor
- Customer due diligence (CDD) and record-keeping measures apply to designated non-financial businesses and professions (such as Dedza) who prepare for or carry out certain transactions on behalf of their clients.
- Esau is a 'politically exposed person' ('PEP' ie an individual who is to be entrusted with prominent public functions in a foreign country).
- Dedza's business relationships with Pholey therefore involve reputational risks similar to those with Esau. In addition to performing normal due diligence measures Dedza should:
  - have risk management systems to have determined that Esau is a PEP;
  - obtain senior partner approval for maintaining business relationships with such customers;
  - take reasonable measures to establish the source of wealth and source of funds;
  - conduct enhanced ongoing monitoring of the business relationship.
- Dedza can choose to decline to act for Pholey and/or Esau (if asked).
- If the business relationship is to be continued senior partner approval should be obtained for any transactions carried out on Pholey's behalf in future.

Tutorial note: *The Pholey family is not described as an audit client therefore no familiarity threat arises in relation to an audit (the family may not have any involvement in entities requiring an audit).*

Marks must only be awarded for points relevant to answering the question set. Unless otherwise indicated, marks should not be awarded for restating the facts of the question.

For most questions you should award ½ a mark for a point of knowledge, increased to 1 mark for the application of knowledge and 1½ marks for a point demonstrating the higher skill expected in the professional level.

The model answers are indicative of the breadth and depth of possible answer points, but may not be not exhaustive.

Most questions require candidates to include a range of points in their answer, so an answer which concentrates on one (or a few) points should normally be expected to result in a lower mark than one which considers a range of points.

In awarding the mark to each part of the question you should consider whether the standard of the candidate's answer is above or below the pass grade. If it is of pass standard it should be awarded a mark of 50% or more, and it should be awarded less than 50% if it does not achieve a pass standard. When you have completed marking a question you should consider whether the total mark is fair.

Finally, in awarding the mark to each question you should consider the pass/fail assessment criteria:
- Adequacy of answer plan
- Structured answer
- Inclusion of significant facts
- Information given not repeated
- Relevant content
- Inferences made
- Commercial awareness
- Higher skills demonstrated
- Professional commentary

In general, the more of these you can assess in the affirmative, the higher the mark awarded should be. If you decide the total mark is not a proper reflection of the standard of the candidate's answer, you should review the candidate's answer and adjust marks, where appropriate, so that the total mark awarded is fair.

1 (a) Principal business risks
Generally ½ *mark* each risk identified and up to 1½ *marks* for a (good) description

max 9

> **Ideas**
> - technological obsolescence (communications industry)
> - competition
> - integration (operations, cultures)
> - operating losses
> - falling ARPC (key performance indicator)
> - sustaining growth
> - exchange rate fluctuations
> - market regulation

(b) Impact on planning of audit
Generally 1 *mark* each point contributing to an explanation to a maximum 3 marks each impact

max 10

> **Impact ideas**
> - group structure
> - materiality assessment (NOT on profit)
> - goodwill arising (amount/amortisation)
> - group (related party) transactions and balances
> - on analytical procedures
> - MTbox on income statement
> - other auditors
>   - ACCA/competent/independent
>   - introductory/co-operation letter
> - group instructions
> - accounting policies (Xstatic & MTbox)
> - timetable
> Note: Two professional marks are included

(c) 'Support letters'
Generally 1 *mark* each point contributing to an explanation of their role as audit evidence

max 6

> **Ideas**
> - Consolidated FS vs entity FS
> - Bank requirement/routine
> - Going concern basis
> - Support by whom?
> - For how long?
> - Formal confirmation of *intent*
> - Approved by board
> - Need for evidence of *ability*

(d) 'Horizontal groups'
Generally 1 *mark* each point contributing to a discussion

max 5

> **Ideas**
> - 'business empires'
> - development (as off-balance sheet vehicles)
> - increased audit risk – related party/confidentiality issues
> - complex fraud risk factor
> - reliance on management representation

30

2 (a) 'Forensic auditing'

Generally *1 – ½ mark* each point

> **Ideas**
> Definition
> - eg of Institut des Fraud Auditeurs de Fraude (IFA-IAF)
> - audit (examination) + forensic (legal)
>
> Application to fraud investigation
> - irregular nature of fraud
> - objective(s)
> - reactive vs proactive (preventative)

(b) Prior to commencing investigation

Generally *1 mark* each matter/procedure

> **Ideas**
> Matters
> - Terms of reference (obtaining is a procedure)
> - Purpose/scope of investigation
>   - possible understatement of inventory at 30/6
>   - high material consumption in quarter to 30/6
>   - to give credence to y/e amount (next quarter to 30/9)
> - Scope of access to records relevant to the investigation (any restriction?)/Information to be supplied
> - Staffing – level/experience/number/availability/other client commitments
> - Degree of reliance to be placed on report
>
> By whom? – insurer?
> - Timeframe – before next (= annual) physical count
> - Form of report required – Any caveats?
>
> Procedures
> - Discuss assignment with directors – responsibilities etc
> - Obtain engagement letter (terms are a matter)
> - Agree investigative fee
> Note: two professional marks are included

Tutorial note: There is no maximum to be awarded for each of matters and procedures as answer points about matters may be constructed as procedures (and vice versa). Marks should be awarded for either/or (not both).

(c) Inventory undervaluation

Generally up to *1½ marks* each matter explained
1 mark each test

> **Ideas**
> (i) matters
> - omission from count
> - cut-off
> - scrap/waste etc
>
> (ii) tests
> - physical inspection
> - arithmetic checks
> - cut-off tests
> - analytical procedures
> - tests on production records/pricing

Tutorial note: Tests must address *under*statement of stock at 30 June.

(d) **High materials consumption**
Generally up to *1½ marks* each matter explained
1 mark each test

> **Ideas**
> (i) matters
> - cut-off
> - losses
> - obsolescence etc
> - major contracts
> - change of supplier
>
> (ii) tests
> - physical inspection
> - arithmetic checks
> - cut-off tests
> - tests of control

Tutorial note: Matters must address *over*statement of materials consumption in the quarter to 30 June.

3 **Implications of findings**
Generally up to *1½ marks* each (good) implication

> **Specific finding ideas**
> - relevant ISAs
>   - (a) APs mandatory at planning stage (520)
>   - (e) subsequent events (560)
> - materiality (ISA 320)
>   - (b) non-current assets 17%
>   - (c) receivables 58%
>   - (d) inventory 2.4%
>   - (e) prior period error 12.5%
> - inappropriate procedures?
>   inventory 'roll back' (immaterial)
> - inappropriate timing
>   external confirmations (ISA 505) – too late?
>
> **QC at audit firm level ideas/Conclusions**
> - professional behaviour
> - skills and competence
> - assignment/delegation
> - consultation
> - acceptance of clients
> - monitoring

(a)	max 4
(b)	max 4
(c)	max 4
(d)	max 3
(e)	max 5
Professional skills	max 4
	Max 20

4 Auditors' reports proposals

Generally *1 mark* each comment on suitability and *1 mark* each conclusion (alternative, if any)

Ideas

(a) Going concern (ISA 570 reporting implications)

(b) Change in accounting policy – inadequate disclosure

(c) 'Other information' (ISA 720)

(b) Subsequent event (ISA 560)

- Disagreement vs limitation
- Material vs pervasive
- Statutory/professional requirements
- Relevant IFRSs (IASs 1, 8, 36, IFRS 3)
- Disclosure (adequate?) ==> disagreement
- Evidence (sufficient?) ==> limitation
- Validity of senior's argument/justification
- Alternative proposal ==> Conclusion

(a)	max 5
(b)	max 6
(c)	max 4
(d)	max 5
	20

5   **(a)**   **Need for ethical guidance for accountants**
Generally *1 mark* a point up to   max 5

> **Ideas (illustrative)**
> * Legal responsibilities
> * Risk of offence
> * Confidentiality
> * Other reporting responsibilities
> * Professional etiquette
> * Accountants working in other jurisdictions

(b)   **Ethical and other professional issues**
Generally ½ *mark* each issue identified + *1 mark* each comment/action

> **Ideas**
> (i)   Tax investigation
> * new client (relatively) – CDD
> * 'professional etiquette' – change in professional appointment
> * quality control eg second review
> * criminal property includes proceeds of tax evasion
> * money laundering offence?
> * suspicion of fraud (intent) vs error in incorrect tax returns
> * disclosure by Dedza vs voluntary (confidentiality)
> * need for STR
>
> (ii)   Advice on payments
> * not a tax issue
> * corruption and bribery/extortion – designated categories of offence
> * clear intent
> * seriousness in context of domestic laws
> * need to report to FIU?
>
> (iii) Financial advisor
> * designated non-financial profession
> * customer due diligence/record keeping
> * politically exposed person (PEP)
> * reputational risk
> * additional measures
> * refusal to act

(a)	max 7
(b)	max 4
(c)	max 4
	15
	20

Professional Level – Options Module

Advanced Audit and Assurance (International)

Monday 2 June 2014

Paper P7 (INT)

Time allowed
Reading and planning: 15 minutes
Writing: 3 hours

This paper is divided into two sections:

Section A – BOTH questions are compulsory and MUST be attempted

Section B – TWO questions ONLY to be attempted

Do NOT open this paper until instructed by the supervisor.
During reading and planning time only the question paper may
be annotated. You must NOT write in your answer booklet until
instructed by the supervisor.
This question paper must not be removed from the examination hall.

The Association of Chartered Certified Accountants

This is a blank page.
The question paper begins on page 3.

Section A – BOTH questions are compulsory and MUST be attempted

1   You are a manager in Dando & Co, a firm of Chartered Certified Accountants responsible for the audit of the Adams Group. Your firm was appointed as auditor in January 2014, and the audit engagement partner, Joss Dylan, has sent you the following email:

To: Audit manager

From: Joss Dylan

Regarding: Adams Group audit planning

Hello

I need you to begin planning the audit of the Adams Group (the Group). As you know, we have been appointed to audit the Group financial statements, and we have also been appointed to audit the financial statements of the parent company and of all subsidiaries of the Group except for an overseas subsidiary, Lynott Co, which is audited by a local firm, Clapton & Co. All components of the Group have the same year end of 31 May, report under IFRS and in the same currency.

I have provided you with some information about the Group's general background and activities, and extracts from the draft financial statements. Using this information, you are required to:

(a) (i) Evaluate the audit risks to be considered in planning the audit of the Group and;   (18 marks)

   (ii) Identify and explain any additional information which would be relevant to your evaluation.   (5 marks)

(b) Explain the matters to be considered, and the procedures to be performed, in respect of planning to use the work of Clapton & Co.   (8 marks)

Please present your response as briefing notes for my attention.

Thank you.

Attachment: Background and structure of the Adams Group

The Group operates in the textile industry, buying cotton, silk and other raw materials to manufacture a range of goods including clothing, linen and soft furnishings. Goods are sold under the Adams brand name, which was acquired by Adams Co many years ago and is held at its original cost in the Group statement of financial position. The Group structure and information about each of the components of the Group is shown below:

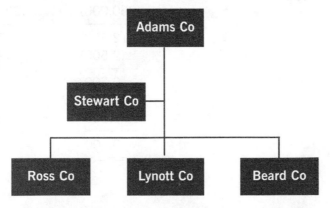

Ross Co, Lynott Co and Beard Co are all wholly owned, acquired subsidiaries which manufacture different textiles. Adams Co also owns 25% of Stewart Co, a company which is classified as an associate in the Group statement of financial position at a value of $12 million at 31 May 2014. The shares in Stewart Co were acquired in January 2014 for consideration of $11·5 million. Other than this recent investment in Stewart Co, the Group structure has remained unchanged for many years.

Information relevant to each of the subsidiaries

Ross Co manufactures luxury silk clothing, with almost all of its output sold through approximately 200 department stores. Ross Co's draft statement of financial position recognises assets of $21·5 million at 31 May 2014. Any silk clothing which has not been sold within 12 months is transferred to Lynott Co, where the silk material is recycled in its manufacturing process.

Lynott Co is located overseas, where it can benefit from low cost labour in its factories. It produces low price fashion clothing for the mass market. A new inventory system was introduced in December 2013 in order to introduce stronger controls over the movement of inventory between factories and stores. Lynott Co is audited by Clapton & Co, and its audit reports in all previous years have been unmodified. Clapton & Co is a small accounting and audit firm, but is a member of an international network of firms. Lynott Co's draft statement of financial position recognises assets of $24 million at 31 May 2014.

Beard Co manufactures soft furnishings. The company is cash-rich, and surplus cash is invested in a large portfolio of investment properties, which generate rental income. The Group's accounting policy is to measure investment properties at fair value. Beard Co's draft statement of financial position recognises assets of $28 million at 31 May 2014, of which investment properties represent $10 million.

Other information

As part of management's strategy to increase market share, a bonus scheme has been put in place across the Group under which senior managers will receive a bonus based on an increase in revenue.

Adams Co imposes an annual management charge of $800,000 on each of its subsidiaries, with the charge for each financial year payable in the subsequent August.

Extracts from draft Group consolidated financial statements

Draft consolidated statement of profit or loss and other comprehensive income

	Year ended 31 May 2014 $'000 Draft	Year ended 31 May 2013 $'000 Actual
Revenue	725,000	650,000
Cost of sales	(463,000)	(417,500)
Gross profit	262,000	232,500
Other income – rental income	200	150
Operating expenses	(250,000)	(225,000)
Profit before tax	12,200	7,650
Income tax expense	(2,500)	(2,000)
Profit for the year	9,700	5,650
Other comprehensive income:		
Gain on investment property revaluation	1,000	3,000
Total comprehensive income	10,700	8,650

Draft consolidated statement of financial position

	31 May 2014 $'000 Draft	31 May 2013 $'000 Actual
Non-current assets		
Property, plant and equipment	50,000	45,000
Investment property	10,000	7,500
Intangible asset – brand name	8,000	8,000
Investment in associate	12,000	–
	80,000	60,500
Current assets		
Inventory	12,000	6,000
Receivables	5,500	6,600
Cash	10,000	22,000
	27,500	34,600
Total assets	107,500	95,100
Equity and liabilities		
Share capital	55,000	55,000
Retained earnings	34,000	24,600
	89,000	79,600
Current liabilities		
Trade payables	16,000	13,500
Tax payable	2,500	2,000
	18,500	15,500
Total equity and liabilities	107,500	95,100

Required:

Respond to the email from the audit partner.   (31 marks)

Note: The split of the mark allocation is shown within the partner's email.

Professional marks will be awarded for the presentation, logical flow and clarity of explanation of the briefing notes.

(4 marks)

(35 marks)

2   You are a manager in Hunt & Co, a firm which offers a range of services to audit and non-audit clients. You have been asked to consider a potential engagement to review and provide a report on the prospective financial information of Waters Co, a company which has been an audit client of Hunt & Co for six years. The audit of the financial statements for the year ended 30 April 2014 has just commenced.

Waters Co operates a chain of cinemas across the country. Currently its cinemas are out of date and use projectors which cannot show films made using new technology, which are becoming more popular. Management is planning to invest in all of its cinemas in order to attract more customers. The company has sufficient cash to fund half of the necessary capital expenditure, but has approached its bank with a loan application of $8 million for the remainder of the funds required. Most of the cash will be used to invest in equipment and fittings, such as new projectors and larger screens, enabling new technology films to be shown in all cinemas. The remaining cash will be used for refurbishment of the cinemas.

The draft forecast statements of profit or loss for the years ending 30 April 2015 and 2016 are shown below, along with the key assumptions which have been used in their preparation. The unaudited statement of profit or loss for the year ended 30 April 2014 is also shown below. The forecast has been prepared for use by the bank in making its lending decision, and will be accompanied by other prospective financial information including a forecast statement of cash flows.

Forecast statement of profit or loss

	Year ended 30 April 2014 Unaudited $'000	Note relevant to forecast information	Year ending 30 April 2015 Forecast $'000	Year ending 30 April 2016 Forecast $'000
Revenue	35,000	1	43,000	46,000
Operating expenses	(28,250)	2	(31,500)	(32,100)
Operating profit	6,750		11,500	13,900
Finance costs	(1,700)		(2,000)	(1,900)
Profit before tax	5,050		9,500	12,000

Note 1: The forecast increase in revenue is based on the following assumptions:

(i)   All cinemas will be fitted with new projectors and larger screens to show new technology films by September 2014.

(ii) Ticket prices will increase from $7·50 to $10 from 1 September 2014.

Note 2: Operating expenses include mainly staff costs, depreciation of property and equipment, and repairs and maintenance to the cinemas.

Required:

(a) (i)   Explain the matters to be considered by Hunt & Co before accepting the engagement to review and report on Waters Co's prospective financial information. (6 marks)

(ii) Assuming the engagement is accepted, describe the examination procedures to be used in respect of the forecast statement of profit or loss. (8 marks)

(b) The audit strategy relevant to the audit of Waters Co concludes that the company has a relatively high risk associated with money laundering, largely due to the cash-based nature of its activities. The majority of customers purchase their cinema tickets and refreshments in cash, and the company transfers its cash to overseas bank accounts on a regular basis.

Required:

(i) Explain the stages used in laundering money, commenting on why Waters Co has been identified as high risk. (5 marks)

(ii) Recommend FOUR elements of an anti-money laundering programme which audit firms such as Hunt & Co should have in place. (6 marks)

(25 marks)

3 **(a)** You are an audit manager in Rose & Co, responsible for the audit of Cooper Co. You are reviewing the audit working papers relating to the financial year ended 31 January 2014. Cooper Co is a manufacturer of chemicals used in the agricultural industry. The draft financial statements recognise profit for the year to 31 January 2014 of $15 million (2013 – $20 million) and total assets of $240 million (2013 – $230 million).

The audit senior, Max Turner, has brought several matters to your attention:

(i) Cooper Co's factories are recognised within property, plant and equipment at a carrying value of $60 million. Half of the factories produce a chemical which is used in farm animal feed. Recently the government has introduced a regulation stipulating that the chemical is phased out over the next three years. Sales of the chemical are still buoyant, however, and are projected to account for 45% of Cooper Co's revenue for the year ending 31 January 2015. Cooper Co has started to research a replacement chemical which is allowed under the new regulation, and has spent $1 million on a feasibility study into the development of this chemical. (8 marks)

(ii) In October 2013, Cooper Co's finance director, Hannah Osbourne, purchased a car from the company. The carrying value of the car at the date of its disposal to Hannah was $50,000, and its market value was $75,000. Cooper Co raised an invoice for $50,000 in respect of the disposal, which is still outstanding for payment. (7 marks)

Required:

Comment on the matters to be considered and explain the audit evidence you should expect to find during your review of the audit working papers in respect of each of the issues described above.

Note: The split of the mark allocation is shown against each of the issues above.

(b) Max noticed that a section of the audit file had not been completed on the previous year's audit. The incomplete section relates to expenditure incurred in the year to 31 January 2013, which appears not to have been audited at all in the prior year. The expenditure of $1·2 million was incurred in the development of an internally generated brand name. The amount was capitalised as an intangible asset at 31 January 2013, and that amount is still recognised at 31 January 2014.

Required:

Explain the implications of this matter for the completion of the audit, and any other professional issues raised, recommending any actions to be taken by the auditor. (5 marks)

(20 marks)

4 You are a manager in Ryder & Co, a firm of Chartered Certified Accountants, and you have taken on the responsibility for providing support and guidance to new members of the firm. Ryder & Co has recently recruited a new audit junior, Sam Tyler, who has come across several issues in his first few months at the firm which he would like your guidance on. Sam's comments and questions are shown below:

(a) I know that auditors are required to assess risks of material misstatement by developing an understanding of the business risks of an audit client, but I am not clear on the relationship between business risk and risk of material misstatement. Can you explain the two types of risk, and how identifying business risk relates to risk of material misstatement? (4 marks)

(b) I worked on the interim audit of Crow Co, a manufacturing company which outsources its payroll function. I know that for Crow Co payroll is material. How does the outsourcing of payroll affect our audit planning? (4 marks)

(c) Crow Co is tendering for an important contract to supply Hatfield Co. I know that Hatfield Co is also an audit client of our firm, and I have heard that Crow Co's management has requested our firm to provide advice on the tender it is preparing. What matters should our firm consider in deciding whether to provide advice to Crow Co on the tender? (5 marks)

(d) I also worked on the audit of Campbell Co, where I heard the managing director, Ting Campbell, discussing a potential new business opportunity with the audit engagement partner. Campbell Co is an events organiser, and is planning to run a programme of nationwide events for accountants, at which speakers will discuss technical updates to financial reporting, tax and audit regulations. Ting proposed that our firm could invest some cash in the business opportunity, supply the speakers, market the events to our audit clients, and that any profit made would be shared between Ryder & Co and Campbell Co. What would be the implications of our firm considering this business opportunity? (7 marks)

Required:

For each of the issues raised, respond to the audit junior, explaining the ethical and professional matters arising from the audit junior's comments.

Note: The split of the mark allocation is shown against each of the issues above.

(20 marks)

5 **(a)** The IAASB has conducted a review of the structure and content of audit reports, including the issuance of an Invitation to Comment on *Improving the Auditor's Report*, in which several suggestions were made with the aim of improving the disclosure of matters included in the auditor's report, including those relating to going concern status.

Required:

Explain the suggestions made by the IAASB in respect of additional disclosures in the auditor's report regarding going concern status, and discuss the benefits of such disclosures. (8 marks)

(b) You are an audit manager in Taylor & Co, a firm of Chartered Certified Accountants, responsible for the audit of Marr Co, with a year ended 28 February 2014. The draft financial statements recognise profit for the year of $11 million. The audit for the year end is nearing completion, and several matters have been highlighted for your attention by the audit senior, Xi Smith. The matters have been discussed with management and will not be adjusted in the financial statements:

1. In January 2014 a major customer went into administration. There was a balance of $2·5 million owing to Marr Co from this customer at 28 February 2014, which is still included in trade receivables.

2. A court case began in December 2013 involving an ex-employee who is suing Marr Co for unfair dismissal. Lawyers estimate that damages of $50,000 are probable to be paid. The financial statements include a note describing the court case and quantifying the potential damages but no adjustment has been made to include it in the statement of financial position or the statement of profit or loss.

Xi Smith has produced a draft audit report for your review, an extract of which is shown below:

Basis for opinion and disclaimer of opinion
We have performed our audit based on a materiality level of $1·5 million. Our audit procedures have proven conclusively that trade receivables are materially misstated. The finance director of Marr Co, Rita Gilmour, has refused to make an adjustment to write off a significant trade receivables balance. Therefore in our opinion the financial statements of Marr Co are materially misstated and we therefore express a disclaimer of opinion because we do not think they are fairly presented.

Emphasis of Matter paragraph
Marr Co is facing a legal claim for an amount of $50,000 from an ex-employee. In our opinion this amount should be recognised as a provision but it is not included in the statement of financial position. We draw your attention to this breach of the relevant IFRS.

Required:

Critically appraise the proposed auditor's report of Marr Co for the year ended 28 February 2014.

Note: You are NOT required to re-draft the extracts from the auditor's report. (12 marks)

(20 marks)

End of Question Paper